ERIK LARSON ...
of Beasts, Th ... *c's Storm,*
which have collectively sold more than nine million copies. *The Devil in the White City* won an Edgar Award and was shortlisted for the Crime Writers' Association Gold Dagger Non-Fiction Award. His books have been published in ...

The #1 *New York Times* Bestseller

One of *Chicago Tribune's* Best Books of the Year

'An enthralling page-turner'   *O: The Oprah Magazine*

'Fresh, fast and deeply moving ... Larson's deft portraits show the essential connection that words created between the powerful and the powerless, capturing the moments that defined life for millions struggling to survive the decisions of a few'   *New York Times Book Review*

'There are countless books about World War II, but there's only one Erik Larson ... There are many things to admire about *The Splendid and the Vile*, but chief among them is Larson's electric writing. The book reads like a novel, and even though everyone (hopefully) knows how the war ultimately ended, he keeps the reader turning the pages with his gripping prose'   *NPR*

'A particularly gripping read, written with bounce and brio. Larson pulls together vivid vignettes – some moving, some amusing, a few grim – to create a collage of what it was like to be alive in Britain at this time, and especially what it was like to be around Churchill. There are some splendid descriptions ... A fine writer of narrative nonfiction history'
                    ROBBIE MILLEN, *The Times*

'Churchill's lessons of resilience and his style of steady-handed leadership are essential to the state of mind of American readers' *Vanity Fair*

'Still, it is a time of sadness, fear, grief and uncertainty for so many, and I find myself comforted by reading about other supremely challenging times in human history, and about resilience, and hope. For this, there is no better book right now than *The Splendid and the Vile* by Erik Larson'
MACKENZIE DAWSON, *New York Post*

'I loved reading *The Splendid and the Vile* by Erik Larson, which is a fascinating look at Winston Churchill and London during the Blitz'
KARIN SLAUGHTER, *Irish Daily Mail*

'This book is peppered with eye-popping details ... A deeply compelling work of history ... Without resorting to heroism, it makes one long powerfully for real leadership' *Lit Hub*

'I have an early copy of this book on my desk and idly began reading the first pages – and suddenly time disappeared' *Seattle Times*

'Larson's skill at integrating vast research and talent for capturing compelling human dramas culminate in an inspirational portrait of one of history's finest, most fearless leaders' *Booklist* (starred review)

'A captivating history of Churchill's heroic year, with more than the usual emphasis on his intimates' *Kirkus Reviews* (starred review)

'Nonfiction king Erik Larson is back' *PopSugar*

'The popular historian Erik Larson has done it again. As I read this book, I kept wondering what the swelling of powerful emotion was that I felt, sometimes in an almost physical sense'

ANDREW ROBERTS, author of *Churchill: Walking with Destiny*, in *Air Mail*

'Delivers the great saga with a novelist's touch. It's like you're watching and hearing the days and nights of 1940 as a passenger on a double-decker London bus'

CHRIS MATTHEWS, *Churchill Bulletin*

'This is a gem of historical writing … Larson evokes the terror of that time magnificently. Using the lens of Winston Churchill's first year as Prime Minister, Larson offers up a narrative that is both panoramic and achingly intimate … [It] will not disappoint fans. Even without the precedent of his previous works, it packs a punch … A wonderful, distressing, yet inspiring read'

GARETH RUSSELL, author of *The Ship of Dreams*

The
SPLENDID
and the VILE

CHURCHILL, FAMILY
AND DEFIANCE DURING
THE BOMBING OF
LONDON

ERIK LARSON

**WILLIAM
COLLINS**

William Collins
An imprint of HarperCollins*Publishers*
1 London Bridge Street
London SE1 9GF

WilliamCollinsBooks.com

First published in Great Britain in 2020 by HarperCollins*Publishers*
First published in the United States in 2020 by Crown
This William Collins paperback edition published in 2021

1

Frontispiece photograph: Central Press/Hulton Archive/Getty Images
Map by Jeffrey L. Ward
Book design by Barbara M. Bachman

A catalogue record for this book is
available from the British Library

ISBN 978-0-00-827498-6

Set in Bembo
Printed and bound in Great Britain by
CPI Group (UK) Ltd, Croydon

MIX
Paper from
responsible sources
FSC™ C007454

This book is produced from independently certified FSC™ paper
to ensure responsible forest management.

For more information visit: www.harpercollins.co.uk/green

To David Woodrum

—for secret reasons

It is not given to human beings—happily for them, for otherwise life would be intolerable—to foresee or to predict to any large extent the unfolding course of events.

—WINSTON CHURCHILL,
EULOGY FOR NEVILLE CHAMBERLAIN,
NOVEMBER 12, 1940

A Note to Readers

I T WAS ONLY WHEN I MOVED TO MANHATTAN A FEW YEARS AGO THAT I came to understand, with sudden clarity, how different the experience of September 11, 2001, had been for New Yorkers than for those of us who watched the nightmare unfold at a distance. This was their home city under attack. Almost immediately I started thinking about London and the German aerial assault of 1940–41, and wondered how on earth anyone could have endured it: fifty-seven consecutive nights of bombing, followed by an intensifying series of nighttime raids over the next six months.

In particular I thought about Winston Churchill: How did he withstand it? And his family and friends? What was it like for him to have his city bombed for nights on end and to know full well that these air raids, however horrific, were likely only a preamble to far worse, a German invasion from the sea and sky, with parachutists dropping into his garden, panzer tanks clanking through Trafalgar Square, and poison gas wafting over the beach where once he painted the sea?

I decided to find out, and quickly came to realize that it is one thing to *say* "Carry on," quite another to do it. I focused on Churchill's first year as prime minister, May 10, 1940, to May 10, 1941, which coincided with the German air campaign as it evolved from sporadic, seemingly aimless raids to a full-on assault against the city of London. The year ended on a weekend of Vonnegutian violence, when the quotidian and the fantastic converged to mark what proved to be the first great victory of the war.

What follows is by no means a definitive account of Churchill's life. Other authors have achieved that end, notably his indefatigable but alas not immortal biographer Martin Gilbert, whose eight-volume study should satisfy any craving for the last detail. Mine is a more intimate account that delves into how Churchill and his circle went about surviving on a daily basis: the dark moments and the light, the romantic entanglements and debacles, the sorrows and laughter, and the odd little episodes that reveal how life was really lived under Hitler's tempest of steel. This was the year in which Churchill became *Churchill,* the cigar-smoking bulldog we all think we know, when he made his greatest speeches and showed the world what courage and leadership looked like.

Although at times it may appear to be otherwise, this is a work of nonfiction. Anything between quotation marks comes from some form of historical document, be it a diary, letter, memoir, or other artifact; any reference to a gesture, gaze, or smile, or any other facial reaction, comes from an account by one who witnessed it. If some of what follows challenges what you have come to believe about Churchill and this era, may I just say that history is a lively abode, full of surprises.

—ERIK LARSON
MANHATTAN, 2020

Contents

THE SPLENDID AND THE VILE

Bleak Expectations

———

N O ONE HAD ANY DOUBT THAT THE BOMBERS WOULD COME. Defense planning began well before the war, though the planners had no specific threat in mind. Europe was Europe. If past experience was any sort of guide, a war could break out anywhere, anytime. Britain's military leaders saw the world through the lens of the empire's experience in the previous war, the Great War, with its mass slaughter of soldiers and civilians alike and the first systematic air raids of history, conducted over England and Scotland using bombs dropped from German zeppelins. The first of these occurred on the night of January 19, 1915, and was followed by more than fifty others, during which giant dirigibles drifting quietly over the British landscape dropped 162 tons of bombs that killed 557 people.

Since then, the bombs had grown bigger and deadlier, and more cunning, with time delays and modifications that made them shriek as they descended. One immense German bomb, a thirteen-foot, four-thousand-pounder named Satan, could destroy an entire city block. The aircraft that carried these bombs had grown larger as well, and faster, and flew higher, and were thus better able to evade home-front defenses. On November 10, 1932, Stanley Baldwin, then deputy prime minister, gave the House of Commons a forecast of what was to come: "I think it is well for the man in the street to realize that there is no power on earth that can protect him from being bombed. Whatever people may tell him, the bomber will always get through." The only effective defense lay in offense, he said, "which means that you have to kill more women and children more quickly than the enemy if you want to save yourselves."

Britain's civil defense experts, fearing a "knock-out blow," predicted that the first aerial attack on London would destroy much if not all of the city and kill two hundred thousand civilians. "It was widely believed that London would be reduced to rubble within minutes of war being declared," wrote one junior official. Raids would cause such terror among the survivors that millions would go insane. "London for several days will be one vast raving bedlam," wrote J.F.C. Fuller, a military theorist, in 1923. "The hospitals will be stormed, traffic will cease, the homeless will shriek for help, the city will be a pandemonium."

The Home Office estimated that if standard burial protocols were followed, casket makers would need twenty million square feet of "coffin wood," an amount impossible to supply. They would have to build their coffins from heavy cardboard or papier-mâché, or simply bury people in shrouds. "For mass burial," the Scottish Department of Health advised, "the most appropriate type of grave is the trench grave, dug deep enough to accommodate five layers of bodies." Planners called for large pits to be excavated on the outskirts of London and other cities, the digging to be done with as much discretion as possible. Special training was to be provided to morticians to decontaminate the bodies and clothing of people killed by poison gas.

When Britain declared war against Germany, on September 3, 1939, in response to Hitler's invasion of Poland, the government prepared in earnest for the bombing and invasion that was sure to follow. The code name for signaling that invasion was imminent or underway was "Cromwell." The Ministry of Information issued a special flyer, Beating the Invader, which went out to millions of homes. It was not calculated to reassure. "Where the enemy lands," it warned, ". . . there will be most violent fighting." It instructed readers to heed any government advisory to evacuate. "When the attack begins, it will be too late to go. . . . STAND FIRM." Church belfries went silent throughout Britain. Their bells were now the designated alarm, to be rung only when "Cromwell" was invoked and the invaders were on their way. If you heard bells, it meant that parachute troops had been sighted nearby. At this, the pamphlet instructed, "disable and hide your bicycle and destroy your maps." If you owned a car: "Remove distributor head and leads and either empty the tank or remove the carburetor. If you don't know how to do this, find out now from your nearest garage."

Towns and villages took down street signs and limited the sale of maps to people holding police-issued permits. Farmers left old cars and trucks in their fields as obstacles against gliders laden with soldiers. The government issued thirty-five million gas masks to civilians, who carried them to work and church, and kept them at their bedsides. London's mailboxes received a special coating of yellow paint that changed color in the presence of poison gas. Strict blackout rules so darkened the streets of the city that it became nearly impossible to recognize a visitor at a train station after dark. On moonless nights, pedestrians stepped in front of cars and buses and walked into light stanchions and fell off curbs and tripped over sandbags.

Suddenly everyone began paying attention to the phases of the moon. Bombers could attack by day, of course, but it was thought that after dark they would be able to find their targets only by moonlight. The full moon and its waxing and waning gibbous phases became known as the "bomber's moon." There was comfort in the fact that bombers and, more importantly, their fighter escorts would have to fly all the way from their bases in Germany, a distance so great as to sharply limit their reach and lethality. But this presumed that France, with its mighty army and Maginot Line and powerful navy, would stand firm and thereby hem in the Luftwaffe and block all German paths to invasion. French endurance was the cornerstone of British defensive strategy. That France might fall was beyond imagining.

"The atmosphere is something more than anxiety," wrote Harold Nicolson, soon to become parliamentary secretary at the Ministry of Information, in his diary on May 7, 1940. "It is one of actual fear." He and his wife, the writer Vita Sackville-West, agreed to commit suicide rather than be captured by German invaders. "There must be something quick and painless and portable," she wrote to him on May 28. "Oh my dear, my dearest, that we should come to this!"

A CONFLUENCE OF UNANTICIPATED forces and circumstances finally did bring the bombers to London, foremost among them a singular event that occurred just before dusk on May 10, 1940, one of the loveliest evenings in one of the finest springs anyone could recall.

1940

Part One

—

THE
RISING
THREAT

May–June

The Coroner Departs

———

THE CARS SPED ALONG THE MALL, THE BROAD BOULEVARD THAT runs between Whitehall, seat of Britain's government ministries, and Buckingham Palace, the 775-room home of King George VI and Queen Elizabeth, its stone facade visible now at the far end of the roadway, dark with shadow. It was early evening, Friday, May 10. Everywhere bluebells and primroses bloomed. Delicate spring leaves misted the tops of trees. The pelicans in St. James's Park basked in the warmth and the adoration of visitors, as their less exotic cousins, the swans, drifted with their usual stern lack of interest. The beauty of the day made a shocking contrast to all that had happened since dawn, when German forces stormed into Holland, Belgium, and Luxembourg, using armor, dive-bombers, and parachute troops with overwhelming effect.

In the rear of the first car sat Britain's topmost naval official, the first lord of the Admiralty, Winston S. Churchill, sixty-five years old. He had held the same post once before, during the previous war, and had been appointed anew by Prime Minister Neville Chamberlain when the current war was declared. In the second car was Churchill's police guardian, Detective Inspector Walter Henry Thompson, of Scotland Yard's Special Branch, responsible for keeping Churchill alive. Tall and lean, with an angular nose, Thompson was omnipresent, often visible in press photographs but rarely mentioned—a "dogsbody," in the parlance of the time, like so many others who made the government work: the myriad private and parliamentary secretaries and assistants and typists who constituted the Whitehall infantry. Unlike most, however, Thompson carried a pistol in the pocket of his overcoat at all times.

Churchill had been summoned by the king. To Thompson, at least, the reason seemed obvious. "I drove behind the Old Man with indescribable pride," he wrote.

Churchill entered the palace. King George was at this point forty-four years old and well into the fourth year of his reign. Knock-kneed, fish-lipped, with very large ears, and saddled with a significant stammer, he seemed fragile, especially in contrast with his visitor, who, though three inches shorter, had much greater width. The king was leery of Churchill. Churchill's sympathy for Edward VIII, the king's older brother, whose romance with American divorcée Wallis Simpson sparked the abdication crisis of 1936, remained a point of abrasion between Churchill and the royal family. The king had also taken offense at Churchill's prior criticism of Prime Minister Chamberlain over the Munich Agreement of 1938, which allowed Hitler to annex a portion of Czechoslovakia. The king harbored a general distrust of Churchill's independence and shifting political loyalties.

He asked Churchill to sit down and looked at him steadily for a while, in what Churchill later described as a searching and quizzical manner.

The king said: "I suppose you don't know why I have sent for you?"

"Sir, I simply couldn't imagine why."

THERE HAD BEEN A rebellion in the House of Commons that left Chamberlain's government tottering. It erupted in the context of a debate over the failure of a British attempt to evict German forces from Norway, which Germany had invaded a month earlier. Churchill, as first lord of the Admiralty, had been responsible for the naval component of the effort. Now it was the British who faced eviction, in the face of an unexpectedly ferocious German onslaught. The debacle sparked calls for a change of government. In the view of the rebels, Chamberlain, seventy-one, variously nicknamed "the Coroner" and "the Old Umbrella," was not up to the task of managing a fast-expanding war. In a speech on May 7, one member of Parliament, Leopold Amery, directed a blistering denunciation at Chamberlain, borrowing words used by Oliver Cromwell in 1653: "You have sat too long here for any good you have been doing! Depart, I say, and let us have done with you! In the name of God, go!"

The House held a vote of confidence, by way of a "division," in which members line up in the lobby in two rows, for yes and no, and file past tellers, who record their votes. At first glance, the tally seemed a victory for Chamberlain—281 ayes to 200 nays—but in fact, compared to prior votes, it underscored how much political ground he had lost.

Afterward, Chamberlain met with Churchill and told him that he planned to resign. Churchill, wishing to appear loyal, persuaded him otherwise. This heartened the king but prompted one rebel, appalled that Chamberlain might try to stay, to liken him to "a dirty old piece of chewing gum on the leg of a chair."

By Thursday, May 9, the forces opposing Chamberlain had deepened their resolve. As the day advanced, his departure seemed more and more certain, and two men rapidly emerged as the candidates most likely to replace him: his foreign secretary, Lord Halifax, and the first lord of the Admiralty, Churchill, whom much of the public adored.

But then came Friday, May 10, and Hitler's blitzkrieg assaults on the Low Countries. The news cast gloom throughout Whitehall, although for Chamberlain it also brought a flicker of renewed hope that he might retain his post. Surely the House would agree that with such momentous events in play, it was foolhardy to change governments. The rebels, however, made it clear that they would not serve under Chamberlain, and pushed for the appointment of Churchill.

Chamberlain realized he had no choice but to resign. He urged Lord Halifax to take the job. Halifax seemed more stable than Churchill, less likely to lead Britain into some new catastrophe. Within Whitehall, Churchill was acknowledged to be a brilliant orator, albeit deemed by many to lack good judgment. Halifax himself referred to him as a "rogue elephant." But Halifax, who doubted his own ability to lead in a time of war, did not want the job. He made this duly clear when an emissary dispatched to attempt to change his mind found that he had gone to the dentist.

It remained for the king to decide. He first summoned Chamberlain. "I accepted his resignation," the king wrote in his diary, "& told him how grossly unfairly I thought he had been treated, & that I was terribly sorry that all this controversy had happened."

The two men talked about successors. "I, of course, suggested Halifax," the king wrote. He considered Halifax "the obvious man."

But now Chamberlain surprised him: He recommended Churchill.

The king wrote, "I sent for Winston & asked him to form a Government. This he accepted & told me he had not thought this was the reason for my having sent for him"—though Churchill, according to the king's account, did happen to have handy the names of a few men he was considering for his own cabinet.

THE CARS CARRYING CHURCHILL and Inspector Thompson returned to Admiralty House, the seat of naval command in London and, for the time being, Churchill's home. The two men left their cars. As always, Thompson kept one hand in his overcoat pocket for quick access to his pistol. Sentries holding rifles with fixed bayonets stood watch, as did other soldiers armed with Lewis light machine guns, sheltered by sandbags. On the adjacent green of St. James's Park, the long barrels of anti-aircraft guns jutted upward at stalagmitic angles.

Churchill turned to Thompson. "You know why I've been to Buckingham Palace," he said.

Thompson did, and congratulated him, but added that he wished the appointment had come sooner, and in better times, because of the immensity of the task that lay ahead.

"God alone knows how great it is," Churchill said.

The two men shook hands, as solemn as mourners at a funeral. "All I hope is that it is not too late," Churchill said. "I am very much afraid that it is. But we can only do our best, and give the rest of what we have—whatever there may be left to us."

These were sober words, although inwardly, Churchill was elated. He had lived his entire life for this moment. That it had come at such a dark time did not matter. If anything, it made his appointment all the more exquisite.

In the fading light, Inspector Thompson saw tears begin to slip down Churchill's cheeks. Thompson, too, found himself near tears.

LATE THAT NIGHT CHURCHILL lay in bed, alive with a thrilling sense of challenge and opportunity. "In my long political experience," he wrote, "I had held most of the great offices of State, but I readily admit that the post which had now fallen to me was the one I liked the best." Coveting power for power's sake was a "base" pursuit, he wrote, adding, "But power in a national crisis, when a man believes he knows what orders should be given, is a blessing."

He felt great relief. "At last I had the authority to give directions over the whole scene. I felt as if I were walking with destiny, and that all my past life had been but a preparation for this hour and for this trial. . . .

Although impatient for the morning I slept soundly and had no need for cheering dreams. Facts are better than dreams."

Despite the doubts he had expressed to Inspector Thompson, Churchill brought to No. 10 Downing Street a naked confidence that under his leadership Britain would win the war, even though any objective appraisal would have said he did not have a chance. Churchill knew that his challenge now was to make everyone else believe it, too—his countrymen, his commanders, his cabinet ministers, and, most importantly, the American president, Franklin D. Roosevelt. From the very start, Churchill understood a fundamental truth about the war: that he could not win it without the eventual participation of the United States. Left to itself, he believed, Britain could endure and hold Germany at bay, but only the industrial might and manpower of America would ensure the final eradication of Hitler and National Socialism.

What made this all the more daunting was that Churchill had to achieve these ends quickly, before Hitler focused his full attention on Britain and unleashed his air force, the Luftwaffe, which British intelligence believed to be vastly superior to the Royal Air Force.

IN THE MIDST OF THIS, Churchill had to cope with all manner of other challenges. An immense personal debt payment was due at the end of the month, one he did not have the money to pay. His only son, Randolph, likewise was awash in debt, persistently demonstrating a gift not just for spending money but also for losing it gambling, at which his ineptitude was legendary; he also drank too much and had a propensity, once drunk, for making scenes and thereby posing what his mother, Clementine, saw as a continual risk that one day he would cause irrevocable embarrassment to the family. Churchill also had to deal with blackout rules and strict rationing and the mounting intrusion of officials seeking to keep him safe from assassination—as well as, not least, the everlasting offense of the army of workmen dispatched to buttress Downing Street and the rest of Whitehall against aerial attack, with their endless hammering, which more than any other single irritant had the capacity to drive him to the point of fury.

Except maybe whistling.

His hatred of whistling, he once said, was the only thing he had in common with Hitler. It was more than merely an obsession. "It sets up an almost psychiatric disturbance in him—immense, immediate, and irrational," wrote Inspector Thompson. Once, while walking together to

Downing Street, Thompson and the new prime minister encountered a newsboy, maybe thirteen years old, heading in their direction, "hands in pockets, newspapers under his arms, whistling loudly and cheerfully," Thompson recalled.

As the boy came closer, Churchill's anger soared. He hunched his shoulders and stalked over to the boy. "Stop that whistling," he snarled.

The boy, utterly unruffled, replied, "Why should I?"

"Because I don't like it and it's a horrible noise."

The boy moved on, then turned and shouted, "Well, you can shut your ears, can't you?"

The boy kept walking.

Churchill was for the moment stunned. Anger flushed his face.

But one of Churchill's great strengths was perspective, which gave him the ability to place discrete events into boxes, so that bad humor could in a heartbeat turn to mirth. As Churchill and Thompson continued walking, Thompson saw Churchill begin to smile. Under his breath, Churchill repeated the boy's rejoinder: "You can shut your ears, can't you?"

And laughed out loud.

CHURCHILL BENT AT ONCE to his new summons, heartening many, but confirming for others their most dire concerns.

A Night at the Savoy

MARY CHURCHILL, SEVENTEEN YEARS OLD, AWOKE THAT MORN-ing, May 10, to the grim news from Europe. The details were terrifying in themselves, but it was the juxtaposition between how Mary had spent her night and what had happened across the English Channel that made it all the more shocking.

Mary was the youngest of Churchill's four children; a fifth child, a daughter named Marigold, the family's beloved "Duckadilly," had died of septicemia in August 1921, at two years and nine months of age. Both parents were present at her death, a moment that drew from Clementine, as Churchill later told Mary, "a succession of wild shrieks, like an animal in mortal pain."

Mary's eldest sister, Diana, thirty, was married to Duncan Sandys, who served as Churchill's "special liaison" to Air Raid Precautions (ARP), the civil defense division of the Home Office. They had three children. The second sister, Sarah, twenty-five, so stubborn that as a child she was nicknamed "Mule," was an actress who, to Churchill's displeasure, had married an Austrian entertainer named Vic Oliver, sixteen years her senior and twice married before he met her. They had no children. The fourth child was Randolph, nearly twenty-nine, who a year earlier had married Pamela Digby, now twenty years old and pregnant with their first child.

Mary was pretty, buoyant, and spirited, described by one observer as "very effervescent." She approached the world with the unabashed enthusiasm of a spring lamb, a guilelessness that a young American visitor, Kathy Harriman, found cloying. "She's a very intelligent girl," Harriman wrote, "but so naive that it hurts. She says such frank things; then people laugh at her, make fun of her, and being super-sensitive, she takes it all to heart." At her birth, Mary's mother, Clementine, had nicknamed her "Mary the mouse."

While Hitler had been inflicting death and trauma on untold millions in the Low Countries, Mary had been out with friends having the time of her life. The evening began with a dinner party for her close friend Judy—Judith Venetia Montagu—a cousin, also seventeen, daughter of the late Edwin Samuel Montagu, former secretary of state for India, and his wife, Venetia Stanley. Theirs had been a marriage steeped in drama and speculation: Venetia married Montagu after carrying on a three-year affair with former prime minister H. H. Asquith, thirty-five years her senior. Whether Venetia and Asquith had ever had a physical relationship remained for all but them an unresolved question, although if word volume alone were a measure of romantic intensity, Asquith was a man lost irreclaimably to love. Over the three years of their affair he wrote at least 560 letters to Venetia, composing some during cabinet meetings, a penchant Churchill called "England's greatest security risk." Her surprise engagement to Montagu crushed Asquith. "No hell could be so bad," he wrote.

A number of other young men and women also attended Judy Montagu's dinner, all members of London's bright set, the offspring of Britain's gentry, who dined and danced and drank champagne at the city's popular nightclubs. The war did not put an end to their revelry, though it injected a somber note. Many of the men had joined some branch of the military services, the RAF being perhaps the most romantic, or were ensconced in military schools like Sandhurst and Pirbright. Some had fought in Norway, and others were now abroad with the British Expeditionary Force. Many of the girls in Mary's group joined the Women's Voluntary Service, which helped resettle evacuees, operated rest centers, and provided emergency food, but also did such varied tasks as spinning dogs' hair into yarn for use in making clothing. Other young women were training to be nurses; some took shadowy posts within the Foreign Office, where, as Mary put it, they pursued "activities not to be defined." But fun was fun, and despite the gathering darkness, Mary and her friends danced, Mary armed with the £5 allowance Churchill gave to her on the first of each month. "London social life was lively," Mary wrote in a memoir. "Despite the blackout, theaters were full, there were plenty of nightclubs for late dancing after restaurants closed, and many people still gave dinner parties, often organized round a son on leave."

A favorite location for Mary and her group of friends was the Players' Theatre, near Covent Garden, where they sat at tables and watched an ensemble of actors, including Peter Ustinov, perform old music-hall songs. They stayed until the theater closed, at two A.M., then walked home through blacked-out streets. She adored the beauty and mystery conjured on nights when the moon was full: "Emerging from streets deep in shadow like dark valleys into the great expanse of Trafalgar Square flooded with moonlight, the classical symmetry of St Martin-in-the-Fields etched in the background and Nelson's Column soaring away up into the night above his guardian lions so formidable and black—it was a sight I shall never forget."

Among the men at Judy Montagu's dinner was a young army major named Mark Howard, whom Mary judged to be handsome and debonair, and whom she "rather fancied." Fated to die in action in four years' time, Howard was a major with the Coldstream Guards, the oldest continuously serving regiment in Britain's regular army. Though an active combat unit, its duties included helping guard Buckingham Palace.

After dinner, Mary, Mark, and their friends went to the famed Savoy Hotel to dance, then moved on to a nightclub favored by London's well-off young men and women, the 400 Club, known as "the night-time headquarters of Society." Situated in a cellar in Leicester Square, the club stayed open until dawn, as guests waltzed and fox-trotted to the music of an eighteen-piece orchestra. "Danced almost exclusively with Mark," Mary wrote in her diary. "V. nice! Home and bed 4 A.M."

That morning, Friday, May 10, she learned of Hitler's lightning attacks in Europe. In her diary she wrote, "While Mark & I were dancing gaily & so unheedingly this morning—in the cold grey dawn Germany swooped on 2 more innocent countries—Holland & Belgium. The bestiality of the attack is inconceivable."

She went to her school, Queen's College, on Harley Street, where, as a part-time "day girl," she studied French, English literature, and history. "A cloud of uncertainty & doubt hung over us all day," she noted. "What would happen to the govt?"

She soon got the answer. In the afternoon, as she customarily did on Fridays, she traveled to the Churchill family estate, Chartwell, about twenty-five miles southeast of London. She had grown up here, raising a menagerie of animals, some of which she sought to sell through an enterprise she named "The Happy Zoo." The house was closed for the war, save for Churchill's study, but a cottage on the grounds remained open, and was now occupied by Mary's beloved former nanny, Maryott

Whyte, Clementine's first cousin, known variously within the family as Moppet or Nana.

It was a warm, summery evening. Mary sat on the cottage steps in the blue dusk—"the gloaming," she called it—and listened to a radio playing within. Around nine o'clock, just before the regular BBC news broadcast, Chamberlain came on and made a brief speech, in which he stated that he had resigned, and that Churchill was now prime minister.

Mary was thrilled. Many others were not.

FOR AT LEAST ONE member of Mary's set who was also present that night at the Savoy and the 400 Club, the appointment was troubling, in terms of both how it would affect the nation and the war, and how it was likely to affect his own life.

Until Saturday morning, May 11, John "Jock" Colville had served as an assistant private secretary to Neville Chamberlain, but now he found himself assigned to Churchill. Given the demands of the job, he faced the prospect of practically living with the man at No. 10. Mary's view of Jock was ambivalent, almost wary: "I suspected him—rightly, on both counts!—of being a 'Chamberlainite' and a 'Municheer.'" He, in turn, was less than enthralled with her: "I thought the Churchill girl rather supercilious."

The job of private secretary was a prestigious one. Colville joined four other newly assigned men who together composed Churchill's "Private Office" and served almost as his deputies, while a cadre of other secretaries and typists managed his dictation and routine clerical tasks. Colville's heritage seemed to predetermine his posting to No. 10. His father, George Charles Colville, was a barrister, and his mother, Lady Cynthia Crewe-Milnes, a courtier, woman of the bedchamber to Mary, the queen mother. She also served as a social worker ministering to the poor in East London and now and then brought Colville along so that he could see the other side of English life. At the age of twelve, Colville became a page of honor to King George V, a ceremonial post that obliged him to appear at Buckingham Palace three times a year, bedecked in knee breeches, lace cuffs, a royal blue cape, and a three-cornered hat with red feathers.

Though only twenty-five, Colville looked older, an effect attributable both to the funereal manner in which he was compelled to dress and to his dark eyebrows and impassive face. Together these conveyed a dour censoriousness, though in fact—as would become apparent in a covertly kept diary of his days at No. 10—he was a precise observer of human behavior who wrote with grace and had a deep appreciation for the ambient beauty in the world at large. He had two older brothers, the eldest, David, in the navy, the other, Philip, an army major serving in France with the British Expeditionary Force, for whom Jock felt great anxiety.

Colville had been schooled in all the right places; this was important among Britain's upper echelons, for whom one's school served as a kind of regimental flag. He went to Harrow and captained its fencing team, then moved on to Trinity College, Cambridge. Harrow in particular had an outsized influence on the fates of young men of Britain's uppermost classes, as evident in the roster of "Old Harrovians," which included seven prime ministers, among them Churchill, a lackluster student said by a staff member to have exhibited "phenomenal slovenliness." Colville learned German and burnished his skills during two stays in Germany, first in 1933, shortly after Hitler became chancellor of Germany, and a second time in 1937, when Hitler was asserting full control. At first Colville found the enthusiasm of the German populace infectious, but over time he grew uneasy. He witnessed a book burning in Baden-Baden and later attended one of Hitler's speeches. "I had never before, and have never since, seen an exhibition of mass-hysteria so universal in its scope," he wrote. That same year he joined the Foreign Office in its diplomatic service division, which supplied No. 10 with its private secretaries. Two years later, he found himself working for Chamberlain, by then engulfed in conflict over his failed Munich Agreement. Churchill, one of Chamberlain's foremost critics, called the agreement "a total and unmitigated defeat."

Colville liked and respected Chamberlain, and feared what might happen now that Churchill was in power. He saw only chaos ahead. Like many others in Whitehall, he considered Churchill to be capricious and meddlesome, inclined toward dynamic action in every direction at once. But the public adored him. Colville, in his diary, blamed Hitler for this surge in popularity, writing, "One of Hitler's cleverest moves has been to make Winston Public Enemy Number One, because this fact has helped to make him Public Hero Number One at home and in the U.S.A."

To Colville, it seemed as though a miasma of dismay settled over Whitehall as the potential consequences of Churchill's appointment began to register. "He may, of course, be the man of drive and energy the country believes him to be and he may be able to speed up our creaking military and industrial machinery," Colville wrote. "But it is a terrible risk, it involves the danger of rash and spectacular exploits, and I cannot help fearing that this country may be manoeuvred into the most danger-ous position it has ever been in."

Colville harbored a quiet wish that Churchill's tenure would be short. "There seems to be some inclination to believe that N.C."—Neville Chamberlain—"will be back before long," he confided in his diary.

One thing seemed certain, however: Colville's posting with Churchill would provide ample material for the diary, which he had begun keep-ing eight months earlier, just after the war began. Only later did it occur to him that doing so was very likely a grave violation of laws governing national security. As a fellow private secretary put it later: "I am filled with amazement at the risks Jock was running in the matter of security, for which he should have been sacked on the spot if he had been caught."

COLVILLE'S DAY-AFTER SKEPTICISM WAS echoed throughout Whitehall. King George VI told his own diary, "I cannot yet think of Winston as P.M." The king encountered Lord Halifax on the grounds of Bucking-ham Palace, through which Halifax had royal permission to walk in his commute from his home in Euston Square to the Foreign Office. "I met Halifax in the garden," the king wrote, "& I told him I was sorry not to have him as P.M."

Halifax, though newly reappointed as foreign secretary, was skeptical of Churchill and the wild energy he seemed likely to bring to No. 10. On Saturday, May 11, the day after Churchill's appointment, Halifax wrote to his own son, "I hope Winston won't lead us into anything rash."

Halifax—whose nickname for Churchill was "Pooh," after the A. A. Milne character Winnie-the-Pooh—grumbled that Churchill's new cabinet appointees lacked intellectual heft. Halifax likened them all to "gangsters," the chief gangster, in his view, being Churchill. "I have seldom met anybody with stranger gaps of knowledge, or whose mind worked in greater jerks," Halifax wrote in his diary that Saturday. "Will it be possible to make it work in orderly fashion? On this much depends."

Churchill's appointment enraged the wife of one member of Parlia-ment, who likened him to Hermann Göring, the obese, brutal chief of the German air force, the Luftwaffe, and the second most powerful man in the Third Reich. "W.C. is really the counterpart of Göring in En-gland," she wrote, "full of the desire for blood, 'Blitzkrieg,' and bloated with ego and over-feeding, the same treachery running through his veins, punctuated by heroics and hot air."

But a civilian diarist named Nella Last had a different view, one she reported to Mass-Observation, an organization launched in Britain two years before the war that recruited hundreds of volunteers to keep daily diaries with the goal of helping sociologists better understand ordinary British life. The diarists were encouraged to hone their observational skills by describing everything on their own fireplace mantels and on the mantels of friends. Many volunteers, like Last, kept their diaries throughout the war. "If I had to spend my whole life with a man," she wrote, "I'd choose Chamberlain, but I think I would sooner have Mr Churchill if there was a storm and I was shipwrecked."

The public and Churchill's allies greeted his appointment with applause. Letters and telegrams of congratulations arrived at Admiralty House in a torrent. Two of these surely tickled Churchill, both from women with whom he had been friends for a long time, and who at varying points may have harbored romantic aspirations. Clementine certainly wondered, and was said to be wary of both women.

"My wish is realized," wrote Violet Bonham Carter, daughter of H. H. Asquith, the former prime minister, who'd died in 1928. "I can now face all that is to come with faith & confidence." She knew Churchill well and had no doubt that his energy and pugnacity would transfigure the office. "I know, as you do, that the wind has been sown, & that, we must all reap the whirlwind," she wrote. "But you will ride it—instead of being driven before it—Thank Heaven that you are there, & at the helm of our destiny—& may the nation's spirit be kindled by your own."

The second letter was from Venetia Stanley, the woman who had carried on the epistolary affair with Asquith. "Darling," Venetia wrote now to Churchill, "I want to add my voice to the great paean of joy which has gone up all over the civilized world when you became PM. Thank God at last." She rejoiced, she told him, in the fact that "you have been given the chance of saving us all."

She added a postscript: "Incidentally how nice to have No. 10 once more occupied by someone one loves."

London and Washington

————

AMERICA LOOMED LARGE IN CHURCHILL'S THINKING ABOUT THE war and its ultimate outcome. Hitler seemed poised to overwhelm Europe. Germany's air force, the Luftwaffe, was believed to be far larger and more powerful than Britain's Royal Air Force, the RAF, and its submarines and surface raiders were by now severely impeding the flow of food, arms, and raw materials that were so vital to the island nation. The prior war had shown how potent the United States could be as a military force, when roused to action; now it alone seemed to have the wherewithal to even the sides.

Just how important America was in Churchill's strategic thinking became evident to his son, Randolph, one morning soon after Churchill's appointment, when Randolph walked into his father's bedroom at Admiralty House and found him standing before a washbasin and mirror, shaving. Randolph was home on leave from the 4th Queen's Own Hussars, Churchill's old regiment, in which Randolph now served as an officer.

"Sit down, dear boy, and read the papers while I finish shaving," Churchill told him.

After a few moments, Churchill made a half turn toward his son. "I think I see my way through," he said.

He turned back to the mirror.

Randolph understood that his father was talking about the war. The remark startled him, he recalled, for he himself saw little chance that Britain could win. "Do you mean that we can avoid defeat?" Randolph asked. "Or beat the bastards?"

At this, Churchill threw his razor into the basin and whirled to face his son. "Of course I mean we can beat them," he snapped.

"Well, I'm all for it," Randolph said, "but I don't see how you can do it."

Churchill dried his face. "I shall drag the United States in."

IN AMERICA, THE PUBLIC had no interest in being dragged anywhere, least of all into a war in Europe. This was a change from early in the conflict, when a Gallup Poll found that 42 percent of Americans felt that if in the coming months France and Britain seemed certain to be defeated, the United States should declare war on Germany and send troops; 48 percent said no. But Hitler's invasion of the Low Countries drastically altered the public's attitude. In a poll taken in May 1940, Gallup found that 93 percent opposed a declaration of war, a stance known as isolationism. The U.S. Congress had previously codified this antipathy with the passage, starting in 1935, of a series of laws, the Neutrality Acts, that closely regulated the export of weapons and munitions and barred their transport on American ships to any nation at war. Americans were sympathetic toward Britain, but now came questions as to just how stable the British Empire was, having thrown out its government on the same day that Hitler invaded Holland, Belgium, and Luxembourg.

On Saturday morning, May 11, President Roosevelt convened a cabinet meeting at the White House at which the UK's new prime minister became a topic of discussion. The central question was whether he could possibly prevail in this newly expanded war. Roosevelt had exchanged communiqués with Churchill a number of times in the past, while Churchill was first lord of the Admiralty, but had kept these secret for fear of inflaming American public opinion. The overall tone of the cabinet meeting was skeptical.

Among those present was Harold L. Ickes, secretary of the interior, an influential adviser to Roosevelt who was credited with implementing Roosevelt's program of social works and financial reforms known as the New Deal. "Apparently," Ickes said, "Churchill is very unreliable under the influence of drink." Ickes further dismissed Churchill as "too old." According to Frances Perkins, secretary of labor, during this meeting Roosevelt seemed "uncertain" about Churchill.

Doubts about the new prime minister, in particular his consumption of alcohol, had been sown well before the meeting, however. In February 1940, Sumner Welles, undersecretary of the U.S. State Department, had set off on an international tour, the "Welles Mission," to meet with leaders in Berlin, London, Rome, and Paris, to gauge political conditions in Europe. Among those he visited was Churchill, then first lord of the Admiralty. Welles wrote about the encounter in his subsequent report: "When I was shown into his office Mr. Churchill was sitting in front of the fire, smoking a 24-inch cigar, and drinking a whiskey and soda. It was quite obvious that he had consumed a good many whiskeys before I arrived."

The main source of skepticism about Churchill, however, was America's ambassador to Britain, Joseph Kennedy, who disliked the prime minister and repeatedly filed pessimistic reports about Britain's prospects and Churchill's character. At one point Kennedy repeated to Roosevelt the gist of a remark made by Chamberlain, that Churchill "has developed into a fine two-handed drinker and his judgment has never proved good."

Kennedy, in turn, was not well liked in London. The wife of Churchill's foreign secretary, Lord Halifax, detested the ambassador for his pessimism about Britain's chances for survival and his prediction that the RAF would quickly be crushed.

She wrote, "I could have killed him with pleasure."

Galvanized

IN HIS FIRST TWENTY-FOUR HOURS IN OFFICE, CHURCHILL REVEALED himself to be a very different kind of prime minister. Where Chamberlain— the Old Umbrella, the Coroner—was staid and deliberate, the new prime minister, true to his reputation, was flamboyant, electric, and wholly unpredictable. One of Churchill's first acts was to appoint himself minister of defense, which prompted an outgoing official to write in his diary, "Heaven help us." The post was a new one, through which Churchill would oversee the chiefs of staff who controlled the army, navy, and air force. He now had full control of the war, and full responsibility.

He moved quickly to build his government, making seven key appointments by noon the next day. He kept Lord Halifax as foreign secretary and, in an act of generosity and loyalty, also included Chamberlain, naming him lord president of the council, a post with a minimal workload that served as a bridge between the government and the king. Rather than evict Chamberlain immediately from the prime ministerial residence at No. 10 Downing Street, Churchill resolved to continue living for a while at Admiralty House, his current home, to give Chamberlain time for a dignified exit. He offered Chamberlain an adjacent townhouse, No. 11 Downing Street, which Chamberlain had occupied in the 1930s while chancellor of the exchequer.

A new electricity surged through Whitehall. Subdued corridors awoke. "It was as though the machine had overnight acquired one or two new gears, capable of far higher speeds than had ever before been thought possible," wrote Edward Bridges, secretary to the War Cabinet.

This new energy, unfamiliar and disconcerting, coursed through all bureaucratic strata, from the lowest secretary to the most senior minister. The effect within No. 10 was galvanic. Under Chamberlain, even the advent of war had not altered the pace of work, according to John Colville; but Churchill was a dynamo. To Colville's astonishment, "respectable civil servants were actually to be seen running along the corridors." For Colville and his fellow members of Churchill's private secretariat, the workload increased to hitherto unimagined levels. Churchill issued directives and commands in brief memoranda known as "minutes," which he dictated to a typist, one of whom was always on hand, from the moment he awoke until he went to bed. He raged at misspellings and nonsensical phrases caused by what he deemed to be misattention, though in fact the challenge of taking dictation from him was made all the harder by a slight lisplike speech impediment that caused him to muddy his *s*'s. In the course of transcribing a twenty-seven-page speech, one typist, Elizabeth Layton, who came to Downing Street in 1941, drew his ire for making a single error, typing "Air *Minister*" instead of "Air *Ministry,*" thereby creating a sentence with an unintended, but robust, visual image: "The Air Minister was in a state of chaos from top to bottom." It could be hard to hear Churchill, however, especially in the morning, when he dictated from bed, according to Layton. Other clarity-distorting factors intruded as well. "There's always that cigar," she remarked, "and usually he paces up and down the room as he dictates, so that sometimes he's behind your chair and sometimes far across the room."

No detail was too small to draw his attention, even the phrasing and grammar that ministers used when writing their reports. They were not to use the word "aerodrome" but, rather, "airfield"; not "aeroplane" but "aircraft." Churchill was particularly insistent that ministers compose memoranda with brevity and limit their length to one page or less. "It is slothful not to compress your thoughts," he said.

Such precise and demanding communication installed at all levels a new sense of responsibility for events, and dispelled the fustiness of routine ministerial work. Churchill's communiqués tumbled forth daily, by the dozens, invariably brief and always written in precise English. It was not uncommon for him to demand an answer on a complex subject before the day was out. "Anything that was not of immediate importance and a concern to him was of no value," wrote General Alan Brooke, known as "Brookie" to the secretarial staff at No. 10 Downing Street. "When he wanted something done, everything else had to be dropped."

The effect, Brooke observed, was "like the beam of a searchlight ceaselessly swinging round and penetrating into the remote recesses of the administration—so that everyone, however humble his rank or his function, felt that one day the beam might rest on him and light up what he was doing."

PENDING CHAMBERLAIN'S DEPARTURE FROM No. 10, Churchill established an office on the ground floor of Admiralty House, where he planned to work at night. A typist and a private secretary occupied the dining room and daily traversed a walkway populated with furniture in a dolphin motif, the backs and arms of chairs rendered in kelp and twisty marine creatures. Churchill's office occupied an inner room. On his desk he kept a miscellany of pills, powders, and toothpicks, as well as cuffs to protect his sleeves and various gold medals, which he deployed as paperweights. Bottles of whiskey stood on an adjacent table. By day he occupied an office in Downing Street.

But Churchill's notion of what constituted an office was expansive. Often generals, ministers, and staff members would find themselves meeting with Churchill while he was in his bathtub, one of his favorite places to work. He also liked working in bed, and spent hours there each morning going through dispatches and reports, with a typist seated nearby. Always present was the Box, a black despatch box that contained reports, correspondence, and minutes from other officials requiring his attention, replenished daily by his private secretaries.

Nearly every morning one visitor in particular came to Churchill's bedroom, Major General Hastings Ismay, newly appointed military chief of staff, known lovingly, and universally, as "Pug" for his likeness to that breed of dog. It was Ismay's job to serve as an intermediary between Churchill and the chiefs of the three military services, helping them to understand him, and him to understand them. Ismay did so with tact, and a diplomat's grace. Immediately he became one of the central members of what Churchill called his "Secret Circle." Ismay came to Churchill's bedroom to discuss matters that would come up later, at the morning meeting of the chiefs of staff. Other times he would simply sit with Churchill, in case he was needed—a warm and calming presence. Pug was a favorite of typists and private secretaries alike. "The eyes, wrinkling nose, mouth and shape of his face produced a canine effect which was entirely delightful," wrote John Colville. "When he smiled his face was alight and he gave the impression that he was wagging an easily imaginable tail."

Ismay was struck by how much the public seemed to need this new prime minister. While walking with him from No. 10 back to Admiralty House, Ismay marveled at the enthusiastic greeting Churchill got from the men and women they passed. A group of people waiting at the private entrance to No. 10 offered their congratulations and encouragement, with cries of "Good luck, Winnie. God bless you."

Churchill was deeply moved, Ismay saw. Upon entering the building, Churchill, never afraid to express emotion, began to weep.

"Poor people, poor people," he said. "They trust me, and I can give them nothing but disaster for quite a long time."

What he wanted most to give them was action, as he made clear from the start—action in all realms, from the office to the battlefield. What he especially wanted was for Britain to take the offensive in the war, to do something, anything, to bring the war directly to "that bad man," his preferred term for Adolf Hitler. As Churchill said on frequent occasions, he wanted Germans to "bleed and burn."

Within two days of his taking office, thirty-seven RAF bombers attacked the German city of München-Gladbach, in Germany's heavily industrialized Ruhr district. The raid killed four people, one of whom, oddly enough, was an Englishwoman. But mere mayhem wasn't the point. This mission and other raids soon to follow were meant to signal to the British public, to Hitler, and especially to the United States that Britain intended to fight—the same message that Churchill sought to convey on Monday, May 13, when he gave his first speech before the House of Commons. He spoke with confidence, vowing to achieve victory, but also as a realist who understood the bleak terrain in which Britain now lay. One line stood out with particular clarity: "I have nothing to offer but blood, toil, tears and sweat."

Although later these words would take their place in the pantheon of oratory as among the finest ever spoken—and years later would even receive praise from Hitler's chief propagandist, Joseph Goebbels—at the time, the speech was just another speech, delivered to an audience made newly skeptical by morning-after remorse. John Colville, who despite his new assignment remained loyal to Chamberlain, dismissed it as "a brilliant little speech." For the occasion, Colville chose to wear "a bright blue new suit from the Fifty-Shilling Tailors"—a large chain of shops that sold low-cost men's clothing—"cheap and sensational looking, which I felt was appropriate to the new Government."

BY NOW, GERMAN FORCES were asserting their hold on the Low Countries with ruthless authority. On May 14, massed bombers of the Luftwaffe, flying at two thousand feet, bombed Rotterdam in what appeared to be an indiscriminate assault, leaving more than eight hundred civilians dead and, in the process, signaling that a similar fate might lie ahead for Britain. What most alarmed Churchill and his commanders, however, was the startling force with which German armor, accompanied by aircraft acting as aerial artillery, were pummeling Allied forces in Belgium and France, causing French resistance to wither and leaving Britain's continental army, the British Expeditionary Force, or BEF, dangerously exposed. On Tuesday, May 14, the French prime minister, Paul Reynaud, telephoned Churchill and begged him to send ten squadrons of RAF fighters to supplement the four already promised, "if possible today."

Germany was already claiming triumph. In Berlin that Tuesday, William Shirer, an American correspondent, heard German newscasters declare victory over and over, interrupting the regular radio programming to crow about the latest advance. First would come a fanfare, then news of the latest success, and after this, as Shirer recorded in his diary, a chorus would sing "the current hit, 'We March on England.'"

At seven-thirty the next morning, Wednesday, May 15, Reynaud called Churchill again, reaching him while he was still in bed. Churchill picked up the phone on his bedside table. Through the scratchy, distant connection he heard Reynaud say, in English: "We have been defeated."

Churchill said nothing.

"We are beaten," Reynaud said. "We have lost the battle."

"Surely it can't have happened so soon?" Churchill said.

Reynaud told him that the Germans had broken the French line in the commune of Sedan, in the Ardennes, near the French border with Belgium, and that tanks and armored cars were pouring through the gap. Churchill tried to calm his French counterpart, pointing out that military experience taught that offensives invariably lose momentum over time.

"We are defeated," Reynaud insisted.

This seemed so unlikely as to defy belief. The French army was large and skilled, the fortified Maginot Line said to be impregnable. British strategic planning counted on France as a partner, without which the BEF had no chance of prevailing.

It struck Churchill that the time had come to make a direct plea for

American assistance. In a secret cable to President Roosevelt dispatched that day, he told the president that he fully expected Britain to be attacked, and soon, and that he was preparing for the onslaught. "If necessary, we shall continue the war alone, and we are not afraid of that," he wrote. "But I trust you realize, Mr. President, that the voice and force of the United States may count for nothing if they are withheld too long. You may have a completely subjugated, Nazified Europe established with astonishing swiftness, and the weight may be more than we can bear."

He wanted material aid, and specifically asked Roosevelt to consider dispatching up to fifty old destroyers, which the Royal Navy would use until its own naval construction program could begin delivering new ships. He also requested aircraft—"several hundred of the latest types"— and anti-aircraft weapons and ammunition, "of which again there will be plenty next year, if we are alive to see it."

Now he came to what he knew to be an especially sensitive matter in dealing with America, given its apparent need always to drive a hard bargain, or at least to be seen as doing so. "We shall go on paying dollars for as long as we can," he wrote, "but I should like to feel reasonably sure that when we can pay no more, you will give us the stuff all the same."

Roosevelt replied two days later, stating that he could not send destroyers without the specific approval of Congress and adding, "I am not certain that it would be wise for that suggestion to be made to the Congress at this moment." He was still wary of Churchill, but even more wary of how the American public would react. At the time, he was mulling whether to run for a third term, though he had yet to declare his interest.

After sidestepping Churchill's various requests, the president added, "The best of luck to you."

EVER RESTLESS, CHURCHILL DECIDED that he needed to meet personally with French leaders, both to better understand the battle underway and to attempt to bolster their resolve. Despite the presence of German fighters in the skies over France, on Thursday, May 16, at three P.M., Churchill took off in a military passenger aircraft, a de Havilland Flamingo, from an RAF airbase in Hendon, roughly seven miles north of Downing Street. This was Churchill's favorite aircraft: an all-metal, twin-engine passenger plane furnished with large upholstered armchairs. The Flamingo promptly joined a formation of Spitfires dispatched to escort it to France. Pug Ismay and a small group of other officials went along.

Upon landing, they realized immediately that things were much worse than they had expected. Officers assigned to meet them told Ismay that they expected the Germans to arrive in Paris within the next few days. Wrote Ismay, "None of us could believe it."

Reynaud and his generals again pleaded for more aircraft. After much agonizing, and with an eye, as always, on history, Churchill promised the ten squadrons. He telegraphed his War Cabinet that night: "It would not be good historically if their requests were denied and their ruin resulted."

He and his party returned to London the next morning.

The prospect of sending so many fighters to France worried John Colville. In his diary he wrote, "This means denuding this country of a quarter of its first-line fighter defense."

AS THE SITUATION IN France degraded, so rose the fear that Hitler would now turn his full attention to Britain. Invasion seemed a certainty. The deep current of appeasement that had persistently flowed within Whitehall and British society began to surface anew, with fresh calls for a peace arrangement with Hitler, the old instinct burbling up like groundwater through a lawn.

In the Churchill household, such defeatist talk inspired only rage. One afternoon, Churchill invited David Margesson, his chief whip in Parliament, for lunch, along with Clementine and daughter Mary. Margesson was one of the so-called Men of Munich, who had previously endorsed appeasement and had supported Chamberlain's 1938 Munich Agreement.

As lunch progressed, Clementine found herself growing more and more unsettled.

Ever since Churchill's appointment as prime minister, she had become his ever-present ally, hosting luncheons and dinners and answering innumerable letters from the public. She often wore a head scarf, wrapped turban-style, that was printed with tiny copies of war posters and slogans exhorting, "Lend to Defend," "Go to It," and the like. She was now fifty-five years old and had been married to Churchill for thirty-two of them. Upon their engagement, Churchill's good friend Violet Bonham Carter had expressed grave doubts about Clementine's worthiness, forecasting that she "could never be more to him than an ornamental sideboard as I have often said and she is unexacting enough not to mind not being more."

Clementine, however, proved to be anything but a "sideboard." Tall, lean, and displaying a "finished, flawless beauty," as Bonham Carter conceded, she was strong-willed and independent, to the point where she often took vacations alone, absent from the family for long periods. In 1935, she traveled solo on an excursion to the Far East that lasted more than four months. She and Churchill kept separate bedrooms; sex happened only upon her explicit invitation. It was to Bonham Carter that Clementine, soon after being wed, revealed Churchill's peculiar taste in underclothes: pale pink and made of silk. Clementine was undaunted by argument, no matter how lofty her opponent, and was said to be the only person who could effectively stand up to Churchill.

Now, over lunch, her anger rose. Margesson espoused a pacifism that she found repulsive. She quickly reached a point where she could stand it no longer, and lit into him for his past role as an appeaser, implicitly blaming him for helping bring Britain to its current dire position. As daughter Mary put it, she "flayed him verbally before sweeping out." This was not uncommon. Family members talked of "Mama's sweeps." Churchill, describing one incident in which the victim received a particularly vivid rebuke, quipped, "Clemmie dropped on him like a jaguar out of a tree."

In this case, she did not sweep out alone. She dragged Mary with her. They had lunch at the Grill in the nearby Carlton Hotel, famous for its gleaming interior rendered in gold and white.

Mary was mortified by her mother's behavior. "I was most ashamed and horrified," she wrote in her diary. "Mummie & I had to go & have lunch at the Carlton. Good food wrecked by gloom."

A visit to church presented Clementine with another opportunity to express her indignation. On Sunday, May 19, she attended a service at St. Martin-in-the-Fields, the famed Anglican church in Trafalgar Square, and there heard a minister deliver a sermon that struck her as being inappropriately defeatist. She stood up and stormed from the church. Upon arriving at Downing Street, she told her husband the story.

Churchill said, "You ought to have cried 'Shame,' desecrating the House of God with lies!"

Churchill then traveled to Chartwell, the family home outside London, to work on his first radio broadcast as prime minister, and to spend a few peaceful moments beside his pond, feeding his goldfish and a black swan.

There had been other swans, but foxes had killed them.

A NEW TELEPHONE CALL from France drew Churchill back to London. The situation was growing dramatically worse, the French army wilting. Despite the grave news, Churchill seemed unfazed, and this caused a further warming in Jock Colville's attitude toward his new employer. In his diary that Sunday, Colville wrote, "Whatever Winston's shortcomings, he seems to be the man for the occasion. His spirit is indomitable and even if France and England should be lost, I feel he would carry on the crusade himself with a band of privateers."

He added: "Perhaps my judgments of him have been harsh, but the situation was very different a few weeks ago."

At a four-thirty meeting of his War Cabinet, Churchill learned that the commander in chief of Britain's forces in France was contemplating a withdrawal toward the channel coast, identifying in particular the port city of Dunkirk. Churchill opposed the idea. He feared that the force would be trapped and destroyed.

Churchill made the decision that, in fact, no fighter aircraft would be sent to France. With that country's fate now seeming so tenuous, there was little point, and every fighter was needed in England to defend against the coming invasion.

He worked on his radio speech until the last minute, from six to nine that night, before settling himself in front of a BBC microphone.

"I speak to you for the first time as Prime Minister in a solemn hour for the life of our country," he began.

He explained how the Germans had broken through the French line, using a "remarkable" combination of aircraft and tanks. However, he said, the French had proven themselves in the past to be adept at raising counteroffensives, and this talent, in tandem with the power and skill of the British Army, could turn the situation around.

The speech set a pattern that he would follow throughout the war, offering a sober appraisal of facts, tempered with reason for optimism.

"It would be foolish to disguise the gravity of the hour," he said. "It would be still more foolish to lose heart and courage."

He left out completely any reference to the possibility, discussed just a few hours earlier with his War Cabinet, that Britain might withdraw the BEF from France.

Next he addressed his main reason for giving the speech: to warn his countrymen of what lay ahead. "After this battle in France abates its force there will come the battle for our Islands, for all that Britain is and all that Britain means," he said. "In that supreme emergency we shall not hesitate to take every step—even the most drastic—to call forth from our people the last ounce and inch of effort of which they are capable."

The speech terrified some listeners, but Churchill's apparent candor—at least on the threat of invasion, if not the true state of the French army—encouraged others, according to the Home Intelligence division of the Ministry of Information. The division went to great lengths to monitor public opinion and morale, publishing weekly reports that drew from more than one hundred sources, including postal and telephone censors, movie-theater managers, and the operators of bookstalls owned by W. H. Smith. After Churchill's broadcast, Home Intelligence conducted a lightning survey of listeners. "Of 150 house-to-house interviews in the London area," it reported, "approximately half said they were frightened and worried by the speech; the rest were 'heartened,' 'made more determined,' 'stiffened.'"

Now Churchill turned again to the agonizing decision about what to do with the hundreds of thousands of British soldiers in France. His inclination was to insist that they take the offensive and fight it out, but the time for such heroics seemed to have passed. The British Expeditionary Force was in full retreat toward the coast, pursued by Germany's armored divisions, which had given Hitler so lethal an advantage in his drive across Europe. The BEF faced the very real prospect of annihilation.

The Churchill who on Sunday had struck Colville as being unfazed was here supplanted by a prime minister who seemed deeply worried about the fate of the empire in his charge. Wrote Colville on Tuesday, May 21, "I have not seen Winston so depressed."

CHURCHILL RESOLVED, AGAINST THE advice of his chiefs of staff and others, to fly to Paris for a second meeting, this time in foul weather.

The visit achieved nothing, except to worry Clementine and daughter Mary. "It was terrible flying weather," Mary wrote in her diary, "and I was so anxious. The news is unbelievably bad—one can only hang on by praying it will come out all right."

SO TENSE WERE THINGS, so high the pressure on all, that members of Churchill's cabinet decided that he ought to have a personal physician, though the patient himself did not agree. The assignment fell to

Sir Charles Wilson, dean of the medical school at St. Mary's Hospital in London. A medical officer in the prior war, he had been awarded a Military Cross in 1916 for bravery in the Battle of the Somme.

Late in the morning on Friday, May 24, Wilson found himself at Admiralty House, being led upstairs to Churchill's bedroom. "I have become his doctor," Wilson wrote in his diary, "not because he wanted one, but because certain members of the Cabinet, who realized how essential he has become, have decided that somebody ought to keep an eye on his health."

It was almost noon by now, but as Wilson entered the room he found Churchill still in bed, seated upright against a bedrest, reading. Churchill did not look up.

Wilson walked to his bedside. Churchill still did not acknowledge his presence. He continued to read.

After a few moments—what to Wilson "seemed quite a long time"—Churchill lowered the document and with impatience said, "I don't know why they are making such a fuss. There's nothing wrong with me."

He resumed reading, with Wilson still at hand.

After another overlong interval, Churchill abruptly shoved away his bedrest, threw off his covers, and barked, "I suffer from dyspepsia"—indigestion, or what later generations would call heartburn—"and this is the treatment."

He launched into a breathing exercise.

Wilson watched. "His big white belly was moving up and down," he recalled later, "when there was a knock on the door, and the P.M. grabbed at the sheet as Mrs. Hill came into the room." This was Kathleen Hill, thirty-nine, his beloved personal secretary. She and her typewriter were ever present, whether Churchill was clothed or not.

"Soon after," Wilson wrote, "I took my leave. I do not like the job, and I do not think the arrangement can last."

FROM JOHN COLVILLE'S PERSPECTIVE, Churchill had no need for a doctor's attention. He seemed fit and was once again in good spirits, having shed his depression of several days earlier. Later that Friday, Colville arrived at Admiralty House to find Churchill "dressed in the most brilliant of flowery dressing-gowns and puffing a long cigar as he ascended from the Upper War Room to his bedroom."

He was about to take one of his daily baths, these prepared with precision—ninety-eight degrees Fahrenheit and two-thirds full—by his valet-butler Frank Sawyers, present at all hours ("the inevitable, egregious Sawyers," as Colville wrote). Churchill took two baths every day, his longtime habit, no matter where he was and regardless of the urgency of the events unfolding elsewhere, whether at the embassy in Paris during one of his meetings with French leaders or aboard his prime ministerial train, whose lavatory included a bathtub.

On this Friday, a number of important telephone calls demanded his attention during his bath hour. With Colville standing by, Churchill took each call, climbing naked from the tub and swathing himself with a towel.

Colville found this to be one of Churchill's most endearing traits—"his complete absence of personal vanity."

Colville witnessed scenes at Admiralty House and Downing Street unlike anything he had encountered while working for Chamberlain. Churchill would wander the halls wearing a red dressing gown, a helmet, and slippers with pom-poms. He was also given to wearing his sky-blue "siren suit," a one-piece outfit of his own design that could be pulled on at a moment's notice. His staff called it his "rompers." At times, according to his security officer, Inspector Thompson, the outfit made Churchill look "so pneumatic as to suggest he might at any moment rise from the floor and sail around over his own acres."

Colville was coming to like the man.

CHURCHILL'S EQUANIMITY WAS ALL the more remarkable given the news emerging that Friday from across the channel. To everyone's continued mystification, the great French army now seemed on the verge of final defeat. "The one firm rock on which everyone was willing to build for the last two years was the French army," wrote Foreign Secretary Halifax in his diary, "and the Germans walked through it like they did through the Poles."

That day, too, Churchill received a sobering document that dared contemplate this hitherto unthinkable outcome, still so beyond imagining that the authors of the report, the chiefs of staff, could not bring themselves to mention it in the title, calling their paper "British Strategy in a Certain Eventuality."

Moondread

———

"THE OBJECT OF THIS PAPER," THE REPORT BEGAN, "IS TO INVESTigate the means whereby we could continue to fight single-handed if French resistance were to collapse completely, involving the loss of a substantial proportion of the British Expeditionary Force, and the French Government were to make terms with Germany."

Labeled "MOST SECRET," it made for a frightening read. One of its fundamental assumptions was that the United States would provide "full economic and financial support." Without this, the report noted in italics, *"we do not think we could continue the war with any chance of success."* It forecast that only a fragment of the BEF could be evacuated from France.

The overriding fear was that if the French did capitulate, Hitler would turn his armies and air force against Britain. "Germany," the report said, "has ample forces to invade and occupy this country. Should the enemy succeed in establishing a force, with its vehicles, firmly ashore—the Army in the United Kingdom, which is very short of equipment, has not got the offensive power to drive it out."

Everything depended "on whether our fighter defenses will be able to reduce the scale of attack to reasonable bounds." Britain's energies were to be concentrated on the production of fighters, the training of crews, and defense of aircraft factories. "The crux of the whole problem is the air defence of this country."

If France fell, the report said, the task would be immeasurably more difficult. Previous plans for homeland defense were based on the assumption—the certainty—that the Luftwaffe would be flying from bases within Germany, and would thus have limited ability to penetrate deep into England. But now British strategists had to face the prospect of German fighters and bombers taking off from airfields along the French coast, just minutes from the English shore, and from bases in Belgium, Holland, Denmark, and Norway. These bases, the report said, would allow Germany "to concentrate a very heavy weight of long and short-range bomber attack over a large area of this country."

A central question was whether the British public would be able to endure what was sure to be a furious assault by the full force of Germany's air force. The morale of the country, the report warned, "will be subjected to a heavier strain than ever before." The authors, however, found reason to believe that the people's morale would hold, "if they realize—as they are beginning to do—that the existence of the Empire is at stake." It was time, the report said, "to inform the public of the true dangers that confront us."

London seemed certain to be Hitler's primary target. In a 1934 speech to the House of Commons, Churchill himself had called it "the greatest target in the world, a kind of tremendous, fat, valuable cow tied up to attract the beast of prey." After one cabinet meeting, Churchill led his ministers out to the street and with a grim half-smile told them, "Take a good look round. I expect all these buildings will look very different in two or three weeks' time."

EVEN THE REPORT from the chiefs of staff, gloomy as it was, did not envision the rapid and complete collapse already underway across the channel. With a German victory in France nearly certain, British intelligence now forecast that Germany might invade Britain immediately, without waiting for a formal French surrender. The British expected that an invasion would begin with a titanic onslaught by the German air force, potentially a "knock-out" blow—or, as Churchill called it, an aerial "banquet"—with as many as fourteen thousand aircraft darkening the sky.

British strategists believed that the Luftwaffe had four times as many aircraft as the RAF. Germany's three main bombers—the Junkers Ju 88, the Dornier Do 17, and the Heinkel He 111—carried bomb loads ranging from two thousand to eight thousand pounds, more than could have been imagined in the prior war. One aircraft was particularly fearsome, the Stuka, its name a contraction of the German word for dive-bomber: *Sturzkampfflugzeug*. The plane looked like a giant bent-wing insect and was equipped with an apparatus, the *Jericho-Trompete* ("Jericho trumpet"), that caused it to emit a terrifying shriek while diving. It could place bombs—up to five at a time—with far more precision than a standard aircraft, and had terrified Allied troops during Germany's blitzkrieg attacks.

As British planners saw it, Germany possessed the ability to bomb Britain to the point where it might have no other option but to surrender, an outcome contemplated long before by theorists of aerial warfare who saw "strategic bombing," or "terror bombing," as a means of subduing an enemy. Germany's bombing of Rotterdam had seemed to validate such thinking. The day after the Luftwaffe's attack, the Dutch surrendered, out of fear that other cities would be destroyed. Britain's ability to defend itself from this kind of campaign depended entirely on the nation's aircraft industries' capacity to produce fighter aircraft—Hurricanes and Spitfires—at a rate high enough not just to compensate for the fast-mounting losses but also to increase the overall number of planes available for combat. Fighters alone in no way could win the war, although Churchill believed that with enough aircraft, Britain might be able to hold Hitler at bay and stave off invasion long enough for the United States to enter the war.

But fighter production lagged. Britain's aircraft plants operated on a prewar schedule that did not take into account the new reality of having a hostile force based just across the channel. Production, though increasing, was suppressed by the fusty practices of a peacetime bureaucracy only now awakening to the realities of total war. Shortages of parts and materials disrupted production. Damaged aircraft accumulated as they awaited repair. Many nearly completed planes lacked engines and instruments. Vital parts were stored in far-flung locations, jealously guarded by feudal officials reserving them for their own future needs.

With all this in mind, Churchill, on his first day as prime minister, created an entirely new ministry devoted solely to the production of fighters and bombers, the Ministry of Aircraft Production. In Churchill's view, this new ministry was the only thing that could save Britain from defeat, and he was confident he knew just the man to run it: his longtime friend and occasional antagonist Max Aitken—Lord Beaverbrook—a man who drew controversy the way steeples draw lightning.

Churchill offered him the job that night, but Beaverbrook demurred. He had made his fortune in newspapers and knew nothing about running factories that manufactured products as complex as fighters and bombers. Moreover, his health was impaired. He was plagued by eye troubles and asthma, so much so that he devoted a room in his London mansion, Stornoway House, to asthma treatments and filled it with kettles to produce steam. Two weeks from turning sixty-one, he had pulled back from direct management of his newspaper empire and was intent on spending more time at his villa at Cap-d'Ail, on the southeast coast of France, though Hitler had killed this plan for the time being. Beaverbrook's secretaries were still composing draft letters of refusal when, on the evening of May 12, apparently on impulse, he accepted the post. He became minister of aircraft production two days later.

Churchill understood Beaverbrook, and knew on an instinctive level that he was the man to jolt awake the still-slumbering aircraft industry. He also understood that Beaverbrook could be difficult—*would* be difficult—and anticipated that he would spark conflict. But it did not matter. As one American visitor put it, "The PM, who has the most kindly feelings toward Beaverbrook, looked at him as an indulgent parent would to a small boy at a party who had said something not quite appropriate, but made no comment."

There was more to Churchill's decision, however. Churchill needed Beaverbrook's presence as a friend, to provide counsel on matters beyond aircraft production. Despite later hagiography, Churchill did not and frankly could not manage the staggering pressure of directing the war by himself. He relied heavily on others, even if sometimes these others merely served as an audience on whom he could test his thoughts and plans. Beaverbrook could be counted on for candor at all times, and to deliver advice without regard for politics or personal feelings. Where Pug Ismay was a calming and cooling influence, Beaverbrook was gasoline. He was also wildly entertaining, a trait that Churchill loved and needed. Ismay sat quietly, ready to offer advice and counsel; Beaverbrook enlivened every room he entered. On occasion he called himself Churchill's court jester.

Canadian by birth, Beaverbrook had moved to England before the previous war. In 1916, he bought the moribund *Daily Express,* and over time he grew its circulation sevenfold, to 2.5 million, cementing his reputation as an ingenious maverick. "Beaverbrook enjoyed being provocative," wrote Virginia Cowles, a prominent chronicler of life in wartime Britain who worked for Beaverbrook's *Evening Standard.* Complacency was as tempting a target to him "as a balloon to a small boy with a pin," Cowles remarked. Beaverbrook and Churchill had been friends for three decades, though the intimacy of their connection had tended to wax and wane.

To the many people who disliked Beaverbrook, his physical appearance seemed a metaphor for his personality. He stood five feet, nine inches—three inches taller than Churchill—with a broad upper body over narrow hips and slender legs. There was something about this combination, tied with his wide and wickedly gleeful smile, his overly large ears and nose, and a scattering of facial moles, that inclined people to describe him as smaller than he was, like some malignant elf from a fairy tale. American general Raymond Lee, stationed in London as an observer, called him "a violent, passionate, malicious and dangerous little goblin." Lord Halifax nicknamed him "the Toad." A few, behind his back, referred to him as "the Beaver." Clementine, in particular, nursed a deep mistrust of Beaverbrook. "My darling—" she wrote to Churchill. "Try ridding yourself of this microbe which some people fear is in your blood—exorcise this bottle imp and see if the air is not clearer and purer."

As a rule, however, women found Beaverbrook attractive. His wife, Gladys, died in 1927, and both during and after their marriage he conducted numerous affairs. He loved gossip, and thanks to his female friends and his network of reporters, he knew many of the secrets of London's uppermost strata. "Max never seems to tire of the shabby drama of some men's lives, their infidelities and their passions," wrote his doctor, Charles Wilson, now also Churchill's physician. One of Beaverbrook's most impassioned enemies, Minister of Labor Ernest Bevin, deployed a gritty analogy to describe the relationship between Churchill and Beaverbrook: "He's like a man who's married a whore: he knows she's a whore, but he loves her just the same."

Churchill saw the relationship in succinct terms. "Some take drugs," he said. "I take Max."

He recognized that by removing the responsibility for aircraft production from the long-established Air Ministry and giving it to Beaverbrook, he was laying the groundwork for a clash of territorial interests, but he failed to anticipate just how much outright bickering Beaverbrook would immediately generate and how great a source of exasperation this would become. The writer Evelyn Waugh, whose comic novel *Scoop* was thought by some to have been inspired by Beaverbrook (though Waugh denied it), once said that he found himself compelled to "believe in the Devil if only to account for the existence of Lord Beaverbrook."

The stakes were indeed high. "It was as dark a picture as any Britain has ever faced," wrote David Farrer, one of Beaverbrook's many secretaries.

BEAVERBROOK EMBRACED HIS NEW task with relish. He loved the idea of being at the center of power and loved, even more, the prospect of disrupting the lives of hidebound bureaucrats. He launched his new ministry from his own mansion and staffed its administrative side with employees pulled from his own newspapers. In a move unusual for the age, he also hired one of his editors to be his personal propaganda and public relations man. Intent on quickly transforming the aircraft industry, he recruited a collection of top business executives to be his senior lieutenants, including the general manager of a Ford Motor Company plant. He cared little about whether they had expertise with airplanes. "They are all captains of industry, and industry is like theology," Beaverbrook said. "If you know the rudiments of one faith you can grasp the meaning of another. For my part I would not hesitate to appoint the Moderator of the General Assembly of the Presbyterian Church to take over the duties of the Pope of Rome."

Beaverbrook convened key meetings in his downstairs library or, on fine days, outside on a balcony off his first-floor ballroom. His typists and secretaries worked upstairs wherever space permitted. The bathrooms had typewriters. Beds served as surfaces for arranging documents. No one left the premises for lunch; at the asking, food prepared by Beaverbrook's chef was delivered on trays. His own typical lunch was chicken, bread, and a pear.

All employees were expected to work the same hours he did, meaning twelve hours a day, seven days a week. He could be unrealistically demanding. One of his most senior men complained about how Beaverbrook gave him an assignment at two in the morning, then called back at eight A.M. to see how much had been accomplished. After a personal secretary, George Malcolm Thomson, took an unscheduled morning off, Beaverbrook left him a note: "Tell Thomson that Hitler will be here if he doesn't look out." Beaverbrook's valet, Albert Nockels, once countered his shouted command "For god's sake, hurry up" with the rejoinder "My lord, I am not a Spitfire."

No matter their value, fighters were still only defensive weapons. Churchill also wanted a steep increase in the production of bombers. He saw these as the only means currently at hand for bringing the war directly to Hitler. For the time being Churchill had to rely on the RAF's fleet of medium bombers, though two four-engine heavy bombers were nearing introduction, the Stirling and the Halifax (named for a town in Yorkshire, not for Lord Halifax), each with the capacity to carry up to fourteen thousand pounds of bombs well into Germany. Churchill acknowledged that Hitler was for the time being free to project his forces in whatever direction he wished, be it eastward or into Asia and Africa. "But there is one thing that will bring him back and bring him down," Churchill wrote in a minute to Beaverbrook, "and that is an absolutely devastating, exterminating attack by very heavy bombers from this country upon the Nazi homeland. We must be able to over-whelm them by this means, without which I do not see a way through."

In his own hand, Churchill added, "We cannot accept any lower aim than air mastery. When will it be obtained?"

Churchill's minister of aircraft production proceeded with the exuberance of an impresario, even designing a special flag for the radiator of his car, with "M.A.P." in red against a blue background. British aircraft plants began turning out fighters at a rate that no one, least of all German intelligence, could have foreseen, and under circumstances that factory managers had never imagined.

THE PROSPECT OF INVASION forced citizens at all levels of British society to contemplate exactly what invasion would mean, not as an abstraction but as something that could happen as you sat at your table reading the *Daily Express* or knelt in your garden pruning your rosebushes. Churchill was convinced that one of Hitler's first goals would be to kill him, with the expectation that whatever government replaced his would be more willing to negotiate. He insisted on keeping a Bren light machine gun in the trunk of his car, having vowed on numerous occasions that if the Germans came for him, he would take as many as possible with him to the grave. He often carried a revolver—and often misplaced it, according to Inspector Thompson. From time to time, Thompson recalled, Churchill would abruptly brandish his revolver and, "roguishly and with delight," exclaim: "You see, Thompson, they will never take me alive! I will get one or two before they can shoot me down."

But he was also ready for worse. According to one of his typists, Mrs. Hill, he embedded a capsule containing cyanide in the cap of his fountain pen.

Harold Nicolson, parliamentary secretary for the Ministry of Information, and his wife, writer Vita Sackville-West, began working out the nitty-gritty details of coping with an invasion, as if preparing for a winter storm. "You will have to get the Buick in a fit state to start with a full petrol-tank," Nicolson wrote. "You should put inside it some food for 24 hours, and pack in the back your jewels and my diaries. You will want clothes and anything else very precious, but the rest will have to be left behind." Vita lived at the couple's country home, Sissinghurst, just twenty miles from the Strait of Dover, the narrowest point between England and France and, thus, a likely pathway for amphibious assault. Nicolson recommended that when the invasion came, Vita should drive to Devonshire, five hours west. "This all sounds very alarming," he added, "but it would be foolish to pretend that the danger is inconceivable."

The lovely weather only heightened the anxiety. It seemed as though nature were conspiring with Hitler, delivering a nearly uninterrupted chain of fine, warm days with calm waters in the channel, ideal for the shallow-hulled barges Hitler would need to land tanks and artillery. Writer Rebecca West described the "unstained heaven of that perfect summer," when she and her husband walked in London's Regent's Park as barrage balloons—"silver elephantines"—drifted overhead. Five hundred and sixty-two of these giant oblong balloons were aloft over London, tethered by mile-long cables to block dive-bombers and keep fighters from descending low enough to strafe the city's streets. West recalled how people sat in chairs among the roses, staring straight ahead, their faces white with strain. "Some of them walked among the rose-beds, with a special earnestness looking down on the bright flowers and inhaling the scent, as if to say, 'That is what roses are like, that is how they smell. We must remember that, down in the darkness.'"

But even invasion fears could not wholly obliterate the sheer seductiveness of those late spring days. Anthony Eden, Churchill's new secretary of war—tall, handsome, and as recognizable as a film star—went for a walk in St. James's Park, sat on a bench, and took an hour-long nap.

WITH FRANCE IN PRECIPITOUS collapse, air raids over England seemed certain, and the moon became a source of dread. The first full moon of Churchill's premiership occurred on Tuesday, May 21, imparting to the streets of London the cool pallor of candle wax. The German raid on Rotterdam lingered as a reminder of what could very soon befall the city. So likely was this prospect that three days later, on Friday, May 24, with the moon still bright—a waning gibbous—Tom Harrisson, director of Mass-Observation's network of social observers, sent a special message to his many diarists: "In the case of air raids observers will not be expected to stand about . . . it will be entirely satisfactory if observers take shelter, so long as they are able to take shelter with *other people*. Preferably *with a lot of other people*."

The opportunity for observing human behavior at its most raw was just too perfect.

Göring

O N THAT FRIDAY, MAY 24, HITLER MADE TWO DECISIONS THAT would influence the duration and character of the coming war.

At noon, on the advice of a trusted senior general, Hitler ordered his armored divisions to halt their advance against the British Expeditionary Force. Hitler agreed with the general's recommendation that his tanks and crews be given a chance to regroup before a planned advance to the south. German forces already had sustained major losses in the so-called campaign in the west: 27,074 soldiers dead, 111,034 more wounded, and another 18,384 missing—a blow to the German public, who had been led to expect a brief, tidy war. The halt order, which gave the British a lifesaving pause, perplexed British and German commanders alike. The Luftwaffe's general field marshal Albert Kesselring later called it a "fatal error."

Kesselring was all the more surprised when suddenly the task of destroying the fleeing British force was assigned to him and his air fleet. Luftwaffe chief Hermann Göring had promised Hitler that his air force could destroy the BEF on its own—a promise that had little grounding in reality, Kesselring knew, especially given the exhaustion of his pilots and the spirited attacks by RAF pilots flying the latest Spitfires.

That same Friday, further swayed by Göring's belief in the near-magical power of his air force, Hitler issued Directive No. 13, one of a series of broad strategic orders he would issue throughout the war. "The task of the Air Force will be to break all enemy resistance on the part of the surrounded forces, to prevent the escape of the British forces across the Channel," the directive read. It authorized the Luftwaffe "to attack the English homeland in the fullest manner, as soon as sufficient forces are available."

GÖRING—LARGE, BUOYANT, RUTHLESS, CRUEL—HAD used his close connection to Hitler to win this commission, deploying the sheer strength of his ebullient and joyously corrupt personality to overcome Hitler's misgivings, at least for the time being. Although on paper Hitler's official number two man was Deputy Führer Rudolf Hess (not to be confused with Rudolf Hoess, who ran Auschwitz), Göring was his favorite. Göring had built the Luftwaffe from nothing into the most powerful air force in the world. "When I talk with Göring, it's like a bath in steel for me," Hitler told Nazi architect Albert Speer. "I feel fresh afterward. The Reich Marshal has a stimulating way of presenting things." Hitler did not feel this way toward his official deputy. "With Hess," Hitler said, "every conversation becomes an unbearably tormenting strain. He always comes to me with unpleasant matters and won't leave off." When the war began, Hitler chose Göring to be his primary successor, with Hess next in line.

In addition to the air force, Göring held enormous power over other realms within Germany, as evident in his many official titles: president of the Defense Council, commissioner for the Four-Year Plan, president of the Reichstag, prime minister of Prussia, and minister of forests and hunting, this last an acknowledgment of his personal love for medieval history. He had grown up on the grounds of a feudal castle that had turrets and walls with machicolations designed for the dispersion of stones and boiling oil onto any assailants below. According to one British intelligence report, "In his childhood games he always played the part of a robber knight or led the village boys in some imitation military manoeuvre." Göring held full control over German heavy industry. Another British assessment concluded that "this man of abnormal ruthlessness and energy now holds almost all the threads of power in Germany."

On the side, Göring ran a criminal empire of art dealers and thugs who provided him with a museum's worth of art that was either stolen or bought at coercively low prices, much of it considered "ownerless Jewish art" and confiscated from Jewish households—in all, fourteen hundred paintings, sculptures, and tapestries, including Van Gogh's *Bridge at Langlois in Arles* and works by Renoir, Botticelli, and Monet. The term "ownerless" was a Nazi designation applied to works of art left behind by fleeing and deported Jews. In the course of the war, while ostensibly traveling on Luftwaffe business, Göring would visit Paris twenty times, often aboard one of his four "special trains," to review and select works gathered by his agents at the Jeu de Paume, a museum in the Jardin des Tuileries. By the fall of 1942, he had acquired 596 works from this source alone. He displayed hundreds of his best pieces at Carinhall, his country home and, increasingly often, his headquarters, named for his first wife, Carin, who had died in 1931. Paintings hung on the walls, from floor to ceiling, in multiple tiers that emphasized not their beauty and worth but, rather, the acquisitiveness of their new owner. His demand for fine things, especially those rendered in gold, was fed as well by a kind of institutional larceny. Every year, his underlings were compelled to contribute money for the purchase of an expensive present for his birthday.

Göring designed Carinhall to evoke a medieval hunting lodge, and built it in an ancient forest forty-five miles north of Berlin. He also erected an immense mausoleum on the grounds for the body of his late wife, framed with large sarsen stones that evoked the sandstone blocks at Stonehenge. He married again, an actress named Emmy Sonnemann, on April 10, 1935, in a ceremony at Berlin Cathedral, attended by Hitler, as formations of Luftwaffe bombers flew overhead.

Göring also had a passion for extravagant sartorial display. He designed his own uniforms, the flashier the better, with medals and epaulettes and silver filigree, often changing clothes multiple times in the course of a day. He was known to wear more eccentric costumes as well, including tunics, togas, and sandals, which he accented by painting his toenails red and applying makeup to his cheeks. On his right hand he wore a large ring with six diamonds; on his left, an emerald said to be an inch square. He strode the grounds of Carinhall like an oversized Robin Hood, in a belted jacket of green leather, with a large hunting knife tucked into his belt, and carrying a staff. One German general reported being summoned for a meeting with Göring and finding him "sitting there dressed in the following way: a green silk shirt embroidered in gold, with gold thread running through it, and a large monocle. His hair had been dyed yellow, his eyebrows were penciled, his cheeks rouged— he was wearing violet silk stockings and black patent leather pumps. He was sitting there looking like a jellyfish."

To outside observers, Göring seemed to have a limited grip on sanity, but an American interrogator, General Carl Spaatz, would later write that Göring, "despite rumors to the contrary, is far from mentally deranged. In fact he must be considered a very 'shrewd customer,' a great actor and professional liar." The public loved him, forgiving his legendary excesses and coarse personality. The American correspondent William Shirer, in his diary, sought to explain this seeming paradox: "Where Hitler is distant, legendary, nebulous, an enigma as a human being, Göring is a salty, earthy, lusty man of flesh and blood. The Germans like him because they understand him. He has the faults and virtues of the average man, and the people admire him for both. He has a child's love for uniforms and medals. So have they."

Shirer detected no resentment among the public directed toward the "fantastic, medieval—and very expensive—personal life he leads. It is the sort of life they would lead themselves, perhaps, if they had the chance."

Göring was revered by the officers who served him—at first. "We swore by the *Führer* and worshipped Göring," wrote one bomber pilot, who attributed Göring's cachet to his performance in the prior war when he was a top ace, legendary for his courage. But some of his officers and pilots were now growing disenchanted. Behind his back they began calling him "the Fat One." One of his top fighter pilots, Adolf Galland, came to know him well and repeatedly clashed with him over tactics. Göring was easily influenced by a "small clique of sycophants," Galland said. "His court favorites changed frequently since his favor could only be won and held by means of constant flattery, intrigue and expensive gifts." More worrisome, in Galland's view, was that Göring seemed not to understand that aerial warfare had advanced radically since the prior war. "Göring was a man with almost no technical knowledge and no appreciation of the conditions under which modern fighter aircraft fought."

But Göring's worst error, according to Galland, was hiring a friend, Beppo Schmid, to head the Luftwaffe's intelligence arm, responsible for determining the day-to-day strength of the British air force—an appointment soon to have grave consequences. "Beppo Schmid," Galland said, "was a complete wash-out as intelligence officer, the most important job of all."

Nonetheless, Göring paid attention only to him. He trusted Schmid as a friend but, more importantly, reveled in the happy news that he seemed always ready to provide.

When Hitler turned to the daunting task of conquering Britain, naturally he came to Göring, and Göring was delighted. In the western campaign, it was the army, especially its armored divisions, that won all the honors, with the air force playing a secondary role, providing air support. Now the Luftwaffe would have its chance to achieve glory, and Göring had no doubt that it would prevail.

Sufficient Bliss

<hr />

A S FRANCE TOTTERED, AND GERMAN PLANES BATTERED BRITISH
and French forces massing at Dunkirk, private secretary John Colville
struggled with a long-standing and, for him, wrenching quandary. He
was in love.

The object of his adoration was Gay Margesson, a student at Oxford
and the daughter of David Margesson, the former appeaser whom Clementine Churchill had savaged over lunch. Two years earlier, Colville had
asked Gay to marry him, but she had declined, and ever since he had felt
both drawn to her and repelled by her unwillingness to return his affections. His disappointment made him look for, and find, faults in her
personality and behavior. This did not stop him, however, from trying
to see her as often as he could.

On Wednesday, May 22, he telephoned her to confirm arrangements
for the coming weekend, when he was to visit her at Oxford. She was
evasive. She told him first that there was no point in his coming because
she would be working, but then changed her story and told him that
there was something she planned to do that afternoon at college. He persuaded her to honor their plans, since they had arranged the visit weeks
earlier. She relented. "She did so with an ill-grace and I felt very hurt that
she [should] prefer some miserable undergraduate arrangement, which
she had made at Oxford, to seeing me," he wrote. "It is extraordinary to
be quite so inconsiderate about other people's feelings when one pretends
to be fond of them."

The weekend began on an optimistic note, however. He drove to Oxford on Saturday morning, through lovely spring weather suffused with

sunshine. But as he arrived, clouds filled the sky. After lunch at a pub, he and Gay drove to Clifton Hampden, a village south of Oxford on the Thames, and spent time lying in the grass, talking. Gay was depressed about the war and the horror that seemed certain to come. "Nevertheless we enjoyed ourselves," Colville wrote, "and for me it was sufficient bliss to be with her."

The next day they walked together in the grounds of Magdalen College and sat for a time talking, but the talk was dull. They went to her room. Nothing happened. She studied French; he took a nap. Later, they clashed over politics, Gay having recently declared herself a socialist. They strolled along the Isis (the name given to the Thames within the bounds of the city of Oxford), with its many punts and painted barges, until toward evening they found themselves at the Trout Inn—"the Trout," for short— a seventeenth-century pub beside the river. The sun emerged and the weather turned "glorious," Colville wrote, producing "a blue sky, a setting sun and enough clouds to make the sun still more effective."

They dined at a table with views of a waterfall, an old bridge, and an adjacent forest, then walked along a towpath as children played nearby and plovers called to one another. "There has never been a more beautiful setting in which to be happy," Colville wrote, "and I have never felt greater serenity or contentment."

Gay felt likewise. She told Colville that "happiness could only be attained if one lived for the moment."

This seemed promising. But then, upon returning to her room, Gay reiterated her decision that she and Colville would never marry. He promised to wait, in case she changed her mind. "She urged me not to be in love with her," he wrote, "but I told her that to have her as my wife was the greatest ambition I had, and that I could not give up crying for the moon, when the moon meant everything in life to me."

He spent Sunday night on a sofa in a cottage on the grounds of a nearby estate owned by the family of a sister-in-law, Joan.

IN LONDON THAT EVENING, May 26, just before seven P.M., Churchill ordered the start of Operation Dynamo, the evacuation of the British Expeditionary Force from the French coast.

IN BERLIN, HITLER DIRECTED his armored columns to resume their advance against the BEF, which now crowded the port city of Dunkirk.

His forces moved more tentatively than expected, content to let Göring's bombers and fighters finish the task at hand.

But Göring harbored a distorted perception of what by now was unfolding off the coast of Dunkirk, as British soldiers—nicknamed Tommies—prepared to evacuate.

"Only a few fishing boats are coming across," he said on Monday, May 27. "One hopes that the Tommies know how to swim."

The First Bombs

THE ESCAPE RIVETED THE WORLD. IN HIS DIARY, THE KING KEPT a daily count of how many men had gotten away. The Foreign Office sent Roosevelt detailed daily updates. Initially the Admiralty had expected that at best 45,000 men would escape; Churchill himself estimated a maximum of 50,000. The tally for the first day—just 7,700 men—seemed to suggest that both estimates were generous. The second day, Tuesday, May 28, was better, with 17,800 men evacuated, but still nowhere near the kind of volume Britain would need to reconstitute a viable army. Throughout, however, Churchill never flagged. Far from it. He seemed almost enthusiastic. He understood, however, that others did not share his positive outlook; this was underlined on that Tuesday when one member of his War Cabinet said the BEF's prospects looked "blacker than ever."

Recognizing that confidence and fearlessness were attitudes that could be adopted and taught by example, Churchill issued a directive to all ministers to put on a strong, positive front. "In these dark days the Prime Minister would be grateful if all his colleagues in the Government, as well as high officials, would maintain a high morale in their circles; not minimizing the gravity of events, but showing confidence in our ability and inflexible resolve to continue the war till we have broken the will of the enemy to bring all Europe under his domination."

Also that day, he sought to put to an end, once and for all, any thought of Britain seeking peace with Hitler. Speaking before twenty-five of his ministers, he told them what he knew about the impending debacle in France and conceded that even he had briefly considered negotiating a peace agreement. But now, he said: "I am convinced that every man of you would rise up and tear me down from my place if I were for one moment to contemplate parley or surrender. If this long island story of ours is to end at last, let it end only when each of us lies choking in his own blood upon the ground."

For a moment, there was stunned silence. Then, to a man, the ministers rose and mobbed him, slapping his back and shouting their approval. Churchill was startled, and relieved.

"He was quite magnificent," wrote one minister, Hugh Dalton. "The man, and the only man we have, for this hour."

Here, as in other speeches, Churchill demonstrated a striking trait: his knack for making people feel loftier, stronger, and, above all, more courageous. John Martin, one of his private secretaries, believed that he "gave forth a confidence and invincible will that called out everything that was brave and strong." Under his leadership, Martin wrote, Britons began to see themselves as "protagonists on a vaster scene and as champions of a high and invincible cause, for which the stars in their courses were fighting."

He did this on a more intimate level as well. Inspector Thompson recalled one summer evening at Chartwell, Churchill's home in Kent, when Churchill was dictating notes to a secretary. At some point he opened a window to admit the cooling country breeze, and in flew a large bat, which began wildly careening through the room, now and then diving at the secretary. She was terrified; Churchill was oblivious. At length he noticed her convulsive ducking and asked if something was wrong. She pointed out the fact that the bat—"a large and extremely hostile bat," Thompson wrote—was in the room.

"Surely you're not afraid of a bat, are you?" Churchill asked.

She was indeed afraid.

"I'll protect you," he said. "Get on with your work."

THE EVACUATION FROM DUNKIRK proved successful beyond imagining, aided by Hitler's pause order and by bad weather over the channel, which thwarted the Luftwaffe. The Tommies did not, after all, have to swim. In the end, 887 vessels carried out the Dunkirk evacuation, of which only a quarter belonged to the Royal Navy. Another 91 were passenger ships, the rest an armada of fishing boats, yachts, and other small craft. In all, 338,226 men got away, including 125,000 French soldiers. Another 120,000 British soldiers still remained in France, including John

Colville's older brother Philip, but were making their way toward evacuation points elsewhere on the coast.

As successful as it was, the evacuation of the BEF was nonetheless deeply frustrating for Churchill. He was desperate to take the offensive. "How wonderful it would be if the Germans could be made to wonder where they were going to be struck next instead of forcing us to try to wall in the Island and roof it over," he wrote to Pug Ismay, his military chief of staff. "An effort must be made to shake off the mental and moral prostration to the will and initiative of the enemy from which we suffer."

It can be no accident that in the midst of the evacuation, Churchill began adding red adhesive labels exhorting "ACTION THIS DAY" to any minute or directive requiring an immediate response. These labels, wrote secretary Martin, "were treated with respect: it was known that such demands from the summit could not be ignored."

On June 4, the last day of the evacuation, in an address to the House of Commons, Churchill again turned to oratory, this time to bolster the empire as a whole. First he applauded the success at Dunkirk, though he added a sober reminder: "Wars are not won by evacuations."

As he neared the conclusion of the speech, he fired his boilers. "We shall go on to the end," he said, in a crescendo of ferocity and confidence. "We shall fight in France, we shall fight on the seas and oceans, we shall fight with growing confidence and growing strength in the air, we shall defend our island, whatever the cost may be. We shall fight on the beaches, we shall fight on the landing grounds, we shall fight in the fields and in the streets, we shall fight in the hills; we shall never surrender—"

As the House roared its approval, Churchill muttered to a colleague, "And . . . we will fight them with the butt end of broken bottles, because that's bloody well all we've got."

His daughter Mary, who sat in the gallery that day, beside Clementine, found the speech breathtaking. "It was now that my love and admiration for my father became enhanced by an increasing element of hero-worship," she wrote. One young navy man, Ludovic Kennedy, later to achieve fame as a journalist and broadcaster, recalled how "when we heard it, we knew in an instant, that everything would be all right."

Harold Nicolson wrote to his wife, Vita Sackville-West, "I feel so much in the spirit of Winston's great speech that I could face a world of enemies." Not, however, to the extent that he abandoned his plan for suicide. He and Vita planned to acquire some form of poison and— borrowing a phrase from *Hamlet*—a "bare bodkin" with which to administer it. He instructed her to keep her bodkin close at hand, "so that you can take your quietus when necessary. I shall have one also. I am not in the least afraid of such sudden and honorable death. What I dread is being tortured and humiliated."

As stirring as Churchill's speech was, it did not win the whole-hearted approval of all. Clementine noted that "a great section of the Tory Party"—the Conservative Party—did not react with enthusiasm, and that some even met the speech with "sullen silence." David Lloyd George, a former prime minister and current Liberal member of Parliament, called the reception "very half-hearted." The next day, Home Intelligence reported that only two newspapers "gave Churchill's speech headline value" and that the speech had done little to fortify the public. "The final evacuation of the BEF has brought with it a certain feeling of depression," the office noted. "There is a deflation of tension without a corresponding increase in resolve." The report found, further, that "some apprehension has been caused throughout the country on account of the PM's reference to 'fighting alone.' This has led to some slight increase in doubt about the intentions of our ally"—meaning France.

One diarist for Mass-Observation, Evelyn Saunders, wrote, "Churchill's speech yesterday hasn't raised my spirits yet, I still feel sick through me."

But the audience Churchill had mainly in mind when he'd crafted his speech was, once again, America, and there it was viewed as an unequivocal success, as might be expected, since the hills and beaches to be fought upon were four thousand miles away. Though he never mentioned America directly, Churchill intended that his speech communicate to Roosevelt and Congress that whatever the setback of Dunkirk, and regardless of what France did next, Britain was wholly committed to victory.

The speech also sent a signal to Hitler, reiterating Churchill's resolve to fight on. Whether the speech had anything to do with it or not, the next day, Wednesday, June 5, German aircraft began bombing targets on the British mainland for the first time—deploying a few bombers, accompanied by clouds of fighters. This raid, and others that immediately followed, perplexed RAF commanders. The Luftwaffe lost aircraft and men largely in vain. In the course of one night's raids, bombs fell onto pastures and forests around Devon, Cornwall, Gloucestershire, and elsewhere, doing little damage.

The RAF presumed these to be practice raids meant to test Britain's defenses in preparation for the invasion to come. Hitler, as feared, seemed now to have turned his gaze toward the British Isles.

Mirror Image

———

ONE THING CHURCHILL DID NOT ADDRESS IN HIS SPEECH WAS an underappreciated element of the Dunkirk evacuation. To those who cared to look, the fact that more than three hundred thousand men had managed to cross the channel in the face of concerted aerial and ground attack carried a darker lesson. It suggested that deterring a massive German invasion force might be more difficult than British commanders had assumed, especially if that force, like the evacuation fleet at Dunkirk, was composed of many hundreds of small ships, barges, and speedboats.

Wrote General Edmund Ironside, commander of Britain's Home Forces, "It brings me to the fact that the Bosches may equally well be able to land men in England despite [RAF] bombing."

He feared, in effect, a reverse Dunkirk.

Apparition

M ONDAY, JUNE 10, FOUND CHURCHILL IN A FOUL MOOD, ONE of those rare times when the war eroded his outward buoyancy. Italy had declared war on Britain and France, drawing from him a minatory quip: "People who go to Italy to look at ruins won't have to go as far as Naples and Pompeii in future."

This and the situation in France combined to make No. 10 Downing Street a stormy place. "He was in a very bad temper," wrote Jock Colville, "snapped almost everybody's head off, wrote angry minutes to the First Sea Lord, and refused to pay any attention to messages given him orally." When Churchill was in such a mood, it was usually the person nearest at hand who caught the brunt of it, and that person was often his loyal and long-suffering detective, Inspector Thompson. "He would turn on any handy person and let off steam," Thompson recalled. "Because I was *always* handy, I got a good many of these scaldings. Nothing I seemed to do appeared correct in his eyes. I bored him. The necessity of my job bored him. My everlasting ubiquity must have bored him to death. It even bored me." Churchill's sniping at times disheartened Thompson, and made him feel a failure. "I kept wishing somebody would attack him so I could shoot the attacker," he wrote.

It was also the case, however, that Churchill's hostile moods faded quickly. He would never apologize, but he managed to communicate through other means that the storm had passed. "He has been accused of being bad-tempered," explained Lord Beaverbrook, who, as minister of aircraft production, was himself often a target of Churchill's ire. "It isn't true. He could get very emotional, but after bitterly criticizing you he had a habit of touching you, of putting his hand on your hand—like that—as if to say that his real feelings for you were not changed. A wonderful display of humanity."

The weather did not help. In a departure from the long stretch of warmth and sun, the day was dark, eerily so. "Pitch dark," wrote Alexander Cadogan, undersecretary of state for foreign affairs, Britain's senior diplomat, a prominent diarist of the era. Another diarist, Olivia Cockett, a clerk with Scotland Yard and a prolific member of the Mass-Observation panel, wrote: "The black heavy clouds continue all day, though no rain falls, and they are the chief subject of conversation. Rather touchy moods all round." She overheard someone say, "The day Christ was crucified it came dark like this, something terrible will happen."

Churchill's main preoccupation was France. It irked him that, despite his several trips to France, he remained powerless to influence events and to ignite a French resurgence. Paris was expected to fall within forty-eight hours, and the French seemed certain to capitulate. He had not yet given up, however. He still believed that with his presence, his encouragement, perhaps some stirring remark or pledge, he might be able to revive the French corpse. He got the chance on Tuesday, June 11, when Prime Minister Reynaud summoned him again, this time to Briare, a small town on the Loire a hundred miles south of Paris. The conference sparked nothing; it merely underscored how bad things had gotten. Hoping to rouse the prime minister, Churchill, in a rush of bad French and good English, vowed to fight on no matter what, alone if necessary— "on and on and on, *toujours,* all the time, everywhere, *partout, pas de grâce,* no mercy. *Puis la victoire!*"

The French were unmoved.

The meeting did succeed, however, in searing into the minds of several French officers a singular image: that of Churchill, angered by the French failure to prepare his afternoon bath, bursting through a set of double doors wearing a red kimono and a white belt, exclaiming, *"Uh ay ma bain?"*—his French version of the question "Where is my bath?" One witness reported that in his fury he looked like "an angry Japanese genie."

So disconsolate were the French, and clearly so close to giving up, that Churchill renewed his determination not to send RAF fighters to help. He told the French he was not being selfish, merely prudent; that only the fighter force could stop the expected assault against Britain. "We grieve that we cannot help more," he said, "but we cannot."

FOR JOCK COLVILLE, THERE was personal anxiety as well. He knew that many of the British soldiers still in France were being evacuated from Cherbourg, and he hoped his brother Philip was among them. Some of Philip's luggage had arrived in London, a hopeful sign, but much danger remained.

With both of his brothers in the war, and so many of his peers, Colville now decided that he, too, needed to join the fight. He believed that the best path lay through the Royal Navy, and he told this to his immediate boss, Eric Seal, Churchill's senior private secretary. Seal promised to help, but found he could do nothing. A lot of young men throughout Whitehall had the same aspirations as Colville, including many in the diplomatic service, and this had become a problem. For the time being, at least, the Foreign Office was refusing to release any of its young men for military duty. Colville resolved to keep trying.

ON WEDNESDAY, JUNE 12, as Churchill and his party concluded their meetings in France, U.S. ambassador Joseph Kennedy sent a confidential cable to his chief, Secretary of State Cordell Hull, offering another jaundiced appraisal of Britain's prospects. The empire's preparedness was, he related, "appallingly weak" relative to Germany's great strength. "Pitiful," he wrote. All Britain possessed was courage. What kept Churchill going, Kennedy stated, was his belief that the United States would enter the war soon after the upcoming presidential election, on November 5, in which Roosevelt seemed increasingly likely to run. Churchill, he wrote, believed "that when the people in the United States see the towns and cities of England, after which so many American cities and towns have been named, bombed and destroyed they will line up and want war."

Kennedy cited a report from a British correspondent in America who had written that all that was needed was "an 'incident' to bring the United States in." Kennedy found this alarming. "If that were all that were needed, desperate people will do desperate things," he warned.

THERE WAS FORBIDDING NEWS from another quarter. That Wednesday morning, June 12, Churchill's newly appointed personal scientific adviser, Frederick Lindemann, known universally as the Prof, convened a meeting with a young scientist from the intelligence branch of the Air Ministry, Dr. Reginald V. Jones, a former student of his who now, at the age of twenty-eight, had the lofty title of deputy director of intelligence research.

The meeting was supposed to focus on whether Germany had succeeded in developing and deploying its own radar system, something the British had done before the war and now used to great, and secret, advantage, with a network of coastal towers—the "Chain Home" stations— that gave accurate advance warning of the approach of German aircraft. The meeting, however, soon veered in another direction, to reveal a terrifying prospect: a technological advance that, if real, would give Germany a huge advantage in the air war.

Part Two

—

A CERTAIN
EVENTUALITY

June – August

The Mystery of Swan Castle

—

THE PROF—LINDEMANN—LISTENED WITH GROWING SKEPTICISM. What Dr. Jones, the young air force intelligence man, was now proposing went against all that physicists understood about the propagation of radio waves over long distances. The bits of intelligence Jones presented were compelling, but they surely meant something other than what Jones imagined.

It was the Prof's job to assess the world with scientific objectivity. Fifty-four years old, an Oxford physicist, he was one of the first men Churchill had brought into his ministry, in accord with the prime minister's belief that in this new war, advances in technology would play an important role. This had already proved the case with radar, a happy by-product of far less successful research into the feasibility of creating a "death ray" capable of destroying aircraft outright. Likewise, the British were becoming adept at intercepting and decrypting Luftwaffe communications, these processed at Bletchley Park, the ultrasecret home of the Government Code and Cypher School, where codebreakers had cracked the secrets of the German "Enigma" encryption machine.

Lindemann had previously run an Admiralty office established to provide Churchill, as first lord, with as rich a grasp as possible of the day-to-day readiness of the Royal Navy. Immediately after becoming prime minister, Churchill put Lindemann in charge of a successor bureau with a much broader purview, the Prime Minister's Statistical Department, and made him his special scientific adviser, with the formal title of personal assistant to the prime minister. Together the two roles gave Lindemann license to explore any scientific, technical, or economic matter that might influence the progress of the war, a compelling mandate but one certain to ignite jealousy within the ministerial fiefdoms of Whitehall.

What further complicated things was Lindemann himself, whose main achievement, according to foreign-affairs undersecretary Cadogan, "was to unite against him any body of men with whom he came in contact."

He was a tall, pale man, given to wearing stiff-fronted "boiled" shirts, rigid collars, and ties knotted to a wasp's waist at his neck. His pallor matched the gray of his suits. He always wore an immense black bowler and an overcoat with a velvet collar, and carried an umbrella. His expression was invariably one of contemptuous appraisal, this imparted by lips perpetually turned down at the ends. He seemed ageless—or, rather, always aged, recalled Lady Juliet Townsend, daughter of Lord Birkenhead, a close friend of Lindemann's and his eventual biographer. "I think he was probably one of those people who got to look quite old quite early on," she said, "and then just went on looking the same for twenty years." It was Townsend who as a child assigned Lindemann the nickname "Prof." Whether one called him Prof or *the* Prof was a matter of personal preference.

Contradiction defined Lindemann. He hated black people, and yet for years played tennis with a doubles partner who was West Indian. He disliked Jews, on one occasion describing a fellow physicist as a "d-dirty l-little Jew," yet counted Albert Einstein as a friend and, during Hitler's rise, helped Jewish physicists escape Germany. He was binary in his affections. His friends could do no wrong, his enemies no right. Once crossed, he remained so, for life. "His memory," wrote John Colville, "was not just comprehensive; in recording past slights it was elephantine."

And yet by all counts, women and children loved him. He was a favorite of Churchill's family and never forgot a birthday. He was beloved in particular by Clementine, who had little affection for most of the ministers and generals with whom Churchill associated. Lindemann's outward austerity masked an inner sensitivity to public perception sufficiently profound that he would never wear a wristwatch, for fear it looked unmanly. He was assiduous about keeping secret the pet name his parents had given him as a child: Peach.

He had to be the best at whatever he pursued and played tennis at a nearly professional level, once even competing in a doubles match at Wimbledon. He often played with Clementine but never exhibited any outward sense of joy, according to his sister, Linda. He seemed always to be fighting some interior battle: "Peach at luncheon shining with quite appalling general knowledge which made all conversation a nightmare of pitfalls. Peach determinedly playing chess, playing tennis, playing the piano. Poor Peach, never really playing at all."

Through an accident of timing that Lindemann attributed to the selfishness of his mother, he was born not in Britain but in Germany, at the spa town of Baden-Baden, on April 5, 1886. "The fact that she knew her time was drawing near and yet chose to give birth to him on German territory was a source of life-long annoyance to Lindemann," wrote Lord Birkenhead. Lindemann saw himself as anything but German and, in fact, loathed Germany, yet because of his birthplace found himself during the past war, and now again during the new one, the target of suspicions as to his national allegiance. Even Colville noted, early on, "His foreign connections are fishy."

Lindemann's mother had another lasting influence that later shaped how people viewed him. It was she who, while he was a child, placed him and his siblings on a strict vegetarian diet. She and the rest soon abandoned the regimen; he alone held to it, and with a vengeful obstinance. Day after day, he consumed enormous quantities of egg whites (never the yolks) and mayonnaise made from olive oil. He also had a sweet tooth of the first magnitude, with a special passion for filled chocolates, in particular Fuller's chocolate creams. By his own careful measure, he consumed up to two hundred grams of sugar a day, equivalent to forty-eight teaspoons.

Lindemann and Churchill first met in the summer of 1921, at a dinner in London, and over time became friends. In 1932, they toured Germany together to visit battlefields fought upon by Churchill's ancestor the Duke of Marlborough, about whom Churchill was then writing a biography. While tooling around the countryside in the Prof's Rolls-Royce (he had inherited great wealth upon the death of his father), they became aware of an undercurrent of bellicose nationalism. Alarmed, they began working together to collect as much information as possible about the rise of militarism in Hitler's Germany, and to awaken Britain to the coming danger. Churchill's home became a kind of intelligence center for amassing inside information about Germany.

Lindemann felt a professional kinship with Churchill. He saw him as a man who should have been a scientist but had missed his vocation. Churchill, in turn, marveled at Lindemann's ability to recall details and to distill complex subjects to their fundamental elements. He often described the Prof as having a "beautiful brain."

LINDEMANN'S MEETING WITH Dr. Jones began, as planned, with the question of whether Germany had mastered the art of detecting aircraft using radio waves. Jones was certain the Germans had done so, and cited intelligence to support his view. As the meeting came to a close, Jones changed the subject. Something had happened earlier that day that troubled him. A colleague, Group Captain L. F. Blandy, head of the RAF unit responsible for listening in on German radio transmissions, had given Jones a copy of a Luftwaffe message deciphered at Bletchley Park.

"Does this mean anything to you?" Blandy had asked. "It doesn't seem to mean much to anybody here."

The message was brief, and included a geographic position rendered in latitude and longitude, along with what appeared to be two German nouns, *Cleves* and *Knickebein*. As best Jones could make out, the message, translated, said: "*Cleves Knickebein* is confirmed [or established] at position 53° 24' north and 1° west."

Jones was startled. The message, he told Blandy, meant *everything* to him.

It fit into a mosaic that lay partially completed at the back of his mind, consisting of fragments of intelligence that had drawn his attention over the preceding months. He had seen the word *Knickebein* once before, on a piece of paper found in the wreckage of a German bomber downed in March 1940; it bore the phrase "Radio Beacon *Knickebein*." More recently, after the RAF's Air Intelligence Branch had made it routine practice to eavesdrop on conversations between prisoners, he had listened to a recording of two captured German fliers discussing what seemed to be a secret wireless navigation system.

And then came this latest message. Jones knew that *Knickebein* in English meant "crooked leg" or "dog's leg," and he believed that *Cleves* most likely referred to a town in Germany, known also by the spelling Kleve. The town had a famous castle, Schwanenburg, or Swan Castle, where supposedly Anne of Cleves resided before heading to England to become the fourth wife of Henry VIII. Swan Castle and the legend of the knight Lohengrin were thought to have influenced Wagner in his creation of the famed opera that bears the knight's name.

Suddenly the pieces fit together in a way that made sense to Jones, though what he concluded seemed improbable. He was twenty-eight years old. If wrong, he would seem a fool. But if he was right, his discovery could save untold numbers of lives.

He knew that the geographic coordinates cited in the newly intercepted message identified a point south of the town of Retford, in England's industrial Midlands. A line drawn from Cleves to Retford would delineate a vector, possibly an aircraft's course or radio transmission—a beam or beacon—as evinced by the phrase "Radio Beacon *Knickebein*." The term "crooked leg" suggested an intersection of some kind and, by Jones's reckoning, raised the possibility that a second beam might intersect the first. This would have the effect of marking a precise geographic location on the ground, perhaps a city or even an individual factory. A technology already existed to guide commercial and military aircraft using radio beams, but only over short distances, to help them land in conditions of limited visibility. Known as the Lorenz blind-landing system, after its inventor, C. Lorenz AG of Germany, the technology was familiar to both sides, and was in use at airports and military airfields in Britain and Germany. It struck Jones that the Luftwaffe might have found a way to project a Lorenz-like beam all the way across the channel to targets in Britain.

The prospect was deeply troubling. As things stood now, bomber pilots flying at night needed clear skies and moonlight if they hoped to achieve any degree of accuracy. With a system of the kind Jones imagined, German bombers could range over Britain on any night, without having to wait for a full moon or its brightest waxing and waning phases, even in weather that would keep RAF fighters grounded. The RAF was confident that it could counter air raids conducted by day, but at night its fighters had little ability to find and engage enemy aircraft, despite Britain's radar network. Combat required visual contact, and ground radar simply was not precise enough to bring RAF pilots close enough to afford it. By the time the pilots received radar fixes from controllers at Fighter Command, the German bombers would already be in a different location, possibly at new altitudes and on different headings.

Now, at his morning meeting with the Prof, Jones laid out his theory. He was excited, certain that he had stumbled on a secret new German technology. But Lindemann—pallid, ascetic, lips turned down, as always—told him that what he proposed was impossible. Conventional blind-landing beams traveled only in straight lines, meaning that, owing to the curvature of the earth, by the time a beam from Germany traveled the needed two hundred or more miles to the skies above a given target in England, it would be beyond the reach of even the highest-flying bomber. This was accepted doctrine. And Lindemann, once convinced of a thing, was a very hard man to bend. As one close associate, Roy Harrod, put it, "I have never met anyone who, when once he was convinced by his own reasonings, was so deeply and unshakably convinced."

Discouraged but not yet vanquished, Jones returned to his office to consider his next move. He arranged a second meeting with Lindemann for the next day.

AT ELEVEN O'CLOCK ON Thursday morning, Churchill again took off for France, for what would prove to be his last face-to-face meeting with French leaders. He brought Pug Ismay, Halifax, Cadogan, and Major General Edward Spears, the British liaison to the French army, and this time even Lord Beaverbrook, once again putting at risk a significant portion of Britain's government. The airfield to which they were headed, at Tours, had been bombed just the night before. For Mary Churchill and her mother, the flight meant another day of anxiety. "I do hate it when he goes," Mary wrote in her diary. "We all have a ghastly premonition that the French are going to give in. O God! France can't do it! She must go on—she must go on."

The field was deserted and desolate, cratered from the night's raid. French fliers lazed among the hangars, showing little interest in the new arrivals. Churchill walked up to a group of airmen and introduced himself, in awful French, as Britain's prime minister. They gave him a small touring car—hard for Churchill to fit into, let alone Halifax, who was six feet five inches tall. Thus crammed into the car, like characters in a slapstick movie, they set off for the local *préfecture,* which housed local representatives of the national government. Here they found just two officials, French prime minister Reynaud and his undersecretary for foreign affairs, Paul Baudouin. Reynaud sat behind a desk; Churchill chose a deep armchair and nearly disappeared from view.

Unlike at the previous meeting in Briare, Churchill made no effort to appear affable. He looked "extremely stern and concentrated," wrote General Spears. Pug Ismay, no longer the lovable human canine, also wore a severe expression. Beaverbrook jingled coins in his pocket, "as if feeling for a coin with which to tip someone," Spears observed. His face was flushed, his hair—what little he had—wild. "His round head looked like a cannon-ball that might be projected at any moment at Reynaud by the powerful spring his small, tense body provided."

The French were clearly bent on surrender and seemed impatient to get the meeting over with. At this point, Reynaud said, everything depended on what the United States would do. He planned to cable Roosevelt immediately. "For the moment," he noted, "the only move open to us is to put the situation to the American President with the greatest frankness."

Churchill promised to do likewise, then asked for a moment alone with his colleagues. *"Dans le jardin!"* he commanded. They retreated to a bleak rectangular garden lined with a narrow path, and marched in repeated circuits. "I believe that everyone was too stunned to speak," Spears wrote. "I certainly was."

Abruptly, Beaverbrook broke the silence. All they could do now, he said, was wait for Roosevelt's response. Fearing that Churchill might rashly promise anew to dispatch squadrons of RAF fighters, Beaverbrook urged him not to make any last-minute pledges. "We are doing no good here," he said. "In fact, listening to these declarations of Reynaud's only does harm. Let's get along home."

They returned to England at dusk.

FOR HIS SECOND MEETING with the Prof, young Dr. Jones came more heavily armed. Jones knew that Britain's top radio-wave expert, Thomas L. Eckersley, a veteran research engineer with the Marconi Company, had once written a short paper in which he'd calculated that a very narrow beam might indeed bend with the curvature of the earth and, therefore, could be marshaled to guide a bomber from Germany to Britain. Now Jones brought along Eckersley's paper, as well as some new bits of intelligence.

By way of further preparation, Jones had contacted a friend and colleague, Group Captain Samuel Denys Felkin, in charge of interrogating Luftwaffe crew members. Jones knew that bombers shot down in recent days had yielded new prisoners for interrogation, so he had asked Felkin to include questions focused specifically on beam-guidance technology.

Felkin did so, but the direct questions yielded nothing new. Felkin, however, had developed an effective new way of harvesting intelligence from prisoners. After an interrogation session, he would reunite the subject with his fellow airmen, then eavesdrop via hidden microphones as they discussed the interview and the questions asked. Felkin returned one of the new prisoners to his cell and listened in as he told a cellmate that no matter how hard the RAF looked, they would never find "the equipment."

Which, of course, piqued Jones's curiosity. The prisoner's remark provided oblique confirmation that Jones was on the right track. It also suggested that the device might in fact be hidden in plain sight.

Jones immediately requested a copy of a technical report made after British investigators had examined a bomber shot down the previous fall, the same kind of bomber in which the prisoner had flown. Jones focused on its radio equipment. One instrument caught his attention: a device identified in the report as a blind-landing receiver. This in itself was not surprising, since all German bombers were equipped with standard Lorenz landing systems. The report showed that the equipment had been closely examined by an engineer at the Royal Aircraft Factory, an experimental aviation unit.

Jones called him.

"Tell me," he said, "is there anything unusual about the blind landing receiver?"

The engineer said no, then qualified his answer. "But now you mention it," he said, "it is much more sensitive than they would ever need for blind landing."

The device could be tuned to particular frequencies, which, Jones reasoned, must be the ranges at which the new beam system operated—provided, of course, that his hunch was correct.

As inclined as Lindemann was to stand his ground, he was also receptive to cool scientific logic. It was one thing to listen to a twenty-eight-year-old scientist propose the existence of a secret new German guidance technology, working from a few pieces of circumstantial evidence, but quite another to see in clear, hard numbers the calculations of a leading expert purporting to prove that the underlying radio physics could permit the creation of such a system. And the new evidence Jones had collected was compelling.

Lindemann now recognized that if the Luftwaffe had managed to harness this new technology, it was indeed a fearsome development. Jones believed the beam could place an aircraft within four hundred yards of a target, a startling degree of precision.

Leveraging the power of his direct connection to Churchill, Lindemann that day composed an urgent minute for delivery direct to the prime minister. It was this intimate Rasputin-like link that raised so much suspicion and jealousy among Lindemann's peers. With his exalted new mandate, anything and everything now came within his purview. He could probe the most remote corners of government and question whatever he wished, even propose new weapons and weigh in on military strategy and, in so doing, upset the lives of bureaucrats both lofty and low. "He was as obstinate as a mule, and unwilling to admit that there was any problem under the sun which he was not qualified to solve," recalled Pug Ismay. "He would write a memorandum on high strategy on one day, and a thesis on egg production on the next." Notes and minutes flew from Lindemann's office—more than 250 by year's end—on such diverse subjects as nitroglycerin, timber supplies, and secret anti-aircraft weapons. These often prompted Churchill to demand some new action from his various ministers, thereby disrupting their already pressured lives. One never knew during a meeting whether Churchill, forearmed by Lindemann, would suddenly flourish a statistical rapier that would eviscerate a demand or argument—or whether Lindemann himself, with his quiet, raspy voice, would conduct the evisceration. As Lindemann grew more comfortable in the job, he would append to his notes a draft of a minute for Churchill to initial, written in a voice approximating Churchill's, careful to mask his own role in the process.

But this was what Churchill wanted from Lindemann: to challenge the orthodox, the tried-and-true, and thereby spark greater efficiency. The Prof delighted in coming up with ideas that turned conventional beliefs upside down. Once, as he was walking with a colleague, Donald MacDougall, he saw a poster that admonished, "Stop that dripping tap," an exhortation meant to conserve water and thereby save the coal that fueled the water-distribution system. As he walked, the Prof began calculating the costs in energy, wood pulp, and shipping needed to produce the paper for the posters. "And of course," MacDougall recalled, "Prof was right in his initial suspicions that it all added up to enormously more than was going to be saved by the posters' advice being followed."

In his minute to Churchill about Dr. Jones's apparent discovery, Lindemann kept his tone dispassionate. "There seems some reason to suppose that the Germans have some type of radio device with which they hope to find their targets," he wrote. The exact nature of the technology was unclear, but might, he hypothesized, involve some kind of beam, or possibly radio beacons installed in Britain by spies. Regardless, Lindemann wrote, "it is vital to investigate and especially to discover what the wave-length is. If we knew this we could devise means to mislead them."

He asked Churchill's permission to "take this up with the Air Ministry and try and stimulate action."

Churchill took the information seriously from the first, later recalling that he received the news as a "painful shock." He forwarded the Prof's minute to Air Ministry chief Archibald Sinclair, with a handwritten note: "This seems most intriguing and I hope you will have it thoroughly examined."

Coming from Churchill, this was like being prodded with a whip. Sinclair acted immediately, though grudgingly, and appointed a senior Air Ministry official to investigate Jones's theory.

NOW CAME MOVING DAY for the Churchills. On Friday, June 14, with deposed prime minister Chamberlain having at last left No. 10, the Churchills began transferring their belongings from Admiralty House into their new residential quarters. Clementine directed the operation.

Moving in any era was a stressful affair, but the strain certainly was amplified by the fact that France was about to fall and invasion loomed. Clementine, however, seemed to weather it well, as her friend Violet Bonham Carter (the once-suspected rival) found when she stopped at Admiralty House for tea just a few days before the move. The house was still fully decorated and furnished. "It was looking cool & delicious— full of flowers—& all their lovely pictures lit up," she wrote in her diary on June 11. "Clemmie was absolutely her normal self—chirrupy—very sweet—& always a little more amusing than one expects to find her."

The move took several days, during which Mary and Clementine stayed at the Carlton Hotel, also the Prof's temporary residence. Choosing to avoid domestic chaos, Churchill stayed with Lord Beaverbrook in his London mansion, Stornoway House, headquarters of the Ministry of Aircraft Production.

The Churchills brought to Downing Street a new family member, the Admiralty's black cat, Nelson, named after Vice Admiral Horatio Nelson, hero of the British naval victory at Trafalgar. Churchill adored the cat and often carried him about the house. Nelson's arrival caused a certain degree of feline strife, according to Mary, for Nelson harassed the cat that already resided at No. 10, whose nickname was "the Munich Mouser."

There was much to arrange, of course, as in any household, but an inventory for No. 10 hints at the complexity that awaited Clementine: wine glasses and tumblers (the whiskey had to go somewhere), grapefruit glasses, meat dishes, sieves, whisks, knives, jugs, breakfast cups and saucers, needles for trussing poultry, bedroom carafes and tumblers, 36 bottles of furniture polish, 27 pounds of carbolic soap, 150 pounds of primrose soap (in bars), and 78 pounds of Brown Windsor soap, a favorite of both Napoleon and Queen Victoria. There were banister brushes, both bristle and whisk; a Ewbank automatic floor sweeper; hearth brushes; kneeling mats; mops and handles for mops and heads for special Do-All mops; as well as chamois leathers, 8 pounds of rags, and 24 dozen matches for lighting hearths and cigars alike.

"The Chamberlains have left the place very dirty," Mary wrote in her diary the next day. "Mummie has left the Admiralty house like a new pin."

Mary loved her new home, particularly its dignified air. The front door was painted with black enamel and had a lion's-head knocker; it was guarded by a uniformed doorman and a police officer. Churchill's private study and the famed Cabinet Room were on the ground floor, where a stately quiet prevailed, as if the clamor of daily life were muffled by the sheer weight of British history. His paintings hung in the halls.

The family quarters were upstairs on the second floor, linked by halls painted eggshell blue with carpet the color of tomatoes. Sashed windows overlooked the garden and the rear entrance of the house and the Horse Guards Parade, a broad, graveled plaza upon which important ceremonial events took place. To Mary, this floor evoked a country home. Here, as at Admiralty House, Churchill and Clementine kept separate bedrooms.

Mary especially liked the rooms assigned to her. "Mummie has given me a lovely bedroom, sitting room & most spacious clothes closet (this latter most <u>Hollywood</u>)," she wrote.

With her father as prime minister, she was at the center of things now. It was all very stirring and romantic. That the Luftwaffe would soon evict Mary from her lovely rooms, and from London itself, was a thought that at this point, judging by the tenor of her diary, never entered her mind.

FULFILLING HIS PROMISE TO the French, late on Saturday afternoon, June 15, Churchill dictated a telegram to President Roosevelt that contained his most ardent plea yet.

The process of dictation invariably strained the patience of whomever was in attendance—typically his primary personal secretary, Mrs. Hill, and a private secretary, in this case John Colville. As Colville wrote later, "To watch him compose some telegram or minute for dictation is to make one feel that one is present at the birth of a child, so tense is his expression, so restless his turnings from side to side, so curious the noises he emits under his breath."

The ritual was especially painstaking for telegrams as sensitive as this one.

"I understand all your difficulties with American public opinion and Congress," Churchill dictated, "but events are moving downward at a pace where they will pass beyond the control of American public opinion when at last it is ripened." France was confronting an existential crisis, and the only force capable of influencing her future was America. "A declaration that the United States will if necessary enter the war might save France," he said. "Failing that, in a few days French resistance may have crumbled and we shall be left alone."

But far more than France was at stake, he added. He raised the specter of Britain, too, succumbing to Hitler's influence and warned that a new and pro-German government might then replace his own. "If we go down you may have a United States of Europe under the Nazi command far more numerous, far stronger, far better armed than the New World."

He reprised his earlier request that the United States send destroyers to bolster the Royal Navy and backed it up with a paper that detailed just how urgently the destroyers were needed in light of the expected invasion. The paper, echoing Home Forces commander General Ironside's earlier concerns about a reverse Dunkirk, warned that a German invasion from the sea "will most certainly be in the form of dispersed landings from a large number of small craft, and the only effective counter to such a move is to maintain numerous and effective destroyer patrols." But the Royal Navy, the report cautioned, had only sixty-eight operational destroyers. The need for more was therefore crucial. "Here," Churchill wrote, "is a definite practical and possible decisive step which can be taken at once and I urge most earnestly that you will weigh my words." He called receipt of the destroyers "a matter of life or death."

After completing this telegram, and another to the prime ministers of Canada and Britain's other dominions, Churchill turned to John Colville and quipped, "If words counted, we should win this war."

Though sympathetic, Roosevelt remained hamstrung by neutrality laws and the isolationist bent of the American public.

SOON AFTERWARD, COLVILLE FOUND himself whisked off to the countryside for a weekend at what was fast becoming for Churchill a kind of secret weapon: the official prime ministerial estate, Chequers, in Buckinghamshire, forty miles northwest of London

The Ghosts of Dull People

THE THREE BLACK DAIMLERS SPED THROUGH THE COUNTRYSIDE, in fading light. Churchill liked to go fast. With luck and daring, his driver could cover the distance from Downing Street to Chequers in an hour; if he did it in fifty minutes, a feat that required running traffic lights and ignoring rights-of-way, he won Churchill's generous praise. On one return trip he was said to have hit seventy miles per hour—this in an age when cars had no seatbelts. Churchill was invariably accompanied in the back seat by a typist, for whom the ride could be hair-raising. Wrote secretary Elizabeth Layton, of a later experience: "One would sit with book balanced on one knee, scribbling hard, one's left hand holding spare pencils, his glasses' case or an extra cigar, sometimes with one's foot keeping open his precious Box, which otherwise would have slammed shut as we swung around a corner." Shorthand was allowed only in cars; the rest of the time, Churchill's dictation had to be typed.

Inspector Thompson came along as well, his anxiety rising as he approached the house, which he deemed an ideal setting for an assassination. Owing to the thoughtful gift of its prior owner, Sir Arthur Lee, the house, a large Tudor mansion of turmeric-hued brick, had been the official country home of British prime ministers since 1917, when Lee gave it to the government. "A police officer, even with his health and a revolver, could feel very alone there," Thompson wrote. "And very unsafe."

The procession entered the grounds through a large wrought-iron gate, which was flanked on both sides by brick lodges. Soldiers of the Coldstream Guards patrolled the grounds; police officers manned the lodges and stopped the cars to check identities. Even Churchill's driver was questioned. The cars then proceeded down a long, straight lane called Victory Way.

Banks of tall windows would, in peacetime, have been filled with a welcoming amber light but now were dark, in accord with the strict blackout rules in place throughout the country. The cars entered a semicircular drive and came to a stop before the main entrance, on the east side of the house, where the party was greeted by Miss Grace Lamont, "Monty," a Scot who had managed the house for its prime ministerial tenants since 1937. Her official title was "lady housekeeper."

The terms of Lee's gift specified that no work was to be done at the house—that it was to be a place of rest and renewal. Lee had written, "Apart from these subtle influences, the better the health of our rulers, the more sanely will they rule and the inducement to spend two days a week in the high and pure air of the Chiltern hills and woods will, it is hoped, result in a real advantage to the nation as well as to its chosen leaders."

It was indeed an idyllic place. "Happy Prime Ministers, whichever way you go fresh beauties meet you," wrote Hubert Astley, a descendant of an early owner. The house stood in a shallow valley of the Chilterns, surrounded on three sides by rising terrain laced with paths that led walkers among yew hedges, ponds, and copses of beech, larch, and holly, delicately patrolled by chalk-blue butterflies. One of the estate's comely forests was the Long Walk Wood, happily and densely populated with rabbits. The immediate grounds had a croquet lawn, which delighted Clementine, an avid and demanding player. Churchill would soon put the croquet lawn to secondary use, testing novel military weapons, some the brainchildren of the Prof. Off the south end of the house was an ancient sundial with a gloomy inscription:

> Ye houres doe flie,
> Full soone we die
> In age secure
> Ye House and Hills
> Alone endure.

The front door opened onto an entry passage that led to the Great Hall, whose walls rose the full height of the house and displayed thirty large paintings, including Rembrandt's *The Mathematician*. (The painting was later determined to have been done by one of Rembrandt's students.) The entire house embodied the grand sweep of British history, but it was in the Long Gallery, on the second floor, that a sense of the past was most palpable. Here stood a table used by Napoleon Bonaparte during his exile on St. Helena. On the mantel of a large fireplace lay two swords once wielded by Oliver Cromwell, one of which supposedly accompanied him into battle at Marston Moor in 1644. To the left of the fireplace hung the cheery letter written by him from the scene with the notable line "God made them as stubble to our Swords."

The house was not to everyone's taste. Lloyd George disliked the fact that it was situated in a hollow and thus afforded only constricted views of the countryside. The house, he said, was "full of the ghosts of dull people," and this, he mused, might explain why his dog, Chong, tended to growl in the Long Gallery. Churchill visited the house during Lloyd George's tenure, in February 1921, a visit that must surely have stoked his lust to one day be prime minister. "Here I am," he wrote to Clementine about his visit. "You [would] like to see this place. Perhaps you will some day! It is just the kind of house you admire—a paneled museum full of history, full of treasures—but insufficiently warmed—Anyhow a wonderful possession."

Churchill quickly demonstrated that he had no intention of honoring Arthur Lee's demand that prime ministers leave their work behind.

DINNER ON THAT SATURDAY, June 15, was to begin at nine-thirty. The cook, alerted that the Prof would be a guest, prepared a special meal for him, suited to his vegetarian palate. He favored asparagus omelettes, lettuce salads, and tomatoes, first peeled, then sliced—anything, basically, that could be matched with eggs and olive oil–based mayonnaise. Clementine did not mind bending the culinary apparatus of the house to accommodate the Prof. "My mother took endless trouble," Mary recalled. "There was always a special, different dish cooked for Prof, endless egg dishes, and he would carefully pick out the yolks and eat the whites." Meals aside, he was an easy guest. "Prof was never a worry," Mary wrote. "He wasn't any trouble to entertain: he would take himself off to play golf, or he was working, or he was enlightening Papa, or he was playing tennis. He was a totally wonderful guest."

As welcome as he was, Mary had her reservations. "I always rather dreaded sitting next to Prof as he didn't make many jokes, and for a young person he was a little boring. I never felt cozy with Prof. He was absolutely charming," she remarked, "but he was a different animal altogether."

Neither Clementine nor Mary was present that Saturday night, presumably having chosen to stay behind to continue the process of moving the family, and Nelson, into No. 10. The guests who would stay the night included Churchill's daughter Diana and her husband, Duncan Sandys, and the ever-present John Colville; the Prof, leery of encountering others while on his way to the bath, never stayed overnight, preferring the privacy and comfort of his rooms at Oxford or his new workday residence at the Carlton Hotel.

Shortly before everyone entered the dining room, Colville received a telephone call from a fellow private secretary on duty in London, reporting the grimmest news from France thus far. The French were now openly demanding to be allowed to make their own peace deal with Hitler, in violation of a prior Anglo-French pact. Colville took the news to Churchill, "who was immediately very depressed." At once the atmosphere at Chequers grew funereal, Colville wrote. "Dinner began lugubriously, W. eating fast and greedily, his face almost in his plate, every now and then firing some technical question at Lindemann, who was quietly consuming his vegetarian diet."

Churchill—troubled and glum—made it clear that, at least for the moment, he had little interest in routine dinner talk and that only Lindemann merited his attention.

At length, the house staff served champagne, brandy, and cigars, and these did wonders to lighten the mood. This revitalization over drink and dinner was something of a pattern, as Lord Halifax's wife, Dorothy, had noted in the past: Churchill would be "silent, grumpy and remote" at the start of a meal, she wrote. "But mellowed by champagne and good food he became a different man, and a delightful and amusing companion." After Clementine once criticized his drinking, he told her, "Always remember, Clemmie, that I have taken more out of alcohol than alcohol has taken out of me."

The talk grew animated. Churchill began reading aloud telegrams of support that had come from far-flung lands within the empire, this by way of cheering himself up and heartening the others in the party as well. He offered a sobering observation: "The war is bound to become a bloody one for us now, but I hope our people will stand up to bombing and the Huns aren't liking what we are giving them. But what a tragedy that our victory in the last war should have been snatched from us by a lot of softies." By "softies," he was referring to supporters of Chamberlain's policy of appeasement.

The group went outside to stroll the grounds, with Churchill, son-in-law Duncan, and Inspector Thompson going to the rose garden, while Colville, the Prof, and Diana headed for the opposite side of the house. The sun had set at nine-nineteen; the moon was up and bright, a waxing gibbous, with a full moon due in five days. "It was light and deliciously warm," Colville wrote, "but the sentries, with tin helmets and fixed bayonets, who were placed all round the house, kept us fully alive to the horrors of reality."

Colville was summoned often to the telephone, and each time set out to find Churchill—"searching for Winston among the roses," as he put it in his diary. The French, he told Churchill, were moving ever closer to capitulating.

Churchill said, "Tell them . . . that if they let us have their fleet we shall never forget, but that if they surrender without consulting us we shall never forgive. We shall blacken their name for a thousand years!"

He paused, then added, "Don't, of course, do that just yet."

DESPITE THE NEWS, CHURCHILL'S mood continued to improve. He passed out cigars; matches flickered in the dark. As the coal ends of cigars glowed, he recited poems and discussed the war with an animation that verged on delight. At intervals he chanted the refrain from a popular song performed by the male duo Flanagan and Allen:

> Bang, bang, bang, bang goes the farmer's gun,
> Run rabbit, run rabbit, run, run, run, run.

The song would become immeasurably more popular later in the war when Flanagan and Allen substituted "Adolf" for "rabbit."

A telephone call arrived for Churchill, from America's ambassador to Britain, Joseph Kennedy. Colville retrieved Churchill from the garden. His demeanor immediately more grave, Churchill unleashed on Kennedy "a flood of eloquence about the part that America could and should play in saving civilization," Colville wrote in his diary. Churchill told the ambassador that America's promises of financial and industrial support constituted "a laughing-stock on the stage of history."

At one A.M., Churchill and his guests gathered in the central hall;

Churchill lay down on a sofa, puffing his cigar. He told a couple of off-color jokes and talked about the importance of increasing the production of fighters for the RAF.

At 1:30 A.M. he rose to go to bed, telling the others, "Good night, my children."

That night in his diary Colville wrote, "It was at once the most dramatic and the most fantastic evening I have ever spent."

CHAPTER

13

Scarification

———

A T SEVEN-THIRTY ON SUNDAY MORNING, UPON LEARNING THAT Churchill was awake, Colville brought him the latest report on the French situation, which had arrived earlier both over the telephone and in the form of a document delivered by courier. Colville brought the messages to Churchill's room. Churchill was in bed, "looking just like a rather nice pig, clad in a silk vest."

Churchill decided to convene a special cabinet meeting at ten-fifteen that morning, in London. As Churchill breakfasted in bed, his valet, Sawyers, ran his bath, and the house roused to action. Mrs. Hill readied her portable typewriter. Inspector Thompson checked for assassins. Churchill's driver prepared the car. Colville raced to dress and pack, and rushed through his breakfast.

They sped back to London through heavy rain, splashing through traffic lights and hurtling along the Mall at high speed, with Churchill all the while dictating minutes to Mrs. Hill and generating a morning's worth of work for Colville and his fellow private secretaries.

Churchill arrived at Downing Street just as his cabinet ministers were gathering. The meeting resulted in a telegram to the French, sent at twelve thirty-five P.M., authorizing France to inquire about the terms of an armistice on its own behalf, "provided, but only provided, that the French Fleet is sailed forthwith for British harbors pending negotiations." The telegram made clear that Britain planned to fight on, and would not participate in any deliberations that France pursued with Germany.

Churchill knew France was lost. What he cared about most, now, was the French fleet. If it fell under Hitler's control, as seemed likely, it would change the balance of power on the high seas, where Britain, at least for the time being, retained superiority.

IN LONDON THAT SUNDAY, the Prof and young Dr. Jones of Air Intelligence attended a meeting of the RAF's Night Interception Committee, convened by Air Marshal Philip Joubert to further consider Jones's apparent discovery of a new German beam navigation system. Churchill, otherwise engaged, did not attend, but the galvanic power of his interest was evident. What had hitherto been the subject of more or less academic interest now became a target of concrete inquiry, with specific tasks assigned to various officers.

"What a change," Jones wrote, "from my inactivity of only a week ago!"

But doubts about Jones's theory persisted. One key participant in the meeting, Air Chief Marshal Hugh Dowding, head of Fighter Command, described Jones's case as consisting of "some rather nebulous evidence." Another, Henry Tizard, a prominent scientific adviser to the Air Ministry, wrote, "I may be wrong, but there seemed to me to be unnecessary excitement about this latest alleged German method for dealing with the country. One cannot possibly get accurate bombing on a selected target in this way."

The Prof, however, was convinced that the matter was urgent. Lindemann again wrote to Churchill, this time urging him to issue a directive "that such investigation take precedence, not only as regards materials but especially the use of men, over any research whose results are not liable to affect production in the next three months."

Churchill agreed. On Lindemann's note he jotted, "Let this be done without fail."

Soon Jones heard a rumor that Churchill considered the matter so grave that he planned to convene a meeting on the subject at No. 10 Downing Street.

To Jones, this seemed implausible, very likely the opening move in a multiple-step practical joke by his colleagues in Air Intelligence, who had elevated the art of pulling pranks to a high level; Jones himself was acknowledged to be a foremost practitioner.

ON MONDAY, JUNE 17, "a certain eventuality" came to pass. France fell. Churchill's cabinet met at eleven A.M. and soon afterward learned that

Marshal Philippe Pétain, who that day replaced Reynaud as leader of France, had ordered the French army to stop fighting.

After the meeting, Churchill walked into the garden at No. 10, alone, and began to pace, head down, hands clasped behind his back—not depressed, and not cowed, but deep in thought. Colville watched him. "He was doubtless considering how best the French fleet, the air force and the Colonies could be saved," Colville wrote. "He, I am sure, will remain undaunted."

Judging by the telegram Churchill sent to Pétain and General Maxime Weygand later that day, this appeared to be the case. Deploying flattery leavened with irony, he began: "I wish to repeat to you my profound conviction that the illustrious Marshal Pétain and the famous General Weygand, our comrades in two great wars against the Germans, will not injure their ally by delivering over to the enemy the fine French Fleet. Such an act would scarify"—*scarify*, a six-hundred-year-old word that only Churchill would use in crucial diplomatic correspondence—"would scarify their names for a thousand years of history. Yet this result may easily come by frittering away these few precious hours when the Fleet can be sailed to safety in British or American ports, carrying with it the hope of the future and the honor of France."

The news about France was first broadcast by the BBC at one o'clock that afternoon. Home Intelligence reported that the reaction by the public "has been one of confusion and shock, but hardly surprise. From all parts come reports of bewilderment and great anxiety." There was widespread fear that the British government might "go abroad" or simply give up. "A few feel all is over." The two questions most on people's minds were what would happen to the soldiers still in France—"Will a second Dunkirk be possible?"—and what would now become of the French air force and navy. It was crucial, the report said, that Churchill or the king come forward that very night to speak.

Olivia Cockett, the Scotland Yard clerk and Mass-Observation diarist, was at work when she heard the BBC broadcast. "Poor France!" she wrote at three-forty P.M. "The 1 o'clock news was a bomb to me. I'd said over and over again that I didn't believe France was ever going to give in to Germany. We all fell very silent." The afternoon tea service arrived. Cockett did not share Britain's national obsession with tea, but today, she said, "I was grateful for a cup, for once." She spent the next hour "quivering and with tears."

But at No. 10 and Buckingham Palace, there was a new and welcome sense of clarity. "Personally," the king wrote, in a letter to his mother,

Queen Mary, "I feel happier now that we have no allies to be polite to & to pamper." Air Marshal Dowding was elated, for it meant the end, at last, of the persistent threat that Churchill, in a rash and generous moment, would send fighters to France and deplete the force needed to repel the massive assault by the German air force that was certain to come now that France had capitulated. Dowding later confessed to Lord Halifax, "I don't mind telling you, that when I heard of the French collapse I went on my knees and thanked God."

But all this relief was tempered by an appreciation of just how radically the French collapse altered the strategic landscape. The Luftwaffe was sure now to move its air fleets into bases along the channel coast. Invasion seemed not only practical but imminent. The British expected it to begin with a massive onslaught by the German air force, the much-feared "knock-out" blow.

MORE BAD NEWS ARRIVED that afternoon. Churchill was seated in the quiet of the Cabinet Room at No. 10 when he was told that a large Cunard liner, the *Lancastria,* which was serving as a troopship and loaded with more than 6,700 British soldiers, air crews, and civilians, had been attacked by German aircraft. Three bombs had struck the ship and set it afire. It sank in twenty minutes, with the loss of at least 4,000 lives, far more than the combined tolls of the *Titanic* and the *Lusitania.*

So wrenching was this news, especially on top of the French debacle, that Churchill barred the press from reporting it. "The newspapers have got quite enough disaster for today at least," he said. This was, however, a misguided attempt at censorship, given that 2,500 survivors soon arrived in Britain. The *New York Times* broke the story five weeks later, on July 26, and the British press followed suit. The fact that the government never acknowledged the sinking caused a surge of distrust among the public, according to Home Intelligence. "The withholding of the news of the *Lancastria* is the subject of much adverse criticism," the agency stated in one of its daily reports. The lack of disclosure raised "fears that other bad news is withheld . . . and the fact that the news was only released after publication in an American paper gives rise to the feeling that it would otherwise have been withheld longer."

As it happened, the death toll was likely much greater than first reported. The actual number of people aboard the ship was never determined but could have been as high as 9,000.

THERE WAS GOOD NEWS, however, from the Ministry of Aircraft Production. On Tuesday, June 18, Lord Beaverbrook gave the War Cabinet his first report on the output of aircraft. The results were stunning: New aircraft were exiting his factories at a rate of 363 a week, up from 245. The production of engines had soared as well—620 new engines a week, compared to 411.

What he did not report, at least not here, was that these gains had come at considerable cost to himself, in terms of stress and health, and to harmony within Churchill's government. Immediately after accepting his new post, Beaverbrook began clashing with the Air Ministry, which he saw as fusty and hidebound in its approach not just to building aircraft but also to deploying and equipping them. He had personal insight into aerial warfare: His son, also named Max, and known as "Little Max," was a fighter pilot, tall and sharply handsome, soon to win the Distinguished Flying Cross. From time to time, Beaverbrook invited him and his fellow pilots to his home for cocktails and conversation. Beaverbrook lived each day in a state of anxiety until about eight o'clock each evening, when Little Max would check in by telephone to let him know he was alive and intact.

Beaverbrook wanted control—of everything: production, repair, storage. The Air Ministry, however, had always considered these its exclusive responsibility. It wanted all the planes it could get, of course, but resented Beaverbrook's intrusions, especially when he sought to dictate even the kinds of guns that should be installed in new aircraft.

Beaverbrook infuriated other ministries as well. He wanted first access to all resources: wood, steel, fabric, drills, milling equipment, explosives—anything needed for the manufacture of bombers and fighters, regardless of the needs and demands of other ministries. He would, for example, commandeer buildings already earmarked for other uses. His direct connection to Churchill made his depredations all the more exasperating. As Pug Ismay saw it, Beaverbrook had more in common with a highwayman than an executive. "In the pursuit of anything which he wanted—whether materials, machine tools, or labor—he never hesitated, so rival departments alleged, to indulge in barefaced robbery."

Two days before submitting his progress report, Beaverbrook had dictated a nine-page letter to Churchill in which he laid out his troubles. "Today," he began, "I find myself frustrated and obstructed, and I ask for your immediate help."

He cited a long list of vexations, including resistance from the Air Ministry to his campaign to salvage and repair downed RAF planes, a province the ministry saw as its own. Beaverbrook recognized from the start that these wrecked planes were a trove of spare components, especially engines and instruments, that could be cobbled together into complete aircraft. Many damaged British fighters managed to crash-land at airfields, farms, and parks, or on other friendly ground, from which they could be readily retrieved. He marshaled the talents of myriad mechanics and small companies to create a repair network so adept at salvage that it could return to battle hundreds of aircraft a month.

Beaverbrook demanded full control of maintenance depots where damaged planes and parts accumulated, and claimed that the Air Ministry, out of territorial pique, tried to stymie him at every turn. In his letter to Churchill, he described how one of his salvage squads had recovered sixteen hundred inoperable Vickers machine guns from one depot and sent them to a factory for repair. He was told there were no more such guns, but this proved not to be true. "Yesterday, after an early morning raid, carried out at my instigation, we recovered another batch of 1,120 guns," he wrote.

His use of the word "raid" was emblematic of his approach. His tactics won him no praise from Air Ministry officials who viewed his emergency salvage crews—his "Action Squads"—as the equivalent of roving bands of pirates, and at one point banned the squads from frontline airfields.

Beaverbrook never sent the nine-page letter. This change of heart was not unusual. He often dictated complaints and attacks, sometimes in multiple drafts, deciding later not to post them. In the personal papers he eventually left to the archives of Parliament, one big file contains unsent mail, a collection that steams with unvented bile.

His dissatisfaction continued to fester and intensify.

"This Queer and Deadly Game"

———

THAT AFTERNOON, TUESDAY, JUNE 18, AT 3:49 P.M., CHURCHILL stood before the House of Commons to address the French debacle, delivering a speech he would repeat that evening in a radio broadcast to the public. This speech, too, would go down as one of the great moments in oratory, at least as he delivered it in the House of Commons.

Churchill spoke of parachute troops and airborne landings and of bombing attacks "which will certainly be made very soon upon us." While Germany had more bombers, he said, Britain had bombers too, and would deploy them "without intermission" to attack military targets in Germany. He reminded his audience that Britain had a navy. "Some people seem to forget that," he said. He made no attempt, however, to skirt the true meaning of the French collapse. The "Battle of France" was over, he said, adding, "I expect that the Battle of Britain is about to begin." At stake was not only the British Empire but all of Christian civilization. "The whole fury and might of the enemy must very soon be turned on us. Hitler knows that he will have to break us in this island or lose the war."

He marched toward his climax: "If we can stand up to him, all Europe may be free, and the life of the world may move forward into broad, sunlit uplands; but if we fail then the whole world, including the United States, and all that we have known and cared for, will sink into the abyss of a new dark age made more sinister, and perhaps more prolonged, by the lights of a perverted science."

He issued an appeal to the greater spirit of Britons everywhere. "Let us therefore brace ourselves to our duty and so bear ourselves that if the

British Commonwealth and Empire lasts for a thousand years, men will still say, 'This was their finest hour.'"

Arguably, this was Churchill's finest as well, and so it would have remained had he taken the recommendation of his minister of information to broadcast the speech live from the chamber. As Home Intelligence had found, the public needed to hear from Churchill himself about the French fiasco and what it meant for Britain's prospects in the war. But the process of arranging a broadcast from the House, including a necessary vote of approval by members, proved too daunting.

Churchill agreed, with reluctance, to do a separate broadcast that night. The ministry expected him to write something new, but, with a child's contrariness, he decided simply to reread the speech he had delivered in the Commons. Although public reaction as measured through Mass-Observation and Home Intelligence reports varied, one consistent theme was criticism of Churchill's delivery. "Some suggested he was drunk," Mass-Observation reported on Wednesday, June 19, "others that he did not himself feel the confidence he was proclaiming. A few thought he was tired. It would seem that the delivery to some extent counteracted the contents of the speech." Cecil King, editorial director of the *Daily Mirror,* wrote in his diary, "Whether he was drunk or all-in from sheer fatigue, I don't know, but it was the poorest possible effort on an occasion when he should have produced the finest speech of his life."

One listener went so far as to send a telegram to No. 10 Downing Street warning that Churchill sounded as though he had a heart condition, and recommended he work lying down.

As it happened, the problem was largely mechanical. Churchill had insisted on reading the speech with a cigar clenched in his mouth.

THE NEXT DAY, CHURCHILL'S top three military commanders—his chiefs of staff—sent a secret note ("To Be Kept Under Lock and Key") to Churchill and his War Cabinet, via Pug Ismay, in which they laid out the coming danger in terms more stark than Churchill had detailed in his speech. "Experience of the campaign in Flanders and France indicates that we can expect no period of respite before the Germans may begin a new phase of the war," the note read. "We must, therefore, regard the threat of invasion as immediate." But first would come an assault from the air, the chiefs explained, one that "will tax our air defenses and the morale of our people to the full."

Hitler would spare nothing, they warned. "The Germans have accepted prodigious losses in France, and are likely to be prepared to face even higher losses and to take even greater risks than they took in Norway to achieve decisive results against this country."

The next three months, they predicted, would determine the outcome of the war.

ON THURSDAY, THERE WERE more rumors that Churchill would hold a meeting devoted solely to beam navigation. The meeting, Dr. Jones now heard, would take place the next morning, Friday, June 21. No one had invited him, however, so on that Friday morning he kept to his usual routine, which involved catching a train from the London Borough of Richmond at nine thirty-five and arriving at work about thirty-five minutes later. When he got to his office, he found a note from a secretary in the Air Intelligence Branch stating that a colleague, Squadron Leader Rowley Scott-Farnie, "has telephoned and says will you go to the Cabinet Room in 10 Downing Street."

AT NO. 10, THE Cabinet Room began filling with officials. Here was the "long table," a twenty-five-foot span of polished wood covered with green cloth, toothed by the backs of twenty-two mahogany chairs. The prime minister's chair—the only armchair—was at the center of one side of the table, in front of a large marble fireplace. Tall windows afforded views of the back garden and, beyond, the Horse Guards Parade and St. James's Park. At each seat was a writing pad, a blotter, and notepaper with "10 Downing Street" embossed in black at the top.

From time to time, Churchill used the room as his base for dictating telegrams and minutes. A secretary would sit opposite him, with a typewriter, sometimes for hours, typing item after item, with Churchill "holding out his hand for it almost before he had finished dictating," wrote Elizabeth Layton. At the ready were his "klop"—his hole punch—and two pens, one with blue-black ink for signing correspondence, one with red ink for initialing minutes. If he needed something, he would hold out a hand and say "Gimme," and Layton was expected to know what device he wanted. He used the same command to summon people. "Gimme Prof" or "Gimme Pug" meant she was to call for Lindemann or General Ismay. During long quiet stretches, she listened to the chimes of Big Ben and the Horse Guards clock, both of which sounded at quarterly intervals, with a pleasing dissonance, the clang of the Horse Guards clock against the stately boom of Big Ben.

The officials took their seats. Here came Churchill, Lindemann, Lord Beaverbrook, and the empire's top aviation officials, including Air Minister Sir Archibald Sinclair and Fighter Command chief Hugh Dowding, a dozen or so men in all. Present as well was Henry Tizard, who advised the government on aeronautical affairs. A onetime friend of Lindemann's, Tizard had become estranged from the Prof, in large part because of the Prof's virtuosity at nursing grudges. No secretaries were present, private or personal, indicating that the meeting was deemed so secret that no written record would be kept.

There was tension in the room. Tizard and Lindemann were feuding over past imagined slights; the animus between them was clearly evident.

Churchill noticed that one key man, Jones, the young scientist whose detective work had caused the meeting to be convened in the first place, was absent. The discussion began without him.

With the fall of France, the urgency of the matter was growing by the day. The Luftwaffe was moving its bases steadily closer to the French coast; its raids over the British mainland were growing in size, severity, and frequency. Two nights earlier, the Luftwaffe had sent 150 aircraft over England, damaging steelworks and a chemical plant, destroying gas and water mains, sinking one merchant ship, and nearly blowing up an ammunition depot in Southampton. Ten civilians were killed. It was all part of the mounting drumbeat of suspense as to when the Germans would invade, like the slow build of a thriller (to use a word that debuted in 1889). The suspense was making people irritable and anxious, as well as more critical of the government, according to a Home Intelligence report.

If German aircraft were indeed being guided, at night, by a secret new navigational system, it was crucial to know that, and to devise some means of countering the technology as soon as possible. This realm of secret science was one in which Churchill took great delight. He loved gadgets and secret weapons, and was an ardent promoter of the novel inventions proposed by the Prof, even those derided by other officials as the dreams of a crackpot. Upon the failure of an early prototype of an explosive device that adhered to the exterior of a tank—and occasionally to the soldier throwing it—Churchill rose to the Prof's defense. In a minute addressed to Pug Ismay but meant for wider distribution, Churchill wrote, "Any chortling by officials who have been slothful in pushing this bomb over the fact that it has not succeeded will be viewed with strong disfavor by me."

The "sticky bomb," as it was known, did eventually reach a point where it could be deployed in the field, despite opposition by the War Office. Churchill overrode the department's objections and gave the weapon his full support. In a June 1, 1940, minute noteworthy for both its precision and its brevity, Churchill commanded, "Make one million. WSC."

When, later, several members of Parliament began to question Lindemann's influence, Churchill bridled. During a contentious "Question Time" in the House of Commons, one member not only asked questions that implicitly criticized Lindemann but made dark allusions to his German heritage, which infuriated Churchill. Afterward, he ran into the critic in the Commons Smoking Room and—"bellowing at him like an infuriated bull," according to one witness—shouted, "Why in Hell did you ask that Question? Don't you know that he is one of my oldest and greatest friends?"

Churchill told the man "to get the hell out" and never to speak to him again.

In an aside to his own parliamentary secretary, Churchill said, "Love me, love my dog, and if you don't love my dog you damn well can't love me."

DR. JONES STILL THOUGHT the meeting at 10 Downing Street might be a prank. He tracked down the secretary who had put the note on his desk that morning. She assured him that the invitation was real. Still unconvinced, Jones paid a call on Squadron Leader Scott-Farnie, the colleague who had telephoned the original message to the secretary. He, too, avowed that this was no prank.

Jones caught a taxi. By the time he reached No. 10, the meeting had been underway for nearly half an hour.

For Jones, this was an unnerving moment. As he entered the room, Churchill and a dozen other men turned his way. Jones was a bit stunned to find himself, all of twenty-eight years old, looking down the center of the legendary long table in the Cabinet Room.

Churchill was seated midway down the left side of the table, flanked by Lindemann and Lord Beaverbrook, the two men antipodes in appearance—Lindemann pale and soap-featured; Beaverbrook, animated and bilious, every bit the scowling elf captured in newspaper photographs. At the other side of the table sat Henry Tizard, Air Minister Sinclair, and Fighter Command's Dowding.

Jones sensed the tension in the room. Lindemann gestured toward the empty seat to his right, the men on Tizard's side signaled that he should come sit with them. For an instant Jones was flummoxed. Lindemann was his former professor and undoubtedly the main reason he had been invited to the meeting in the first place; but the Air Staff men were his colleagues, and by all rights he should sit with them. What further complicated the moment was that Jones was well aware of the ill feeling between Tizard and Lindemann.

Jones resolved the quandary by taking a chair at the end of the table, in what he called "the no-man's land" between the two delegations.

He listened as the others renewed their conversation. He judged by their comments that the group had only a partial understanding of the beam situation and its implications for aerial warfare.

At one point Churchill addressed a question directly to him, to clarify a detail.

Instead of merely answering, Jones said, "Would it help, sir, if I told you the story right from the start?" In retrospect, he was startled by his own sangfroid. He attributed his calmness in part to the fact that his summons to the meeting had so taken him by surprise that he had not had an opportunity to let his anxiety build.

Jones told it as a detective story, describing the early clues and the subsequent accumulation of evidence. He revealed, as well, some fresh intelligence, including a note pulled just three days earlier from a downed German bomber that seemed to confirm his hunch that the *Knickebein* system deployed not just one beam but two, with the second one intersecting the first over the intended target. The note pegged the second beam's point of origin as Bredstedt, a town in Schleswig-Holstein, on Germany's north coast. It also provided what appeared to be the frequencies of the beams.

Churchill listened, rapt, his fascination for secret technologies in full flare. But he also realized the bleak significance of Jones's discovery. It was bad enough that the Luftwaffe was establishing itself at bases on captured territory just minutes from the English coast. But now he understood that the aircraft at those bases would be able to bomb accurately even on moonless nights and in overcast weather. To Churchill, this was dark news indeed, "one of the blackest moments of the war," as he later put it. Until this point, he had been confident that the RAF could hold its own, despite being, as Air Intelligence believed, vastly outnumbered by the Luftwaffe. In daylight, RAF pilots were proving adept at bringing down Germany's slow-moving bombers and besting their fighter escorts, which were hamstrung by having to hang back to protect the slower aircraft and by fuel limitations that gave the fighters only ninety minutes of flying time. At night, however, the RAF was powerless to intercept German aircraft. If the German planes could bomb accurately even in heavy overcast and on the darkest nights, they would no longer need their swarms of fighter escorts, and no longer be restrained by the fighters' fuel limits. They could traverse the British Isles without restriction, a tremendous advantage in laying the groundwork for invasion.

Jones talked for twenty minutes. When he was done, Churchill recalled, "there was a general air of incredulity" in the room, though some at the table were clearly concerned. Churchill asked, What should now be done?

The first step, Jones said, was to use aircraft to confirm that the beams actually existed, and then to fly among them to understand their character. Jones knew that if indeed the Germans were using a Lorenz system like that employed by commercial airliners, it had to have certain characteristics. Transmitters on the ground would send signals through two separate antennae. These signals would spread and become diffuse at long distances, but where they overlapped they would form a strong, narrow beam, in the way that two shadows become darker at the point where they intersect. It was this beam that commercial pilots would follow until they saw the runway below. The transmitters sent a long "dash" signal through one antenna and a shorter "dot" signal through the other, both made audible by the pilot's receiver. If the pilot heard a strong dash signal, he knew to move to the right, until the dot signal gained strength. When he was centered on the correct approach path, where both dashes and dots had equal strength—the so-called equi-signal zone—he heard a single continuous tone.

Once the nature of the beam system was known, Jones told the men in the meeting, the RAF could devise countermeasures, including jamming the beams and transmitting false signals to trick the Germans into dropping their bombs too early or flying along the wrong course.

At this, Churchill's mood improved—"the load was once again lifted," he later told Jones. He ordered the search for the beams to begin immediately.

He also proposed that such beams made it all the more important to press ahead with one of the Prof's pet secret weapons, the "aerial mine," which Lindemann had been promoting since well before the war, and which had become an obsession for him and Churchill alike. These mines were small explosive devices hung by wire from parachutes that could be dropped by the thousands in the path of German bomber formations, to be snagged by wings and propellers. Lindemann went so far as to propose a plan to protect London by raising a nightly "mine-curtain" nearly twenty miles long, replenished by successive flights of mine-dispensing aircraft that would drop 250,000 mines per six-hour night.

Churchill fully endorsed Lindemann's mines, although most everyone else doubted their worth. At Churchill's insistence, the Air Ministry and Beaverbrook's Ministry of Aircraft Production had developed and tested prototypes, but only halfheartedly, and this caused Churchill great frustration. The inevitable Luftwaffe assault demanded the thorough examination of every possible means of defense. Now, at the meeting, his frustration blazed anew. It seemed clear to him that the existence of German navigation beams, if proven, added new urgency to fulfilling the Prof's dream, because if these beams could be located, suddenly the placement of aerial mines along the paths of inbound bombers would become much more precise. But so far the whole program seemed bogged down in studies and minutes. He banged on the table. "All I get from the Air Ministry," he growled, "is files, files, files!"

Tizard, in part driven by his hostility toward Lindemann, scoffed at Jones's story. But Churchill, convinced about "the principles of this queer and deadly game," declared that the existence of the German beams should be treated as established fact. He understood that soon Hitler would turn the full strength of the Luftwaffe against Britain. Work on countering the beams was to be given precedence over all else, he said, and "the slightest reluctance or deviation in carrying out this policy" was to be reported to him.

Tizard, his objections ignored and his loathing for Lindemann inflamed anew, took this as a personal affront. Shortly after the meeting, he resigned both from his position as chairman of the Scientific Advisory Committee and as an adviser to the Air Staff.

It was in such moments that Churchill most appreciated the Prof. "There were no doubt greater scientists," Churchill acknowledged. "But he had two qualifications of vital consequence to me." First was the fact that Lindemann "was my friend and trusted confidante of twenty years," Churchill wrote. The Prof's second qualification was his ability to distill arcane science into simple, easy-to-grasp concepts—to "decipher the signals from the experts on the far horizons and explain to me in lucid, homely terms what the issues were." Once thus armed, Churchill could turn on his "power-relay"—the authority of office—and transform concepts into action.

A search flight to attempt to locate the beams was scheduled for that evening.

Jones got little sleep that night. He had put his career on the line before the prime minister and Lindemann and the most senior men of the Royal Air Force. His mind paged back through the entire meeting, one detail to the next. "Had I, after all," he wondered, "made a fool of myself and misbehaved so spectacularly in front of the Prime Minister? Had I jumped to false conclusions? Had I fallen for a great hoax by the Germans? Above all, had I arrogantly wasted an hour of the Prime Minister's time when Britain was about to be invaded or obliterated from the air?"

CHURCHILL HAD FURTHER CAUSE for relief that day, a kind of financial Dunkirk. As the war deepened and the demands on him intensified, he wrestled with a personal problem that had dogged him through much of his career, a lack of money. He wrote books and articles to supplement his official income. Until his appointment as prime minister, he had written columns for the *Daily Mirror* and *News of the World* and had done broadcasts for American radio, also for the money. But it had never been enough, and now he was nearing a financial crisis, unable to fully pay his taxes and routine bills, including those from his tailors, his wine supplier, and the shop that repaired his watch. (He had nicknamed his watch the "turnip.") What's more, he owed his bank—Lloyds—a lot of money. His account statement for Tuesday, June 18, had cited an overdraft amounting to over £5,000. An interest payment on this was due at the end of the month, and he lacked the money to pay even that much.

But that Friday of the beam meeting, a check in the amount of £5,000 mysteriously, and conveniently, turned up in his Lloyds account. The name on the deposited check was that of Brendan Bracken, Churchill's parliamentary private secretary, but the true source was Bracken's wealthy co-owner of the *Economist* magazine, Sir Henry Strakosch. Three days earlier, upon receiving a statement from Lloyds listing his overdraft, Churchill had called Bracken to his office. He was fed up with the distraction and pressure caused by his financial troubles and had far more important matters to confront. He told Bracken to fix the situation, and Bracken did. The Lloyds payment did not get Churchill out of debt entirely, but it removed the immediate risk of an embarrassing personal default.

THE NEXT DAY, SATURDAY, Dr. Jones attended a meeting convened to hear the results of the previous night's flight to search for German beams. The pilot, Flight Lieutenant H. E. Bufton, appeared in person and delivered a concise report, with three numbered items. He and an observer had taken off from an airfield near Cambridge with instructions only to fly north and look for transmissions like those generated by a Lorenz blind-landing system.

First, Bufton reported finding a narrow beam in the air a mile south of Spalding in Lincolnshire, close to the North Sea coast. The flight detected transmissions of dots just south of the beam and dashes to the north, as would be expected with a Lorenz-style beacon.

Second, Bufton reported that the frequency of the detected beam was 31.5 megacycles per second, the frequency previously identified in one of the notes retrieved by Air Intelligence.

And then came the best news of all, at least for Jones. The flight had detected a second beam, with similar characteristics, that crossed the first at a point near Derby, home to a Rolls-Royce factory that produced all the Merlin engines for the RAF's Spitfires and Hurricanes. This second beam, on a different frequency, would necessarily intersect the first shortly before the target, to give the German crew time to drop their bombs.

Despite the fact that the point of intersection seemed to indicate that the Rolls factory was a target, there was jubilation. For Jones, especially, it was a great relief. The officer in charge of the meeting, Jones recalled, was "actually skipping round the room in delight."

Now came the urgent effort to find an effective way of countering the beams. *Knickebein* received the code name "Headache"; the potential countermeasures, "Aspirin."

First, though, Jones and a colleague walked to nearby St. Stephen's Tavern, a popular Whitehall pub situated a hundred yards from Big Ben, and got drunk.

CHAPTER

15

London and Berlin

———

A T 6:36 P.M., SATURDAY, JUNE 22, THE FRENCH SIGNED AN armistice with Hitler. Britain was now officially alone. At Chequers the next day, the news about France soured the atmosphere. "A wrathful & gloomy breakfast downstairs," Mary wrote in her diary.

Churchill was in a black mood. What consumed his thoughts and darkened his spirits was the French fleet. Germany had not immediately disclosed the precise terms of the armistice, and thus the official fate of the fleet remained a mystery. That Hitler would annex its ships seemed certain. The effect would be catastrophic, likely both to change the balance of power in the Mediterranean and to make a German invasion of England even more certain.

Churchill's behavior annoyed Clementine. She sat down to write him a letter, recognizing, as always, that the best way to get his attention for anything was in writing. She began, "I hope you will forgive me if I tell you something that I feel you ought to know."

She completed the letter, but then tore it up.

IN BERLIN, VICTORY SEEMED NEAR. On Sunday, June 23, Joseph Goebbels, whose official title was minister for popular enlightenment and propaganda, convened the regular morning meeting of his chief propaganda operatives, this one to address the new direction of the war now that France had made its capitulation official.

With France quelled, Goebbels told the group, Britain must now become the focus of their attention. He warned against doing anything that would cause the public to believe that a quick victory would follow. "It is still impossible to say in what form the fight against Britain will now be continued, and on no account, therefore, must the impression be created that the occupation of Britain is about to start tomorrow," Goebbels said, according to minutes of the meeting. "On the other hand, there can be no doubt that Britain will receive the same sentence as France if she persists in closing her mind to sensible considerations"—meaning a peace agreement.

With Britain now casting itself as the last guardian of European liberty, Goebbels said, Germany must stress in reply that "we are now the leaders in the clash between continental Europe and the plutocratic British island people." Germany's foreign-language transmitters must henceforth "deliberately and systematically operate with slogans on the lines of 'Nations of Europe: Britain is organizing your starvation!' etc."

In a remark not recorded in the minutes but later quoted by a member of the Reich press office, Goebbels told the group, "Well, this week will bring the great swing in Britain"—meaning that with France fallen, the British public would now, surely, clamor for peace. "Churchill, of course, can't hold on," he said. "A compromise government will be formed. We are very close to the end of the war."

The Red Warning

IN LONDON ON MONDAY, JUNE 24, CHURCHILL'S WAR CABINET met three times, once in the morning and twice that night, the last meeting beginning at ten-thirty P.M. Most of the time was spent discussing what the Permanent Undersecretary for Foreign Affairs Sir Alexander Cadogan called "the awful problem of the French fleet."

Earlier that day, the *Times* of London had revealed the terms of the French armistice, which Germany had not yet formally disclosed. German forces would occupy the northern and western tiers of France; the rest of the country would be administered by a nominally free government based in Vichy, about two hundred miles south of Paris. It was Article 8 that Churchill read most intently: "The German Government solemnly declare that they have no intention of using for their own purposes during the war the French Fleet stationed in ports under German control except those units necessary for coast surveillance and minesweeping." It also called for all French ships operating outside French waters to return to France, unless they were needed to protect French colonial holdings.

The clause as later published by Germany included this sentence: "The German Government further solemnly and expressly declare that they do not intend to claim the French Fleet on the conclusion of peace."

Churchill did not for an instant believe that Germany would honor this declaration. Hitler's persistent dishonesty aside, the language of the article by itself seemed to offer great leeway in how he deployed French ships. What exactly did "coast surveillance" entail? Or "minesweeping"? Churchill scoffed at Germany's "solemn" promise. As he later told Parliament, "Ask half a dozen countries what is the value of such a solemn assurance."

Despite the three cabinet meetings, the ministers made little progress toward shaping a final course of action.

Just after the last meeting came to an end, at one-fifteen on Tuesday morning, air-raid sirens began to howl, the city's first "red warning" since the previous September, when the war began. The alert meant an attack was imminent, but no bombers appeared. The warning had been triggered by a civilian aircraft.

While waiting for the all-clear siren to sound, Mass-Observation diarist Olivia Cockett opened her diary and wrote, "The night is very still. The clock ticks loudly. Four bowls of roses and one of tall white lilies scent the air deliciously." As her family watched, she took the lilies and lay down on the rug, propping them on her chest in funereal fashion. "All laughed," she wrote, "but not very uproariously."

Home Intelligence reported that Tuesday that 10 to 20 percent of London's population failed to hear the air-raid warning. "Many people did not leave their bedrooms," the report said, "and parents were reluctant to awaken children." A seven-year-old girl came up with a term for the sirens: the "Wibble-Wobbles."

THE THREAT OF INVASION seemed to grow daily. On Friday, June 28, Churchill received a note from Dr. Jones of Air Intelligence, who seemed to have a talent for delivering disconcerting news. In this note, Jones reported that the same "unimpeachable source" who had provided critical information about the German beams had learned that an anti-aircraft unit of the German air force known as Flakkorps I was requesting eleven hundred maps of England of various scales for immediate shipment to its headquarters. Jones pointed out that this could indicate "an intention to land motorized AA units in both England and Ireland." Such a force would be necessary to help an invading army protect itself from the RAF and consolidate its hold on captured ground.

Churchill knew that the "unimpeachable source" was not in fact a human spy but, rather, the elite codebreaking unit at Bletchley Park. He was one of the few senior officials in Whitehall who knew of the unit's existence; Jones, as deputy director of Air Intelligence, also knew. Bletchley's secrets were delivered to Churchill in a special yellow despatch box, separate from his regular black box, that only he was authorized to open. The intercepted map request was troubling in that it was the kind of concrete preparatory measure that would be expected before an invasion. Churchill immediately sent copies of the message to the Prof and Pug Ismay.

The next three months, Churchill judged, were the period when the threat of invasion would be greatest, after which the weather would become progressively more hostile and, thus, a deterrent.

The tone of his minutes grew more urgent, and more precise. Prodded by the Prof, he told Pug Ismay that trenches were to be dug across any open field more than four hundred yards long, to defend against tanks and landings by troop-carrying aircraft, specifying that "this should be done simultaneously throughout the country in the next 48 hours." In a separate note, on Sunday, June 30, he ordered Pug to see that a study was made of tides and moon phases in the Thames Estuary and elsewhere, to determine on "which days conditions will be most favorable to a seaborne landing." Also that Sunday, he sent Pug a minute on a subject of particular sensitivity: the use of poison gas against invading forces. "Supposing lodgments were effected on our coast, there could be no better points for application of mustard than these beaches and lodgments," he wrote. "In my view there would be no need to wait for the enemy to adopt such methods. He will certainly adopt them if he thinks it will pay." He asked Ismay to determine whether "drenching" the beaches with gas would be effective.

Another threat caused him particular worry: German parachutists and fifth columnists in disguise. "Much thought," he wrote, "must be given to the trick of wearing British uniform."

THE STRESS OF MANAGING the war began to take its toll on Churchill, and Clementine grew alarmed. During the previous weekend at Chequers, he had been a boor. Having discarded her first letter on the subject, she now wrote to him again.

She reported that a member of Churchill's inner circle, whom she did not identify, "has been to me and told me there is a danger of your being generally disliked by your colleagues & subordinates because of your rough sarcastic & overbearing manner." She assured her husband that the source of this complaint was "a devoted friend," with no ax to grind.

Churchill's private secretaries, she wrote, seemed to have resolved simply to take it and shrug it off. "Higher up, if an idea is suggested (say at a conference) you are supposed to be so contemptuous that presently no ideas, good or bad, will be forthcoming."

Hearing this shocked and hurt her, she said, "because in all these years I have been accustomed to all those who have worked with & under you, loving you." Seeking to explain the degradation in Churchill's behavior, the devoted friend had said, "No doubt it's the strain."

But it was not just the friend's observations that drove Clementine to write her letter. "My Darling Winston," she began, "—I must confess that I have noticed a deterioration in your manner; & you are not so kind as you used to be."

She cautioned that in possessing the power to give orders and to "sack anyone & everyone," he was obliged to maintain a high standard of behavior—to "combine urbanity, kindness and if possible Olympic calm." She reminded him that in the past he had been fond of quoting a French maxim, *"On ne règne sur les âmes que par le calme,"* meaning, essentially, "One leads by calm."

She wrote, "I cannot bear that those who serve the Country & yourself should not love you as well as admire and respect you." She warned, "You won't get the best results by irascibility & rudeness. They <u>will</u> breed either dislike or a slave mentality—(Rebellion in War time being out of the question!)"

She closed, "Please forgive your loving devoted & watchful Clemmie."

At the bottom of the page she drew a caricature of a cat at rest, with a curled tail, and added a postscript: "I wrote this at Chequers last Sunday, tore it up, but here it is now."

The irascible Churchill she depicted was not, however, what John Colville encountered that morning when, at ten o'clock, he entered Churchill's bedroom at 10 Downing Street.

The prime minister seemed remarkably at ease. He lay in bed, propped up by his bedrest. He wore a bright red dressing gown and was smoking a cigar. Beside him was a large chrome cuspidor for his expended cigars (a Savoy Hotel ice bucket) and the Box, open and half full of papers. He was dictating to Mrs. Hill, who sat at the foot of the bed with her typewriter. Cigar smoke misted the room. Churchill's black cat, Nelson, lay also at the foot of the bed, in full cat sprawl, the portrait of peace and repose.

Now and then Churchill gazed adoringly at the cat and murmured, "Cat, darling."

"Tofrek!"

AS A REFUGE FROM THE PRESSURES AND DISTRACTIONS OF WEEK-days in London, Chequers was proving a godsend to Churchill. By now it had become his country command post, to which he summoned legions of guests—generals, ministers, foreign officials, family, staff—who were invited to dine, to sleep, or to "dine and sleep." He brought a private secretary (leaving others on duty in London), two typists, his valet, his chauffeur, two telephone operators, and, always, Inspector Thompson. Barbed wire surrounded the grounds; soldiers of the Coldstream Guard patrolled its hills and vales and boundaries; sentries guarded all access points and demanded passwords from everyone, including Churchill himself. Every day, messengers delivered reports and minutes and the latest intelligence, all to be placed in his black box, or in his top-secret yellow box. He received eight daily and Sunday newspapers, and read them. Although he took time out for meals, walks, baths, and his nap, he spent most of the day dictating minutes and discussing the war with his guests, much as he did at 10 Downing Street, but here with a crucial difference: The house fostered an easier and more candid exchange of ideas and opinions, encouraged by the simple fact that everyone had left their offices behind and by a wealth of novel opportunities for conversation—climbs up Beacon and Coombe Hills, walks in the rose garden, rounds of croquet, and hands of bezique, further leavened by free-flowing champagne, whiskey, and brandy.

The talk typically ranged well past midnight. At Chequers, visitors knew they could speak more freely than in London, and with absolute confidentiality. After one weekend, Churchill's new commander in chief of Home Forces, Alan Brooke, wrote to thank him for periodically inviting him to Chequers, and "giving me an opportunity of discussing the problems of the defense of this country with you, and of putting some of my difficulties before you. These informal talks are of the very greatest help to me, & I do hope you realize how grateful I am to you for your kindness."

Churchill, too, felt more at ease at Chequers, and understood that here he could behave as he wished, secure in the knowledge that whatever happened within would be kept secret (possibly a misplaced trust, given the memoirs and diaries that emerged after the war, like desert flowers after a first rain). This was, he said, a *"cercle sacré."* A sacred circle.

General Brooke recalled one night when Churchill, at two-fifteen A.M., suggested that everyone present retire to the great hall for sandwiches, which Brooke, exhausted, hoped was a signal that soon the night would end and he could get to bed.

"But, no!" he wrote.

What followed was one of those moments often to occur at Chequers that would remain lodged in visitors' minds forever after.

"He had the gramophone turned on," wrote Brooke, "and, in the many-colored dressing-gown, with a sandwich in one hand and watercress in the other, he trotted round and round the hall, giving occasional little skips to the tune of the gramophone." At intervals as he rounded the room he would stop "to release some priceless quotation or thought." During one such pause, Churchill likened a man's life to a walk down a passage lined with closed windows. "As you reach each window, an unknown hand opens it and the light it lets in only increases by contrast the darkness of the end of the passage."

He danced on.

ON THAT LAST WEEKEND in June, the house filled to bursting. At least ten guests came, some to dine, some to dine and sleep. Lord Beaverbrook arrived, brimming with exuberance and bile. Alexander Hardinge, private secretary to the king, came for tea only. Churchill's son, Randolph, and his twenty-year-old wife, Pamela, also arrived, to spend the weekend. Now, too, came General Bernard Paget, chief of the general staff of the Home Forces, and Leopold Amery, the Conservative member of Parliament whose stirring Cromwellian cry "In the name of God, go!" had helped put Churchill in power.

The conversation traversed a broad terrain: aircraft production; the novelty of German armored warfare; the French failure; how to manage the Duke of Windsor, whose abdication to marry Wallis Simpson, four years earlier, continued to cause much upheaval; and where and how invading forces were likely to land. One guest, General Augustus Francis Andrew Nicol Thorne, commander of forces assigned to defend the English coast where the channel was at its narrowest, declared himself convinced that his zone was the prime target and that Germany would attempt to put eighty thousand men on its beaches.

On Saturday afternoon, June 29, while Churchill and Beaverbrook talked privately and, as it happened, heatedly, John Colville took advantage of the respite and spent the afternoon, sunny and warm, in the garden with Clementine and daughter Mary, "whom I find very much nicer on closer acquaintance," he wrote.

Tea followed, after which Randolph Churchill provided Colville with a glimpse of a coarser side to Churchill family life. "I thought Randolph one of the most objectionable people I had ever met: noisy, self-assertive, whining and frankly unpleasant," wrote Colville. "He did not strike me as intelligent." Indeed, Randolph had a reputation as a rude house guest. He was known to start verbal fights with even the most august of dinner companions, and seemed intent on antagonizing all around. He waged what Colville called "preventive war," denouncing guests for what he expected them to say, rather than what they actually said. Often he started fights with Churchill himself, to Churchill's great embarrassment. It did not help that he routinely picked his nose in public and coughed in relentless gusts. "His coughing is like some huge dredger that brings up sea-changed things," wrote Lady Diana Cooper, wife of Minister of Information Duff Cooper, who professed to be a friend of Randolph's. "He spews them out into his hand."

Things got worse at dinner, Colville wrote. Randolph "was anything but kind to Winston, who adores him." He "made a scene" in front of Home Forces staff chief Paget, criticizing generals, lack of equipment, and government complacency.

As the day's consumption of alcohol caught up with him, Randolph grew noisier and still more objectionable.

RANDOLPH'S WIFE, PAMELA, WAS his antithesis: charming, lighthearted, and flirtatious. Though only twenty, she exhibited the sophistication and confidence of an older woman, as well as a degree of sexual knowingness unusual for her circle. This had been apparent even two years earlier, when Pamela had "come out" as a debutante. "Pam was terribly sexy and very obvious," a fellow debutante said. "She was very plump and so bosomy we all called her 'the dairy maid.' She wore high heels and tossed her bottom around. We thought she was quite outrageous. She was known as hot stuff, a very sexy young thing." An American visitor, Kathy Harriman, wrote, "She's a wonderful girl, my age, but one of the wisest young girls I've ever met—knows everything political and otherwise."

Through her marriage, Pamela grew close to the Churchills; she was also befriended by Lord Beaverbrook, who valued her ability to circulate at the highest levels of society. "She passed everything she knew about anybody to Beaverbrook," said American broadcaster Reagan McCrary, better known as Tex, a columnist for William Randolph Hearst's *New York Daily Mirror*. "Beaverbrook was a gossipmonger and Pamela was his bird dog."

Pamela and Randolph had gotten married on October 4, 1939, after a brief courtship whose haste was at least partly driven by Randolph's desire to have a child—a son to be his heir—before being shipped off to battle and dying, an outcome he believed to be inevitable. He proposed to Pamela on their second date, and she, matching impulse for impulse, accepted. He was nearly a decade older and stunningly handsome, but the thing that appealed most to her was that he was a Churchill, at the center of power. Although Clementine did not approve of the marriage, Churchill, calling Pamela "a charming girl," opened his arms wide and saw no problem with the speed at which the relationship had advanced. "I expect that he will be in action in the early spring," Churchill wrote to a friend, shortly before the wedding, "and therefore I am very glad that he should be married before he goes."

Churchill believed marriage to be a simple thing and sought to dispel its mysteries through a series of aphorisms. "All you need to be married are champagne, a box of cigars, and a double bed," he said. Or this: "One of the secrets of a happy marriage is never to speak to or see the loved one before noon." Churchill had a formula for family size as well. Four children was the ideal number: "One to reproduce your wife, one to reproduce yourself, one for the increase in population, and one in case of accident."

Clementine's unease about the marriage stemmed more from her concerns about her son than about Pamela. Clementine's relationship with Randolph had always been a tense one. As a child, he was difficult. "Combative," according to one headmaster. He once pushed a nanny into a filled bathtub; on another occasion, he telephoned the Foreign Office and pretended to be Churchill. One account holds that he encouraged a cousin to empty a chamber pot through an open window onto Lloyd George. When he was nine years old, Clementine, during a school visit, slapped him, an act that Randolph later identified as the moment when he realized she hated him. He was an unremarkable student and drew frequent criticism from Churchill for his lack of scholarly rigor. Churchill condemned even his penmanship, and once returned the boy's loving letter home with editorial corrections marked in red. Randolph got into Oxford only through the kindly intercession of Frederick Lindemann, the Prof, who treated him like a beloved nephew. There, too, he failed to excel. "Your idle & lazy life is [very] offensive to me," Churchill wrote. "You appear to be leading a perfectly useless existence." Churchill loved him, John Colville wrote, but over time "liked him less and less." Clementine, meanwhile, was by any standard a remote parent who expressed little maternal warmth. "That was one of the reasons he was such a nightmare," a friend told Christopher Ogden, Pamela's biographer. "He never got any maternal love at all. Clemmie hated Randolph all his life."

Mary Churchill offered a more nuanced analysis of her brother, observing that "as his personality developed it produced features of character and outlook too dissimilar from his mother's whole nature and attitude to life." As Mary saw it, Randolph "manifestly needed a father's hand; but the main task of controlling him fell almost entirely upon Clementine and so right from the early days she and Randolph were at loggerheads."

He was loud, lacked tact, drank too much, spent beyond his income—his army pay and the salary he received as a correspondent for Beaverbrook's *Evening Standard*—and gambled with startling ineptitude. Even as Churchill tried to stabilize his own financial condition that spring, Randolph asked for help paying his debts, which Churchill agreed to do. "It was indeed generous of you to say that you would meet £100 of my bills," Randolph wrote to his father on June 2. "I do hope it is not very inconvenient for you to do this. I enclose the two most urgent."

More troubling, in terms of the couple's marital future, was Randolph's attitude toward women and sex. To him, fidelity was a fungible condition. He loved sexual conquest, whether his target was married or not, and he took full advantage of the wicked centuries-old custom at country homes whereby hosts arranged guest accommodations to foster sexual liaisons. Randolph once bragged that he would enter the rooms of women without invitation, just in case his presence might be welcomed.

He told this to a female friend, who quipped sardonically, "You must get a lot of rebuffs."

He said, laughing, "I do, but I get a lot of fucking too."

From the start Randolph demonstrated that he was anything but an ideal husband. Though he conveyed an image of dash and charm, he also had a tedious side. During their honeymoon, while in bed at night, he would read to Pamela from *The History of the Decline and Fall of the Roman Empire* by Edward Gibbon. He read lengthy passages and treated Pamela more like a distracted pupil than a marital bedmate, asking at intervals, "Are you listening?"

Yes, she would answer.

But he wanted proof. "Well, what was the last sentence?"

For the moment, all this was eclipsed by the fact that Pamela was now six months pregnant. It was very reassuring: Here, in the midst of a world conflagration, came proof that the greater rhythms of life persisted and that a future lay ahead, despite the uncertain prospects of the moment. If all went well—if Hitler did not invade, if poison gas did not come seeping through the windows, if a German bomb did not obliterate the landscape—the child would arrive in October. Pamela called the fetus her "Baby Dumpling."

AFTER DINNER—AFTER MORE WINE and champagne—Colville took a walk with Mary and another guest, Mary's friend Judy Montagu, and received a reminder that as bucolic and lovely as the estate was, there was a war underway and Chequers was under close guard. The three found themselves "challenged in the most alarming way by ferocious sentries," Colville wrote. Happily they knew the day's password, "Tofrek," apparently a reference to a nineteenth-century battle in the Sudan.

Later, upon checking in with the Air Ministry in London for details on German raids that night, Colville learned that a fleet of enemy planes had just been reported very near to Chequers. Colville relayed this to Churchill, who told him, "I'll bet you a monkey to a mouse-trap they don't hit the house."

Excited at the prospect of action, Churchill rushed out of the building, past a sentry, while shouting, "Friend—Tofrek—Prime Minister," which left the guard slack-jawed with surprise.

Colville and General Paget, the Home Forces staff chief, followed at a slower pace. Paget, amused, said, "What a wonderful tonic he is."

All this was heady stuff for Colville, always present yet always in the background, and the next morning, Sunday, June 30, as he sat in a chair in the sun, he reflected in his diary on the strangeness of his situation. "It is a curious feeling to stay for the week-end in a country house, not as a guest and yet, for a number of reasons, on fairly close terms with the family. It was much like any week-end party except for the conversation which, of course, was brilliant. It is a pleasure to hear really well-informed talk, unpunctuated by foolish and ignorant remarks (except occasionally from Randolph), and it is a relief to be in the background with occasional commissions to execute, but few views to express, instead of being expected to be interesting because one is the P.M.'s Private Secretary."

THAT DAY, AS A herald of the invasion that seemed soon to come, the Germans seized and occupied Guernsey, a British dependency in the Channel Islands off the coast of Normandy, less than two hundred air miles from Chequers. It was a minor action—the Germans held the island with only 469 soldiers—but troubling all the same.

Resignation No. 1

———

As if war and invasion were not enough to think about, that same day, Sunday, June 30, Churchill's close friend and counselor and industrial miracle worker, Lord Beaverbrook, submitted his resignation.

The letter began with the happy reminder that in the seven weeks since Beaverbrook had become minister of aircraft production, the output of aircraft had increased at a near-inconceivable rate: The RAF now had at its disposal 1,040 aircraft ready for service, compared with 45 when he took over—though how he derived these numbers would soon become a matter of dispute. He had done what he set out to do; it was time for him to go. His conflict with the Air Ministry had become so profound as to impede his ability to perform.

"It is now imperative that the Ministry of Aircraft Production should pass into the keeping of a man in touch and sympathy with the Air Ministry and the Air Marshals," he wrote. He blamed himself, declaring he was not suited to working with Air Ministry officials. "I am certain that another man could take up the responsibilities with hope and expectation of that measure of support and sympathy which has been denied to me."

He asked to be relieved of his duties as soon as his successor had been fully briefed on his ministry's ongoing operations and projects.

"I am convinced," he wrote, "that my work is finished and my task is over."

John Colville guessed that Beaverbrook's true motive was a wish to quit "at the peak of his success, before new difficulties arise." Colville considered this an unworthy reason. "It is like trying to stop playing cards immediately after a run of luck," he wrote in his diary.

Churchill, clearly annoyed, sent Beaverbrook his reply the following day, Monday, July 1. Instead of addressing him as Max, or simply Beaverbrook, he began his letter with a frosty "Dear Minister of Aircraft Production."

"I have received your letter of June 30, and hasten to say that at a moment like this when an invasion is reported to be imminent there can be no question of any Ministerial resignations being accepted. I require you, therefore, to dismiss this matter from your mind, and to continue the magnificent work you are doing on which to a large extent our safety depends."

In the meantime, Churchill told him, "I am patiently studying how to meet your needs in respect of control of the over-lapping parts of your Department and that of the Air Ministry, and also to assuage the unfortunate differences which have arisen."

A partly chastened Beaverbrook replied immediately. "I will certainly not neglect my duties here in the face of invasion. But it is imperative—and all the more so because of this threat of armed attack upon our shores—that the process of turning over this Ministry should take place as soon as possible."

He again aired his frustrations: "I cannot get information which I require about supplies or equipment. I cannot get permission to carry out operations essential to strengthening our reserves to the uttermost in readiness for the day of invasion.

"It is not possible for me to go on because a breach has taken place in the last five weeks through the pressure I have been compelled to put upon reluctant officers."

This breach, he wrote, "cannot be healed."

But he no longer threatened immediate resignation.

Churchill was relieved. Beaverbrook's departure at this time would have left an unfillable absence in the skein of counsel and succor that surrounded the prime minister. This would become apparent late that night when, with the threat of resignation for now stifled, Churchill felt compelled to summon Beaverbrook to 10 Downing Street to address a matter of greatest urgency.

Force H

T HE NIGHT WAS EXCEPTIONALLY DARK, WITH ALMOST NO MOON; a brisk wind shook the windows at 10 Downing Street. Churchill needed the counsel of a friend—a decisive, clear-eyed friend.

It was just after midnight when he called Beaverbrook to the Cabinet Room. There was no doubt that Beaverbrook would still be awake and alert. As minister of aircraft production, he kept the same hours as Churchill, prodding and cajoling his staff to find ways to get Britain's aircraft factories to accelerate production. Beaverbrook's brief insurrection had been a schoolboy's pout aimed at eliciting Churchill's support against the Air Ministry, rather than a serious attempt at abandoning his job.

Already present for the meeting were Churchill's top two Admiralty men, First Lord A. V. Alexander and his operations chief, First Sea Lord Sir Dudley Pound. There was tension in the room. The matter of what to do about the French fleet had come down to a yes or no question—whether or not to attempt to seize the fleet to keep it out of Hitler's hands. The Royal Navy was poised to execute a newly devised plan for "the simultaneous seizure, control, or effective disablement of all the accessible French fleet," meaning any ships in such English ports as Plymouth and Southampton, as well as those moored at French bases in Dakar, Alexandria, and Mers el-Kébir, in Algeria. One element of the plan, code-named Operation Catapult, focused on the most important base, Mers el-Kébir, and a smaller annex three miles away at Oran, where some of the French navy's most powerful ships lay at anchor, among them two modern battle cruisers, two battleships, and twenty-one other ships and submarines.

Time was short. These ships could sail any day, and once under the control of Germany, would shift the balance of power at sea, especially in the Mediterranean. No one expected for a moment that Hitler would adhere to his promise to leave the French fleet idle for the duration of the war. An ominous development seemed to confirm the Admiralty's fears: British intelligence learned that the Germans now possessed and were using French naval codes.

Once Operation Catapult got underway, Churchill knew, its commander might have to use force if the French did not willingly relinquish or disable their ships. The man placed in charge was Vice Admiral Sir J. F. Somerville, who earlier had met with his superiors in London to discuss the plan. For Somerville, the idea of firing on the French was deeply unsettling. Britain and France had been allies; together they had declared war against Germany, and their troops had fought side by side, enduring thousands of casualties in the vain attempt to stop Hitler's onslaught. And then there was the fact that the officers and crew on the French ships were fellow navy men. Sailors of all nations, even when at war, felt a strong kinship to one another, as brothers for whom the sea, with all its rigors and dangers, was a common opponent. They recognized a duty to rescue anyone cast adrift, whether by mishap, storm, or warfare. On Monday afternoon, Somerville had telegraphed the Admiralty, urging "that the use of force should be avoided at all costs."

He was prepared, however, to carry out his orders to the fullest, and he possessed the wherewithal to do so. The Admiralty had placed under his command a persuasive battle fleet, code-named Force H, consisting of seventeen ships, including a battle cruiser, HMS *Hood,* and an aircraft carrier, HMS *Ark Royal*. By Monday night, when Churchill summoned Beaverbrook, the force was already gathered at Gibraltar, ready to sail for Mers el-Kébir.

All Admiral Somerville needed now was a final order.

AT 10 DOWNING STREET that blustery night, First Sea Lord Pound declared himself in favor of attacking the French ships. First Lord Alexander at first expressed uncertainty, but he soon sided with Pound. Churchill was still tormented. He called the matter "a hateful decision, the most unnatural and painful in which I have ever been concerned." He needed Beaverbrook's clarity.

And true to form, Beaverbrook showed no hesitation. He urged attack. There could be no doubt, he argued, that Hitler would appropriate the French ships, even if their captains and crews balked. "The Germans will force the French Fleet to join the Italians, thus taking command of the Mediterranean," he said. "The Germans will force this by threatening to burn Bordeaux the first day the French refuse, the next day Marseilles, and the third day Paris."

This persuaded Churchill, but just after he gave the order to proceed, the magnitude of what might soon unfold overwhelmed him. He grabbed Beaverbrook by the arm and dragged him into the garden behind 10 Downing Street. It was almost two A.M. The wind blew strong. Churchill sped through the garden, with Beaverbrook behind, struggling to keep up. Beaverbrook's asthma spiked. As he stood wheezing and gulping air, Churchill affirmed that the only path was indeed attack, and began to weep.

Somerville received his final orders at 4:26 A.M., on Tuesday, July 2. The operation was to begin with the delivery of an ultimatum from Somerville to the French admiral in command at Mers el-Kébir, Marcel Gensoul, that set out three alternatives: to join Britain in fighting Germany and Italy; to sail to a British port; or to sail to a French port in the West Indies where the ships could be stripped of armament or transferred to the United States for safekeeping.

"If you refuse these fair offers," Somerville's message stated, "I must with profound regret require you to sink your ships within six hours. Finally, failing the above, I have the orders of His Majesty's Government to use whatever force may be necessary to prevent your ships from falling into German or Italian hands."

Force H left Gibraltar at dawn. That night, at ten fifty-five, Admiral Pound, at Churchill's behest, telegraphed Somerville: "You are charged with one of the most disagreeable and difficult tasks that a British Admiral has ever been faced with, but we have complete confidence in you and rely on you to carry it out relentlessly."

IN BERLIN THAT DAY, Tuesday, July 2, Hitler asked the commanders of his army, navy, and air force to evaluate the feasibility of a full-on invasion of Britain, the first concrete indication that he had begun seriously to contemplate such an attack.

Until now he had shown little interest in invasion. With the fall of France and the disarray of Britain's army after Dunkirk, Hitler had assumed that Britain, in one way or another, would withdraw from the war. It was crucial that this happen, and soon. Britain was the last obstacle in the west, one Hitler needed to eliminate so that he could concentrate on his long-dreamed-of invasion of Soviet Russia and avoid a two-front war, a phenomenon for which the word-minting power of the German language did not fail: *Zweifrontenkrieg*. He believed that even Churchill, at some point, would have to acknowledge the folly of continuing to oppose him. The war in the west was, in Hitler's view, all but over. "Britain's position is hopeless," he told his head of Army High Command, General Franz Halder. "The war is won by us. A reversal in the prospects of success is impossible." So confident was Hitler that Britain would negotiate, he demobilized forty Wehrmacht divisions—25 percent of his army.

But Churchill was not behaving like a sane man. Hitler sent a series of indirect peace feelers through multiple sources, including the king of Sweden and the Vatican; all were rejected or ignored. To help avoid scuttling any opportunity for a peace deal, he forbade Luftwaffe chief Hermann Göring from launching air raids against civilian districts of London. Invasion was a prospect he contemplated with anxiety and reluctance, and with good reason. Early studies conducted independently by the German navy well before Hitler himself began to ponder invasion highlighted grave obstacles, mostly centered on the fact that Germany's relatively small navy was ill-equipped for any such enterprise. The army, too, saw dangerous hurdles.

Hitler's uncertainty was evident in how he now couched this new request to his commanders. He emphasized that "the plan to invade England has not taken any definite shape" and that his request merely contemplated the possibility of such an invasion. He was definitive on one point, however: Any such invasion could succeed only if Germany first achieved complete air superiority over the RAF.

AT THREE A.M. ON Wednesday, July 3, as Admiral Somerville's Force H neared Oran in the Mediterranean Sea, a destroyer in the group was sent out ahead with three officers, to open a communications channel with the French. Nearby stood the ruins of an ancient Roman town with the disconcerting name of Vulturia. Soon afterward, a message was sent to the French admiral in charge, Gensoul, requesting a meeting. The message began with a salvo of flattery: "The British Navy hopes that their proposals will enable you and the valiant and glorious French Navy to be by our side." It assured the French admiral that if he chose to sail with the Royal Navy, "your ships would remain yours and no one need have anxiety for the future."

The message closed: "A British Fleet is at sea off Oran waiting to welcome you."

The admiral refused to meet with the British officers, who now sent him a written copy of the full ultimatum. The time was 9:35 A.M. Britain's Admiral Somerville signaled the French: "We hope most sincerely that the proposals will be acceptable and that we shall have you by our side."

Reconnaissance planes from the *Ark Royal,* the aircraft carrier assigned to Force H, reported signs that the French ships were preparing to sail, "raising steam and furling awnings."

At ten A.M., the French admiral delivered a message affirming that he would never let the French ships fall under German control but also vowing, in light of the ultimatum, that his ships would fight back if the British used force. He repeated this vow an hour later, pledging to spare nothing to defend his fleet.

Tension mounted. At eleven-forty, the British sent a message stating that no French ship would be allowed to leave the harbor unless the terms of the ultimatum were accepted. British air reconnaissance reported further signs that the French fleet was getting ready to put to sea. The ships' bridges were fully manned.

Admiral Somerville ordered that aircraft from the *Ark Royal* begin depositing mines at the mouth of the harbor.

Somerville was just about to send a message telling the French that he would begin bombarding their ships at two-thirty that afternoon when word arrived from the French admiral, agreeing to a face-to-face conference. By this point, Somerville suspected that the French were merely stalling for time, but he dispatched an officer all the same. The meeting, aboard the French flagship, *Dunkerque,* began at four-fifteen, by which time the French ships were fully primed to sail, with tugboats in position.

Somerville ordered the placement of more mines, these to be dropped in the nearby harbor at Oran.

ABOARD THE *DUNKERQUE,* the meeting went badly. The French admiral was "extremely indignant and angry," according to the British emissary. The talk continued for an hour, achieving nothing.

IN LONDON, CHURCHILL AND the Admiralty grew impatient. The French admiral was clearly stalling for time, and so, it seemed, was Somerville. His reluctance to attack was understandable; nevertheless, the time for action had come. Nightfall was approaching. "There was nothing for it but to give [Somerville] a peremptory order to carry out the repugnant task without further question," wrote Pug Ismay. "But all who were present when that message was drafted could not but feel sad and, in a sense, guilty." Pug had initially opposed attacking the French fleet, out of both moral scruple and fear that France might declare war on Britain. "To kick a man when he is down is unattractive at any time," he wrote. "But when the man is a friend who has already suffered grievously, it seems almost to border on infamy."

The Admiralty wired Somerville, "Settle the matter quickly or you may have French reinforcements to deal with."

At four-fifteen P.M., while the meeting aboard the *Dunkerque* was just getting underway, Somerville signaled the French that if they did not accept one of the options set out in the original British ultimatum by five-thirty, he would sink their ships.

Force H prepared for battle. The French did likewise. As the British emissary left the *Dunkerque,* he heard alarms behind him sounding "Action." He reached his ship at five twenty-five P.M., five minutes before Somerville's deadline.

The deadline came—and went.

IN PORTSMOUTH AND PLYMOUTH, where the operation to seize French ships was also underway, British forces faced little resistance. "The action was sudden and necessarily a surprise," Churchill wrote. "Overwhelming force was employed, and the whole transaction showed how easily the Germans could have taken possession of any French warships lying in ports which they controlled."

Churchill described the action in British ports as having been mostly "amicable," with some French crews actually glad to leave their ships behind. One vessel resisted—the *Surcouf,* an immense submarine named for an eighteenth-century French privateer. As a British squad raced aboard, the French sought to burn manuals and scuttle the submarine. Gunfire left one French sailor dead, three British. The *Surcouf* surrendered.

IN THE MEDITERRANEAN OFF Mers el-Kébir, Admiral Somerville at last gave the order to open fire. The time was 5:54 P.M., nearly a half hour past his deadline. His ships were positioned at "maximum visibility range" of 17,500 yards, just shy of ten miles.

The first salvo fell short. The second struck a breakwater, blasting loose chunks of concrete, some of which struck the French ships. The third was on target. A large French battleship, the *Bretagne,* with a crew of twelve hundred men, exploded, sending a great orange plume of fire and smoke hundreds of feet into the sky. A destroyer also blew up. Smoke filled the harbor, blocking the view of British spotters aboard their ships and in the air.

One minute after the British began firing, the French began to fire back, using big shipboard guns and other heavy guns on shore. Their shells fell closer and closer to the British ships, as their gunners adjusted their aim.

Somerville sent a message by wireless to London: "Am being heavily engaged."

At 10 Downing Street, Churchill told First Lord Alexander that "the French were now fighting with all their vigor for the first time since war broke out." Churchill fully expected France to declare war.

British shells struck another French battleship, drawing forth a cascade of orange flames. A large destroyer received a direct hit as it tried to flee the harbor.

In all, the ships of Force H fired thirty-six salvos of shells, each fifteen inches in diameter and packed with high explosives, until the French guns went quiet. Somerville gave the order to cease fire at 6:04 P.M., just ten minutes after the action began.

As the smoke cleared, Somerville saw that the battleship *Bretagne* had disappeared. The attack and the secondary actions killed 1,297 French officers and sailors. To the statistically inclined, that worked out to roughly 130 lives per minute. Nearly a thousand of the dead had been aboard the *Bretagne*. Somerville's Force H suffered no casualties.

AT 10 DOWNING STREET, news of the fighting began to arrive. Churchill paced his office, and kept repeating, "Terrible, terrible."

The battle affected him deeply, as daughter Mary observed in her diary. "It is so terrible that we should be forced to fire on our own erst-while allies," she wrote. "Papa is shocked and deeply grieved that such action has been necessary."

Strategically, the attack yielded obvious benefits, partially crippling the French navy, but to Churchill what mattered just as much or more was what it signaled. Until this point, many onlookers had assumed that Britain would seek an armistice with Hitler, now that France, Poland, Norway, and so many other countries had fallen under his sway, but the attack provided vivid, irrefutable proof that Britain would not surrender—proof to Roosevelt and proof, as well, to Hitler.

THE NEXT DAY, THURSDAY, July 4, Churchill revealed the story of Mers el-Kébir to the House of Commons, telling it as a kind of maritime thriller, recounting the battle as it had unfolded, in direct terms, not shying from details. He called it a "melancholy action" but one whose necessity was beyond challenge. "I leave the judgment of our action, with confidence, to Parliament. I leave it to the nation, and I leave it to the United States. I leave it to the world and to history."

The House roared its approval, rising in a wild tumult, Labour, Liberals, and Conservatives alike. Churchill's great trick—one he had demonstrated before, and would demonstrate again—was his ability to deliver dire news and yet leave his audience feeling encouraged and uplifted. "Fortified" is how Harold Nicolson put it in his diary that day. Despite the grim circumstances, and the grimmer potential that France might now declare war on Britain, Nicolson felt something akin to elation. "If we can stick it," he wrote, "we really shall have won the war. What a fight it is! What a chance for us! Our action against the French Fleet has made a tremendous effect throughout the world. I am as stiff as can be."

The applause lasted for several minutes. Churchill wept. Amid the tumult, John Colville overheard him say, "This is heartbreaking for me."

The public applauded as well. The Home Intelligence survey for July 4 reported that news of the attack "has been received in all Regions with satisfaction and relief. . . . It is felt that this strong action gives welcome evidence of Government vigor and decision." A Gallup Poll for July 1940 found that 88 percent of Britons approved of the prime minister.

Within the Admiralty itself, however, there was condemnation. The senior officers involved in the attack called it "an act of sheer treachery." French naval officers sent Somerville a scathing letter that, according to Pug Ismay, accused the admiral "of having brought disgrace on the whole naval profession." Outwardly, Somerville seemed to brush off the rebuke, but, wrote Ismay, "I am sure it cut him to the quick."

The episode caused a tense moment over lunch at Downing Street soon afterward. Word came to Clementine that one of the expected guests, General Charles de Gaulle, now lodged in England, was in an even more obstreperous mood than usual, and that she should make sure everyone at lunch was on their best behavior. Pamela Churchill was among those invited.

At Clementine's end of the table, the conversation lurched into dangerous territory. She told de Gaulle that she hoped the French fleet would now join with Britain in the fight against Germany. "To this," Pamela recalled, "the General curtly replied that, in his view, what would really give the French fleet satisfaction would be to turn their guns 'On *you*!'" Meaning against the British fleet.

Clementine liked de Gaulle, but, keenly aware of how deeply her husband grieved having to sink the French ships, she now rounded on the general and, in her perfect French, took him to task "for uttering words and sentiments that ill became either an ally or a guest in this country," as Pamela put it.

Churchill, at the far side of the table, sought to dispel the tension. He leaned forward and, in an apologetic tone, in French, said, "You must excuse my wife, my General; she speaks French too well."

Clementine glared at Churchill.

"No, Winston," she snapped.

She turned back to de Gaulle and, again in French, said, "That is not the reason. There are certain things that a woman can say to a man that a man cannot say. And I am saying them to you, General de Gaulle."

The next day, by way of apology, de Gaulle sent her a large basket of flowers.

Berlin

———

Hitler was serious about seeking an agreement with Britain that would end the war, though he grew convinced that no such thing could be achieved while Churchill was still in power. Britain's attack on the French fleet at Mers el-Kébir had proved that beyond doubt. In July, Hitler met with his deputy, Rudolf Hess, and told him of his frustration, conveying his "wish" that Hess find a way of engineering the removal of Churchill as prime minister so as to clear a path for negotiations with a presumably more pliable successor. As Hess saw it, Hitler was assigning him the great mandate of securing peace in the west.

To Hess, it was a welcome honor. For a time, he had been closer to Hitler than any other party member. For eight years he served as Hitler's private secretary, and, following the abortive Nazi putsch of 1923, was incarcerated with Hitler at Landsberg Prison, where Hitler began writing *Mein Kampf*. Hess typed the manuscript. Hess understood that a central tenet of Hitler's geopolitical strategy set out in the book was the importance of peace with Britain, and he knew how strongly Hitler believed that in the prior war Germany had made a fatal mistake in provoking Britain to fight. Hess considered himself so much in tune with Hitler that he could execute his will without being commanded to do so. Hess hated Jews, and orchestrated many restrictions on Jewish life. He cast himself as the embodiment of the Nazi spirit and made himself responsible for perpetuating national adoration of Hitler and ensuring party purity.

But with the advent of war, Hess began to lose prominence, and men like Hermann Göring began to ascend. To have Hitler now assign so important an undertaking must certainly have reassured Hess. There was little time, however. With France now fallen, Britain must either agree to stand down or face extinction. One way or another, Churchill had to be removed from office.

In his conversation with Hess, Hitler expressed his frustration at Britain's intransigence in a way that, given events soon to occur, would seem at least superficially prophetic.

"What more can I do?" Hitler asked. "I can't fly over there and beg on bended knee."

THE ATTACK AT MERS EL-KÉBIR had indeed taken Nazi leaders by surprise, but Propaganda Minister Joseph Goebbels now saw that the incident opened a new path for waging Germany's propaganda war against Britain. At his morning meeting on July 4, he told his lieutenants to use the incident to show that once again France was bearing the brunt of the war, even as Britain claimed that the attack was in France's interest. "Here," he told the group, "Britain has really revealed herself without her mask."

All efforts were to be made to continue stoking hatred of Britain, and of Churchill in particular, but not to the point of sparking popular demand for an all-out attack. Goebbels knew that Hitler remained ambivalent about invasion and still favored a negotiated resolution. "It is therefore necessary to mark time, since we cannot anticipate any decisions by the *Führer*," Goebbels said. "The mood, as far as possible, must be kept on the boil until the *Führer* himself has spoken."

And Hitler did plan to speak, soon, as Goebbels knew. Anticipating his remarks, Goebbels, at a meeting two days later, emphasized that for the time being the ministry's propaganda should promote the idea that the British "should be given one last chance of getting off comparatively slightly."

Goebbels believed that Hitler's coming speech could alter the course of the war, possibly even end it—and, failing that, would at least offer a rich new avenue for igniting public hatred of Churchill.

AT 10 DOWNING STREET THAT WEEK, anxiety intensified as to whether the French might yet declare war against Britain, and whether Germany would now invade. On July 3, a report by the chiefs of staff warned that "major operations against this country either by invasion and/or heavy air attack may commence any day from now onwards." It listed ominous developments detected by reconnaissance and intelligence sources, among them certain "secret sources," a reference undoubtedly to Bletchley Park. In Norway, German forces were requisitioning and arming vessels; the country had eight hundred fishing boats. The Luftwaffe was transferring troop-carrying aircraft to its first-line air bases. The German navy held an amphibious-landing exercise on the Baltic coast, and two regiments of parachute troops moved to Belgium. Perhaps most ominous: "Information from a most reliable source is to the effect that the Germans will hold a parade of their armed forces in PARIS some time after 10th July." Hitler, it seemed, considered victory to be certain.

"I have the impression," John Colville wrote, "that Germany is collecting herself for a great spring; and it is an uncomfortable impression."

Fueling his concerns was a German action that had taken place a few days earlier, on the day of Churchill's speech about the battle at Mers el-Kébir. Twenty German dive-bombers had attacked targets on the Isle of Portland, which juts into the channel off England's south coast. They escaped without interception by the RAF—"a bad look-out for the future if this can be done with impunity in broad daylight," Colville wrote.

Champagne and Garbo

O N WEDNESDAY, JULY 10, GAY MARGESSON VISITED COLVILLE IN London. They saw the Strauss operetta *Die Fledermaus,* performed in English. Most of the audience loved the humor; Colville and Gay did not, and left in the middle of the third act. "In the intervals," he wrote in his diary, "Gay insisted on talking politics, about which she is as ignorant as she is prejudiced, and indulging in recriminations of Chamberlain and his Government. For the first time since I have known her I found her definitely tedious and puerile."

As Colville himself admitted, by looking for faults in Gay he hoped to ease the hurt of her steadfast unwillingness to return his affections. But he could not help it: He was still in love.

They moved on to the Café de Paris, a popular nightclub, and there "her charms and real lovableness reasserted themselves and I forgot the somewhat unpleasant impression I had been forming." They talked, drank champagne, and danced. An impersonator did renditions of Ingrid Bergman and Greta Garbo.

Colville was back in his own bed—alone—at two A.M., content in the belief that Gay might be warming to him at last.

Have We Sunk So Low?

———

ENGLAND BRACED FOR INVASION. TROOPS PILED SANDBAGS AND built machine-gun nests near the Palace of Westminster, home to Parliament and Big Ben. In Parliament Square, a small fortified redoubt— a pillbox—was disguised as a W. H. Smith book kiosk. Sandbags and guns adorned the grounds of Buckingham Palace, where the masses of tulips in the palace gardens were, according to *New Yorker* writer Mollie Panter-Downes, "exactly the color of blood." The queen began taking lessons in how to shoot a revolver. "Yes," she said, "I shall not go down like the others." In Hyde Park, soldiers dug anti-tank trenches and erected obstacles to prevent German gliders from landing troops in the heart of London. A government pamphlet on how to behave during an invasion warned citizens to stay in their homes and not attempt to run, "because, if you run away, you will be machine-gunned from the air, as were civilians in Holland and Belgium."

Every day, more and more of the British public bore direct witness to the war as German bombers, accompanied by masses of fighters, extended their forays deeper and deeper into the realm. Just that week, a lone bomber attacked Aberdeen, dropping ten bombs that killed thirty-five people yet never triggered an air-raid alert. The same night, other bombers struck Cardiff, Tyneside, and near Glasgow. Forty dive-bombers with fighter escorts attacked the harbor at Dover; bombs and incendiaries fell on Avonmouth, Colchester, Brighton, Hove, and the Isle of Sheppey. Churchill made sure that Roosevelt knew about all of them. By now the Foreign Office was dispatching daily telegrams to the president on the "war situation," matter-of-fact accountings of actions in all theaters, delivered through Britain's ambassador in Washington. These had a dual purpose: to keep the president up to date and, more importantly, to make sure that Roosevelt understood that Britain's need for American aid was real and urgent.

Often the German sorties were met by British fighters, which gave the civilians below a close-up look at aerial warfare. The RAF's fighter pilots were fast becoming the heroes of the age, as were their counterparts in RAF Bomber Command. Established on April 1, 1918, in the waning months of the prior war, the RAF consolidated disparate air units operated by the army and navy in order to better defend against aerial attack. It was now acknowledged to be the first line of defense against Germany.

To Mary Churchill and her friend Judy Montagu, the pilots were gods. The two girls were spending the "high summer" together at Judy's country home, Breccles Hall, in Norfolk, where nearly every afternoon they flirted with bomber crews from nearby air bases. In the evening they attended squadron dances, which Mary described as "very jolly and noisy and pretty drunken affairs, with sometimes an undercurrent of tension (especially if planes had failed to return)." They made "special friends," as Mary put it, and Judy invited them back to the house "to play tennis, swim, lark about, indulge in snogging sessions in the hayloft, or just sit in the garden gossiping." The men were for the most part in their twenties, middle-class, unmarried. Mary found them charming. She delighted in the occasions in which the pilots engaged in bouts of "beating up"— flying over Breccles at treetop level. On one occasion, crews from the nearby base at Watton "gave us the most superb aerial beating up that anyone could possibly conceive," Mary wrote in her diary. "A flight of Blenheims appeared & one after another swooped down to within 25 or 30 feet of the ground. We all nearly passed out with excitement."

Every day these same pilots took part in life-or-death sorties that, as far as Churchill was concerned, would determine the fate of the British Empire. Civilians watched air battles unfold from the safety of their gardens or while strolling village streets and picnicking in bucolic meadows, as circular contrails filled the sky above. At dusk these caught the last of the day's sunlight and turned a luminescent amber; at dawn, they became mother-of-pearl spirals. Aircraft crashed into pastures and forests; pilots tumbled from cockpits and drifted to earth.

On July 14, a mobile BBC radio team stationed itself on the Dover cliffs in hopes of capturing an aerial battle as it occurred, and gave its listeners an account that for some proved too enthusiastic. The BBC announcer, Charles Gardner, turned the battle into a blow-by-blow account that had more in common with a soccer commentary than a report on a mortal encounter over the channel. This struck many listeners as unseemly. A London woman wrote to the *News Chronicle,* "Have we really sunk so low that this sort of thing can be treated as a sporting event? With cries of glee, we were told to listen for the machine-gunning, we were asked to visualize a pilot, hampered by his parachute, struggling in the water." She warned, with a degree of prescience, "If this sort of thing is allowed to go unchecked we shall soon have microphones installed in any available front line, with squared diagrams printed in the 'Radio Times' to help us follow the action." Mass-Observation diarist Olivia Cockett also found it repellent. "It <u>shouldn't be allowed</u>," she insisted. "It makes play and sport of agonies, not to help people bear them, but to pander to the basest, crudest, most-to-be-wiped-out feelings of cruel violence."

What made it worse, one woman told a Home Intelligence survey taker, was the announcer's "callous Oxford accent."

But a Home Intelligence report released the next day, July 15, after a quick poll of three hundred Londoners, stated that "a considerable majority spoke enthusiastically of the broadcast." *New Yorker* writer Panter-Downes suspected that most listeners reveled in the drama. She wrote in her diary, "The majority of decent citizens, possibly less squeamish, sat by their radios, hanging onto their seats and cheering."

What especially heartened the public was that the RAF appeared consistently to best the Luftwaffe. In the battle off Dover, as Churchill told Roosevelt in one of the Foreign Office's daily telegraphic updates, the Germans suffered six confirmed losses (three fighters, three bombers); the British lost a single Hurricane. The July 15 Home Intelligence report found that for the public watching from below, "the bringing down of raiders . . . has a psychological effect immensely greater than the military advantage gained."

Churchill himself found it all thrilling. "After all," he told an interviewer with the *Chicago Daily News* later that week, "what more glorious thing can a spirited young man experience than meeting an opponent at four hundred miles an hour, with twelve or fifteen hundred horse power in his hands and unlimited offensive power? It is the most splendid form of hunting conceivable."

IN JULY, WITH HIS aborted resignation forgiven and forgotten, Lord Beaverbrook returned with gusto to the production of fighters. He built planes at a furious pace and made enemies just as fast, but he also became the adored son of Britain. Though a brigand in the view of his antagonists, Lord Beaverbrook had a subtle grasp of human nature, and was adept at marshaling workers and the public to his cause. Case in point was his "Spitfire Fund."

Without prompting by him or the Air Ministry, the citizens of Jamaica (a British colony until 1962) contributed money for the building of a bomber and sent it to Beaverbrook, via the island's major newspaper, the *Daily Gleaner*. This tickled Beaverbrook, who made sure that the gift and his telegram of thanks got widespread attention.

Soon other gifts began to arrive, from places as far away as America and Ceylon, and once again Beaverbrook sent thank-you telegrams and made sure the messages got national coverage. Soon it occurred to him that this civic generosity could be harnessed not just to generate much-needed cash to build airplanes but also to boost engagement with the war effort among the public and, importantly, among workers in his aircraft plants, whom he believed to be plagued by a persistent "lack of drive."

He never issued a direct public plea for contributions; instead, he made a deliberate show of acknowledging those that arrived. When donations reached a certain level, the contributors could choose to name a specific fighter; a richer total allowed the donors to name a bomber. "The naming of a whole squadron became the goal," recalled David Farrer, one of Beaverbrook's secretaries. Soon the BBC began announcing the names of contributors on the air during its nightly news broadcasts. At first Beaverbrook wrote a personal letter to every donor, but when this became too big an obligation, he directed his secretaries to choose the gifts most worthy of attention, whether because of the amount or the story behind the gift. A child giving up a few pence was as likely to get a letter as was a rich industrialist.

A torrent of money began to flow toward the Ministry of Aircraft Production, mostly in small amounts, and accumulated in what the donors themselves began calling the Spitfire Fund, owing to their preference for the fighter that had become the icon of the air war (even though the RAF had more Hurricanes than Spitfires). Although Beaverbrook's detractors dismissed the fund as just another of his "stunts," in fact it soon began drawing contributions at a rate of £1 million per month. By May 1941, the total collected would reach £13 million, at which point, wrote Farrer, "practically every big town in Britain had its name on an aircraft."

The fund had only a marginal effect on the overall production of fighters and bombers, but Beaverbrook saw a much greater value in its spiritual influence. "To countless men and women," secretary Farrer wrote, "he made easy the way to a more personal interest in the war and to an enthusiastic contribution to its waging."

Beaverbrook found other means of achieving this heightened engagement as well, these just as oblique. Like Churchill, he recognized the power of symbols. He sent RAF pilots to factories, to establish a direct connection between the work of building airplanes and the men who flew them. He insisted that these be actual fighting pilots, with wings on their uniforms, not merely RAF officials paroled briefly from their desks. He also ordered that the husks of downed German planes be displayed around the country, and in such a way that the public would not suspect the hand of the minister of aircraft production. He saw great benefit in having flatbed trucks carry the downed aircraft through bombed-out cities. This "circus," as he called it, was always well received, but especially so in the most heavily mauled locations. "The people appeared very pleased to see the aircraft," Beaverbrook told Churchill, "and the circus had a great effect."

When complaints arrived from farmers, village elders, and golf course operators about German aircraft on their fields, squares, and greens, Beaverbrook resolved to take his time having the planes removed—the opposite of the haste with which he recovered salvageable RAF fighters. After a complaint from one golf course, he ordered that the German plane be left where it was. "It will do the players good to see the crashed machine," he told his publicity man. "It will make them conscious of the battle."

OUTRAGED BY CHURCHILL'S RESISTANCE and rhetoric, Hitler ordered the very thing Britain had feared, a full-on assault from the sea. Until now, there had been no concrete plan for an invasion of England, scientific or otherwise. On Tuesday, July 16, he issued Directive No. 16, entitled "On Preparations for a Landing Operation Against England," and code-named the plan Seelöwe, or Sea Lion.

"Since England, in spite of her hopeless military situation, shows no signs of being ready to come to an understanding," the directive began, "I have decided to prepare a landing operation against England and, if necessary, to carry it out."

He anticipated a vast seaborne attack: "The landing will be in the form of a surprise crossing on a wide front from about Ramsgate to the area west of the Isle of Wight." This encompassed a swath of English coastline that included beaches on the Strait of Dover, the narrowest part of the English Channel. (His commanders envisioned as many as sixteen hundred vessels delivering a first wave of one hundred thousand men.) All planning and preparation for Sea Lion were to be completed by mid-August, Hitler wrote. He identified objectives that had to be achieved before an invasion could begin, foremost among them: "The English Air Force must be so reduced morally and physically that it is unable to deliver any significant attack against the German crossing."

What's in a Name?

A SMALL BUT PRESSING CRISIS ABRUPTLY AROSE IN THE CHURCHILL family.

By July, Pamela Churchill was convinced that her baby was going to be a boy, and she set her heart on naming the child Winston Spencer Churchill, after the prime minister. But that same month, the Duchess of Marlborough, whose husband was a cousin of Churchill's, gave birth to a boy and claimed the full name for her son.

Pamela was crushed and angry. She went to Churchill in tears and pleaded with him to do something. He agreed that the name was rightfully his to bestow, and that it would be more appropriate to give it to a grandson than a nephew. He called the duchess and told her bluntly that the name was his, and it was to be given to Pamela's new son.

The duchess protested that Pamela's child had not even been born yet; obviously there was no certainty that it would be a boy.

"Of course it will," Churchill snapped. "And if it isn't this time, it will be next time."

The duke and duchess renamed their son Charles.

The Tyrant's Appeal

O N FRIDAY, JULY 19, HITLER STRODE TO THE ROSTRUM OF THE Kroll Opera House, in Berlin, to address the Reichstag, Germany's legislature, which had been meeting in that building ever since the eponymous 1933 fire that had made the body's official home unusable. On the dais, near Hitler, sat Luftwaffe chief Göring, large and merry, "like a happy child playing with his toys on Christmas morning," wrote correspondent William Shirer, who witnessed the speech. In an aside, Shirer added, "Only how deadly that some of the toys he plays with, besides the electric train in the attic of Carinhall, happen to be Stuka bombers!" Göring and a dozen generals were to receive their own promotions that night, the generals to the rank of field marshal, and Göring, already a field marshal, to the newly created rank of *Reichsmarschall*. Hitler knew his man. He understood Göring's need for special attention and gleaming medals.

Earlier that Friday, Propaganda Minister Joseph Goebbels had centered his regular morning meeting on the speech and its potential effect, according to minutes of the session. He cautioned that foreign reaction would likely not reach full flower for two or three days but that it was certain to polarize public opinion within Britain, even to the point of forcing Churchill's resignation. The meeting minutes stated: "The Minister emphasizes that Britain's fate will be decided this evening."

AS HITLER BEGAN SPEAKING, Shirer, seated in the audience, was struck anew by his rhetorical skills: "So wonderful an actor," Shirer wrote in his diary, "so magnificent a handler of the German mind." He marveled at how Hitler managed to cast himself as both conqueror and humble supplicant for peace. He noticed, too, that Hitler spoke in a lower register than was typical, and without his usual histrionics. He used his body to underscore and amplify the thoughts he sought to convey, cocking his head to impart irony, moving with a cobra's grace. What especially caught Shirer's attention was the way Hitler moved his hands. "Tonight he used those hands beautifully, seemed to express himself almost as much with his hands—and the sway of his body—as he did with his words and the use of his voice."

First Hitler ran through the history of the war thus far, laying the blame for it on Jews, Freemasons, and Anglo-French "warmongers," foremost among them Churchill. "I feel a deep disgust for this type of unscrupulous politician who wrecks entire nations and States," Hitler said. He framed the war as a quest to restore Germany's honor and rescue the nation from the oppression of the Treaty of Versailles. He congratulated his army and generals, commending many by name, singling out as well Rudolf Hess, his official deputy; Heinrich Himmler, chief of Hitler's protective force, the S.S.; Joseph Goebbels; and Göring, clearly his favorite among the four, to whom he devoted several minutes of fulsome praise.

"Throughout Hitler's speech," Shirer observed, "Göring leaned over his desk chewing his pencil, and scribbling out in large, scrawly letters the text of his remarks which he would make after Hitler finished. He chewed on his pencil and frowned and scribbled like a schoolboy over a composition that has got to be in by the time class is ended." At intervals Göring grinned and applauded, thudding his big hands together with exaggerated force. Hitler announced Göring's promotion and handed him a box containing the requisite new insignia for his uniform. Göring opened the box, peeked in, then went back to chewing his pencil. His "boyish pride and satisfaction was almost touching, old murderer that he is," Shirer wrote.

Hitler turned to the future. He proclaimed his army to be at its most powerful and promised to respond to British air raids on Germany in a manner that would bring "unending suffering and misery" to Britain— though probably not to Churchill himself, he said, "for he no doubt will already be in Canada where the money and the children of those principally interested in the war already have been sent. For millions of other persons, great suffering will begin."

Now came the portion of the speech that Goebbels believed would determine Britain's fate. "Mr. Churchill," Hitler said, ". . . for once believe me when I predict a great empire will be destroyed, an empire that it was never my intention to destroy or even to harm."

The only possible result of the war, he warned, was the annihilation of either Germany or Britain. "Churchill may believe this will be Germany," he said. "I know it will be Britain." With his hands and body he conveyed with clarity that this was no mere threat. "In this hour I feel it to be my duty before my own conscience to appeal once more to reason and common sense in Great Britain as much as elsewhere. I consider myself in a position to make this appeal, since I am not the vanquished, begging favors, but the victor speaking in the name of reason."

Abruptly the conqueror gave way to the humble *Führer*. "I can see no reason why this war must go on," he said. "I am grieved to think of the sacrifices it will claim. I should like to avert them."

OVERHEAD, GERMAN ACE Adolf Galland and his squadron flew a protective screen above Berlin's opera house to guard against RAF bombers, a choice assignment meant to honor their performance in the French campaign.

Though only twenty-eight years old, Galland was by now a seasoned combat pilot, commander of his own fighter group. Big-eared, dark, with a black mustache and a broad smile, he had none of the Nordic iciness that the Nazi Party held dear; nor was he an ardent believer in party ideology. He cut a rakish figure, often wearing his officer's cap cocked at an angle. Just the day before the speech, he had been promoted to the rank of major and awarded his third Knight's Cross, for shooting down seventeen aircraft and providing effective support for Germany's ground forces. By the time his commander, Albert Kesselring, physically presented the award, however, Galland's total of verified kills had risen to thirty. His role as aerial guardian during Hitler's speech was not wholly honorific, he wrote later: "One bomb on the Kroll Opera House would actually have eliminated the entire German High Command at one fell swoop, so the precaution seemed well justified."

Galland's journey to this moment embodied the broader story of the creation and flowering of the Luftwaffe as a whole. Galland became obsessed with aviation early in his youth, his imagination fired by postwar accounts of the aerial exploits of Baron von Richthofen. At age seventeen, he began flying gliders. His father pressed him to join the army, but Galland just wanted to fly, and sought a way of making a living in the air.

What he most wanted was to fly powered aircraft. He saw only one path: to become a pilot with Germany's newly founded airline, Deutsche Luft Hansa, soon to be known simply as Lufthansa. But every other young flying enthusiast seemed also to share this ambition. Galland's application to the German Airline Pilot School was one of twenty thousand, from which the school chose one hundred candidates. Only twenty made the final cut, Galland among them. By the end of 1932, he had earned a preliminary flying certificate.

Now things took an unexpected turn. Galland and four other students received orders to report to a flying school in Berlin, where they were invited to join a secret course in flying military aircraft—secret, because Hitler at this time was beginning his campaign to rearm Germany in defiance of the Treaty of Versailles, which had ended the Great War. All five accepted the offer; they traveled in civilian clothes to an airfield near Munich, where they attended lectures on tactics and spent twenty-five hours flying old biplanes, learning such techniques as how to fly in formation and strafe targets on the ground. The high point, Galland recalled, was a visit from Hermann Göring, who had embarked, secretly, on building a new air force.

After a brief stint as a copilot on a commercial airliner, Galland in December 1933 was summoned back to Berlin and invited to join Göring's still secret force, the Luftwaffe; the following fall he was posted to its first fighter unit. When the air force began flying combat missions in Spain's Civil War, on behalf of General Francisco Franco's Nationalist forces, and pilots came back with stories that depicted a life of romance and derring-do, Galland volunteered. He soon found himself aboard a tramp steamer bound for Spain, along with 370 other Luftwaffe members, all again dressed in civilian clothing and carrying papers that indicated they were civilians. In Spain, Galland was disappointed to find himself placed in charge of a fighter group equipped with biplanes, while his fellow pilots flew the latest fighter, the Messerschmitt Me 109.

The Luftwaffe's Spanish experience taught many valuable lessons about aerial warfare, but it also lodged a misconception in the minds of Göring and other senior officers. The bombers Germany deployed in Spain happened to be faster than the antiquated enemy fighters they encountered, and this conjured a wishful conviction, early on, that bombers did not require fighter escorts.

Galland went on to participate in each of Hitler's lightning invasions and at last was assigned to a fighter group that flew the newest fighters.

Soon he had his first encounters with British RAF pilots flying the latest Hurricanes and Spitfires. He immediately understood that from this point onward he would be facing an opponent unlike any he had encountered thus far—the kind of combat he claimed to wish for, "when each relentless aerial combat was a question of 'you or me.'"

The first-line fighter planes of both sides were more or less evenly matched, though each had attributes that gave it an advantage under particular conditions. Britain's Spitfires and Hurricanes were more heavily armed and more maneuverable, but the German Messerschmitt Me 109 performed better at higher altitudes and carried more protective armor. The Spitfire had eight machine guns, the Me 109 only two, but it also had two cannons that fired exploding shells. All three fighters were mono-wing, single-engine planes capable of flying at unheard-of speeds—well over three hundred miles an hour—but all had the same limitation: Their fuel capacity gave them only about ninety minutes of flying time, barely enough to get to London and back. Overall, the Messerschmitt was considered to be the superior aircraft, but a more important advantage was the fact that German pilots, like Galland, had far more experience with aerial combat. The average age of a Luftwaffe fighter pilot was twenty-six; his RAF counterpart, twenty.

With each rapid victory of the German army, Galland's fighter group moved to a new airfield to keep up with the advancing front and, therefore, moved closer to the French coast, closer to England. Every advance meant an increase in the amount of time a fighter could engage in combat over the British mainland. Barring a peace agreement between Churchill and Hitler, the next phase of the war would begin. In Galland's view, the outcome was certain: Britain would be crushed.

THE FIRST REPLY FROM Britain to Hitler's speech came an hour after its conclusion, in the form of a commentary broadcast by the BBC, without prior authorization by either Churchill or Foreign Secretary Halifax. The commentator, Sefton Delmer, did not mince words. "Let me tell you what we here in Britain think of this appeal to what you are pleased to call our reason and common sense," he said. "Herr *Führer* and Reich Chancellor, we hurl it right back into your evil-smelling teeth!"

William Shirer was present at the German radio center in Berlin, getting ready to broadcast his own report on Hitler's speech, when he heard the BBC reply. The various officials present in the studio "could not believe their ears," Shirer wrote. One shouted, "Can you make it out? Can you understand those British fools? To turn down peace now? . . . They're crazy."

Britain's official response came three days later, but not from Churchill. "I do not propose to say anything in reply to Herr Hitler's speech, not being on speaking terms with him," he quipped. Foreign Secretary Halifax gave the reply on Monday, July 22, at nine-fifteen P.M. His message was clear. "We shall not stop fighting," he said, "until freedom, for ourselves and others, is secure."

Propaganda Minister Goebbels instructed the German press to describe Halifax's official rejection as a "war crime." At his morning meeting on Wednesday, July 24, Goebbels outlined how Germany's propaganda apparatus would now proceed: "Mistrust must be sown of the plutocratic ruling caste, and fear must be instilled of what is about to befall. All this must be laid on as thick as possible."

The ministry's array of "secret transmitters," masquerading as British radio stations but based in Germany, were now to be deployed, "to arouse alarm and fear among the British people." They were to take pains to disguise their German origins, even to the point of starting broadcasts with criticism of the Nazi Party, and fill their reports with grisly details of air-raid deaths and injuries, so that when the first air raids against Britain took place, the populace would be primed for panic. Goebbels also ordered broadcasts that outwardly would appear to be classes on how to prepare for an air raid but whose precise details were, in fact, meant to further terrorize British listeners.

Seeking also to leverage British anxiety about invasion, Goebbels directed his transmitters to report, falsely, that the German army had found one hundred thousand British uniforms left behind at Dunkirk. "At the right moment the secret transmitters should then put out the story that parachutists have been dropped over Britain wearing these uniforms."

BY NOW NEARLY ALL of Germany's fighter aircraft were massed at airfields in France along the channel coast, including those of Adolf Galland's group, based at an airfield near Calais, just one hundred air miles from central London.

The Prof's Surprise

THROUGHOUT WHITEHALL, THE PROF—FREDERICK LINDEMANN— was fast gaining a reputation for being difficult. Brilliant, yes, but time and again he demonstrated an annoying proclivity for disrupting the working lives of others.

On the night of Saturday, July 27, Lindemann joined the Churchills for dinner at Chequers. As usual, the house was full of guests: Beaverbrook, Ismay, Churchill's daughter Diana and her husband, Duncan Sandys, as well as various senior military officials, including Field Marshal Sir John Dill, chief of the Imperial General Staff, and Sir James Marshall-Cornwall, commander of the British Army's III Corps, most having come to dine and sleep. Mary Churchill was absent, still summering at the Norfolk estate of her cousin and friend Judy Montagu. As always, the guests dressed for dinner, the women in gowns, the men in dinner jackets; Lindemann wore his usual morning coat and striped pants.

Churchill was in high spirits—"bubbling over with enthusiasm and infectious gaiety," wrote General Marshall-Cornwall later. The general sat between Churchill and the Prof, with Field Marshal Dill directly across the table. Churchill liked to refer to Dill by the four-letter abbreviation of his title, CIGS.

Champagne arrived, and immediately Churchill began quizzing Marshall-Cornwall about the status of the two divisions under his command, which had escaped Dunkirk with little or no equipment. The general got off to a good start by telling Churchill that his first task had been to emphasize taking the offensive. Until now, he explained, his corps had been "obsessed with defensive tactical ideas, the main object of everyone being to get behind an anti-tank obstacle." The corps' new slogan, he said, was "Hitting, not Sitting."

Churchill was delighted. "Splendid!" he told the general. "That's the spirit I want to see." Marshall-Cornwall's apparent confidence prompted Churchill to ask another question: "I assume then that your Corps is now ready to take the field?"

"Very far from it, sir," Marshall-Cornwall said. "Our re-equipment is not nearly complete, and when it is we shall require another month or two of intensive training."

Churchill's mood deflated. With a disbelieving glower, he reached into a pocket of his dinner jacket and withdrew a bundle of papers, the Prof's latest "State of Readiness" charts. These were statistical compilations that Lindemann's office had begun producing earlier that month, at Churchill's request; they purported to show the state of readiness of every army division on a weekly basis, down to the level of rifles, machine guns, and mortars. These compilations had become a source of irritation around Whitehall. "We are aware," said one senior War Office official, "that figures have in the past been used by Professor Lindemann's department in such a way as possibly to convey a wrong impression to the Prime Minister."

Churchill opened the sheaf of statistics he had just withdrawn from his pocket and pointedly asked General Marshall-Cornwall, "What are your two Divisions?"

"The 53rd (Welsh) and the 2nd London," the general replied.

With one pudgy finger Churchill grubbed among the entries in the Prof's tables until he found the two divisions.

"There you are," Churchill said. "One hundred percent complete in personnel, rifles and mortars; fifty percent complete in field artillery, anti-tank rifles and machine-guns."

This startled the general. His divisions were anything but ready. "I beg your pardon, Sir," he said. "That state may refer to the weapons which the ordnance depots are preparing to issue to my units, but they have not yet reached the troops in anything like those quantities."

Churchill glared and, "almost speechless with rage," as Marshall-Cornwall put it, threw the papers across the table toward General Dill, chief of the Imperial General Staff.

"CIGS!" he said. "Have those papers checked and returned to me tomorrow."

For a moment, all conversation ceased. "A diversion seemed called for," Marshall-Cornwall wrote. And Churchill supplied it. He leaned toward the Prof, who was seated on Marshall-Cornwall's other side.

"Prof!" he bellowed. "What have *you* got to tell me today?"

For all Lindemann's apparent self-effacement—his pale appearance, quiet voice, and less-than-ebullient personality—he in fact liked being the center of attention, and understood that by leveraging his apparent blandness, he could amplify the impact of the things he said and did.

Now, at the table, Lindemann reached slowly into the pocket of his tailcoat and, with a magician's flourish, pulled out a hand grenade of a type known colloquially as a Mills bomb, the classic grooved "pineapple," with a levered handle and circular metal pull ring.

This got everyone's attention. A look of concern spread around the table.

Churchill shouted, "What's that you've got, Prof, what's that!"

"This," Lindemann said, "is the inefficient Mills bomb, issued to the British infantry." It was constructed of a dozen different parts, he explained, each of which had to be crafted by a different machining process. "Now *I* have designed an improved grenade, which has fewer machined parts and contains a fifty percent greater bursting charge."

Churchill, always willing to embrace a new gadget or weapon, exclaimed, "Splendid, Prof, splendid! That's what I like to hear." To General Dill he said, "CIGS! Have the Mills bomb scrapped at once and the Lindemann grenade introduced."

Dill, according to Marshall-Cornwall, "was completely taken aback." The army had already contracted with manufacturers in Britain and America to build millions of the old grenade. "But the Prime Minister would not listen," Marshall-Cornwall said.

A more level appraisal appears to have taken place at some point after the dinner, however, for the Mills bomb would remain in service, with various modifications, for another three decades. Whether the grenade that Lindemann flourished at dinner was a live bomb or not is a detail lost to history.

Now Churchill pointed toward Beaverbrook, at the other side of the table. "Max!" he cried. "What have *you* been up to?"

In gentle mockery of the Prof and his numbers, Beaverbrook answered, "Prime Minister! Give me five minutes and you will have the latest figures."

He left the table and walked to a telephone at one end of the room. He returned a few moments later with a grin on his face that telegraphed mischief afoot.

He said, "Prime Minister, in the last forty-eight hours we have increased our production of Hurricanes by fifty percent."

White Gloves at Dawn

I N HIS COMMUNICATIONS WITH PRESIDENT ROOSEVELT, CHURCHILL found himself compelled to walk a very fine line.

On the one hand, he had to make the president understand how urgent things had become. At the same time, he had to avoid making Britain's situation seem *so* bleak that Roosevelt might balk at providing significant aid for fear that if Britain fell, the American supplies would be abandoned or destroyed—or, worse, captured and turned eventually against American forces. The thousands of trucks, guns, and supplies abandoned at Dunkirk provided vivid testament to the high material costs of defeat. It was crucial now, Churchill knew, to shore up Britain's own confidence in ultimate victory and, above all, to quash any manifestations of official pessimism. This was especially important with regard to the ultimate disposition of the British fleet. With concerns about the French navy in large part assuaged by the action at Mers el-Kébir, the United States wanted assurances that Britain would never surrender its own fleet to Germany, and considered hinging the donation of destroyers on an agreement that if defeat became inevitable, the British fleet would be placed under American control.

Churchill abhorred the idea of using the fleet as a negotiating lever to secure the destroyers. In an August 7 cable he urged his ambassador to America, Lord Lothian, to resist any discussion of even the possibility of such an agreement, fearing that it would send a defeatist message, "the effect of which would be disastrous." A week later, Churchill struck the same theme in a meeting of his War Cabinet, whose minutes record him as saying, "Nothing must now be said which would disturb morale or lead people to think that we should not fight it out here."

In his cable to Lothian, however, he did allow that if the United States entered the war and became a full-fledged ally, the fleet would be open to whatever strategic disposition both sides deemed necessary "for the final effectual defeat of the enemy." He saw a positive side to America's interest in the fleet, for it indicated that Roosevelt took seriously his previous warnings that a defeated Britain under Nazi control would pose a grave danger to America. As Churchill saw it, a little apprehension on America's part was to be welcomed. He told Lothian, "We have no intention of relieving [the] United States from any well-grounded anxieties on this point."

Churchill also understood that American public opinion was split sharply between isolationists, who wanted nothing to do with the war, and those who believed war would come eventually and that the longer America waited, the more costly intervention would be. But it also galled Churchill that Roosevelt was unable to see forward with that same dreadful clarity. Churchill had first asked about the possible loan of fifty obsolete destroyers back in May, and he had repeated his request on June 11, stating, "The next six months are vital." But America still had not delivered the ships. Churchill knew that Roosevelt was an ally in spirit, but like many of his fellow countrymen, Churchill imagined the president to have more power than he did. Why could Roosevelt not do more to translate that spiritual allegiance into material aid, even direct intervention?

Roosevelt, however, faced a political landscape of daunting complexity. Congress was already riven with countervailing passions, raised by the introduction of a bill calling for national conscription, the first peacetime draft in history. Roosevelt saw it as a necessity. When the war in Europe began, the U.S. Army had only 174,000 men, equipped with obsolete weapons, including Springfield rifles that dated to 1903. In May, a military maneuver involving 70,000 soldiers conducted in the South had revealed the sorry state of this army to fight a war—especially a war against a juggernaut like Hitler's heavily mechanized army. As *Time* magazine put it, "Against Europe's total war, the U.S. Army looked like a few nice boys with BB guns."

To send Britain the fifty destroyers would, Roosevelt believed, require congressional approval, owing to a clause in the federal Munitions Program of 1940 which held that before the United States could ship military supplies abroad, Congress first had to confirm that the supplies were not needed by America's own armed forces. Given the passions already aroused by the debate over conscription, Roosevelt believed such approval to be unlikely, even though the ships were in fact obsolete—so much so that earlier in the year Congress had considered scrapping them. But the navy had intervened, arguing that these very destroyers were in fact vital assets.

What further confounded things was that 1940 was a presidential election year, and Roosevelt had decided to run for an unprecedented third term. He had accepted the Democratic nomination on July 18 at the party's convention in Chicago. He was sympathetic to Britain's plight and favored doing all he could to send aid, but he also understood that many in America were deeply opposed to joining the war. For the time being, at least, both he and his Republican opponent, Wendell Willkie, were treating the issue with circumspection.

For Churchill, however, the war grew ever more threatening. The German navy was on the verge of launching two brand-new battleships, the *Bismarck* and the *Tirpitz,* both of which Churchill identified as "targets of supreme consequence." Air and U-boat attacks against inbound merchant convoys and British destroyers were growing increasingly effective, destroyers being, as Churchill cabled Roosevelt, "frighteningly vulnerable to Air bombing." The American destroyers would be vital now not just for helping protect convoys but for guarding home waters and perhaps buying time as Britain struggled to organize and reequip its forces evacuated from Dunkirk. But Roosevelt remained maddeningly aloof.

Churchill would never stoop to pleading, although at the end of July, he came close. In a cable to Roosevelt on Wednesday, July 31, he wrote that the need for the destroyers, as well as other supplies, was now "most urgent." This was a crucial moment, he warned. The mere presence or absence of the American ships—"this minor and easily remediable factor"—could decide "the whole fate of the war." In his draft telegram, he pressed the point in a tone he had not previously used with the president—"I cannot understand why, with the position as it is, you do not send me at least 50 or 60 of your oldest destroyers"—but he omitted this phrase from the final cable. Churchill promised to outfit the ships immediately with submarine-finding sonar and to deploy them against U-boats in the Western Approaches, the shipping lanes that converged on the western entrance to the channel. The destroyers also would be essential in helping repulse the expected amphibious invasion. "Mr. President, with great respect I must tell you that in the long history of the world, this is a thing to do now."

In his own later retelling, Churchill italicized "*now*."

ROOSEVELT DID UNDERSTAND THE urgency of Churchill's demand for destroyers, and on Friday, August 2, he convened a cabinet meeting to find a way to give Britain the ships without running afoul of American neutrality laws.

In the course of the meeting, his secretary of the navy, Frank Knox, proposed an idea: Why not structure the transfer as a trade, in which America would give Britain the destroyers in return for access to British naval bases on various islands in the Atlantic, including Newfoundland and Bermuda? The law allowed the transfer of war materials if the result was an improvement in America's security. The gain of strategic bases in return for obsolete destroyers seemed to meet the requirement.

Roosevelt and the cabinet approved but, given the political climate, agreed that the exchange would still need the approval of Congress.

Roosevelt asked a friendly senator, Claude Pepper, to introduce a bill authorizing the trade. For it to have any chance at all, it would need the endorsement of the Republican Party, but with so many Americans adamantly opposed to going to war, and an election on the horizon, this proved impossible to attain.

Pepper told Roosevelt the bill had "no chance of passing."

ON THAT FRIDAY, CHURCHILL made Beaverbrook a full member of his War Cabinet and, soon afterward, of his defense committee. Beaverbrook joined with reluctance. He loathed committees—of any kind, at any level. A sign in his office shouted, "COMMITTEES TAKE THE PUNCH OUT OF WAR."

Meetings were the last thing he needed. "I was driven all through the day at the Aircraft Ministry with the need for more production," he wrote in a private recollection. "I was harassed by the fear that our Air Force would go short of supplies. I was required to attend innumerable Cabinet meetings, and if I absented myself the Prime Minister would send for me." Churchill would summon him for meetings of the defense committee that would extend late into the night, after which Churchill would retain him and continue the discussion in his sitting room.

"The burden was too heavy," Beaverbrook wrote. And Churchill, he noted, had an unfair advantage: his naps.

ON SUNDAY, AUGUST 4, Churchill's son, Randolph, returned home to 10 Downing Street, on leave from his army unit, the 4th Queen's Own Hussars, looking lean and fit in his uniform.

The first night began on a happy note, with a joyful dinner at Downing Street with Pamela, Clementine, and Churchill, everyone in good spirits. After dinner, Churchill went back to work and Clementine retired to her bedroom, where she spent many evenings alone. She disliked many of her husband's friends and colleagues and much preferred dining in her room, an austere chamber with a single bed and a sink; Churchill, meanwhile, held or attended dinners as often as five nights a week.

Despite this being Randolph's first night home in a while, he set off after dinner for the Savoy Hotel, by himself. He planned to meet a friend, H. R. Knickerbocker, an American journalist, and assured Pamela that he would be gone only a short time. The two men drank together until the hotel bar closed, then went to Knickerbocker's room, where they polished off at least one bottle of brandy. Randolph returned to Downing Street at six-ten the next morning, his arrival witnessed by Churchill's security man, Inspector Thompson. Randolph stumbled from his car and made his way to Pamela's room, too drunk even to change into his nightclothes.

Thompson inspected the car.

FOR PAMELA, RANDOLPH'S DRUNKENNESS and disheveled appearance were mortifying enough, but about an hour later, around seven-thirty A.M., a maid knocked on Pamela's door and presented a note from Clementine, demanding to see her immediately.

Clementine was livid. When angry, she had a habit of donning white gloves. She was wearing them now.

"Where was Randolph last night?" she asked. "Do you have any idea what has happened?"

Pamela knew, of course, that her husband had come home drunk, but judging by Clementine's demeanor, there was more to come. At this point, Pamela began to cry.

Clementine told her that Inspector Thompson, upon checking Randolph's car, had discovered a collection of secret military maps inside, accessible to any passerby, a serious violation of security protocols.

"What is going on?" Clementine asked.

Pamela confronted Randolph, who offered fervent apologies. Shamefaced, he told her all that had occurred, and then told his father. Randolph apologized and promised to give up drinking. Clementine's fury remained unabated: She banished Randolph from No. 10, forcing him to take up temporary residence at his men's club, White's, a seventeenth-century haven for many a disgraced husband, especially those, like Randolph, who were inclined toward gambling.

His promise to quit drinking proved to be one of many pledges he could not keep.

Directive No. 17

—————

As PLANNING FOR THE INVASION OF BRITAIN PROGRESSED, HITLER issued a new directive, No. 17, which called for an all-out assault on the RAF. "The German Air Force is to overpower the English Air Force with all the forces at its command, in the shortest possible time," Hitler wrote. "The attacks are to be directed primarily against flying units, their ground installations, and their supply organizations, but also against the aircraft industry, including that manufacturing anti-aircraft equipment."

Hitler reserved to himself "the right to decide on terror attacks as measures of reprisal." His continued reluctance to authorize raids against central London and the civilian districts of other big cities had nothing to do with moral distaste but, rather, stemmed from his continued hope for a peace deal with Churchill and a wish to avoid reprisal raids on Berlin. This new campaign against the RAF was a milestone in the history of warfare, according to the Luftwaffe's own later assessment. "For the first time . . . an air force was going to conduct, independent of operations by other services, an offensive which aimed at decisively smashing the enemy air force." The question was, Could air power alone "undermine the general fighting power of the enemy by massed air attacks until he is ready to sue for peace?"

The task of planning and executing this new strategic-bombing offensive fell to Hermann Göring, who code-named the launch date *Adlertag*, or Eagle Day. He set it first for August 5, then pushed it back to August 10, a Saturday. He had absolute confidence that his air force would fulfill Hitler's wish. On Tuesday, August 6, he met with his senior air commanders at his country estate, Carinhall, to fashion a plan for the new campaign.

Until now, the Luftwaffe had engaged in limited operations against Britain, intended to probe its air defenses and draw out RAF fighters. German bombers conducted short, isolated raids against communities in Cornwall, Devon, South Wales, and elsewhere. But now Göring, given as always to flamboyant gestures, envisioned a mass attack unlike anything history had seen, aimed at delivering an annihilating blow to Britain's air defenses. He expected little resistance. According to reports by his intelligence chief, Beppo Schmid, the RAF had already been badly mauled, and could not possibly produce enough new aircraft to compensate for its losses. This meant the RAF's strength was decreasing by the day. In Schmid's appraisal, soon the RAF would have no serviceable aircraft at all.

Goaded by Göring and fortified by Schmid's reports, the air force commanders gathered at Carinhall decided they would need only four days to destroy what remained of the RAF's fighter and bomber operations. After this, the Luftwaffe would proceed step by step, in day and night raids, to eliminate air bases and aircraft manufacturing centers throughout Britain—a bold plan, with one very large indeterminate and crucial variable: weather.

Göring transferred hundreds of bombers to bases along the channel coast of France and in Norway. He planned an initial attack involving fifteen hundred aircraft, a modern armada meant to surprise and overwhelm the British. Once airborne, Göring's bombers would need only six minutes to cross the channel.

What Beppo Schmid's reports depicted, however, was very different from what Luftwaffe pilots were experiencing in the air. "Göring refused to listen to his fighter commanders' protests that such claims were not realistic," Luftwaffe ace Galland later told an American interrogator. In encounters with the RAF, German pilots found no hint of diminished strength or resolve.

The big attack was to begin that coming Saturday. If all went well, invasion soon would follow.

"Oh, Moon, Lovely Moon"

ONE OF THE MOST DISTINCTIVE ASPECTS OF CHURCHILL'S APproach to leadership was his ability to switch tracks in an instant and focus earnestly on things that any other prime minister would have found trivial. Depending on one's perspective, this was either an endearing trait or a bedevilment. To Churchill, *everything* mattered. On Friday, August 9, for example, amid a rising tide of urgent war matters, he found time to address a minute to the members of his War Cabinet on a subject dear to him: the length and writing style of the reports that arrived in his black box each day.

Headed, appropriately enough, by the succinct title "BREVITY," the minute began: "To do our work, we all have to read a mass of papers. Nearly all of them are far too long. This wastes time, while energy has to be spent in looking for the essential points."

He set out four ways for his ministers and their staffs to improve their reports. First, he wrote, reports should "set out the main points in a series of short, crisp paragraphs." If the report involved discussion of complicated matters or statistical analysis, this should be placed in an appendix.

Often, he observed, a full report could be dispensed with entirely, in favor of an aide-mémoire "consisting of headings only, which can be expanded orally if needed."

Finally, he attacked the cumbersome prose that so often marked official reports. "Let us have an end to phrases such as these," he wrote, and quoted two offenders:

"It is also of importance to bear in mind the following considerations . . ."

"Consideration should be given to the possibility of carrying into effect . . ."

He wrote: "Most of these woolly phrases are mere padding, which can be left out altogether, or replaced by a single word. Let us not shrink from using the short expressive phrase, even if it is conversational."

The resulting prose, he wrote, "may at first seem rough as compared with the flat surface of officialese jargon. But the saving of time will be great, while the discipline of setting out the real points concisely will prove an aid to clear thinking."

That evening, as he had done almost every weekend thus far, he set off for the country. The private secretary on Chequers duty that weekend was John Colville, who rode in a separate car with Clementine and Mary. Other guests had already gathered at the house, or soon would, including Anthony Eden, Pug, and two key generals, who all converged to dine and sleep. Churchill also invited First Sea Lord Dudley Pound but failed to tell anyone else, which, as Colville noted, "occasioned some hectic rearranging of the dinner table."

After the meal, Mary and Clementine left the dining room, as per custom and Clementine's preference.

Among the men, the talk turned to the threat of invasion, and to measures taken to defend Britain. Anti-tank mines had been secreted along many of the country's beaches, and these, wrote Colville, "had been shown to be most devastating." Indeed, he noted, they had claimed the lives of a number of British citizens. Churchill told the story, possibly apocryphal, of an ill-starred golfer who managed to direct a golf ball onto an adjacent beach. Colville summarized the denouement in his diary: "He took his niblick down to the beach, played the ball, and all that remained afterward was the ball, which returned safely to the green."

After dinner, Churchill, the generals, and Admiral Pound moved to the Hawtrey Room, where large timbers had been installed to brace the structure against explosion. Within the room were innumerable treasures, among them a book dating to 1476. Meanwhile, Colville read memoranda and arranged the papers in Churchill's black box.

At one point, a German aircraft flew overhead. With Churchill in the lead, the group charged out into the garden to try to catch a glimpse of the plane.

To the amusement of all, Admiral Pound tripped while descending the steps. Wrote Colville, "The First Sea Lord fell down first one flight of steps and then, having picked himself up disconsolately, he tumbled down another, ending in a heap on the ground where a sentry threatened him with a bayonet."

Pound righted himself, muttering, "This is not the place for a First Sea Lord."

Churchill, amused, said, "Try and remember you are an Admiral of the Fleet and not a Midshipman!"

SATURDAY MORNING BROUGHT MORE work for Colville, in the form of cables to send and minutes to relay. He then had lunch *"en famille,"* with Churchill, Clementine, and Mary, "and it could not have been more enjoyable." Churchill was "in the best of humors," Colville wrote. "He talked brilliantly on every topic from Ruskin to Lord Baldwin, from the future of Europe to the strength of the Tory Party." He complained about the dire lack of munitions and weapons for the army he was trying to build. "We shall win," he declared, "but we don't deserve it; at least, we do deserve it because of our virtues, but not because of our intelligence."

The talk turned silly. Colville began reciting bits of doggerel. One quatrain gave Churchill particular delight:

> Oh, Moon, lovely Moon, with thy beautiful face
> Careering throughout the boundaries of space
> Whenever I see thee, I think in my mind
> Shall I ever, oh ever, behold thy behind.

After lunch Colville, Clementine, and Mary climbed one of the adjacent hills. Colville and Mary turned the walk into a race, to see who could reach the top first. Colville won, but ended up "feeling iller than I have ever felt and was quite unable to see or think."

Mary's appraisal of Colville was steadily improving, though she still had reservations. In her diary for Saturday, August 10, she wrote, "I like Jock but I think he is very 'wet.'" For his part, Colville continued warming to Mary as well. In his diary the next day he wrote, "Even though she takes herself a little seriously—as she confesses—she is a charming girl and very pleasant to look upon."

FOR HERMANN GÖRING THAT Saturday, there was disappointment: This was the day he had designated as Eagle Day, the start of his all-out campaign against the RAF, but bad weather over the south of England forced him to cancel the attack. He set the new start for the next morning, Sunday, August 11, but then postponed it again, to Tuesday, August 13.

One consolation: With the moon by then well into its waxing gibbous phase, rising toward a full moon the coming weekend, those sorties designated to take place at night would be easier and more successful. Germany's beam-navigation technology had reduced the Luftwaffe's dependence on moonlight, but its pilots remained wary of the new system and still preferred attacking in clear weather over a landscape agleam with lunar light.

IN BERLIN, WORKERS CONTINUED building grandstands in Pariser Platz, at the center of the city, to prepare for the victory parade that would mark the end of the war. "Today they painted them and installed two huge golden eagles," wrote William Shirer in his diary entry for Sunday. "At each end they also are building gigantic replicas of the Iron Cross." His hotel was on the same square, at one end of which stood the Brandenburger Tor—the Brandenburg Gate—through which the victorious army was to pass.

Within Nazi Party circles, Shirer found, there was talk that Hitler wanted the stands ready before the end of the month.

Part Three

—

DREAD

August —
September

Eagle Day

———

A T DAWN ON TUESDAY, AUGUST 13, TWO GROUPS OF GERMAN bombers totaling about sixty aircraft rose into the skies over Amiens, climbing in broad ascending circles to flight altitude, where they assembled in battle formations. This took half an hour. Getting so many planes into position was difficult even on clear days, but this morning the challenge was compounded by an unexpected change in the weather. A high-pressure zone over the Azores that had seemed poised to deliver fair weather in Europe had abruptly dissipated. Now heavy clouds covered the channel and the coasts of France and England, and fog clung to many German airfields. Over England's southeastern coast, the ceiling was as low as four thousand feet.

A third group of aircraft, with one hundred bombers, rose over Dieppe; a fourth, with forty planes, assembled north of Cherbourg; a fifth gathered over the Channel Islands. Once in formation, numbering well over two hundred bombers, the planes began making their way toward England.

This was to be Hermann Göring's big day, *Adlertag,* Eagle Day, the start of his all-out assault on the RAF to gain control of the air over England, so that Hitler could launch his invasion. Over the previous week, the Luftwaffe had launched lesser attacks, including forays against England's chain of coastal radar stations, but it was time now for the main event. Göring planned to blacken the sky with aircraft in a display of aerial might that would stun the world. For this purpose, and for the sake of drama, he had amassed a force totaling twenty-three hundred aircraft, including 949 bombers, 336 dive-bombers, and 1,002 fighters. At last he would show Hitler, and the world, what his air force truly could do.

No sooner did the attack begin, however, than the weather forced Göring to call it off. Although the Luftwaffe's secret navigational beams now permitted its bombers to fly in overcast weather, a raid of this size and importance required good visibility. Fighters and bombers could not find each other in clouds; nor could they communicate directly with one another, and fighters lacked the equipment needed to follow the beams. The cancellation order failed to reach many of Göring's units. In one case, a formation of eighty bombers set out for England while their designated escorts, which did receive the order, returned to base, leaving the bombers dangerously exposed. Their commander continued onward, apparently in the belief that the overcast skies would limit the RAF's ability to find his force in the first place.

As one group approached its target, a swarm of RAF Hurricanes appeared, their arrival so unexpected, their attack so furious, that the bombers dropped their munitions and fled into the clouds.

Göring gave orders to resume the offensive at two o'clock that afternoon.

AMONG THE PILOTS TAKING part was Adolf Galland, who by now held a near-mythic reputation not only within the Luftwaffe but also among RAF pilots. Like Churchill, his signature was the cigar. He smoked Havanas, twenty a day, which he lit using a cigar lighter scavenged from a car, and was the only pilot authorized by Göring to smoke while in the cockpit. Hitler, however, forbade him from being photographed while he smoked, fearing the influence such publicity might have on the morals of German youths. Galland and his group were now based at a field in Pas-de-Calais, on the French coast. For the Luftwaffe, accustomed to the easy victories of the early phase of the war, this period was, Galland said, "a rude awakening."

The ninety-minute flying time of his group's Me 109 fighters was proving an even greater liability than usual, given the half hour needed to assemble formations of bombers and escorts over the French coast before heading to England. Galland's fighters had an operational range of only 125 miles, or roughly the distance to London. "Everything beyond was practically out of reach," he wrote. He likened German fighters to a dog on a chain, "who wants to attack the foe but cannot harm him, because of the limitation of his chain."

The Luftwaffe also was fast discovering the limitations of its Stuka dive-bomber, which had been one of its most potent weapons in the western campaign of May and June. It could place a bomb with far more precision than a standard aircraft, but owing in part to its external bomb load, it flew at about half the speed of a Spitfire. It was most vulnerable while diving, a trait British pilots quickly exploited. Wrote Galland, "These Stukas attracted Spitfires and Hurricanes as honey attracts flies."

Germany's larger bombers also flew at relatively slow speeds. In Spain and Poland, those speeds were fast enough to avoid effective interception, but not now, against the latest British fighters. The bombers needed a big protective escort. How this could be provided was a growing source of conflict between the fighter pilots and Göring, who insisted that the fighters fly "close escort," staying level with and close to the bombers all the way to their targets and back. This meant the pilots had to fly at the bombers' much slower speeds, not only making themselves more vulnerable to attack but also limiting their opportunities to accumulate kills, which was all any fighter pilot really wanted. One pilot recalled the frustration of looking up and seeing the "bright blue bellies" of British fighters and not being allowed to go after them. "We clung to the bomber formation in pairs—and it was a damned awkward feeling," he wrote. Galland favored looser patterns that allowed fighter pilots to fly their planes as they were meant to be flown, with some flying slow and close but others weaving among the bombers at high speeds, while still more flew high above the bomber formation, providing "top cover." But Göring refused to listen. Galland and his fellow pilots increasingly saw him as being out of touch with the new realities of aerial combat.

Although popular perception—influenced by Göring's self-promotion—portrayed the Luftwaffe as a nearly invincible force with a might far greater than the RAF's, in fact Galland recognized that the British had several major advantages that he and his fellow pilots could do nothing to neutralize. Not only did the RAF fly and fight over friendly territory, which ensured that surviving pilots would fight again; its pilots also fought with the existential brio of men who believed they were battling a far larger air force with nothing less than Britain's survival at stake. RAF pilots recognized the "desperate seriousness of the situation," as Galland put it, while the Luftwaffe operated with a degree of complacency, conjured by easy past successes and by faulty intelligence that portrayed the RAF as a desperately weakened force. German analysts accepted without challenge reports from Luftwaffe pilots of downed British aircraft and crippled airfields. In fact, the bases often resumed operation within hours. "At Luftwaffe HQ, however, somebody took the reports of the bomber or Stuka squadron in one hand and a thick blue pencil in the other and crossed the squadron or base in question off the tactical map," Galland wrote. "It did not exist any more—in any case not on paper."

The RAF's greatest advantage, Galland believed, was its deft use of radar. Germany possessed similar technology but, thus far, had not deployed it in a systematic manner, in the belief that British bombers would never be able to reach German cities. "The possibility of an Allied air attack on the Reich was at the time unthinkable," Galland wrote. German pilots saw the tall radar towers along England's coastline as they crossed the channel and occasionally attacked them, but the stations invariably returned to operation soon afterward, and Göring lost interest. Yet day after day, Galland was struck by the uncanny ability of British fighters to locate German formations. "For us and for our Command this was a surprise and a very bitter one," Galland wrote.

Göring himself was proving to be a problem. Easily distracted, he was unable to commit to a single, well-defined objective. He became convinced that by attacking a multitude of targets across a broad front, he could not only destroy RAF Fighter Command but also cause such widespread chaos as to drive Churchill to surrender.

THE ATTACK RESUMED. As Eagle Day progressed, nearly five hundred bombers and one thousand fighters entered the skies over England. In the aerial parlance of the day, this was called "landfall."

Perplexity

ONCE AGAIN, BRITAIN'S CHAIN HOME RADAR NETWORK DETECTED the approach of German aircraft, but this time the number of bombers and fighters exceeded anything the radar operators had seen before. At about three-thirty P.M., they identified three formations of German aircraft with some thirty bombers, each crossing the channel from bases in Normandy. Then came two more formations, totaling roughly sixty aircraft. RAF sector commanders ordered their fighter squadrons into the air. At about four P.M., more than one hundred RAF fighters were airborne and racing toward the attackers, guided by ground controllers using location information provided by the radar stations and by ground observers, who began reporting the types of approaching aircraft and their altitude, speed, and location. A massive formation of German fighters flew well ahead of the approaching bombers. Both forces met in a tumult of roaring engines and chattering machine guns, maneuvering wildly through a scree of heavy-caliber bullets and cannon fire. The bombers continued forward. Bombs fell on Southampton and a range of other locations, in Dorset, Hampshire, Wiltshire, Canterbury, and Castle Bromwich.

British observers were mystified. Bombs fell everywhere, on airfields, harbors, and ships, but with no clear pattern or focus. And strangely, the bombers left London untouched, a surprise, since the Germans had shown no such reticence in their attack on Rotterdam.

By late afternoon, the fighting in the skies over Britain had reached an intensity not previously experienced. Wave after wave of German bombers and fighters were met by RAF Hurricanes and Spitfires flying seven hundred distinct sorties, guided by radar. The Air Ministry reported that the RAF destroyed seventy-eight German bombers, at a cost of three of its own pilots.

At 10 Downing Street, there was jubilation. But there was unease, too: The intensity of the day's raids seemed to signal an increase in the size and violence of Germany's aerial attacks. What the RAF did not yet understand was that this was the start of a major German offensive, the beginning of what later became known as the "Battle of Britain," though that phrase would enter common usage only early the next year, with publication by the Air Ministry of a thirty-two-page thusly titled pamphlet that sought to capture the drama of the campaign and sold a million copies. But on Tuesday, August 13, 1940, none of this was clear. For now, the day's raids merely seemed to be the latest episode in an intensifying and perplexing pattern of aerial attack.

"The question everyone is asking today is, what is the motive of these gigantic daylight raids, which cost so much and effect so little?" wrote John Colville in his diary. "Are they reconnaissance in force, or a diversion, or just the cavalry attack before the main offensive. Presumably the next few days will show."

As it happened, the day's score proved to be exaggerated, a common problem in the immediate aftermath of battle, but the ratio still seemed propitious: The Luftwaffe lost forty-five planes in all, the RAF thirteen, for a ratio of over three to one.

IN WASHINGTON THAT DAY, Roosevelt met with key members of his cabinet and told them he had reached a decision on how he would transfer the fifty aging destroyers to Britain. He would use his executive powers to authorize the ships-for-bases deal without seeking congressional approval. Moreover, he would not tell Congress about it until the deal became final. Roosevelt informed Churchill of his plan in a telegram that reached London that night.

Churchill was delighted, but now he had to find a way to make the deal palatable to his own government and to the House of Commons, where the idea of leasing the islands—sovereign territory—aroused "deep feelings." Churchill understood that "if the issue were presented to the British as a naked trading-away of British possessions for the sake of fifty destroyers it would certainly encounter vehement opposition."

He urged Roosevelt not to announce it to the public as a this-for-that exchange but, rather, to frame the destroyer transfer and the leases as completely separate agreements. "Our view is that we are two friends in danger helping each other as far as we can," he cabled Roosevelt. The gift of the destroyers would be, he wrote, "entirely a separate spontaneous act."

Churchill feared that casting the deal as a commercial transaction might cause him grave political harm, for it clearly favored America, in that it provided ninety-nine-year leases of British territory, while the U.S. Navy was handing over a flotilla of obsolete ships that Congress had once wanted to scrap. To frame it publicly as a contract, with the destroyers as payment for territory, would inevitably raise questions about which party had gotten the better deal, and it would quickly become clear that America had come out much the winner.

But Roosevelt had worries of his own. His decision carried with it the potential to derail his campaign to win a third term as president, especially at a time when the conscription bill in Congress was already inflaming passions on both sides of the aisle. To give a gift of fifty destroyers *spontaneously* would constitute a clear violation of neutrality laws and stretch the bounds of executive authority. It was crucial for the American public to recognize not only that the deal had resulted from some hard and savvy bargaining but also that it increased the security of the United States.

As to security, there was little debate—provided the agreement itself did not drag America into the war. "The transfer to Great Britain of fifty American warships was a decidedly un-neutral act by the United States," Churchill wrote later. "It would, according to all the standards of history, have justified the German Government in declaring war upon them."

THE NEXT DAY, WEDNESDAY, August 14, was supposed to be the second day of Göring's promised four-day drive to destroy the RAF, but once again he was thwarted by the weather, which was even worse than the day before, and kept most of his planes on the ground. Nonetheless, some bomber groups managed to carry out sorties against targets scattered throughout western England.

Adolf Galland was delighted to receive orders to fly "detached escort" for a formation of eighty Stuka dive-bombers. His was one of an equal number of fighters assigned to protect the bombers, of which about half would fly well ahead, like Galland, while the rest stayed close to the formation. As Galland and his wingman walked to their Me 109s, Galland said he could tell it was going to be a good day—what he called a "hunter's day." The bombers were to approach England over the Strait of Dover, the narrowest point in the channel. To Galland, this meant he and his squadron would have plenty of time for combat before their fuel limits drove them back across the channel. That the RAF would make an appearance seemed to Galland beyond question. And, in fact, British radar in Dover detected him and his group even as they massed over France. Four squadrons of RAF fighters rose to meet them. Galland saw them in the distance well before his plane passed over the famous chalk cliffs at Dover.

Galland dove headlong into the phalanx of fighters and picked out an RAF Hurricane, off by itself, but the pilot was too quick. He rolled his plane, then plunged in a fast dive toward the sea, pulling up only at the last second. Galland chose not to follow. Instead, he gunned his engine and climbed one thousand feet, in order to get a better look at the unfolding fight. He rolled his plane 360 degrees to give him a full view, his trademark maneuver.

He spotted a Hurricane fighter that was clearly about to attack one of the Stuka bombers, which was lumbering along at a pace that made it an easy target. Galland fired at long range. The Hurricane bolted into a cloud. Acting on a hunch, Galland positioned himself near where he guessed the British plane would emerge, and an instant later the Hurricane popped from the cloud right in front of him. Galland fired, blasting away for three full seconds, a minor eternity in a dogfight. The Hurricane spiraled to the ground. Galland returned safely to France.

In the course of this second day of air battles, the Luftwaffe lost nineteen aircraft, the RAF eight.

Göring was very unhappy.

Göring

———

THE WEATHER CONTINUED TO DISRUPT GÖRING'S GRAND PLAN FOR the annihilation of the RAF, grounding most of his aircraft. On Thursday, August 15, the day his bombers and fighters should have nearly completed the campaign, he used the lull to summon his top officers to his country estate, Carinhall, and reproach them for their lackluster performance thus far.

Late that morning, however, as his inquisition progressed, the weather suddenly improved, yielding clear skies, prompting his field commanders to launch a colossal attack involving more than twenty-one hundred aircraft. Forever after, within the Luftwaffe, the day would be known as "Black Thursday."

One incident seemed emblematic. The Luftwaffe believed that with so many German aircraft approaching from the south, the RAF would dispatch as many fighters as possible to England's southern coast to defend against the coming onslaught, including fighters that were usually based in northern England, thereby leaving the north unprotected.

This presumption, coupled with intelligence that described the RAF as a severely eroded force, prompted one Luftwaffe commander to order a raid against RAF bases in northern England, using bombers from Norway. Ordinarily a raid like this, in daylight, would have been foolhardy, since Germany's best fighters, the Me 109s, did not have the range to escort the bombers all the way across the North Sea.

The mission was a gamble but, given the underlying assumptions, seemed tactically sound. So it was that at twelve-thirty that afternoon a force of sixty-three German bombers approached England's northeast coast, escorted by a skimpy force of two-man, twin-engine fighters, the only kind capable of flying so long a distance but far less agile than the single-engine Me 109, and thus more vulnerable to attack.

The RAF, however, did not behave as expected. While Fighter Command had indeed concentrated its forces in the south, it had kept some northern squadrons in place to defend against precisely this kind of strike.

The German bombers were about twenty-five miles offshore when the first Spitfires arrived, flying three thousand feet above the formation. As one RAF pilot looked down, he saw the bombers silhouetted against gleaming white cloud tops and exclaimed through his radio, "There's more than a hundred of them!"

The Spitfires dove through the formation, blasting away with terrifying effect. The bombers scattered, seeking shelter in the clouds six hundred feet below. They jettisoned their cargoes, scattering bombs over the coastal countryside, and turned back, never having reached their targets. In this one encounter, the Luftwaffe lost fifteen aircraft, the RAF none.

And this was just one of thousands of aerial battles that took place that Thursday alone, the Luftwaffe flying eighteen hundred sorties, the RAF a thousand. It proved to be the last day of life for a young Luftwaffe lieutenant who piloted one of the twin-engine Me 110s. The second seat was occupied by a wireless telegraph operator, who also manned a machine gun. RAF intelligence recovered the pilot's diary, which told worlds about the harrowing life of German air crews. His very first "war flight" had taken place the previous month, on July 18, during which he had fired two thousand rounds of machine-gun ammunition and his plane had been hit by opposing fire three times. Four days later, he learned that his best friend, a fellow airman, had been killed. "I have known him since he was eleven and his death shook me considerably." A week after this, his own fighter got hit thirty times and his wireless operator was nearly killed. "He has got a wound as big as my fist because bits of the machine were driven in by the bullet," the pilot wrote. Over the next couple of weeks, more of his friends died, one killed when the control column of his Me 109 broke off as he tried to pull out of a dive.

RAF intelligence provided the last entry in the young pilot's diary on Thursday, August 15, for him indeed the blackest of Thursdays, just twenty-eight days after his first combat flight. A notation reads: "The writer of this diary was killed in S9 + TH." The code was the Luftwaffe's identifier for the pilot's aircraft.

The Bomber in the Pasture

T HROUGHOUT THURSDAY, JOHN COLVILLE FOUND HIMSELF ONCE again called upon to deliver the latest count of downed aircraft.

The tally of successes seemed incredible. The RAF claimed its fighters shot down 182 German aircraft for certain, and possibly another 53. Churchill, caught up in the excitement, commandeered Pug Ismay for a visit to the RAF operations room at Uxbridge, which directed fighters attached to No. 11 Group, charged with defending London and southeast England. In the car afterward, he admonished Pug, "Don't speak to me; I have never been so moved."

After a few minutes, Churchill broke the silence, saying, "Never in the field of human conflict has so much been owed by so many to so few."

The remark had such power that Ismay quoted it to his wife after returning home. He had no idea that Churchill would soon deploy the line in one of his most famous speeches.

In reality, once again, the day's score was not quite as brilliant as Churchill had been told. The Luftwaffe lost 75 aircraft, the RAF 34. The original numbers, however, had been so widely reported and lauded that they became fixed in the popular imagination. "RAF exploits continue to arouse intense satisfaction," Home Intelligence proclaimed. Alexander Cadogan, foreign-affairs undersecretary, wrote in his diary, "This was to be the day Hitler was to be in London. Can't find him."

The focus on keeping score masked a graver reality, however, as the Prof, ever ready to dampen any inclination toward ecstasy, made clear in his relentless, unflinching production of histograms, stacked area charts, and Venn diagrams, some quite beautiful, with proportions represented in crimson and lovely shades of green and blue. The Prof reminded everyone concerned that the much-touted tallies of losses in the air did not include the number of British aircraft destroyed on the ground. On Friday, August 16, the Luftwaffe attacked the important RAF base at Tangmere, five miles inland from the channel, and destroyed or crippled fourteen aircraft, including six bombers and seven first-line fighters. Later that day, a German raid on an RAF base west of Oxford destroyed forty-six planes used for flight training. The score also omitted British bombers shot down or damaged during raids over Germany. On Friday night, August 16, for example, RAF Bomber Command dispatched 150 bombers and lost seven.

At Chequers the next day, with the Prof in attendance, Churchill composed a minute to Chief of the Air Staff Sir Cyril Newall. "While our eyes are concentrated on the results of the air fighting over this country," he wrote, "we must not overlook the serious losses occurring in the bomber command." These casualties, combined with the number of aircraft destroyed on the ground and the tally of fighters lost in combat, added up to a rather different ratio of British and German losses. "In fact, on the day, we have lost two to three," Churchill wrote.

It was only now that British air officials began to realize that something new was occurring, and that the RAF itself was the target. Over the preceding week, air intelligence had noted only a general increase in activity by the German air force. Bad weather and the seemingly random selection of targets had masked the all-out nature of the campaign, but now the awareness grew that this was indeed different, and that it might well be a preamble to the expected invasion. A British intelligence report for the week ended August 22 noted that fifty RAF fields had been attacked in raids involving an average of seven hundred aircraft a day. The report warned that if Germany succeeded in hobbling these defenses, an intense bombing campaign was likely to follow, conducted by Germany's long-range bombing force, "which would then be free to operate by day without serious opposition."

For the public, too, this perception of increasing ferocity was slow to crystallize. Memories of the previous war, with its grotesque land battles, were still fresh in the British psyche, and this new war in the sky bore little comparison. If the battles occurred at low altitude, people on the ground might hear machine guns and engines; if at high altitude, they heard and saw almost nothing. Clouds often masked the action overhead; on clear days, contrails etched spirals and loops against the sky.

On one sunny day in August, journalist Virginia Cowles found herself watching a major air battle while lying on the grass atop Shakespeare Cliff, near Dover. "The setting was majestic," she wrote. "In front of you stretched the blue water of the Channel and in the distance you could distinguish the hazy outline of the coast of France." Houses lay below. Boats and trawlers drifted in the harbor, agleam with sun. The water sparkled. Above hung twenty or more immense gray barrage balloons, like airborne manatees. Meanwhile, high above, pilots fought to the death. "You lay in the tall grass with the wind blowing gently across you and watched the hundreds of silver planes swarming through the heavens like clouds of gnats," she wrote. "All around you, anti-aircraft guns were shuddering and coughing, stabbing the sky with small white bursts." Flaming planes arced toward the ground, "leaving as their last testament a long black smudge against the sky." She heard engines and machine guns. "You knew the fate of civilization was being decided fifteen thousand feet above your head in a world of sun, wind and sky," she wrote. "You knew it, but even so it was hard to take it in."

Now and then, an onlooker might catch sight of a British pilot still in flight gear hailing a cab for the ride back to his airfield. For parachutists who survived the descent, there was another danger: trigger-happy members of the Home Guard. The danger was particularly acute for German airmen. One Luftwaffe bomber pilot, Rudolf Lamberty, had a singularly vivid encounter with British defenders, both in the air and on the ground. First his bomber collided with a cable shot into the sky by a rocket and suspended there from a small parachute. Climbing to escape further entanglement, he was hit by anti-aircraft fire, then machine-gunned by British fighters, before finally crash-landing amid a hail of Home Guard bullets. Taken prisoner, he found himself dodging bombs dropped by his own side. He survived. Seven of the nine bombers assigned to his squadron failed to return to base.

The thousands of battles fought by the RAF and the Luftwaffe filled the skies with bits of metal—machine-gun bullets, anti-aircraft shrapnel, fragments of aircraft—all of which had to go somewhere. Remarkably, most of it ended up falling harmlessly into fields, forests, or the sea, but not always, as became chillingly clear to Harold Nicolson's wife, Vita Sackville-West. In a letter to her husband, sent from their country home, Sissinghurst, she told him she had found a heavy-caliber bullet that had passed through the roof of their garden shed. "So, you see," she scolded, "I am right to tell you to keep indoors when they fight just overhead. They are nasty pointed things."

Among residents of London, there was a mounting sense that the air raids were coming closer to the city—that something big was about to occur. On Friday, August 16, bombs fell on the London suburb of Croydon, killing or badly wounding eighty people and damaging two of Lord Beaverbrook's factories. That same day, bombers struck Wimbledon, killing fourteen civilians and wounding fifty-nine. Londoners were on edge. In the city, warning sirens became commonplace. The Ministry of Information stated in its Friday intelligence report that residents were beginning to shed their conviction that Germany would never dare bomb the city. An unpleasant aspect of the tension, wrote Mass-Observation diarist Olivia Cockett, was that "one thinks every noise now will be a siren or plane." At the slightest sound, everyone adopted "that 'listening look.'"

Moonlight was a particular source of dread. That Friday, August 16, Cockett wrote in her diary, "With this gorgeous moon we all expect more tonight."

THIS DID NOT KEEP John Colville from setting out that evening for a weekend in the country and a much-needed break from the exhausting demands of Churchill. A red alert was still in effect as he left 10 Downing Street and began the two-hour drive to Stansted Park, in West Sussex near Portsmouth; he was headed for the estate of Vere Ponsonby, 9th Earl of Bessborough, whose daughter, Moyra, and son Eric were friends of his.

Here stood Stansted House, a comely three-story Edwardian box of red-ocher brick fronted by a portico of six Ionic columns. The estate was historically noteworthy for the fact that in 1651 King Charles II had passed through its grounds while making his escape after his army had been crushed by Cromwell in the last big battle of the English Civil War. The nearby city of Portsmouth, an important naval base, had of late become a favorite target of the Luftwaffe. Situated on the Solent, the boomerang-shaped strait separating England's southern coast from the Isle of Wight, the base was the home port for destroyer flotillas charged with protecting merchant shipping and defending Britain against invasion. An RAF airfield occupied nearby Thorney Island, separated from the mainland by a narrow channel eerily named the Great Deep.

When Colville arrived, he found only Lord Bessborough's wife, Roberte, and daughter, Moyra, at home, Eric being away with his regiment and Bessborough himself delayed by a bomb on the railway over which his train was to pass. Colville, Moyra, and Lady Bessborough dined by themselves, tended by servants. Colville joked that his main reason for coming was "to see one of these great air battles."

He awoke the next morning, Saturday, August 17, to a hot and sunny day "devoid of aerial activity." He and Moyra took a walk in one of the estate's gardens to gather peaches, then continued on until they came to the wreckage of a German bomber, a twin-engine Junkers Ju 88, one of the mainstays of the Luftwaffe, easily recognized in the air by its bulbous cockpit set forward of the wings, which gave it the look of a very large dragonfly. A torn and twisted portion of the aircraft had come to rest in a pasture upside down, exposing the underside of a wing and one wheel of its landing gear.

For Colville, this was an odd moment. It was one thing to experience the war at a ministerial remove, quite another to see firsthand evidence of its violence and cost. Here was a German bomber lying in country-side as classically English as any traveler could imagine, an undulating topography of meadow, forest, and farmland that sloped gently toward the south, with vestiges of medieval forest once used for hunting and the harvest of timber. Exactly how the bomber came to be here, Colville could not have said. But here it was, an alien mechanical presence, its body dark green, its underwing gray, splashed here and there with yellow and blue insignia, like random flowers. A white starfish gleamed from the center of a blue shield. Once a terrifying symbol of modern warfare, the bomber lay emasculated in a field, a mere relic to view before returning home for tea.

As it happened, the plane had been shot down six days earlier, at twelve-fifteen P.M., a mere forty-five minutes after leaving its airfield outside Paris. An RAF fighter intercepted it at nine thousand feet, killing its radioman and striking an engine, causing the aircraft to enter a spin. As the bomber's pilot fought to regain control, the plane broke apart, with its tail and rear-gun assembly tumbling onto Thorney Island, the tail portion landing just outside the airfield's operations room. The bulk of the bomber, the portion seen by Colville and Moyra, landed at Horse Pasture Farm, at the edge of Stansted's parklands. In all, three of the crew, aged twenty-one to twenty-eight, were killed, the youngest just two weeks shy of his birthday. A fourth crewman, though wounded, managed to parachute to a safe landing and was taken prisoner. In the course of the war, Stansted became something of a magnet for bombs and fallen aircraft, with a total of eighty-five bombs and four planes landing on its grounds.

The rest of Saturday unfolded without event. But the next day, as Colville put it, "I got my wish."

COLVILLE AWOKE TO ANOTHER perfect summer day, just as warm and sunny as the one before. Throughout the morning, air-raid sirens warned of attack, but none came, and no aircraft appeared in the skies overhead. After lunch, however, this changed.

Colville and Moyra were seated on the south-facing terrace of the house, which offered a distant view of the Solent and Thorney Island. To the right, woodlands occupied the foreground, beyond which they could just see the barrage balloons meant to protect Portsmouth from low-altitude attack by dive-bombers.

"Suddenly we heard the sound of A.A. fire and saw puffs of white smoke as the shells burst over Portsmouth," Colville wrote. Anti-aircraft explosions pocked the sky. From off to the left came a crescendo of aircraft engines and machine-gun fire, rising to a roar.

"There they are," Moyra cried.

Shading their eyes against the sun, they spotted twenty aircraft in heated combat, breathtakingly close, offering the two what Colville called a "grandstand view." A German bomber arced from the sky trailing a plume of smoke, then disappeared beyond the trees. "A parachute opened," Colville wrote, "and sank gracefully down through the whirling fighters and bombers."

A dive-bomber, probably a Stuka, broke loose, "hovered like a bird of prey," and entered a steep dive in the direction of Thorney Island. Other dive-bombers followed.

Now came the far-off thunder of high explosives; smoke blossomed from the island, where hangars appeared to have been set aflame; four of the Portsmouth barrage balloons exploded and sagged from view— all this as Colville and Moyra watched at a distance through the pretty August haze.

They remained on the terrace, "in high spirits, elated by what we had seen," Colville wrote. By his estimate, the battle lasted all of two minutes.

Afterward, they played tennis.

Berlin

I

N BERLIN ON SATURDAY MORNING, JOSEPH GOEBBELS FOCUSED HIS regular propaganda meeting on how best to take advantage of what he believed must certainly be a rising sense of dread among Britain's civilian population.

"The important thing now," he told the gathering, "is to intensify as far as possible the mood of panic which is undoubtedly slowly gaining ground in Britain." Germany's secret transmitters and foreign-language service were to continue describing the "frightful effects" of air raids. "The secret transmitters, in particular, should marshal witnesses who must give horrifying accounts of the destruction they have seen with their own eyes." This effort, he instructed, should also include transmissions warning listeners that fog and mist would not protect them from aerial attack; bad weather merely confused the aim of German bombers and made it more likely that bombs would fall on unintended targets.

Goebbels warned the heads of his foreign and domestic press departments to prepare for a drive by the British to use atrocity stories about the bombing deaths of old men and pregnant women to arouse the world's conscience. His press chiefs were to be ready to counter these claims at once, using pictures of children killed in a May 10, 1940, air raid on Freiburg. What he did not tell the meeting was that this raid, which killed twenty children on a playground, was carried out in error by German bombers whose crews believed they were attacking the French city of Dijon.

Hitler still would not allow bombers to attack London itself. The main goal was to put the British on edge, Goebbels said. "We must continue to emphasize that even the present attacks are a mere foretaste of what is yet to come."

Ol' Man River

F OR CHURCHILL, THE CHALLENGE OF SELLING THE DESTROYERS-for-bases deal to the House of Commons rankled anew. Roosevelt had declined his proposal that both countries frame the deal as the spontaneous result of a mutual wish to help each other. In the judgment of the State Department, American neutrality laws made it "utterly impossible" to make a spontaneous gift of the destroyers, or pretty much anything else. There had to be some sort of this-for-that payment.

Killing the deal was out of the question. Britain's maritime losses were mounting. In the preceding six weeks, eighty-one merchant ships had been sunk by submarines, mines, and aircraft. And this was just one theater of a fast-expanding world conflagration. It was clear by now that the Luftwaffe was waging all-out war against the RAF—and equally clear that despite RAF successes in the air, the intensity of German raids and the precision brought by beam navigation had begun doing serious damage to British air bases and to Lord Beaverbrook's network of aircraft factories. Invasion seemed not just likely but imminent, so real a prospect that no one would have been surprised to look up and see German paratroopers drifting past Nelson's Column in Trafalgar Square. Citizens brought gas masks to church and began wearing small metal identity disks on bracelets, in case they got blown into unidentifiable pieces. Civil defense pamphlets arrived in mailboxes, describing what to do if a panzer tank appeared in the neighborhood. One tip: Jab a crowbar into the point where the tank's steel tread passed over a guide wheel.

Seeing no other choice, Churchill accepted Roosevelt's position but resolved to use his own approach in describing the deal to Parliament and the public. He planned a lengthy speech on the "war situation," in which he would include his first formal remarks on the agreement. He worked on the speech throughout the afternoon of Monday, August 19.

When John Colville read the initial draft, he realized he had heard bits of it before, as Churchill tested ideas and phrases in the course of ordinary conversation. The prime minister also kept snippets of poems and biblical passages in a special "Keep Handy" file. "It is curious," Colville wrote, "to see how, as it were, he fertilizes a phrase or a line of poetry for weeks and then gives birth to it in a speech."

The next morning, Tuesday, Churchill worked on it some more, but found his concentration broken by the sound of hammering coming from construction underway in the Horse Guards Parade, where workers were busy shoring up the Cabinet War Rooms (later named the Churchill War Rooms), situated in the basement of a large government office building a short walk from No. 10 Downing Street. At nine A.M. he ordered Colville to find the source and stop it. "This is an almost daily complaint," Colville wrote, "and must cause considerable delay in the measures being taken to defend Whitehall."

EVERY DAY SOME NEW obstacle arose to thwart Lord Beaverbrook's production goals. U-boats sank ships loaded with vital parts, tools, and raw materials. Bombs fell on factories. Frightened workers walked off the job. False alarms shut down plants for hours. The Luftwaffe, aware of this, routinely sent solo bombers over factory districts to set off air-raid sirens, causing Beaverbrook endless exasperation. And now even God threatened to upset his plans.

On Tuesday, August 20, the Church of England proposed that all munitions plants close for a National Day of Prayer, to be held three weeks hence, on Sunday, September 8, 1940, to mark the passage of a year of war. (A previous day of prayer had been held on May 26, when British troops seemed on the verge of being exterminated at Dunkirk.) The church wanted to give all factory workers a chance to attend church. "We feel that the material loss would be small while the spiritual gain would be incalculable," wrote Herbert Upward, editor of the church's newspaper, in a letter to the prime minister.

Churchill rejected a total shutdown but agreed that factories should reconfigure their hours on that Sunday so that workers had time in the morning or evening to go to church. Which irked Beaverbrook no end. "We have already many interruptions to contend with," he complained to Churchill, citing his usual tormentors: air raids, air-raid sirens, and La-bor Minister Ernest Bevin, a former union organizer. "I hope very much that these troubles will not be reinforced by Providence."

But, he wrote, "since the workers in the munition factories should have the same opportunity to pray against the enemy as anyone else, perhaps the clergy could be brought to the works instead of taking the workers to the churches.

"Such a decision would ensure more widespread invocations. And they should be no less effective."

IN LONDON, ON TUESDAY, August 20, Churchill began his "war situa-tion" speech at 3:52 P.M., before a House of Commons made sleepy by the August heat. He made no mention of the destroyers at all—only the leases, couching these as an act of goodwill on the part of his govern-ment meant to address Roosevelt's anxiety about American security in the North Atlantic and the West Indies. To hear Churchill tell it, the of-fer of the leases was simply a magnanimous act to help out a friend and likely future ally. "There is, of course, no question of any transference of sovereignty," Churchill assured the House.

He portrayed the lease grants as having a value for Britain far greater than what the actual details might at first indicate. He pitched them as a kind of maritime engagement ring that enmeshed the interests of Brit-ain and America. "Undoubtedly," he said, "this process means that these two great organizations of the English-speaking democracies, the British Empire and the United States, will have to be somewhat mixed up to-gether in some of their affairs for mutual and general advantage."

He told the House that he had no "misgivings" about this—an arch comment, given that he wanted nothing more than for the United States to be wholly, utterly mixed up in the war, ideally as a full-fledged com-batant. And even if he did have concerns, he said, the process of enmesh-ment would continue regardless. "I could not stop it if I wished; no one can stop it. Like the Mississippi, it just keeps rolling along. Let it roll," he said, as he brought his speech rumbling to an end. "Let it roll on full flood, inexorable, irresistible, benignant, to broader lands and better days."

CHURCHILL WAS PLEASED WITH the speech. Throughout the drive back to 10 Downing Street, he sang an exuberant but off-key rendition of "Ol' Man River."

To Colville, however, the speech lacked Churchill's usual verve. "On the whole, except for bright patches . . . the speech seemed to drag and the House, which is not used to sitting in August, was languid." What most drew the members' interest, Colville noted, was the closing portion about the island bases.

Yet this was also the speech in which Churchill, while lauding the achievements of the RAF, offered what history would later appraise as one of the most powerful moments in oratory—the very line Churchill had tried out in the car with Pug Ismay during the fierce air battles of the previous week: "Never in the field of human conflict was so much owed by so many to so few." Like many other diarists of the era, Colville made no reference to the line in his diary; he wrote, later, that "it did not strike me very forcibly at the time."

More important to Colville, as far as diary-worthy matters were concerned, was a dinner date that night at a restaurant called Mirabelle, where he dined with Audrey Paget, a young woman who, as his dream of marrying Gay Margesson faded, had begun increasingly to draw his attention, even though she was only eighteen years old. What made this new flirtation still more problematic was that Audrey was a daughter of Lord Queenborough, a Conservative MP with fascist leanings. He was considered a tragic figure: He had longed for a son, but his first marriage, to an American woman, yielded only two daughters; his second marriage, again to an American, brought him three more daughters, including Audrey, all, in Colville's words, "exceptionally pretty." Their mother, Edith Starr Miller, seemed a match for Queenborough. An anti-Semite, she described herself as an "international political investigator" and wrote a seven-hundred-page volume entitled *Occult Theocrasy,* in which she sought to expose an international conspiracy by Jews, Freemasons, the Illuminati, and others "to penetrate, dominate and destroy not only the so-called upper classes, but also the better portion of all classes."

To Colville, entranced by a young woman's beauty, none of this seemed to matter. In his diary he described Audrey as "very attractive and refreshing with her enthusiasm for life and her passion for enjoyment. She has plenty of conversation and though strikingly 'ingenue' is evidently not stupid." She was also, he noted elsewhere, "seductively pretty."

Now, on that strangely warm night of Tuesday, August 20, Colville found himself delighting in a dinner alone with Audrey, interrupted at one point when Lord Kemsley, owner of the *Sunday Times,* stopped by their table and with no preamble handed Colville a giant cigar.

After dinner, Colville took Audrey to Wyndham's Theatre on Charing Cross Road to watch a play, *Cottage to Let,* a comic spy thriller. They closed the evening at a nightclub, the Slippin', an unfortunate choice. Colville found it "empty, dull and sordid."

But he was enthralled by Audrey. "We flirted more brazenly than ever and at one moment it looked like becoming more than a flirtation; but I feel a little conscience-stricken about committing the crime for which Socrates was condemned"—a reference to Audrey's youth.

Colville was all of twenty-five.

Berlin

IN BERLIN ON THAT TUESDAY, AUGUST 20, HITLER EXPRESSED HIS disappointment that the Luftwaffe had not yet fulfilled Hermann Göring's promise to gain air superiority over England. He told his headquarters staff, "The collapse of England in the year 1940 is under present circumstances no longer to be reckoned on." But he made no move to cancel Operation Sea Lion, the invasion of Britain, now set for September 15.

Göring still believed that his air force alone could bring Britain to heel, and blamed his own fighter squadrons for lacking the courage and skill to protect his bomber force. On Tuesday, he ordered his officers to finish off the RAF once and for all, through "ceaseless attacks." London itself remained off-limits, by Hitler's explicit command.

Over the next few nights, Göring's bombers and fighters flew thousands of sorties over England—so many aircraft from so many directions that at times they threatened to overwhelm England's coastal radar network and the ability of RAF trackers to accurately dispatch squadrons to meet them.

And then, on the night of Saturday, August 24, came a navigational error destined to change the nature of the entire war—"a piece of carelessness" that Basil Collier, a leading Battle of Britain historian, pegs as the moment that set the world inexorably on the march toward Hiroshima.

Teatime

———

BUT FIRST CAME TEA, TO WHICH THE PROF NOW TURNED HIS attention.

His enemies made him out to be a statistical incubus who lived a life stripped clean of warmth and compassion. In fact, he often did kind things for employees and strangers, preferring to keep his role in such deeds secret. In one case, he paid the medical bills of a young female employee of his laboratory who suffered a fractured skull when, under blackout conditions, she rode her bicycle into a hole on her way to work. Upon hearing that an elderly former nurse had fallen "upon evil days," as a charitable organization put it, he established a pension for the woman. He was especially generous with his valet, Harvey. On one occasion Lindemann gave him a motorcycle, but then, worried that Harvey would get hurt in an accident, he provided a car to use instead.

He expressed broader concerns as well. Despite his standoffishness and his love of fine things—his big cars, his chocolates, his Merton coats—the Prof often demonstrated a caring for the common man's experience of the war. Such was the case that summer when he wrote to Churchill to oppose a proposal by the Ministry of Food to reduce the ration of tea to a mere two ounces a week.

The one universal balm for the trauma of war was tea. It was the thing that helped people cope. People made tea during air raids and after air raids, and on breaks between retrieving bodies from shattered buildings. Tea bolstered the network of thirty thousand observers who watched for German aircraft over Britain, operating from one thousand observation posts, all stocked with tea and kettles. Mobile canteens dispensed gallons of it, steaming, from spigots. In propaganda films, the making of tea became a visual metaphor for carrying on. "Tea acquired almost a magical importance in London life," according to one study of London during the war. "And the reassuring cup of tea actually did seem to help cheer people up in a crisis." Tea ran through Mass-Observation diaries like a river. "That's one trouble about the raids," a female diarist complained. "People do nothing but make tea and expect you to drink it." Tea anchored the day—though at teatime, Churchill himself did not actually drink it, despite reputedly having said that tea was more important than ammunition. He preferred whiskey and water. Tea was comfort and history; above all, it was British. As long as there was tea, there was Britain. But now the war and the strict rationing that came with it threatened to shake even this most prosaic of pillars.

The Prof saw danger.

"The wisdom of a 2 ounce tea ration is open to serious doubt," Lindemann wrote, in a memorandum to Churchill. "A large proportion of the population consisting of the working class women who do all their own housework, and charwomen, rely exclusively on tea for stimulant. It would be an understatement to call tea their principal luxury; it is their sole luxury."

It was customary for such people to keep a kettle on hand at all times, he wrote, and to prepare a cup of tea once every couple of hours. "Frequent air-raid warnings," he wrote, "are likely to strengthen the appetite." Limiting this luxury could have far-reaching consequences, he warned. "It is this class which suffers most from the war. They meet the direct impact of high prices and scarcities. The blackout and, in certain cases, evacuation impose further hardships. And they lack the compensation of new interests and adventure."

This class of tea drinkers was also "the least educated and least responsible in the country," Lindemann wrote. "They have little stake in the good things of a free democratic community. They can say with some truth, and often do say, that it would make no difference to them if Hitler were in charge."

Tea underpinned morale. "If the whole of this class lost heart completely they might infect their menfolk and undermine morale, especially if intense air bombardment added to their present troubles."

In this case, Lindemann's intercession did not succeed, despite his direct connection to Churchill. The tea ration, eventually raised to three ounces a week, would remain in effect until 1952.

In the meantime, people dried their used tea leaves so they could steep them again.

The Lost Bombers

———

O N THE NIGHT OF SATURDAY, AUGUST 24, A FORMATION OF GERMAN
bombers lost its way. Their intended targets were aircraft factories and an
oil depot east of London, over which the crews believed they were now
flying. In fact, they were over London itself.

The RAF tracked the planes from the moment they left France but
could do nothing to stop them. As yet, the British had no effective means
for intercepting intruders after dark. Although ground radar could direct
a fighter to a bomber's general location, it offered imprecise details about
the plane's altitude and whether it was just one bomber or one of a fleet
of twenty. About four minutes elapsed between the time a plane was first
detected and when its coordinates were plotted by Fighter Command
controllers, during which time the enemy aircraft would have moved
well across the channel and to a different altitude. Pilots needed to see
their targets in order to attack. The RAF was struggling to modify aircraft for fighting at night and to equip them with experimental air-to-air
radar; so far, however, these efforts had proven ineffective.

Researchers were also racing to find ways of jamming and bending
German navigational beams. The first jammers were crude modifications
of medical devices used in the practice of diathermy, the application of
electromagnetic energy for treatment of various conditions. By August,
these had been largely supplanted by more effective jammers and by a
system for masking the German beacons—"meaconing"—and retrans-
mitting them to confuse or divert the bombers following them. But these
measures were just beginning to show promise. Otherwise, the RAF relied on barrage balloons and anti-aircraft guns guided by searchlights.

The guns at this point were almost comically inaccurate. A study by the Air Ministry would soon find that only one enemy aircraft was downed for every six thousand shells fired.

As the bombers approached, sirens began to sound throughout London. On the steps of St. Martin-in-the-Fields, a radio reporter for CBS News, Edward R. Murrow, began a live broadcast. "This," he said, his voice deep, his tone composed, "is Trafalgar Square." From where he stood, Murrow told his audience, he was able to see Nelson's Column and the admiral's statue on top. "That noise that you hear at the moment is the sound of air-raid sirens," he said. A searchlight came on in the distance, then another closer at hand, behind Nelson's statue. Murrow paused to let listeners hear the chilling contrapuntal wail of several sirens as they filled the night with sound. "Here comes one of those big red buses around the corner," he said. "Double-deckers they are. Just a few lights on the top deck. In this blackness it looks very much like a ship that's passing in the night and you just see the portholes."

Another bus passed. More searchlights came on. "You see them reach straight up into the sky and occasionally they catch a cloud and seem to splash on the bottom of it." A traffic signal turned red, the light barely visible through the cross-shaped aperture of blackout plates installed over the bulbs. Incredibly, under the circumstances, the traffic came to an obedient stop. "I'll just ooze down in the darkness here along these steps and see if I can pick up the sound of people's feet as they walk along," Murrow said. "One of the strangest sounds one can hear in London these days, or rather these dark nights, is just the sound of footsteps walking along the street, like ghosts shod with steel shoes."

In the background, the sirens wobbled continuously up and down the scale, before at last dying away, leaving London under a state of alert pending the sounding of the all-clear signal. During the broadcast, Murrow did not see or hear any explosions, but just east of where he stood bombs began to fall onto neighborhoods in central London. One damaged St. Giles's Church in Cripplegate; others fell on Stepney, Finsbury, Tottenham, Bethnal Green, and adjacent neighborhoods.

The damage was minimal, casualties few, but the raid sent a tremor of terror throughout the city. No one in Britain knew as yet that the bombs were strays, dropped in error, against Hitler's explicit orders, or that early on Sunday morning Göring sent an irate message to the bomber wing involved, saying, "It is to be reported forthwith which crews dropped bombs in the London prohibited zone. The Supreme Commander"—

Göring—"reserves to himself the personal punishment of the commanders concerned by re-mustering them to the infantry."

To Londoners, the attack seemed to herald a new phase of the war. For Mass-Observation diarist Olivia Cockett, it conjured visions of fresh horrors ahead. "I suppressed a horrid fantasy of fears on the lines of—sewers and water mains gone; gas gone; daren't drink water (typhoid); then gas from cruising planes; and nowhere to go. Endless possibilities of horrors, difficult to dismiss during those listening hours in the night."

She experienced mounting anxiety. "My heart misses a beat whenever a car changes gear-up, or when someone runs, or walks very quickly, or suddenly stands still, or cocks their head on one side, or stares up at the sky, or says 'Sshh!' or whistles blow, or a door bangs in the wind or a mosquito buzzes in the room. So taken all round my heart seems to miss more beats than it ticks!!"

THE SATURDAY NIGHT RAID on London infuriated Churchill, but it also eased his growing frustration at not being able to go on the offensive and bring the war to Germany itself. The RAF had already bombed industrial and military targets along the Ruhr River and elsewhere, but these had minimal impact in terms of both damage and psychological effect. The attack on London gave him the pretext he had been waiting for: moral justification for an attack on Berlin itself.

CHAPTER
38

Berlin

THE NEXT NIGHT, AT TWELVE-TWENTY A.M., BERLINERS WERE SHOCKED
to hear air-raid sirens go off throughout the city as British bombers
droned overhead, a scenario their leaders had assured them was impossible. Anti-aircraft guns tore the sky apart. "The Berliners are stunned,"
correspondent Shirer wrote the next day. "They did not think it could
happen. When this war began, Göring assured them it couldn't. He
boasted that no enemy planes could ever break through the outer and
inner rings of the capital's anti-aircraft defense. The Berliners are a naïve
and simple people. They believed him."

The raid caused only minor damage and killed no one, but it posed
a fresh challenge for Propaganda Minister Joseph Goebbels. The "wild-
est rumors" had begun circulating, he told the attendees at his morning
meeting. One rumor making the rounds held that the paint on British
bombers had somehow made them invisible to searchlights; how else
could they have made it to Berlin without being shot down?

Goebbels instructed that rumors were to be countered with "a precise
statement" setting out in detail how little damage had been done.

He advocated more forceful action as well: "Unofficial measures are
to be taken by way of the Party to ensure that rumor-mongers from
among the decent circles of the population are dealt with rigorously and
on occasion, if necessary, can even be roughed up."

Ah, Youth!

————

T HAT HITLER WOULD RETALIATE SEEMED A CERTAINTY, AND GIVEN Germany's penchant for massed raids, the attack was likely to be a big one. Thus when air-raid sirens sounded in London on the following Monday morning, August 26, Churchill ordered John Colville and everyone else at 10 Downing Street to go into the building's air-raid shelter.

The alert proved to be a false alarm.

Churchill knew that the RAF planned a raid on Leipzig that night, but he felt Leipzig was a pale target. He telephoned Sir Cyril Newall, chief of the Air Staff, to express his displeasure. "Now that they have begun to molest the capital," Churchill told him, "I want you to hit them hard—and Berlin is the place to hit them."

The sirens sounded in London again that night, just as Colville was finishing dinner with a friend, a member of the King's Guard, in the guards' dining room at St. James's Palace. The men had moved on to cigars; a bagpiper was marching around the table playing "Speed Bonnie Boat." At the sound of the alert, the men calmly put out their cigars and moved to the palace shelter, where they changed from their formal blue dining uniforms into battle dress and helmets.

No bombs fell, but the alert continued. At length Colville left and made his way back to No. 10. By twelve-thirty A.M., the all clear still had not sounded. Now and then Colville heard airplane engines and the sharp report of anti-aircraft guns. Churchill, still up and active, again ordered his staff to the shelter, but he himself remained at work, along with Colville, the Prof, and several other officials and secretaries.

At one point, finding himself in the rare position of having nothing to do, Colville walked into the walled garden at the back of the house. The night was soft, suffused with mist rising from the warm city around him. Searchlights cast pillars of pale light far into the sky. Only a few aircraft had come and still no bombs had fallen, but the mere presence of the planes had shut down the city. This made for an oddly serene moment. "I stood in the garden, heard midnight strike on Big Ben, watched the searchlight display and wondered at the unaccustomed stillness of London. Not a sound, and scarcely a breath of air. Then suddenly the noise of an engine and the flash of a distant gun."

Churchill changed into his nightclothes and, carrying a helmet, came downstairs in what Colville described as a "particularly magnificent golden dragon dressing-gown." He, too, entered the garden, where he paced back and forth for a time, a stubby round figure in flaming gold, until he at last moved down to the shelter to spend the night.

Churchill slept well, not even waking when the all clear sounded at three forty-five A.M. He always slept well. His ability to sleep anywhere, anytime, was his particular gift. Wrote Pug Ismay, "His capacity for dropping off into a sound sleep the moment his head touched the pillow had to be seen to be believed."

Not so for Colville, who, like many others in London, having managed finally to fall asleep after the initial alert, was awakened by the steady one-note wail of the all clear. This, Colville wrote, "is the double sting about air-raids at night."

Among the public at large, for the moment, morale remained high, at least as gauged by a Postal and Telegraph Censorship Department study of mail bound for America and Ireland, intercepted and read by the bureau. The report, released on Friday, August 30, quoted a correspondent from North Wembley who wrote, "I would not be anywhere in the world but here, for a fortune." The censors claimed to have detected a paradox, that "morale is highest in places that have been most badly bombed." Upon noting this, however, the censors' report took on a distinctly censorious tone: "There is a general complaint of lack of sleep, but writers who speak of shattered nerves would appear to be people who are normally uncourageous, and where mention is made of children's terror it would seem in most cases, to be the fault of the mother."

That said, the civilian districts of London and other big cities had thus far gone largely unscathed.

Overnight, the RAF launched a second raid against Berlin and killed its first Berliners, ten of them, and wounded another twenty-one.

WHILE LONDON BRACED FOR Hitler's reprisal, Mary Churchill and her mother were savoring the peace of a warm summer night at Breccles Hall, the country home of Mary's friend Judy Montagu, where Mary was supposed to spend another few weeks. Clementine planned shortly to return to London.

Here, in these rural lands at the edge of Thetford Forest in Norfolk, among its 102 acres of fields, moors, and pinelands, the air war, with its bombs and aerial battles, seemed especially remote, as Mary recorded in her diary. The house itself dated to the mid-1500s, and was said to be visited now and then by a beautiful ghost in a coach and four whose gaze caused instant death to anyone who gazed back. The girls rode bicycles and horses, played tennis, swam, went to the movies, and danced with airmen at nearby RAF bases, occasionally bringing them back for the now-familiar "snogging" sessions in the hayloft, all of which prompted Mary one day to exclaim in her diary, "Ah '*la jeunesse—la jeunesse.*'"

Judy's mother, Venetia, made it her mission to balance the laziness of these summer days by engaging the girls in various intellectual pursuits. She read them the works of Jane Austen, likening Mary and Judy to those "giddy girls" from *Pride and Prejudice,* Kitty and Lydia Bennett, "who were forever off to Meryton to see what regiments had appeared locally!" as Mary later wrote.

The girls also resolved to learn the sonnets of William Shakespeare and to commit one to memory each day—a task at which they failed, though Mary would retain the ability to recite several for years afterward.

Now and then the war intruded, as when her father telephoned with news about a big German raid on Ramsgate, on the Strait of Dover, that destroyed seven hundred homes. The raid was particularly intense, with five hundred high-explosive bombs falling in the space of just five minutes. The news was jarring for Mary, who wrote, "Down here—despite air activity & especially during this lovely day one had almost forgotten the war."

The news intensified the dissonance she felt between the life she was leading at Breccles Hall and the greater reality of the war, and this prompted her, on Monday, September 2, to write to her mother to plead for permission to return home to London. "I am indulging in escapism down here," she wrote. "For quite a long time on end I have forgotten the war completely. Even when we are with the airmen one forgets—because they are so gay." With millions of people throughout Europe "starving and bereaved and unhappy," she wrote, "somehow it's all wrong. May I please come back to you and Papa as soon as possible? I really won't let the air raids rattle me—and I care so terribly about the war and everything, and I should like to feel that I was risking something."

Her parents had a different, distinctly parental view. "It makes me glad that you are having a happy care-free spell in the country," Clementine wrote in reply. "You must not feel guilty about it. Being sad and low does not help anyone."

She told Mary about life at No. 10 since the Saturday night attack. "We have got quite used to the Air Raid Warnings, & when you come back you will find a comfortable little bunk in the Shelter. There are 4, one for Papa, one for me, one for you & one for Pamela"—a reference to Pamela Churchill, now eight months pregnant. "The top ones are quite difficult to climb into. Twice we have spent the whole night there as we were asleep when the 'All Clear' went. Down there you can hear nothing."

It doubtless did not help ease Mary's guilt that in this letter Clementine called her "my Darling Country Mouse."

But one visit to a nearby RAF base made Mary's pangs grow still more acute. There were the usual frivolities—lunch, tennis, tea—but then came "the highlight of the whole afternoon," a tour of a Blenheim bomber.

"It was thrilling," she wrote, although, she added, "It made me feel very useless. There can never be a true measure of my love for England— because I am a woman & I feel passionately that I would like to pilot a plane—or risk everything for something which I believe in so entirely & love so very deeply."

Instead, she wrote, "I must lick down envelopes & work in an office & live a comfortable—happy life."

WITH THE PROSPECT OF raids on London itself, U.S. ambassador Joseph Kennedy decamped. To the great disdain of many in London, he began conducting his ambassadorial affairs from his home in the country. Within the Foreign Office, a joke began to circulate: "I always thought my daffodils were yellow until I met Joe Kennedy."

Foreign Secretary Halifax found the joke "unkind but deserved." He took a certain satisfaction from the fact that one German raid came dangerously close to destroying Kennedy's country home. Halifax, in his diary entry for Thursday, August 29, called this "a judgment on Joe."

LORD BEAVERBROOK WAS TIRED. His asthma dogged him, and as always, he was annoyed—annoyed that air-raid sirens robbed his factories of countless hours of work, that German bombers seemed able to come and go at will, that a single bomb could knock out production for days. Still, despite all these obstacles, and although his factories were under nightly assault by the Luftwaffe, his manufacturing and salvage empire managed to produce 476 fighters in August, nearly 200 more than the total previously projected by the chiefs of staff.

Lest Churchill have somehow overlooked this feat, Beaverbrook wrote to him on Monday, September 2, to remind him of his own success. He also took the opportunity to express a degree of self-pity as to how much struggle these gains had required, closing his note with a lyric from an American folk spiritual: "Nobody knows the trouble I've seen."

By way of reply, Churchill the next day returned Beaverbrook's note with a two-word rejoinder jotted at the bottom:

"I do."

Berlin and Washington

THE ATTACKS ON BERLIN DID INDEED ENRAGE HITLER. ON SATUR-day, August 31, he shed his prior reluctance and ordered his air chief, Göring, to begin preparations for an assault on London itself. The attack, Hitler instructed, was to reduce enemy morale while still maintaining focus on targets of strategic value. He did not, as yet, wish to cause "mass panic." But Hitler understood as well as anyone that given the inherent inaccuracy of bombing, attacks against strategic targets within London would be tantamount to targeting civilian districts outright.

Two days later, Göring issued a directive to the Luftwaffe. Once again he envisioned a cataclysmic raid of such extraordinary proportion that Churchill would capitulate or be evicted from office. Göring craved revenge on the British for humiliating his air force, and was delighted at the prospect of unleashing the full power of his armada against the UK's capital. This time he would bring Britain to heel.

AS GÖRING READIED HIS aerial onslaught, and preparations continued for the invasion of Britain, Hitler's deputy, Rudolf Hess, grew increasingly concerned about the intensifying conflict. Thus far he had made no progress in fulfilling Hitler's wish that he somehow bring about the collapse of Churchill's government. That the two empires should clash struck Hess as fundamentally wrong.

On August 31, he met with a friend and mentor, Professor Karl Haushofer, a leading political scientist whose theories informed Hitler's worldview but whose personal life placed him on precarious ground: His wife was half Jewish. To protect Haushofer's two sons, Hess, despite his own hatred of Jews, had declared both to be "honorary Aryans."

Hess and Haushofer spoke for nine hours, during which Hess alerted his friend to the increasing likelihood that Germany would invade Britain. The two discussed the idea of delivering a peace proposal to London through a British intermediary, someone with close connections among appeasement-minded members of Churchill's government, with the goal of sparking a parliamentary rebellion against the prime minister.

Three days after this meeting, Professor Haushofer wrote a delicately worded letter to one of his sons, Albrecht, who was an important adviser to both Hitler and Hess, and an Anglophile who spoke perfect English. The elder Haushofer expressed his concerns about the looming invasion and asked his son if it might not be possible to arrange a meeting in a neutral location with an influential middleman to discuss ways of averting further conflict with Britain. He knew that his son had befriended a prominent Scotsman, the Duke of Hamilton, and now suggested approaching him.

It was important to act quickly. "As you know," Professor Haushofer wrote, "everything is so prepared for a very hard and severe attack on the island in question that the highest ranking person only has to press a button to set it off."

IN THE UNITED STATES, a final obstacle to the destroyers-for-bases deal was cleared when a lawyer with the State Department came up with a compromise that would let both Churchill and Roosevelt portray the arrangement in the manner each deemed most palatable to his countrymen.

The Newfoundland and Bermuda bases would be classified as a gift granted in acknowledgment of Britain's "friendly and sympathetic interest in the national security of the United States." Leases on the remaining bases would serve as payment for the destroyers, but no cash value would be assigned to any particular asset, thereby limiting each side's ability to calculate comparative worth. It was clear enough that America was getting the better deal, without providing critics too easy an opportunity to demonstrate the disparity with hard numbers. And, indeed, the American press hailed it as a coup for the president, the kind of hard bargain that appealed to America's sense of itself as a nation adept at doing things in a businesslike manner. As the Louisville *Courier-Journal* put it, "We haven't had a better bargain since the Indians sold Manhattan Island for $24 in wampum and a demi john of hard liquor."

Britain's ambassador, Lord Lothian, and U.S. secretary of state Cordell Hull signed the agreement on Monday, September 2. Two days later, the first eight destroyers were moored in Halifax Harbor, at which point their new British crews began to appreciate how much work was needed just to make them seaworthy, let alone battle-ready. As one American officer put it, their hulls were barely thick enough "to keep out the water and small fish."

For Churchill, however, the quality of the destroyers was to a large extent beside the point. As a navy man, he had to have known that the ships were too antique to be of much use. What mattered, rather, was that he had gotten Roosevelt's attention, and perhaps nudged him a step closer to full involvement in the war. Just how much longer Roosevelt would be president, however, was an open question. The American presidential election was to take place two months hence, on November 5, and Churchill fervently hoped Roosevelt would win, but this outcome was by no means certain. A Gallup Poll released on September 3 showed that 51 percent of Americans favored Roosevelt in the upcoming election; 49 percent preferred Wendell Willkie. Given margins of error in polling, the two candidates were running neck and neck.

But in America, the tilt toward isolationism was gaining momentum and intensity. On September 4, a group of Yale Law students founded the America First Committee to oppose involvement in the war. The organization grew quickly, winning the energetic support of no less a celebrity than Charles Lindbergh, a national hero ever since his 1927 flight across the Atlantic. And Willkie, urged by Republican leaders to do whatever he could to pull ahead in the presidential election, was about to change strategy and make the war—and fear—the central issue in the campaign.

He Is Coming

ON WEDNESDAY, SEPTEMBER 4, HITLER STEPPED TO THE ROSTRUM at the Berlin Sportpalast, where some years earlier he had made his first speech as chancellor of Germany. Now he prepared to speak to a huge audience of female social workers and nurses, ostensibly to honor the opening of the year's War Winter Relief campaign—Kriegswinterhilfswerk—to raise money to provide food, heat, and clothing to impoverished Germans. He used the opportunity, however, to launch a tirade against Britain for its recent air attacks against Germany. "Mr. Churchill," he said, "is demonstrating his new brain child, the night air raid."

Hitler decried such raids as being cowardly, unlike the daylight sorties conducted by the Luftwaffe. He told his audience that thus far he had tempered his reaction to the British raids, in hopes that Churchill would reconsider and halt them. "But Herr Churchill saw in this a sign of weakness," Hitler said. "You will understand that we are now answering, night for night. And when the British air force drops two or three or four thousand kilograms of bombs, then we will in one night drop 150- 230- 300- or 400,000 kilograms."

At this, wrote American correspondent William Shirer, a great roar rose from the crowd and forced Hitler to pause.

He waited for the clamor to subside, then said, "When they declare that they will increase their attacks on our cities, then we will raze *their* cities to the ground." He vowed to "stop the handiwork of these air pirates, so help us God."

The women leapt to their feet, Shirer wrote in his diary, "and, their breasts heaving, screamed their approval."

Hitler continued: "The hour will come when one of us will break, and it will not be National Socialist Germany."

The crowd erupted in a deafening tumult, crying "NEVER! NEVER!"

"In England, they're filled with curiosity and keep asking: 'Why doesn't he come?'" Hitler said, infusing every gesture with irony. "Be calm. Be calm. He's coming! He's coming!"

The laughter from the audience verged on the maniacal.

Churchill offered a bloody rejoinder: That night an RAF bomb fell on Berlin's lovely main park, the Tiergarten, killing a policeman.

AT CARINHALL, IN THE peaceful German countryside, Hermann Göring and his Luftwaffe commanders mapped out a concise, tersely worded plan of attack for "the destruction of London."

The initial raid was scheduled to begin at six P.M., followed by "the main attack" at six-forty. The purpose of the first raid was to draw RAF fighters into the air, so that by the time the main wave of bombers arrived, the British defenders would be running out of fuel and ammunition.

Three fleets of bombers, guarded by a large screen of fighters, would set out from three locations on the channel's French coast and proceed on a straight-line course to London. The fighters would accompany the bombers all the way to the city and back. "In view of the fact that the fighters will be operating at the limit of their endurance," the plan said, "it is essential that direct courses be flown and the attack completed in minimum time." The plan called for maximum force, with aircraft flying at staggered altitudes. "The intention is to complete the operation in a single attack."

With so many aircraft in the air, it was imperative that the pilots also know how to orchestrate their return. After dropping their bombs, the formations were to turn left and return along a course different from the one they had followed to England, to avoid colliding with bombers still making their approach.

"To achieve the necessary maximum effect it is essential that units fly as highly concentrated forces during approach, attack, and especially on return," the plan said. "The main objective of the operation is to prove that the Luftwaffe can achieve this."

The date was set for September 7, 1940, a Saturday. Göring told Goebbels the war would be over in three weeks.

AMONG THE BOMBER GROUPS assigned to take part was a special unit called KGr 100, one of three groups known as "pathfinders." Its crews were specialized in flying along Germany's navigational beams, taking advantage of a technology even more advanced than the *Knickebein* system, which was proving problematic. The genius of *Knickebein* was its simplicity and the fact that it used familiar technology. Every German bomber pilot knew how to use ordinary Lorenz blind-landing equipment when approaching an airfield, and every bomber had the system aboard. To use *Knickebein*, pilots just had to fly higher and follow the central beam for longer distances. But something seemed to have gone amiss. Pilots reported mysterious beam distortions and lost signals, and were growing distrustful of the system. A major raid against Liverpool on the night of August 29 had been severely and mysteriously disrupted, with only about 40 percent of the dispatched bombers reaching their targets. It seemed likely that British intelligence had discovered the *Knickebein* secret.

Happily, another technology, this one even more advanced, remained as secret as ever, as best anyone could tell. German scientists had developed another method of beam navigation, called *X-Verfahren*, or "X-system," that was much more precise but also much more complicated. It, too, relied on the transmission of Lorenz-like dash and dot signals, but instead of just one intersecting beam, it incorporated three, these much narrower, and thought to be harder for RAF listeners to detect. The first beam to cross the bomber's course was merely a warning signal, meant to alert its wireless operator that a second, more crucial intersection was coming soon. Upon hearing that second signal, a crew member turned on a mechanism that calibrated the plane's exact ground speed. Soon afterward the bomber crossed a third, and final, intersecting beam, at which point the crew started a timer that controlled the plane's bomb-release mechanisms so that the plane would disgorge its bombs at exactly the moment necessary to hit the target.

The system was effective, but because it demanded highly skilled and trained crews, the Luftwaffe formed a special bomber group, KGr 100, to use it. For the system to work, the aircraft had to fly precisely on course, at a steady speed and at the calibrated altitude, until it reached its target, leaving it vulnerable to attack. This made for some hair-raising moments, but bombers using the system flew at very high altitudes to pick up the beam, well beyond the range of searchlights and barrage balloons, and had little risk, at least at night, of being intercepted by RAF fighters. The group's aircraft were painted matte black on every surface to make them all the more difficult to locate in darkness; this also imparted an aura of menace. Trials at a test range on a lake near Frankfurt found that crews could place bombs within a hundred yards of a target. As early as December 1939, the group had made three test flights to London with no bombs aboard.

Over time the Luftwaffe developed a new tactic to take advantage of KGr 100's special abilities. The group's bombers would take the lead during raids, arriving first to mark targets by dropping a mix of incendiary and high-explosive bombs that ignited immense fires to guide the pilots following behind. The glow was visible even through clouds. The group's zone of operations was expanded to include London.

Ominous Doings

O N FRIDAY EVENING, SEPTEMBER 6, CHURCHILL LEFT 10 DOWNING
Street for Chequers, where, after his usual nap, he had dinner with Pug
Ismay and his two top generals, John Dill, chief of the Imperial General
Staff, and Alan Brooke, commander in chief of Home Forces.

Dinner began at nine. The talk centered on the potential for invasion, and there was much to discuss. Intercepted signals and reconnaissance photos suggested that concrete preparations for an invasion had
begun and were rapidly progressing. That weekend, British intelligence
counted 270 barges at the Belgian port city of Ostend, where just a week
earlier there had been only 18. One hundred barges arrived at Flushing (Vlissingen) on Holland's North Sea coast. Reconnaissance aircraft
spotted many more vessels converging on channel ports. Britain's Joint
Intelligence Committee assessed that the coming days—in particular,
September 8 through 10—would present a combination of moon and tide
that would be especially conducive to an amphibious landing. On top of
this came reports of increased bombing activity. That day alone, three
hundred long-range bombers accompanied by four hundred fighters attacked targets in Kent and the Thames Estuary.

The conversation became animated. "PM warmed up and was most
entertaining for rest of evening," Brooke wrote in his diary. "First of all
he placed himself in the position of Hitler and attacked these isles while
I defended them. He then revised the whole of the Air Raid Warning
system and gave us his proposals to criticize. Finally at 1:45 A.M. we got
off to bed!"

In his diary the next day Brooke wrote, "All reports look like invasion getting nearer." For him, as the general in charge of defending Britain from attack, the tension was great. "I do not think I can remember any time in the whole of my career when my responsibilities weighed heavier on me than they did during those days of the impending invasion," he wrote later. The survival of Britain would rest on his preparations and his ability to direct his forces, despite what he knew to be their shortcomings in training and armament. All this, he wrote, "made the prospect of the impending conflict a burden that was almost unbearable at times." Compounding this was the fact that he felt he could not reveal his inner concerns. Like Churchill, he understood the power and importance of outward appearance. He wrote, "There was not a soul to whom one could disclose one's inward anxieties without risking the calamitous effects of lack of confidence, demoralization, doubts, and all those insidious workings which undermine the power of resistance."

On that Saturday, September 7, the question before Brooke and the chiefs of staff was whether to issue the official alert, code-named "Cromwell," that would indicate that invasion was imminent and require Brooke to mobilize his forces.

Cap Blanc-Nez

O N SATURDAY MORNING, GÖRING AND TWO SENIOR LUFTWAFFE
officers made their way along the French coast in a motorcade consisting of three large Mercedes-Benzes led by soldiers on motorcycles. His
"special train" had brought him from his temporary headquarters at The
Hague to Calais, so that he could travel in comfort and examine new
troves of art along the way, accompanied always by a detachment of
twenty plainclothes members of Heinrich Himmler's Sicherheitsdienst,
the state security service, or SD; if he saw something he liked, he could
have it packed aboard immediately. Göring exhibited an "all-embracing
acquisitiveness," according to a later report by U.S. investigators. "There
were no limits to his desires as far as the Collection was concerned." His
long leather coat made him look immense; underneath, he wore his medals and his favorite white uniform.

The cars climbed to the top of Cap Blanc-Nez, one of the highest
points on the French coast and, in more peaceful times, a popular picnic
ground. Here the officers set up tables and chairs and laid out a meal of
sandwiches and champagne. The chairs were collapsible, and care was
taken to ensure that the one given to Göring was as sturdy as possible.
The officers were here to watch the start of the Luftwaffe's attack on
London, set to begin that afternoon.

At about two o'clock continental time, Göring and the others heard
the first sounds of the bombers, a low hum rising to the north and south.
Officers stood on their toes to scan the horizons. Göring raised his bin-
oculars. An officer called out and pointed down the coast. Soon the sky
was filled with bombers and their fighter escorts, and high above them,

barely visible, additional waves of single-engine Messerschmitt 109s, positioned to take on the British fighters that, without doubt, would rise to meet the assault. German ace Galland and his squadron were assigned to sweep the English coastline for RAF interceptors.

So confident was Göring that the day would bring the Luftwaffe a stunning success, he announced to a group of radio reporters present on the cliff that he had taken personal command of the attack. This was the kind of moment Göring adored: the grand coup, with him the center of attention. "This moment is a historic one," he told the correspondents. "As a result of the provocative British attacks on Berlin on recent nights, the *Führer* has decided to order a mighty blow to be struck in revenge against the capital of the British Empire. I personally have assumed the leadership of this attack, and today I have heard above me the roaring of the victorious German squadrons."

The mood on the clifftop was one of elation. Barely able to restrain his glee, Göring grasped the shoulder of an officer next to him and, beaming, shook it hard, as if acting in a film for Goebbels's Ministry of Popular Enlightenment and Propaganda.

Part Four

—

BLOOD
AND DUST

September —
December

On a Quiet Blue Day

THE DAY WAS WARM AND STILL, THE SKY BLUE ABOVE A RISING haze. Temperatures by afternoon were in the nineties. People thronged Hyde Park and lounged on chairs set out beside the Serpentine. Shoppers jammed the stores of Oxford Street and Piccadilly. The giant barrage balloons overhead cast lumbering shadows on the streets below. After the August air raid when bombs first fell on London proper, the city had retreated back into a dream of invulnerability, punctuated now and then by false alerts whose once-terrifying novelty was muted by the failure of bombers to appear. The late-summer heat imparted an air of languid complacency. In the city's West End, theaters hosted twenty-four productions, among them the play *Rebecca,* adapted for the stage by Daphne du Maurier from her novel of the same name. Alfred Hitchcock's movie version, starring Laurence Olivier and Joan Fontaine, was also playing in London, as were the films *The Thin Man* and the long-running *Gaslight.*

It was a fine day to spend in the cool green of the countryside.

Churchill was at Chequers. Lord Beaverbrook departed for his country home, Cherkley Court, just after lunch, though he would later try to deny it. John Colville had left London the preceding Thursday, to begin a ten-day vacation at his aunt's Yorkshire estate with his mother and brother, shooting partridges, playing tennis, and sampling bottles from his uncle's collection of ancient port, in vintages dating to 1863. Mary Churchill was still at Breccles Hall with her friend and cousin Judy, continuing her reluctant role as country mouse and honoring their commitment to memorize one Shakespeare sonnet every day. That Saturday she chose Sonnet 116—in which love is the "ever-fixed mark"—and recited it to her diary. Then she went swimming. "It was so lovely—joie de vivre overcame vanity."

Throwing caution to the winds, she bathed without a cap.

IN BERLIN THAT SATURDAY morning, Joseph Goebbels prepared his lieu-tenants for what would occur by day's end. The coming destruction of London, he said, "would probably represent the greatest human catas-trophe in history." He hoped to blunt the inevitable world outcry by casting the assault as a deserved response to Britain's bombing of German civilians, but thus far British raids over Germany, including those of the night before, had not produced the levels of death and destruction that would justify such a massive reprisal.

He understood, however, that the Luftwaffe's impending attack on London was necessary and would likely hasten the end of the war. That the British raids had been so puny was an unfortunate thing, but he would manage. He hoped Churchill would produce a worthy raid "as soon as possible."

Every day offered a new challenge, tempered now and then by more pleasant distractions. At one meeting that week, Goebbels heard a re-port from Hans Hinkel, head of the ministry's Department for Special Cultural Tasks, who'd provided a further update on the status of Jews in Germany and Austria. "In Vienna there are 47,000 Jews left out of 180,000, two-thirds of them women and about 300 men between 20 and 35," Hinkel reported, according to minutes of the meeting. "In spite of the war it has been possible to transport a total of 17,000 Jews to the south-east. Berlin still numbers 71,800 Jews; in future about 500 Jews are to be sent to the south-east each month." Plans were in place, Hinkel re-ported, to remove 60,000 Jews from Berlin in the first four months after the end of the war, when transportation would again become available. "The remaining 12,000 will likewise have disappeared within a further four weeks."

This pleased Goebbels, though he recognized that Germany's overt anti-Semitism, long evident to the world, itself posed a significant pro-paganda problem. As to this, he was philosophical. "Since we are being opposed and calumniated throughout the world as enemies of the Jews," he said, "why should we derive only the disadvantages and not also the advantages, i.e. the elimination of the Jews from the theater, the cinema, public life and administration. If we are then still attacked as enemies of the Jews we shall at least be able to say with a clear conscience: It was worth it, we have benefited from it."

THE LUFTWAFFE CAME AT TEATIME.

The bombers arrived in three waves, the first composed of nearly a thousand aircraft—348 bombers and 617 fighters. Eight specially equipped Heinkel bombers of the KGr 100 "pathfinder" group led the way, carrying a combination of standard high-explosive bombs, incendiary oil bombs (*Flammenbomben*), and bombs with time-delayed fuses meant to keep firefighting crews at bay. Despite clear weather and daylight, they used the X-system of beams to navigate. In London the first siren sounded at 4:43 P.M.

Writer Virginia Cowles and a friend, Anne, were staying at the home of a British press baron, Esmond Harmsworth, in the village of Mereworth, about thirty miles southeast of central London. They were having tea on the lawn, enjoying the warmth and sun, when a low thrum rose from the southeast. "At first we couldn't see anything," Cowles wrote, "but soon the noise had grown into a deep, full roar, like the faraway thunder of a giant waterfall." She and her friend counted more than 150 planes, the bombers flying in formation, with fighters surrounding them in a protective shield. "We lay in the grass, our eyes strained towards the sky; we made out a batch of tiny white specks, like clouds of insects moving northwest in the direction of the capital."

She was struck by the fact that they proceeded without interference from the RAF, and guessed that somehow the German planes had broken through England's defenses.

"Poor London," her friend said.

Cowles was correct in observing that the German planes met little resistance, but not about the reason. The RAF, alerted by radar that a huge force of bombers was crossing the channel, had dispersed its fighter squadrons to take up defensive positions over key airfields, in the assumption that these would yet again be the principal targets. Likewise, anti-aircraft guns had been withdrawn from London to protect the airfields and other strategic targets. Only ninety-two guns were positioned to protect central London.

As soon as the RAF realized that the city was in fact the target, its fighters began converging on the German raiders. One RAF pilot, upon spotting the attackers, was shocked by what he saw. "I'd never seen so many aircraft," he wrote. "It was a hazy sort of day to about 16,000 feet.

As we broke through the haze, you could hardly believe it. As far as you could see there was nothing but German aircraft coming in, wave after wave."

The perspective from the ground was equally stunning. One young man, Colin Perry, eighteen, was on his bicycle when the first wave passed overhead. "It was the most amazing, impressive, riveting sight," he wrote later. "Directly above me were literally hundreds of planes, Germans! The sky was full of them." The fighters stuck close, he recalled, "like bees around their queen."

In the Plumstead district of southeast London, architecture student Jack Graham Wright and his family had settled in their parlor for tea. His mother brought it out on a tray edged with silver, along with cups, saucers, a small jug containing milk, and a teapot under a cozy meant to help the beverage retain heat. The sirens sounded. At first the family felt little concern, but when Wright and his mother looked out the door, they saw the sky full of planes. His mother noted the descent of "little bright things" and realized these were bombs. The two ran for cover under a stairway. "We all became conscious of a growing crescendo of noise drowning the growl of the planes, and then a series of enormous thuds growing nearer," Wright recalled.

The house shuddered; its floorboards heaved. Shock waves transmitted from the ground rose upward through their bodies. Wright steadied himself against a doorjamb. Then came a surge of noise and energy more powerful than anything before it. "The air of the parlor condensed and became opaque as if turned instantaneously to a red-brown fog," he wrote. The heavy brick "party wall" that separated his house from the next seemed to flex, and his doorjamb shimmied. Slates torn from the roof crashed through the glass of the family's conservatory. "I could hear doors and windows crashing all over the place," he wrote.

The heaving stopped; the wall still stood. "The brown fog had gone, but everything was covered with a heavy brown dust, which lay so thickly on the floor that it concealed the carpet." A detail became lodged in his memory: "The little china milk jug was lying on its side, and the spilt milk lay in a rivulet dripping over the edge of the table to a white pool in that thick layer of dust below."

It was this dust that many Londoners remembered as being one of the most striking phenomena of this attack and of others that followed. As buildings erupted, thunderheads of pulverized brick, stone, plaster, and mortar billowed from eaves and attics, roofs and chimneys, hearths and furnaces—dust from the age of Cromwell, Dickens, and Victoria. Bombs often detonated only upon reaching the ground underneath a house, adding soil and rock to the squalls of dust coursing down streets, and permeating the air with the rich sepulchral scent of raw earth. The dust burst outward rapidly at first, like smoke from a cannon, then slowed and dissipated, sifting and settling, covering sidewalks, streets, windshields, double-decker buses, phone booths, bodies. Survivors exiting ruins were coated head to toe as if with gray flour. Harold Nicolson, in his diary, described seeing people engulfed in a "thick fog which settled down on everything, plastering their hair and eyebrows with thick dust." It complicated the care of wounds, as one physician, a Dr. Morton, quickly discovered that Saturday night. "What struck one was the tremendous amount of dirt and dust, the dirt and dust of ages blown up in every incident," she wrote. Her training in keeping the wounded free of infection proved useless. "Their heads were full of grit and dust, their skin was engrained with dust, and it was completely impossible to do anything much about antisepsis at all."

Particularly jarring was the sight of blood against this gray background, as writer Graham Greene observed one night after watching soldiers emerge from a bombed building, "the purgatorial throng of men and women in dusty torn pajamas with little blood splashes standing in doorways."

AT 5:20 P.M. ON SATURDAY, Pug Ismay and the chiefs of staff met and debated the meaning of the raid. At 6:10 P.M., the all clear sounded, but at eight o'clock British radar identified a second wave of German aircraft assembling over France, consisting of 318 bombers. At 8:07 P.M., the chiefs of staff agreed that the time had come to issue the "Cromwell" alert, notifying Home Forces that invasion was imminent. Some local commanders went so far as to order the ringing of church bells, the signal that parachutists had been spotted in mid-descent, even though they personally had not seen anything of the kind.

By 8:30 that night, bombs were falling in London's Battersea district, but the city's anti-aircraft guns remained strangely silent, not firing until half an hour later, and then only at sporadic intervals. As night fell, RAF fighters returned to base and stayed there, made helpless by the dark.

BOMBS FELL THROUGHOUT THE NIGHT. Anyone venturing outside saw the sky glowing red. Fire crews fought immense blazes but made little headway, thereby ensuring that German pilots would have no trouble finding the city. German radio rejoiced. "Thick clouds of smoke spread over the roofs of the greatest city in the world," an announcer said, noting that pilots could feel the shock waves of detonations even in their planes. (When dropping their biggest bombs, the "Satan" weapons, crews were instructed to stay above two thousand meters—sixty-five hundred feet—lest they, too, be blown from the sky.) "The heart of the British Empire is delivered up to the attack of the German Air Force," the announcer said. One German airman, in a report that bore a whiff of propaganda, wrote, "A blazing girdle of fire stretched round the city of millions! In a few minutes we reached the point where we had to drop our bombs. And where are Albion's proud fighters to be found?"

For Londoners, it was a night of first experiences and sensations. The smell of cordite after a detonation. The sound of glass being swept into piles. London resident Phyllis Warner, a teacher in her thirties who kept a detailed journal of life during the war, heard the sound of a bomb falling for the first time, "an appalling shriek like a train whistle growing nearer and nearer, and then a sickening crash reverberating through the earth." As if it would do any good, she put her pillow over her head. Writer Cowles recalled "the deep roar of falling masonry like the thunder of breakers against the shore." The worst sound, she said, was the low, droning noise made by the masses of aircraft, which reminded her of a dentist's drill. Another writer present in London that night, John Strachey, recalled the olfactory impact of an explosion, describing it as "an acute irritation of the nasal passages from the powdered rubble of dissolved homes," followed by the "mean little stink" of leaking gas.

It was also a night for putting things in context. One woman, Joan Wyndham, later to become a writer and memoirist, retreated to an air-raid shelter in London's Kensington neighborhood, where, around midnight, she decided the time had come to cease being a virgin, and to employ her boyfriend, Rupert, in the venture. "The bombs are lovely," she wrote. "I think it is all thrilling. Nevertheless, as the opposite of death is life, I think I shall get seduced by Rupert tomorrow." She possessed a condom (a French "thingummy") but planned to go with a friend to a pharmacy for a popular spermicide called Volpar, in case the condom failed. "The all clear went at five A.M.," she wrote. "All clear for my lovely Rupert, I thought."

The next afternoon she followed through on her decision, but the experience fell well short of what she had hoped for. "Rupert slipped off his clothes, and I suddenly realized he looked terribly funny in the nude and began laughing helplessly."

"What's the matter, you don't like my cock?" he asked, according to her later recollection.

"It's all right, just a bit lopsided!"

"Most people's are," Rupert said. "Never mind, take your clothes off."

Later she reflected, "Well, that's done, and I'm glad it's over! If that's really all there is to it I'd rather have a good smoke or go to the pictures."

DAWN ON SUNDAY, SEPTEMBER 8, brought the jarring juxtaposition of clear summer skies and a black wall of smoke in the East End. Residents of Mornington Crescent, in Camden Town, awoke to find a double-decker bus protruding from the second-story window of a house. Overhead, and as far as one could see, hundreds of barrage balloons, drifting with untroubled ease, turned a comely pink in the rising light. At 10 Downing Street, the private secretary on duty, John Martin, walked outside after spending the night in the building's underground shelter, surprised "to find London still there."

The night's raids killed over four hundred people and caused severe injuries to sixteen hundred more. For many residents, the night brought another first: the sight of a corpse. When eighteen-year-old Len Jones ventured into the rubble behind his family's home, he spotted two heads protruding from the wreckage. "I recognized one head in particular; it was a Chinese man, Mr. Say, he had one eye closed, and then I began to realize that he was dead." Here, in what hours earlier had been a peaceful London neighborhood. "When I saw the dead Chinese, I just convulsed and couldn't get my breath. I was shaking completely. Then I thought well I must be dead, as they were, so I struck a match, and tried to burn my finger, I kept doing this with a match to see if I was still alive. I could see, but I thought I cannot be alive, this is the end of the world."

The Luftwaffe lost forty aircraft, the RAF twenty-eight, with another sixteen fighters badly damaged. To German ace Adolf Galland, this was a success. "The day," he said, "passed off with ridiculously few losses." His commander, Field Marshal Albert Kesselring, judged the raid to be a major victory, though he recalled with displeasure how Göring, on the cliff at Cap Blanc-Nez, "let himself be carried away in a superfluous bombastic broadcast to the German people, an exhibition distasteful to me both as a man and as a soldier."

As the sun rose, Churchill and his entourage—his detective, typist, secretary, soldiers, perhaps Nelson the cat—raced in from Chequers, Churchill intent on touring the damaged parts of the city and, most importantly, doing so as visibly as possible.

Beaverbrook, too, sped back to the city. He persuaded his secretary, David Farrer, working on a book about the Ministry of Aircraft Production, to depict him as having been in the city throughout the raid.

Farrer resisted at first. He tried to make Beaverbrook relent by reminding him that many of his own staff had heard him announce his departure for his country home right after lunch on the Saturday of the raid. But Beaverbrook insisted. In a later memoir Farrer wrote, "It was, I think, inconceivable to him in retrospect that he, the Minister of Aircraft Production, should not have been witness to this cataclysmic moment in air warfare; so he was there—and that was all there was to it."

Unpredictable Magic

FIRES STILL BURNED AND CREWS WERE STILL DIGGING BODIES from wrecked buildings when Churchill arrived in the East End, accompanied, as always, by Inspector Thompson, alert to the risks that such a visit posed. Pug Ismay came too, his kind canine face worn by lack of sleep and by grief for the stunned souls the procession encountered along the way. "The destruction was much more devastating than I had imagined it would be," Ismay wrote. "Fires were still raging all over the place; some of the larger buildings were mere skeletons, and many of the smaller houses had been reduced to piles of rubble." He was struck in particular by the sight of paper Union Jacks planted in mounds of shattered lumber and brick. These, he wrote, "brought a lump to one's throat."

Churchill understood the power of symbolic acts. He stopped at an air-raid shelter where a bomb had killed forty people and a large crowd was gathering. For a moment, Ismay feared that the onlookers might resent Churchill's arrival, out of indignation at the government's failure to protect the city, but these East Enders seemed delighted. Ismay heard someone shout, "Good old Winnie! We thought you'd come and see us. We can take it. Give it 'em back." Colin Perry, who had witnessed the raid from his bicycle, saw Churchill and wrote in his diary, "He looked invincible, which he is. Tough, bulldogged, piercing."

Tough, yes, but at times weeping openly, overcome by the devastation and the resilience of the crowd. In one hand he held a large white handkerchief, with which he mopped his eyes; in his other he grasped the handle of his walking stick.

"You see," an elderly woman called out, "he really cares; he's crying."

When he came to a group of dispirited people looking over what remained of their homes, one woman shouted, "When are we going to bomb Berlin, Winnie?"

Churchill whirled, shook his fist and walking stick, and snarled, "You leave that to me!"

At this, the mood of the crowd abruptly changed, as witnessed by a government employee named Samuel Battersby. "Morale rose immediately," he wrote. "Everyone was satisfied and reassured." It was the perfect rejoinder for the moment, he decided. "What could a Prime Minister at that time and in such desperate conditions say that was not pathetically inadequate—or even downright dangerous?" To Battersby, it typified "the uniquely unpredictable magic that was Churchill"—his ability to transform "the despondent misery of disaster into a grimly certain stepping stone to ultimate victory."

Churchill and Ismay continued touring the East End well into the evening, causing the dock officials there, and Inspector Thompson, to grow anxious. After nightfall, the fires would serve as a beacon for what surely would be another attack. The officials told Churchill he must leave the area immediately, but, Ismay wrote, "he was in one of his most obstinate moods and insisted that he wanted to see everything."

The evening darkened, and the bombers did indeed return. Churchill and Ismay got into their car. As the driver struggled to negotiate blocked and obstructed streets, a cluster of incendiaries landed just ahead, sparking and hissing, as if someone had upended a basket of snakes. Churchill— "feigning innocence," Ismay believed—asked what the fallen objects were. Ismay told him and, aware that the Luftwaffe used incendiaries to light targets for bombers soon to follow, added that it meant their car was "in the middle of the bull's-eye."

The fires already burning would have achieved the same end, however. The Luftwaffe had timed the first raid on Saturday afternoon to give its bomber pilots plenty of daylight to find London by dead reckoning, without the help of navigation beams. The fires they ignited burned throughout the night, serving as visual guides for each successive wave of bombers. Even so, most bombs missed their targets and fell in random patterns throughout the city, prompting American air force observer Carl Spaatz to write in his diary, "Apparently indiscriminate bombing of London has started."

Churchill and Ismay made it back to 10 Downing Street late that night to find its central hall crowded with staff members and ministers who had grown anxious about Churchill's failure to return before nightfall.

Churchill walked past them without a word.

The group then pilloried Ismay for exposing the prime minister to such danger. To which Ismay replied that "anybody who imagined that he could control the Prime Minister on jaunts of this kind was welcome to try his hand on the next occasion." Ismay, in recounting this, noted that the actual language he deployed was much rougher.

CONCERNED THAT INVASION HYSTERIA could confuse things, General Brooke, commander of Home Forces, had on Sunday morning issued an instruction to his commanders that they could order the ringing of church bells only if they themselves actually *saw* twenty-five or more parachutists descending, and not because they heard bells ringing elsewhere or because of secondhand reports.

The Cromwell alert remained in effect. Concern about invasion intensified.

BEAVERBROOK SAW GRAVE WARNING in the September 7 attack. Upon his return to London, he convened an emergency meeting of his top men, his council, and ordered a tectonic change in the structure of the nation's aircraft industry. Henceforth, large centralized manufacturing centers would be broken up and dispersed to nodes spread throughout the country. A Spitfire plant in Birmingham was divided into twenty-three buildings in eight towns; a large Vickers plant that employed ten thousand workers was dispersed into forty-two locations, none with more than five hundred employees. In a move certain to ignite new bureaucratic strife, Beaverbrook commandeered for himself the authority to requisition manufacturing space at will, no matter its location, provided it was not currently occupied or designated for some crucial war-related function.

Beaverbrook also grew concerned about how his newly built aircraft were stored before being transferred to combat squadrons. Up until this point, new aircraft had been housed in large storage buildings, typically at RAF airfields, but now Beaverbrook ordered that these aircraft be scattered throughout the countryside, tucked into garages and barns, to prevent the catastrophic losses that even a single lucky pilot could produce. He had been concerned about such an event since July, when he'd visited a storage depot at Brize Norton, west of Oxford, and found a large number of aircraft packed closely together, "dangerously exposed to enemy attack," as he put it in a note to Churchill. Six weeks later, his concerns had proved justified, when a raid against the base carried out by just two German aircraft destroyed dozens of planes. The new shelters became known as "Robins' Nests."

Beaverbrook's dispersion program raised a surge of bureaucratic outrage. He seized buildings that other ministries had earmarked for their own use. "It was high-handed, it was . . . the height of piracy," wrote his secretary, David Farrer. But to Beaverbrook the logic of dispersion was overpowering, no matter the degree of opposition. "It secured him premises for the duration," Farrer wrote, "and enemies for life."

It also slowed the output of new aircraft, although this seemed a small cost relative to the assurance that no single raid could cause lasting damage to future production.

ON SUNDAY, HITLER'S DEPUTY, Rudolf Hess, summoned Albrecht Haushofer for a meeting at the town of Bad Godesberg, on the Rhine. Unlike Hess's previous nine-hour summit with Albrecht's father, this meeting lasted a meager two hours. "I had the opportunity to speak in all frankness," Albrecht wrote later, in a memorandum on the conversation. The two discussed how to communicate to influential officials in Britain that Hitler really was interested in a peace arrangement. According to Hess, Hitler did not want to destroy the British Empire. Hess asked, "Was there not somebody in England who was ready for peace?"

Secure in his friendship with the deputy, Albrecht felt free to speak with a bluntness that might have gotten another man shipped to a concentration camp. The English, he said, would need assurance that Hitler would honor a peace agreement, because "practically all Englishmen who mattered, regarded a treaty signed by the *Führer* as a worthless scrap of paper."

This perplexed Hess. Albrecht gave him examples, and then asked the deputy: "What guarantee did England have that a new treaty would not be broken again at once if it suited us? It must be realized that, even in the Anglo-Saxon world, the *Führer* was regarded as Satan's representative on earth and had to be fought."

At length the conversation turned to the potential use of an intermediary and a meeting in a neutral country. Albrecht suggested his friend the Duke of Hamilton, "who has access at all times to all important persons in London, even to Churchill and the King." Whether Albrecht knew it or not, the duke was now also an RAF sector commander.

Four days later, a letter was on its way to him, via an oblique route devised by Hess and Albrecht. The letter suggested, in veiled prose, that the duke and Albrecht meet on neutral ground, in Lisbon. Albrecht signed the letter with the initial "A," in the expectation that the duke would understand who had sent it.

The duke did not reply. As the silence from Britain grew long, Hess realized that a more direct approach to him would be necessary. He believed, too, that a mysterious hand was now guiding him. As he wrote later to his son, Wolf, nicknamed Buz:

"Buz! Take notice, there are higher, more fateful powers which I should point out to you—let us call them divine powers—which intervene, at least when it is time for great events."

IN AN ILL-TIMED MANEUVER, Mary Churchill, in the midst of her summer idyll at Breccles Hall, chose that Sunday, September 8, the day after the immense raid on London, to renew her plea to her parents that she be allowed to return to the city.

"I think of you all so often," she wrote in a letter to Clementine, "—and I hate to be separated from you and Papa in these dark days. Please—oh—please, Mummie darling, let me come back."

She hungered to start working for the Women's Voluntary Services, the WVS, and already had a posting assigned to her in London, arranged by her mother earlier that summer, but she was not scheduled to begin the job until after her Breccles holiday. "I would so like to be with you and take my share, and also I do want to begin my work," Mary wrote. She urged Clementine to please not "make Kitten into 'evacuee Kit'!"

THE BOMBERS RETURNED TO London that night and again the next day, Monday, September 9. A bomb struck writer Virginia Woolf's house in Bloomsbury, which served as the headquarters of her Hogarth Press. A second bomb also struck the house but did not immediately explode; it detonated a week later, completing the destruction of her home. Bombs landed in London's West End for the first time. One struck the grounds of Buckingham Palace, but it did not explode until 1:25 the next morning, propelling shattered glass throughout the royal apartments. The king and queen, however, were not present; they spent each night at Windsor

Castle, twenty miles due west of the palace, and commuted to London each morning.

With London now under attack, Mary's parents, unswayed by her latest plea, decided to have her spend the winter at Chequers, where she could work full-time for the Women's Voluntary Service in the nearby village of Aylesbury, instead of London. Clementine apparently arranged the change in location without first consulting Mary. "The 'ordering' of my life must have been settled over the telephone," Mary wrote.

On Wednesday, September 11, the eve of Mary's departure for Chequers, her cousin Judy and Judy's mother, Venetia, threw a combined birthday and going-away party for her and invited a number of RAF airmen. The party continued well past midnight; in her diary, Mary called it "the best one I've been to for ages" and described an encounter with a young pilot named Ian Prosser. "He gave me such a sweet romantic kiss as he left—starlight & moonlight—my—my—REAL ROMANTIC ATMOSPHERE."

That night her father gave a radio address from the underground Cabinet War Rooms, using the BBC's special link to the fortified chamber. The complex was a five-minute walk from Downing Street through the heart of Whitehall.

The subject of his broadcast was invasion, which seemed ever more imminent. As always, he proffered a mix of optimism and unglazed realism. "We cannot tell," he said, "when they will come; we cannot be sure that in fact they will try at all; but no one should blind himself to the fact that a heavy, full-scale invasion of this island is being prepared with all the usual German thoroughness and method, and that it may be launched now—upon England, upon Scotland, or upon Ireland, or upon all three."

If Hitler did plan to invade, Churchill warned, he would have to do so soon, before the weather worsened, and before attacks by the RAF on Germany's assembled invasion fleet grew too costly. "Therefore, we must regard the next week or so as a very important period in our history. It ranks with the days when the Spanish Armada was approaching the Channel . . . or when Nelson stood between us and Napoleon's Grand Army at Boulogne." But now, he warned, the outcome was "of far more consequence to the life and future of the world and its civilization than these brave old days of the past."

Lest his remarks send people cowering en masse, Churchill offered grounds for hope and heroism. The RAF, he said, was more potent than ever, and the Home Guard now numbered a million and a half men.

He called Hitler's bombing of London an attempt "to try to break our famous island race by a process of indiscriminate slaughter and destruction." But the attempt, by "this wicked man," had backfired, Churchill said. "What he has done is to kindle a fire in British hearts, here and all over the world, which will glow long after all traces of the conflagration he has caused in London have been removed."

The speech was a gloomy one, but it took place on a night when Londoners otherwise felt suddenly heartened, even though German bombers again arrived in force. This new surge in morale had nothing to do with Churchill's speech and everything to do with his gift for understanding how simple gestures could generate huge effects. What had infuriated Londoners was that during these night raids the Luftwaffe seemed free to come and go as it wished, without interference from the night-blind RAF and the city's strangely quiescent anti-aircraft guns. Gun crews were under orders to conserve ammunition and fire only when aircraft were sighted overhead and, as a consequence, did little firing at all. On Churchill's orders, more guns were brought to the city, boosting the total to nearly two hundred, from ninety-two. More importantly, Churchill now directed their crews to fire with abandon, despite his knowing full well that guns only rarely brought down aircraft. The orders took effect that Wednesday night, September 11. The impact on civic morale was striking and immediate.

Crews blasted away; one official described it as "largely wild and uncontrolled shooting." Searchlights swept the sky. Shells burst over Trafalgar Square and Westminster like fireworks, sending a steady rain of shrapnel onto the streets below, much to the delight of London's residents. The guns raised "a momentous sound that sent a chattering, smashing, blinding thrill through the London heart," wrote novelist William Sansom. Churchill himself loved the sound of the guns; instead of seeking shelter, he would race to the nearest gun emplacement and watch. The new cacophony had "an immense effect on people's morale," wrote private secretary John Martin. "Tails are up and, after the fifth sleepless night, everyone looks quite different this morning—cheerful and confident. It was a curious bit of mass psychology—the relief of hitting back." The next day's Home Intelligence reports confirmed the effect. "The dominating topic of conversation today is the anti-aircraft barrage of last night. This greatly stimulated morale: in public shelters people cheered and conversation shows that the noise brought a shock of positive pleasure."

Even better, on that Wednesday when Churchill spoke and the

guns raged, news arrived that the RAF had hit Berlin in force the night before—"the severest bombing yet," wrote William Shirer in his diary. For the first time, the RAF dropped large numbers of incendiaries on the city, Shirer noted. Half a dozen landed in the garden of Dr. Joseph Goebbels.

Sleep

———

IN LONDON, AS THE RAIDS CONTINUED, THE MUNDANE CHALLENGES of daily life became wearing, like the endless dripping of rainwater through roofs perforated by shrapnel. A shortage of glass meant windows had to be patched with wood, cardboard, or canvas. Churchill believed that with winter approaching, part of Luftwaffe chief Göring's plan was "to smash as much glass as possible." Electricity and gas outages were regular occurrences. Commuting to work became a long and tedious process, with a one-hour journey potentially expanding to four hours or more.

One of the worst effects was lack of sleep. Sirens and bombs and anxiety tore the night apart, as did the newly exuberant anti-aircraft guns. According to Home Intelligence, "People living near guns are suffering from serious lack of sleep: a number of interviews made round one gun in West London showed that people were getting much less sleep than others a few hundred yards away." But no one wanted the guns to stop. "There is little complaint about lack of sleep, mainly because of the new exhilaration created by the barrage. Nevertheless this serious loss of sleep needs watching."

Those Londoners who fled to public shelters found them poorly equipped for slumber, because prewar civil defense planners had not anticipated that air raids would occur at night. "It's not the bombs I'm scared of any more, it's the weariness," wrote a female civil servant in her Mass-Observation diary—"trying to work and concentrate with your eyes sticking out of your head like hat-pins, after being up all night. I'd die in my sleep, happily, if only I *could* sleep."

A survey found that 31 percent of respondents reported getting no sleep on the night of September 11. Another 32 percent got less than four hours. Only 15 percent said they slept more than six. "Conversation was devoted to one topic only: where and how to sleep," wrote Virginia Cowles. The "where" part was particularly challenging. "Everyone had theories on the subject: some preferred the basement, others said the top of the house was safer than being trapped under debris; some recommended a narrow trench in the back garden, and still others insisted it was best to forget it and die comfortably in bed."

A small percentage of Londoners used the Underground for shelter, though popular myth would later convey the impression that all of London flocked to the system's deep subway stations. On the night of September 27, when police counted the highest number of people sheltering in these "tube" stations, the total was 177,000, or about 5 percent of the population then remaining in London. And Churchill, at first, wanted it this way. Having a lot of people concentrated in stations conjured for him the nightmare of hundreds of lives, possibly thousands, lost to a single bomb, should one penetrate to the train platforms far below ground. And, indeed, on September 17, a bomb would strike the Marble Arch tube stop, killing twenty people; in October, four direct hits on stations would kill or wound six hundred. It was the Prof, however, who persuaded Churchill that deep shelters that could house large numbers of people were necessary. "A very formidable discontent is now arising," the Prof told him; people wanted "a safe and quiet night."

A November survey, however, found that 27 percent of London's residents used their own domestic shelters, mostly so-called Anderson shelters, named for John Anderson, minister for Home Security. These were metal enclosures designed to be buried in yards and gardens, billed as being able to protect occupants from all but a direct hit, though protecting them from flooding, mold, and bone-chilling cold was proving a confounding challenge. Many more Londoners—by one estimate, as many as 71 percent—just stayed in their homes, sometimes in their basements, often in their beds.

Churchill slept at 10 Downing Street. When the bombers came, much to the consternation of Clementine he climbed to the roof to watch.

ON THURSDAY, SEPTEMBER 12, a four-thousand-pound bomb, apparently of the "Satan" variety, landed in front of St. Paul's Cathedral and penetrated the ground to a depth of twenty-six feet but did not detonate.

Men tunneled to reach it, and hauled it gingerly to the surface three days later. The tunnelers were among the first to win a new award for civilian bravery created at the request of the king: the George Cross.

The next day bombs again struck Buckingham Palace, this time a near miss for the royal couple. They had driven in from Windsor Castle, through weather that suggested that raids would be unlikely, with rain falling from a thickly overcast sky. The couple were speaking with the king's private secretary, Alec Hardinge, in an upstairs room overlooking the large open quadrangle at the center of the palace, when they heard the roar of an aircraft and saw two bombs fly past. Two explosions shook the palace. "We looked at each other, & then we were out into the passage as fast as we could get there," the king wrote in his diary. "The whole thing happened in a matter of seconds. We all wondered why we weren't dead." He was convinced the palace was the intended target. "The aircraft was seen coming straight down the Mall below the clouds having dived through the clouds & had dropped 2 bombs in the forecourt, 2 in the quadrangle, 1 in the Chapel & the other in the garden." A police constable guarding the palace told the queen it had been "a magnificent piece of bombing."

Though the bombing itself quickly became public knowledge, the narrowness of the royal couple's escape was kept secret, even from Churchill, who learned of it only well afterward while writing his personal history of the war. The episode left the king shaken. "It was a ghastly experience & I don't want it to be repeated," he confided in his diary. "It certainly teaches one to 'take cover' on all future occasions, but one must be careful not to become 'dugout minded.'" For a time, however, he remained uneasy. "I quite disliked sitting in my room on Monday & Tuesday," he wrote the following week. "I found myself unable to read, always in a hurry, & glancing out of the window."

The bombing had a positive side. The attack, the king observed, made him and his wife feel a closer connection to the masses. The queen put it succinctly: "I'm glad we've been bombed. It makes me feel I can look the East End in the face."

As the weekend neared, invasion fears became acute. With the moon almost full and favorable tides in the offing, Londoners began calling it "Invasion Weekend." On Friday, September 13, Home Forces commander General Brooke wrote in his diary, "Everything looks like an invasion starting tomorrow from the Thames to Plymouth! I wonder whether we shall be hard at it by this time tomorrow?"

Sufficiently grave were these concerns that on Saturday Churchill sent a directive to Pug Ismay, War Cabinet secretary Edward Bridges, and other senior officials, asking them to visit a special fortified compound established in northwest London called the "Paddock," where if worst came to worst, the government could retreat and still function. The idea of the government evacuating Whitehall was anathema to Churchill, who feared the defeatist signal this would send to the public, to Hitler, and especially to America. But now he saw a new urgency. In his minute he directed his ministers to examine the quarters designated for them, and to "be ready to move there at short notice." He insisted they avoid all publicity while making these preparations.

"We must expect," he wrote, "that the Whitehall-Westminster area will be the subject of intensive air attack any time now. The German method is to make the disruption of the Central Government a vital prelude to any major assault upon the country. They have done this everywhere. They will certainly do it here, where the landscape can be so easily recognized and the river and its high buildings affords a sure guide both by day and night."

THOUGH INVASION ANXIETY SOARED and rumors flew, scores of parents in London and elsewhere in Britain felt a new sense of peace that weekend. With great relief, these parents settled their children aboard a ship named the *City of Benares,* in Liverpool, to evacuate them to Canada, in the hope of keeping them safe from bombs and the impending German invasion. The ship carried ninety children, many accompanied by their mothers, the rest traveling alone. The passenger manifest included one boy whose parents feared that since he had been circumcised at birth, he might be ruled a Jew by the invading forces.

Four days after the ship's departure, six hundred miles out at sea, with a gale raging, the ship was torpedoed by a U-boat and sunk, killing 265 souls, including seventy of the ninety children on board.

Terms of Imprisonment

AT CHEQUERS, MARY CHURCHILL SETTLED HERSELF INTO A BEDROOM on the third floor of the house, which could be reached by a secret spiral staircase from the Hawtrey Room below. A more conventional path, via an ordinary hallway, also gave access to the room, but Mary preferred the stairs. The room was isolated, on an otherwise unoccupied floor, and tended to be cold and drafty, exposed to winds that "wuthered"—her term—around the outside walls. It had sloping ceilings and a large fireplace that did little to dispel the cold. She loved it.

The room was imbued with mystery, and like everything else at Chequers, it evoked the distant past. For centuries, it had been known as the Prison Room, its name deriving from an episode that occurred in 1565, an era when royal displeasure could yield deeply unpleasant outcomes. That prisoner, another Mary—Lady Mary Grey, younger sister of Lady Jane Grey, famously executed in 1554—decided to marry, in secret, a commoner named Thomas Keyes, who managed security for Queen Elizabeth I. The marriage offended the queen for a variety of reasons, not least of which was the likelihood that it would bring ridicule to the royal household, owing to the fact the bride was tiny, perhaps a dwarf, and the groom enormous, said to be the largest man in the court. The queen's secretary, Sir William Cecil, described the match as "monstruoos." The queen threw Keyes into Fleet Prison and ordered the then owner of Chequers, William Hawtrey, to lock Lady Mary in the house and keep her there until further notice, except for occasional ventures outside for air. She was released two years later, her husband a year after that, but they never saw each other again.

Two small windows provided a view of Beacon Hill. At night, even though Chequers was forty miles from London, modern Mary saw the distant flare of anti-aircraft guns and heard their distinctive crump and rumble. Often aircraft passed over the house, prompting her at times to hide her head under the covers.

The house, Mary saw, threatened to be very quiet on weekdays, though she was delighted that her parents had imported "Nana" Whyte, her childhood nanny, from Chartwell, for that first weekend. It helped, too, that her sister-in-law, Pamela Churchill, was now also ensconced in the house, "waiting impatiently for little Winston," Mary observed in her diary.

The house enlivened markedly that Friday, September 13, with the arrival of Churchill, Clementine, and the private secretary on duty, John Martin, and with the happy prospect of Mary celebrating her eighteenth birthday on Sunday.

The weekend would also present what Mary called "gripping distractions."

CHURCHILL AND CLEMENTINE STAYED at Chequers through lunch on Saturday but drove to London in the afternoon. Churchill planned to come back the next day for the party; Clementine returned that evening, with a surprise. "Mummie had ordered a lovely cake for me despite raids!" Mary wrote in her diary. "How sweet she is!"

That night Mary mused upon her own advancing age in a lengthy entry in her diary, describing Saturday as "the last day that I shall be 'sweet seventeen'!" There was war, yes, but she could not help herself: She exulted in her life. "What a wonderful year it has been!" she wrote. "I think it will always stand out in my memory. It has been very happy for me too—despite the misery & unhappiness in the world. I hope that does not mean that I am unfeeling—I really don't think I am, but somehow I just haven't been able to help being happy."

She acknowledged a heightened sensitivity to the world around her. "I think I have felt fear & anxiety & sorrow in small doses for the first time in my life. I do so love being young & I don't very much want to be 18. Although I often behave in a completely idiotic & 'haywire' fashion—yet I feel I have grown up quite a lot in the last year. I am glad of it."

She went to bed as gunfire lit the sky over distant London.

CHURCHILL RETURNED TO CHEQUERS on Sunday, in time for lunch. Afterward, observing that "the weather on this day seemed suitable to the enemy," he set out with Clementine, Pamela, and secretary Martin to pay another visit to the Fighter Command operations center at Uxbridge. Upon arrival Churchill, Clementine, and the others were led down stairways fifty feet underground to the Operations Room, which looked to Churchill like a small theater, two stories high and sixty feet across. The room was quiet at first. Earlier in the day, a major air battle had taken place after more than two hundred bombers and their fighter escorts had crossed the coastline, but this had subsided. As Churchill and the others made their descent, the commander of No. 11 Group, Air Vice Marshal Keith Park, said, "I don't know whether anything will happen today. At present all is quiet."

The family took seats in what Churchill called "the Dress Circle." Below was a vast map on a table, attended by twenty or so men and women and various assistants answering telephones. The opposite wall was taken up entirely by a light board with banks of colored bulbs that denoted the status of each squadron. Red lights indicated fighters in action; another bank showed those returning to their airfields. Officers in a glass-enclosed control room—Churchill called it a "stage-box"—evaluated information phoned in from radar operators and the Air Ministry's thirty-thousand-strong network of human observers.

The quiet did not last. Radar detected aircraft massing over Dieppe, on the French coast, and advancing toward England. Initial reports put the total of attacking planes at "40 plus." Lights began to glow in the board on the far wall, showing that RAF fighter squadrons were now "Standing By," meaning ready to take off on two minutes' notice. More reports came in of German aircraft approaching, and these were announced as blandly as if they were trains arriving at a station:

"Twenty plus."

"Forty plus."

"Sixty plus."

"Eighty plus."

The staff attending the map table began sliding disks across its surface, toward England. These represented the approaching German forces. On the far wall, red lights blinked on as hundreds of Hurricanes and Spitfires took to the air from bases throughout southeast England.

The German disks shifted steadily forward. On the light board, the bulbs that indicated aircraft held in reserve went dark, meaning every single fighter in No. 11 Group was now engaged. Messages from observers on the ground poured in via telephone, reporting sightings of German aircraft, their type, number, direction, and approximate altitude. During a typical raid, thousands of these messages would arrive. A single young officer directed the group's fighters toward the intruders, his voice, as Churchill recalled, "a calm, low monotone." Vice Marshal Park was clearly anxious, and walked back and forth behind the officer, now and then preempting him with orders of his own.

As the battle progressed, Churchill asked, "What other reserves have we?"

Park answered: "There are none."

Long a student of war, Churchill knew well that this meant the situation was very grave. The RAF's fighters carried only enough fuel to keep them aloft for about an hour and a half, after which they had to land to refuel and reload their guns. On the ground they would be dangerously vulnerable.

Soon the light board showed the RAF squadrons returning to base. Churchill's anxiety rose. "What losses should we not suffer if our refuelling planes were caught on the ground by further raids of '40 plus' or '50 plus!' " he wrote.

But the German fighters, too, were reaching their operational limits. The bombers they accompanied could have stayed aloft far longer, but, like their RAF counterparts, the Luftwaffe fighters had only ninety minutes of endurance, which included the time they needed to make their way back across the English Channel to their coastal bases. The bombers could not risk flying without protection and, therefore, had to return as well. These limitations, according to German ace Adolf Galland, "became more and more of a disadvantage." During one raid, his own group lost a dozen fighters, five of which had to make what were known as "pancake" landings on French beaches, the other seven forced to ditch in the channel itself. An Me 109 could float for up to a minute, which Galland counted as "just about long enough for the pilot to unstrap himself and to scramble out," at which point he would deploy his "Mae West" life preserver or a small rubber dinghy and fire a flare, in hopes of being rescued by the Luftwaffe's Air Sea Rescue Service.

As Churchill watched, the light board indicated more and more RAF squadrons returning to their fields. But now, also, the staff at the map table began moving the disks representing German bombers back toward the channel and the French coast. The battle was over.

The Churchills climbed up to the surface just as the all clear sounded. Awed by the idea of so many young pilots dashing headlong into battle, Churchill, in the car, said aloud to himself, "There are times when it is equally good to live or to die."

They returned to Chequers at four-thirty P.M., Churchill exhausted, only to learn that a planned Allied assault on the West African city of Dakar, to be commanded by General de Gaulle using British and Free French troops, was threatened by the unexpected appearance of warships that had escaped British confiscation and were now under the control of the pro-German Vichy government. After a quick call to London at five-fifteen P.M., during which he recommended that the operation, code-named "Menace," be canceled, he went to bed for his afternoon nap.

Ordinarily, his naps lasted an hour or so. This day, drained by the drama of the afternoon's air battle, he slept until eight P.M. Upon waking, he summoned the duty secretary, Martin, who brought him the latest news from all quarters. "It was repellent," Churchill recalled. "This had gone wrong here; that had been delayed there; an unsatisfactory answer had been received from so-and-so; there had been bad sinkings in the Atlantic."

Martin reserved the good news until the end.

"However," he now told Churchill, "all is redeemed by the air. We have shot down one hundred and eighty-three for a loss of under forty."

These numbers were so extraordinary that throughout the empire, September 15 became known as Battle of Britain Day, although this count too proved to be incorrect, greatly inflated by the usual heat-of-battle exaggeration.

THERE WAS MORE JOY that Sunday night at Chequers when Mary's birthday celebration got underway. Her sister Sarah brought her a leather writing portfolio. A friend sent chocolates and silk stockings; cousin Judy sent a congratulatory telegram. Mary was delighted by the attention. "How sweet everyone is in these terrible times to remember me being 18!" she wrote that night in her diary. "I do appreciate it terribly."

She closed the entry: "I went to bed eighteen—very happy." She was delighted too by the prospect of starting work the next day with the Women's Voluntary Service at Aylesbury.

Berlin

FOR HERMANN GÖRING, THE LOSSES IN SUNDAY'S AIR BATTLE WERE shocking and humiliating. His commanders knew soon afterward the true extent of their losses, by the number of aircraft that failed to return. Even though far short of the 183 victories claimed by the RAF, the number of downed German planes was hard to fathom: 60 aircraft, 34 of which were bombers. The loss was even more grave than this, however, for the tally did not reflect the fact that another 20 bombers had been badly damaged, and that many members of the returning crews had been pulled from their planes dead, maimed, or otherwise wounded. The RAF, by final count, had lost only 26 fighters.

Up to this point, Göring had promoted the idea that his bomber crews were more courageous than their British counterparts because they attacked in broad daylight as well as at night, unlike the cowardly British, who conducted their raids against Germany only under cover of darkness. But now he halted all major daylight attacks (though later that week there would be one more large, and, for the Luftwaffe, extremely costly daytime raid against London).

"We lost our nerve," said Field Marshal Erhard Milch, in a later interrogation. Milch, described by British intelligence in August 1940 as "a vulgar little man" who revered medieval gods and ceremonies, had been instrumental in helping Göring build the Luftwaffe. The losses were unnecessary, Milch said. He cited two main causes: "a) the bombers flew in a frightful formation, b) the fighter escort was never where it should have been. It wasn't disciplined flying." The fighters, he said, "didn't stick to fighter escort work; they were more for freelance fighter activity, as they wanted to shoot aircraft down."

That the Luftwaffe had failed was clear to all, especially to Göring's patron and master, Adolf Hitler.

PROPAGANDA CHIEF GOEBBELS, MEANWHILE, wrestled with yet another propaganda challenge: how to cool the outcry caused by the Luftwaffe's bombing of Buckingham Palace the preceding Friday, which was proving to be a public relations debacle.

In war, inhumane things happened every day, but to the world at large, the attack seemed mean-spirited and gratuitous. What would help blunt the outrage, Goebbels knew, would be a revelation that the palace had itself become a storage depot for munitions or that a significant warehouse or power station or other target was located near enough to make it seem plausible that the palace had been hit by stray bombs—even though the nature of the attack, with a bomber diving through rain and clouds and flying along Whitehall toward one of the largest, most recognizable landmarks in London, made this defense seem singularly feeble.

At his Sunday propaganda meeting, Goebbels turned to Major Rudolf Wodarg, the Luftwaffe's liaison to his ministry, and directed him "to ascertain whether there are any military targets in the vicinity of Buckingham Palace."

If not, Goebbels said, German propaganda must make them up, specifically by asserting "that secret military stores are concealed in its immediate neighborhood."

Fear

M ARY'S FIRST WEEK WITH THE WOMEN'S VOLUNTARY SERVICE brought home to her the real impact of the war. The country mouse found herself assigned to help find places to live for families who had been bombed out of their London homes or were fleeing the city out of fear that this fate would befall them. They arrived in a flood, bringing terrifying tales of their experiences in London. The number of refugees far outstripped the available billets, which caused the WVS to politely but firmly appeal to citizens in the area to open their homes to the new-comers. Special emergency laws passed when the war began gave the government the power to commandeer homes, but the WVS was reluctant to invoke it, for fear of generating resentment and exacerbating already simmering class hostility—dockworker meets country gentleman—at a time when there was plenty of tension to go around.

For Mary, the contrast between what she now encountered and how she had spent her summer at Breccles Hall was almost incomprehensible. Just two weeks earlier, she and Judy Montagu had been bicycling happily through the countryside, bathing in the estate's pond, and dancing and flirting with young officers of the RAF, the war distant and out of frame. Even the guns at night were more a source of comfort than terror.

But now:

"This is the twentieth century—" Mary wrote in her diary that weekend. "Look on London—look at the crowds of homeless destitutes and weary people in Aylesbury alone—

"I have seen more suffering & poverty this week than ever before.

"I cannot find words to describe my feelings about it. I only know I am moved to a greater & wider realization of the suffering war brings. I only know that I have learnt more about human suffering & anxiety than ever before.

"O God, be with the homeless and anxious

"I have seen so many worried & sad & lost expressions—& a great deal of courage & optimism & good sense."

Two days later, on Monday, September 23, Mary read the news about the sinking of the *City of Benares,* and the deaths of so many of the children aboard. "May God rest their souls," she wrote in her diary that night, "and help us to wipe the curse of Hitler & the vilest burden mankind has ever born[e] from the world." Her father ordered that in view of the sinking, "the further evacuation overseas of children must cease."

In the distance, guns fired and shells burst, but in the Prison Room at Chequers, there was peace and history and the benign presence of Lady Mary's ghost. No matter how harsh the stories Mary heard each day, she was able to retreat each night to her lovely home, to be looked after by Monty—Grace Lamont, the Chequers housekeeper—and kept company by Pamela, as the latter awaited the arrival of her baby. Unexpectedly, Pamela's doctor, Carnac Rivett, also now made himself a more or less full-time inhabitant, much to Clementine's displeasure. She found his presence both oppressive and embarrassing, especially since Chequers was not the Churchills' private property but belonged to the government. She told Pamela, "My darling, you must realize this is an official house and it is rather awkward having the doctor every night at the dinner table."

Rivett often stayed the night, arguing that his presence was required because the baby could come at any time.

Pamela suspected that Rivett was driven by a different motive: fear. He was, she believed, terrified of the bombing in London and came to Chequers to be safe.

Her baby was due in three weeks.

JOHN COLVILLE LEFT CHEQUERS Sunday afternoon, after tea, and traveled to London to have dinner at his family's home in Eccleston Square, near Victoria Station. Just before they sat down to eat, the sirens rang out, and soon came the sound of German bombers overhead. Colville went up to a bedroom. With the lights off behind him, he knelt by a window to watch the raid unfold. It was all very surreal—bombs falling into the heart of one's capital city, one's home—but it also had a certain beauty, which he attempted to describe in his diary before going to bed.

"The night," he wrote, "was cloudless and starry, with the moon rising over Westminster. Nothing could have been more beautiful and the searchlights interlaced at certain points on the horizon, the star-like flashes in the sky where shells were bursting, the light of distant fires, all added to the scene. It was magnificent and terrible: the spasmodic drone of enemy aircraft overhead; the thunder of gunfire, sometimes close sometimes in the distance; the illumination, like that of electric trains in peace-time, as the guns fired; and the myriad stars, real and artificial, in the firmament. Never was there such a contrast of natural splendor and human vileness."

Hess

———

T HE LETTER WAS A CURIOUS ONE. BRITAIN'S NETWORK OF CENSORS kept close watch on all mail entering and leaving the country, and this letter, mailed from Germany on September 23, immediately drew their attention. The outer envelope was addressed to an elderly British woman, a "Mrs. V. Roberts," but it contained a second envelope and instructions to send that one to a prominent Scotsman, the Duke of Hamilton.

Inside this second envelope, the censors found a letter that seemed disconcertingly cryptic, proposing a meeting in a neutral city, perhaps Lisbon. The letter was signed only with the initial "A."

The censors gave the letters to Britain's domestic counterintelligence agency, MI5, and there they remained. The duke would not learn of their existence until the following spring, six months after they were posted.

Sanctuary

———

GERMANY'S ASSAULT ON LONDON GREW IN INTENSITY, AS GÖRING sought to dispel the taint of failure that had gathered around him like a fog, dulling the gleam of his white uniforms and glinting medals. Every night scores of bombers advanced on London in waves, bombing with abandon, though officially Germany still clung to its claim that the Luftwaffe was only going after targets of military significance.

In practice, however, it waged war more openly against the city's civilian population than ever before. For one thing, the Luftwaffe was deploying increasing numbers of bombs known as "parachute mines," which drifted wherever the wind carried them. Loaded with fifteen hundred pounds of high explosives, they could destroy everything and everyone within a five-hundred-yard radius. Originally designed to destroy ships, they were first used over land on September 16, when twenty-five were dropped on London, descending on the city in eerie silence. The terror they raised was amplified when seventeen of them failed to explode, forcing evacuations of whole neighborhoods until the weapons could be disarmed by specially trained technicians from the Royal Navy.

The mines soon began falling in increasing numbers. In a note to Pug Ismay on September 19, a day when the Luftwaffe set loose thirty-six such weapons, Churchill wrote that dropping mines by parachute "proclaims the enemy's entire abandonment of all pretense of aiming at military objectives." He proposed to retaliate by dropping similar weapons on German cities, matching one for one. With ruthless glee, he also suggested publishing in advance a list of the German cities to be targeted, to build foreboding. "I do not think they would like it," he wrote, "and there is no reason why they should not have a period of suspense."

With the German shift to night raids, life in London became compressed into the hours of daylight, which, as autumn advanced, began to shrink with a dreadful ineluctability, all the faster because of the city's northern latitude. The raids generated a paradox: The odds that any one person would die on any one night were slim, but the odds that someone, somewhere in London would die were 100 percent. Safety was a product of luck alone. One young boy, asked what he wanted to be when he grew up, a fireman or pilot or such, answered:

"Alive."

Scores of residents did die, and the onset of night became a source of dread, but by day, life took on a strange normalcy. The shops of Piccadilly and Oxford Street still teemed with customers, and Hyde Park still filled with sunbathers, more or less confident that German bombers would not pass overhead until after dusk. A pianist, Myra Hess, held daily concerts in the National Gallery, on Trafalgar Square, during lunch hour to avoid the nightly raids. The hall filled to capacity, many attendees sitting on the floor, gas masks at hand just in case. Audiences edged toward tears, the applause "tremendous and moving," observed Mollie Panter-Downes, the *New Yorker* writer. From time to time the pianist showed off her dexterity by playing music with an orange under each hand. Afterward, everyone hurried away, Panter-Downes wrote, "shouldering their gas masks and looking all the better for having been lifted for an hour to a plane where boredom and fear seem irrelevant."

Even night came to seem less intimidating, despite the escalating violence and spreading destruction. At one point, Mass-Observation diarist Olivia Cockett and a friend, Peg, went for a stroll *during* an air raid. "Walked out into the light of the full moon," Cockett wrote. "Were so thrilled with its beauty we walked to Brixton, through gunfire and all, admiring the effects of shadow and light and liking the empty quiet of the streets. As Peg said, the war and the guns did seem trivial, essentially frivolous, against that solemn splendor." Another diarist, also a young woman, described her own surprise at how she felt while lying in bed after a near miss by a bomb. "I lay there feeling indescribably happy and triumphant," she wrote. " 'I've been *bombed*!' I kept saying to myself, over and over again—trying the phrase on, like a new dress, to see how it fitted. 'I've been *bombed*! . . . *I've* been bombed—*me*!' " Many people had probably been killed or wounded during the raid, she acknowledged, "but never in my whole life have I ever experienced such *pure and flawless happiness.*"

Diarist Phyllis Warner found that she and fellow Londoners were surprised by their own resilience. "Finding we can take it is a great relief to most of us," she wrote on September 22. "I think that each one of us was secretly afraid that he wouldn't be able to, that he would rush shrieking to shelter, that his nerve would give, that he would in some way collapse, so that this has been a pleasant surprise."

But the persistence of the raids and the increasing destruction also had a darker effect. Wrote novelist Rose Macaulay, on Monday, September 23: "I am getting a burying-phobia, result of having seen so many houses and blocks of flats reduced to piles of ruins from which people can't be extracted in time to live, and feel I would rather sleep in the street, but know I mustn't do this." Harold Nicolson had a similar fear, which he confided to his diary the next day. "What I dread," he wrote, "is being buried under huge piles of masonry and hearing the water drip slowly, smelling the gas creeping towards me and hearing the faint cries of colleagues condemned to a slow and ungainly death."

Many Londoners began complaining of gastrointestinal distress, a condition called "Siren Stomach."

RATIONING REMAINED AN IRRITANT, especially the total absence of eggs in stores, but here too one could adapt. Families raised hens in their yards, a tactic adopted by the Prof, who kept chickens at his laboratory and in the Christ Church Meadow at Oxford. A Gallup Poll found that 33 percent of the public had begun growing their own food or raising livestock.

The Churchills were subject to rationing rules but managed to live well all the same, thanks, in part, to the generosity of others. (Churchill seemed to attract charitable offerings by friends. In 1932, upon returning to London after a lecture tour during which he was struck by a car in New York and hospitalized, he was given a new Daimler automobile, paid for by donations from 140 contributors, including Lord Beaverbrook.) The Prof, being a vegetarian, did not consume his allotted rations of meat and bacon, and ceded these to the Churchills for their use. At Chequers, food was always a welcome hostess gift. The king sent venison, pheasants, partridges, and hares from the royal hunting grounds at Balmoral and Sandringham. The provincial government of Quebec sent chocolate; the Duke of Westminster sent salmon, via fast train, marked "DELIVER IMMEDIATELY."

Churchill was, of course, the prime minister, and with this came a degree of privilege denied the common man—as in the case of that most precious of commodities, gasoline. The Ford automobile kept at Chequers, license plate DXN 609, consumed gasoline at a rate higher than Churchill's allocation of eighty gallons, which was supposed to have lasted from June 1 through July. By late June, it became apparent that a good deal more fuel was necessary. An ordinary Londoner would have been out of luck; all Churchill had to do was ask for more. "If you would also be careful to star your letter it will receive my immediate personal attention," wrote Harry B. Hermon Hodge, a divisional petroleum officer for the Mines Department, which oversaw gasoline rationing. The necessary coupons were issued to caretaker Grace Lamont—Monty—for another fifty-eight gallons.

When Churchill realized, early on, that his allotted food rations could not possibly feed the many official guests he now entertained, he simply requested extra coupons. On June 30, private secretary John Martin wrote to the Ministry of Food, "Both at Chequers and at No. 10 Downing Street the rationing restrictions make it very difficult to entertain officially to the extent which the Prime Minister finds necessary." The ministry agreed to help. "We think that the simplest way to meet the position would be to follow the procedure adopted in the case of Foreign Ambassadors to whom we have issued special ration books covering meat, butter, sugar, bacon and ham, the coupons being used for official guests entertained by the Ambassadors. A set of books is enclosed." Churchill also wanted extra diplomatic coupons for tea and "cooking fats." These, too, were supplied. To make sure the foods were available for the coming weekend at Chequers, the ministry instructed its local "food executive officer" to notify nearby stores that these unfamiliar coupons might be coming their way. "I hope that the arrangements now made will be satisfactory," wrote the Food Ministry's R.J.P. Harvey, "but if there is any further difficulty, perhaps you will let us know."

Happily for Churchill, rationing rules did not apply to certain critical commodities. He found no shortage of Hine brandy, Pol Roger champagne, or Romeo y Julieta cigars, though the money to pay for these was, as usual, never quite sufficient, especially when it came to covering the costs of hosting the many visitors who came to Chequers each weekend. The Chequers Trust, which paid the wages of Chequers' staff and the routine costs of maintaining the estate, donated £15 for each weekend, about half of what Churchill actually spent—or, as he once put it, just about enough to cover the cost of feeding the chauffeurs of his guests. For the period from June through December 1940, his costs at Chequers exceeded the trust's overall contributions by £317.

Wine was a significant expense, just as it had been when he was first lord of the Admiralty; at Chequers, now, he spent twice as much. The Government Hospitality Fund agreed to chip in wines and spirits, with the caveat that these were to be served only when entertaining foreign visitors. Churchill took enthusiastic advantage of the program. One Chequers order consisted of:

> 36 bottles of Amontillado—Duff Gordon's V.O.;
> 36 bottles, white wine—Valmur, 1934 [Chablis];
> 36 bottles, port—Fonseca, 1912;
> 36 bottles, claret—Château Léoville Poyferré, 1929;
> 24 bottles, whisky—Fine Highland Malt;
> 12 bottles, brandy—Grande Fine Champagne, 1874
> [66 years old, same as Churchill];
> 36 bottles of champagne—Pommery et Greno, 1926
> [Pol Roger, however, remained his favorite].

The wines were promptly stocked at Chequers by the fund's own "Government Hospitality Butler," a Mr. Watson, who noted their exact positions in the cellar's bins. He also complained that the bins were haphazardly marked; special cards to correct this deficiency were sent forthwith. The fund's administrator, Sir Eric Crankshaw, laid out the precise rules for using the bottles in a letter to Grace Lamont. The wines were to be served only when "Foreign, Dominion, Indian or Colonial guests" were being entertained. Before each event, the Churchills were to consult with Crankshaw, "and I will let you know whether or not Government Hospitality wines are to be used during the visit." Crankshaw instructed Miss Lamont to keep precise records in a "cellar book" provided by the fund, including the names of visitors and the wines consumed; the book would be audited every six months. The record keeping did not stop there, however. "After the Luncheons or Dinners held," Crankshaw wrote, "would you please complete a form, specimen of which is attached, to show the nature of the entertainment, the number of guests and the amount of the various wines consumed, and return the form to me for record and accounting purposes."

Many other products, while not rationed, were nonetheless in short supply. A visiting American found that he could buy chocolate cake and a lemon meringue pie at Selfridges, but cocoa was impossible to find. Shortages made some realms of hygiene more problematic. Women found tampons increasingly difficult to acquire. At least one brand of toilet paper was also in perilously short supply, as the king himself discovered. He managed to sidestep this particular scarcity by arranging shipments direct from the British embassy in Washington, D.C. With kingly discretion, he wrote to his ambassador, "We are getting short of a certain type of paper which is made in America and is unprocurable here. A packet or two of 500 sheets at intervals would be most acceptable. You will understand this and its name begins with B!!!" The paper in question was identified by historian Andrew Roberts as Bromo soft lavatory paper.

WITH RAIDS SO LIKELY and so predictable, Londoners inclined to use public shelters found themselves following a new and novel routine, leaving their chosen shelter for work in the morning, returning at dusk. Some shelters began publishing their own journals and bulletins, with names like *Subway Companion, Station Searchlight,* and the *Swiss Cottager,* this last named for a newly built, deep-level tube station, Swiss Cottage, which now served as a shelter. The station, in turn, had been named for a nearby pub, whose exterior evoked a Swiss chalet. "Greetings to our nightly companions," the *Cottager's* inaugural bulletin began, "our temporary cave dwellers, our sleeping companions, somnambulists, snorers, chatterers, and all who inhabit the Swiss Cottage Station of the Bakerloo, nightly from dusk to dawn." The editor, shelter resident Dore Silverman, promised to publish only intermittently—at a rate "as spasmodic as Hitler's hallucinations"—and hoped the publication would have a very short life.

Full of cautions and advice, the *Cottager* warned shelterers not to bring camp beds or deck chairs, as these took up too much room; begged all inhabitants to be less "generous" with their litter; and pledged that soon the shelter would provide hot tea, though how soon could not be determined—and anyway, "while you sit, read or sleep in quietness and comfort, other things than tea may be brewing up in the streets." In an item entitled "ARE YOU NERVOUS?" the *Cottager's* second issue sought to address anxiety caused by the deployment of heavier anti-aircraft guns in the neighborhood above, noting that subway tunnels tended to amplify noise. Here the bulletin offered a bit of what it called expert advice: "Vibration due to heavy gunfire or other causes will be felt much less if you do not lie with your head against the wall."

In shelters, the danger posed by poison gas was a particular concern. People were encouraged to wear their gas masks for thirty minutes a day, so that they would grow accustomed to their use. Children took part in gas-attack drills. "All the little children of five have Mickey Mouse gas-masks," wrote Diana Cooper in her diary. "They love putting them on for drill and at once start trying to kiss each other, then they march into their shelter singing: 'There'll always be an England.'"

THE RAIDS CREATED A difficult situation for the city's hotels, especially the grand ones—the Ritz, Claridge's, the Savoy, and the Dorchester—which housed all manner of visiting dignitaries, including diplomats, monarchs in exile, and government ministers, many of whom made the hotels their full-time residences. These hotels prided themselves on meeting the whims of their guests, but providing safe shelter from falling bombs and flying shrapnel posed a challenge for which they were at first unprepared—though here the Dorchester, situated on Park Lane in Mayfair, opposite Hyde Park, had a significant advantage.

Nine stories tall and built of reinforced concrete, it was an anomaly in London; its opening, in 1931, had raised fears that Park Lane might soon come to resemble New York's Fifth Avenue. It was also considered indestructible and, as a consequence, was particularly popular with senior officials, who closed up their homes and became full-time residents, among them Lord Halifax and Minister of Information Duff Cooper. (A previous full-time inhabitant was Somerset Maugham; and during the 1930s, the hotel's nightly cabaret featured a young American entertainer named David Kaminsky, later better known by his screen name, Danny Kaye.) Cooper and his wife, Diana, lived in a suite on the top floor, even though this was considered the only floor in the hotel vulnerable to bombs. It did have a view, however, as Diana recalled in her diary: "From its high windows one could scan nearly all London beyond the green sea of Hyde Park, sprawled out for slaughter, dense with monuments, landmarks, tell-tale railway-lines and bridges. How red would the flames be, I wondered, when our hour struck?" She could also see the building that housed her husband's ministry. "The high white building," she wrote, "became symbolic to me, like Dover's cliffs."

The Dorchester's first floor was considered especially resistant to bomb damage, given that it was roofed by a massive concrete slab that supported the building above. To absorb blast forces and prevent the intrusion of shrapnel, the Dorchester piled sandbags outside its front entrance so densely that they resembled a giant honeycomb. The hotel turned its expansive Turkish bath into a luxurious shelter with cubicles reserved for guests staying in the regular rooms upstairs, including Lord Halifax and his wife. In a stroke of marketing élan, the Dorchester published a brochure that touted the new shelter as a prime reason for booking the hotel in the first place. "Experts agree," the brochure proclaimed, "the shelter is absolutely safe against even a direct hit." At least one woman—Phyllis de Janzé, a friend of Evelyn Waugh's—placed so much trust in the Dorchester that she lived in her own home by day and transferred to the hotel at night. Guests called it the Dorm and often appeared there in evening dress. To Cecil Beaton, famed for his eerie nocturnal photographs of bomb-ravaged London, it was "reminiscent of a transatlantic crossing in a luxury liner, with all the horrors of enforced jocularity and expensive squalor."

Even in the shelter, Halifax fell asleep readily, according to Lady Alexandra Metcalfe, a fellow hotel guest in whom Halifax had a romantic interest. "Edward only takes three minutes before he is asleep but manages to yawn loudly and incessantly as a prelude to dropping off into this bottomless, childlike slumber, out of which nothing wakes him." The Coopers occupied an adjacent cubicle, and would listen to the various noises the Halifaxes made as they awoke and dressed each morning. "Between 6 and 6:30 we start getting up one by one," Diana Cooper wrote in her diary. "We wait until they have all gone. They each have a flashlight to find their slippers with, and I see their monstrous forms projected caricatureishly on the ceiling magic-lanternwise. Lord Halifax is unmistakeable. We never actually meet."

At Claridge's and the Ritz, when sirens sounded, guests brought their mattresses and pillows down to the lobby. This made for moments of egalitarian comedy, as journalist Virginia Cowles discovered upon finding herself raid-bound in the Ritz lobby. "They wandered about," she observed, "in all forms of odd attire: beach pajamas, slacks, siren suits, and some just in ordinary wrappers with their night-dresses trailing on the floor." While crossing the lobby, Cowles encountered a member of the royal family of Albania: "I tripped over King Zog's sister, who was sleeping peacefully outside the door of the Ritz restaurant."

On Wednesday night, September 18, during a raid that would destroy the famous John Lewis department store, Cowles again found herself marooned in a hotel lobby, this time Claridge's as it rapidly filled with guests, many of whom were dressed for bed. "Everyone talked to everyone else, a round of drinks was ordered, and from the general merriment you might have thought an enjoyable (if somewhat odd) costume party was going on."

At one point an elderly woman dressed in a black hat, long black coat, and smoked glasses descended the stairs, along with three women whom Cowles described as ladies-in-waiting.

The lobby went quiet.

The woman in black was Wilhelmina, exiled queen of Holland. After she and her retinue passed, the clamor resumed.

For one contingent of working-class citizens from the hard-hit East End, the glamour of all this hotel sheltering became too much. On Saturday, September 14, a group of up to seventy people from Stepney, an impoverished district situated between Whitechapel and Limehouse, marched to the Savoy Hotel, on the Strand, a short walk from Trafalgar Square. Here Churchill often had lunch, favoring table Number Four, and attended meetings of his "Other Club," a dining society he co-founded in 1911. The club met in the hotel's Pinafore Room, where a wooden sculpture of a black cat, named Kaspar, was always in attendance, with a cloth napkin around its neck. The Savoy shelter was by now renowned for its opulence, with sections painted pink, green, and blue, with matching bedding and towels, and furnished with comfortable armchairs and the elsewhere-forbidden deck chairs.

The marchers entered the hotel, occupied the chairs, and vowed not to leave, despite attempts by Scotland Yard to persuade them to go. Wrote Phil Piratin, a Communist politician and organizer of the march: "We decided that what was good enough for the Savoy Hotel parasites was reasonably good enough for Stepney workers and their families." With the start of the night's raid, the hotel's managers realized they could not expel the crowd, and instead had the staff feed them bread and butter and, of course, tea.

AS THE NIGHTLY RAIDS continued, strange effects and odd moments accumulated. A bomb might demolish one home and leave the one next door unscathed. Similarly, entire blocks remained untouched, as if the war were happening in another country, while other blocks, especially those visited by a parachute mine, were reduced to mounds of brick and lumber. After one raid set London's Natural History Museum on fire, water from firemen's hoses caused seeds in its collection to germinate, among them those from an ancient Persian silk tree, or mimosa—*Albizia julibrissin*. The seeds were said to be 147 years old. A raid on September 27 damaged the city's zoo and set loose a zebra. Residents saw a black-and-white specter tearing through the streets, until the animal was captured in Camden Town. Early in the war, the zoo had killed its poisonous snakes and spiders, anticipating that if their enclosures were destroyed, these creatures would pose a significantly greater hazard than, say, a fugitive koala bear.

One air-raid warden had a profoundly unsettling experience when, upon crawling into a deep crater to search for bodies, he came across the ruins of what had once been a sculptor's studio. The building had previously housed a variety of marble statues, fragments of which now protruded from the crater. The moon bathed the landscape with a blue-white light that caused the fragments to luminesce. "Among the heaps of brick one would suddenly see a white hand sticking up in the moon-light, or a piece of a trunk, or a face," the warden wrote in his Mass-Observation diary. "The effect was uncanny."

WHAT THE ATTACKS ON London seemed clearly to unleash was a new sexuality, as Joan Wyndham's lover, Rupert, had already found. As bombs fell, libidos soared. "No one wanted to be alone," wrote Virginia Cowles. "You heard respectable young ladies saying to their escorts: 'I'm not going home unless you promise to spend the night.'" One young American woman newly arrived in London marveled at the vibrance of her social life, despite bombs and fire. "Every night next week is booked up already and the weekend hasn't started," she wrote, in a letter home. "The only thing people seem scared about here is being lonely, so they date up way ahead of time to ensure against an evening alone."

Condoms were readily available; diaphragms too, though the fitting process was problematic. A popular guide to sex was Frank Harris's memoir *My Life and Loves,* full of explicit, and often innovative, erotic endeavors. The book was officially banned in Britain and the United States—which, of course, enhanced its popularity and made it easy to acquire. Everyone was in love with "life and living," wrote actress Theodora Rosling, who later, under her married name, FitzGibbon, would achieve acclaim as a writer of cookbooks. "For the young it was undeniably exciting and stimulating. It was God's gift to naughty girls, for from the moment the sirens went, they were not expected to get home until morning when the 'all clear' sounded. In fact, they were urged to stay where they were. . . . Young people were reluctant to contemplate death without having shared their bodies with someone else. It was sex at its sweetest: not for money or marriage, but for love of being alive and wanting to give."

Affairs involving married women and men became commonplace. "The normal barriers to having an affair with somebody were thrown to the winds," wrote William S. Paley, founder of the Columbia Broadcasting System, who spent much of the war in London. "If it looked pretty good, you felt good, well what in Hell was the difference." Sex became a refuge, but that did not guarantee that the sex would be fulfilling. Mass-Observation diarist Olivia Cockett, in the midst of an affair with a married man, noted in passing that during a weeklong bout of lovemaking, she and her lover had sex six times, but "only one complete for me."

There may have been a lot of sex, but lingerie wasn't selling. Maybe it seemed too much of a luxury for wartime, or maybe in that supercharged sexual milieu the added oomph of sexy lingerie was perceived as unnecessary; whatever the cause, demand dwindled. "I have never in all my life experienced or thought of experiencing such a terrible season," said the owner of one lingerie shop. "We don't have a customer all day, hardly. It's heartbreaking."

One man who seemed immune to this sexual conflagration was the Prof, who, in keeping with his propensity for making binary decisions that lasted forever, had decided some years earlier that henceforth romance was not something he would pursue. He had come close, having fallen for a certain Lady Elizabeth Lindsay. He was forty-nine at the time, she twenty-seven. Twice before he had been rejected by women, but this friendship seemed to advance in satisfactory fashion—until one cruel day in February 1937, when he received news from Lady Elizabeth's father that while traveling in Italy she had become ill with pneumonia and died. She was buried in Rome.

Apparently that was enough for Lindemann, who deposited romance and marriage into the same vault that housed his many other grudges and grievances.

At a party at Blenheim Palace, during a discussion of sex, a woman so notorious for her sexual appetite that she was nicknamed "the Bedbug" turned to the Prof and said, "Now come on, Prof, tell us when you last slept with a woman."

Silence followed.

Berlin

F
IGHTER ACE ADOLF GALLAND, STILL ALIVE, AND FAST ACCUMULATING
aerial victories, posed a problem for Hermann Göring, chief of the Luftwaffe.

Galland's record was of course to be celebrated, and rewarded, but
Göring held firm to his belief that Galland and his fellow fighter pilots
had failed him. He blamed them—their inability and unwillingness to
provide effective close escort for his bombers—for the grave losses sustained by the Luftwaffe and for the consequent shift to night bombing,
which had brought its own costs in terms of missed targets and scores
of accidents and collisions, the incidence of which promised only to increase as winter approached. (In the first three months of the coming
year, accidents would damage or destroy 282 Luftwaffe bombers, nearly
70 percent of the total lost to all causes.) Göring had promised Hitler he
would bring Britain to its knees in four days, but even after four weeks of
nightly attacks on London and raids against a host of other targets, there
was still no sign that Churchill was beginning to waver.

Göring summoned Galland to his hunting lodge in East Prussia, the
Reichsjägerhof, to air his complaints about the fighter force. Galland
stopped first in Berlin to accept his latest decoration, Oak Leaves added
to his Knight's Cross, then flew to East Prussia for his meeting with
Göring. At the heavily timbered gate to the compound, Galland encoun-
tered a friend, fellow ace and archrival Werner Mölders, making his exit.
Mölders had received the same medal as Galland three days earlier, in
Berlin, and was now hurrying back to his base, annoyed at having lost

three days that otherwise could have been spent in the air shooting down planes and adding to his tally of victories.

Just before setting off, Mölders called out to Galland, "The Fat One promised me he would detain you at least as long as he did me." Galland continued on to the entrance to the lodge, a large and gloomy structure built of immense logs, roofed with thatch, and set among tall, slender trees. Göring came out to greet him, looking like a character from a Brothers Grimm fable. He wore a silk shirt with butterfly sleeves, a green suede hunting jacket, and high boots. Tucked into his belt was a large hunting knife that resembled a medieval sword. Göring seemed in a good humor. After congratulating Galland on his new decoration, he told him that he had another honor to confer: a chance to hunt one of the lodge's prized stags. Göring knew these animals the way other men knew their dogs, and had assigned each a name. He told Galland he would have plenty of time for the hunt, because he had promised Mölders to keep him at the lodge for at least three days. Galland killed his stag the next morning, "really a royal beast, the stag of a lifetime." The head, with its great rack of antlers, was removed for Galland to keep as a trophy.

Galland saw no reason to linger further, but Göring insisted on honoring the promise he had made to Mölders.

That afternoon, reports came in about a big raid on London, one of the last conducted in daylight, in which the Luftwaffe suffered major losses. "Göring was shattered," Galland wrote. "He simply could not explain how the increasingly painful losses of bombers came about."

To Galland, the answer was obvious. What he and fellow pilots had been trying to get their superiors to understand was that the RAF was just as strong as ever, fighting with undiminished spirit in a seemingly endless supply of new aircraft. A week earlier, Göring had announced that the RAF had only 177 fighters left, but this did not tally with what Galland saw in the air. Somehow the British were managing to produce fighters at a rate that outpaced their losses.

With Göring so distracted by the day's misfortune, Galland again asked permission to return to his unit. This time Göring did not object, despite his promise to Mölders.

Galland left, hauling the hugely antlered stag's head along with him. For part of the journey, he and the head traveled aboard a train, where, Galland said, "the stag caused more sensation than the oak leaves to my Knight's Cross."

There was big news elsewhere: During Galland's stay at the lodge, Japan signed the Tripartite Pact to ally itself formally with Germany and Italy.

IN BERLIN, AT ABOUT this time, a member of a Luftwaffe bomber crew stopped by William Shirer's apartment for a discreet chat. The airman was a confidential source who, at great personal risk, kept Shirer informed about life within the German air force. The source told Shirer that he and his fellow crew members felt a high degree of admiration for pilots of the RAF, especially one jaunty pilot who always had a cigarette jutting from the side of his mouth and whom they had vowed to hide and protect if he ever got shot down over German-controlled territory.

Night bombing, the airman said, was causing profound stress on the crews. Bombers had to fly on a strict schedule and along carefully choreographed routes to avoid collisions between outbound and inbound aircraft. The crews often flew four nights out of seven and were growing tired, he told Shirer. They were surprised that the raids on London had thus far produced so little visible effect. The airman "was impressed by the size of London," Shirer wrote in his diary. "He said they've been pounding away on it for three weeks and he is amazed that so much of it is left! He said they were often told before taking off that they would find their target by a whole square mile of the city on fire. When they got there they could find no square mile on fire; only a fire here and there."

In another entry, Shirer noted that a joke had begun making its way around the more cynical quarters of Berlin:

"An airplane carrying Hitler, Göring and Goebbels crashes. All three are killed. Who is saved?"

Answer: "The German People."

AS THE DAYS PASSED, Propaganda Minister Joseph Goebbels grew perplexed. None of it made sense. He could not fathom why Churchill had not yet conceded defeat, given the nightly pounding of London. Reports from Luftwaffe intelligence continued to indicate that the RAF was critically wounded, down to its last hundred or so fighters. Why was London still standing, Churchill still in power? Britain showed no outward signs of distress or weakness. Far from it. At his propaganda meeting on October 2, Goebbels told his lieutenants that "an unmistakable wave of optimism and make-believe is at present being spread by London over the whole of Britain and possibly also over the world as a whole."

Britain's apparent resilience was having unexpected—and troubling—repercussions at home, among the German public. With Britain still fighting, Germans realized that a second winter of war was inevitable; discontent was growing. In recent days, news that the German government had ordered the mandatory evacuation of children from Berlin had caused a surge in popular anxiety, for it contradicted Goebbels's own reassuring propaganda about the Luftwaffe's prowess at defending Germany against air raids. The evacuations were voluntary, Goebbels insisted at his next meeting, Thursday, October 3, and vowed that anyone spreading rumors to the contrary "must expect to find himself in a concentration camp."

Target Churchill

WITH THE BOMBING OF LONDON CAME INCREASED FEARS FOR Churchill's safety, a concern that he himself appeared not to share. No raid was too fierce to stop him from climbing to the nearest roof to watch. On one cold night while watching a raid from the roof of the building that capped the Cabinet War Rooms, he sat on a chimney to keep warm, until an officer came up to ask him politely to move—smoke was backing up into the rooms below. Churchill, enthralled by gunfire, continued to visit anti-aircraft installations even as German bombers flew overhead. When raids occurred, he dispatched his staff to the shelter below but did not himself follow, returning instead to his desk to continue working. At night and for naps, he slept in his own bed. When a large unexploded bomb was discovered in St. James's Park, perilously near 10 Downing Street, Churchill stayed put, expressing concern only for "those poor little birds"—the pelicans and swans—in the lake. Even near misses seemed not to ruffle him. John Colville recalled how one night as they were walking through Whitehall, two bombs came whistling to earth nearby. Colville dove for cover; Churchill continued on, "striding along the middle of King Charles Street, his chin stuck out and propelling himself rapidly with his gold-headed walking stick."

Churchill's disregard for his own safety drew an exasperated plea from Air Minister Sinclair. "One thing worries me these days—that you stay at Downing Street without a proper shelter." He urged Churchill to take up residence in the Cabinet War Rooms, or in some other well-protected place. "You are making us ridiculous if you insist on us living in basements & refuse to do it yourself!" Churchill's great friend Violet Bonham Carter told him that she had urged Clementine to restrain him from venturing into dangerous zones. "It may be fun for you—but it is terrifying for the rest for us. Please realize that for most of us this war is a One-Man Show (unlike the last) & treat your life like a guarded flame. It does not belong to you alone but to all of us."

Others stepped in to take measures to protect him. Blast shutters were installed over windows to block shrapnel and keep glass from disintegrating into flesh-rending shards. The Ministry of Works began construction of a concrete-and-steel shield to reinforce the ceiling of the Cabinet War Rooms. The rising danger also led the government to begin constructing a new, blastproof flat in the building above the war rooms; designed for the Churchills, the apartment became known as the No. 10 Annexe, or, simply, "the Annexe." As always, the associated hammering drove Churchill wild. He routinely sent his private secretaries to find the source and stop it, thereby causing what Colville believed to be a significant delay in the project's completion.

No. 10 Downing Street, which Churchill once described as "rickety," at least had the advantage of being tucked away among larger buildings, within a zone protected by a concentration of anti-aircraft batteries and barrage balloons. His prime ministerial country home, Chequers, was another story. About all that had been done so far to protect the house itself against aerial attack was to install the timbers in the Hawtrey Room. When Chequers' previous owner, Arthur Lee, first saw these arrangements, he was appalled. "When I was at Chequers," he wrote, "I was, I must confess somewhat flabbergasted by the Office of Works conception of bombproof chambers inside the house; fortified by piles of decaying sandbags against the brickwork outside." The sandbags had since been removed; the timbers remained.

Churchill himself was fully prepared to fight it out among the Cromwellian artifacts, should German invaders enter the house, and expected his family to do likewise. At one gathering he said, "If the Germans come, each one of you can take a dead German with you."

"I don't know how to fire a gun," protested daughter-in-law Pamela.

"You could go into the kitchen and get a carving knife."

She had no doubt that he meant it. "He was in dead earnest," she recalled later, "and I was terrified." Four helmets, known universally as "tin hats," were allotted to Chequers, to be used by caretaker Grace Lamont, Churchill's chauffeur, Clementine, and Pamela. Mary had her own helmet, and full uniform, from the Women's Voluntary Service.

It was private secretary Eric Seal who first seemed to recognize the vulnerability of Chequers. In a discreet note to Pug Ismay he aired his fears, and Ismay in turn grew concerned. That the Germans knew the location of the house was beyond doubt. Three years earlier, Hitler's foreign minister, Joachim von Ribbentrop, then ambassador to Britain, had visited the property while Stanley Baldwin was prime minister. With the advent of the air war over Britain, Ismay realized that Chequers would make a choice target, both for the Luftwaffe and for parachute troops dropped into adjacent fields, though he did not realize just how vulnerable it was until the RAF produced a series of reconnaissance photos of the estate to see how it might appear to German pilots.

Taken from an altitude of ten thousand feet, these photographs (and others shot later at five thousand and fifteen thousand feet) revealed an aspect of the house and its orientation in the landscape that was thoroughly startling. The long entry road, Victory Way, intersected a U-shaped drive that led to the front and rear entrances of the house. The lanes were surfaced with light-colored gravel that contrasted sharply with the adjacent greenery. From the air, the effect was uncanny: The long white length of Victory Way looked like an arrow pointing at the house. At night, when the moon caused the pale gravel to luminesce, the effect was even more pronounced, so much so that it seemed a marvel that the Luftwaffe hadn't attacked the house already.

Compounding Ismay's worries was the fact that an aerial photograph of Chequers from a private source had already been published in the press, and was, as Ismay told the Ministry of Home Security in a letter dated August 29, "therefore, likely to be in possession of the Germans." He enclosed a copy of the photograph, in which the house did indeed appear to be a distinctive target, and wrote: "In view of the fact that the Prime Minister goes there most week-ends, it is very important that early action should be taken to render it less easily identified."

The ministry's Camouflage Branch proposed a number of solutions, including paving the lanes with the same material used to surface tennis courts and erecting raised nets tufted with steel wool, but decided that the best, and least costly, means of masking the lanes would be to cover them with turf. Clementine wanted this done quickly. Her youngest daughter and pregnant daughter-in-law were now at the house, and increasingly Churchill himself seemed to be the target of the Luftwaffe, as suggested by the apparent rise in aerial attacks on Whitehall.

Ismay was concerned about other dangers as well. A security assessment had warned that Chequers required protection against all kinds of threats, ranging from lone assassins in disguise to squads of parachutists. The house and grounds were currently watched over by a platoon of Coldstream Guards consisting of four noncommissioned officers and thirty soldiers, but Ismay wanted this expanded to a company of 150. The guardsmen were housed in tents on the grounds; Ismay recommended a more permanent arrangement, with huts and a mess room hidden in the trees at the back of the estate. Sewage could be a problem, he acknowledged. "Chequers drains would have to be used, and they may be overloaded."

In mid-September, as invasion fears intensified, Home Forces stationed a Lanchester armored car at Chequers, for Churchill's use, along with two officers to operate it. The Home Forces general staff recommended that the officers be armed with Thompson submachine guns. "These would provide greater striking power than pistols in the event of opposition from enemy agents or parachute troops." On weekdays, the car would reside in London; Churchill's personal chauffeur was to be offered instruction in how to drive it.

The Prof, for his part, was particularly concerned about the dangers posed by the many cigars Churchill received as gifts from citizens and foreign emissaries, not because smoking was yet perceived to be bad, but for fear the sender or an infiltrator might lace the cigar with poison. All it would take was a tiny amount inserted into just one cigar out of fifty. Only a tested cigar could be ruled absolutely safe, but the testing process inevitably destroyed the sample. One detailed assay uncovered a Cuban cigar that contained "a small black and flattened mass of vegetable debris containing much starch and two hairs," this ruled to be the fecal pellet of a mouse. Nicotine itself, MI5's chief tester, Lord Rothschild, pointed out, was a dangerous poison, though he noted, after testing one group of gift cigars, "I should say that it would be safer to smoke the rest than to cross a London street."

At one point Churchill threw caution to the winds. He received an entire chest full of Havana cigars as a gift from the president of Cuba. He showed this to his ministers one night after dinner, before the resumption of a particularly fraught cabinet meeting. "Gentlemen," he said, "I am now going to try an experiment. Maybe it will result in joy. Maybe it will end in grief. I am about to give you each one of these magnificent cigars."

He paused.

"It may well be that these each contain some deadly poison."

Another dramatic beat.

"It may well be that within days I shall follow sadly the long line of coffins up the aisle of Westminster Abbey."

He paused again.

"Reviled by the populace; as the man who has out-Borgia-ed Borgia."

He handed out the cigars; the men lit them; all survived.

A week later, however, John Colville notified Churchill that he was sending one cigar from each donated box to be tested by MI5. The Prof, he told Churchill, "hopes that you will not smoke any of the cigars until the result of the analysis is known. He points out that there has just been a round-up of undesirable elements in Cuba, which has shown that a surprisingly large number of Nazi agents and sympathizers exist in that country."

Lindemann would have preferred that Churchill not smoke any cigar donated from abroad, as Colville reported in a separate note: "The Professor thought however that you might like to let them accumulate in a safe and dry place until after the war, when you might feel justified in taking the risk involved in smoking them if you wished to do so."

This was the Prof's coolly scientific way of saying that by then, if a cigar killed him, it wouldn't matter.

BEAVERBROOK GREW INCREASINGLY FRUSTRATED with the amount of work lost to air raids, false alerts, and visits by lone bombers whose mission clearly was simply to trigger sirens and drive workers into shelters. On a single day, two solo aircraft making separate flights over London triggered alerts that caused a six-hour delay in production at the city's factories. In the week ending Saturday, September 28, raids and warnings reduced by half the working hours at seven major aircraft plants. The cost of these lost hours was compounded by the fact that workers who spent the night in shelters were less efficient the next day. When bombs did strike, the secondary effects were even more profound. Workers stayed home; night shifts became hard to staff. The risks, however, were real. In July, one company, Parnall Aircraft Ltd., a maker of gun turrets, lost seventy-three thousand hours of work to false alarms. Seven months later more than fifty of the plant's workers were killed in a single daylight raid.

Beaverbrook came to loathe the wail of air-raid sirens. "The sirens, it must be admitted, became almost an obsession with him," wrote David Farrer, his personal secretary. Beaverbrook deluged Churchill with complaints and hectored him to ban warning sirens altogether. "The decision might cost the country some lives," he wrote. "But if we persist in the warnings we shall probably pay a higher price in lives through the impairment of our aircraft production."

Beaverbrook laid some of the blame for lost production at the feet of his favorite antagonist, Air Minister Archie Sinclair, accusing him of failing to provide adequate protection for factories and for failing to defend them even after receiving advance warning that a raid was likely to occur. He wanted more barrage balloons hung over factories, and more antiaircraft guns, and went so far as to demand that the Air Ministry assign one Spitfire to protect each complex.

He did not believe for a moment that such measures would indeed protect a factory, according to secretary Farrer: "It was the appearance, not the reality of safety that he was after." His interest was not in saving workers but in keeping them at their posts, wrote Farrer, adding, "He was fully prepared to risk lives in order to produce more aircraft."

Beaverbrook also railed against other threats to production, and saw such threats everywhere. When Herbert Morrison, minister for Home Security, and Home Secretary, proposed to allow shopkeepers to work only five days a week and to close their stores at three P.M., to give them time to get home or to a shelter before the night raids began, Beaverbrook objected, on the grounds that factory workers would then demand to do likewise. "This, of course, would be disastrous," he wrote.

Beaverbrook warned, too, that if British factory workers did not work their machine tools twenty-four hours a day, America would notice, and would be disinclined to send more tools. That Beaverbrook actually cared about American perceptions is doubtful. He wanted production, at all costs. For this he needed Churchill's attention, and raising the specter of disillusioning Roosevelt was one way to get it. "The American claim that we have more machine tools than we require will be completely justified," he wrote.

By way of encouraging others to ignore air-raid alerts, Beaverbrook resolved to remain at his desk when the sirens rang out. He was, however, terrified. "Beaverbrook is a man of nervous temperament," wrote secretary Farrer. "He was thoroughly scared by the noise of a falling bomb. But his sense of urgency prevailed over his fears."

THE PROF, MEANWHILE, PEPPERED Churchill with notes and minutes on far-flung topics and novel weapons. His penchant for viewing all things through the icy lens of science caused some of his proposals to veer toward the ruthless. In one memorandum, he recommended poisoning water wells used by Italian troops in the Middle East. He suggested using calcium chloride, "extremely convenient since only 1 lb of material should be required for every 5,000 gallons." He was not unaware of the importance of public perception, however, and thus shied from recommending poisons of a more lethal nature, like arsenic, since they raised "undesirable associations in the public mind."

He expressed no such restraint, however, with regard to simply incinerating columns of enemy soldiers. "In my view burning oil has great possibilities in warfare provided it is used on a large scale," he told Churchill a week later. Flaming oil could be deployed for stopping an advancing force or "better still burning up a whole column of troops or vehicles," he wrote. "All that need be done is to run a couple of pipes along [the] side of the road concealed in a hedge with holes bored in them pointing towards the road. A pipe is carried away some hundreds of yards to a supply of oil. At the crucial moment when a column of armored vehicles is on the road the oil is turned on and ignited producing a flaming furnace over the whole prepared length of road."

MARY CHURCHILL STILL RESENTED being tucked away for safekeeping in the countryside by "excessively protective" parents and not being able to share in the experience of war. On the night of Wednesday, September 25, she got an opportunity. One of the Luftwaffe's giant parachute mines drifted into Aylesbury and exploded so near the offices of the Women's Voluntary Service as to render them unusable. Nineteen staff members were injured.

The excitement was eclipsed by heartbreak, as a tidal surge of criticism broke over her father and his government. Bowing to confident assurances from his top military advisers, Churchill had reinstated Operation Menace, the seizure of Dakar, in West Africa, by a mixed force of British and Free French soldiers led by General de Gaulle. The attack, which began earlier in the week, at first seemed certain to yield an easy victory, but a combination of factors, including an unexpectedly strong defense by Vichy forces in control of the port, produced only spectacular failure—an operation so confused and inept that it became a parody of the stirring offensive coup Churchill had hoped for. Once again British forces were compelled to withdraw, prompting critics to portray the incident as only the most recent of a chain of failures that included

Norway, Dunkirk, and—for those who cared to look back further— Gallipoli during Churchill's initial tenure as first lord of the Admiralty, when his attempt to land an army on the Turkish peninsula had also ended in evacuation. That debacle, far bloodier than Dakar, had cost him his post. A Home Intelligence report summed up popular reaction to the Dakar failure: "Another victory for evacuation."

Mary knew how desperately her father wanted to launch offensive operations against Germany, beyond merely bombing the country. Churchill's initial instinct to cancel the operation, after his visit to the RAF operations center at Uxbridge a week earlier, had been a good one, but he had allowed himself to be overruled by the confident dissent of senior commanders. In her diary, Mary rose to her father's defense: "I don't see how in the course of having to make endless decisions one can avoid some mistakes."

Within the Churchill household, the failure of Operation Menace was perceived to be sufficiently grave as to pose a threat to Churchill's government.

"O god—somehow this minor reversal has cast a shadow over everything," Mary wrote. "I do hope the government will pull through—All my feelings are so mixed. Of course I want Papa to pull it off but not only for personal reasons—but also if he went WHO IS TO COME??"

The next day, Friday, September 27, was no better. "All today seemed overcast with the gloom of the Dakar affair," Mary observed. "It certainly does seem that there was misjudgment somewhere. Oh I am so anxious for Papa. He loves the French so much, & I know longs for them to do something grand & spectacular—but I fear he will take rather a bump over this." She was shocked by the vitriol from the press. The *Daily Mirror,* in particular, seemed to have gone mad over the episode. " 'The Gallipoli touch?' " Mary wrote, quoting the paper. "Oh—how unkind."

On top of it all, compounding the suspense that already pervaded the house, her pregnant sister-in-law, Pamela, was feeling ill, sick on Thursday, sicker on Friday. And the ministrations of Pamela's doctor, Carnac Rivett, including his apparent obsession with keeping her on her feet and walking, were becoming suffocating, prompting Mary to exclaim in her diary, "Why can't Mr. Rivett let the poor girl alone."

DESPITE THE FACT THAT the baby was due any day, on Tuesday, October 8, Pamela and Clementine set out from Chequers for London, to attend the swearing-in of Pamela's husband, Randolph, as a new member of the House of Commons, a post he would hold while also retaining his commission in the 4th Hussars and continuing as a correspondent for Beaverbrook's *Evening Standard*.

They drove to London knowing full well that the Luftwaffe would likely pound the city again that night, as it had done every night since September 7, and despite the fact that invasion fears remained high. As Churchill told Roosevelt on Friday, October 4: "I cannot feel that the invasion danger is past." Referring to Hitler, he wrote, "The gent has taken off his clothes and put on his bathing suit, but the water is getting colder and there is an autumn nip in the air." If Hitler planned to make his move, Churchill knew, he would have to do it soon, before the weather worsened. He told Roosevelt, "We are maintaining the utmost vigilance."

Pamela and Clementine carried a tank of laughing gas in the car, to administer to Pamela if she happened to go into labor. But it was to Mary, who remained behind at Chequers, that the day would yield the greatest drama.

AT CHEQUERS THAT NIGHT, Mary found herself the guest of the officers of the Coldstream Guards unit assigned to defend the house. She loved the party and the attention—until the Luftwaffe intervened.

The dinner was in full sway when she and the others heard the unmistakable whistle of a falling bomb. They all ducked, by instinct, and waited what seemed an inordinate amount of time for the detonation. When the explosion came, it was oddly muted; it left the guests "rather breathless but intact & morale on all sides good," Mary wrote.

Her hosts rushed her outside into a deep air-raid trench, whose base was full of mud, which destroyed her beloved suede shoes. Once the raid was judged to have ended, the men escorted her home. "They were all sweet to me," she wrote in her diary, "—and I was feeling terribly excited & rather breathless—but thank god—not all white & trembly as I so often feared & imagined I would be."

She added: "Damn those Bloody Huns for breaking up an enjoyable party."

The next day, Wednesday, October 9, Mary discovered that the bomb had left a huge crater only one hundred yards from the guards' mess, in a muddy field. The mud, she reasoned, probably explained why the explosion had sounded so muted.

In her diary she wrote, "I am not feeling so ignored by the war."

EARLY ON THURSDAY MORNING, at Chequers, Pamela, attended by the fearful and ever-present Dr. Rivett, gave birth to a son. A young nurse was present as well. Pamela was just coming out of an anesthetic haze when she heard the nurse say, "I've told you five times that it's a boy. Will you please believe me?"

Pamela, dazed, needed reassurance. "It can't change now," she said. "No. It can't change now."

She was assured that indeed the baby's sex would not change.

Clementine entered the news in the Chequers visitors' book. "October 10th 4.40 A.M.—Winston." This was the first birth in the house in over a century.

"Winston Churchill Junior arrived," Mary wrote in her diary. "Hooray."

She added:

"Pam weak but happy

"Baby not at all weak & only partially happy!"

Pamela's husband, Randolph, newly minted member of Parliament, missed the birth. He was in London, in bed with the wife of an Austrian tenor, whose monocled image appeared on cigarette trading cards.

THE NEXT MORNING, in London, Churchill, working from his bed at 10 Downing Street, learned that two bombs had fallen on the Horse Guards Parade adjacent to the house but had failed to detonate. He asked Colville, "Will they do us any damage when they explode?"

"I shouldn't think so, Sir," Colville said.

"Is that just your opinion, because if so it's worth nothing," Churchill said. "You have never seen an unexploded bomb go off. Go and ask for an official report."

Which reinforced for Colville the folly of offering opinions in Churchill's presence, "if one has nothing with which to back them."

CHURCHILL MET HIS NEW grandson that weekend when he again traveled to Chequers, bringing with him, as always, numerous guests, including Pug Ismay and General Brooke. Churchill was "utterly delighted, and he used to come and watch the baby, feed him, and was just thrilled to death with him," Pamela said.

While baby Winston was the main attraction, Churchill's attention also was drawn to the crater left by the bomb that had interrupted Mary's dinner party. After lunch, he and Ismay, along with Colville and other guests, gave it a close inspection, and debated whether the bomb's proximity to the house was mere accident. Colville judged it a chance event; Churchill and Pug disagreed, and posited that it might have been a deliberate attempt to strike the house.

"Certainly there is a danger," Colville mused in his diary that night. "In Norway, Poland and Holland the Germans showed it was their policy to go all out for the Government, and Winston is worth more to them than the whole Cabinets of those three countries rolled into one." His colleague Eric Seal, principal secretary, reiterated his own concerns in a private letter to the new chief of the Air Staff, Charles Portal, who replaced Cyril Newall. "We have established a Military guard there which should be adequate for all emergencies likely to arise by land," he wrote. "But I am not at all sure whether he is really safe from bombing attack." Emphasizing that he had said nothing about this as yet to Churchill, Seal added, "I should myself be much happier if it were possible for him to have several other retreats which could be used irregularly so that the enemy would never know where he was."

Chequers was too valuable an asset for Churchill to abandon entirely, but he agreed that spending every weekend at the house might pose too great a security risk, at least when the sky was clear and the moon was in its fullest phases. He himself had expressed concern about the safety of Chequers. "Probably, they don't think I am so foolish as to come here," he said. "But I stand to lose a lot, three generations at a swoop."

Simply staying in the city, however, was not a consideration. Churchill needed his weekends in the country, and believed he knew of a house that was ideally suited to the role of moonlight surrogate.

He invited its owner, Ronald Tree, to his office. Tree was a friend of long standing who had shared Churchill's prewar concerns about the rise of Hitler. Now he was a Conservative member of Parliament and parliamentary secretary to Minister of Information Duff Cooper. From a financial standpoint, Tree needed neither post: He had inherited great wealth as a scion of the Marshall Field's empire in Chicago. His wife, Nancy, was American, a niece of Lady Astor. They owned Ditchley, an eighteenth-century house in Oxfordshire, about seventy-five miles from 10 Downing Street.

Churchill was direct. He told Tree that he wished to spend the upcoming weekend at Ditchley, and that he would be arriving with a number of guests and a full complement of staff and protective guard.

Tree was delighted; his wife, thrilled. Whether they quite knew what they were in for is open to question. Churchill's descent upon the house had more in common with one of Hitler's blitzkriegs than a tranquil arrival for a weekend in the country.

"It is quite a business," wrote Harold Nicolson in his diary, after taking part in one such Ditchley invasion. "First come two detectives who scour the house from garret to cellar; then arrive valet and maid with much luggage; then thirty-five soldiers plus officers turn up to guard the great man through the night; then two stenographers with masses of papers." Next, the guests arrive: "The great mass of the house is dark and windowless, and then a chink in the door opens and we enter suddenly into the warmth of central heating, the blaze of lights and the amazing beauty of the hall."

The decor of the house was by now legendary, and was fast becoming the model for a style of country home decor that emphasized color, comfort, and lack of formality. Its popularity prompted Mrs. Tree to create a home-design firm around the concept. Her future business partner would later describe her aesthetic as one of "pleasing decay."

The Trees did not mind the sudden siege of their home. Far from it. "I have always been one of your greatest if most humble admirers," Mrs. Tree wrote to Churchill after his initial visit, "—and I meant to tell you how delighted and honored we all were to have you come to Ditchley. If it is convenient for you at any time to use no matter how short the notice—it is at your disposal."

It was indeed convenient. Churchill came the following weekend as well, and over the next year or so, he would occupy the house on more than a dozen additional weekends, including one of the most momentous of the war.

One advantage became immediately apparent to Churchill: Ditchley had a home cinema, which the prime minister so enjoyed that in due course, to the dismay of fire inspectors who later deemed it a "grave fire risk," he ordered one installed at Chequers. Beaverbrook arranged it, and made sure Churchill received the latest movies and newsreels. "Max knows how to do these things," Churchill said. "I do not."

Two projectionists joined the weekly Chequers entourage.

Spendthrift

AS IF THE WAR WEREN'T TRIAL ENOUGH, PAMELA'S MARRIAGE to Randolph grew increasingly strained: unpaid bills accumulated and his gambling and drinking continued unabated. He dined often at his club, White's, and at various restaurants favored by London's young and rich, and was always quick to pick up the dinner check, even when his companions were far richer than he. He bought tailor-made shirts and suits. Pamela begged Churchill for help. He agreed to settle the couple's debts, but on the condition that no more bills would accumulate. "Yes," Pamela assured him, "this is the end." Many shops and department stores, however, allowed customers to buy things on credit and billed at three-month intervals or longer, causing a lag between the time of purchase and the arrival of the quarterly invoice. "Then, my God!" Pamela said. "There would be more and more bills."

The couple's expenses outstripped Randolph's income, even though by the standards of the day he made a good deal of money. Between his army salary, lecture fees, the pay he received from Parliament and Beaverbrook's *Evening Standard,* and other sources of income, he was taking in a robust £30,000 a year. Beaverbrook alone paid him £1,560 a year. It wasn't enough, and his creditors were losing patience. One day during a shopping trip to Harrods, the luxurious department store in London's Knightsbridge district, Pamela was told, to her great humiliation, that her credit had been rescinded. This, she said, "was horrifying for me."

She left the store weeping. Back at 10 Downing Street, she told the story to Clementine, who had no illusions about her own son. His spending had long been a problem. When Randolph was twenty years old,

Churchill wrote to urge him to pay off his debts and resolve a conflict with his bank. "Instead of this," Churchill told his son, "you seem to be spending every penny you get and more in a most reckless manner involving yourself in endless worry and possibly in some lamentable incident & humiliation."

Randolph's proclivity for insulting others and provoking argument was also a persistent source of conflict. After Churchill found himself the target of a particularly cutting remark, he wrote to Randolph to cancel a planned lunch together, "as I really cannot run the risk of such insults being offered to me, & do not feel I want to see you at the present time." Churchill tended to forgive his son, always ending his letters—even this one—with the closing, "Your loving father."

Clementine was not so charitable. Her relationship with Randolph had been marked by outright hostility ever since his childhood, a rift that only grew wider with age. Early in Pamela's marriage, during a difficult period, Clementine gave her some strategic advice for dealing with Randolph: "Leave and just go away for three or four days, don't say where you are going. Just leave. Leave a little note that you are gone." Clementine said she had done likewise with Churchill and added, "It was very effective." Now, hearing about Pamela's ordeal at Harrods, Clementine was sympathetic. "She was wonderfully comforting and wonderfully kind and thoughtful, but she was very nervous also," Pamela said.

Clementine harbored a persistent anxiety that one day Randolph would do something to cause grave embarrassment to his father, and this fear, Pamela knew, was more than justified. Especially when Randolph drank. "I mean, I came of a family that was really teetotaler," Pamela said. "My father was a teetotaler. My mother maybe had a glass of sherry and that was it." Life with a drinker proved startling. With alcohol, the already unpleasant aspects of Randolph's personality became amplified. He would provoke arguments with whomever happened to be at hand, be it Pamela, friends, or hosts; some nights he would leave the table in a fury and stalk away. "I was sort of challenged as to whether to remain or walk out with him and I found all this very unsettling and unhappy," Pamela said.

Soon, she knew, she would have to face the inrush of bills by herself. In October, Randolph transferred from the 4th Hussars to a new commando unit being formed by a member of his club. He expected resistance from the Hussars but, to his dismay, got none: His fellow officers were only too glad to see him go. As a cousin recalled later, "What a shock it was to be told that the other officers disliked him, that they were fed up with his diatribes and could hardly wait for him to get some job elsewhere."

Randolph left for Scotland in mid–October to begin his commando training. Pamela did not want to continue living at Chequers alone, on the Churchills' charity, and hoped to find an inexpensive house somewhere, where she and Randolph and Winston Junior could be a family. Brendan Bracken, Churchill's jack of all tasks, found for her an old rectory house in Hitchin, Hertfordshire, about thirty miles north of London, that she could rent for a mere £52 a year. To further pare costs, she invited Randolph's older sister, Diana, and her children, to live there as well, and also recruited her own childhood governess, Nanny Hall, to help with the baby. She wrote to her husband shortly before his departure, "Oh! Randy everything would be so nice, if only you were with us all the time." She was overjoyed to at last have a home of her own, and could not wait to move in. "Oh my darling isn't it rather thrilling—our own family life—no more living in other people's houses."

The house needed work, which the war repeatedly disrupted. Her curtain installer disappeared before completing the job. His phone was dead, and Pamela presumed that his London home had been bombed. A carpenter hired to make cupboards got called away for a government job. He promised to find someone else to finish the work, but he had doubts as to whether his successor would even be able to find the necessary wood, a commodity made scarce by the war.

The house had nine bedrooms, and these soon filled. There was Nanny; Diana and her family; a housekeeper; several other employees; and, of course, soon, Pamela and the baby, whom she dubbed variously "Baby Dumpling" and "Baby P.M." In addition, Randolph's secretary, Miss Buck, had invited her own neighbors to stay at the rectory after their house was bombed. Miss Buck was very apologetic, but Pamela professed to be delighted. "It is a very good thing from our point of view," she wrote in a letter to Randolph, "as the local authorities tried yesterday to billet 20 children on us, & Miss Buck was able to say we were full."

Still, being away from the house made her uneasy. "I wish I could go over & see what is happening," she told him. "I am delighted to have evacuees as I can do so little to help anybody in my present state, but I would like to be running it myself, & secretly hope they're not pigging up our lovely home."

As cheap as the rent was, the house was expensive to operate. The curtains alone were slated to cost £162. Happily, Clementine had agreed to contribute the full cost. Financial pressures mounted. "Please darling pay the telephone account," Pamela wrote to Randolph.

His own spending while in Scotland became a worry as well. He lived and trained with the very wealthy members of his club, White's, who had formed the commando unit together, and therein lay danger. "Darling," Pamela wrote, "I know it is difficult now you are living with so many rich people, only do try & save a bit on your messing bills, etc. Remember baby Winston & I are willing to starve for you, but we would prefer not to."

ON THE EVENING OF Monday, October 14, 1940, while Churchill was dining with guests in the newly fortified Garden Rooms at 10 Downing Street, a bomb fell so close to the building that it blew out windows and destroyed the kitchen and a sitting room. Soon after the bombing, Clementine, in a letter to Violet Bonham Carter, wrote, "We have no gas or hot water and are cooking on an oil stove. But as a man called to Winston out of the darkness the other night, 'It's a grand life if we don't weaken!'"

The same night 10 Downing Street was struck, bombs also caused major damage to the nearby Treasury building, and a direct hit destroyed the Carlton Club, popular with senior members of Churchill's government, some of whom were present in its dining room when the blast occurred. Harold Nicolson got a full account from one guest, future prime minister Harold Macmillan. "They heard the bomb screaming down and ducked instinctively," Nicolson recorded in his diary on October 15. "There was a loud crash, the main lights went out and the whole place was filled with the smell of cordite and the dust of rubble. The side-lights on the tables remained alight, glimmering murkily in the thick fog which settled down on everything, plastering their hair and eye-brows with thick dust." There were about 120 people in the club when the bomb detonated, but none was seriously hurt. "An astonishing escape," wrote Nicolson.

With Britain's seat of government seemingly under fire, prudence dictated a fresh retreat to Chequers. Cars and secretaries were marshaled. The usual convoy set off, moving slowly through rubble-strewn streets. A dozen or so miles out, Churchill abruptly asked, "Where is Nelson?" Meaning, of course, the cat.

Nelson was not in the car; nor did he appear to be in any of the other vehicles.

Churchill ordered his driver to turn around and go back to No. 10. There, a secretary cornered the terrified cat and trapped him under a wastebasket.

With Nelson safely aboard, the cars resumed their journey.

IN LONDON THAT FOLLOWING Saturday night, October 19, John Colville experienced firsthand the Luftwaffe's apparent new focus on bombing Whitehall. After having dinner at his home, he set out to return to work, riding in a car the army had lately made available to Churchill's staff. Up ahead, the sky was suffused with an orange glow. He directed the driver to turn onto the Embankment, along the Thames, and saw that a warehouse on the far bank was wholly aflame, just beyond County Hall, the immense Edwardian escarpment that housed London's local government.

Colville understood at once that the fire would serve as a beacon for the bombers above. His driver headed for Downing Street at high speed. The car entered Whitehall just as a bomb exploded on the Admiralty building, which fronted the Horse Guards Parade.

The driver stopped the car near the entrance to a passage that led to the Treasury building. Colville leapt out and headed toward No. 10 on foot. A few moments later, incendiaries began to land all around him. He dropped to the ground and lay flat.

The roof of the Foreign Office building caught fire. Two incendiaries fell into the already heavily damaged Treasury building; others landed on open ground.

Colville, heart pounding, raced to No. 10 and entered through an emergency exit. He spent the evening in Churchill's reinforced dining room, on the basement level. The rest of the night was peaceful, despite an electric fan that sounded to Colville exactly like a German airplane.

WHILE COLVILLE WAS DODGING incendiaries in Whitehall, Churchill was at Chequers, in a dispirited mood. He and Pug Ismay sat alone in the Hawtrey Room, neither speaking. Ismay often found himself in this role, serving as a quiet presence, ready to offer advice and opinions when asked, or to listen as Churchill tried out ideas and lines for upcoming speeches, or simply to sit with him in companionable silence.

Churchill looked tired, and was clearly deep in thought. The Dakar episode weighed on him. When would the French stand and fight? Elsewhere, U-boats were taking a staggering toll in ships and lives, with eight ships sunk on the previous day alone, and ten more that day. And the continuing cycle of air-raid warnings and bombs, and the disruption they brought, appeared for once to be wearing him down.

It was hard for Ismay to see Churchill so tired, but, as he recalled later, a positive outcome also occurred to him: Maybe, at last, just this one night, Churchill would go to bed early, thereby freeing Ismay to do likewise.

Instead, Churchill suddenly jumped to his feet. "I believe that I can do it!" he said. In an instant, his tiredness seemed dispelled. Lights came on. Bells rang. Secretaries were summoned.

CHAPTER 55

Washington and Berlin

I N AMERICA, THE PRESIDENTIAL ELECTION TURNED UGLY. REPUB-
lican strategists persuaded Willkie that he was being too much the gentleman, that the only way to increase his standing in the polls was to make
the war the central issue; he needed to portray Roosevelt as a warmon-
ger and himself as an isolationist. Willkie assented with reluctance but
plunged in with enthusiasm, waging a campaign designed to spike fear
throughout America. If Roosevelt was elected, he warned, the country's
young men would be on their way to Europe within five months. His
poll numbers improved immediately.

In the midst of this, on October 29, just a week before Election Day,
Roosevelt presided over a ceremony at which the first lottery number
of the new draft was selected. Given America's isolationist bent, it was
a risky thing to do, even though Willkie also endorsed selective service
as an important step in improving America's ability to defend itself. In
a broadcast that night, Roosevelt chose his words carefully, avoiding altogether "conscription" and "draft," using instead the more neutral, historically resonant term "muster."

But otherwise, Willkie abandoned all restraint. One Republican
broadcast aimed at America's mothers said, "When your boy is dying on
some battlefield in Europe—or maybe in *Martinique*"—a Vichy French
stronghold—"and he's crying out, 'Mother! Mother!'—don't blame
Franklin D. Roosevelt because he sent your boy to war—blame YOUR-
SELF, because YOU sent Franklin D. Roosevelt back to the White
House!"

Willkie's sudden strength in the polls prompted Roosevelt to counter with an adamant declaration of his own wish to avoid war. "I have said this before," he told an audience in Boston, "but I shall say it again and again and again: Your boys are not going to be sent into any foreign wars." The official Democratic platform added the phrase "except in case of attack," but now he left it out, an omission surely meant to appeal to isolationist voters. Challenged on this by one of his speechwriters, the president replied testily, "Of course we'll fight if we're attacked. If somebody attacks us, then it isn't a foreign war, is it? Or do they want me to guarantee that our troops will be sent into battle only in the event of another Civil War."

The results of Gallup's final "presidential trial heat" for 1940, conducted October 26–31 and released the day before the election, showed Roosevelt leading Willkie by only four percentage points, down from twelve points earlier in the month.

IN BERLIN, THE LUFTWAFFE prepared to execute a new shift in strategy ordered by its master, Hermann Göring, that would bring an even greater swath of Britain's civilian population into its bombsights.

A month earlier, after reviewing the Luftwaffe's failure to bring Churchill to heel, Hitler had postponed Operation Sea Lion, without setting a future date, though he contemplated revisiting the idea in the spring. He and his commanders had always been uneasy about the prospect of such an assault. Had Göring's beloved Luftwaffe achieved air superiority over the British Isles as promised, invasion might have seemed a more comely prospect, but with the RAF still in control of the air, it would be foolhardy.

Britain's resilience raised a forbidding prospect for Hitler. As long as Churchill stood fast, intervention by the United States on Britain's behalf seemed increasingly likely. Hitler saw Churchill's destroyer deal as concrete evidence of the growing bond between the two. But he feared worse: that once America entered the war, Roosevelt and Churchill would then seek an alliance with Stalin, who had demonstrated a clear appetite for expansion and was fast strengthening his military forces. Although Germany and Russia had signed a nonaggression pact in 1939, Hitler harbored no illusions that Stalin would honor it. An alliance between Britain, America, and Russia would create, Hitler said, "a very difficult situation for Germany."

The solution, as he saw it, was to eliminate Russia from the equation, and thereby protect his eastern flank. War with Russia also promised to fulfill his longtime imperative, espoused since the 1920s, to crush Bolshevism and acquire "living space," his cherished *Lebensraum*.

His generals were still concerned about the dangers of a two-front war, the avoidance of which had always been a bedrock principle in Hitler's strategic thinking; now, however, he appeared to cast aside his own misgivings. Compared to a cross-channel invasion of Britain, war against Russia seemed easy, the kind of campaign at which his forces had thus far demonstrated great proficiency. The worst of the fighting would be over in six weeks, he predicted, but he stressed that the attack on Russia must begin soon. The longer he put it off, the more time Stalin would have to bolster his forces.

In the meantime, to block Churchill from interfering, he ordered Göring to step up his air campaign. "The decisive thing," he said, "is the ceaseless continuation of air attacks." He still held out the hope that the Luftwaffe would at last deliver on its promises and by itself drive Churchill to seek peace.

Göring fashioned a new plan. He would still hammer London but would target other urban centers as well, with the intent to annihilate them and, in so doing, crush Britain's resistance at last. He himself selected the targets and issued the code name for the first attack, "Moonlight Sonata," playing off the popular name for a haunting piano work by Beethoven.

What he prepared to launch now was a raid that the RAF, in a later report, would describe as a milestone in the history of air warfare. "For the first time," the report said, "air power was massively applied against a city of small [proportions] with the object of ensuring its obliteration."

The Frog Speech

AT CHEQUERS, DESPITE THE LATE HOUR, CHURCHILL BEGAN dictating at once. His plan: to speak directly to the French public, in both English and French, in a broadcast from the BBC's new radio studio at the Cabinet War Rooms in London. Uneasy about the possibility that the Vichy government in charge of unoccupied France might formally ally its armed forces with Germany's, Churchill hoped to assure French people everywhere, including in France's colonies, that Britain was wholly on their side and to rouse them to acts of resistance. For the time being, to his great frustration, he could offer nothing more. He proposed to write the French version himself.

He dictated slowly, without notes. Pug Ismay stayed with him, the hoped-for early bedtime lost. Churchill spoke for two hours, well into Sunday morning. He notified the Ministry of Information that he planned to make his broadcast the following night, Monday, October 21, and would speak for a total of twenty minutes—ten in French, ten in English. "Make all necessary arrangements," he directed.

On Monday, while still at Chequers, he continued working on the speech, still intent on drafting the French version himself but finding the going harder than his ego had led him to expect. The Ministry of Information dispatched to Chequers a young staff member with an academic competence in French to translate the text, but the man made no headway. He was "terrified," according to John Peck, the private secretary on duty at Chequers that day. The would-be translator found himself confronting a prime minister who had again changed his mind and was trying anew to work up his own French draft, and was adamant about doing so. The young man was shipped back to London.

The ministry sent a new translator, Michel Saint-Denis, "a charming, avuncular, truly bilingual Frenchman . . . unearthed from the BBC," according to Peck. Churchill acknowledged the man's obvious expertise, and relented.

By now Churchill had begun referring to the text as his "frog speech," "frog" being an unhappy nickname for a Frenchman. The speech was of sufficient importance that Churchill actually rehearsed it. Ordinarily this would have drawn forth his streak of stubborn childishness, but translator Saint-Denis, to his relief, encountered a tolerant, mostly obedient prime minister. Churchill had difficulty with certain French linguistic maneuvers, in particular rolling his *r*'s, but Saint-Denis found him to be a willing student, later recalling, "He relished the flavor of some words as though he was tasting fruit."

Churchill and Saint-Denis drove to London. The speech was now scheduled for nine o'clock that night. This being the BBC's accustomed news hour, Churchill was guaranteed a vast listenership in Britain and France and, via illicit radios, in Germany.

AN AIR RAID WAS underway when Churchill, wearing his pale blue siren suit, left 10 Downing Street to head for the war rooms, followed by various staff members and Saint-Denis. Ordinarily the walk was a pleasant one, but the Luftwaffe once again seemed to be targeting government buildings. Searchlights sabered the sky, illuminating the condensation trails of bombers above. Anti-aircraft guns blasted away, sometimes with a single report, sometimes a brisk sequence, at two rounds a second. The shells exploded far overhead, showering the streets with steel splinters that whistled as they fell. Churchill walked briskly; his translator ran to keep up.

Inside the BBC's broadcast chamber, Churchill settled in to begin his speech. The room was cramped, with a single armchair, a desk, and a microphone. The translator, Saint-Denis, was to introduce him to listeners, but found he had no place to sit.

"On my knees," Churchill said.

He leaned back and patted his thigh. Wrote Saint-Denis, "I inserted a leg between his and next moment had seated myself partly on the arm of the chair and partly on his knee."

"Frenchmen!" Churchill began. "For more than thirty years in peace and war I have marched with you, and I am marching still along the same road." Britain, too, was under attack, he said, referring to the nightly air raids. He assured his audience that "our people are bearing up unflinchingly. Our Air Force has more than held its own. We are waiting for the long-promised invasion. So are the fishes."

What followed was a plea for the French to take heart and not make things worse by impeding Britain's fight—this clearly a reference to Dakar. Hitler was the true enemy, Churchill stressed: "This evil man, this monstrous abortion of hatred and defeat, is resolved on nothing less than the complete wiping out of the French nation, and the disintegration of its whole life and future."

Churchill urged resistance, including within "so-called unoccupied France," another reference to Vichy-administered territory.

"Frenchmen!" he declaimed. "Rearm your spirits before it is too late."

He promised that he and the British Empire would never give up until Hitler was beaten. "Good night, then," he said. "Sleep to gather strength for the morning. For the morning will come."

At Chequers, Mary listened with great pride. "Tonight Papa spoke to France," she wrote in her diary. "So frankly—so encouragingly—so nobly & tenderly.

"I hope his voice reached many of them, and that its power & richness will have brought them new hope & faith." She felt moved to inscribe in her diary the chorus to "La Marseillaise," in French, which begins, *"Aux armes, citoyens . . ."* To arms, citizens.

"Dear France," she ended, "—so great & glorious be worthy of your noblest song and of that right cause you twice bled for—Liberty."

In the Cabinet War Rooms, when the broadcast came to an end, there was silence. "Nobody moved," translator Saint-Denis recalled. "We were deeply stirred. Then Churchill stood up; his eyes were full of tears."

Churchill said, "We have made history tonight."

IN BERLIN, A WEEK later, Goebbels began his morning meeting by bemoaning the fact that the German public appeared to be listening to the BBC "on an increasing scale."

He ordered "heavy sentences for radio offenders" and told his propaganda lieutenants that "every German must be clear in his mind that listening in to these broadcasts represents an act of serious sabotage."

As it happened, according to an RAF report summarizing intelligence gathered from captured Luftwaffe airmen, this injunction "in the long run worked in the opposite sense to that which was intended; it produced an irresistible urge to listen to them."

The Ovipositor

ELECTION NIGHT, NOVEMBER 5, WAS TENSE ON BOTH SIDES OF the Atlantic. The early returns, delivered to Roosevelt at his home in Hyde Park, New York, showed Willkie doing better than expected. But by eleven P.M., it became clear that Roosevelt would win. "It looks all right," he told a crowd gathered on his lawn. The final tally showed that he had won the popular vote by fewer than ten percentage points. In the electoral college, however, he won by a landslide: 449 to 82.

The news brought joy throughout Whitehall. "It is the best thing that has happened to us since the outbreak of war," wrote Harold Nicolson. "I thank God." Upon hearing the results, he said, "my heart leapt like a young salmon." Home Intelligence reported that throughout England and Wales, the result "has been greeted with overwhelming satisfaction."

Mary Churchill, at Chequers, wrote, "Glory hallelujah!!"

With Roosevelt reelected, the hoped-for payoff—America joining the war as a full partner—seemed much less distant.

Churchill needed the help more than ever. The chancellor of the exchequer now informed him that Britain would soon run out of money to pay for the weapons, food, and other aid it needed to survive.

CHURCHILL SENT HIS CONGRATULATIONS to Roosevelt in a floridly disingenuous telegram, in which he confessed that he had prayed for his victory and was thankful for the outcome. "This does not mean," he wrote, "that I seek or wish for anything more than the full, fair and free play of your mind upon the world issues now at stake in which our two nations have to discharge their respective duties." He claimed that he merely looked forward to being able to exchange thoughts about the war. "Things are afoot which will be remembered as long as the English language is spoken in any quarter of the globe, and in expressing the comfort I feel that the people of the United States have once again cast these great burdens upon you, I must avow my sure faith that the lights by which we steer will bring us all safely to anchor."

Roosevelt neither acknowledged the telegram nor replied.

This galled Churchill and worried him, though he was reluctant to do anything about it. At last, after nearly three weeks, he cabled his ambassador in Washington, Lord Lothian, and, with the guardedness of a snubbed suitor, quietly raised the issue. "Would you kindly find out for me most discreetly whether [the] President received my personal telegram congratulating him on re-election," he wrote. "It may have been swept up in electioneering congratulations. If not I wonder whether there was anything in it which could have caused offense or been embarrassing for him to receive."

He added, "Should welcome your advice."

THE PROF, AT LEAST, provided some good news. In a November 1, 1940, minute to Churchill, he reported that his aerial mines had finally claimed a victim, this during the first operational test of parachute-tethered mines released from an RAF aircraft in front of Luftwaffe bombers.

Radar tracked the German bomber to the curtain of drifting parachutes, at which point the plane's radar echo vanished "and did not reappear." Lindemann saw this as proof of success.

He did note, however, that there had been a malfunction involving the apparatus through which the mines were expelled, which Lindemann dubbed the "ovipositor," borrowing a biological term for the organ an insect or fish uses to deposit its eggs. The failure caused one of the mines to explode against the fuselage of the RAF plane that dropped it, an event that most certainly raised a degree of consternation among the crew but that otherwise caused "no serious damage."

Still, the Prof worried about how this would affect the Air Ministry's already jaundiced appraisal of the weapon, and he wanted reassurance of Churchill's continued support. He wrote, "I trust this unlikely accident will not be allowed to prejudice immediate continuance of these trials which seem to have had such an auspicious beginning after so many years."

Churchill's faith in the weapon, and the Prof, did not waver.

The Prof, meanwhile, seemed bent on further vexing the Air Ministry. In late October he had written to Churchill about something else that had become one of his obsessions: the German navigational beams. The Prof saw the development of electronic countermeasures to jam and bend the beams as vital to Britain's defense, and he believed the Air Ministry was dragging its feet in developing and deploying the needed technologies. He complained to Churchill.

Again invoking his "power-relay," Churchill took this up immediately and forwarded the Prof's minute to Charles Portal, chief of the Air Staff, who replied with an account of all that had been done, including development of jamming devices and decoy fires set along the paths of beams to trick German pilots into dropping their bombs. These fires were called "Starfish," owing to their appearance from the air at night, and were proving effective, as gauged by the number of bombs falling into empty fields adjacent to the fires. In one notable case, a decoy fire outside Portsmouth drew 170 high-explosive bombs and 32 parachute mines.

With evident irritation, but ever mindful of the Prof's special connection to the prime minister, Portal wrote: "Professor Lindemann implies in his Minute that we are not pressing on with our radio countermeasures to the German beam system as fast as we might. I can assure that this is not the case." The effort, Portal said, "is being given the highest possible priority."

The Prof also inflicted added work on Pug Ismay, who, as Churchill's military chief of staff, already was fully occupied, and appeared to be feeling the strain. This new sally, too, involved navigational beams.

On the night of November 6, a bomber from the Luftwaffe's secretive KGr 100 unit, thought to be expert at flying along beams, went down in the sea off Bridport, on the south coast, mostly intact and very near shore. A navy salvage squad wanted to retrieve the bomber while it was still readily accessible, but army officials claimed it was their jurisdiction, "the result being that the Army did not make any attempt to secure it and the heavy seas soon wrecked the aircraft," according to an RAF intelligence report on the incident, which was sent to Lindemann. The Prof made sure that Churchill knew about the debacle. In a note with the RAF report attached he sniffed: "It is a very great pity that inter-service squabbles resulted in the loss of this machine, which is the first of its kind to come within our grasp."

Churchill promptly dispatched a personal minute to Pug Ismay on the matter, saying, "Pray make proposals to ensure that in future immediate steps are taken to secure all possible information and equipment from German aircraft which come down in this country or near our coasts, and that these rare opportunities are not squandered through departmental differences."

Which was, of course, just exactly what Ismay needed to make his day complete. Ismay relayed this to the chiefs of staff, who reviewed the existing protocols for handling downed aircraft. The airplane had been lost, Ismay told Churchill, "through a stupidly rigid interpretation of these orders." He assured Churchill that new instructions were being issued and that safeguarding downed aircraft was of paramount importance. He noted, in closing, that the radio equipment the RAF had most hoped to salvage from the bomber had ultimately been washed up from the wreckage, and recovered.

Lost in this acerbic interchange was the reason why this plane had crash-landed in the first place. Thanks to continued prodding by the Prof and the inventive attentions of Dr. R. V. Jones and the RAF's No. 80 Wing countermeasures unit, as well as deft interrogation of captured German airmen, the RAF now knew of the existence of the Luftwaffe's "X-system" of navigation, enough to build transmitters, code-named "Bromides," capable of redirecting—"meaconing"—the system's beams. The first such transmitter had been installed five days before the German bomber's flight.

The bomber's crew, flying at night through heavily overcast skies, had expected to pick up their designated guidance beam over the Bristol Channel, and then to follow it to their target, a factory in Birmingham, but they could not find the signal. To proceed without the beam with such bad visibility would have been foolhardy, so the pilot decided to change the plan and instead bomb the dockyards in Bristol. He hoped that by descending beneath the clouds, he would find a visual landmark to establish his new course. But the cloud ceiling was very low, and visibility under it was extremely poor due to darkness and weather. The pilot, Hans Lehmann, realized that he was lost.

Soon, however, his wireless operator began picking up strong signals from the Luftwaffe's standard radio beacon at St. Malo, on the Brittany coast. Lehmann decided to turn around and use this to help guide him back to his base. When he reached St. Malo, he reported his position and the course he would now follow. Contrary to standard practice, he received neither a confirmation that his message had been received nor the usual landing instructions.

Lehmann continued on and began his descent, hoping soon to be able to see familiar terrain below, but he found only water. On the assumption that he had overshot his airfield, he turned around and tried another approach. By now he was low on fuel. His bomber had been aloft, and lost, for over eight hours. Lehmann decided that his only option now was to beach the plane on the French coast. Visibility was so poor that he landed instead in the sea, near the shore. He and two other crewmen managed to reach dry ground, but the fourth failed to appear.

Lehmann thought he had landed in France, perhaps on the Bay of Biscay. Instead, he had put the plane down just off the Dorset coast. What he had believed to be the St. Malo guide point was in fact an RAF masking beacon transmitted by a meaconing station in the village of Templecombe, in Somerset, thirty-five miles south of Bristol.

Lehmann and his men were promptly captured and shipped off to an RAF interrogation center outside London, where air intelligence was delighted to learn that they were members of the mysterious KGr 100.

Our Special Source

E NGLAND'S WEATHER DEGRADED. GALES RAKED THE LANDSCAPE and roiled the surrounding seas, making an amphibious landing by German forces seem less and less likely. Fragments of intelligence from Bletchley Park—which Air Ministry officials referred to only as "our special source"—suggested that Hitler might have postponed his planned Operation Sea Lion. Yet the Luftwaffe continued to pummel London with nightly raids, and now appeared to be expanding its range of targets elsewhere in Britain. Clearly something new was afoot, and the implications were troubling. London had shown itself able to withstand nightly attack, but how would the rest of the country fare, as more and more civilians were killed or injured and bombed from their homes?

The details of the Luftwaffe's new campaign were starting to come into focus. On Tuesday, November 12, intelligence officers listened in as a newly captured German airman conversed with another prisoner in a room fitted with a hidden microphone. "He believes," the officers reported, "that riots have broken out in London and that Buckingham Palace has been stormed and that 'Hermann'"—a reference to Luftwaffe chief Hermann Göring—"thinks the psychological moment has come for a colossal raid to take place between the 15th and the 20th of this month at the full moon and that Coventry and Birmingham will be the towns attacked."

The scenario described by the prisoner was chilling. For this raid, the Luftwaffe planned to deploy every available bomber and use every navigational beam. The planes would carry fifty-kilogram (110-pound) "shrieking" bombs. The prisoner, according to the report, said the bombers were to concentrate on destroying working-class neighborhoods, where the populace was believed to be on the verge of revolt.

The report cautioned that the new prisoner might not be very reliable, and recommended that his remarks be treated with circumspection. What had prompted air intelligence to relay them now, the report said, was its receipt that afternoon of information from the special source that indicated the Germans were planning "a gigantic raid," code-named Moonlight Sonata. The special source believed the target was not Coventry or Birmingham but, rather, London. The attack would likely take place three days hence, on Friday, November 15, when the moon was full, and would involve up to eighteen hundred German aircraft, including bombers from KGr 100, the elite fire-starter unit, whose incendiaries would further light the target. One indication of the singular importance of the raid was the fact that Göring himself planned to direct the operation.

If all this was true, it raised the specter of the massive knock-out raid—Churchill's aerial "banquet"—that civil defense officials had expected and feared ever since the start of the war.

The Air Ministry circulated a "minute sheet," on which officials offered their thoughts about the bits of intelligence known thus far. In an entry marked "MOST SECRET," an RAF wing commander wrote that the exact date of the raid would probably be signaled by a flight in the afternoon by bombers from KGr 100; their goal would be to check on weather conditions over the selected target and make sure the navigational beams were positioned properly. He proposed that the word "sonata" might itself be significant. In music, sonatas were traditionally structured around three movements. This suggested that the attack might occur in three phases. The exact target was still not clear, but intercepted instructions showed that the Luftwaffe had selected four possible areas, among them London.

The information in hand was deemed reliable enough to cause Air Ministry officials to begin planning a response. A counter-operation intended to pour "cold water" on the German attack began to take shape; appropriately enough, it was code-named "Cold Water." One official proposed that the best response, from the point of view of the British public, would be to launch a massive RAF strike against a target in Germany. He suggested a "big bang" on targets along the Ruhr River, or even Berlin itself, and recommended, as well, that the bombs used be fitted with the RAF's version of Germany's "Jericho trumpet," to make each bomb howl on its way down. "The whistles for our bombs," he noted, "have already gone out to Depots and there should be no trouble in getting them fitted to our 250 and 500 lb. bombs for an occasion of this kind. If the big bang is to achieve the best moral effect we suggest we should do this."

Operation Cold Water also called for the RAF's new countermeasures squadron, No. 80 Wing, established in July, to do all it could to disrupt the skein of navigational beams transmitted by the Germans. Two specially equipped bombers were to fly back along a key beam transmitted from Cherbourg and bomb the transmitter. They would know they were over the target because previous electronic reconnaissance had shown that the beams disappeared directly above the transmitting stations. The RAF referred to this dead space as "the silent zone," "the cut-out," and, yes, "the cone of silence."

No word of the possible German attack, as yet, was conveyed to Churchill.

AT SEVEN O'CLOCK ON Wednesday night, air intelligence gave RAF commanders a new update on Moonlight Sonata from the special source, which confirmed that the raid would indeed have three parts, though whether these were three phases in one night or over three nights was not clear. The source supplied the code names for two of the three phases, the first being *Regenschirm,* or "Umbrella," the second *Mondschein Serenade,* or "Moonshine Serenade." The name for the third was not yet known. One of the Air Ministry's most senior men, William Sholto Douglas, deputy chief of the Air Staff, doubted that the Germans planned an attack over three nights: "How can even the optimistic Boche hope to get 3 successive nights of fine weather?"

Typically news about the day-to-day activities of German forces did not get sent to Churchill, but with the scale of the attack expected to be so great, on Thursday, November 14, the Air Ministry prepared a special "MOST SECRET" memorandum for the prime minister. This, in turn, was placed in his special yellow box, reserved for the most secret messages.

As best anyone could tell, the raid would not occur until the next night, Friday, November 15, which promised to be nearly ideal for flying, with cold, mostly clear skies and a full moon that would light the landscape below to a brightness approaching that of daylight.

But this supposition was incorrect, as soon became apparent.

———

AT NOON ON THURSDAY, Colville made his way to Westminster Abbey, where he was to be an usher at the funeral service for former prime minister Neville Chamberlain, who had died the week before. Churchill was a pallbearer, as was Halifax. A bomb had blown out the windows of the chapel; there was no heat. Government ministers filled the seats in the choir. Everyone wore coats and gloves, but froze all the same. The chapel was only partly full, owing to the fact that the time and place for the funeral had been kept secret—a prudent measure, Colville noted, "for a judiciously placed bomb would have had spectacular results."

Colville's gaze fell on Duff Cooper, minister of information, whose face bore a "look of blank indifference, almost of disdain." A few ministers sang hymns. No sirens wailed; no German aircraft appeared overhead.

LATER THAT AFTERNOON, at 10 Downing Street, Churchill, his detective, his typist, and the rest of his usual weekend platoon walked through the back garden and entered the usual cars; they settled in for the drive to the country, this time to Ditchley, Churchill's full-moon house.

Just before departure, the private secretary assigned to weekend duty, John Martin, handed Churchill the yellow box containing his most secret communications and joined him in the back seat. The cars set off at high speed and moved west along the Mall, past Buckingham Palace, and along the southern border of Hyde Park. A few minutes into the drive, Churchill opened the box and there found a secret memorandum dated that day that described, in three dense pages, a possibly imminent Luftwaffe operation called Moonlight Sonata.

The report proceeded to detail what air intelligence had learned and how the RAF planned to respond; it named four possible target areas, with Central London and Greater London mentioned first. The report stated that London seemed the likely choice.

Then came the most troubling phrase in the memorandum: "The whole of the German long range Bomber Force will be employed." The raid, moreover, would be directed—"we think"—by Hermann Göring himself. The intelligence "comes from a very good source indeed." Churchill, of course, knew that this source had to be Bletchley Park.

Far more satisfactory were the next two pages of the report, which detailed the RAF's planned response, Operation Cold Water, and stated that RAF Bomber Command would follow a "knock-for-knock policy," with bombers concentrating on a single city in Germany, maybe Berlin but possibly Munich or Essen, the choice to be determined by the weather.

By this point, Churchill and his entourage, en route to Ditchley but still within the city, were just passing Kensington Gardens. Churchill ordered his driver to turn around. Wrote secretary Martin, "He was not going to sleep quietly in the country while London was under what was expected to be a heavy attack."

The cars sped back to 10 Downing Street. So grave was the apparent threat that Churchill ordered his female staff to leave before nightfall and directed them to go home or to the "Paddock," the fortified emergency headquarters in Dollis Hill. He told John Colville and another private secretary, John Peck, to spend the night at the Down Street station, a luxurious shelter built by the London Passenger Transport Board that Churchill occasionally occupied. He called it his "burrow." Colville did not object. He and Peck dined "apolaustically," as Colville put it, using a ten-penny word meaning "with great enjoyment." The shelter's stock of luxuries included caviar, Havana cigars, brandy dating to 1865, and, of course, champagne: Perrier-Jouët 1928.

Churchill went to the Cabinet War Rooms to await the raid. He did many things well, but waiting was not one of them. Growing impatient, he climbed to the roof of the nearby Air Ministry building to watch for the attack, bringing Pug Ismay with him.

AIR INTELLIGENCE AT LAST identified the target. In the afternoon, members of the RAF's radio countermeasures unit detected new beam transmissions from German transmitters in France. Wireless operators listening in on German communications intercepted the expected Luftwaffe advance reconnaissance reports, as well as messages from a control center at Versailles from which the raid was to be directed. Together these offered strong evidence that Moonlight Sonata would occur that night, November 14, a day earlier than intelligence had first suggested.

At 6:17 P.M., roughly an hour after sunset, the first German bombers—thirteen of them—crossed the southern coast of England, at Lyme Bay. These were the bombers of KGr 100, so adept at finding and flying along radio beams. They carried more than ten thousand individual incendiary canisters, to illuminate the target for the bombers that soon would follow.

A few aircraft did pass over London, at 7:15 P.M. and again ten minutes later, setting off sirens and driving people into shelters, but these aircraft continued on without event, leaving behind a silent city made ghostly by moonlight. As it happened, these were feints, meant to convince the RAF that the big raid was indeed targeting the capital.

A Coventry Farewell

BY THREE O'CLOCK THAT THURSDAY AFTERNOON, THE RAF'S RADIO countermeasures group knew that German navigational beams were intersecting not over London but above Coventry, a center for arms manufacturing in the Midlands, nearly one hundred miles away. Industry aside, Coventry was best known for its medieval cathedral and for hosting, according to legend, the drafty eleventh-century ride of Lady Godiva (and, as a by-product, giving rise to the term "Peeping Tom," after a man named Thomas was said to defy an edict ordering citizens not to peek at the passing countess). For reasons unclear, the news that Coventry was the intended target was not relayed to Churchill, waiting impatiently on the Air Ministry roof.

The RAF's radio countermeasures group struggled to determine the exact frequencies needed to jam or distort the navigational beams aimed toward the city. Only a few jamming transmitters were available, and by now the sky was scored with invisible beams. One beam passed right over Windsor Castle, west of London, prompting concern that the Luftwaffe might have targeted the royal family itself. A warning was relayed to the castle. Air Raid Precautions (ARP) officials assigned to its defense manned the battlements as if awaiting a medieval siege, and they soon saw bombers overhead, black against the nearly full moon, in a procession that seemed endless.

No bombs fell.

AT 5:46 P.M., COVENTRY entered its blackout period; the moon was already up and visible, having risen at 5:18 P.M. Citizens closed their blackout blinds and curtains; the lights at train stations were turned off. This was routine. But even with the blackout underway, the streets were agleam with light. The moon was dazzling, the sky exceptionally clear. Leonard Dascombe, a tool setter at an arms factory, was on his way to work when he realized how brilliantly it shone, its light "glistening from on the house-tops." Another man observed that the moon made the headlights on his car unnecessary. "We could almost have read a newspaper, it was such a wonderful night," he said. Lucy Moseley, a daughter of the city's newly elected mayor, John "Jack" Moseley, recalled, "It really was unnaturally light outside; hardly ever before or since have I seen such a brilliant November night." As the Moseleys settled in for the evening, a family member called it "a huge, really horrible 'bomber's moon.'"

At 7:05 P.M., an ARP message arrived at the local civil defense control room, stating "Air Raid Message Yellow." This meant that aircraft had been detected heading in the direction of Coventry. Then came "Air Raid Message Red," the signal to turn on the sirens.

Coventry had experienced air raids before. The city had taken them in stride. But Thursday night felt different, as many residents later recalled. Suddenly flares appeared in the sky, drifting under parachutes, further lighting streets already luminescent with moonglow. At 7:20, incendiary bombs began to fall, with what one witness described as "a swishing sound like heavy rain." Some of the incendiaries seemed to be a new variety. Instead of simply igniting and starting fires, they exploded, sending incendiary material in all directions. A number of high-explosive bombs fell as well, including five four-thousand-pound "Satans," with the apparent intent of destroying water mains and keeping firefighting teams from getting to work.

Then came the full rain of high-explosive bombs, as the pilots above "bombed the fires." They dropped parachute mines as well, 127 in all, of which 20 failed to explode, either because of a malfunction or a time-delay fuse, something the Luftwaffe seemed to delight in deploying. "The air was filled with the crash of guns, the whine of bombs and the terrific flash and bang as they exploded," recalled one police constable. "The sky seemed to be full of planes." The raid came so suddenly and with such strength that a group of women at a YWCA hostel had no time to escape to a nearby shelter. "For the first time in my life," one wrote, "I knew what it was like to shake with fear."

Bombs struck several shelters. Teams of soldiers and ARP men worked through the rubble by hand, for fear of causing harm to survivors. One refuge had clearly been destroyed by a direct hit. "After a time we came to the occupants of the shelter," wrote one rescuer. "Some were quite cold and others were still warm, but they were all dead."

A bomb landed close to a shelter into which Dr. Eveleen Ashworth and her two children had retreated. First came "a shattering noise," she wrote, then the blast, "and a land wave which rocked the shelter." The blast blew off the shelter door.

Her seven-year-old said, "That nearly blew my hair off."

Her three-year-old: "It nearly blew my head off!"

At one city hospital, Dr. Harry Winter climbed to the roof to help extinguish incendiary bombs before they set the hospital on fire. "I could hardly believe my eyes," he said. "All round the hospital grounds glowed literally hundreds of incendiary bombs, like lights twinkling on a mammoth Christmas tree."

Within the building, women in the maternity ward were placed under their beds, with mattresses over their bodies. One patient was a German airman, injured and convalescing in a bed on the top floor. "Too much bomb—too long!" he moaned. "Too much bomb!"

Casualties began to arrive at the hospital. Dr. Winter and his fellow surgeons went to work in three operating theaters. Most of the injuries were damaged limbs and severe lacerations. "The complication with bomb lacerations, however, is that you get a small wound on the surface but extensive disruption underneath," Dr. Winter wrote later. "Everything is pulped together. It's no use fixing the surface wound without doing a major cutting job on the inside."

At another hospital, a nurse in training found herself confronting an old terror. "During the course of my training I had always the fear of being left with the limb of a patient in my hand after amputation and had so far managed to be off-duty when amputations were taking place," she wrote. The attack "changed all that for me. I didn't have time to be squeamish."

Now the city bore what many considered its most traumatic wound. Incendiaries salted the roofs and grounds of the city's famed Cathedral of St. Michael, the first descending at around eight o'clock. One landed on the roof, which was made of lead. The fire burned through the metal, causing molten lead to fall onto the wooden interior below, igniting it as well. Witnesses called for fire trucks, but all of the trucks were engaged fighting fires throughout the city. The first truck to reach the cathedral arrived an hour and a half later, having come from the town of Solihull, fourteen miles away. Its crew could do nothing but watch. A bomb had shattered a critical water main. An hour later, water at last began to flow, but with very low pressure, and soon that, too, waned to nothing.

As the fire advanced and began consuming chancel and chapels and the heavy wood beams of the roof, church employees rushed inside to rescue all that they could—tapestries, crosses, candlesticks, a wafer box, a crucifix—and brought them to the police station in a solemn procession. Reverend R. T. Howard, provost of the cathedral, watched it burn from the police station porch, as an orange fist engulfed its ancient pipe organ, once played by Handel. "The whole interior was a seething mass of flame and piled up blazing beams and timbers, interpenetrated and surmounted with dense bronze-colored smoke," Howard wrote.

The rest of Coventry seemed to be on fire as well. The glow was visible thirty miles away, spotted in fact by Minister of Home Security Herbert Morrison, who was a guest at a distant country home. A German pilot shot down soon after the raid told RAF interrogators that he could see the glow a hundred miles off as he flew over London on his return leg. In Balsall Common, eight miles west of Coventry, diarist Clara Milburn wrote, "When we went out the searchlights were probing the clear sky, the stars looked very near, the air was so clear and the moonlight was brilliant. I have never seen such a glorious night. Wave after wave of aircraft came over, and heavy gunfire followed."

All through the night, for eleven hours, the bombers came, and incendiaries and bombs fell. Witnesses told of familiar odors raised from the flames that would have been comforting if not for the cause. A fire consuming a tobacco store filled the surrounding area with the scent of cigar smoke and burning pipe tobacco. A burning butcher shop raised the aroma of roast meat and brought to mind the comforts of the traditional Sunday evening "joint."

The bombs fell until 6:15 A.M. The blackout ended at 7:54. The moon still shone in the clear dawn sky, but the bombers were gone. The cathedral was a ruin, with melted lead still dripping from its roofs, and fragments of charred timber now and then coming loose and falling to the ground. Throughout the city, the most common sound was that of broken glass crunching under people's shoes. One news reporter observed glass "so thick that looking up the street it was as if it was covered with ice."

Now came scenes of horror. Dr. Ashworth reported seeing a dog running along a street "with a child's arm in its mouth." A man named E. A. Cox saw a man's headless body beside a bomb crater. Elsewhere, an exploded land mine left behind a collection of charred torsos. Bodies arrived at a makeshift morgue at a rate of up to sixty per hour, and here morticians had to deal with a problem they had rarely, if ever, been compelled to confront: bodies so mangled that they were unrecognizable as bodies. Between 40 and 50 percent were classified as "unidentifiable owing to mutilation."

Those bodies that were mostly intact received luggage tags, stating where the body had been found and, when possible, the likely identification, and were stacked in multiple tiers. Survivors were permitted to walk through and look for missing friends and kin, until a bomb struck an adjacent natural gas storage facility, causing an explosion that tore the roof off the morgue. Rain fell, distorting the luggage tags. The process of identification was so macabre, so fruitless, with sometimes three or four people identifying the same body, that visits were halted and identifications made by examining personal belongings collected from the dead.

A sign went up outside the morgue, stating: "It is greatly regretted that the pressure at the mortuary is such that it is not possible for relatives to view any of the bodies."

LORD BEAVERBROOK HURRIED TO the city, unwilling to be perceived as missing another cataclysmic raid. His visit was not well received. He focused on restoring production in factories damaged in the attack. During a meeting with officials, he tried out a bit of Churchillian rhetoric. "The roots of the Air Force are planted in Coventry," he said. "If Coventry's output is destroyed the tree will languish. But if the city rises from the ashes then the tree will continue to burgeon, putting forth fresh leaves and branches." He was said to have shed tears upon seeing the destruction, only to be brought up "sharply," according to Lucy Moseley, the mayor's daughter. Tears, she wrote, had no value. Beaverbrook had hectored the factories for maximum production, and now much of the city was in ruins. "He'd asked Coventry's workers for an all-out effort," Moseley wrote, "and what had they got for it?"

Minister of Home Security Herbert Morrison came too, and found himself blamed for failing to better protect the city, and for the fact that the German bombers had arrived virtually without challenge by the RAF. And, indeed, the RAF, though it had made 121 sorties during the night, using dozens of fighters equipped with air-to-air radar, reported only two "engagements" and failed to destroy a single bomber, once again underscoring the persistent difficulty of fighting in darkness. Operation Cold Water took place but with minimal effect. British bombers struck airfields in France and military targets in Berlin, losing ten bombers in the process. The RAF's countermeasures group, No. 80 Wing, used jammers and beam-bending transmitters to distort and divert German beams, but these were thought to have had little effect, according to an air force analysis, "since the night was so clear and bright that radio navigational aids were not essential." The unit did succeed in dispatching a pair of bombers to follow two German beams back to their home transmitters in Cherbourg, where they knocked both out of action. The failure to down any aircraft, however, prompted an angry telegram from the Air Ministry to Fighter Command, asking why there had been so few interceptions despite "fine weather, moonlight and considerable fighter effort exerted."

The city offered a much warmer welcome to the king, who arrived on Saturday morning for an unannounced visit. Mayor Moseley had learned of the impending honor only late the previous day. His wife, who was in the midst of gathering up the family's personal belongings for a move to a relative's home outside the city, burst into tears. These were not tears of joy. "Oh dear!" she cried. "Doesn't he understand we're in too much of a mess and have so much to do without him coming?"

The king met first with the mayor in his formal mayor's parlor, now lighted only by candles stuck in the mouths of beer bottles. Afterward, accompanied by other officials, the two men set out to tour the devastation, and soon, without warning, the king began turning up in the most prosaic places. At one stop, a stunned group of weary elderly people jumped to their feet and sang "God Save the King." Elsewhere, a worker who had sat down on a curb for a brief rest, grubby and tired, still wearing his helmet, looked up to see men approaching on the street. As the group passed, its apparent leader said, "Good morning" and nodded. Only after they moved on did the man on the curb realize it was the king. "I was so taken aback, flabbergasted, amazed, overwhelmed that I couldn't even answer him."

At the cathedral, the king was introduced to provost Howard. "The king's arrival took me completely by surprise," Howard wrote. He heard cheering and saw the king enter through a door at the southwest end of the church. Howard greeted him. They shook hands. "I stood with him watching the ruins," Howard wrote. "His whole attitude was one of intense sympathy and grief."

A team of Mass-Observation researchers, experienced in chronicling the effects of air raids, had arrived on Friday afternoon. In their subsequent report they wrote of having found "more open signs of hysteria, terror, neurosis" than they had seen over the prior two months of chronicling air-raid effects. "The overwhelmingly dominant feeling on Friday was the feeling of utter *helplessness*." (The italics were theirs.) The observers noted a widespread sense of dislocation and depression. "The dislocation is so total in the town that people feel that *the town itself is killed*."

In order to help stem the surge of rumors arising from the raid, the BBC invited Tom Harrisson, the twenty-nine-year-old director of Mass-Observation, to do a broadcast on Saturday night, at nine o'clock, during its prime Home Service news slot, to talk about what he had seen in the city.

"The strangest sight of all," Harrisson told his vast audience, "was the Cathedral. At each end the bare frames of the great windows still have a kind of beauty without their glass; but in between them is an incredible chaos of bricks, pillars, girders, memorial tablets." He spoke of the absolute silence in the city on Friday night as he drove around it in his car, threading his way past bomb craters and mounds of broken glass. He slept in the car that night. "I think this is one of the weirdest experiences of my whole life," he said, "driving in a lonely, silent desolation and drizzling rain in that great industrial town."

The broadcast became a topic of earnest conversation at the Monday, November 18, meeting of Churchill's War Cabinet. Anthony Eden, secretary of state for war (soon to become foreign secretary) called it "a most depressing broadcast." Others agreed, and wondered whether it would dampen public morale. Churchill, however, argued that on balance the broadcast had done little harm, and might even have done some good by drawing attention to the attack among listeners in the United States. This proved to be the case in New York, where the *Herald Tribune* described the bombing as an "insane" barbarity and proclaimed: "No means of defense which the United States can place in British hands should be withheld."

IN GERMANY, SENIOR OFFICIALS were anything but alarmed by the publicity given the attack on Coventry. Goebbels called it an "exceptional success." In his diary entry for Sunday, November 17, he wrote, "The reports from Coventry are horrendous. An entire city literally wiped out. The English are no longer pretending; all they can do now is wail. But they asked for it." He saw nothing negative in the worldwide attention the attack had drawn, and in fact thought the raid could signal a turning point. "This affair has aroused the greatest attention all over the world. Our stock is on the rise again," he wrote in his diary, on Monday, November 18. "The USA is succumbing to gloom, and the usual arrogant tone has disappeared from the London press. All we need is a few weeks of good weather. Then England could be dealt with."

Luftwaffe chief Göring hailed the raid as a "historic victory." Adolf Galland's commander, Field Marshal Kesselring, lauded the "exceptionally good results." Kesselring shrugged off the mass of civilian deaths as simply a cost of war. "The unpredictable consequences of even a precision bombing attack are much to be regretted," he wrote later, "but are inseparable from any attack in force."

For some Luftwaffe pilots, however, the raid seemed to have crossed a line. "The usual cheers that greeted a direct hit stuck in our throats," wrote one bomber pilot. "The crew just gazed down on the sea of flames in silence. Was this really a military target?"

IN ALL, THE COVENTRY RAID killed 568 civilians and seriously wounded another 865. Of the 509 bombers ultimately dispatched by Göring to attack the city, some were deterred by anti-aircraft fire, others turned back for other reasons; 449 actually made it. Over eleven hours, Luftwaffe crews dropped 500 tons of high explosives and 29,000 incendiaries. The raid destroyed 2,294 buildings and damaged 45,704 more, such thorough devastation that it gave rise to a new word, "coventration," to describe the effect of massed air raids. The RAF made Coventry the standard by which to estimate the total of deaths likely to occur during its own raids on German towns, with the results rated as "1 Coventry," "2 Coventries," and so on.

The sheer volume of bodies, many still unidentified, caused city officials to forbid individual burials. The first mass funeral and burial, for 172 victims, was held on Wednesday, November 20; the second, for 250 more, took place three days later.

There were no public calls for reprisals against Germany. At the first of the funerals the bishop of Coventry said, "Let us vow before God to be better friends and neighbors in the future, because we have suffered this together and have stood here today."

Distraction

———

JOHN COLVILLE WAS ENTRANCED. BOMBS FELL AND CITIES BURNED, but there was his love life to attend to. As he endured the persistent aloofness of his yearned-for Gay Margesson, he found himself increasingly drawn to eighteen-year-old Audrey Paget. On Sunday, November 17, a brilliant fall day, the two went riding on the expansive grounds of the Paget family's estate, Hatfield Park, roughly an hour's drive north of central London.

He described the afternoon in his diary: "Mounted on two spirited and good-looking horses, Audrey and I rode for two hours in brilliant sunshine, galloping through Hatfield Park, walking through the woods and bracken, careening wildly over fields and ditches; and all the time I found it hard to take my eyes off Audrey, whose slim figure, sweetly disordered hair and flushed cheeks made her seem a woodland nymph, too lovely for the world of reality."

He was torn. "Actually," he wrote the next day, "if I were not in love with Gay, and if I thought Audrey would marry me (which she certainly would not just at present) I should not at all mind having a wife so beautiful, so vivacious and whom I genuinely like as well as admire.

"But still Gay with all her faults is Gay, and it would be silly to get married—even if I could—at this moment of European History."

FOR PAMELA CHURCHILL, there was mounting anxiety about money. On Tuesday, November 19, she wrote to her husband, Randolph, to ask him to pay her an additional £10 a week in allowance. "I enclose a sketch of the expenses here which I hope you will look into carefully," she wrote. "I don't want to be mean & beastly, but my darling, I am doing everything I can to run your home & look after your son economically, but I can't do the impossible." She listed all the family's expenses, down to the cost of cigarettes and drinks. Together these consumed nearly all the income she received from Randolph and from other sources, namely the rent her sister-in-law Diana paid and an allowance from her own family.

These, however, were merely the expenses she could anticipate with reasonable accuracy. Her deep fear was about Randolph's spending and his weakness for alcohol and gambling. "So try & limit your expenses to £5 a week in Scotland," she wrote. "And darling, surely you're not ashamed of saying you're too poor to gamble. I know you love Baby Winston & me, & won't mind making a sacrifice for us."

She cautioned that it was vital for them to get control of their expenditures. "I simply can't be happy, when I'm sick with worry all the time," she wrote. She was by now deeply disappointed in her marriage, but not yet irrevocably. She softened her tone. "Oh! my darling Randy," she wrote, "I wouldn't worry if I didn't love you so deeply & so desperately. Thank you for making me your wife, & for letting me have your son. It is the most wonderful thing that has happened in my life."

CHURCHILL'S WEEKEND STAYS AT Chequers and Ditchley provided him with invaluable opportunities for distraction. They took him away from the increasingly dreary streetscape of London, where each day another fragment of Whitehall was incinerated or blown away.

During one weekend at Ditchley, his full-moon refuge, he and his guests watched a film in the mansion's home cinema, Charlie Chaplin's *The Great Dictator*. Late the next night, exhausted, Churchill mistimed his landing on a chair and fell between it and an ottoman, wedging himself with his rear on the floor and his feet in the air. Colville witnessed the moment. "Having no false dignity," Colville wrote, "he treated it as a complete joke and repeated several times, 'A real Charlie Chaplin!' "

THE WEEKEND OF NOVEMBER 30 brought two particularly welcome diversions. That day, Saturday, the family gathered at Chequers to celebrate Churchill's sixty-sixth birthday; the next, the christening of Pamela and Randolph Churchill's new son, Winston. The child was round and robust and from early on struck private secretary John Martin as being "absurdly like his grandfather," which prompted one of Churchill's daughters to quip, "So are all babies."

First came a service at the little parish church in nearby Ellesborough, where Clementine was a regular attendee. This was Churchill's first visit. Their three daughters came—Mary despite a sore throat—as did the baby's four godparents, among them Lord Beaverbrook and reporter Virginia Cowles, a close friend of Randolph's.

Churchill wept throughout the service, now and then saying, softly, "Poor infant, to be born into such a world as this."

Then came lunch back at the house, attended by the family, the godparents, and the church rector.

Beaverbrook stood up to propose a toast to the child.

But Churchill rose immediately and said, "As it was *my* birthday yesterday, I am going to ask you all to drink to *my* health first."

A wave of good-natured protest rose from the guests, as did shouts of "Sit down, Daddy!" Churchill resisted, then took his seat. After the toasts to the baby, Beaverbrook raised a glass to honor Churchill, calling him "the greatest man in the world."

Again Churchill wept. A call went up for his reply. He stood. As he spoke, his voice shook and tears streamed. "In these days," he said, "I often think of Our Lord." He could say no more. He sat down and looked at no one—the great orator made speechless by the weight of the day.

Cowles found herself deeply moved. "I have never forgotten those simple words and if he enjoyed waging the war let it be remembered that he understood the anguish of it as well."

The next day, apparently in need of a little attention himself, Beaverbrook resigned again.

BEAVERBROOK WROTE THE LETTER on Monday, December 2, from his country home, Cherkley, "where I am alone, and where I have had time to think about the direction which I believe our policy should take." Further dispersal of aircraft factories was vital, he wrote, and required an aggressive new push, though this would certainly mean a temporary decline in production. "This bold policy," he warned, "means much interference with other Ministries, on account of the need for suitable premises already earmarked for other services."

But then he wrote: "I am not now the man for the job. I will not get the necessary support."

Once again he veered toward self-pity, citing how his reputation had diminished as the fighter crisis had begun to ease. "In fact, when the reservoir was empty, I was a genius," he wrote. "Now that the reservoir has some water in it, I am an inspired brigand. If ever the water slops over, I will be a bloody anarchist."

Someone new must now take over, he said; he made a couple of recommendations. He suggested that Churchill explain his resignation to others as having been prompted by ill health, "which I regret to say is more than justified."

As always he ended with flattery, applying what he often called "the oil can." He wrote: "I cannot conclude this very important letter without emphasizing that my success in the past has come from your support. Without that backing, without that inspiration, without that leadership, I could never have accomplished the tasks and duties you set me."

Churchill knew that Beaverbrook's asthma had flared anew. He felt sympathy for his friend, but he was losing patience. "There is no question of my accepting your resignation," he wrote the next day, Tuesday, December 3. "As I told you, you are in the galleys and will have to row on to the end."

He suggested that Beaverbrook take a month to recuperate. "Meanwhile I will certainly support you in carrying out your dispersal policy, which seems imperative under the heavy attacks to which we are subjected," Churchill wrote. He told Beaverbrook that he regretted the return of his asthma, "because it always brings great depression in its train. You know how often you have advised me not to let trifles vex and distract me. Now let me repay the service by begging you to remember only the greatness of the work you have achieved, the vital need of its continuance, and the goodwill of—

"Your old and faithful friend,

"Winston Churchill."

Beaverbrook returned to the galleys, and took up his oar once again.

IN THE MIDST OF it all, everyone got sick. A cold raced through the family. Mary sensed its onset on Monday night, December 2. "Have temperature," she wrote in her diary. "Oh hell."

Churchill caught her cold, or another, on December 9.

Clementine, on December 12.

Bombs fell all the same.

Special Delivery

———

Bᴿɪᴛɪꜱʜ ꜰᴏʀᴄᴇꜱ ᴀᴛ ʟᴀꜱᴛ ᴡᴏɴ ᴀ ᴠɪᴄᴛᴏʀʏ, ᴛʜɪꜱ ᴀɢᴀɪɴꜱᴛ ᴛʜᴇ Italian army in Libya, but merchant ships carrying crucial supplies continued to sink at an alarming rate, British cities to burn. The nation's financial crisis worsened daily, prompting Churchill to compose a long letter to President Roosevelt about the gravity of Britain's position and what it needed from America if it was to prevail. In writing the letter, which totaled fifteen pages, Churchill once again had to find the right balance of confidence and need, as captured in the minutes of a meeting of his War Cabinet: "The Prime Minister said that if the picture was painted too darkly, elements in the United States would say that it was useless to help us, for such help would be wasted and thrown away. If too bright a picture was painted, then there might be a tendency to withhold assistance."

The whole thing, Churchill grumbled, on Friday, December 6, was a "bloody business."

Later, and with good reason, Churchill would call this letter to Roosevelt one of the most important he had ever written.

ᴛʜᴀᴛ ꜱᴀᴛᴜʀᴅᴀʏ, ᴅᴇᴄᴇᴍʙᴇʀ 7, at Chequers, Churchill convened a secret meeting to try to come up with a definitive estimate of German air strength and Germany's capacity for producing more planes in the future. Deeming the matter to be of utmost importance, he invited the Prof, War Cabinet secretary Bridges, and five others, including members of the Ministry of Economic Warfare (MEW) and the intelligence arm of the Air Staff. Churchill did not invite Pug Ismay, however, in order to give him a rest—on Pug's part, a rare absence.

For more than four hours, the group debated available statistics and intelligence, and succeeded only in confirming that no one had a precise sense of how many aircraft the Luftwaffe possessed, let alone how many were available for frontline action and how many more could be manufactured in the coming year. Even more frustrating, no one seemed to know how many aircraft the RAF itself was able to marshal. The two agencies—MEW and air intelligence—came up with different numbers and different approaches to calculating these figures, a confusion compounded by the Prof's sallies into both sets of estimates. Churchill was vexed. "I have not been able to reach a conclusion as to which are right," he wrote in a minute to Air Minister Sinclair and Chief of the Air Staff Portal. "Probably the truth lies mid-way between them. The subject is of capital importance to the whole future picture we make to ourselves of the war."

Most galling was that his own Air Ministry appeared to be unable to account for 3,500 airplanes out of 8,500 frontline and reserve aircraft believed ready, or nearly ready, for service. "Surely there is in the Air Ministry an account kept of what happens to every machine," Churchill complained in a subsequent minute. "These are very expensive articles. We must know the date when each one was received by the RAF and when it was finally struck off, and for what reason." After all, he noted, even automaker Rolls-Royce kept track of each of car it sold. "A discrepancy of 3,500 in 8,500 is glaring."

The summit convinced Churchill that the issue could be resolved only by the intercession of a clear-eyed outsider. He decided to subject the matter to the equivalent of a court trial, complete with a judge, to hear evidence from all parties involved. He selected Sir John Singleton, a justice of the King's Bench Division who was best known for presiding over the 1936 trial of Buck Ruxton in the notorious "Bodies Under the Bridge" case, in which Ruxton was convicted of killing his wife and housemaid and butchering them into more than seventy pieces, most of these later found in a bundle under a bridge. The case was also known as "the Jigsaw Murders," an allusion to the heroic forensic effort to piece together the victims' bodies.

Both sides agreed that recruiting Mr. Justice Singleton was a wise thing to do, and Singleton accepted the task, perhaps allowing himself to imagine that this endeavor would be a lot more straightforward than assembling mutilated corpses.

———

IN LONDON, THE TOLL on lovely things mounted. On the night of Sunday, December 8, a bomb destroyed the cloisters in St. Stephen's Chapel in Westminster Palace, one of Churchill's favorite places. The next day, parliamentary secretary Chips Channon came upon Churchill walking among the ruins.

Churchill had spent the weekend at Chequers but had come back to the city, despite his incipient cold. He wore a coat with a fur collar; a cigar jutted from his mouth. He picked his way through shattered glass and mounds of debris.

"It's horrible," he said mushily, around the cigar.

"They would hit the best bit," Channon said.

Churchill grunted. "Where Cromwell signed King Charles's death warrant."

THAT MONDAY, CHURCHILL'S LONG letter to Roosevelt, sent by cable to Washington, reached the president aboard a U.S. Navy cruiser. The *Tuscaloosa* was in the midst of a ten-day voyage through the Caribbean, ostensibly to visit the British West Indies bases to which the U.S. Navy now had access but mainly as a chance for the president to relax—to rest in the sun, watch movies, and fish. (Ernest Hemingway sent him a message saying that large fish could be found in the waters between Puerto Rico and the Dominican Republic, and recommending that he use pork rind as bait.) Churchill's letter arrived in a navy seaplane, which landed near the ship to deliver the latest White House mail.

"As we reach the end of this year," the letter began, "I feel you will expect me to lay before you the prospects for 1941." Churchill made it clear that where he most needed assistance was in maintaining the flow of food and military supplies to Britain, and emphasized that whether the nation endured or not could also determine the fate of America. He saved the crux of the problem for last: "The moment approaches when we shall no longer be able to pay cash for shipping and other supplies."

In closing he urged Roosevelt to "regard this letter not as an appeal for aid, but as a statement of the minimum action necessary to achieve our common purpose."

Churchill, of course, did want American aid. Masses of it: ships, planes, bullets, machine parts, food. He simply didn't want to have to pay for it and, indeed, was fast running out of the means to do so.

Three days later, on Thursday, December 12, Churchill's ambassador to America, Lord Lothian, abruptly died of uremic poisoning. He was fifty-eight years old. A Christian Scientist, he had been ill for two days but had declined medical aid, which prompted Foreign Secretary Halifax to write, "Another victim for Christian Science. He will be very difficult to replace." Wrote Diana Cooper: "Orangeade and Christian Science quite vanquished him. An untimely end indeed."

Churchill traveled to Chequers that day. Lothian's death cast the house into an intemperate gloom. Only Mary and John Colville joined him for dinner. Clementine, suffering a migraine and a sore throat, skipped the meal and went to bed.

The atmosphere was not helped by a soup course that Churchill found so inadequate that it launched him into the kitchen, in a fury, his brilliantly hued dressing gown flapping over his light blue siren suit. Wrote Mary in her diary, "Papa in very bad mood over food, and of course I couldn't control him & he was very naughty & rushed out & complained to the cook about the soup, which he (truthfully) said was tasteless. I fear the domestic apple-cart may have been upset. Oh dear!"

At length, after listening to her father expound on the poor quality of food at Chequers, Mary left the table; Churchill and Colville remained. Gradually, Churchill's mood improved. Over brandy he savored the recent Libyan victory and talked as if the end of the war were near. Colville went to bed at one-twenty A.M.

EARLIER THAT NIGHT, IN London, Churchill's War Cabinet had met in great secrecy to consider a new tactic in the RAF's strategy for bombing targets in Germany, which Churchill had endorsed as a response to the Luftwaffe's massed attack on Coventry and subsequent intense raids against Birmingham and Bristol. The goal was to deliver the same kind of obliterative assault—a "crash concentration"—against a German city.

The cabinet determined that such an attack would rely mainly on fire and should target a densely built town that had not been previously raided by the RAF, thereby ensuring that its civil defense services would be inexperienced. High-explosive bombs were to be used to produce craters that would hamper the response of fire crews. "Since we aimed at affecting the enemy's morale, we should attempt to destroy the greater part of a particular town," the cabinet minutes said. "The town chosen should therefore not be too large." The cabinet approved the plan, which received the code name "Abigail."

As John Colville noted in his diary the next day, Friday, December 13, "The moral scruples of the Cabinet on this subject have been overcome."

ROOSEVELT HAD RECEIVED CHURCHILL'S letter aboard the *Tuscaloosa*. He read it, but kept his impression of it to himself. Even Harry Hopkins, his friend and confidant, who was traveling with him aboard the *Tuscaloosa,* could not gauge his reaction. (Hopkins, in failing health, caught a twenty-pound grouper but was too weak to reel it in and had to pass his fishing rod to another passenger.) "I didn't know for quite awhile what he was thinking about, if anything," Hopkins said. "But then—I began to get the idea that he was refueling, the way he so often does when he seems to be resting and carefree. So I didn't ask him any questions. Then, one evening, he suddenly came out with it—the whole program."

Directive

———

MASS-OBSERVATION SENT OUT ITS "DECEMBER DIRECTIVE," asking its many diarists to express their feelings about the coming year.

"How do I feel about 1941?" wrote diarist Olivia Cockett. "I stopped typing for two minutes to listen to an extra noisy enemy plane. It dropped a bomb which puffed my curtains in and made the house shiver (I am in bed under the roof) and now the guns are galoomphing at its back. There are craters at the bottom of my garden, and a small unexploded bomb. Four windows are broken. Can see the ruins of 18 houses within five minutes walk. Have two lots of friends staying with us whose homes have been wrecked.

"About 1941, I feel that I shall be damned glad if I'm lucky enough to see it at all—and that I'd rather like to see it." At root she felt "cheerful," she wrote. "But I THINK differently, think we'll be hungrier (haven't been hungry yet), think many of our young men will die abroad."

That Silly Old Dollar Sign

Roosevelt RETURNED TO WASHINGTON ON MONDAY, DECEMber 16, looking "tanned and exuberant and jaunty," according to his speechwriter, Robert E. Sherwood, a playwright and screenwriter. The president convened a press conference the next day, smoking a cigarette as he greeted reporters. Mischievous as always with the press, he told them, "I don't think there is any particular news"—and then proceeded to introduce the idea that had come to him aboard the *Tuscaloosa,* which historians would later judge to be one of the most important developments of the war.

He began, "There is absolutely no doubt in the mind of a very overwhelming number of Americans, that the best immediate defense of the United States is the success of Britain in defending itself.

"Now, what I am trying to do is eliminate the dollar sign. That is something brand new in the thoughts of everybody in this room, I think—get rid of the silly, foolish, old dollar sign.

"Well, let me give you an illustration," he said, and then deployed an analogy that distilled his idea into something both familiar and easy to grasp, something that would resonate with the quotidian experience of countless Americans. "Suppose my neighbor's home catches fire, and I have got a length of garden hose four or five hundred feet away: but, my Heaven, if he can take my garden hose and connect it up with his hydrant, I may help him put out the fire. Now, what do I do? I don't say to him before that operation, 'Neighbor, my garden hose cost me $15; you have got to pay me $15 for it.' What is the transaction that goes on? I don't want $15—I want my garden hose back after the fire is over. All right. If it goes through the fire all right, intact, without any damage to it, he gives it back to me and thanks me very much for the use of it. But suppose it gets smashed up—holes in it—during the fire; we don't have to have too much formality about it, but I say to him, 'I was glad to lend you that hose; I see I can't use it any more, it's all smashed up.'

"He says 'How many feet of it were there?'

"I tell him, 'There were 150 feet of it.'

"He says, 'All right, I will replace it.'"

That became the kernel of an act introduced in Congress soon afterward, numbered H.R. 1776 and titled "A Bill Further to Promote the Defense of the United States, and for Other Purposes," soon to receive its lasting byname, the Lend-Lease Act. Central to the proposal was the idea that it was in the best interests of the United States to provide Britain, or any ally, with all the aid it needed, whether it could pay or not.

The bill immediately met pitched resistance from senators and congressmen who believed it would bring America into the war, or as one opponent vividly predicted—also deploying an analogy that would resonate in America's heartland—that it would result in "ploughing under every fourth American boy." The remark infuriated Roosevelt, who called it "the most untruthful, the most dastardly, unpatriotic thing that has been said in public life in my generation."

That Roosevelt's idea would ever be more than an idea was, by Christmas 1940, anything but certain.

HARRY HOPKINS GREW CURIOUS about Churchill. According to Sherwood, the eloquent power of the prime minister's letter to Roosevelt sparked in Hopkins "a desire to get to know Churchill and to find out how much of him was mere grandiloquence and how much of him was hard fact."

Hopkins soon would get that chance and, in the process, despite his ill health and fragile frame, shape the future course of the war—while spending much of his time freezing to death in bomb-torn London.

A Toad at the Gate

WITH CHURCHILL'S COURTSHIP OF ROOSEVELT IN SO SENSITIVE a phase, choosing an ambassador to replace Lord Lothian became a critical matter. His craftier instincts told him that Lothian's death might in fact offer him an opportunity to strengthen his hold on his own government. Banishing men to far-flung posts was for Churchill a familiar and effective tactic for muting political dissent. Two men stood out as potential sources of future opposition, former prime minister Lloyd George and Churchill's foreign secretary, Lord Halifax, the also-ran for his own job.

That his first choice among the two men was Lloyd George suggests that he saw him as the more immediate and serious threat. Churchill sent Lord Beaverbrook as intermediary to offer him the post. This was awkward for Beaverbrook, because he himself would have liked to be made U.S. ambassador, but Churchill believed he was too valuable an asset, both as minister of aircraft production and as a friend, confidant, and adviser. Lloyd George declined the offer, citing his doctor's concerns about his health. He was, after all, seventy-seven years old.

The next day, Tuesday, December 17, Churchill again summoned Beaverbrook, this time to discuss the possibility of sending Halifax to Washington, and he again dispatched Beaverbrook to make the offer, or at least propose the idea. What Churchill clearly knew from their long friendship was that Beaverbrook had a knack for, and delighted in, making people do what he wanted them to do. Halifax biographer Andrew Roberts called Beaverbrook a "born schemer." Beaverbrook's own biographer, A.J.P. Taylor, wrote, "There was nothing Beaverbrook liked better in politics than moving men about from one office to another or in speculating how to do it."

Offering the job to Halifax required a certain brutality. By any standard, the post was a demotion, no matter how important it was that Britain win America's eventual participation in the war. But Churchill also knew well that if his own government faltered, the king would likely turn to Halifax to replace him, having favored Halifax initially. Which was precisely why Churchill decided that Halifax should go, and why he sent Beaverbrook to propose that he do so.

ON TUESDAY, DECEMBER 17, after doing a broadcast at the BBC, Beaverbrook made his way to the Foreign Office to meet with Halifax, who was immediately on his guard. He knew that Beaverbrook lived for intrigue and that he had been waging a war of whispers against him. Beaverbrook offered him the job on Churchill's behalf. In his diary that Tuesday night, Halifax expressed uncertainty as to whether Churchill really thought he was the best choice or merely wanted to get him out of the Foreign Office, out of London.

Halifax did not want to go, and told Beaverbrook as much, but Beaverbrook reported back to Churchill that Halifax had replied with an unhesitant "yes." Wrote biographer Roberts, "He returned to Churchill with a completely fabricated story about Halifax's reaction to the offer."

Churchill and Halifax met at eleven-forty the next morning on an unrelated matter, during which Halifax explained his reluctance. He did so again the next day, Thursday, December 19. The conversation was a tense one. Halifax tried to persuade Churchill that sending a foreign secretary to Washington as an ambassador might appear to be an act of desperation—of trying too hard to please Roosevelt.

Halifax returned to the Foreign Office feeling that he had succeeded in sidestepping the appointment. He was, however, mistaken.

WITH THE COMING OF WINTER, the immediate threat of invasion diminished, though no one doubted this was only a temporary easement. Now another, more amorphous danger took its place. As the Luftwaffe expanded its attacks and sought to replicate the Coventry raid in attacks on other British cities, the matter of morale rose to the fore. London had thus far proven resilient, but London was an immense city, immune to the Luftwaffe's new obliterative tactics. Would the rest of the country prove as tough if more cities experienced "coventration"?

The attack on Coventry had shaken that city to the core, causing morale to falter. Home Intelligence observed that "the shock effect was greater in Coventry than in the East End [of London] or any other bombed area previously studied." A pair of subsequent raids on Southampton, also intense, likewise shattered the public psyche. The bishop of Winchester, whose diocese included the city, observed that people were "broken in spirit after the sleepless and awful nights. Everyone who can do so is leaving the town." Each night hundreds of residents vacated the city and slept in their cars in open country before returning to work the next day. "For the time," the bishop reported, "morale has collapsed." After a series of raids on Birmingham, the city's American consul wrote to his superiors in London that while he had seen no sign of disloyalty or defeatism among residents, "to say that their mental health is not being undermined by bombing is to talk nonsense."

These new attacks threatened to bring about the wholesale collapse of national morale that defense planners long had feared, and to so intensify public dismay as to threaten Churchill's government.

The arrival of winter made the matter even more acute, for it multiplied the daily hardships imposed by the German air campaign.

Winter brought rain, snow, cold, and wind. Asked by Mass-Observation to keep track of the factors that most depressed them, people replied that weather topped the list. Rain dripped through roofs pierced by shrapnel; wind tore past broken windows. There was no glass to repair them. Frequent interruptions in the supply of electricity, fuel, and water left homes without heat and their residents without a means of getting clean each day. People still had to get to work; their children still needed to go to school. Bombs knocked out telephone service for days on end.

What most disrupted their lives, however, was the blackout. It made everything harder, especially now, in winter, when Britain's northern latitude brought the usual expansion of night. Every December, Mass-Observation also asked its panel of diarists to send in a ranked list of the inconveniences caused by the bombings that most bothered them. The blackout invariably ranked first, with transport second, though these two factors were often linked. Bomb damage turned simple commutes into hours-long ordeals, and forced workers to get up even earlier in the darkness, where they stumbled around by candlelight to prepare for work.

Workers raced home at the end of the day to darken their windows before the designated start of the nightly blackout period, a wholly new
class of chore. It took time: an estimated half hour each evening—more
if you had a lot of windows, and depending on how you went about it.
The blackout made the Christmas season even bleaker. Christmas lights
were banned. Churches with windows that could not easily be darkened
canceled their night services.

The blackout also imposed new dangers. People routinely crashed
into lampposts or rode their bikes into obstacles. Cities used white paint
to try to ameliorate the most obvious problems, applying it to curbs,
steps, and the running boards and bumpers of cars. Trees and lampposts
received rings of white paint. And the police enforced special blackout
speed limits, issuing 5,935 tickets in the course of the year. But people
still drove into walls and tripped over obstacles, and stumbled into one
another. Dr. Jones, the Air Intelligence man who'd discovered Germany's
secret beams, discovered the value of white paint—or, rather, the dangers of its absence. When driving to London one night after giving a
lecture at Bletchley Park, he crashed into a truck left standing in the road.
The rear end had been painted white, but the paint was now obscured by
mud. Jones was driving at only fifteen miles an hour, but he still went
hurtling through the windshield and lacerated his forehead. Authorities in Liverpool implicated the blackout in the deaths of fifteen dock-
workers, who died by drowning.

But the blackout also was a vector for humor. Blackout material used
on train windows became a "scribbling pad," wrote Mass-Observation
diarist Olivia Cockett. She noted how someone had altered the notice
"Blinds must be kept down after dark" to "Blonds must be kept down
after dark," which was subsequently amended to "Knickers must be kept
down after dark." For a degree of relief from the blackout and the other
new burdens of life, Cockett turned to smoking. "One new habit since
the war—enjoying cigarettes," she wrote. "Used to smoke occasionally,
but now three or four a day regularly, and with pleasure! Inhaling makes
the difference, and the nicotine-treat which just detaches one's mind
from one's body for a second or two after each breath."

The greatest threat to morale in London was deemed to arise from
the tens of thousands of citizens bombed out of their homes or otherwise compelled to use public shelters, where the conditions within were
drawing widespread condemnation.

The mounting outcry prompted Clementine Churchill to venture
into the shelters to see them for herself, often accompanied by John

Colville. She began visiting what she believed to be "a fairly representative cross-section" of shelters.

On Thursday, December 19, for example, she toured shelters in Bermondsey, an industrial district that in the preceding century had housed a notorious slum, Jacob's Island, where Charles Dickens, in *Oliver Twist,* had killed off the malignant Bill Sikes. What Clementine found repulsed her. The occupants of shelters spent "perhaps fourteen hours out of the twenty-four in really horrible conditions of cold, wet, dirt, darkness and stench," she wrote in notes to her husband. The worst shelters escaped reform because officials judged them so awful as to be beyond redemption but too necessary to close immediately. As a consequence, Clementine found, they just grew worse.

One object of her ire was the way in which shelters, trying to adapt to night bombing by installing permanent sleeping accommodations, tried to cram as many beds as possible into the allocated space by stacking bunks in threes. "The more one sees of the 3-tier bunks," Clementine wrote, "the worse one feels them to be. They are, of course, much too narrow; an extra 6 inches would have made all the difference between great discomfort and comparative comfort."

The bunks were also too short. Feet touched feet; feet touched heads; heads touched heads. "In the case of heads touching there is great danger of lice spreading," Clementine wrote. And lice posed a serious problem. Although lice were to be expected—"war entails lice," she wrote—their presence raised the potential for outbreaks of typhus and trench fever, both louse-borne diseases. "It seems that if these started they would rage through the poorer population of London like wildfire," she noted. "If there was tremendous mortality among the workers war output would be seriously diminished."

By far the worst trait of the three-tier bunk, as Clementine saw it, was the limited vertical space between tiers. "I wonder people do not die for lack of air," she wrote. "Where mothers have their babies sleeping with them it must be quite intolerable, as the baby has to sleep on top of the mother as the bunk is too narrow for it to sleep by her side." She feared that many more three-tiered bunks had been ordered, and asked Churchill if these orders could be stopped until the bunks were redesigned. As to the bunks already installed, the solution, she argued, was simply to remove the middle tier. Doing so, she noted, would have the "satisfactory effect" of reducing the number of people crowding the worst shelters by one-third.

Her greatest concern was sanitation. She was horrified to find that there were very few toilets in shelters and that, overall, sanitation conditions were abysmal. Her reports reveal not just a willingness to venture into unaccustomed realms but an eye for Dickensian detail. The latrines, she wrote, "are often among the bunks and have skimpy canvas curtains which do not cover the opening. These curtains are often foul at the bottom. The latrines should be <u>away</u> from the bunks and the entrances turned to a wall so as to ensure a little privacy." The worst conditions she encountered were on Philpot Street, at the Whitechapel synagogue, "where people were sleeping absolutely opposite the latrines with their feet almost inside the canvas curtains and where the stench was intolerable."

She recommended that the number of latrines be doubled or tripled. "This is easy," she noted, "as they are mostly buckets." She observed that these were often placed on porous ground, into which waste seeped and accumulated. One solution, she wrote, would be to place these "on big sheets of tin with turned-up edges like trays. These tin trays could be washed." Separate latrines should be installed for children, with shorter buckets, she wrote. "The ordinary buckets are too high for them." And, she found, the buckets received little attention. "The buckets should, of course, be emptied before they are full, but in some places, I am told, this is done only once in twenty-four hours, which is not soon enough."

She was especially appalled to find that latrines were often unlit. "The prevailing darkness merely hides and, of course, encourages the dirty conditions."

The winter rain and cold had made bad conditions worse. In her tours of shelters, she found water "dripping through the roof and seeping through the walls and floors." She reported hearing examples of earthen floors turned to mud, and water accumulating to such a degree that it needed to be removed with pumps.

She isolated another problem: Most shelters had no provision for making tea. "For this purpose," she wrote, "the minimum requirement would be an electric power plug and a boiler."

She told Churchill that she believed the problem with the worst shelters was that responsibility for them was apportioned among too many agencies with overlapping authority, and as a result, nothing was done. "The only way to get the matter straightened out is to have one authority for safety, health, and everything else," she wrote in a brief minute in which she addressed her husband not as Winston but as "Prime Minister." "Division of authority is what is preventing improvement."

Her investigations had an effect. Churchill, aware that how the public felt about shelters would influence how they viewed his government, made shelter reform a priority for the coming year. In a minute to his minister of health and his home secretary, he wrote, "Now is the time to begin a radical improvement in the shelters, so that by next winter there may be more safety, more comfort, warmth, light and amenities for all who use them."

That the shelters would still be needed at the end of 1941 was, to Churchill, a certainty.

ON FRIDAY MORNING, DECEMBER 20, Halifax's undersecretary, Alexander Cadogan, picked him up at the Foreign Office and together they went to Westminster Abbey to attend the memorial service for Lord Lothian. Cadogan noted in his diary that Halifax's wife was already seated, and clearly unhappy. "Furious," he wrote. She vowed to talk to Churchill herself.

After the service, she and her husband set off for No. 10. Barely banking her anger, Dorothy told Churchill that if he sent her husband to America, he would lose a loyal colleague who could marshal strong allies to support him should a political crisis arise. She suspected the hand of Beaverbrook.

Halifax, looking on with bemusement, wrote that Churchill could not have been kinder, but "he and Dorothy were certainly talking a different language." Halifax later wrote to former prime minister Stanley Baldwin, "You can guess how mixed my feelings are. I don't think it is particularly my line of country and I have never liked Americans, except odd ones. In the mass I have always thought them dreadful!"

By Monday, December 23, the deal was done, the assignment announced, Halifax's replacement as foreign secretary chosen. Anthony Eden would succeed him. At a noon cabinet meeting, Churchill spoke of his gratitude to Halifax for taking on so vital a mission. Cadogan was present as well. "I looked up and saw the Beaver opposite me, hugging himself, beaming and almost winking."

The king sought to console Halifax, when Halifax paid him a visit at Windsor Castle on Christmas Eve. "He was very unhappy at the thought of leaving here now, & was perplexed at what might happen if anything happened to Winston," the king wrote in his diary. "The team was not a strong one without a leader, & there were some hot heads among it. I told him he could always be recalled. By way of helping him I suggested that the post of my Ambassador in U.S.A. was more important at this moment than the post of Foreign Secy, here."

This was scant relief for Halifax, who by now understood not only that his removal as foreign secretary was recompense for his being perceived to be a likely successor to Churchill, but also that the engineer behind the plan's execution was indeed—to use his favored nickname for Beaverbrook—"the Toad."

Weihnachten

C HURCHILL'S RESILIENCE CONTINUED TO PERPLEX GERMAN leaders. "When will that creature Churchill finally surrender?" wrote propaganda chief Joseph Goebbels in his diary, after noting the latest Coventry-style attack against Southampton and the sinking of another fifty thousand tons of Allied shipping. "England cannot hold out for ever!" He vowed that air raids would continue "until England falls on her knees and begs for peace."

But England seemed far from doing so. The RAF made a succession of raids against targets in Italy and Germany, among them an attack against Mannheim by more than one hundred bombers that killed thirty-four people and destroyed or damaged some five hundred structures. (This was the Operation Abigail raid in retaliation for Coventry.) The raid itself was not particularly troubling to Goebbels, who called it "easily bearable." What he found disconcerting, however, was the fact that Britain still felt confident enough to conduct the raid at all, and that the RAF was able to muster so many aircraft. Bombers also struck Berlin, prompting Goebbels to write, "It seems that the English have found their touch again."

But now it was more vital than ever that Churchill somehow be made to exit the war. On December 18, Hitler issued Directive No. 21, "Case Barbarossa," his formal order to his generals to begin planning for an invasion of Russia. The directive began: "The German Armed Forces must be prepared, even before the conclusion of the war against England, *to crush Soviet Russia in a rapid campaign.*" The italics were Hitler's. The directive detailed the roles to be played by the German army, air force, and navy—especially the army's armored units—and envisioned the occupation of Leningrad and Kronstadt, as well as, eventually, Moscow. "The bulk of the Russian Army stationed in Western Russia will be destroyed by daring operations led by deeply penetrating armored spearheads."

Hitler directed his commanders to produce plans and timetables. It was crucial that the campaign begin soon. The longer Germany delayed, the more time Russia would have to build up its army and air force, and Britain to recoup its strength. German forces were to be ready by May 15, 1941.

"It is of decisive importance," the directive said, "that our intention to attack should not be known." During these preparations, the Luftwaffe was to continue its attacks against Britain without restraint.

GOEBBELS, MEANWHILE, FRETTED ABOUT moral decay. In addition to guiding Germany's propaganda program, he served as minister of popular culture, and saw it as his mission to vanquish forces that threatened to undermine public morality. "No strip dancers are to perform in rural areas, in small towns, or in front of soldiers," he told the staff at one of his December propaganda meetings. He called on his assistant, Leopold Gutterer, a baby-faced thirty-nine-year-old, to compose a circular addressed to all "compères," masters of ceremonies at cabarets and the like. "The circular is to be in the form of a categorical final warning, forbidding compères to make political wisecracks or to use lewd erotic jokes in their performances."

Goebbels also brooded about Christmas. Germans loved Christmas—Weihnachten—more than any other holiday. They sold Christmas trees on every corner, sang carols, danced, and drank to excess. He warned his lieutenants against the creation of "a sentimental Christmas atmosphere" and condemned the "blubbing and mourning" that Christian holidays induced. It was "unsoldierly and un-German," he said, and must not be allowed to extend through the whole period of Advent. "This must be confined exclusively to Christmas Eve and Christmas Day," he told the group. And even then, he said, Christmas was to be framed in the context of the war. "A sloppy Christmas tree atmosphere lasting several weeks is out of tune with the militant mood of the German people."

At his own home, however, Goebbels found himself increasingly mired, not unhappily, in preparations for the holiday. He and his wife, Magda, had six children, all of whose names began with *H*: Helga, Hildegard, Helmut, Holdine, Hedwig, and Heidrun, the last just a month and a half old. The couple also had an older son, Harald, from Magda's previous marriage. The children were excited, as was Magda, "who thinks about nothing but Christmas," Goebbels wrote.

Diary, December 11: "A lot of work with the Christmas parcels and gifts. I have to distribute them to the 120,000 soldiers and flak gunners in Berlin alone. But I enjoy it. And then the host of personal commitments. These are increasing from year to year."

December 13: "Choose Christmas gifts! Make Christmas arrangements along with Magda. The children are sweet. Unfortunately, one or the other of them is always ill."

On December 22, two RAF air raids drove the family into a shelter until seven A.M. "Not pleasant with all the children, some of whom are still sick," Goebbels wrote. "Only two hours' sleep. I am so tired." Not too tired, however, to muse upon his favorite pastime. "A Jew Law has been passed by the Sobranje [Bulgaria's parliament]," he wrote. "Not a radical measure, but nevertheless something. Our ideas are on the march throughout the whole of Europe, even without compulsion."

The next day, RAF bombers killed forty-five Berliners.

"So considerable losses, after all," Goebbels wrote on Christmas Eve.

He authorized Christmas bonuses for his colleagues. "They must have some sort of compensation for all their work and their ceaseless dedication."

WITH RUSSIA NOW IN Hitler's sights, deputy Rudolf Hess was more anxious than ever to engineer a settlement with Britain and fulfill the "wish" of his *Führer*. He still had not received a response from the Duke of Hamilton, in Scotland, but continued to see the duke as a source of hope.

An idea came to Hess, and now, December 21, his plane stood ready at the Augsburg airfield of the Messerschmitt Works, near Munich, even though more than two feet of snow lay on the ground.

The aircraft was a Messerschmitt Me 110, a twin-engine fighter-bomber modified for long-distance flying. Ordinarily it carried two men, but it could easily be flown solo. Hess was an accomplished pilot; nevertheless, he had needed to learn the peculiarities of the Me 110, and took lessons with an instructor. After proving himself capable, he was given exclusive use of a brand-new model, a privilege accorded him because he was, after all, Hitler's deputy and, depending on perspective, either the second or third most powerful man in the Third Reich. Power had its limits, however: Hess's first choice of aircraft, a single-engine Me 109, was denied. He kept his new plane at the Augsburg airfield and flew it often. No one questioned—at least not openly—why so senior an official would want to do so, nor why he kept requesting additional modifications to the aircraft that would increase its range, nor why he kept asking his secretary to get him the latest aviation weather forecasts for the British Isles.

He acquired a map of Scotland and mounted it on the wall of his bedroom, so that he could memorize prominent elements of the terrain. He delineated a mountainous zone in red.

Now, on December 21, with the runway cleared of snow, Hess took off.

Three hours later, he was back. At some point during the flight, his emergency flare pistol had become entangled in the cables that controlled the plane's vertical stabilizers, the two upright fins at the rear of the fuselage, causing them to jam. That he was able to land at all, and in such snowy conditions, was a testament to his skill as a pilot.

Rumors

———

AS CHRISTMAS NEARED, RUMORS FLOURISHED. AIR RAIDS AND the threat of invasion left fertile ground for the propagation of false tales. To combat them, the Ministry of Information operated an Anti-Lies Bureau, for countering German propaganda, and an Anti-Rumors Bureau, for dealing with rumors of local origin. Some were detected by the Postal Censorship bureau, which read people's mail and listened in on telephone conversations; managers of bookstalls owned by W. H. Smith reported rumors as well. Anyone spreading false stories could be fined or, in egregious cases, imprisoned. The rumors covered a broad range:

—In the Orkney Islands, the Shetlands, Dover, and elsewhere, intercepted letters reported that thousands of bodies had washed ashore after a failed invasion attempt. This rumor was particularly persistent.

—German parachute troops dressed as women were said to have landed in Leicestershire, in the Midlands, and Skegness, on the North Sea coast. This proved not to be true.

—German planes were believed to be dropping poison cobwebs. "This rumor is rapidly dying," Home Intelligence reported.

—A rumor circulating in Wimbledon held "that the enemy is preparing to use a high explosive bomb of terrifying dimensions which is destined to wipe the suburb off the map." Wrote one official, "I am seriously informed that it has taken an unhealthy grip on Wimbledonian imagination." No such bomb existed.

—A particularly gruesome, and common, rumor in circulation during the week before Christmas held "that large numbers of corpses in bombed public shelters are to remain there, the shelters being bricked up to form communal catafalques." This rumor proved stubborn as well, reincarnated afresh after each new air raid.

Christmas

CHRISTMAS WAS ON EVERYONE'S MIND. THE HOLIDAY WAS IM-
portant for morale. Churchill decided that the RAF would not conduct
bombing operations against Germany on Christmas Eve or Christmas
Day, unless the Luftwaffe attacked Britain first. Colville found himself
saddled with addressing "the vexed question," raised in the House of
Commons, of whether the custom of ringing church bells on Christmas
should be suspended, owing to the fact that church bells were the designated warning that invasion was underway. At first Churchill recommended that the bells be rung. He changed his mind after talking with
his Home Forces commander, General Brooke.

Colville by then had prepared what he considered to be a strong argument for ringing the bells, but now he backed off, noting in his diary
that "the thought of the responsibility that would be mine if any disaster
occurred on Christmas Day made me pause."

Colville and his fellow private secretaries, having worked a succession
of two A.M. nights, hoped to have a week off for the holiday. Principal
secretary Eric Seal crafted a delicately phrased minute asking permission.
The request "incensed" Churchill, according to Colville.

Scrooge-like, Churchill scrawled "No" on the document itself. He
told Seal that his own plan for the holiday, which fell on a Wednesday,
was to spend it either at Chequers or in London, working "continuously." He hoped, he wrote, "that the recess may be used not only for
overtaking arrears, but for tackling new problems in greater detail."

He did, however, concede that each member of his staff could have one week off between then and March 31, provided the weeks were "well spread."

On Christmas Eve, in the afternoon, he signed copies of his own books to distribute as gifts to Colville and the other secretaries. He also sent Christmas presents to the king and queen. He gave the king a siren suit like his own, the queen a copy of Henry Watson Fowler's famous 1926 guide to the English language, *A Dictionary of Modern English Usage*.

The private secretaries, meanwhile, scrambled to find something that would make a suitable gift for Churchill's wife. Despite the war and the threat of air raids, London's commercial streets were crowded, even though stores were meagerly stocked. Wrote American observer General Lee in his diary, "There may not be a great deal in the shops and there may be a great many people out of London, but to try to buy anything today was like swimming against Niagara. The streets were packed with traffic, both foot and motor."

The secretaries first considered getting flowers for Clementine, but they found that the flower vendors had only sparse inventory, and nothing suitable. "Apparently," wrote John Martin in his diary, "those bowls of hyacinths that used to appear at Christmas were Dutch"—and Holland was now firmly under German control. Their thoughts turned next to chocolate. Here, too, the big stores had been mostly denuded, "but in the end we found one that could produce a large box." It doubtless helped that the intended recipient was the wife of the prime minister.

Churchill left for Chequers, calling out as he made his exit, "A busy Christmas and a frantic New Year!"

IT WAS OF COURSE on Christmas Eve, with snow falling and the night skies quiet, that Colville first heard a rumor that his beloved Gay Margesson had become engaged to Nicholas "Nicko" Henderson, who, decades later, would become Britain's ambassador to America. Colville pretended not to care. "But it gave me a pang and worries me, even though I am fairly confident Gay will take no sudden leap—she is much too indecisive."

He could not understand why he persisted in loving Gay, with so little likelihood that she would ever return his affections. "So often I despise her for her weakness of character, unobservancy, selfishness and inclination to moral and mental defeatism. Then I tell myself it is all selfishness on my part, that I find faults in her as a cover for her lack of interest in me, that instead of trying to help her—as I should, if I really loved her—I seek relief for my feelings in bitterness or contempt."

He added, "I wish I understood the true state of my feelings."

There was something about Gay that made her different from every other woman he knew. "I sometimes think I should like to marry; but how can I even think of it when the possibility of my marrying Gay, however distant, remains in being? Only time can solve this problem, and patience!"

THAT NIGHT, LATE, LORD Beaverbrook discovered that one of his most valued men was still in his office. The man had been working six or seven days a week, arriving in the morning before sunup, leaving well after nightfall, remaining at his desk even after sirens warned of imminent attack. And here it was Christmas Eve.

At length, the man got up and left his office to go to the washroom before departing for the night.

When the man returned, there was a small package on his desk. He opened it, and found a necklace.

There was also a note from Beaverbrook: "I know what your wife must be feeling. Please give her this with my regards. It belonged to *my* wife." He'd signed it "B."

FOR MARY CHURCHILL, THIS was a Christmas of unexpected and unparalleled joy. The entire family—even Nelson, the cat—gathered at Chequers, most arriving on Christmas Eve. Sarah Churchill's husband, Vic Oliver, whom Churchill disliked, also came. For once there were no official visitors. The house was warmed by holiday decorations: "The great gloomy hall glowed with the lighted, decorated tree," Mary wrote in her diary. Fires burned from every grate. Soldiers patrolled the grounds with rifles and bayonets, breathing steam into the cold night air, and aircraft spotters stood freezing on the roof, but otherwise the war had gone quiet, with Christmas Eve and Christmas Day devoid of air or sea battles.

On Christmas morning Churchill had breakfast in bed, with Nelson lounging on the bedclothes, as he worked through the papers in his regular black box and in his yellow box of secrets, dictating replies and comments to a typist. "The Prime Minister has made a great point of working as usual over the holiday," wrote John Martin, the private secretary on duty at Chequers that weekend, "and yesterday morning was like almost any other here, with the usual letters and telephone calls and of course many Christmas greeting messages thrown in." Churchill gave him a signed copy of his own *Great Contemporaries,* a collection of essays about two dozen famous men, including Hitler, Leon Trotsky, and Franklin Roosevelt, this last entitled "Roosevelt from Afar."

"From lunchtime on less work was done and we had a festive family Christmas," wrote Martin, who was treated as if he were a member of the family. Lunch centered on a ration-times luxury, an immense turkey—"the largest turkey I have ever seen," Martin wrote—sent from the farm of Churchill's late friend Harold Harmsworth. The newspaper magnate had died a month before and among his last wishes had directed the bird's final disposition. Lloyd George sent apples picked from the orchards at his estate, Bron-y-de, in Surrey, where in addition to growing Bramleys and Cox's Orange Pippins he cultivated his long-standing love affair with his personal secretary, Frances Stevenson.

The family listened to the king's "Royal Christmas Message," an annual custom, broadcast over the radio since 1932. The king spoke slowly, clearly fighting the speech impediment that long had harried him—for example, a strangled start to the word "unstinted," followed by its perfect execution—but this added to the gravity of his message. "In the last great war the flower of our youth was destroyed," he said, "and the rest of the people saw but little of the battle. This time we are all in the front lines and in danger together." He predicted victory, and invited his audience to look forward to a time "when Christmas days are happy again."

And now the fun began. Vic Oliver sat down at the piano; Sarah sang. A cheery dinner followed, and after this came more music. Champagne and wine put Churchill in a buoyant mood. "For once the shorthand writer was dismissed," wrote John Martin, "and we had a sort of singsong until after midnight. The PM sang lustily, if not always in tune, and when Vic played Viennese waltzes he danced a remarkably frisky measure of his own in the middle of the room."

All the while, Churchill held forth, expounding on this and that until two in the morning.

"This was one of the happiest Christmases I can remember," Mary wrote in her diary late that night, in the Prison Room. "Despite all the terrible events going on around us. It was not happy in a flamboyant way. But I've never before seen the family look so happy—so united—so sweet. We were complete, Randolph and Vic having arrived this morning. I have never felt the 'Christmas feeling' so strongly. Everyone was kind—lovely—gay. I wonder if we will all be together next Christmas. I pray we may. I pray also next year it may be happier for more people."

The unofficial Christmas truce held. "*Heilige Nacht* in truth *stille Nacht,*" John Martin wrote—holy night, silent night—calling this "a relief and rather touching."

In Germany and Britain, no bombs fell, and families everywhere were reminded of how things once had been, except for the fact that no church bells rang and a great many Christmas tables had empty chairs.

IN LONDON, HAROLD NICOLSON, of the Ministry of Information, spent Christmas Day alone, his wife safely lodged at their country home. "The gloomiest Christmas Day that I have yet spent," he wrote in his diary. "I get up early and have little work to do." He read various memoranda and had lunch by himself, during which he read a book, *The War Speeches of William Pitt the Younger,* published in 1915. Later he met his friend and sometime lover, Raymond Mortimer, at the Ritz Bar, after which the two dined at Prunier, the famed French restaurant. At day's end Nicolson attended a ministry party, which included the showing of a movie. He returned to his Bloomsbury flat through a landscape made desolate by previous bombs and fires and melting snow, the night extraordinarily dark because of the blackout and the absence of moonlight, a new moon due in three days.

"Poor old London is beginning to look very drab," he wrote. "Paris is so young and gay that she could stand a little battering. But London is a char-woman among capitals, and when her teeth begin to fall out she looks ill indeed."

And yet, in places the city still managed to raise a good deal of Christmas cheer. As one diarist noted, "The pubs were all full of happy, drunken people singing 'Tipperary' and the latest Army song which goes 'Cheer up my lads, fuck 'em all.'"

Egglayer

O N FRIDAY, DECEMBER 27, 1940, THE ADMIRALTY CONDUCTED
its first full-scale test of the Prof's aerial mines, a new iteration that involved small bombs carried aloft by balloons. The balloons—nine hundred of them—were readied for launch as German planes approached. Officials gave the signal for their release.

No balloons rose.

The release team did not receive the message to launch for half an hour.

What followed was no more encouraging. "About a third of the nine-hundred-odd balloons inflated proved defective," wrote Basil Collier, the air-war historian; "others exploded early in their flight or descended prematurely in unexpected places."

No bombers appeared; the test was suspended two hours later.

Still Churchill and the Prof were not deterred. They insisted that the mines were not merely viable but crucial to air defense. Churchill ordered more mines produced, more trials conducted. By now, presumably with no intent at humor, the mines program had been assigned the official code name "Egglayer."

Work proceeded, as well, on improving the RAF's ability to locate the Luftwaffe's beams and jam or mask them, but German engineers kept devising new variants and transmission patterns and building more transmitters. German pilots, meanwhile, were growing uneasy about the possibility that the RAF might use the same beams to locate their bombers and set up an aerial ambush.

They gave the RAF too much credit. Despite refinements of air-to-air radar and tactics, Fighter Command was still effectively blind after dark.

Auld Lang Syne

On the night of Sunday, December 29, Roosevelt pressed his case for aid to Britain in a "Fireside Chat," the sixteenth of his presidency. With his reelection achieved, he now felt able to speak more freely about the war than thus far had been the case. He used the word "Nazi" for the first time and described America as the "arsenal of democracy," a phrase suggested by Harry Hopkins.

"No man can tame a tiger into a kitten by stroking it," Roosevelt said. "There can be no appeasement with ruthlessness." If Britain were to be defeated, the "unholy alliance" of Germany, Italy, and Japan—the Axis—would prevail, and "all of us, in all the Americas, would be living at the point of a gun"— "a Nazi gun," he specified later in the speech.

Hopkins had also urged him to leaven his talk with something optimistic. Roosevelt settled on this: "I believe that the Axis powers are not going to win this war. I base that belief on the latest and best information."

As it happened, that "latest and best information" was merely his own instinct that his lend-lease plan not only would pass in Congress but also would change the balance of the war in Britain's favor. Speechwriter Robert Sherwood called it Roosevelt's "own, private confidence that Lend Lease would go through and his certainty that this measure would make Axis victory impossible."

Millions of Americans heard the broadcast, and so did millions of Britons—at three-thirty in the morning. In London, however, there was a good deal of distraction. That night, possibly in hopes of blunting the power of Roosevelt's planned Fireside Chat, the Luftwaffe launched one of its biggest raids thus far. The raid targeted London's financial district, known as the City. Whether the intent truly was to counter Roosevelt's broadcast is unclear, but other elements of its timing were deliberate. The bombers came on a Sunday night, during Christmas week, when all City offices, shops, and pubs would be closed, thus ensuring that few people would be around to spot and extinguish falling incendiaries. The Thames was at low tide, thereby limiting the supply of water to fight fires. It was also a night with no moon—the astronomical new moon had occurred the night before—all but guaranteeing little or no resistance from the RAF. The Luftwaffe's fire-starter group, KGr 100, guided precisely by radio beacons, dropped incendiaries to light the target, and high-explosive bombs to destroy water mains and expose more fuel to the resulting fires. A brisk wind intensified the conflagration, producing what became known as "the Second Great Fire of London," the first having occurred in 1666.

The raid caused fifteen hundred fires and destroyed 90 percent of the City. Two dozen incendiaries landed on St. Paul's Cathedral. With its dome at first obscured by smoke from the surrounding fires, the cathedral was feared lost. It survived with relatively little damage. The raid was otherwise so effective that RAF planners adopted the same tactics for future fire raids against German cities.

IN BERLIN, JOSEPH GOEBBELS, writing in his diary, gloated over the attack, but first he addressed Roosevelt's Fireside Chat. "Roosevelt," he wrote, "makes a scurrilous speech aimed against us, in which he slanders the Reich and the Movement in the most boorish fashion and calls for the most extensive support for England, in whose victory he firmly believes. A model of democratic distortion. The *Führer* still has to decide what to do about it. I would be in favor of a really tough campaign, of finally pulling no punches towards the USA. We are not getting far at present. One must defend oneself sometime, after all."

With evident satisfaction, he turned next to the Luftwaffe and its recent successes. "London trembles under our blows," he wrote. The American press, he contended, was stunned and impressed. "If only we could keep up bombing on this scale for four weeks running," he wrote. "Then things would look different. Apart from this, there are heavy shipping losses, successful attacks on convoys, and so on. London has nothing to smile about at the moment, that is for sure."

ON THAT SCORE, CHURCHILL begged to differ. The timing of the "Great Fire" raid, in terms of sparking American sympathy, was perfect, as Alexander Cadogan observed in his diary: "This may help us enormously in America at a most critical moment. Thank God—for all their cunning and industry and efficiency—the Germans are fools."

Death and damage aside, Churchill was thrilled with Roosevelt's Fireside Chat. On New Year's Eve he met with Beaverbrook and his new foreign secretary, Anthony Eden, to craft a response. Churchill's senior-most finance minister, Kingsley Wood, chancellor of the exchequer, was also present.

The cable began, "We are deeply grateful for all you said yesterday."

But Churchill, as much as any man alive, understood that at this point Roosevelt's speech was just a collection of well-chosen words. It raised many questions. "Remember, Mr. President," he dictated, "we do not know what you have in mind, or exactly what the United States is going to do, and we are fighting for our lives."

He warned of the financial pressures bearing down on Britain, with many supplies on order as yet unpaid for. "What would be the effect upon the world situation if we had to default in payments to your contractors, who have their workmen to pay? Would not this be exploited by the enemy as a complete breakdown in Anglo-American co-operation? Yet, a few weeks' delay might well bring this upon us."

IN THE BACK OF her diary, on blank pages allocated for notes and addenda to earlier entries, Mary quoted books, songs, and her father's speeches, and wrote out snippets of doggerel. She kept a list of the dozens of books she had read in 1940, which included Hemingway's *A Farewell to Arms,* du Maurier's *Rebecca,* and Dickens's *The Old Curiosity Shop,* which she started but did not finish. "Just couldn't take that ruddy little Nell & her old grandpop," she wrote. She also read Aldous Huxley's *Brave New World,* noting, "I thought it sounded bloody."

She wrote out the lyrics of a song, "A Nightingale Sang in Berkeley Square," the lovers' anthem of the day, recorded most recently—on December 20, 1940—by the American singer Bing Crosby. One portion, as Mary remembered it:

The moon was shining up above,
Poor puzzled moon he wore a frown!

How could he know we were so in love
That the whole darned world seemed upside down?

IN BERLIN, JOSEPH GOEBBELS worked a full day, then drove to his country home on the Bogensee, a lake north of the city, through "a savage snowstorm." The snow, the snugness of the house—despite its seventy rooms—and the fact it was New Year's Eve (in Germany, *Silvester*) put him in a reflective mood.

"Sometimes I hate the big city," he wrote in his diary that night. "How beautiful and cozy it is out here.

"Sometimes I would like to never have to go back.

"The children are waiting for us at the door with hurricane lanterns.

"The snowstorm rages outside.

"All the better to chat by the fireside.

"It troubles my conscience that we have things so good out here."

IN THE CABINET WAR ROOMS, in London, John Colville handed a glass of champagne to his fellow private secretary John Martin, this after both had consumed multiple brandies served by Pug Ismay. They climbed to the roof, the night black and nearly moonless, and toasted the New Year.

AS OF MIDNIGHT, GERMAN RAIDS over London alone in 1940 had killed 13,596 citizens, and caused serious injury to another 18,378. And more was yet to come, including the single worst raid of all.

1941

Part Five

—

THE
AMERICANS

January – March

Secrets

———

THE FIRST SIX DAYS OF JANUARY WERE COLD IN A WAY THAT WAS atypical for the British Isles. At West Linton, near Edinburgh, temperatures stayed below freezing from January first through the sixth. Temperatures tumbled to six degrees below zero Fahrenheit in the English hamlet of Houghall. Snow fell at intervals throughout the month, with accumulations of fifteen inches in Birmingham and drifts near Liverpool up to ten feet deep. Powerful gales scoured the countryside, bringing winds that gusted to over seventy miles an hour; one gust tore through the port of Holyhead at eighty-two.

In London, the wind and cold made for icy streets, and produced miserable conditions for the many Londoners whose homes had been perforated by shrapnel and lacked heat and window glass. Even Claridge's was uncomfortable, its heating system unable to cope with such depths of cold. One guest, General Lee, the American military attaché, reported on January 4 that his rooms "are like an icebox," though a coal fire eventually provided warmth.

Snow fell on the night of January 6, obscuring for a time the jagged remains of obliterated homes, and turning London beautiful. "What a nice wintry morning this was!" General Lee wrote in his journal the next day. "When I arose and looked out of my window, which is up pretty high, I could see all the streets and roofs covered with clean white snow." The view over London evoked for him a Christmas card depicting a snow-covered city in Central Europe, "with its chimney pots and angles picked out in black against the white snow coverlet and the gray sky above."

———

BEAVERBROOK RESIGNED AGAIN, ONE of a number of vexations that inaugurated the New Year for Churchill. This resignation came after he asked Beaverbrook to take on an additional job that he deemed crucial to Britain's survival.

One of Churchill's top priorities was to increase imports of food, steel, and myriad other civilian and material supplies, whose delivery, owing to Germany's intensified U-boat attacks, was more endangered than ever. To better direct, coordinate, and increase the flow of materials, Churchill established an "Import Executive," and decided the best man to run it was Beaverbrook, who had so radically increased the production of fighters for the RAF. On January 2, he offered Beaverbrook the chairmanship with the idea that Beaverbrook would continue as minister of aircraft production but would expand his portfolio to oversee the government's three supply ministries. His hope was that here, too, Beaverbrook would serve as a catalytic force, to prod them into producing a greater flow of goods and materials. The post would give Beaverbrook greater power, which he had long claimed to want, but it would also put him in the position of being, essentially, a committee chairman, and Beaverbrook, as Churchill well knew, loathed committees.

Sensing that Beaverbrook might resist the idea, Churchill imbued his pitch with flattery and an uncharacteristic woe-is-me needfulness.

"Nothing can exceed the importance of the tasks you are about to assume," Churchill began, in the apparent presumption that Beaverbrook would of course take the job. "I want to point out to you that I am placing my entire confidence and to a large extent the life of the State, upon your shoulders."

If Beaverbrook chose not to take the job, Churchill wrote, he himself would have to do it. "This would not be the best arrangement, as it is bound to distract my thought from the military side of our affairs," he wrote. "I mention this to you because I know how earnestly you wish to help me, and there is no way in which you can help me so much as in making a happy solution of our Import, Shipping and Transport problems."

Beaverbrook was unmoved. Professing deep regret, he rejected the chairmanship and made it clear that his resignation also applied to the Ministry of Aircraft Production. "I am not a committee man," he wrote on January 3. "I am the cat that walks alone."

He offered his own sad-sack closing: "This letter does not need any answer. I will find my own way about."

Churchill took Beaverbrook's resignation as a slight against both himself and Britain. For Beaverbrook to leave now would be a betrayal. His energy and rapacious ingenuity had driven aircraft production to levels that seemed nearly miraculous, and were crucial in helping the country to withstand Germany's aerial onslaught and Churchill to maintain his own confidence in ultimate victory. Moreover, Churchill needed him personally: his knowledge of political undercurrents, his counsel, and just generally his presence, which enlivened the day.

"My dear Max," Churchill dictated on January 3. "I am very sorry to receive your letter. Your resignation would be quite unjustified and would be regarded as desertion. It would in one day destroy all the reputation that you have gained and turn the gratitude and goodwill of millions of people to anger. It is a step you would regret all your life."

Again Churchill struck a note of self-pity: "No Minister has ever received the support which I have given you, and you know well the burden which will be added to my others by your refusal to undertake the great commission with which I sought to entrust you."

He awaited Beaverbrook's reply.

CHURCHILL HAD FURTHER CAUSE for annoyance. He had learned of two lapses in secrecy, and these troubled him. In one case, an American correspondent telegraphed secret information about the Vichy government to her newspaper, the *Chicago Daily News*. What made this especially galling for Churchill was that the reporter, Helen Kirkpatrick, had gleaned the information from a conversation during one of his own dinner parties at Ditchley, his full-moon retreat, where the unwritten law against divulging country house confidences held sway. The secret—that the Vichy government would not provide direct military assistance to Germany—was divulged over dinner by a French pianist, Ève Curie, daughter of the famous physicist.

"Mademoiselle Curie, who is a woman of distinction, should have had the good sense not to gossip about it at a country house party," Churchill wrote to Anthony Eden, now his foreign secretary. "Miss Helen Kirkpatrick has betrayed the confidence for journalistic profit. Both these women should be questioned by MI5 at the earliest moment, and their explanations obtained." He told Eden that Kirkpatrick should be ejected from the country immediately. "It is very undesirable to have a person of this kind scouting about private houses for copy regardless of British interests."

This, and a second incident involving the publication of secret aircraft details in an American aviation magazine, prompted Churchill to send a directive to Pug Ismay, as well as others, on the subject of secrecy in general. "With the beginning of the New Year, a new intense drive must be made to secure greater secrecy in all matters relating to the conduct of the war," he wrote. He ordered tighter limits on the circulation of secret materials and on what kind of information was made available to reporters. "We are having trouble through the activities of foreign correspondents of both sexes," he wrote. "It must be remembered that everything said to America is instantly communicated to Germany and that we have no redress."

Churchill's ire about secrecy caused John Colville anxiety about his own diary, which, filled as it was with operational secrets and insights into Churchill's behavior, would have been a prize for any German agent who happened across it. Colville well understood that the act of keeping so precise a record was very likely illegal. "The P.M. has circulated a minute about preserving the secrecy of documents which suddenly makes me feel rather conscience-stricken about this diary," he wrote in it on New Year's Day. "I haven't the heart to destroy it and shall compromise by keeping it locked up here, even more strictly than hitherto."

As that first day of 1941 began to wane, Churchill invited Colville on a tour of the construction underway to bombproof the ceiling of the Cabinet War Rooms. So anxious was Churchill to get up among the girders and falsework that he decided to set off with only the flashlight in the top of his walking stick to guide them and, Colville wrote, promptly "sank up to his ankles in thick liquid cement."

MOST ANNOYING OF ALL, apart from falling bombs and torpedoed ships, was a preliminary report Churchill received from Mr. Justice Singleton on his inquiry into the comparative strengths of the RAF and the Luftwaffe. Churchill had hoped it would resolve the issue and end the bickering and sniping among the various parties involved.

It did not.

Singleton wrote that in the course of his investigation he had spent five days hearing evidence about numbers of fighters, bombers, aircraft "wastage," reserves, and planes used as trainers. The document he submitted on that Friday, January 3, was merely an interim report—interim because he, too, was flummoxed. "At one time," he wrote in his opening paragraph, "I hoped that some measure of agreement might be reached but it now seems unlikely that there will be agreement on the main factors."

He accepted the Prof's reasoning, put forth the previous spring, that the German experience of aerial warfare—losses, reserves, rates of new production—could not be all that different from the British experience, and that therefore it was crucial first to know exactly what the British experience was. But precise numbers were elusive. Even after his painstaking analysis, more than three thousand RAF planes remained unaccounted for. Singleton was unable to provide an accurate portrait of the British air force, let alone the German; nor was he able to bring into agreement the figures put forth by various ministries. "I feel it will be extraordinarily difficult to arrive at any figure of German strength," he wrote. "I can say no more at this stage than that I do not think it is as high as claimed by Air Staff (Intelligence)."

Churchill found this deeply unsatisfying and exasperating, especially the failure of the Air Ministry to keep accurate records of its own aircraft. Singleton continued his investigation, as yet more conflicting numbers came into his possession.

BEAVERBROOK STOOD FAST. With a schoolboy's petulance, he told Churchill on Monday, January 6, that he had never wanted to be a minister in the first place. "I did not want to join the Government," he wrote. "The place in the Cabinet was undesired and was, indeed, resisted by me." He reiterated his rejection of the new chairmanship and his resignation as minister of aircraft production. "It is because my usefulness has come to an end. I have done my job." The ministry, he wrote, "is better off without me." He thanked Churchill for his support and friendship and closed the letter with a metaphoric hanky in hand. "On personal grounds," he wrote, "I hope you will permit me to see you sometimes and to talk with you occasionally on the old terms."

This was too much. "I have not the slightest intention of letting you go," Churchill wrote in reply. "I sh'd feel myself struck a most cruel blow if you were to persist in so morbid & unworthy an intention." In places, Churchill's letter read more like the missive of a forsaken lover than a prime ministerial communication. "You have no right in the height of a war like this to put yr burdens on me," he wrote. ". . . No one knows better than you how much I depend on you for counsel & comfort. I cannot believe that you will do such a thing." He suggested that *if* Beaverbrook's health required it, he should take a few weeks to recuperate. "But abandon the ship now—never!"

At midnight, Churchill again wrote to Beaverbrook, this time in longhand and summoning the judgment of history: "You must not forget in the face of petty vexations the vast scale of events and the brightly-lighted stage of history upon which we stand." He closed by quoting a remark that Georges Danton, a leader of the French Revolution, made to himself just before being guillotined in 1794: "'Danton no weakness.'"

This skirmish with Beaverbrook was mostly stage combat. Having been friends for so long, they knew well how to jolt each other's composure, and when to stop. This was one reason Churchill liked having Beaverbrook in his government and found such value in his near-daily presence. Beaverbrook was never predictable. Exasperating, yes, but always a source of energy and cold-eyed clarity, with a mind like an electric storm. Both men took a certain delight in dictating letters to each other. To both it was like acting—Churchill strutting about in his gold-dragon nightclothes and jabbing the air with a dead cigar, savoring the sound and feel of words; Beaverbrook like a knife thrower at a carnival, hurling whatever cutlery came to hand. The physical character of the resulting letters revealed the men's contrapuntal natures. Where Churchill's paragraphs were long and precisely worded, full of complex grammatical structures and historical allusions (in one note to Beaverbrook he used the word "ichthyosaurus"), each of Beaverbrook's paragraphs was a single, brief knife thrust serrated with short, crisp words, not so much savored as sputtered.

"The truth is that they both enjoyed it, and of course neither found the writing, or usually the dictating, of letters laborious," wrote A.J.P. Taylor, Beaverbrook's biographer. "Beaverbrook liked parading his troubles and liked still more winding up with a display of emotional attachment which for the moment, while he was dictating the letter, he really felt."

THAT FIRST WEEK OF 1941 ended on a more positive note, with Churchill, at two A.M. on Tuesday, January 7, climbing into bed in good spirits. More good news had come from Libya, where British forces were continuing to batter the Italian army. And Roosevelt, on Monday evening—early Tuesday in Britain—gave his State of the Union Address, in which he presented his lend-lease plan to Congress, declaring that "the future and the safety of our country and of our democracy are overwhelmingly involved in events far beyond our borders." He described a world to come that would be founded upon "four essential human freedoms": speech, worship, and freedom from want and fear.

Churchill recognized that a long fight lay ahead to secure passage of the Lend-Lease Bill, but he was heartened by Roosevelt's clear and public declaration of sympathy for Britain. Even better, Roosevelt had decided to send a personal emissary to London, who was due to arrive in a few days. At first, the man's name drew a blank: Harry Hopkins. On hearing it, Churchill asked pointedly, "*Who*?"

Now, however, he understood that Hopkins was so close a confidant of the president that he lived in the White House, in a second-floor suite that had once served as Abraham Lincoln's office, just down the corridor from the president's own quarters. Churchill's aide Brendan Bracken called Hopkins "the most important American visitor to this country we have ever had" and deemed him capable of influencing Roosevelt "more than any living man."

When Churchill did at last go to bed that night, it was with a great deal of satisfaction and optimism. He was smiling "as he snuggled beneath the bed clothes," Colville wrote in his diary, and "had the grace for once to apologize for keeping me up so late."

FOR PAMELA CHURCHILL, the year began on a bittersweet note. She missed Randolph. "Oh! I wish you were here to cuddle me," she told him in a letter on New Year's Day. "I would be so happy then. I get panicky here alone & think if you are away long enough you will forget me, & I can't bear it. Please try not to forget me Randy."

She told him as well that a special gas mask had arrived for baby Winston. "He goes into it entirely," she said, adding that she planned, soon, to attend a lecture on poison gas to be given at the local hospital.

BEAVERBROOK STAYED ON AS minister of aircraft production, but he did not become chairman of the Import Executive. Neither did Churchill, despite his threat to martyr himself by doing so.

The Eleven-thirty Special

T HE MAN WHO WALKED INTO 10 DOWNING STREET ON THE MORNING of Friday, January 10, appeared to be unwell. His complexion was sallow, his overall aspect one of fragility and wear, the effect amplified by a very large overcoat. Pamela Churchill noticed that he seemed never to take the coat off. She was shocked by his appearance at their first meeting, her impression of ill health reinforced by the crumpled, unlit cigarette he held in his mouth. The day before, upon arriving at the seaplane port at Poole, a hundred or so miles from London, he had been so exhausted that he had been unable to remove his seatbelt. "He was as unlike one's picture of a distinguished envoy as it was possible to be," wrote Pug Ismay. "He was deplorably untidy; his clothes looked as though he was in the habit of sleeping in them, and his hat as though he made a point of sitting on it. He seemed so ill and frail that a puff of wind would blow him away."

Yet this was Harry Hopkins, the man Churchill would later describe as playing a decisive part in the war. Hopkins was fifty years old, and now served as Roosevelt's personal adviser. Before this point, he had led three major programs of Roosevelt's Depression-era New Deal, including the Works Progress Administration, or WPA, which put millions of unemployed Americans to work. Roosevelt named him secretary of commerce in 1938, a post he held well into 1940 despite declining health. Surgery for stomach cancer had left him plagued by a mysterious suite of ailments that in September 1939 led his doctors to give him only a few weeks to live. He rallied, and on May 10, 1940, the day Churchill became prime minister, Roosevelt invited him to stay at the White House. The arrangement became permanent. "His was a soul that flamed out of a frail and failing body," Churchill wrote. "He was a crumbling lighthouse from which there shone the beams that led great fleets to harbor."

All this flaming and beaming would come later, however. First, before meeting Churchill, Hopkins got a tour of 10 Downing Street, with Brendan Bracken as his guide. The famed prime ministerial residence was so much smaller and less imposing than the White House, and seemed much the worse for wear. "Number 10 Downing is a bit down at the heels because the Treasury next door has been bombed more than a bit," Hopkins wrote in a message to Roosevelt later that day. Bomb damage marked every floor. Most of the windows had been blown out, and workers were busy throughout making repairs. Bracken led Hopkins downstairs to the new armored dining room in the basement and poured him a glass of sherry.

At length, Churchill arrived.

"A rotund—smiling—red-faced gentleman appeared—extended a fat but none the less convincing hand and wished me welcome to England," Hopkins told Roosevelt. "A short black coat—striped trousers—a clear eye and a mushy voice was the impression of Britain's leader as he showed me with obvious pride the photographs of his beautiful daughter-in-law and grandchild." This last was a reference to Pamela and young Winston. "The lunch was simple but good—served by a very plain woman who seemed to be an old family servant. Soup—cold beef—(I didn't take enough jelly to suit the PM and he gave me some more)—green salad—cheese and coffee—a light wine and port. He took snuff from a little silver box—he liked it."

Right off, Hopkins addressed a matter that had pinched relations between America and Britain. "I told him there was a feeling in some quarters that he, Churchill, did not like America, Americans or Roosevelt," Hopkins recalled. Churchill denied it, emphatically, and blamed Joseph Kennedy for promulgating so incorrect an impression. He directed a secretary to retrieve the telegram he had sent to Roosevelt the previous fall, in which he congratulated the president on his reelection—the one Roosevelt had never answered or acknowledged.

This initial awkwardness was quickly eclipsed, as Hopkins explained that his mission was to learn all he could about Britain's situation and needs. The conversation ranged wide, from poison gas, to Greece, to North Africa. John Colville noted in his diary that Churchill and Hopkins "were so impressed with each other that their tête-à-tête did not break up till nearly 4:00."

It was getting dark. Hopkins left for his hotel, Claridge's. With the moon nearly full, Churchill and his usual weekend entourage set off for Ditchley, where Hopkins was to join them the next day, Saturday, to dine and sleep.

COLVILLE AND BRACKEN DROVE to Ditchley together, and discussed Hopkins. It was Bracken who had first realized how important Hopkins was to Roosevelt.

As they drove and chatted, visibility diminished. Even on clear nights, driving was difficult because of the blackout, with headlamps reduced to slits of light, but now "an icy mist descended," Colville wrote, "and we collided with a fish-and-chips wagon which burst into flames. Nobody was hurt and we arrived safely at Ditchley."

It was a fitting punctuation point for a day of heartbreak for Colville. While Churchill had been having lunch with Hopkins, Colville had been dining with his beloved Gay Margesson, at the Carlton Grill, in London. By coincidence, this was the two-year anniversary of his first proposal to marry her. "I tried to be reasonably aloof and not too personal," he wrote, but the conversation soon veered into philosophical approaches to leading one's life and, thus, into more intimate realms. She looked lovely. Sophisticated. She wore a silver fox; her hair hung below her shoulders. She wore too much rouge, however, Colville noted with satisfaction— his accustomed means of easing the pain of her unattainability by noting her imperfections. "Certainly she was not the Gay of Jan. 10, 1939," he wrote, "and I do not think the influence of Oxford has improved her."

After lunch they went to the National Gallery, where they met Elizabeth Montagu—Betts—and Nicholas "Nicko" Henderson, the man rumored to have captured Gay's heart. Colville sensed a strong connection between Nicko and Gay, and this raised in him a "queer nostalgia," which he likened to jealousy.

"I went back to No. 10 and tried to think how immaterial it all was in comparison with the great issues that I see daily there, but it was no good: love dies slowly with me, if at all, and I felt sick at heart."

MARY CHURCHILL DID NOT join the family at Ditchley; she planned instead to spend the weekend with a friend, Elizabeth Wyndham, the adopted daughter of Lord and Lady Leconfield, at Petworth House, their Baroque country home in the South Downs region of West Sussex, southwest of London. A mere fourteen miles from the channel coast, this was invasion country. Mary planned to take a train to London first, do a little shopping with her former nanny, Maryott Whyte, then catch a second train to the southwest. "Looking forward to it so much," she wrote in her diary.

At Chequers the Prison Room was cold, the day outside laced with ice and very dark. Winter mornings always were dark at this latitude, but a change in how Britain kept time during the war made the mornings darker than ever. The previous fall the government had invoked "double British summer time" to save fuel and give people more time to get to their homes before the blackout began each day. The clocks had *not* been turned back in the fall, as per custom, and yet would still be turned forward again in the spring. This created two extra hours of usable daylight during the summer, rather than just one, but also ensured that winter mornings would be long, black, and depressing, a condition that drew frequent complaints in civilian diaries. Wrote Clara Milburn, the diarist from Balsall Common, near Coventry, "It is so dreadfully dark in the mornings that it seems hopeless to get up early and barge about unable to see to do anything properly."

Snug in the dark and cold, Mary overslept. She had expected someone to wake her, but no one had. She felt poorly. The roads were pale with ice; bomb damage along the regular route required a time-consuming detour. She reached the station just in time for her train.

This was her first visit to London since August, and she arrived "feeling strange—country-cousinish & very flustered," she wrote.

In the intervening months, the city had been transmogrified through the dark magic of bombs and fire but was still familiar to her. "And as I drove through the well remembered streets—and saw the scars & wounds—I felt I loved London very deeply. Shorn of her smartness—in war time attire—I suddenly loved her very much."

It evoked for her Proustian memories of how the city had moved her in the past: a bicycle ride on a hot summer afternoon through Hyde Park, when she paused on a bridge and watched people in the boats below; a view of the rooftops of Whitehall, "rising above the trees in the evening sun like distant domes of a magic city"; and a moment when she admired "the perfect beauty" of a tree beside the lake in St. James's Park.

She made a brief stop at the No. 10 Annexe, Churchill's new flat above the Cabinet War Rooms, where she marveled at how homey her mother had made the place, waving her "magic wand," as Mary put it, over rooms that previously had been mundane offices. Clementine had the walls painted in pale hues and filled the rooms with well-lit paintings and the family's own furniture. The flat straddled a passage that ran between government offices, and here, Mary wrote in a memoir, "embarrassed officials would often encounter Winston, robed like a Roman emperor in his bath towel, proceeding dripping from his bathroom across the main highway to his bedroom."

Mary reached Petworth early that afternoon and found a large party underway, with many young friends and strangers on the scene, both male and female. She judged her friend Elizabeth now to be "silly & affected," adding, "I don't really like her." She was delighted, however, with Elizabeth's mother, Violet, who was renowned for leading the charge into new kingdoms of fashion. "Violette [sic] was in excellent form dressed in a pale blue V-necked jumper—loaded with jewelry & wearing scarlet corduroy slacks!!"

Many of the guests left to see a movie, but Mary, still under the weather, decided to sequester herself in her assigned room. Later, rejuvenated by tea, she dressed for the night's ball. "I wore my new cherry red with the silver-embroidered belt & diamond (paste!) earrings."

First came a dinner party, then the dance, which she deemed heavenly: "Positively pre-war."

She danced with a Frenchman, Jean Pierre Montaigne. "I felt incredibly gay—I waltzed with Jean Pierre incovertly, wildly & very fast—great fun. I missed only a few dances."

She got to bed at four-thirty A.M., "footsore & weary but very happy." And quite ill.

AT DITCHLEY ON SATURDAY, the Churchills and the estate's owners, Ronald and Nancy Tree, prepared a gleaming evening for their guest of honor, the American emissary Harry Hopkins. Assorted other guests arrived, among them Oliver Lyttelton, president of the Board of Trade.

"Dinner at Ditchley takes place in a magnificent setting," John Colville wrote in his diary that Saturday night. The only illumination was candlelight, with candles mounted on the walls and in a large chandelier overhead. "The table is not over-decorated: four gilt candle sticks with tall yellow tapers and a single gilt cup in the center." Dinner itself was lavish, the food "in keeping with the surroundings," Colville judged, though he guessed that the meal was less elaborate than would have been the case before a recent campaign against "over-feeding" by the Ministry of Food.

After dinner, Nancy and Clementine and the other female guests left the dining room. Over cigars and brandy, Hopkins unveiled a capacity for charm that belied his death's-door appearance. He praised Churchill for his speeches and said they played very well in America. At one cabinet meeting, he said, Roosevelt had even directed that a radio be brought into the room so that everyone could hear an example of his fine rhetoric. "The P.M.," Colville wrote, "was touched and gratified."

Thus inspired, and warmed by the brandy, Churchill unfurled his sails and embarked on a monologue in which he recounted the life-and-death saga of the war as it had unfolded thus far, as candlelight glinted in the brandy-moist eyes of his guests. At length, he turned to the matter of Britain's war aims and the world of the future. He presented his vision of a United States of Europe, with Britain as its architect. He might have been speaking before the House of Commons, rather than to a small group of men fogged by cigars and alcohol in a quiet country house. "We seek no treasure," Churchill said, "we seek no territorial gains, we seek only the right of man to be free; we seek his right to worship his God, to lead his life in his own way, secure from persecution. As the humble laborer returns from his work when the day is done, and sees the smoke curling upwards from his cottage home in the serene evening sky, we wish him to know that no rat-a-tat-tat"—here Churchill knocked loudly on the table—"of the secret police upon his door will disturb his leisure or interrupt his rest." He said Britain sought only government by popular consent, freedom to say whatever one wished, and the equality of all people in the eyes of the law. "But war aims other than these we have none."

Churchill stopped. He looked at Hopkins. "What will the president say to all this?"

Hopkins paused before answering. Shards of twisty candlelight sparked off the crystal and silver. His silence lasted so long as to become uncomfortable—nearly a minute, which in that intimate context seemed a very long time. Clocks ticked; a fire hissed and seethed in the hearth; the candle flames did their quiet Levantine dance.

At last Hopkins spoke.

"Well, Mr. Prime Minister," he began, in an exaggerated American drawl. "I don't think the President will give a dam' for all that."

Privy councillor Oliver Lyttelton felt a jolt of anxiety, as he noted in his diary. Had Churchill miscalculated? "Heavens alive," he thought, "it's gone wrong . . ."

Hopkins let his second pause linger.

"You see," he drawled, "we're only interested in seeing that that God-dam sonofabitch Hitler gets licked."

Loud laughter amplified by relief convulsed the table.

MRS. TREE ENTERED AND GENTLY but resolutely directed Churchill and the rest of the group toward the Ditchley home cinema, for a movie—a film released the prior year called *Brigham Young,* in which Dean Jagger played the Mormon leader, and Tyrone Power one of his followers. (The film's premiere in Salt Lake City had caused a sensation, drawing 215,000 people at a time when the city's population totaled 150,000.) Next came German newsreels, including one that featured the March 18, 1940, meeting between Hitler and Mussolini at the Brenner Pass, in the Alps between Austria and Italy, "which with all its salutes and its absurdity," Colville wrote, "was funnier than anything Charlie Chaplin produced in *The Great Dictator.*"

Churchill and his guests retired at two A.M.

THAT NIGHT IN LONDON, during an intense German air raid, a bomb struck the Bank Underground station, killing fifty-six of the people sheltering within, throwing some in front of an approaching train. The dead ranged in age from fourteen to sixty-five and included a police officer named Beagles, a sixty-year-old Russian national named Fanny Ziff, and a sixteen-year-old with the grimly apt name of Harry Roast.

South of the Thames, the air was infused with the scent of incinerated coffee, as one hundred tons of it burned in a warehouse in Bermondsey.

This was the added cruelty of air raids. In addition to killing and maiming, they destroyed the commodities that kept Britain alive, and that already were tightly rationed. In the week that ended Sunday, January 12, bombs and fire destroyed 25,000 tons of sugar, 730 tons of cheese, 540 tons of tea, 288 tons of bacon and ham, and, perhaps most barbaric of all, an estimated 970 tons of jams and marmalade.

ON SUNDAY NIGHT AT DITCHLEY, Churchill kept Hopkins up even later, until four-thirty A.M. Hopkins wrote about the night in a letter to Roosevelt, which he composed on demure squares of Claridge's stationery. The letter's contents would have delighted the prime minister. "The people here are amazing from Churchill down," Hopkins told Roosevelt, "and if courage alone can win—the result will be inevitable. But they need our help desperately and I'm sure you will permit nothing to stand in the way." Churchill, he wrote, held sway over the entire British government and understood every aspect of the war. "I cannot emphasize too strongly that he is the one and only person over here with whom you need to have a full meeting of minds."

Hopkins emphasized the urgency of the moment. "This island needs our help now, Mr. President, with everything we can give them."

In a second note, Hopkins emphasized the sense of impending threat that pervaded Churchill's government. "The most important single observation I have to make is that most of the Cabinet and all of the military leaders here believe that invasion is imminent." They expect it before May 1, he wrote, and "believe it will certainly be an all-out attack, including the use of poison gas and perhaps some other new weapons that Germany may have developed." He pressed Roosevelt to act soon. "I . . . cannot urge too strongly that any action you may take to meet the immediate needs here must be based on the assumption that invasion will come before May 1."

That Churchill saw poison gas as a grave and real threat was evident in his insistence that Hopkins be issued a gas mask and a helmet, his "tin hat." Hopkins wore neither. From a sartorial perspective, this was prudent: He and his immense overcoat already resembled something an American farmer might stick in a field to scare away birds.

Hopkins told Roosevelt, "The best I can say for the hat is that it looks worse than my own and doesn't fit—the gas mask I can't get on—so I am all right."

Upon finishing this note Tuesday morning, Hopkins set out through the icy cold to meet Churchill, Clementine, Pug Ismay, American observer Lee, and Lord and Lady Halifax, for a journey to the far north, to the British naval base at Scapa Flow, off the northern tip of Scotland. There, the Halifaxes and General Lee were to board a battleship bound for America.

The journey to Scapa was itself part of Churchill's effort to win Hopkins to Britain's cause. Ever since his arrival, Hopkins had become Churchill's near-constant companion, a broken shadow in an oversized coat. Hopkins realized later that in his first two weeks in Britain, he had spent a dozen evenings with the prime minister. Churchill "scarcely let him out of his sight," wrote Pug Ismay.

Still not wholly versed in the geographic idiosyncrasies of London,

Hopkins made his way toward what he *thought* was King's Cross station, where Churchill's train would be waiting. He had been warned to refer to the train only as the "eleven-thirty special," to keep Churchill's presence a secret.

The train was indeed waiting at King's Cross. Hopkins was not. He had gone to Charing Cross instead.

To Scapa Flow

———

WHEN CHURCHILL AWOKE THAT TUESDAY MORNING, JANUARY 14, in his bombproofed bedroom at the No. 10 Annexe, he looked and sounded terrible. His cold—apparently the one he'd contracted in December—had deepened into a bronchitis he could not shake. (Mary was back at Chequers, where on Monday night her own cold had driven her to bed exhausted and coughing.) Clementine was concerned about her husband, especially in light of his plans to set out that morning for Scapa Flow to bid goodbye to Halifax and his wife, Dorothy. She summoned Sir Charles Wilson, Churchill's doctor, who had last visited him the previous May, just after Churchill became prime minister.

At the main door to the Annexe, a member of Churchill's staff greeted Wilson and told him that Clementine wanted to see him immediately, before he saw Churchill.

She told the doctor that Churchill was going to Scapa Flow.

"When?" Wilson asked.

"Today at noon," she said. "There is a blizzard there, and Winston has a heavy cold. You must stop him."

The doctor found Churchill still in bed and advised him not to make the trip. "He became very red in the face," Wilson recalled.

Churchill threw off his bedclothes. "What damned nonsense!" he said. "Of course I am going."

Wilson reported this to Clementine, who was not pleased. "Well," she snapped, "if you cannot stop him, the least you can do is to go with him."

Wilson consented, and Churchill agreed to bring him along.

Not expecting this denouement from a simple house call, Wilson of course had not packed a bag. Churchill loaned him a heavy coat with an astrakhan collar. "He said it would keep out the wind," Wilson recalled.

Wilson understood that the stated purpose of the trip was to see off the new ambassador, but he suspected another motive: that Churchill really just wanted to see the ships at Scapa Flow.

AT THE STATION, the members of Churchill's party found a long line of Pullman cars, which suggested that the group would be a large one. His "special train" typically consisted of a coach for his use, containing a bedroom, bath, and lounge, and an office; a dining car with two sections, one for Churchill and his designated guests, the other for staff; and a sleeping car with a dozen first-class compartments, each allocated for a particular guest. The staff members had less luxurious accommodations. Churchill's butler, Sawyers, was invariably aboard, as were police detectives, including Inspector Thompson. Churchill kept in constant touch with his office in London through whatever private secretary happened to be on duty at 10 Downing Street—in this case, John Colville. The train carried a scrambling telephone that would be connected to phone lines at a station or siding. All the secretary on the train had to do was tell the operator the number, Rapid Falls 4466, and the call would automatically be directed to the prime minister's office.

The secrecy afforded the eleven-thirty special proved to be of little value. As the passengers arrived, many easily recognizable from press photographs and newsreels, a crowd gathered. A number of ministers, including Beaverbrook and Eden, had come as well, to say goodbye— Beaverbrook's presence unwelcome, at least to Lady Halifax, who believed he had engineered her husband's appointment as ambassador. Neither she nor Halifax wanted to leave London. "We both felt Beaverbrook had suggested it and I had no trust in him of any sort," Lady Halifax wrote later. "In the end we had to go and I don't think that I have ever been more miserable."

General Lee watched the luminaries arrive. "Lord and Lady Halifax, he so tall and she so small, came down the platform and endured their farewells and then the PM with his round fat face, snub nose and twinkling eyes in a semi-nautical attire of double-breasted blue coat and peaked cap, with Mrs. Churchill, tall and smart-looking." Pug Ismay walked with them. Churchill, despite being obviously ill with a cold, "was in high good humor," Lee wrote. The crowd outside cheered.

When Ismay stepped onto the train, he was surprised to see that Churchill's doctor, Sir Charles Wilson, was already aboard. "He looked miserable," Ismay wrote, "and I asked him why he was there."

Wilson told him about his morning encounter with the Churchills. "So here I am," Wilson said, "without even a toothbrush."

At the last minute, Hopkins came rushing along the platform, his great overcoat flapping. There was no danger that the train would leave without him, however. Churchill would have held it for his American talisman no matter how much time was lost.

IN THE DINING CAR that evening, General Lee found himself seated next to Lord Halifax, opposite Clementine and the Canadian minister of munitions. "We really had a pleasant time," Lee wrote. "Mrs. Churchill is a tall and handsome woman and had a fine scarlet cloak which started me off in high good humor." At one point Halifax asked, in all seriousness, why the White House was called the White House, which prompted Clementine to joke that this was something Halifax indeed ought to know before he got to America.

Now General Lee weighed in, and described how the original presidential mansion had been burned by the British in the War of 1812. "Lord Halifax looked shocked and puzzled," Lee wrote later, "and I got the distinct idea that he did not know the War of 1812 had ever happened."

Churchill dined with Lady Halifax, Ismay, and, of course, Hopkins. Churchill was the only member of the party to wear a dinner jacket, a contrast to Hopkins, who looked as unkempt as ever. After dinner, Churchill and the others moved into the lounge.

Despite his bronchitis, Churchill stayed up until two A.M. "He was enjoying himself and with his vast knowledge of history, his power of expression and his huge energy, putting up a show for Hopkins," General Lee wrote. "Hopkins is really the first representative of the president he has had a fair go at. I'm sure he never confided in or even cared for [Joseph] Kennedy."

When Churchill and the others arose the next morning, they found that a derailment somewhere up ahead had forced their train to a halt a dozen miles shy of their final stop at Thurso, where they were to proceed by ship to the waters of Scapa Flow. Outside was a frozen landscape— a "deserted heath," wrote John Martin, the private secretary assigned to the trip, "the ground white with snow and a blizzard howling at the windows." Britain's Meteorological Office reported snowdrifts in the area up to fifteen feet deep. The wind keened among the cars, blowing snowy spindrift horizontally across the plain. For Hopkins, this was a landscape of despair, capping a week in which he had felt only cold.

Churchill, however—though hoarse and obviously ill—"came beaming into the breakfast car, where he consumed a large glass of brandy," Charles Peake, Halifax's personal assistant, wrote in his diary. The prime minister was eager to get out on the water, despite a susceptibility to seasickness. At one point he declared, "I'll go and get my Mothersills," a reference to a popular drug favored by queasy travelers.

He began discoursing on the wonders of an experimental anti-aircraft weapon that launched multiple small rockets at a time. An early iteration was already in place at Chequers for defense against low-flying aircraft, but now the navy was seeking to adapt the weapon to protect its ships. While at Scapa Flow, Churchill planned to test-fire a prototype, and the prospect delighted him—until a senior Admiralty official traveling with the group interjected that each firing cost about £100.

As Peake watched, "The smile faded from the PM's lips and the corners of his mouth turned down like a baby."

"What, not fire it?" Churchill asked.

Clementine cut in: "Yes, darling, you may fire it just once."

"Yes, that's right," Churchill said, "I'll fire it just once. Only once. That couldn't be bad."

Wrote Peake, "Nobody had the heart to say that it would be bad, and he was soon beaming again."

As they all would discover the next day, it would indeed be bad.

CHAPTER
73

"Whither Thou Goest"

———

WITH THE TRAIN STALLED OUTSIDE THURSO, THE WEATHER AWFUL, and Churchill so ill, debate arose as to whether to proceed or not. Clementine worried about her husband's bronchitis, and so did his doctor. "There was much discussion as to what we should do," wrote secretary Martin, "for the sea was stormy and my master had a bad cold."

Churchill broke the impasse. He put on his hat and coat, exited the train, and marched to a car that had drawn up near the tracks. He planted himself firmly in the back seat and vowed that he was going to Scapa Flow, no matter what.

The rest of the party followed, climbing into other cars, and the procession set off over snow-scoured roads for a little harbor called Scrabster, there to board a small vessel that would then take them to larger ships waiting farther out. "The land is bleak, forbidding," General Lee recalled. "The only living things were herds of bundles resembling sheep and I reflected that these animals had to grow Harris tweed or freeze to death." While some in the party boarded a pair of minesweepers, Churchill, Clementine, Hopkins, Ismay, and Halifax transferred to a destroyer, HMS *Napier.* The ship moved through a tormented seascape of opaque snow squalls intermixed with brilliant sun, the sea a striking cobalt against the gleam of the snow-covered shore.

For Churchill, bronchitis aside, this was pure delight—enhanced, no doubt, by the drama of entering Scapa Flow through a succession of antisubmarine nets, which had to be pulled open by guard ships and swiftly closed again, lest a U-boat sneak in behind. (Early in the war, on October 14, 1939, a U-boat had torpedoed the battleship HMS *Royal Oak* in Scapa

Flow, killing 834 of its 1,234 crew, prompting the navy to install a series of protective causeways dubbed "Churchill Barriers.") As the *Napier* and the two minesweepers entered the central waters of Scapa, the sun again emerged, casting diamond light on the moored ships and snowy hills.

Pug Ismay found it breathtaking, and went off in search of Hopkins. "I wanted Harry to see the might, majesty, dominion and power of the British Empire in that setting and to realize that if anything untoward happened to these ships, the whole future of the world might be changed, not only for Britain but ultimately for the United States as well." Here Ismay was exaggerating a bit, because at this moment there were only a few important ships in the roadstead, the bulk of the fleet having been sent to the Mediterranean or dispatched to protect convoys and hunt German commerce raiders.

Ismay found Hopkins, "disconsolate and shivering," in a wardroom. The American seemed exhausted. Ismay gave him one of his own sweaters and a pair of boots lined with fur. This cheered Hopkins a bit, but not enough for him to accept Ismay's recommendation that they both take a brisk walk around the ship. "He was too cold to be enthusiastic about the Home Fleet," Ismay wrote.

Ismay strode off alone, as Hopkins looked for a place to shelter himself from the cold and wind. He found a spot that seemed ideal, and sat down.

A chief petty officer approached him. "Excuse me, sir," the officer said, "—but I don't think you should sit just there, sir—that, sir, is a depth charge."

CHURCHILL AND COMPANY NOW boarded the ship that would take the Halifaxes and General Lee to America, a new and impressive battleship christened the *King George V.* Even Churchill's choice of this ship for Halifax's voyage had been calculated to help woo Roosevelt. Churchill knew that the president loved ships and shared his own avid interest in naval affairs. Indeed, by now, Roosevelt had amassed a collection of more than four hundred ship models, large and small, many of which would go on display at the FDR Presidential Library in Hyde Park, New York, upon its opening in June 1941. "No lover ever studied every whim of his mistress as I did those of President Roosevelt," Churchill said. He chose the *King George V,* he wrote, "in order to clothe the arrival of our new Ambassador, Lord Halifax, in the United States with every circumstance of importance."

After lunch aboard the ship, all said their goodbyes. Hopkins handed General Lee his letters to Roosevelt.

Churchill and the stay-behinds climbed down into a small boat that would take them to their destination for the night, an old battleship named *Nelson*. Churchill was careful, as always, to adhere to naval protocol, which required that the senior officer—in this case, himself—leave the ship last. Swells heaved; the wind scoured the darkling sea. From the *King George V*'s deck, Lee watched the little boat depart, "in a shower of spray." The time was four-fifteen, by Lee's watch, and the northern sunset was fast approaching.

The *King George V* departed, with General Lee and the Halifaxes aboard. Wrote Lee, "There was no noise, no music, no guns; up came the anchor and we stood out to sea."

In the fading light, the little boat with Churchill and Hopkins aboard returned to the *Nelson,* where they and the others spent the night.

THE NEXT DAY, THURSDAY, January 16, aboard the *Nelson,* Churchill got his chance to fire the new anti-aircraft weapon. Something went awry. "One of the projectiles got entangled in the rigging," secretary Martin recalled. "There was a loud explosion and a jam-jar-like object flew towards the bridge, where we were standing. Everyone ducked and there was a great bang, but no serious damage was done." As Hopkins later told the king, the bomb landed five feet from where he was standing. He was unhurt, and found the incident funny. Churchill, apparently, did not.

At length, Churchill and his party left the *Nelson* and traveled in the admiral's barge back to the destroyer *Napier,* which would return them to their train. The weather was worse than it had been the day before, the sea rougher, and this made climbing from the barge to the destroyer's deck a precarious venture. Here naval protocol called for a reversal in the order of boarding, with Churchill first to ascend. The two vessels rose and fell with the swells. Wind ripped the gunwales. As Churchill climbed, he talked the whole while, much at ease. Pug Ismay, on the barge below, heard one of the steps of the ladder crack "ominously" under Churchill's weight, but the prime minister kept going and was soon aboard. Wrote Ismay, "I was careful to avoid that particular rung when my turn came, but Harry Hopkins was not so lucky."

Hopkins began to climb, his coat billowing in the wind. The step broke, and he began to fall. Roosevelt's confidant, Britain's potential savior, was about to plummet onto the boat below or, worse, into the tortured chasm of sea between the barge and the hull, which moved against each other like the jaws of a vise.

Two seamen caught him and held him by his shoulders, dangling above the barge.

Churchill shouted encouragement of sorts: "I shouldn't stay there too long, Harry; when two ships are close together in a rough sea, you are liable to get hurt."

ON THE WAY BACK to London, Churchill's train stopped in Glasgow, where he reviewed legions of civilian volunteers, including fire brigades, police officers, and members of the Red Cross, the Air Raid Precautions service (ARP), and the Women's Voluntary Service, all drawn up in ranks for Churchill's inspection. Whenever he reached a new group, he paused and introduced Hopkins, calling him the personal representative of the president of the United States, which heartened the members of each service but depleted Hopkins's last reserves.

He hid, camouflaging himself among the crowds of spectators who had gathered to see Churchill.

"But there was no escape," Pug Ismay wrote.

Churchill, noting Hopkins's absences, called out each time, "Harry, Harry, where are you?"—forcing Harry to return to his side.

It was here in Glasgow that the most important moment of Hopkins's stay in Britain would occur, though it was kept secret, for the time being, from the public.

The group gathered at the Station Hotel in Glasgow for a small dinner party with Tom Johnston, a member of Parliament and a prominent journalist, soon to be named secretary of state for Scotland. Churchill's doctor, Wilson, sat beside Hopkins, and was struck anew by how disheveled the man looked. Speeches followed. At length it was Hopkins's turn.

Hopkins stood and, as Ismay recalled it, first made "a tilt or two at the British Constitution in general, and the irrepressible Prime Minister in particular." Then he turned to face Churchill.

"I suppose you wish to know what I am going to say to President Roosevelt on my return," he said.

This was an understatement. Churchill was desperate to know how well his courtship of Hopkins was progressing, and what indeed he would tell the president.

"Well," Hopkins said, "I'm going to quote you one verse from that

Book of Books in the truth of which Mr. Johnston's mother and my own
Scottish mother were brought up—"

Hopkins dropped his voice to a near whisper and recited a passage
from the Bible's Book of Ruth: "Whither thou goest, I will go; and
where thou lodgest, I will lodge: thy people shall be my people, and thy
God my God."

Then, softly, he added: "Even to the end."

This was his own addition, and with it a wave of gratitude and relief
seemed to engulf the room.

Churchill wept.

"He knew what it meant," his doctor wrote. "Even to us the words
seemed like a rope thrown to a drowning man." Wrote Ismay: "It may
have been indiscreet for [Hopkins] to show his partisanship in this way,
but it moved us all deeply."

ON SATURDAY, JANUARY 18, as Churchill and Hopkins made their way
back to London, Colville set out by car for Oxford and lunch with Gay
Margesson, camouflaging his romantic interest with the minor deception
that it was prime ministerial business that was bringing him to town.
London was covered in snow, and more fell as he drove. He feared—or
perhaps hoped—that Oxford, by now, would have changed her for the
worst, her newly long hair being a symbol of Oxford's effect, but when
they talked in her room after lunch he saw that she was just as captivating
as always.

"I found her charming and not so changed as I had feared," he wrote,
"but I did not make very much headway. We always talk so fluently, but
I can never succeed in being anything but 'the same old Jock' and until
I become—or appear to become—different, I shall have no chance of
making a new impression on Gay."

Soon it was time to depart. Snow fell. Gay said goodbye and invited
Colville to come visit her again, and there in the snow, as he wrote with
evident sorrow, "Gay looked as beautiful as she ever has, her long hair
half hidden by a handkerchief and her cheeks flushed by the cold."

He drove back to London, through snow and ice, pronouncing the
journey "a nightmare."

Upon his return, he decided enough was enough. He composed a
letter to Gay confirming "that I was still in love with her and saying that
the only solution from my point of view was to cut the Gordian Knot
and see her no more. I should leave no serious gap in her life, though

I believed she was fond of me, but I could not hang around her as a rejected suitor, haunted by memories of what had been and dreams of what might have been."

He knew, however, that really this was just a gambit, one deployed by doomed lovers in every age, and that he did not truly intend that the knot remain severed forever. "So perhaps weakly," he wrote in his diary, after setting the letter aside, "I postponed the project and decided to 'hang around' for some time yet. History is full of lessons about the redemption of Lost Causes."

THAT SATURDAY, HITLER'S DEPUTY, Rudolf Hess, once again traveled to the Messerschmitt Works airfield at Augsburg, accompanied by a driver, a police detective, and one of his adjutants, Karl-Heinz Pintsch. Hess gave Pintsch two letters and instructed him to open one of them after he had been gone for four hours. Pintsch waited the four hours and threw in an additional fifteen minutes just to be safe, then opened the letter. He was stunned. Hess, he read, was on his way to Britain to try to bring about a peace agreement.

Pintsch told the detective and the driver about what he had just read. They were discussing it, no doubt with great anxiety for their own lives and futures, when Hess's fighter returned to the airport. He had been unable to find a radio signal necessary for keeping the plane on course.

Hess and the others drove back to Munich.

HOPKINS'S VISIT TO BRITAIN was supposed to last two weeks; it expanded to over four, most of which he spent with Churchill against a backdrop of mounting suspense with regard to the Lend-Lease Bill, whose passage by Congress was anything but certain. In that time, Hopkins managed to endear himself to nearly everyone he met, including the valets at Claridge's, who took an extra effort to make him look presentable. "Oh yes," Hopkins told one valet. "I've got to remember I'm in London now—I've got to look dignified." From time to time, the valets would find secret documents tucked into his clothing or discover that he had left his wallet in a pants pocket. A hotel waiter said Hopkins was "very genial—considerate—if I may say so, lovable—quite different from other Ambassadors we've had here."

Churchill displayed Hopkins to the public whenever he could, both to hearten his British audience and to afford himself the opportunity to reassure Hopkins and America that he was not asking the United States to go to war—though privately he dearly wished Roosevelt could simply decide to do so without the bother of first winning over Congress. On Friday, January 31, Churchill took Hopkins with him to tour neighborhoods in Portsmouth and Southampton that had been heavily bombed, after which they drove again to Chequers, to dine with Clementine, Ismay, private secretary Eric Seal, and others. Churchill "was in great form," Seal wrote to his wife that evening. "He gets on like a house afire with Hopkins, who is a dear, & is universally liked."

Hopkins brought out a box of gramophone records containing American songs and other music having "Anglo-American significance," as Seal put it, and soon the music filled the Great Hall, where the gramophone was located. "We had these until well after midnight, the PM walking about, sometimes dancing a *pas seul,* in time with the music," Seal wrote. In the midst of his circling and dancing, Churchill would pause now and then to comment on the growing bond between Britain and America, and his appreciation of Roosevelt. "We all got a bit sentimental & Anglo-American, under the influence of the good dinner & the music," Seal wrote. Something ineffable crept into the Great Hall. "It was at the time very pleasant & satisfying—but difficult to convey in words, especially within the confines of a letter," Seal told his wife. "Everyone present knew & liked each other—it is quite extraordinary how Hopkins has endeared himself to everyone here he has met."

Directive No. 23

————

W ITH PLANNING FOR HIS INVASION OF RUSSIA—OPERATION
Barbarossa—well underway, Hitler found Britain's continued resistance
galling. He would require every available soldier, tank, and aircraft for
the campaign, after which he would be free to focus his attentions on the
British Isles. Until then, however, he needed to negotiate a peace or otherwise neutralize Britain as a viable foe, and it was here, with an invasion
at least temporarily out of consideration, that the Luftwaffe continued to
play the most critical role. Its failure to achieve the victory promised by
Hermann Göring was undoubtedly a source of frustration for Hitler, but
he remained hopeful that his air force would prevail.

On Thursday, February 6, he issued a new directive, No. 23, in which
he ordered the air force and navy to further intensify their attacks against
Britain, ideally to cause Churchill to surrender but, short of that, to at
least weaken British forces to the point where they could not disrupt
his Russian campaign. With Russia now thought to be speeding production of aircraft, tanks, and munitions, the longer he waited, the harder it
would be to achieve his vision of utter annihilation.

The increased intensity of attacks, the directive said, would have the
secondary benefit of creating the illusion that a German invasion of Britain was imminent, and thereby force Churchill to continue allocating
forces for home defense.

GÖRING WAS DISMAYED.

"The decision to attack the East made me despair," he later told an
American interrogator.

He tried to dissuade Hitler, he claimed, by quoting Hitler's own book, *Mein Kampf,* which warned of the dangers of a two-front war. Göring was confident that Germany could readily defeat the Russian army, but he believed the timing was wrong. He told Hitler that his air force was on the verge of bringing about Britain's collapse and surrender. "We've got England where we want her and now we have to stop."

Hitler replied: "Yes, I shall need your bombers for just three or four weeks, after that you can have them all back again."

Hitler promised that once the Russian campaign ended, all newly freed resources would be poured into the Luftwaffe. As one witness to the conversation reported, Hitler promised Göring that his air force would be "trebled, quadrupled, quintupled."

Recognizing that he could push Hitler only so far, and always covetous of his favor, Göring resigned himself to the fact that the invasion of Russia would indeed occur, and that he needed to play a key role in its execution. He convened a meeting of military planners at the Gatow Air Academy, outside Berlin, to begin detailed preparations for Barbarossa.

It was "strictly top secret," wrote Luftwaffe field marshal Kesselring. "Nothing leaked out. Staffs were as much in ignorance of what was in the wind as the troops."

Or so the German High Command imagined.

IN ACCORD WITH DIRECTIVE No. 23, the Luftwaffe stepped up its attacks against Britain, hampered only by bouts of bad winter weather. Its pilots encountered little resistance. They could tell from their daily experiences that the British still had not found an effective means of intercepting aircraft at night.

The Coming Violence

ON SATURDAY, FEBRUARY 8—THE DAY HOPKINS WAS TO BEGIN his long journey back to America—the news arrived that the Lend-Lease Bill had overcome its first important hurdle, gaining passage in the U.S. House of Representatives, by a vote of 260 to 165. Hopkins went to Chequers that day to say goodbye to Churchill and Clementine; later he would take a train to Bournemouth to catch a flight to Lisbon. He found Churchill hard at work preparing a speech for broadcast the next evening, Sunday, February 9.

Churchill paced; a secretary typed. Hopkins watched, enthralled. The speech was ostensibly an address to the British public, but both men understood that it was also to be a tool for bolstering American support for the Lend-Lease Bill, which now had to go before the U.S. Senate. Hopkins urged Churchill to make the argument that far from dragging America into the war, the bill presented the best way to stay out. Churchill agreed. He also planned to make use of a note from Roosevelt, in which the president, in longhand, had written five lines from a poem by Longfellow.

Hopkins left Churchill a thank-you note. "My dear Prime Minister," he wrote, "I shall never forget these days with you—your supreme confidence and will to victory—Britain I have ever liked—I like it the more.

"As I leave for America tonight I wish you great and good luck—confusion to your enemies—victory for Britain."

Late that night Hopkins boarded a train for Bournemouth; he arrived at the nearby seaplane port at Poole the next morning, Sunday, to find that bad weather had forced the postponement of his flight to Lisbon. Brendan Bracken had come along to see him off. Hopkins was accompanied as well by a British security agent assigned to watch over him all the way to Washington, owing to his habit of leaving confidential papers lying around his hotel room. The agent was to stay particularly close in Lisbon, by now notorious as a center for espionage.

On Sunday evening, Hopkins, Bracken, and others convened in the bar of the Branksome Tower Hotel in Poole, to listen to Churchill's broadcast.

Later, Home Intelligence would report that elements of the speech "made some people's flesh creep."

CHURCHILL OPENED BY OFFERING praise to the citizens of London and elsewhere who had withstood German raids, noting that the German air force had dropped "three or four tons of bombs upon us for every ton we could send to Germany in return." He singled out the police for special acclaim, noting that they "have been in it everywhere, all the time, and as a working woman wrote to me: 'What gentlemen they are!'" He applauded successes against Italy in the Middle East; he cited Hopkins's visit as a mark of America's sympathy and goodwill. "In the last war," Churchill said, launching into a passage clearly inspired by Hopkins's advice, "the United States sent two million men across the Atlantic. But this is not a war of vast armies, firing immense masses of shells at one another. We do not need the gallant armies which are forming throughout the American Union. We do not need them this year, nor next year, nor any year that I can foresee." What he did need, he said, were supplies and ships. "We need them here and we need to bring them here."

With the passing of winter, he continued, the threat of invasion would arise anew, in a different, potentially more dangerous form. "A Nazi invasion of Great Britain last autumn would have been a more or less improvised affair," he said. "Hitler took it for granted that when France gave in we should give in; but we did not give in. And he had to think again." Now, Churchill said, Germany will have had time to plan and to build the necessary equipment and landing craft. "We must all be prepared to meet gas attacks, parachute attacks, and glider attacks, with constancy, forethought and practiced skill." For the fact remained: "In order to win the war Hitler must destroy Great Britain."

But no matter how far Germany advanced or how much more territory it seized, Hitler would not prevail. The might of the British Empire—"nay, in a certain sense, the whole English-speaking world"—was on his trail, "bearing with them the swords of justice."

By implication, one of those sword-bearers was America, and now, rearing toward his closing, Churchill quoted the handwritten note sent to him by Roosevelt.

"Sail on, O Ship of State!" Churchill rumbled. "Sail on, O Union, strong and great!

> Humanity with all its fears,
> With all the hopes of future years,
> Is hanging breathless on thy fate!

Churchill asked his listeners how he should respond. "What is the answer that I shall give, in your name, to this great man, the thrice-chosen head of a nation of a hundred and thirty millions? Here is the answer . . ."

MOST OF BRITAIN WAS LISTENING: 70 percent of potential listeners. At the Branksome Tower Hotel, Hopkins listened. Colville, with a rare weekend off, listened too, after dining with his mother and brother at Madeley Manor, his grandfather's country home in North Staffordshire, 140 miles from London. The night was cold and rainy, but numerous fireplaces made the house feel cozy.

This was Churchill at his most deft—candid yet encouraging, grave but uplifting, seeking to bolster his own people while reassuring, albeit somewhat disingenuously, the great mass of Americans that all he wanted from the United States was material aid.

Goebbels, listening too, called it "insolent."

CHURCHILL ENTERED HIS CLOSING rhetorical drive.

"Here is the answer which I will give to President Roosevelt: Put your confidence in us," Churchill said. "Give us your faith and your blessing, and, under Providence, all will be well.

"We shall not fail or falter; we shall not weaken or tire. Neither the sudden shock of battle, nor the long-drawn trials of vigilance and exertion will wear us down.

"Give us the tools, and we will finish the job."

THAT WEEKEND KING GEORGE came to a new realization. In his diary he wrote, "I could not have a better Prime Minister."

IN THE AMERICAN CONGRESS, nothing happened.

By mid-February Roosevelt's Lend-Lease Bill still had not been approved by the Senate. Churchill was frustrated, as were the British people, who were growing impatient with what Home Intelligence called the "apparently interminable discussions" about the bill.

Churchill was also more convinced than ever that the Luftwaffe was making a deliberate effort to kill him and fellow members of his government. The Cabinet War Rooms were being reinforced, but, as he told Sir Edward Bridges, secretary to the War Cabinet, in a minute on Saturday, February 15 (one of at least eighteen minutes Churchill composed that day), he was concerned that the headquarters building for Britain's Home Forces was uniquely vulnerable to attack. German bombs seemed to be coming closer, and to be concentrating on Whitehall. "How many bombs have been thrown within a thousand yards of the [war rooms]?" Churchill asked Bridges.

In fact, by this point at least forty raids had struck Whitehall, with 146 bombs landing within a one-thousand-yard radius of the Cenotaph, the national war monument located a block and a half from 10 Downing Street, at the heart of Whitehall.

That same day, Churchill wrote to Pug Ismay on the subject of invasion. Despite intelligence reports suggesting that Hitler had put off his plan to invade Britain, Churchill still believed the threat had to be taken seriously. (The public agreed: In January, a Gallup Poll had found that 62 percent of respondents expected Germany to invade in the coming year.) That Hitler would have to dispose of Britain at some point was clear, as was the reality that he would need to do so soon, before the country grew too strong. Britain was stepping up its production of weapons and equipment and, if Roosevelt's Lend-Lease Bill became law, would soon be receiving a great surge of supplies from America. Churchill's senior commanders believed that Hitler had no choice but to invade, and saw Germany's renewed bombing of London and other British cities as an ominous indication of a revived interest in doing so.

Churchill was less convinced, but agreed to the extent that he believed it imperative that Home Forces and civilians be as ready as possible to repel a German assault, and to Churchill this meant that England's beaches and beach communities had to be cleared of civilians. "We must begin persuading the people to go away," he wrote to Pug Ismay, ". . . and explain to those who wish to stay what is the safest place in their houses, and that they will not be able to leave after the flag falls."

Beaverbrook, in turn, hectored his factory managers with calls to step up their operations. "The need for sustained and increasing efforts on the part of all concerned with aircraft production remains vital to the security of the country in face of threatening invasion when the weather mends," he wrote in a telegram to 144 companies involved in the manufacture of airframes. "I ask therefore for your assurance that work will in future continue at your factory throughout Sundays so that the maximum output may be obtained." He sent a similar telegram to sixty companies that made gas-decontamination equipment. "The decontamination devices are needed so urgently that I have to request you to work night and day shifts and especially to work on Sundays."

AS LUCK WOULD HAVE IT, the departure of Harry Hopkins coincided with the arrival of a period of warm, springlike weather, with melting snow and crocuses peeking from the grass in Hyde Park. Wrote Joan Wyndham, out for a stroll with her "lovely Rupert," he of the lopsided appendage: "Sunny day like spring, blue sky, wonderful feeling of exhilaration. . . . That afternoon was one of the happiest we'd ever spent together. We were two minds with a single thought, or rather lack of thought."

That week, too, Randolph Churchill and his new unit, No. 8 Commando, set out for Egypt aboard a ship called the *Glenroy*. By now the unit had more than five hundred soldiers, plus an assortment of officers and liaison men, one of whom was the writer Evelyn Waugh, also a member of Randolph's social club, White's. Randolph and Pamela hoped this hiatus would give them a chance to stabilize their finances, a task that was all the more vital now, as she believed she might be pregnant with their second child. "Well, it is hell to be parted," Randolph told her, before departure, ". . . at least, we'll get our debts sorted out."

But the voyage was long and Randolph's weakness for gambling, profound.

London, Washington, and Berlin

F OR CHURCHILL, THE FIRST WEEK OF MARCH WAS A TENSE ONE. The Lend-Lease Bill still had not passed, and there were signs that support for its passage was beginning to soften. The latest Gallup Poll showed that 55 percent of Americans favored making the bill law, down from 58 percent in the poll that had preceded it. This may have contributed to Churchill's bad mood at the start of a lunch on Thursday, March 6, held in the newly armored basement dining room at No. 10 Downing Street, in honor of another visiting American, James Conant, president of Harvard.

Churchill was not yet present when Clementine, Conant, and a number of other guests made their way into the dining room. The Prof arrived, tall and doleful, as did a friend of Clementine's, Winnifreda Yuill. Also on hand was Charles Eade, a prominent newspaper editor and compiler of collections of Churchill's speeches.

Clementine served sherry and resolved that the meal should begin without her husband. She wore her war-slogan head scarf wrapped to form a turban.

The first course had not yet been served when Churchill at last arrived. Upon entering, he kissed Winnifreda's hand, a cordial enough beginning, but a disgruntled quiet followed. Churchill was still suffering from bronchitis and was clearly in a grumpy mood. He looked tired and seemed unwilling to converse.

Hoping to lighten the atmosphere, Conant decided to make clear from the start that he was an ardent supporter of the Lend-Lease Bill. He also told Churchill that he had testified in the Senate that the United

States should intervene directly in the war. At which point, Conant noted in his diary, Churchill became more talkative.

First, and with evident joy, the prime minister described a successful British raid on the Lofoten Islands of Norway, carried out two days earlier by a group of British commandos and Norwegian soldiers. Dubbed Operation Claymore, it succeeded in destroying factories that made cod-liver oil, crucial to helping Germany supply much-needed vitamins A and D to its populace, and glycerin, a component of explosives. The commandos captured more than two hundred German soldiers and a few Norwegian collaborators, dubbed "Quislings," after Vidkun Quisling, a Norwegian politician who had sought to ally Norway with Germany.

This was the public story. Churchill, however, knew a secret, one he did not reveal to his luncheon guests. In the course of the raid, the commandos had succeeded in capturing a key component of a German Enigma cipher machine and a document containing the cipher keys the German navy would use in the coming months. Now the codebreakers at Bletchley Park would be able to read not just Luftwaffe communications but also those of the German navy, including orders transmitted to U-boats.

Next Churchill raised the matter most on his mind: lend-lease. "This bill has to pass," he told Conant. "What a state it would leave all of us in if it doesn't; what a state it would leave the President in; what a failure he would appear before history if this bill is not passed."

JOHN COLVILLE, STILL KEEN to quit his job and join the war, came up with a new plan.

On Monday morning, March 3, he had gone riding in Richmond Park, near the Royal Botanical Gardens in Kew, using a horse borrowed from a friend, Louis Greig, personal assistant to Air Minister Sinclair. Afterward, Colville gave Greig a lift back to London, and during the drive, without prior thought, told Greig that he wanted to join a bomber crew. He had the vague idea that Churchill might be more inclined to let him go to the RAF than to the navy or army.

Greig promised to set him up for the first stage of the RAF enlistment process, a medical "interview." Colville was delighted. Whether he was aware of it or not, the life expectancy of a new member of a bomber crew was about two weeks.

IN WASHINGTON, THE WAR Department pored over a report assessing Britain's prospects, written by its own War Plans Division. "It is impossible to predict," the report said, "whether or not the British Isles will fall or if so when."

The coming year was crucial: British production of war materials was climbing and American aid increasing, while German resources, taxed by ten months of war and occupation, would only decline further from their prewar peak. Within a year, the report said, the two sides would approach parity—provided Britain survived that long. The gravest threat "is greatly intensified air, surface, and subsurface activity coincident with or followed by an attempted invasion."

Whether Britain could withstand this combined assault was open to question, the report warned. "During this critical period, the United States cannot afford to base its military program on the assumption that the British Isles will not succumb as a result of blockade, or that they cannot be successfully invaded. The critical period is assumed to be from the present moment until November 1st, 1941."

HITLER WANTED STILL MORE force applied against Britain. America seemed increasingly likely to enter the war but would do so only, he reasoned, if Britain continued to exist. On March 5 he issued another directive, No. 24, this signed by Field Marshal Wilhelm Keitel, chief of the High Command of the Armed Forces (OKW), aimed mainly at how Germany and Japan might coordinate strategy under the Tripartite Pact, which both had signed with Italy the preceding fall.

The goal, the directive said, "must be to *induce Japan to take action in the Far East* as soon as possible. This will tie down strong English forces and will divert the main effort of the United States of America to the Pacific." Beyond this Germany had no particular interest in the Far East. "The *common aim* of strategy," the directive stated, "must be represented as the swift conquest of England in order to keep America out of the war."

Saturday Night

———

T HAT WEEKEND WAS TO BE A BIG ONE FOR MARY CHURCHILL—
another chance to escape the Prison Room, this time to drive into London with her mother for the event that even now, in wartime, kicked
off London's social season: Queen Charlotte's Annual Birthday Dinner
Dance, the city's yearly debutante ball, set for the night of Saturday,
March 8. Afterward, Mary and her friends planned to continue the fun
well into the next morning, dancing and drinking at one of the city's
popular nightclubs, the Café de Paris.

The weather promised to be lovely: clear, under a moon that was
three-quarters full, a waxing gibbous. Excellent weather for young
women in their finest silk, men in their evening suits and silk top hats.
And for German bombers.

Gun and searchlight crews braced for what was almost certain to be a
very long night.

AT THE CAFÉ DE PARIS, on Coventry Street in Piccadilly, owner Martin
Poulsen looked forward to a busy night. Saturdays always drew the biggest crowds to the club, but this particular Saturday promised to bring a
larger and noisier throng than most, owing to the debutante ball taking
place nearby at the Grosvenor House Hotel. The debs and their dates and
their friends—the most attractive men were called "debs' delights"—
would doubtless come to the club afterward and pack the place full. It
was one of the most popular clubs in the city, alongside the Embassy
Club and the 400, and was known to have some of the best jazz bands and

most charismatic bandleaders. Owner Poulsen had hired a particularly popular front man to close out the night, Kenrick "Snakehips" Johnson, a lithe, black twenty-six-year-old dancer and conductor from British Guiana—"slim grey beautiful Snakehips," as one woman described him. No one actually called him Kenrick. It was always Ken. Or just Snakehips.

Poulsen himself was known for his optimism and his always cheerful personality, which struck some as an anomaly, given the fact that he was Danish—"the least melancholy Dane in history," as the club's biographer put it. Poulsen had been the headwaiter at another popular club before founding the Café de Paris in what had been a downtrodden, largely empty restaurant in the basement below a theater, the Rialto Cinema. Its new interior was meant to evoke the glamour and luxury of the *Titanic*. With the advent of war, the club's subsurface location gave Poulsen a marketing edge over his competitors. He advertised it as "the safest and gayest restaurant in town—even in the air raids. *Twenty feet below ground*." In reality, however, it was no safer than any other building in the neighborhood. The club was indeed underground, but it had an ordinary ceiling and, above that, only the glass roof of the Rialto.

But, again, Poulsen was an optimist. Just a week earlier, he'd told a golfing companion that he was so convinced the war would end soon that he'd ordered twenty-five thousand bottles of champagne, the drink of choice among his guests. Magnums were the preferred size. "I don't know why people are making such a fuss over the blitz," he told a female friend. "I'm absolutely certain it will be over in a month or two. In fact, I am so sure of this that I am going to order neon lights to put outside the Café de Paris."

The club was already busy at eight-fifteen that Saturday night when air-raid sirens began to sound. No one paid attention. The first band played. Snakehips was due to arrive soon to take the stage for his first number, at nine-thirty P.M.

JOSEPH GOEBBELS SPENT SATURDAY night in Berlin before heading to his country home on the Bogensee the next day. His wife, Magda, was struggling with a prolonged case of bronchitis.

In his diary on Saturday, Goebbels acknowledged that the British raid on Norway's Lofoten Islands "was more serious than at first thought." In addition to destroying factories, fish oil, and glycerin, the attackers had sunk fifteen thousand tons of German shipping. "Espionage by the Norwegians was involved," he wrote, and noted that Josef Terboven, Reich Commissar for Norway, a German and a staunch party loyalist, had been dispatched to punish the islanders for aiding the attackers. On Saturday, Terboven telephoned Goebbels to report on what he had accomplished thus far, as Goebbels summarized in his diary:

"He has established a punitive court of the harshest kind on the Lofoten island which aided the English and betrayed Germans and Quisling's people to them. He has ordered saboteurs' farms to be put to the torch, hostages to be taken, etc."

Goebbels approved. In his diary he wrote, "This Terboven fellow is all right."

There had been progress elsewhere. "There have also been a mass of death sentences in Amsterdam," Goebbels wrote. "I argue in favor of the rope for Jews. Those fellows must learn their lesson."

He closed the night's entry: "It gets so late. And I am so tired."

IN WASHINGTON, THE PROSPECTS of the Lend-Lease Bill improved. One important factor was a decision by Wendell Willkie, Roosevelt's past opponent, to throw his full support behind the bill. (Willkie dismissed his own former fear crusade as "a bit of campaign oratory.") It now seemed that the bill would indeed be passed by the Senate, and soon—and without being crippled by amendments designed to undermine its effectiveness. Passage could come any day.

So likely did this now seem that Roosevelt prepared to dispatch another emissary to London, this man the antithesis of the frail Harry Hopkins and soon to influence the lives of both Mary Churchill and her sister-in-law, Pamela.

The Tall Man with the Smile

R OOSEVELT AND A GUEST SETTLED IN FOR LUNCH AT THE PRES-
ident's desk in the Oval Office of the White House. Roosevelt was recovering from a cold and seemed woozy.

"An extraordinary meal," his guest wrote later. By "extraordinary,"
he meant extraordinarily awful.

"Spinach soup—" he began.

The guest was William Averell Harriman, known variously as Averell, or Ave, or Bill, depending on who was speaking. Wealthy beyond
measure, he was the scion of the Union Pacific rail empire, built by his
father. He joined its board of directors while a senior at Yale, and now, at
the age of forty-nine, was its chairman. In the mid-1930s, to encourage
rail travel to the West, he directed the construction of a vast ski resort
in Idaho, called Sun Valley. He was handsome by any standard, but the
two things that made him especially so were his smile, which was large
and white, and the easy, athletic grace with which he moved. He was an
expert skier and polo player.

Harriman was to leave for London several days later, on Monday,
March 10, there to coordinate the delivery of American aid once the
Lend-Lease Bill finally passed. Like Hopkins before him, Harriman was
to serve as Roosevelt's looking glass into how Britain was faring, but he
also had the more formal responsibility of making sure that Churchill
got the aid he most needed and, once he got it, made the best use of it.
In announcing the appointment, Roosevelt gave him the title "defense
expediter."

Harriman dipped his spoon into a watery green liquid.

"—didn't taste bad but looked like hot water poured over chopped up spinach," he wrote in a note for his own files. "White toast and hot rolls. Main dish—cheese soufflé with spinach!! Dessert—three large fat pancakes, plenty of butter and maple syrup. Tea for the president and coffee for myself."

Harriman took particular note of this lunch because of Roosevelt's cold. He wrote, "It struck me as the most unhealthy diet under the circumstances, particularly as we discussed the British food situation and their increasing needs for vitamins, proteins and calcium!!"

Roosevelt wanted Harriman to make Britain's food supply a priority, and spent a long while—too long, from Harriman's perspective—talking about the specific foods the British would need to survive. Harriman found this ironic. "As the President was obviously tired and mentally stale, in the British interest it struck me that fortification of the President's diet should be first priority."

Harriman came away from the meeting concerned that Roosevelt did not yet truly grasp the gravity of Britain's position and what it meant for the rest of the world. Harriman himself was publicly on record as favoring American intervention in the war. "All in all I left feeling that the President had not faced what I considered to be the realities of the situation—namely that there was a good chance Germany, without our help, could so cripple British shipping as to affect her ability to hold out."

Later that day, at about five-thirty P.M., Harriman met with Secretary of State Cordell Hull, who was also suffering from a cold and looked tired. The two discussed the broader naval situation, in particular the threat to Singapore posed by the rising power and aggression of Japan. The U.S. Navy had no plans to interfere, Hull told him, but he personally believed that the navy should deploy some of its most powerful ships to the waters of the Dutch East Indies in a display of force, in the hopes—as Harriman paraphrased his remarks—"that by bluff the Japs could be kept within bounds."

By sitting back, Hull said, America risked the "ignominious result" of having Japan seize key strategic points in the Far East, while America kept its ships safely moored at their big Pacific base. Obviously tired and befogged by his cold, Hull could not for the moment remember its exact location.

"What is the name of that harbor?" Hull asked.

"Pearl Harbor," Harriman said.

"Yes," Hull said.

———

AT FIRST, HARRIMAN HAD only a vague sense of exactly what his mission was supposed to accomplish. "No one has given me any instructions or directions as to what my activities should be," he wrote in another memo for his files.

In exploratory conversations with U.S. naval and army officials, Harriman found a deep reluctance to send weapons and matériel to the British without a clearer understanding as to what they planned to do with them. Harriman faulted Hopkins for this. Hopkins had seemed to have only an impressionistic sense of what the British needed and how those needs fit into Churchill's war strategy. The military leaders Harriman spoke to expressed skepticism and seemed unsure of Churchill's competence. "Such remarks are made as, 'We can't take seriously requests that come late in the evening over a bottle of port,' which, without mentioning names, obviously refers to evening conversations between Hopkins and Churchill."

The skepticism Harriman encountered in Washington now made his task clear, he wrote. "I must attempt to convince the Prime Minister that I or someone must convey to our people his war strategy or else he cannot expect to get maximum aid."

HARRIMAN BOOKED A SEAT on Pan American Airways' *Atlantic Clipper,* scheduled to depart at nine-fifteen A.M., Monday, March 10, from the Marine Air Terminal at New York Municipal Airport, known informally as LaGuardia Field. (Only later, in 1953, would the name LaGuardia Airport become official and permanent.) Under the best conditions, the journey would take three days, with multiple stops, first in Bermuda, a six-hour flight away, then a fifteen-hour leg to Horta, in the Azores. From there the *Clipper* would fly to Lisbon, where Harriman was to catch a KLM flight to the Portuguese city of Porto, lay over for an hour, then proceed by plane to Bristol, and catch a British passenger flight to London.

Harriman initially reserved a room for himself at Claridge's hotel, then canceled and booked the Dorchester. Notoriously frugal (he rarely carried cash and never picked up a dinner check; his wife, Marie, called him a "cheap old bastard"), he telegraphed Claridge's on Saturday, March 8: "Cancel my reservation but reserve cheapest room my Secretary."

Just two days earlier, the Dorchester had come up during Churchill's lunch with Harvard president Conant, who was staying at Claridge's. Clementine suggested that for the sake of safety, Conant should move to the Dorchester—at which point Clementine and her friend Winnifreda burst out in earthy knowing laughter and, as another guest recalled, "explained to Dr. Conant that although his life may be in greater danger at Claridge's, his reputation may be in greater danger at the Dorchester."

Conant replied that as president of Harvard, "he would rather risk his life than his reputation."

Snakehips

———

QUEEN CHARLOTTE'S DANCE WAS HELD IN THE UNDERGROUND ballroom at the Grosvenor House Hotel, opposite the eastern border of Hyde Park. The Dorchester was several blocks south; the U.S. embassy, an equal distance to the east. Large Daimlers and Jaguars, their headlights reduced to slender crosses of light, eased their way slowly toward the hotel. Despite the likelihood of an air raid on such a clear, moonlit night, the hotel was thronged with young women in white—150 debutantes— and the many parents, young men, and post-debs who had come to launch them into society with a night of dining and dancing.

Mary Churchill, who had been "presented" the year before, spent Saturday with friends. She shopped with Judy Montagu: "Bought pretty nightdresses & lovely dressing gown." She found the city busy and thronged with shoppers. "I do find London shops so gay & pretty now," she wrote. She and Judy and two other friends went to lunch, then attended a rehearsal for the ball's traditional cake-cutting ceremony, where the new debs practiced curtsying toward a giant white cake. This was no mere curtsy but, rather, a carefully choreographed maneuver—left knee behind right, head erect, hands at side, smooth descent—taught by dance teacher Dame Marguerite Olivia Rankin, better known as Madame Vacani.

Mary and her friends watched in cold appraisal. "I must say," Mary wrote, "we all agreed this year's 'debs' aren't much to write home about."

After the rehearsal, Mary and another friend had tea at the Dorchester ("Great fun") and later a manicure, then dressed for the ball. Mary wore blue chiffon.

Her mother and two other lofty society women had secured a table for themselves and their families and friends. As the dinner was about to begin, and just as Mary was going down the stairs to the ballroom, air-raid sirens began to sound. Then came "3 loud bangs," these probably from an emplacement of heavy anti-aircraft guns across the street in Hyde Park, in a glade beyond the trees.

No one seemed to notice or care, though the rising clamor outside certainly provided an extra frisson of excitement that had been absent in prior years. In the ballroom, Mary wrote, "everything was gay & carefree & happy." Deeming the underground ballroom to be as safe as a bomb shelter, Mary and the other attendees took their seats, and the dinner got underway. The band played; women and the debs' delights began sweeping across the dance floor. No jazz here: That would come later, at the Café de Paris.

Mary could just make out the muffled sounds of anti-aircraft bursts and exploding bombs, which she described as "odd bumps and thuds above our chatter and the music."

WHEN THE RED ALERT SOUNDED, Snakehips Johnson was having a drink with friends at the Embassy Club, after which he planned to take a cab to the Café de Paris for the start of his turn on the dais. Once outside, however, he found that there were no cabs, the drivers having sought shelter from the raid. His friends told him to stay and not risk going to the café in the midst of what clearly was a major raid. But Snakehips insisted on honoring his commitment to the club's owner, Martin Poulsen, the cheery Dane, who had given him permission to play ten one-night stands at clubs outside London for some extra income. He set off at a run, joking as he left about his own very black skin: "Nobody will notice me in the dark."

Snakehips reached the club by nine forty-five, dashing through the black Blitz curtains at the top of the stairwell just inside the street entrance, and down the steps.

Tables surrounded a large dance floor in the shape of an oval, arrayed along a north-south axis, with a raised platform at the southern end for the band. Beyond this lay a large kitchen, which supplied ration-busting meals that included caviar, oysters, steaks, grouse, iced melon, sole, and peach melba, all to be accompanied by champagne. Two open stairways flanked the bandstand and led up to a balcony that ran along the walls of the club and held more tables, many of these favored by regulars for their views of the dance floor below and secured by large tips to Charles, the headwaiter. There were no windows.

The club was half full but was certain to fill to capacity by midnight. One guest, Lady Betty Baldwin, was the daughter of former prime minister Stanley Baldwin. She and a female friend had come to the club with two Dutch officers. At first peeved at not being given her favorite table, she and her date were now making their way to the dance floor. "The men, almost all in uniform, seemed extraordinarily handsome, the young women very beautiful, the whole atmosphere one of great gaiety and youthful charm," she said later.

The couple was just moving past the bandstand when Snakehips arrived, still winded from his run.

At this moment, twenty-one cooks and helpers were at work in the kitchen. Ten showgirls were preparing to dance out onto the floor. A waiter on the balcony pulled a table away from the wall in order to seat a newly arrived party of six. Harry MacElhone, the bartender, the former proprietor of Harry's New York Bar in Paris, now in exile, was in the midst of mixing drinks for a group of eight. A woman named Vera Lumley-Kelly was putting coins into a pay phone to call her mother and warn her to stay in the hall of her home until the raid was over. The band began to play a rousing jazz piece, "Oh Johnny, Oh Johnny, Oh!" A guest named Dan wrote a special request on a menu. "Ken," it said, meaning Snakehips. "It is my sister's birthday. Do you think you can squeeze in 'Happy Birthday' in a foxtrot? Thanks, Dan."

Snakehips approached the right side of the bandstand. As always, he wore a sleek tux and a red carnation. Poulsen, the owner, and Charles, the headwaiter, stood together on the balcony.

A woman on the dance floor did a brisk dance step, jabbed her hand into the air, and called out, "Wow, Johnny!"

AT THE GROSVENOR HOUSE HOTEL, Queen Charlotte's ball continued without pause.

Mary wrote: "It seemed so easy to forget—there in the light & warmth & music—the dark deserted streets—the barking of the guns— the hundreds of men & women ready at their posts—the bombs & death & blood."

Outside, the raid worsened. The night sky filled with aircraft, and with sallow beams of light, as hot bright daisies flared against a black velvet canvas. The bombers dropped 130,000 incendiaries and 130 tons of high explosives. Fourteen high-explosive bombs fell across Buckingham Palace and Green Park, immediately to the north. Twenty-three bombs fell on or near the city's Liverpool Street train station, including one that landed between platforms 4 and 5. An unexploded bomb forced doctors at Guy's Hospital to evacuate the surgical ward. Another destroyed a police station in the City—the financial district—killing two, wounding twelve. Fire brigades reported encountering a new kind of incendiary: Upon landing, it launched flaming rockets two hundred feet into the air.

One bomb, weighing 110 pounds, fell through the roof of the Rialto Cinema, penetrated all the way to the basement dance floor of the Café de Paris, and exploded. It was nine-fifty P.M.

NO ONE IN THE CLUB heard the detonation, but everyone saw it and felt it: a bright flash; an extraordinary flash; a blue flash. Then a choking cloud of dust and cordite, and coal-black darkness.

A saxophone player named David Williams was torn in two. One of the Dutch officers in Betty Baldwin's party lost his fingers. Six guests at one table died with no sign of external injury, and remained seated. The headwaiter, Charles, was thrown from the balcony to the floor, where he came to rest against a pillar on the other side of the room, dead. One young woman had her stockings torn off by the blast but otherwise was fine. Vera Lumley-Kelly, about to dial her mother on the pay phone, calmly hit the button marked "B," which returned her change.

At first there was silence. Then came muffled voices and the sound of shifting debris as survivors attempted to move. Pulverized plaster filled the air and turned hair white. Faces were blackened with cordite.

"I was blown off my feet," said one guest, "but the sensation was that of being pressed down by a great hand." A band member named Yorke de Souza said, "I was watching the dance floor through half-shut eyes when there was a blinding flash. I found myself covered with rubble, plaster and glass on the band stand under the piano. I was choking on cordite. It was black as night." His eyes adjusted. A light came from the kitchen. De Souza and another band member, named Wilkins, began looking for survivors and came across a body lying facedown. "Wilkins and I tried to lift him up but the top of his body came away in our hands," de Souza said. "It was Dave Williams"—the saxophonist—"I was violently sick as I let go of him. My eyes were blurred. I was walking in a haze."

Lady Baldwin found herself sitting on the floor, with one foot pinned under debris. "It felt very hot," she said. "I thought I was pouring with sweat." Blood spilled from a jagged wound in her face. "A light appeared at the top of the stairs and I could see people going up the staircase carrying victims on their backs." She and her Dutch officer found a cab and directed the driver to take her to her doctor's office.

The driver said, "Kindly don't bleed on the seat."

The twenty-one kitchen workers survived unhurt, as did the ten dancers waiting to perform. An initial count placed the death toll at thirty-four; another eighty were injured, many maimed and gashed.

Snakehips was dead, his head severed from his body.

AT LENGTH, THE DANCE at the Grosvenor House Hotel subsided and the all clear sounded; the basement ballroom began to empty. Mary, with her mother's permission, set out with friends and several mothers (not Clementine) to continue the fun. They headed toward the Café de Paris.

As the cars carrying Mary's party neared the club, they found their approach blocked by bomb debris, ambulances, and fire engines. Air-raid wardens diverted traffic onto adjacent streets.

Among Mary's group, the pressing question became, If they couldn't reach the Café de Paris, where then should they try instead? They drove to another club and spent the rest of the night dancing. At some point, they learned about the bombing. "Oh it was so gay our party . . . and suddenly it all seemed wrong & a mockery," Mary wrote in her diary.

Until now, the guns, the crews manning them, and the distant sounds and flashes had all seemed very remote, outside the bounds of daily life. "Somehow," she wrote, "these last did not seem real—of course it is only a terrible dream or figment of the imagination.

"But now—it is real—the Café de Paris hit—many fatal & serious casualties. They were dancing & laughing just like us. They are gone now in a moment from all we know to the vast, infinite unknown."

One friend in her group, Tom Shaughnessy, sought to place the tragedy in context: "If those people who have been killed at the Café suddenly came back now & saw us all here—they would all say, 'Go on—strike up the band—Carry on London.'"

And so they did, dancing, laughing, and joking until six-thirty on

Sunday morning. "Recalling it now," Mary wrote years later, "I am a little shocked that we headed off to find somewhere else to twirl whatever was left of the night away."

In the night's incident report, London civil defense authorities called it "the worst raid since early January."

AT THREE A.M., HARRY HOPKINS telephoned Chequers from Washington, D.C., and told John Colville that the U.S. Senate had passed the Lend-Lease Bill. The margin was 60 to 31.

Bayonet Quadrille

F OR CHURCHILL, THE CALL FROM HARRY HOPKINS WAS WELCOME indeed, "a draught of life." The next morning, he cabled Roosevelt: "Our blessings from the whole British Empire go out to you and the American nation for this very present help in time of trouble."

His high spirits reached full blaze that evening, despite his bronchitis. Though plainly ill, he had worked all day at his usual heroic pace, reading papers and the latest intercepts from Bletchley Park and firing off various minutes and directives. Chequers was packed with guests, some of whom had stayed the night, others who'd arrived that day. Most of Churchill's inner circle was present, including the Prof, Pug Ismay, and Colville. Here, too, were Churchill's daughter Diana and her husband, Duncan Sandys, and Pamela Churchill. (Pamela typically left baby Winston back home in the Hitchin rectory, with his nanny.) An American observer, Colonel William Donovan, came on Sunday; Charles de Gaulle left that morning. The loftiest guest was Australian prime minister Robert Menzies, who stayed the weekend. Mary and Clementine returned from London, bearing accounts of the horrors and glories of Saturday night.

The party was in full swing, without Churchill, when just before dinner he at last came downstairs, wearing his sky-blue siren suit.

Over dinner the talk veered wildly, with what Colville described as "a lot of flippant conversation about metaphysics, solipsists and higher mathematics." Clementine skipped dinner and spent the evening in bed; according to Mary, she had a bronchial cold. Mary was concerned, as well, about her father's health. "Papa not at all well," she wrote in her diary. "V. worrying."

But Churchill stormed on. After dinner, fueled with champagne and brandy, he fired up the Chequers gramophone and began to play military marches and songs. He brought out a big-game rifle, probably his Mannlicher, and began to march to the music, one of his favorite evening pastimes. He then executed a series of rifle drills and bayonet maneuvers, looking in his rompers like a fierce pale blue Easter egg gone to war.

General Brooke, commander in chief of Home Forces, found it both startling and hilarious. "The evening remains very vivid in my mind," he wrote later, in an addendum to his published diary, "as it was one of the first occasions on which I had seen Winston in one of his real light-hearted moods. I was convulsed watching him give the exhibition of bayonet exercises with his rifle, dressed up in his romper suit and standing in the ancestral hall of Chequers. I remember wondering what Hitler would have thought of this demonstration of skill at arms."

For Churchill, this was an early night, his sole concession to his bronchitis. His guests were grateful. "To bed at the record hour of 11:30 P.M.," Colville wrote in his diary. General Brooke observed: "Luckily PM decided to go to bed early and by midnight I was comfortably tucked away in an Elizabethan four poster bed dated 1550. I could not help wondering, as I went to sleep, what wonderful stories the bed could tell of its various occupants during the last 400 years!"

IN BERLIN, JOSEPH GOEBBELS made note in his diary of the new "punishing attacks" on London, adding, "There will be worse to come."

The Gambler

———

To AVOID THE THREAT OF SUBMARINE AND AERIAL ATTACK IN THE Mediterranean, Randolph Churchill's ship, the *Glenroy,* took the long way to Egypt, down the west coast of Africa and then back up, to the Gulf of Aden, the Red Sea, and the Suez Canal. The voyage was long and tedious—thirty-six days to reach the entrance to the canal, on March 8. Finding little else in the way of distraction, Randolph turned to one his favorite pursuits. "There was very high gambling, poker, roulette, chemin-de-fer, every night," Evelyn Waugh wrote in a memorandum about the commando unit. "Randolph lost £850 in two evenings." In a letter to his own wife, Waugh remarked, "Poor Pamela will have to go to work."

As the voyage progressed, Randolph's losses deepened, until he owed his fellow voyagers £3,000. Half of that was owed to just one man: Peter Fitzwilliam, a member of one of the richest families in England, soon to inherit Wentworth Woodhouse, a vast mansion in Yorkshire thought by some to be the inspiration for Jane Austen's Pemberley in *Pride and Prejudice.*

Randolph broke the news to Pamela in a telegram, in which he instructed her to pay off the debt in any way she could. He suggested she send each man £5 or £10 a month. "Anyway," he concluded, "I leave it up to you, but please don't tell my mother and father."

Pamela, certain now that she was indeed again pregnant, was stunned and frightened. This was "the breaking point," she said. At £10 a month, she would have needed a dozen years just to resolve the debt to Fitzwilliam. The amount was unfathomable, so much so that it brought into focus how fundamentally defective her marriage was. "I mean, that was the first realization in my life that I was totally on my own and that the future of my son was dependent entirely on me and my future was dependent on me, that I couldn't rely ever again on Randolph," she said.

She recalled thinking, "What the hell do I do? I can't go to Clemmie and Winston."

Almost immediately, Beaverbrook came to mind. "I liked him enormously, admired him tremendously," she said. She considered him a close friend and, along with baby Winston, had spent a number of weekends at his country home, Cherkley. He felt the same way, although those who knew Beaverbrook understood that he saw a value in their connection that went beyond mere friendship. She was a conduit of gossip from within the loftiest circle in the land.

She called Beaverbrook and sobbed into the phone, "Max, can I come see you?"

She got into her Jaguar and drove to London. It was morning, the risk of being bombed therefore slight. She drove through streets made drab by destruction and dust but colored here and there by flashes of wallpaper, paint, and fabric from the exposed interiors of houses. She met Beaverbrook at the new offices of the Ministry of Aircraft Production, now situated in a large oil-company building on the Thames Embankment.

She told him about the gambling debt and about her marriage, warning that he was not to divulge any of it to Clementine or to Churchill, whom she knew to be Beaverbrook's closest friend. Of course he assented: Secrets were his favorite possessions.

She asked him right off whether he would consider giving her a year's advance on Randolph's salary. It seemed to her an easy request, one that Beaverbrook would surely fulfill. After all, Randolph's job with the *Evening Standard* was more sinecure than anything else. With the immediate crisis averted, she could get on with the larger question of how, or even whether, to proceed with her marriage.

Beaverbrook looked at her. "I won't advance Randolph a single penny of his salary," he said.

She was shocked. "I remember being absolutely astonished," she said later, "It never occurred to me that he wouldn't. It seemed such a little thing to ask."

But now Beaverbrook surprised her again. "If you want me to give you a check for £3,000," he said, "I will do it, for you." But it would be a present, he emphasized, from him, to her.

Pamela grew wary. "Max had to have control of the people around him, whether it was Brendan Bracken or even Winston Churchill," she said. "I mean, he had to be in the driver's seat and he just smelled [of] danger for me." On past occasions, Randolph had warned her about Beaverbrook, telling her never to allow herself to fall under his sway. "Never," Randolph had stressed. "Don't you ever get into Max Beaverbrook's control."

Now, in Beaverbrook's office, she said, "Max, I can't do that."

She still needed his help, however. She knew she had to find a job, in London, to begin paying off the debts.

Beaverbrook offered a compromise. She could move her son and nanny into his country home, and he would make sure to look after them. She would then be free to move to London.

She accepted the arrangement. She leased her house in Hitchin to a nursery school that had been evacuated from London (and made a profit, charging £2 more per week than she herself paid). In London she took a room on the top floor of the Dorchester, sharing it with Churchill's niece, Clarissa. "Not as glamorous or as expensive as that might sound," Clarissa wrote later, "since it was not a popular floor to be on during the constant air raids." They paid £6 a week. Clarissa liked Pamela but noted that she "had no sense of humor." What she did have was a gift for making the most of a situation. "She combined a canny eye for chances with a genuinely warm heart," Clarissa wrote.

Soon after moving in, Pamela found herself at a luncheon at 10 Downing Street, seated beside the minister of supply, Sir Andrew Rae Duncan, to whom she mentioned her hope of finding a job in the city. Within twenty-four hours, she had one, in a division of his ministry that was devoted to establishing hostels for munitions workers assigned to factories far from home.

Securing meals for herself was a problem, at first. Her room rate at the Dorchester included only breakfast. She had lunch at the Supply Ministry. For dinner, she tried as much as possible to dine at No. 10 or with well-off friends. She found herself compelled to "hustle" for these dinner invitations, but this proved to be an art at which she excelled. It helped, of course, that she was the daughter-in-law of the most important man in Britain. In short order, she and Clarissa had "friends and acquaintances on every floor," Clarissa recalled.

The two often sheltered from air raids in the room of another resident, Australian prime minister Menzies, whom Pamela had come to know well because of her connection to the Churchills. Menzies occupied a large suite on the Dorchester's much-coveted first floor. The women spent nights on mattresses laid out in its windowless entry alcove.

Now came the "tricky" matter of keeping Randolph's gambling fiasco a secret from her in-laws, "because I couldn't really tell Clemmie and Winston why suddenly, from living happily in Hitchin with my baby I suddenly up, separated myself from my baby and wanted a job in London."

To help cover expenses and begin paying off the debt, Pamela sold her wedding presents, "including," she said later, "some diamond earrings and a couple of nice bracelets." In the midst of all this she lost her new pregnancy, and blamed the loss on the stress and turmoil in her life. She knew by this point that her marriage was over.

She began to feel a new sense of freedom, helped too by the fact that soon, on March 20, 1941, she would celebrate her twenty-first birthday. She had no inkling, of course, that in a very short while she would fall in love with a handsome older man living a few stories below, on one of the safest floors in the safest hotel in London.

A Treat for Clementine

I N NEW YORK, ON MONDAY MORNING, MARCH 10, AVERELL HARRIMAN boarded the *Atlantic Clipper* at LaGuardia's Marine Air Terminal, accompanied by his personal secretary, Robert P. Meiklejohn. The skies were clear, the waters of Flushing Bay a hard, crystalline blue, with the temperature at eight A.M. a brisk twenty-nine degrees. The plane he stepped into was a Boeing 314 "flying boat"—essentially a giant hull with wings and engines—and, indeed, the boarding process had more in common with climbing onto a ship than an airplane, including a walk over water on a pierlike boarding ramp.

As would have been the case had he been traveling first-class on a transatlantic ocean liner, Harriman received a manifest that identified his fellow passengers. The list was like something from a novel by the new international literary sensation Agatha Christie, whose bestselling thriller *And Then There Were None* had been published in the States a year earlier. (The British version had the abysmal title *Ten Little ——*, the third word being a crude term for blacks in common usage at the time in Britain and America.) The manifest included Antenor Patiño, identified as a Bolivian diplomat, but better known the world over as "the Tin King," and Anthony J. Drexel Biddle Jr., who had been ambassador to Poland during the Nazi invasion and was now to serve as envoy to various exiled governments in London, traveling with his wife and secretary. There were other British and American diplomats on the list, as well as two couriers and various staff members. A passenger named Antonio Gazda, described as an engineer from Switzerland, was in fact an international arms dealer, engaged in selling guns to both sides.

Each passenger was allowed sixty-six pounds of luggage free of charge. Harriman and his secretary brought two bags each; Ambassador Biddle brought thirty-four bags and shipped another eleven on a separate flight.

The *Clipper* pulled away from its moorage, entered Long Island Sound off Queens, and began its takeoff run, bumping across a mile-long fetch of open water before at last lifting off, shedding water like a breaching whale. With a cruising speed of 145 miles per hour, the plane would need about six hours to reach its first stop, Bermuda. It flew at eight thousand feet, which pretty much ensured that it would encounter every cloud and storm in its path. There would be turbulence but also luxury. White-jacketed stewards served full meals on china in a dining compartment with tables, chairs, and tablecloths. At dinner men wore suits, women dresses; at night the stewards made up beds in curtained berths. Honeymooners could book a private suite in the plane's tail and swoon at the moonglade on the sea below.

As the plane approached Bermuda, stewards closed all the shades, a security measure to keep passengers from surveying the British naval base below. Anyone who peeked was subject to a $500 fine, about $8,000 today. Upon landing, Harriman learned that the next leg of his flight would be delayed until the next day, Tuesday, March 11, owing to bad weather in the Azores, where Clippers had to land on an exposed stretch of the Atlantic.

As Harriman waited for the weather to improve, Roosevelt signed the Lend-Lease Bill into law.

IN LISBON, HARRIMAN FACED another delay. The KLM flight to Bristol was in high demand, and passengers with the most senior official rank, like Ambassador Biddle, took priority. The delay lasted three days. Harriman did not suffer, however. He stayed at the Hotel Palácio, in Estoril, on the Portuguese Riviera, known both for its luxury and for being a cradle of espionage. Here, in fact, he met briefly with Colonel Donovan, who was now, after his Sunday at Chequers, on his way back to Washington, where he would soon become head of America's top wartime spy agency, the Office of Strategic Services.

Ever striving for efficiency, Harriman decided to take advantage of the delay by having the hotel clean his traveling clothes, against the advice of secretary Meiklejohn, who later wrote, ruefully, "Mr. Harriman in a rash moment sent his laundry out while he was at the hotel, first receiving a solemn promise that it would be returned before his departure for England."

At some point, Harriman went shopping. Given the nature of his mission, he was more aware than most people of the intricacies of Britain's food shortages and rationing rules, and bought a bag of tangerines to give to Churchill's wife.

CHEQUERS AND ITS FULL-MOON SURROGATE, Ditchley, were by now a regular weekend ritual for Churchill. These brief sojourns took him away from the increasingly dreary, bomb-worn vistas of London, and salved that need within his English soul for trees, hollows, ponds, and birdsong. He planned to return to Chequers on Friday, March 14, just three days after his last stay, there to receive Roosevelt's latest emissary, if the man ever managed to arrive.

Meanwhile, there was much afoot to cause him worry. Bulgaria had just joined the Axis, and soon afterward German forces entered the country, making a feared invasion of Greece, on its southern border, much more likely. After a period of anguished debate, Churchill decided to honor an existing defense pact with Greece and on March 9 dispatched British troops to help fend off the expected onslaught—a risky venture, for it weakened British forces still in Libya and Egypt. The expedition seemed to many to be a lost cause, but at least an honorable one, and—as Churchill saw it   an important assertion of Britain's loyalty and its will to fight. As Foreign Secretary Anthony Eden telegraphed from Cairo, "We were prepared to run the risk of failure, thinking it better to suffer with the Greeks than to make no attempt to help them."

Meanwhile, a new German general had appeared in the deserts of Libya, with hundreds of panzer tanks at his command and with orders to bolster Italian forces and win back territory lost to the British. General Erwin Rommel, soon to be nicknamed "the Desert Fox," had already proven himself in Europe, and now commanded a new army group, the Afrika Korps.

HARRIMAN AT LAST SECURED a seat on the flight from Lisbon to Bristol on Saturday, March 15. His laundry had not been returned. He left instructions with the hotel to forward his clothes to London.

As he walked to his plane, a KLM DC-3, he had what he called an "eerie experience." He spotted a German aircraft on the tarmac, his first visible marker of the war. Painted black from nose to tail, save for a white swastika, the plane was a jarring presence in that otherwise sun-struck landscape, like a blackened tooth in a gleaming smile.

IN GERMANY, HERMANN GÖRING took advantage of a period of fine weather to launch his new campaign against the British Isles, with massed raids that ranged from southern England to Glasgow. On Wednesday, March 12, a force of 340 German bombers carrying high-explosive bombs and incendiaries attacked Liverpool and its surrounding districts, killing more than five hundred people. Over the next two nights the Luftwaffe struck Clydeside, the region encompassing Glasgow, killing 1,085. These raids demonstrated anew the capricious nature of death from the air. A single parachute mine, drifting aimlessly with the wind, destroyed a tenement building and killed eighty-three civilians; a lone bomb killed eighty more when it penetrated an air-raid shelter at a shipyard.

Joseph Goebbels, writing in his diary on Saturday, March 15, exulted. "Our fliers are talking of two new Coventrys. We shall see how long Britain can put up with this." To him, as to Göring, the fall of Britain seemed more likely now than ever, despite the new show of support from America. "We are slowly choking England to death," Goebbels wrote. "One day she will lie gasping on the ground."

None of this distracted Luftwaffe chief Göring from his pursuit of art. On Saturday, March 15, he oversaw delivery of a vast shipment of works seized in Paris and packed onto a train that comprised twenty-five baggage cars, transporting four thousand individual pieces ranging from paintings to tapestries to furniture.

HARRIMAN ARRIVED IN ENGLAND on Saturday afternoon, five days after departing LaGuardia. His KLM flight landed at an airfield outside Bristol at three-thirty, in bright and clear weather, as barrage balloons drifted over the adjacent city. He found that Churchill had engineered a surprise. Harriman was supposed to transfer to a British passenger plane for the final flight to London, but instead Churchill had arranged to have him met by his own naval aide-de-camp, Commander Charles Ralfe "Tommy" Thompson, who tucked Harriman into Churchill's favorite aircraft, his Flamingo. Escorted by two Hurricane fighters, they flew through the waning light over English countryside softened by the first buds and blooms of spring, direct to an airfield near Chequers, where they arrived just in time for dinner.

Churchill and Clementine welcomed Harriman with warmth, as if they had known him forever. He presented the tangerines he had bought for Clementine in Lisbon. "I was surprised to see how grateful Mrs. Churchill was," he wrote, later. "Her unfeigned delight brought home to me the restrictions of the dreary British wartime diet."

AFTER DINNER, CHURCHILL AND HARRIMAN sat down for their first detailed conversation about how Britain was holding up against Hitler. Harriman told the prime minister that he could be useful in promoting Churchill's interests only to the extent that he understood Britain's true condition and the kind of aid Churchill most wanted and what he planned to do with it.

"You shall be informed," Churchill told him. "We accept you as a friend. Nothing will be kept from you."

Churchill proceeded to assess the threat of invasion, noting how the Germans had assembled fleets of barges at ports in France, Belgium, and Denmark. His biggest concern for the time being, however, was the German submarine campaign against British shipping, which he called "the Battle of the Atlantic." In February alone, U-boats, aircraft, and mines had destroyed four hundred thousand tons of shipping, he told Harriman, and the rate was increasing. Losses per convoy were running at about 10 percent; the rate at which ships sank was two to three times faster than the rate at which Britain could build new ones.

It was a dire portrait, but Churchill seemed undeterred. Harriman was struck by his resolve to continue the war alone, if need be, and by his frank avowal that without America's eventual participation, Britain had no hope of achieving a final victory.

A sense of great and fateful change imbued the weekend, and left Mary Churchill feeling a kind of awe at being allowed to witness such grave talk. "The weekend was thrilling," she wrote in her diary. "Here was the hub of the Universe. For many billions of destinies may perhaps hang on this new axis—this Anglo-American–American-Anglo friendship."

WHEN HARRIMAN AT LAST reached London itself, he found a landscape of contrasts. In one block, he saw untouched homes and clear sidewalks;

in the next, mounds of rubble and vertical claws of wood and iron, and half-broken houses with personal belongings splayed across their facades like the battle flags of a lost regiment. Everything was coated with light gray dust, and the scent of combusted tar and wood suffused the air. But the sky was blue, and trees were starting to green, and mists rose off the grass of Hyde Park and the waters of the Serpentine. Commuters streamed from tube stations and double-decker buses, carrying briefcases, newspapers, and lunchboxes, but also gas masks and helmets.

The ambient sense of threat insinuated itself into everyday choices and decisions, such as the importance of leaving work before nightfall, and identifying the nearest shelter, and Harriman's selection of the Dorchester Hotel. The hotel first assigned him a large suite on its sixth floor, rooms 607 through 609, but he deemed this too near the roof (there were only two stories above him), as well as too large and too expensive, and asked to be moved to a smaller suite on the third floor. He directed his secretary, Meiklejohn, to haggle for a cheaper rate. Meanwhile, Meiklejohn quickly found that even his "cheapest room" at Claridge's was beyond his means. "Will have to move out of this place . . . or starve to death," he wrote in his diary, after his first night in the hotel.

He moved from Claridge's to an apartment that seemed likely to withstand attack. In a letter to a colleague back in the States, he described his satisfaction with the place. He occupied a four-room flat on the eighth floor of a modern building made of steel and brick, with a protective shield of two more floors above. "I even have a view," he wrote. "Opinion differs as to whether it is safer to go in a cellar and have the building fall on you in a raid or live upstairs and fall on the building. At least if you are upstairs you can see what hits you—if there's any comfort in that."

He had expected the nightly blackouts to be particularly daunting and depressing but found this not to be the case. The blackout did make life easier for the pickpockets who frequented train stations and for the looters who plucked valuables from damaged homes and shops, but otherwise, bombs aside, the streets were fundamentally safe. Meiklejohn liked walking in the darkness. "Most impressive thing is the silence," he wrote. "Almost everybody walks about like a ghost."

HARRIMAN ACTED QUICKLY TO establish his office. Although news accounts portrayed him as a lone paladin striding through chaos, in fact, the "Harriman Mission," as it became known, soon became a minor empire, with Harriman, Meiklejohn, seven more senior men, and a battalion of staff that included fourteen stenographers, ten messengers, six file clerks, two telephone operators, four "charwomen," and one chauffeur. A benefactor loaned Harriman a Bentley, said to cost £2,000. Harriman specified that some of the stenographers and clerks had to be American, for handling "confidential matters."

The mission was lodged first in the U.S. embassy, at No. 1 Grosvenor Square, but then moved to an adjacent apartment house, where a passage was constructed to link the two buildings. Describing Harriman's office to a friend, Meiklejohn wrote, "Mr. Harriman achieves a somewhat Mussolini-like effect—not at all to his liking—by reason of his office being a very large room that used to be the living room of a rather elegant flat." Meiklejohn was especially pleased that his own office occupied what had once been the flat's dining room and adjoined a kitchen with a refrigerator, whose proximity made it easier for him to maintain a supply of foods to help his boss manage periodic flareups of a stomach ulcer that had long plagued him.

The office itself felt something like a refrigerator. In a letter to the building's manager, Harriman complained that the ambient temperature in the office was sixty-five degrees, compared to seventy-two in the embassy next door.

There was still no sign of his laundry.

THE WARMTH OF CHURCHILL'S initial greeting was repeated throughout London, with invitations arriving at Harriman's office for lunches, dinners, and weekends in country homes. His desk calendar filled with appointments, first and foremost with Churchill, but also with the Prof, Beaverbrook, and Ismay. His schedule quickly grew complex, and soon his calendar marked out a geographic rhythm repeated over and over—Claridge's, the Savoy, the Dorchester, Downing Street—with no written indication of any care given to the possibility of being blown off the planet by the Luftwaffe, save for the monthly, moon-governed shift to Ditchley.

One of the first invitations to arrive, which Harriman received as soon as he got to London, came from David Niven, who at age thirty-one was already an accomplished actor, with film roles ranging from an uncredited slave in the 1934 film *Cleopatra* to the namesake star in 1939's *Raffles*. Upon the outbreak of war, Niven had resolved to put his acting career on hold and rejoin the British Army, in which he had served previously, from 1929 to 1932. He now was assigned to a commando unit. Niven's decision earned him direct praise from Churchill when the two met at a dinner party while Churchill was still first lord of the Admiralty. "Young man," Churchill said, shaking his hand, "you did a very fine thing to give up a most promising career to fight for your country." He paused, and with what Niven described as a cheery glint in his eye, added, "Mark you, had you not done so—it would have been despicable!"

Niven had met Harriman at Sun Valley and had written now because he was coming to London soon on leave and wanted to know if Harriman would be available for "a meal and a laugh." Niven also offered Harriman a temporary membership in Boodle's, his club, with the caveat that for the time being all Boodle's members were using the Conservative Club, as Boodle's had just received "a visiting card" from the Luftwaffe.

Boodle's, Niven wrote, "is very old and very sedate and the Scarlet Pimpernel used to be a member but in spite of all that you can still get the best dinner and are still served by the best staff in London."

Harriman held his first press conference on Tuesday, March 18, his second day in London, and spoke to fifty-four reporters and photographers. The crowd included twenty-seven British and European reporters, seventeen Americans—among them Edward R. Murrow of CBS—and ten photographers, armed with cameras and flash guns, and with pockets full of one-use bulbs. Like Churchill, Harriman was very aware of public perception and how important it would be during his tenure in London, so much so that after the press conference he asked the editors of two of Beaverbrook's newspapers to canvass their reporters to get their candid impressions of how he had done—without letting them know it was he who was asking. The editor of the *Daily Express,* Arthur Christiansen, replied the next day, with "the 'cold' report" Harriman had requested.

"Mr. Harriman was too cagey," Christiansen wrote, quoting the *Express* correspondent who had covered the conference. "While his quick smile and great courtesy gave the reporters the impression that he was pleasant and likable, it was evident that he was not going to say anything which could possibly cause him embarrassment at home. . . . A bit too slow in his replies, which increased the atmosphere of caution."

Harriman asked for a similar report from Frank Owen, editor of Beaverbrook's *Evening Standard,* who passed along comments his news editor had gathered that morning from six reporters. "Of course," Owen wrote, "they did not know what the comment was for. They were gossiping quite candidly."

Among the remarks:

"Too legal and dry."

"More like a successful English barrister than an American."

"Too meticulous: he searches too long for the exact phrase which will convey his meaning. This is rather dull."

That he was an attractive presence was clear to all. After one later press conference, a female reporter told Harriman's daughter Kathy, "For g. sake tell your father next time I have to cover his conference to wear a gas mask so's I can concentrate on what he's saying."

THAT EVENING, WEDNESDAY, MARCH 19, at eight-thirty, Harriman joined Churchill for dinner at 10 Downing Street, in its armored basement dining room, and almost immediately gained a close-up appreciation for two things he so far had only heard about: what it was like to experience a major air raid and the sheer courage of the prime minister.

Men

—

WHEN IT CAME TO HIS DINING TIMETABLE, CHURCHILL MADE no compromise for bombers. He always had dinner late, as was the case that Wednesday night, when he and Clementine welcomed Harriman to the basement dining room at No. 10, along with two other guests, Ambassador Anthony Biddle and his wife, Margaret, both of whom had been aboard Harriman's *Atlantic Clipper* flight from New York to Lisbon.

The night was clear and warm, lighted by a half-moon. Dinner was underway when air-raid sirens began their octave-scaling wail, as the first of what would prove to be five hundred bombers entered the skies over London's dock district, in the city's East End, carrying high-explosive bombs, parachute mines, and more than one hundred thousand incendiary canisters. One bomb destroyed a shelter, killing forty-four Londoners in an instant. The big parachute mines drifted to earth in Stepney, Poplar, and West Ham, where they destroyed whole blocks of homes. Two hundred fires began blazing.

Dinner proceeded as if no raid were occurring. After the meal, Biddle told Churchill that he would like to see for himself "the strides which London had made in air-raid precautions." At which point Churchill invited him and Harriman to accompany him to the roof. The raid was still in progress. Along the way, they put on steel helmets and collected John Colville and Eric Seal, so that they, too, as Colville put it, could "watch the fun."

Getting to the roof took effort. "A fantastic climb it was," Seal said in a letter to his wife, "up ladders, a long circular stairway, & a tiny manhole right at the top of a tower."

Nearby, anti-aircraft guns blasted away. The night sky filled with spears of light as searchlight crews hunted the bombers above. Now and then aircraft appeared silhouetted against the moon and the starlit sky. Engines roared high overhead in a continuous thrum.

Churchill and his helmeted entourage stayed on the roof for two hours. "All the while," Biddle wrote, in a letter to President Roosevelt, "he received reports at various intervals from the different sections of the city hit by the bombs. It was intensely interesting."

Biddle was impressed by Churchill's evident courage and energy. In the midst of it all, as guns fired and bombs erupted in the distance, Churchill quoted Tennyson—part of an 1842 monologue called *Locksley Hall,* in which the poet wrote, with prescience:

> Heard the heavens fill with shouting,
> and there rain'd a ghastly dew
> From the nations' airy navies
> grappling in the central blue.

On the roof, at least, all survived, but in the course of the six-hour raid, five hundred Londoners lost their lives. In the city's West Ham district alone, bombs killed 204 people, all taken to the Municipal Baths Mortuary on Romford Road, where, according to a Scotland Yard inspector's report, "the mortuary men, heedless of time and food and in the stench of flesh and blood, classifying and taking descriptions of the mutilated human remains and fragments of bodies and limbs," managed to identify all but three victims.

Later, Ambassador Biddle sent Churchill a note thanking him for the experience and complimenting him on his leadership and courage. "It was grand being with you," he said.

It was a measure of the ambient courage of London in 1941 that Harriman now decided to invite his daughter Kathy, a twenty-three-year-old reporter and recent Bennington College graduate, to come live with him in Britain.

THERE WAS COURAGE; there was despair. On Friday, March 28, the writer Virginia Woolf, her depression worsened by the war and the destruction of both her house in Bloomsbury and her subsequent residence, composed a note to her husband, Leonard, and left it for him at their country home in East Sussex.

"Dearest," she wrote, "I feel certain that I am going mad again. I feel we can't go through another of those terrible times. And I shan't recover this time. I begin to hear voices, and I can't concentrate. So I am doing what seems the best thing to do."

Her hat and cane were found on a bank of the nearby River Ouse.

AT CHEQUERS, THE TURF applied to the entry lanes during the preceding winter had succeeded in making them invisible from the air. But now, in March, a new problem arose.

While flying over Chequers, two pilots from the RAF's Photographic Reconnaissance Unit made a startling discovery. Someone had plowed up the U-shaped area formed where the lanes arced to the front and back of the house, leaving a broad half-moon of pale earth. The plowing, moreover, had been done in "a most peculiar way," as though the plow-man were deliberately trying to depict the head of a trident aimed at the house. The pale, raw soil nullified the camouflage effect of the turf, "thus putting us back more or less where we were at the start, but if anything rather more so," wrote an official of the Ministry of Home Security's Civil Defence Camouflage Establishment.

So deliberate did this first seem that Detective Inspector Thompson, Churchill's security man, suspected foul play. He made "enquiries" on the morning of March 23 and located the culprit, a tenant farmer named David Rogers, who explained that he had plowed the area, hoping only to make maximum use of all available ground. He was simply trying to grow as much food as possible for the war effort, under the "Grow More Food" campaign. Thompson decided that the man was in fact not a fifth columnist and that he had produced the pattern by accident, according to a report on the matter.

On Monday, March 24, workers using heavy-duty tractors resolved the problem by plowing adjacent terrain so that from the air the plowed land looked like an ordinary rectangular field. "The ground, naturally, will show up very white for some days," the report said, "but the directional indication will be completely obliterated and the ground will be sown with quick-growing seeds."

Another problem remained: the inevitable presence of the many parked cars when Churchill was at the house. The phenomenon often thwarted camouflage efforts, wrote Philip James, of the camouflage establishment. "Not only would a number of cars outside Chequers clearly indicate the probable presence of the Prime Minister, but it might equally draw the attention of an enemy airman, who would otherwise have passed by without giving any particular attention to the house."

He urged that cars either be covered or parked under trees.

The fact remained that Chequers was a clear and obvious target, well within the reach of German bombers and fighters. Given the Luftwaffe's prowess at low-altitude bombing, it seemed something of a miracle that Chequers was standing at all.

THAT THE AIR WAR would continue throughout the year and into the next seemed obvious to Churchill, as did the fact that continued bombardment posed a political hazard. Londoners had proven they could "take it," but how much longer would they be able to do so? Having deemed the reform of air-raid shelters to be crucial, he hectored his minister of health, Malcolm MacDonald, to make a wide range of improvements before the next winter. He wanted particular attention paid to flooring and drainage, and urged that shelters be equipped with radios and gramophones.

In a second memorandum that weekend, this to both MacDonald and Minister of Home Security Morrison, Churchill also emphasized the need for inspecting the personal Anderson air-raid shelters Londoners had installed in their gardens and told the ministers "those that are waterlogged should either be removed or their owners helped to give them a good foundation."

One result of Churchill's interest was a pamphlet that advised citizens on how best to use their Anderson shelters. "A sleeping bag with a hot bottle or brick in it will keep you beautifully warm," it said, and recommended bringing in a tin of biscuits during air raids, "in case the children wake up hungry in the night." Oil lamps posed a danger, it warned, "as they may get spilled either by shock from a bomb or by accident." The pamphlet also had advice for dog owners: "If you take your dog into your shelter, you should muzzle him. Dogs are liable to become hysterical if bombs explode nearby."

As Churchill said later, "If we can't be safe, let us at least be comfortable."

THAT WEEKEND, MARY CHURCHILL and a friend, Charles Ritchie, set off by train for a visit to Stansted Park, the home of Lord Bessborough, where John Colville and Bessborough's daughter, Moyra, had investigated a fallen bomber the previous summer. Mary and Charles and other young people in their circle were massing at the house for the weekend, in order to attend a big dance at the Tangmere RAF base, one of the most important, and most heavily bombed, airfields in England, about a half-hour's drive away. The RAF was perhaps banking on the night's new moon, the phase when the moon is utterly black, to reduce the likelihood of German attack during the dance.

Mary and Charles took a train from London's Waterloo station, riding in first class, snug under throw blankets. "We rather monopolized" the carriage, she wrote in her diary, "by putting our feet up & covering ourselves with rugs." At one station a woman looked into their compartment and gave them a knowing look. "Oh, I won't disturb you," the woman said, then rushed away.

"Dear me," Mary wrote.

They arrived at Stansted Park in time for afternoon tea. Mary met Moyra for the first time and was pleasantly surprised. "I was rather alarmed by what I had been previously told—but she turned out to be the best of company. Reserved but gay."

She also met Moyra's brother Lord Duncannon—Eric. An officer in the Royal Artillery, he was nine years older than she, and a survivor of the Dunkirk evacuation. She looked him over and, in her diary, pronounced him "good looking in rather a lyrical way—very beautiful grey, wideset eyes, melodious voice. Charming & easy." John Colville knew him, and had a contrasting opinion. Eric, he wrote, "cannot avoid saying things of such futile egotism that he makes even Moyra blush. He is indeed a fantastic creature."

After tea, Mary, Moyra, Eric, and the other young guests—"La jeunesse," Mary wrote—got ready for the dance, then gathered downstairs. They were on the verge of departure when a bank of nearby anti-aircraft guns began to fire. Once the noise subsided, they set out for the air base. With no moon, the night was especially dark, barely penetrated by the slit-eyed headlights of the cars.

At the party, she met one of the RAF's most famous aces, Squadron Leader Douglas Bader, thirty-one years old. He had lost both legs in an air crash a decade earlier, but with the advent of war and the shortage of pilots, he had been approved for combat, and quickly accumulated victories. He walked with two prosthetic legs and never used crutches or a walking stick. "He's marvelous—" Mary wrote. "I danced with him &

he's so extraordinarily good. He is exemplary of the triumph of life & mind & personality over matter."

But the man who most commanded her attention was Eric. She danced with him throughout the night, and after noting this in her diary, she quoted Hilaire Belloc's very short 1910 poem, "The False Heart":

> I said to Heart,
> "How goes it?"
> Heart replied:
> "Right as a Ribstone, Pippin!"
> But it lied.

Mary added: "No comment."

Late in the party, the lights failed and the dance floor went dark—"not an altogether unwelcome event to many I think." It was all great fun, she wrote, "but distinctly an orgy and rather bizarre."

They returned to Stansted under a sable sky flecked with planets and stars.

SATURDAY NIGHT IN LONDON was exceptionally dark—so much so that when Harriman's secretary, Meiklejohn, went to Paddington station to meet a new member of the mission's staff, the combination of no moon and blacked-out platforms made it impossible to see who was getting off the trains. The secretary had brought a flashlight, and wore a coat with a fur collar, which the new man had been told to look for. After searching in vain for a while, Meiklejohn got the idea to situate himself in a prominent spot and use his light to illuminate his collar. The man found him.

Harriman left the city that night for another stay at Chequers, this time accompanied by America's new ambassador, John G. Winant, appointed by Roosevelt to replace Joseph Kennedy, who, increasingly out of favor, had resigned late the previous year. Both Winant and Harriman came to dine and sleep. Over dinner, Harriman sat opposite Churchill's daughter-in-law, Pamela. In describing the moment later, she wrote: "I saw the best-looking man I had ever seen."

He was much older than she, she acknowledged. But from early on she had recognized in herself an affinity for older men. "I wasn't amused or interested in people my own age," she said. "What attracted me was much older men and I felt very at ease with them." She had never felt wholly comfortable with members of her own generation. "Luckily for me, the war came, so then it sort of didn't matter, and I immediately spent time with people much older than myself and found myself quite happily entertaining whoever it might be."

That Harriman was married struck her as irrelevant. It struck him the same way. By the time of his arrival in London, his marriage had stalled on a plateau of mutual respect and sexual disinterest. His wife, Marie Norton Whitney, was a dozen years younger and ran an art gallery in New York. They had met in 1928, while she was married to a rich New York playboy, Cornelius Vanderbilt Whitney. She and Harriman married in February 1930, after Harriman divorced his first wife. By now, however, both had begun having affairs. Mrs. Harriman was widely thought to be sleeping with Eddy Duchin, a handsome and trim New York bandleader. Duchin, too, was married.

Pamela's own marriage was in lightning decline, and as it devolved her sense of freedom grew. A more exciting life seemed certain to lie ahead. She was young and beautiful, and at the center of Churchill's circle. She wrote, "It was a terrible war, but if you were the right age, [at] the right time and in the right place, it was spectacular."

Given Harriman's ubiquity within Churchill's circle, it was clear that Pamela and he would encounter each other again, and often—much to the glee of Max Beaverbrook, minister of aircraft production and collector of secrets, known to some as "the Minister of Midnight."

THE MOOD AT CHEQUERS that weekend was bright for other reasons as well. Over the preceding days, British forces had seized important ground in Eritrea and Ethiopia, and an anti-German coup in Yugoslavia had installed a new government, which promptly nullified the country's existing pact with Hitler. On Friday, March 28, Churchill sent a cheery telegram to Harry Hopkins in Washington, stating, "Yesterday was a grand day" and noting, too, that he was "in closest touch with Harriman." John Colville, in his diary, wrote that Churchill "has spent much of the weekend pacing—or rather tripping—up and down the Great Hall to the sound of the gramophone (playing martial airs, waltzes and the most vulgar kind of brass-band songs) deep in thought the while."

Sunday brought still more good news: In a battle off Cape Matapan, Greece, the Royal Navy, aided by intelligence from Bletchley Park, had engaged and effectively crippled the Italian navy, already shaken by a defeat the previous fall.

Mary Churchill, still at Stansted Park and savoring the delights of the prior night's dance, was elated by the news. "All day we felt jubilant," she wrote in her diary. That afternoon she and Eric Duncannon took a long walk through the fragrant spring landscape of the estate's parklands. "I think he is charming," she wrote.

As Eric left that day to return to his unit, he said those fatal words: "May I ring you up?"

TWO MEETINGS, TWO COUNTRY homes, one lovely weekend in March, with victory suddenly seeming a bit more near: Of such moments are great family upheavals sown.

Part Six

—

LOVE AMID
THE FLAMES

April – May

CHAPTER
84

Grave News

On Tuesday, April 1, Mary's room at Chequers, the prison Room, was exceptionally cold. The promise of spring had given way to a reprise of winter, as noted in her diary: "Snow—sleet—cold—not funny." She went to work at her Women's Voluntary Service office, then had lunch with her sister Sarah, who told her a bit of gossip about Eric Duncannon and another woman. "Very interesting," Mary wrote.

Two days later, Thursday, April 3, she received a letter from Eric. "A very sweet letter at that," she wrote. She counseled herself: "Now—Mary—take a hold on yourself—my little plum."

And shortly after this, she received a second letter from him, this one inviting her out to dinner the following week.

"Oh heaven," she wrote.

The next day, Sunday, another bitterly cold day, Eric telephoned, sending a tremor of intrigue tingling through the house, which, as always, was well populated with guests, including Harriman, Pamela, Pug Ismay, Air Marshal Sholto Douglas, and others. Eric and Mary spoke for twenty minutes. "He is v. charming I think & has a very beautiful voice," Mary wrote in her diary. "Oh dear—have I fallen, or have I?"

For Mary, these communications offered a sparkle of relief from the downhearted atmosphere that otherwise suffused the house, the result of a sudden reversal of fortune in the Middle East and bad news from the Balkans. Where just a week earlier, the mood at Chequers had been confident and bright, now there was gloom. A sudden German advance had forced the British to abandon Benghazi, yet one more evacuation. And at dawn that Sunday, April 6, before Eric called, German forces had staged a full-scale invasion of Yugoslavia, code-named Operation Retribution, as punishment for turning against Hitler, and also attacked Greece.

Troubled by these events and by their likely effect on her father, Mary decided to brave the frozen weather and attend a morning service in nearby Ellesborough. "Went to church & found great comfort & encouragement there," she wrote in her diary. "Prayed v. hard for Papa." The next morning, before leaving for work, she stopped by Churchill's office to say goodbye and found him reading documents. "He looked tired, I thought—grim—sorrowful." He told her he expected this to be a week of very bad news, and urged her to keep up her morale. "Darling—" she wrote in her diary, "I will try, perhaps I can help in that way."

But she felt this to be a pale contribution. "It is thwarting to feel so ardently about our Cause & yet to be so unavailing. And so weak— for I—who am really very happy & comfortable—have gay friends & rather a butterfly disposition—little or no cares—I allow myself to feel despondent—gloomy."

Not entirely gloomy, however. She spent a good deal of time musing about Eric Duncannon, who now occupied an inordinate share of her imagination, even though she had met him just nine days earlier. "I wish I knew whether I am in love with Eric rather—or whether I simply have a crush."

THE WEEK DID BRING bad news, as Churchill had predicted. In Libya, Erwin Rommel's tanks continued to gain ground against British forces, prompting the British general in command, Archibald Wavell, to cable on April 7 that conditions had "greatly deteriorated." Churchill urged Wavell to defend the port city of Tobruk at all costs, calling it "a place to be held to the death without thought of retirement."

So intent was Churchill on this, and on personally understanding the battlefield, that he ordered Pug Ismay to deliver to him plans and a model of Tobruk, adding, "Let me have meanwhile the best photographs available both from the air and from the ground." News arrived, too, of the toll wrought by Hitler's Operation Retribution against Yugoslavia. Designed to send a message to any vassal state that sought to resist—and also, perhaps, to show Londoners what lay ahead for them—the aerial assault, which began on Palm Sunday, leveled the capital, Belgrade, and killed seventeen thousand civilians. This news struck close to home, for that same week, in an unfortunate confluence, British officials announced that the total number of civilian deaths in Britain caused by German air raids had reached 29,856, and this was just the number of lives lost. Injuries, many catastrophic and disfiguring, far outnumbered the death toll.

On top of this came renewed fears that Hitler might yet invade Britain. Hitler's apparent new focus on Russia, as revealed by intelligence intercepts, did not in itself guarantee that the danger had passed. In a note to Edward Bridges, secretary to the War Cabinet, on Tuesday, April 8, Churchill ordered all his ministers to coordinate their vacations for the upcoming Easter holiday to ensure that key offices were manned and that the ministers themselves were readily available by telephone. "I am told," Churchill wrote, "that Easter is a very good time for invasion." Over the Easter weekend, the moon would be full.

In a speech the next day on the "war situation," which he had scheduled originally to congratulate British forces on their victories, he talked of the new reversals and of the war spreading to Greece and the Balkans. He emphasized the importance of American aid, especially a "gigantic" increase in America's construction of merchant ships. He also raised the specter of invasion. "That is an ordeal from which we shall not shrink," he told the House, but added that Germany clearly had designs on Russia, in particular the Ukraine and oil fields in the Caucasus. He ended on an optimistic note, proclaiming that once Britain had overcome the submarine menace and American lend-lease supplies began to flow, Hitler could be sure that "armed with the sword of retributive justice, we shall be on his track."

The bad news, however, was too overwhelming to be countered by a mere gleam of optimism. "The House is sad and glum," Harold Nicolson wrote in his diary. What seemed clear to Nicolson was that Churchill, more than ever, was staking his hopes and Britain's future on Roosevelt. Nicolson took note of the prime minister's several references to America, seeing in them grave meaning: "His peroration implies that we are done without American help."

HARRIMAN WATCHED THE SPEECH from the Distinguished Strangers' Gallery in the House. Afterward, he wrote a lengthy letter to Roosevelt in which he marveled at "the extent to which the faith and hopes for the future of the people here are bound up in America and in you personally."

He noted that the coming weekend would be his fifth in Britain and the fourth he would spend with Churchill. "He seems to get confidence in having us around," Harriman said, "feeling perhaps that we represent you and the aid that America is to give." Churchill placed much weight on Roosevelt's assurances, Harriman observed: "You are his one strong dependable friend."

Harriman closed his letter with a brief paragraph, one he appeared to add as an afterthought: "England's strength is bleeding. In our own interest I trust our navy can be directly employed before our partner is too weak."

FOR MARY, THE NEWS from the Balkans was particularly distressing. The depth of misery Hitler had inflicted on Yugoslavia seemed almost beyond fathoming. "If one could really completely imagine the full horror of the struggle all the time—I suppose life would be unsupportable," she wrote. "As it is, moments of realization are bad enough."

The news left her feeling "gloomed up," she wrote on Thursday, April 10, though she was still excited about seeing Eric that evening. He brought her a copy of the works of John Donne.

Even more exciting was the prospect of setting off that night with her parents on one of Churchill's damage tours, first to the badly bombed Welsh city of Swansea and then to Bristol, where her father, in his titular role as chancellor of the city's namesake university, was also scheduled to confer a number of honorary degrees.

Earlier that day, though, Mary and her parents had received some wrenching family news: Her sister Diana's husband, Duncan Sandys, had been seriously hurt in a car accident. "Poor Diana—" she wrote. "However—thank God—it seems it is not quite as serious as we thought at first." Churchill wrote about the crash in a letter to his son, Randolph, in Cairo. "You know Duncan had a frightful accident. He was going down in a car from London to Aberporth, and was lying down asleep with his shoes off. He had two drivers, but both fell asleep simultaneously. The car ran into a stone bridge which narrowed the road suddenly, and both his feet are smashed up, also some injury to his spine." Whether Sandys would be able to return to his duties as a colonel in the Anti-Aircraft Command was unclear, Churchill wrote, "but it is possible he may be able to return to his duties by hobbling about." If not, Churchill added, with a wry quip, "there is always the House of Commons."

In the evening, Mary and her parents—"Papa" and "Mummie"—

boarded Churchill's special train, where they were joined by other invited travelers: Harriman, Ambassador Winant, Australian prime minister Menzies, Pug Ismay, John Colville, and several senior military officials. The Prof was supposed to go, too, but was laid up with a cold. They arrived in Swansea at eight o'clock the next morning, Good Friday, and set off to tour the city in a caravan of cars, with Churchill seated in an open Ford with a cigar clenched between his teeth. They traveled through a landscape of utter destruction. "The devastation in parts of the town is ghastly," Mary wrote in her diary. But now she witnessed firsthand the extent to which the city's populace needed this visit from her father, and how they seemed to revere him. "Never have I seen such courage—love—cheerfulness & confidence expressed as by the people today. Wherever he went they swarmed around Papa—clasping his hand—patting him on the back—shouting his name."

She found it very moving, but also disconcerting. "It is rather frightening how terribly they depend on him," she wrote.

The train took them next to an experimental weapons testing station on the Welsh coast, where Churchill and his party were to observe trials of various aerial mines and rocket launchers. The prospect at first delighted Churchill, appealing to the little boy that lurked in his soul, but the tests did not go well. "The firing of the rockets was bad," John Colville wrote, "and at the first display a childishly easy target was repeatedly missed; but the multiple projectors seemed promising; so did the aerial mines descending with parachutes."

It was when the train arrived at Bristol the next day, Saturday, April 12, that the journey turned surreal.

THE TRAIN STOPPED FOR the night on a siding outside the city—a prudent measure, given the recent intensification of German air raids and the fact that the night was clear, the moon at its fullest. And indeed, starting at ten P.M., 150 German bombers, guided both by navigation beams and by moonlight reckoning, began attacking the city, first with incendiaries, then with high explosives, in one of the most severe raids Bristol had suffered thus far. The raid—subsequently dubbed "the Good Friday Raid"—lasted six hours, during which the bombers dropped nearly two hundred tons of high explosives and thirty-seven thousand incendiary bombs, killing 180 civilians and wounding another 382. A single bomb killed ten rescue workers; it blew three of the victims onto the adjacent tarmac road, where they were partially absorbed into its suddenly molten surface. They were later discovered by an unlucky ambulance driver, who had the unenviable task of prying their bodies loose.

Aboard the train, Churchill and his party heard the distant guns and detonations. Wrote Pug Ismay, "It was clear that Bristol was getting it hot." The next morning, Saturday, the train pulled into the Bristol station as fires still burned and smoke bloomed from demolished buildings. At least a hundred bombs had failed to explode either because of malfunction or by design, thereby hampering rescue crews and fire squads, and making Churchill's choice of route through the city a risky and problematic matter.

The morning was gray and cold, as Mary recalled it, and wreckage was strewn everywhere. She saw men and women heading off to their jobs, as on any other day, but clearly worn by the night's raid. "Rather strained pale faces—weary—silent," she wrote.

First Churchill and company went to the city's Grand Hotel. The building had survived the night's raid unscathed, but prior raids had inflicted considerable damage. "It had a sense of lean to it, as if it needed shoring up in order to stay in business," wrote Inspector Thompson.

Churchill requested a bath.

"Yes, sir!" the desk manager said brightly, as if this posed no challenge whatsoever—when, in fact, prior raids had left the hotel with no hot water. "But somehow, somewhere, in but a few minutes," Thompson said, "an amused procession of guests, clerks, cooks, maids, soldiers, and walking wounded materialized out of some mystery in the back part of the building, and went up the stairs with hot water in all types of containers, including a garden sprinkler, and filled the tub in the Prime Minister's room."

Churchill and the others convened for breakfast. Harriman noticed that the hotel staff seemed to have been up all night. "The waiter serving breakfast had been working on the roof of the hotel and had helped to put a number of incendiaries out," he wrote in a letter to Roosevelt. After breakfast, the group set out to tour the city, with Churchill seated on the folded canvas top of an open touring car (in British English, this was the "hood"). The devastation, wrote John Colville, was "such as I had never thought possible."

Churchill's visit was unannounced. As he drove through the streets, people turned to watch. First came recognition, Mary saw, then surprise and delight. Mary rode in the same car as Harriman. She liked him. "He has the root of the matter in him," she wrote. "He feels & works for us so much."

The caravan moved past residents who stood in front of their newly ruined houses, examining the remains and retrieving belongings. Upon seeing Churchill, they came running to his car. "It was unbelievably moving," Mary wrote.

Churchill toured the worst-hit areas on foot. He walked briskly. This was not the halting meander that might have been expected of an overweight sixty-six-year-old man who spent many of his waking hours drinking and smoking. Newsreel footage shows him charging along at the head of his entourage, smiling, scowling, now and then doffing his bowler hat, even executing an occasional snappy pirouette to acknowledge a remark from a bystander. In his long overcoat, over his round frame, he looked like the top half of a very large bomb. Clementine and Mary walked a few steps behind, both looking happy and cheerful; Pug Ismay and Harriman followed as well; Inspector Thompson stayed close, one hand in his pistol pocket. When engulfed by a crowd of men and women, Churchill took off his bowler and put it on top of his walking stick, then held it aloft so that those outside the immediate crush could see it and know he was there. "Stand back, my men," Harriman heard him say, "let the others see."

Harriman noticed that as Churchill moved among the crowds, he used "his trick" of making direct eye contact with individuals. At one point, believing Churchill to be out of earshot, Harriman told Pug Ismay, "The Prime Minister seems popular with the middle-aged women."

Churchill heard the remark. He whirled to face Harriman. "What did you say? Not only with the middle-aged women; with the young ones too."

THE PROCESSION MOVED ON to Bristol University for the degree ceremony. "Nothing could have been more dramatic," Harriman wrote.

The building next door was still in flames. Churchill, in full academic regalia, sat on the dais among similarly attired university officials, many of whom had spent the night helping fight fires. Despite the raid and the wreckage outside, the hall filled. "It was quite extraordinary," Mary wrote. "People kept on arriving late with grime on their faces half washed off, their ceremonial robes on over their fire-fighting clothes which were still wet."

Churchill conferred degrees upon Ambassador Winant and Australian prime minister Menzies, and, in absentia, on Harvard president James Conant, who had returned to America. Before the ceremony, he'd quipped to Harriman, "I'd like to give you a degree, but you're not interested in that sort of thing."

Later in the ceremony, Churchill rose and gave an impromptu speech. "Many of those here today have been all night at their posts," he said, "and all have been under the fire of the enemy in heavy and protracted bombardment. That you should gather in this way is a mark of fortitude and phlegm, of a courage and detachment from material affairs worthy of all that we have learned to believe of Ancient Rome or of modern Greece." He told the audience that he tried to get away from "headquarters" as much as possible to visit bombed areas, "and I see the damage done by the enemy attacks; but I also see side by side with the devastation and amid the ruins quiet, confident, bright and smiling eyes, beaming with a consciousness of being associated with a cause far higher than any human or personal issue. I see the spirit of an unconquerable people."

Afterward, as Churchill, Clementine, and the others emerged on the steps of the university, a large crowd surged forward, cheering. And at that instant, in a singular moment of meteorological synchronicity, the sun broke through the clouds.

AS THE CARS HEADED back to the train station, the crowd followed. For all the laughing and cheering, it could have been a city festival from more peaceful times. Men, women, and children walked beside Churchill's car, their faces gleaming with delight. "These are not mere fairweather friends," Mary wrote in her diary. "Papa has served them with his heart [and] his mind always through peace & wars—& they have given him in his finest & darkest hour their love & confidence." She was struck by this strange power of her father to bring forth courage and strength in the most trying of circumstances. "Oh please dear God," she wrote, "preserve him unto us—& lead us to victory & peace."

As the train departed, Churchill waved at the crowd from the windows, and kept waving until the train was out of sight. Then, reaching for a newspaper, he sat back and raised the paper to mask his tears. "They have such confidence," he said. "It is a grave responsibility."

THEY ARRIVED AT CHEQUERS in time for dinner, where they were joined by a number of new guests, including Foreign Secretary Anthony Eden and his wife and General Dill, chief of the Imperial General Staff.

The atmosphere was somber—at first—as Churchill, Dill, and Eden grappled with the latest news from the Middle East and the Mediterranean. German forces in Greece were advancing quickly toward Athens, and threatened to overwhelm Greek and British defenders, raising the prospect of yet another evacuation. Rommel's tanks in Libya continued to pummel British forces, forcing them to retreat toward Egypt and to concentrate in Tobruk. That night Churchill sent a cable to General Wavell, commander of British forces in the Middle East, telling him that he, Dill, and Eden had "complete confidence" in him, and emphasizing how important it was for Wavell to resist the German advance. "This," Churchill wrote, "is one of the crucial fights in the history of the British Army."

He also urged Wavell to "please spell" Tobruk with a *k,* as opposed to such other spellings as "Tubruq" and "Tobruch."

A telegram from Roosevelt dissipated the gloom. The president notified Churchill that he had decided to extend the American naval security zone in the North Atlantic to include all waters between the U.S. coast and the 25th meridian west—roughly two-thirds of the Atlantic Ocean—and to take other measures, which "will favorably affect your shipping problem." He planned to do so immediately. "It is important for domestic political reasons which you will readily understand that this action be taken by us unilaterally and not after diplomatic conversations between you and us."

U.S. ships and aircraft would now patrol these waters. "We will want in great secrecy notification of movement of convoys so our patrol units can seek out any ships or planes or aggressor nations operating west of the new line of the security zone," Roosevelt stated. The United States would then convey to the Royal Navy the locations of any enemy vessels they encountered.

Churchill was elated. On Easter Sunday, April 13, from Chequers, he sent his thanks to the president. "Deeply grateful for your momentous cable," he wrote; he called the move "a long step towards salvation."

Colville asked Harriman whether it meant that America and Germany would now go to war.

Harriman said, "That's what I hope."

SO MOVED WAS HARRIMAN by his experience at Bristol that he overcame his pinchpenny nature and made an anonymous donation to the city, in the amount of £100. To keep his role confidential, he asked Clementine to forward the money to the city's mayor.

In a handwritten thank-you on Tuesday, April 15, she told him, "whatever happens we do not feel alone any more."

THAT DAY, TOO, HARRIMAN learned that his daughter Kathy, thanks to the intercession of Harry Hopkins, had at last received approval by the State Department to travel to London.

"Thrilled," he telegraphed immediately. "When are you coming— Bring all possible nylon stockings for your friends here also dozen packs Stimudent for another friend."

Here he was referring to Stim-U-Dent, a toothpick-like product used to clean between teeth and stimulate blood flow in the gums, once so popular that the Smithsonian eventually acquired a specimen for its permanent collection. In another cable Harriman urged, "Don't forget stimudents." He told Kathy to bring whatever lipstick she favored, but also to include a few tubes of "green top" lipstick by Guerlain.

His insistent pleas for the Stim-U-Dents drew the bemused attention of his wife, Marie. "We're all dying to know who the peeress with the decayed teeth is who's in such a lather about her toothpicks," she wrote.

She added: "After your third cable about them we decided the situation must be critical."

GLOOM SETTLED OVER MEETINGS of the War Cabinet. The loss of Benghazi and the seemingly imminent fall of Tobruk were especially disheartening. A melancholy suffused Britain that was all the more pronounced because of the contrast between the hopes raised by the winter's victories and the deflation that accompanied the new reversals, and by the intensified German air raids, some of which were even deadlier and more damaging than those of the prior fall. German bombers again struck Coventry, and the next night Birmingham. Darkness continued to stymie the RAF.

Within the House of Commons, discontent deepened. At least one prominent member, Lloyd George, was growing concerned about whether Churchill was indeed the man to wage this war to victory.

Scorn

AT HIS MORNING MEETING ON TUESDAY, APRIL 15, JOSEPH GOEBBELS instructed his propagandists to concentrate on deriding Britain for its imminent retreat from Greece. "Churchill should be pilloried as a gambler, as a character more at home at the tables in Monte Carlo than in the seat of a British prime minister. A typical gambler's nature—cynical, ruthless, brutal, staking the blood of other nations in order to save British blood, riding roughshod over the national destinies of small states."

The press was to repeat over and over, "with savage scorn," the slogan "Instead of butter—Benghazi; instead of Benghazi—Greece; instead of Greece—nothing."

He added: "This then is the end."

HERMANN GÖRING CERTAINLY HOPED that Britain was at last near surrender, and set about making sure that he and his beloved air force would get the credit. But the RAF was causing him grief.

A week earlier, British bombers had struck at the heart of Berlin, shattering the city's finest avenue, the Unter den Linden, and destroying the State Opera House, shortly before a much-anticipated guest performance by an Italian opera company. "Hitler was outraged," wrote Nicolaus von Below, his Luftwaffe liaison, "and as a result he had a furious argument with Göring."

Hitler's fury, and Göring's resentment, both likely played a part in the ferocity with which Göring now proposed to execute a series of new attacks on London, the first set to take place on Wednesday, April 16.

———

CHURCHILL WAS ANNOYED.

Nearly two weeks earlier, he had dispatched a cryptic warning to Stalin hinting at Hitler's invasion plans—cryptic, because he did not want to reveal that Bletchley Park was the source of his own detailed knowledge about Operation Barbarossa. He sent the message to his ambassador to Russia, Sir Stafford Cripps, with instructions to deliver it in person.

Now, in that week after Easter, Churchill learned that Cripps had never delivered it. Angered by this apparent act of insubordination, Churchill wrote to the ambassador's boss, Foreign Secretary Anthony Eden. "I set special importance on the delivery of this personal message from me to Stalin," he wrote. "I cannot understand why it should be resisted. The Ambassador is not alive to the military significance of the facts. Pray oblige me."

By now it was clear to anyone who worked with Churchill that any request beginning with "pray" was a direct and nonnegotiable command.

Cripps at last delivered Churchill's warning. Stalin did not reply.

That Night at the Dorchester

———

AVERELL HARRIMAN LEFT HIS OFFICE EARLY THAT WEDNESDAY, April 16, to get a haircut. Barbershops closed at six-thirty P.M. He was to attend a formal dinner that night at the Dorchester Hotel, honoring Fred Astaire's sister, Adele. This had been a big day for the Harriman Mission: In Washington, Roosevelt had signed off on the first transfer of food under the Lend-Lease Act: eleven thousand tons of cheese, eleven thousand tons of eggs, and one hundred thousand cases of evaporated milk.

Harriman's early departure from the office gave his secretary, Robert Meiklejohn, a chance to have an early dinner for once. The evening was lovely and clear.

AT NINE O'CLOCK, an hour after sunset, air-raid sirens activated throughout London. They drew little attention at first. The sound of sirens was by now a commonplace event. The only thing that distinguished this alert from those of the prior days was its timing, an hour earlier than usual.

In Bloomsbury, flares began to fall, flooding the streets with brilliant light. Author Graham Greene, whose novel *The Power and the Glory* had been published the previous year, was just finishing dinner with his mistress, writer Dorothy Glover. Both were about to go on duty, he as an air-raid warden, she as a fire watcher. Greene accompanied her to her assigned lookout. "Standing on the roof of a garage we saw the flares come slowly floating down, dribbling their flames," Greene wrote in his journal. "They drift like great yellow peonies."

The moon-flushed sky filled with the silhouettes of hundreds of aircraft. Now bombs fell, of all sizes, including giant parachute mines, gargantuan parodies of the Prof's own aerial mines. There was confusion—dust, fire, broken glass. A mine landed on the Victoria Club, in Malet Street, where 350 Canadian soldiers were sleeping. Greene arrived and found chaos: "Soldiers still coming out in grey blood-smeared pajamas; pavements littered by glass and some were barefooted." Where the building had stood there was now a jagged, twenty-foot escarpment that seemed to extend deep into the foundation. The bombers overhead droned without interruption. "One really thought that this was the end," Greene wrote, "but it wasn't exactly frightening—one had ceased to believe in the possibility of surviving the night."

Incidents accumulated. A bomb destroyed a Jewish girls' club, killing thirty people. A parachute mine destroyed an anti-aircraft outpost in Hyde Park. In the ruins of a pub, a priest crawled under a billiard table to take confession from the owner and his family, trapped by debris.

Despite the ongoing raid, John Colville left 10 Downing Street and climbed into Churchill's armored car, which then took him through newly blasted and flaming streets to the American embassy, in Grosvenor Square. He met with U.S. ambassador Winant to discuss a telegram Churchill planned to send to Roosevelt. At one forty-five A.M., he left the embassy to return to 10 Downing Street, this time on foot. Bombs fell around him "like hailstones," he wrote.

He added, with a degree of understatement, "I had quite a disagreeable walk."

HARRIMAN'S SECRETARY, ROBERT MEIKLEJOHN, having finished dinner, went to the roof of the American embassy, along with members of the embassy staff. He climbed to the highest point, which gave him a 360-degree view of the city. Now, for the first time since he had arrived in London, he heard the whistling sound made by falling bombs.

He did not like it.

"More scary than actual explosions," he wrote in his journal. He added, "Did a couple of tumbling acts, in which I had plenty of company, to dodge bombs that fell blocks away."

Immense explosions, likely from parachute mines, occurred within view, shaking the earth. "It looked as if whole houses were sailing up in the air," he wrote. At one point, Ambassador Winant and his wife came to the roof, but did not linger. They took mattresses from their flat on the fifth floor of the embassy and carried them to the first.

Meiklejohn saw a bomb detonate at the Battersea Power Station, in the distance. The bomb ignited a large gas storage tank, which "blew up in a column of fire that seemed to go up miles."

He went back to his own flat and tried to sleep, but after an hour he gave up. Nearby detonations caused the building to shudder and sent shrapnel clattering against his windows. He climbed to his roof and there "was met by the most amazing sight I have ever seen in my life. A whole section of the city north of the financial district was a solid mass of flames, leaping hundreds of feet in the air. It was a cloudless night but the smoke covered half of the sky and was all red from the fires below." Now and then bombs tumbled into structures that were already on fire and raised "regular geysers of flame."

Among the people around him he saw only an interested calm, which astonished him. "They acted," he wrote, "as if the bombing were like a thunderstorm."

Nearby at Claridge's hotel, General Lee, the American military attaché, now back in London, went down to the first-floor room of a member of the U.S. embassy's diplomatic staff, Herschel Johnson. As bombs fell and fires burned, they discussed literature, mainly the works of Thomas Wolfe and Victor Hugo's novel *Les Misérables*. The conversation shifted to Chinese art; Herschel brought out a collection of fine porcelain objects.

"All this time," Lee wrote, "I had the sickening feeling that hundreds of people were being murdered in a most savage way almost within a stone's throw, and there was nothing to do about it."

NINE BLOCKS AWAY, at the Dorchester, Harriman and other guests from the Fred Astaire dinner watched the raid from the hotel's eighth floor. Among them was Pamela Churchill, who had turned twenty-one a month earlier.

As she walked down a corridor toward the dinner party, she reflected on her new sense of freedom and her new confidence. Later she recalled thinking, "You know, I am really on my own and my life is going to change totally now."

She had met Harriman before, at Chequers, and now found herself seated beside him. They talked at length, mostly about Max Beaverbrook. Harriman saw Beaverbrook as the man, after Churchill, whom he most needed to befriend. Pamela tried to convey a sense of Beaverbrook's character. At some point, Harriman said to her, "Well, would you, you know, why won't you come back to my apartment and we can talk easier and you can tell me more about these people."

They went down to his apartment. She was in the midst of providing various insights into Beaverbrook when the raid began.

Flares lit the city outside so brightly that Harriman, in a later letter to his wife, Marie, described it as looking "like Broadway and 42nd Street."

Bombs fell; clothes were shed. As a friend later told Pamela's biographer Sally Bedell Smith, "A big bombing raid is a very good way to get into bed with somebody."

THE RAID TOOK A GREAT TOLL in lives and landscape. It killed 1,180 people and injured far more, making it the worst attack thus far. Bombs struck Piccadilly, Chelsea, Pall Mall, Oxford Street, Lambeth, and Whitehall. An explosion tore a great gash into the Admiralty building. Fire destroyed Christie's auction house. At St. Peter's Church in Eaton Square, a bomb obliterated the vicar, Austin Thompson, as he stood on the church steps beckoning people to come inside for safety.

The next morning, Thursday, April 17, after having breakfast at 10 Downing Street, John Colville and Eric Seal took a walk onto the Horse Guards Parade to examine the damage. "London looks bleary-eyed and disfigured," Colville wrote in his diary that day.

He noted as well that he "found Pamela Churchill and Averell Harriman also examining the devastation." He made no further comment.

HARRIMAN WROTE TO HIS WIFE about the raid. "Needless to say, my sleep was intermittent. Guns were going all the time and airplanes overhead."

The White Cliffs

———

AT A CABINET MEETING AT ELEVEN-THIRTY THAT THURSDAY morning, Churchill, who had worked through much of the night's raid, noted—accurately—that the damage to the Admiralty building had improved his view of Nelson's Column in Trafalgar Square.

It perturbed him, however, that once again the bombers had come with virtually no interference from the RAF. Darkness remained the Luftwaffe's best defense.

Perhaps by way of offering encouraging news, the Prof that day sent Churchill a report on the latest tests of his anti-aircraft mines, these involving a variant in which the mines—tiny microbombs—were attached to small parachutes and then dropped from planes. The RAF "Egglayers" had made twenty-one sorties during which they managed to set out six curtains of mines. These, the Prof claimed, had destroyed at least one German bomber, but perhaps as many as five.

In this, the Prof was engaging in an uncharacteristic behavior: wishful thinking. The only evidence that the bombers had been destroyed was the disappearance of their radar echoes. The action had taken place over the sea. No witnesses provided visual confirmations. No wreckage was found. It was "clearly not feasible to get the evidence we might have demanded overland," he acknowledged.

He saw none of this, however, as sufficient cause to stop him from claiming all five German bombers as successful kills.

ON THURSDAY, APRIL 24, Mary raced home to Chequers from her volunteer work in Aylesbury and had tea with a friend, Fiona Forbes. She and Fiona then rushed off, with piles of luggage, to catch an evening train to London.

Mary looked forward to a relaxing bath at the Annexe before dressing for the night's fun, but telegrams and telephone calls from friends intervened. She stopped in to talk with "Papa." At seven-forty she at last got her bath, though it was less leisurely than she had hoped. She and Fiona were due to attend a party set to begin at eight-fifteen but planned first to have dinner at the Dorchester with Eric Duncannon and other friends, as well as Mary's sister Sarah and her husband, Vic.

She was quite taken with her date. In her diary she wrote, "Oh *tais-toi mon coeur*." ("Be quiet, my heart.")

They moved on to the party, at a club, and danced until the band stopped playing at four A.M. Mary and Fiona returned to the Annexe by dawn, with Mary recounting to her diary, "It really was a completely perfect party."

She spent the next day, Saturday, at a friend's country home in Dorset, recuperating in leisurely fashion, in bed—"Very long delicious 'lie'"— and reading a long poem by Alice Duer Miller, "The White Cliffs," about an American woman who falls in love with an Englishman only to have him die in France in the Great War. In the poem, aptly enough, the woman chronicles her love affair and rails against America for failing to immediately join the war. The poem ends:

> I am American bred,
> I have seen much to hate here—much to forgive,
> But in a world where England is finished and dead,
> I do not wish to live.

Mary wept.

IN LONDON THAT FRIDAY, John Colville had his medical interview with the RAF. He underwent more than two hours of medical testing and passed every category except eyesight, for which he was rated as being "borderline." He was told, however, that he might yet be able to fly, if he got fitted for contact lenses. He would have to pay for that himself, and even then there was no guarantee that he would succeed.

But staying at 10 Downing Street no longer seemed appropriate. The more he thought about joining the RAF, the more dissatisfied he felt, and the more he needed to get away. He pursued it now the way he pursued Gay Margesson, with a futile mix of longing and despair. "For the first time since war broke out I feel discontented and unsettled, bored by most people I meet and destitute of ideas," he told his diary. "I certainly need a change and think an active, practical life in the RAF is the real solution. I am not anxious to immolate myself on the altar of Mars, but have reached the stage of thinking that nothing matters."

Berlin

———

OVERALL, JOSEPH GOEBBELS FELT CONTENT ABOUT THE WAY the war was going. As best he could tell, morale in Britain was slipping. A big air raid on Plymouth was reported to have caused outright panic. "The effect is devastating," Goebbels wrote in his diary. "Secret reports from London tell of a collapse of morale, principally caused by our air raids." In Greece, he wrote, "the English are in full flight."

Best of all, Churchill himself appeared to be growing increasingly pessimistic. "He is said to be in a very depressed state, spending the entire day smoking and drinking," Goebbels wrote in his diary. "This is the kind of enemy we need."

His diary crackled with enthusiasm for the war, and for life. "What a glorious spring day outside!" he wrote. "How beautiful the world can be! And we have no chance to enjoy it. Human beings are so stupid. Life is so short, and they then go and make it so hard for themselves."

This Scowling Valley

ON APRIL 24 AND 25, SEVENTEEN THOUSAND BRITISH TROOPS fled Greece. The next night, another nineteen thousand also evacuated. In Egypt, Rommel's tanks continued their advance. Within Britain concern grew that maybe the country was incapable of taking the offensive and holding territory gained. This was the third major evacuation since Churchill had become prime minister—first Norway, then Dunkirk, now Greece. "That's all we're really good at!" sniped Alexander Cadogan in his diary.

Sensing that the latest military setbacks might be rattling the public and the United States, Churchill made a broadcast on Sunday night, April 27, from Chequers. He framed his recent visits to bomb-damaged cities as having been conducted expressly to gauge the national sentiment. "I have come back not only reassured, but refreshed," he said. He reported that popular morale was high. "Indeed," he said, "I felt encompassed by an exaltation of spirit in the people which seemed to lift mankind and its troubles above the level of material facts into that joyous serenity we think belongs to a better world than this."

Here he may have laid it on a bit too thick. "His statement that morale was best in the worst-bombed areas took some swallowing," wrote one Mass-Observation diarist, from his hospital bed. He heard another patient say, "You —— liar!"

Churchill told his listeners that he felt a deep responsibility to bring them safely "out of this long, stern, scowling valley" and offered cause for optimism. "There are less than seventy million malignant Huns— some of whom are curable and others killable," he said. Meanwhile, he pointed out, "The peoples of the British Empire and of the United States number nearly two hundred million in their homelands and in the British Dominions alone. They have more wealth, more technical resources, and they make more steel, than the whole of the rest of the world put together." He urged his audience not to lose its "sense of proportion and thus become discouraged or alarmed."

THOUGH HAPPY WITH THE SPEECH, Churchill understood that he could not afford further setbacks, especially in the Middle East, where success had once gleamed so brightly. In a "MOST SECRET" directive to his War Cabinet on Monday, April 28, he demanded that all ranks recognize "that the life and honor of Great Britain depends upon the successful defense of Egypt." All precautionary plans that contemplated the evacuation of Egypt or the scuttling of the Suez Canal were to be withdrawn from circulation immediately and locked away, with access closely controlled. "No whisper of such plans is to be allowed," he wrote. "No surrenders by officers and men will be considered tolerable unless at least 50 percent casualties are sustained by the Unit or force in question." Any general or staff officer who found himself facing imminent capture by the enemy was to shoot it out with his pistol. "The honor of a wounded man is safe," he wrote. "Anyone who can kill a Hun or even an Italian has rendered good service."

As always, one of his prime concerns was how Roosevelt would perceive further foundering. "The failure to win the battle of Egypt would be a disaster of the first magnitude to Great Britain," Churchill wrote on Wednesday, April 30, in a minute addressed to Pug Ismay, Lord Beaverbrook, and senior Admiralty officials. "It might well determine the decisions of Turkey, Spain and Vichy. It might strike the United States the wrong way, i.e., they might think we are no good."

But America wasn't his only problem. His broadcast did little to cool the discontent that simmered among his opponents, chief among them Lloyd George, who would soon have an opportunity to express that opposition. On Tuesday, April 29, Hastings Lees-Smith, acting chair of the Parliamentary Labour Party, invoked Parliament's "private notice" provision to place a question immediately before Churchill, asking "when a Debate on the war situation will take place."

Churchill replied that not only would he schedule a debate; he would invite the Commons to vote on a resolution: "That this House approves the policy of His Majesty's Government in sending help to Greece, and declares its confidence that our operations in the Middle East and in all other theaters of war will be pursued by the Government with the utmost vigor."

It would, of course, constitute a referendum on Churchill himself. The timing struck some as symbolic, if not ominous, with the debate set to occur exactly one year after the vote that unseated former prime minister Chamberlain and brought Churchill to power.

IN BERLIN, JOSEPH GOEBBELS contemplated the motivation behind Churchill's broadcast, and its potential effect. He kept careful watch on the evolving relationship between America and Britain, weighing how his propagandists might best influence the outcome. "The battle over intervention or non-intervention continues to rage in the USA," he wrote in his diary on Monday, April 28, the day after the broadcast. The outcome was hard to predict. "We are active to the best of our ability, but we can scarcely make ourselves heard against the deafening Jew-chorus. In London they are placing all their last hopes in the USA. If something does not happen soon, then London is faced with annihilation." Goebbels sensed mounting anxiety. "Their great fear is of a knock-out blow during the next weeks and months. We shall do our best to justify these fears."

He instructed his operatives on how best to use Churchill's own broadcast to discredit him. They were to mock him for saying that after he visited bombed areas, he came back to London "not merely reassured but even refreshed." In particular, they were to seize on how Churchill had described the forces he had transferred from Egypt to Greece to confront the German invasion. Churchill had said: "It happened that the divisions available and best suited to this task were from New Zealand and Australia, and that only about half the troops who took part in this dangerous expedition came from the Mother Country." Goebbels leapt on this with glee. "Indeed, it so happened! It invariably 'so happens' that the British are in the rear; it always so happens that they are in retreat. It so happened that the British had no share in the casualties. It so happened that the greatest sacrifices during the offensive in the West were made by the French, the Belgians and the Dutch. It so happened that the Norwegians had to provide cover for the British flooding back from Norway."

He ordered his propagandists to emphasize that Churchill, in choosing a public broadcast, had avoided questioning in the House of Commons. "There, he might have been challenged after his speech, and awkward questions might have been asked." In his diary Goebbels wrote, "He is frightened of Parliament."

DESPITE THE PRESSURES OF war and politics, Churchill took time to write a letter of condolence to Hubert Pierlot, the exiled prime minister of Belgium.

Even in wartime, tragedies occurred that had nothing to do with bullets and bombs, and these tended to be forgotten in the daily crush of grim events. Two days earlier, at about three-thirty in the afternoon, the driver of an express train en route from Kings Cross to Newcastle noticed a slight drag on his engine's pulling power, indicating that an emergency brake had been activated somewhere on the train. He continued on, planning to stop beside a nearby signal box in case he needed to telephone for assistance. After a second emergency cord was pulled, he brought the train to a full stop—which, given the train's speed and the fact that it was on a long downgrade, took about three minutes.

The last three cars of the eleven-car train were occupied by a hundred boys returning to Ampleforth College, a Catholic boarding school situated in a lovely vale in Yorkshire. The train had been about halfway to Ampleforth, moving at over fifty miles an hour, when some of the boys, apparently bored, had begun flicking lighted matches at each other. One match fell between a seat and a wall. The seats were made of plywood, with cushions stuffed with horsehair; the coaches were timber enclosures fastened to steel chassis. A fire began to burn between the seat and the wall, and continued burning for a time without detection. The fire intensified and soon, fed by the breeze blown through open ventilation ports, began to ascend the wall. In short order the fire engulfed the car and filled it with dense smoke.

The fire killed six boys and injured seven. Two of the dead were sons of the Belgian prime minister.

"My dear Excellency," Churchill wrote on Wednesday, April 30, "The official burdens on your shoulders are indeed heavy. I write to tell you how deeply I sympathize with you in having to bear this new burden of personal loss and sorrow."

THAT DAY, AT THE MESSERSCHMITT airfield outside Munich, Rudolf Hess was ready to try again. He was in his plane, engines on, waiting for permission to take off, when one of his adjutants, Pintsch, came running up to the aircraft. Pintsch gave him a message from Hitler, ordering Hess to stand in for him at a ceremony the next day, May 1—Labor Day—at the Messerschmitt Works, where he was to honor several men, including Willy Messerschmitt himself, as "Pioneers of Labor."

Hess, of course, complied with Hitler's request. The *Führer* was everything to him. In a later letter to Hitler, Hess wrote that "in the last two decades you have fulfilled my life." He saw Hitler as Germany's savior. "After the 1918 collapse you made it worth living again," he wrote. "For you and also for Germany, I have been reborn and able to start once more. It has been a rare privilege for me, as well as your other subordinates, to serve such a man and to follow his ideas with such success."

He climbed down from the cockpit and returned to Munich to prepare his remarks.

Gloom

Also that Wednesday, Lord Beaverbrook submitted yet another resignation to Churchill. "I have taken the decision to retire from the Government," he wrote. "The only explanation I will offer is ill health."

He tempered this with an acknowledgment of their long-standing friendship. "It is with devotion and with affection that I bring my official association to a close."

He added: "Leave me still the personal relations."

Churchill at last assented. As minister of aircraft production, Beaverbrook had succeeded beyond all expectations, while also poisoning beyond salvation the relationship between MAP and the Air Ministry. The time had indeed come for Beaverbrook to leave the post, but Churchill was not yet willing to let his friend make a complete exit, and Beaverbrook, as so often before, was not yet willing, either.

On Thursday, May 1, Churchill appointed him to the post of "Minister of State," and Beaverbrook, after further protest—"You will just have to let me go"—accepted the job, though he recognized that the title was as vague as its underlying mandate, which was to oversee the committees that governed all of Britain's production supply ministries. "I'm ready to be minister of church as well," he quipped.

Though his new appointment was undoubtedly greeted with dread by many within Whitehall, it was well received among the public, according to New Yorker writer Mollie Panter-Downes, who wrote that people "anxious to see the war won as quickly as possible, are hoping that the newly resurrected title of Minister of State carries with it a roving commission to kick inefficiency and departmental dawdling hard wherever it is encountered. The appointment was received with cheers."

That evening after dinner, Churchill and Clementine set off by overnight train on yet another expedition to a devastated city, this time to Plymouth, which had just endured the last of a sequence of five intense night raids conducted over nine days. Home Intelligence put it bluntly: "For the present, Plymouth as a business and commercial center of a prosperous countryside has ceased to exist."

The visit shook Churchill in a way that none of his tours of other bombed cities thus far had, and left him deeply affected. The sheer devastation caused by five nights of bombing eclipsed anything he had seen before. Whole neighborhoods had been obliterated. In the city's Portland Square district, a direct hit on an air-raid shelter had killed seventy-six people in an instant. Churchill visited the city's naval base, where many sailors had been wounded or killed. Forty of the injured lay on cots in a gymnasium, while across the room, behind a low curtain, men hammered the lids onto coffins containing their less lucky brethren. "The hammering must have been horrible to the injured men," wrote John Colville, who accompanied Churchill, "but such has been the damage that there was nowhere else it could be done."

As Churchill's car rolled past the camera of a British Pathé newsreel crew, he stared into the lens with a look that seemed to express a mix of surprise and grief.

HE RETURNED TO CHEQUERS at midnight, exhausted and saddened by what he had seen, and was met by a groundswell of fresh bad news: One of the Royal Navy's precious destroyers had been sunk at Malta and now blocked the entrance to the Grand Harbour; engine trouble had stalled a transport carrying tanks to the Middle East; and a British offensive in Iraq was encountering unexpectedly potent resistance from the Iraqi army. Most disheartening of all was a long, discouraging telegram from Roosevelt, in which the president seemed to dismiss the importance of defending the Middle East. "Personally I am not downcast by more spread of Germany for additional territories," Roosevelt wrote. "There is little of raw materials in all of them put together—not enough to maintain nor compensate for huge occupation forces."

Roosevelt added a callow rejoinder: "Keep up the good work."

The insensitivity of Roosevelt's reply startled Churchill. The subtext seemed clear: Roosevelt was concerned only about assistance that would directly help sustain the safety of the United States from German attack, and cared little whether the Middle East fell or not. Churchill wrote to Anthony Eden, "It seems to me as if there has been a considerable recession across the Atlantic, and that quite unconsciously we are being left very much to our fate."

Colville noted how the accumulation of bad news that night left Churchill "in worse gloom than I have ever seen him."

Churchill dictated a reply to Roosevelt in which he sought to frame the importance of the Middle East in terms of the long-range interests of the United States itself. "We must not be too sure that the consequences of the loss of Egypt and the Middle East would not be grave," he told Roosevelt. "It would seriously increase the hazards of the Atlantic and the Pacific, and could hardly fail to prolong the war, with all the suffering and military dangers that this would entail."

Churchill was growing weary of Roosevelt's reluctance to commit America to war. He had hoped that by now the United States and Britain would be fighting side by side, but always Roosevelt's actions fell short of Churchill's needs and expectations. It was true that the destroyers had been an important symbolic gift, and that the lend-lease program and Harriman's efficient execution of its mandate were a godsend; but it had become clear to Churchill that none of it was enough—only America's entry into the war would guarantee victory in any reasonable period of time. One result of Churchill's long courtship of Roosevelt, however, was that now at least the prime minister felt able to express his concerns and wishes with more candor, directly, without fear of driving America away altogether.

"Mr. President," Churchill wrote, "I am sure that you will not misunderstand me if I speak to you exactly what is in my mind. The one decisive counterweight I can see to balance the growing pessimism in Turkey, the Near East and in Spain would be if [the] United States were immediately to range herself with us as a belligerent Power."

Before going to bed, Churchill gathered Harriman, Pug Ismay, and Colville for a late-night talk by the fire, a kind of geopolitical ghost story, in which he described, as Colville recalled, "a world in which Hitler dominated all Europe, Asia and Africa and left the U.S. and ourselves no option but an unwilling peace." If Suez should fall, Churchill told them, "the Middle East would be lost, and Hitler's robot new order would receive the inspiration which might give it real life."

The war had reached a decisive point, Churchill said—not in terms of determining ultimate victory but, rather, concerning whether the war would be short or very long. If Hitler were to attain control over Iraqi oil and Ukrainian wheat, "not all the staunchness 'of our Plymouth brethren' will shorten the ordeal."

Colville attributed Churchill's gloom mainly to his experience in Plymouth. At intervals throughout the night Churchill repeated, "I have never seen the like."

Eric

———

SATURDAY MORNING BROUGHT DAZZLING SUN BUT A DEEP CHILL. That first week of May was unusually cold, marked by periods of morning frost. "The cold is incredible," Harold Nicolson wrote in his diary. "It is like February." Harriman's secretary, Meiklejohn, took to filling the bathtub in his flat with hot water so that the steam would drift into his sitting room. "It has a good psychological effect," he remarked, "if nothing else." (It was cold, too, in Germany. "Outside, the countryside is covered by deep snow," complained Joseph Goebbels. "And it is supposed to be almost summer!") The many trees at Chequers were just beginning to show their first, almost translucent leaves, and these imparted to the landscape a pointillist effect, as if the grounds had been brushed by Paul Signac. The two nearby hills, Coombe and Beacon, were a soft green. "Everything is very late," John Colville wrote, "but the trees are at last beginning to come out."

Churchill was unusually crabby. "Too little sleep made the P.M. irritable all morning," Colville wrote. By lunch, he was "morose." The proximate cause had nothing to do with the war or Roosevelt but, rather, with his discovery that Clementine had used his treasured honey, sent to him from Queensland, Australia, for the frivolous objective of sweetening rhubarb.

That afternoon Mary Churchill's suitor Eric Duncannon arrived, accompanied by his sister, Moyra Ponsonby, the young woman with whom Colville had examined the downed German bomber at Stansted Park. Duncannon's arrival was a surprise to all, Mary included, and was not wholly welcome: He had been invited only for lunch the following day, Sunday, but was now pretending that he had been asked to stay for the whole weekend.

His presence added new tension to the day. Eric clearly was courting Mary, and seemed likely that weekend to ask her to marry him. Mary was willing but unhappy with the lack of enthusiasm expressed by members of her family. Her mother objected; her sister Sarah openly ridiculed the idea. Mary was just too young.

In the afternoon, Churchill settled in the garden and worked on various notes and minutes. The destruction of Plymouth remained vivid in his mind. It galled him that the Germans had managed to attack the city on five nights out of nine, with minimal interference by the RAF. He still placed great faith in the Prof's aerial mines, though everyone else seemed to view them with derision. Clearly frustrated, Churchill dictated a note to Air Chief Marshal Charles Portal and to John Moore-Brabazon, the new minister of aircraft production, asking why the RAF squadron charged with deploying aerial mines did not yet have its full complement of eighteen aircraft.

"How is it that only 7 are available for supply in view of the fact that they are hardly ever allowed to go up into the Air? Why is a town like Plymouth left to be subjected to five raids on successive nights, or almost successive, without this device being used?" And why, he asked, were aerial mines not being launched across the German radio beams that guided bombers to their targets? "I do not feel this device is yet free from the many years of obstruction which have hampered its perfection," he wrote. "Recent action by the [Royal] Air Force against the night raider has flagged sadly, and you cannot afford to neglect a method which for the number of times it has been used has produced an extraordinarily high percentage of results."

Exactly what he was referring to here is unclear. The mines had yet to be deployed in routine service. Air Ministry researchers were focusing their attentions more on improving air-to-air radar to help fighters locate targets at night and—led by Dr. R. V. Jones—on perfecting technologies for finding and manipulating German navigational beams. In this they were making advances, to the point where, according to interrogation reports, German pilots were growing increasingly distrustful of the beams. The RAF was becoming adept at diverting beams and using Starfish decoy fires to then convince German pilots that they had reached the right targets. Luck still played an inordinately large role in determining whether these measures could be deployed with enough precision to disrupt attacks like those leveled at Plymouth, but clear progress was being made.

Aerial mines, however, had proven to be nothing but problematic, and no one other than Churchill and the Prof seemed to think them worthwhile. Only Churchill's enthusiasm—his "power-relay"—drove their continued development.

Churchill's mood improved that evening. A fierce battle was taking place at Tobruk, and nothing thrilled him more than spirited warfare and the prospect of military glory. He stayed up until three-thirty, in high spirits, "laughing, chaffing and alternating business with conversation," wrote Colville. One by one his official guests, including Anthony Eden, gave up and went to bed. Churchill, however, continued to hold forth, his audience reduced to only Colville and Mary's potential suitor, Eric Duncannon.

Mary by this point had retired to the Prison Room, aware that the next day held the potential to change her life forever.

IN BERLIN, MEANWHILE, HITLER and Propaganda Minister Joseph Goebbels joked about a newly published English biography of Churchill that revealed many of his idiosyncrasies, including his penchant for wearing pink silk underwear, working in the bathtub, and drinking throughout the day. "He dictates messages in the bath or in his underpants; a startling image which the *Führer* finds hugely amusing," Goebbels wrote in his diary on Saturday. "He sees the English Empire as slowly disintegrating. Not much will be salvageable."

ON SUNDAY MORNING, a low-grade anxiety colored the Cromwellian reaches of Chequers. Today, it seemed, would be the day Eric Duncannon proposed to Mary, and no one other than Mary was happy about it. Even she, however, was not wholly at ease with the idea. She was eighteen years old and had never had a romantic relationship, let alone been seriously courted. The prospect of betrothal left her feeling emotionally roiled, though it did add a certain piquancy to the day.

New guests arrived: Sarah Churchill, the Prof, and Churchill's twenty-year-old niece, Clarissa Spencer-Churchill—"looking quite beautiful," Colville noted. She was accompanied by Captain Alan Hillgarth, a raffishly handsome novelist and self-styled adventurer now serving as naval attaché in Madrid, where he ran intelligence operations; some of these were engineered with the help of a lieutenant on his staff, Ian Fleming, who later credited Captain Hillgarth as being one of the inspirations for James Bond.

"It was obvious," Colville wrote, "that Eric was expected to make advances to Mary and that the prospect was viewed with nervous pleasure by Mary, with approbation by Moyra, with dislike by Mrs. C. and with amusement by Clarissa." Churchill expressed little interest.

After lunch, Mary and the others walked into the rose garden, while Colville showed Churchill telegrams about the situation in Iraq. The day was sunny and warm, a nice change from the recent stretch of cold. Soon, to Colville's mystification, Eric and Clarissa set off on a long walk over the grounds by themselves, leaving Mary behind. "His motives," Colville wrote, "were either Clarissa's attraction, which she did not attempt to keep in the background, or else the belief that it was good policy to arouse Mary's jealousy." After the walk, and after Clarissa and Captain Hillgarth had left, Eric took a nap, with the apparent intention (as Colville saw it) of later making a "dramatic entry" in the Long Gallery, where the family and guests, including Eden and Harriman, were to gather for afternoon tea. Colville wrote, "I think all this is a flutter, which pleases Eric's theatrical feelings and stirs Mary's youthful emotions, but will have no serious consequence."

Churchill settled himself in the garden for an afternoon's work, to take advantage of the warmth of the day as he went through the top-secret papers in his yellow box. Colville sat nearby.

Now and then Churchill glanced at him with a look of suspicion, "in the belief that I was trying to read the contents of his special buff boxes."

ERIC TOOK MARY ASIDE in the White Parlor.

"This evening Eric proposed to me," Mary wrote in her diary. "I'm in a daze—I think I've said 'yes'—but O dear God I'm in a muddle."

CHURCHILL WORKED LATE INTO the night. Colville and the Prof—pale, quiet, looming—joined him in his room, where Churchill climbed into bed and began making his way through the day's accumulation of reports and minutes. The Prof sat nearby while Colville stood at the foot of the bed to collect materials as Churchill went through them. This continued until after two in the morning.

Colville returned to London the next day, Monday, May 5, "in a state of exhaustion."

Le Coeur Dit

Mary, Monday, May 5.

"I've struggled all day within myself.
"Mummie came back again—Nana came.
"I must keep calm. Long walks in the garden—
finally succumbed to tears—but happy."

Of Panzers and Pansies

———

THE GREAT PARLIAMENTARY DEBATE ON CHURCHILL'S HANDLING of the war opened on Tuesday, May 6, with a lackluster speech by Foreign Secretary Anthony Eden, who began by saying, "There is much that I would like to tell which, perforce, I am unable to tell at the present time." He then proceeded to say little and to say it badly. "He sat down amidst complete silence," wrote Chips Channon, Eden's parliamentary private secretary. "I have never heard an important speech so badly delivered." A succession of short speeches followed, delivered by members from throughout the realm. One persistent theme was dismay at the fact that Churchill had made this a vote of confidence when all the House had asked for was a debate on the war. "Why should my right hon. Friend the Prime Minister challenge us with this Motion?" said one member. "Does he regard criticism as unseemly?"

A socialist member from Glasgow, John McGovern, delivered the most pointed attack of the day, going so far as to criticize Churchill's practice of visiting bombed cities. He said, "When we have got to the stage when the Prime Minister has to parade himself through every bombed area in the country, and has to sit on the back of a wagonette waving his hat on a stick like a 'Doodles' at the circus—well, it has come to a very sad state of affairs when representatives of the Government are not so sure of the opinions of the people of the country." McGovern professed to have no confidence in the war or the government, adding, "And, while I have a tremendous admiration for the oratorical powers of the Prime Minister, who can almost make you believe that black is white, I have no faith in his achieving anything of lasting benefit to humanity."

Most speakers, however, were careful to leaven their criticism with praise for the prime minister, which at times veered toward the mawkish. "In my lifetime," said one, "I cannot remember any Minister who has inspired such confidence and enthusiasm as our present Prime Minister." Another member, Major Maurice Petherick, avowing that all he wanted was for the government to be "a bit stronger and more powerful," offered one of the more memorable statements of the debate: "We want a panzer and not a pansy Government."

The main criticism throughout the two-day debate was the government's apparent failure to wage war effectively. "It is of but momentary utility to have striking power if you cannot hold what you conquer," said Leslie Hore-Belisha, who had headed Chamberlain's War Office. He also criticized Churchill's growing dependence on America. "Are we relying on winning this war by our own efforts," he asked, "or are we putting off anything that can be done in the belief that the United States will supply the defects? If so we are misguided. We ought to thank God for President Roosevelt every day, but it is unfair to him and to his country to overstate what is possible."

Though Churchill had asked for the vote of confidence, it galled him to have to listen to speech after speech carping on the alleged failings of his government. He was thick-skinned, but only to a point. Even Averell Harriman's daughter Kathy recognized this, after spending a later weekend at Chequers. "He hates criticism," she wrote. "It hurts him as it would a child being unjustly spanked by a mother." On one occasion he told his great friend Violet Bonham Carter, "I feel very biteful & spiteful when people attack me."

The most wounding speech, however, did not come until later.

Mary, Tuesday, May 6:

> "Feel calmer today—
> "I really can't write all I think and feel.
> "I only know I am most seriously & deeply looking
>   at every aspect of it.
> "The trouble is I have so little to judge by.
> "And yet I do love Eric—I know I do.
> "The family have been quite wonderful. So helpful &
>   understanding.
> "I wish I could write about all that has happened in
>   detail—but somehow—it all seems too unreal &

strange. And too important & pent up to write
down calmly."

THE ATTACK CAME ON the second day of debate, Wednesday, May 7,
and it came from David Lloyd George, of all people. One year earlier he
had been instrumental in helping Churchill become prime minister. The
war, he said now, had entered "one of its most difficult and discouraging phases." This in itself was not a surprise, he noted; setbacks were to
be expected. "But we have had our third, our fourth great defeat and
retreat. We have trouble now in Iraq and Libya. We have the German seizure of the islands"—the Channel Islands, of which Guernsey and Jersey
were the largest. "We have tremendous havoc among our shipping, not
merely in losses but in what has not been taken enough into account, in
damage." He called for "an end of the kind of blunders which have dis-
credited and weakened us."

He singled out what he saw as the government's failure to provide
adequate information about events. "We are not an infantile nation," he
said, "and it is not necessary to withhold unpleasant facts from us, so
as not to frighten us." And he accused Churchill of failing to install an
effective War Cabinet. "There is no doubt about his brilliant qualities,"
Lloyd George said, "but for that very reason, if he will allow me to say
so, he wants a few more ordinary persons." Lloyd George spoke for an
hour, "weak at times," wrote Chips Channon, "at others sly and shrewd,
and often vindictive as he attacked the Government." Churchill, Channon wrote, "was obviously shaken, for he shook, twitched, and his hands
were never still."

But now, at just after four o'clock, it was *his* turn to speak. He exuded
energy and confidence, as well as pugnacious good cheer. He held the
House "from the very first moment," wrote Harold Nicolson in his diary: "very amusing . . . very frank."

He was also merciless. He directed his opening salvo at Lloyd George.
"If there were any speech which I felt was not particularly exhilarat-
ing," he said, "it was the speech of my right hon. Friend the Member
for Carnarvon Boroughs." Churchill condemned it as being unhelpful
during a time that Lloyd George himself had described as discouraging
and disheartening. "It was not the sort of speech which one would have
expected from the great war leader of former days, who was accustomed
to brush aside despondency and alarm, and push on irresistibly towards

the final goal," Churchill said. "It was the sort of speech with which, I imagine, the illustrious and venerable Marshal Pétain might well have enlivened the closing days of M. Reynaud's Cabinet."

He defended his decision to ask for a vote of confidence, "because after our reverses and disappointments in the field, His Majesty's Government have a right to know where they stand with the House of Commons, and where the House of Commons stands with the country." In a clear allusion to the United States, he said, "Still more is this knowledge important for the sake of foreign nations, especially nations which are balancing their policy at the present time and who ought to be left in no doubt about the stability or otherwise of this resolved and obstinate war Government."

As he neared his close, he reprised the speech he had made one year earlier in his first address to the House as prime minister. "I ask you to witness, Mr. Speaker, that I have never promised anything or offered anything but blood, tears, toil and sweat, to which I will now add our fair share of mistakes, shortcomings and disappointments and also that this may go on for a very long time, at the end of which I firmly believe—though it is not a promise or a guarantee, only a profession of faith—that there will be complete, absolute and final victory."

Acknowledging that one year, "almost to a day," had passed since his appointment as prime minister, he invited his audience to consider all that had occurred during that time. "When I look back on the perils which have been overcome, upon the great mountain waves in which the gallant ship has driven, when I remember all that has gone wrong, and remember also all that has gone right, I feel sure we have no need to fear the tempest. Let it roar, and let it rage. We shall come through."

As Churchill made his exit, the House erupted in cheers, which continued outside the chamber, in the Members' Lobby.

And then came the vote.

THAT DAY HARRIMAN COMPOSED a letter to Roosevelt, to convey some of his impressions about Churchill and Britain's ability to endure the war. Harriman had no illusions as to why Churchill held him so close and took him along on so many inspections of bombed cities. "He thinks it of value to have an American around for the morale of the people," Harriman told Roosevelt. But Harriman understood that this was only a secondary consideration. "He also wants me to report to you from time to time."

By now, what had long been clear to Churchill was also clear to Harriman: that Britain had no hope of winning the war without the direct intervention of the United States. Harriman understood that it was his own role to serve as a lens through which Roosevelt could see beyond censorship and propaganda into the heart of Britain's war-making architecture. He knew aircraft totals, production rates, food reserves, and the disposition of warships; and, thanks to the many visits to bombed cities, he knew the scent of cordite and decomposing bodies. Just as important, he understood the interplay of personalities around Churchill.

He knew, for example, that Max Beaverbrook, Churchill's newly designated minister of state, was now charged with doing for tanks what he had done for fighters when he was minister of aircraft production. Britain had neglected the matter of tanks and was paying the price in the Middle East. "The Libyan campaign in both directions was a rude shock to many and there will be great pressure for increased production both in England and America," Harriman wrote. More and better tanks were also needed for Britain's defense against invasion, if its home forces were to be able to resist incursions by Hitler's armored units. "Those in charge of tanks tell me it is rather ironic that Beaverbrook is now to help them as he has been the worst offender in stealing things they have needed"—meaning materials and tools. "Beaverbrook is not personally liked but people know he is the only man who can really cut the red tape and he is welcomed as an ally."

Now, however, Beaverbrook's health was becoming a factor. "He is none too well, suffering from asthma and an eye affliction," Harriman told Roosevelt. Nevertheless, Harriman expected that Beaverbrook would stay on and would succeed. "I gather from conversations with both the Prime Minister and Beaverbrook that he will end by being the number one trouble shooter."

It was obvious to Harriman that Churchill dearly hoped America would intervene in the war, but that he and others in the government were being careful not to push too hard. "It is natural that they hope for a belligerent status," he told Roosevelt, "but I am surprised how understanding all are of the psychology of the situation at home."

Mary, Wednesday, May 7:

> "Had made up my mind.
> "Eric rang up in P.M."

STILL DETERMINED TO ESCAPE 10 Downing Street, John Colville sought to further improve his odds by again asking Churchill's fixer, Brendan Bracken, to intercede on his behalf, but again Bracken failed. Churchill simply would not let him go.

No one seemed willing to support him. Opposition by the Foreign Office grew more stern, now that Eric Seal, Churchill's lead private secretary, was being dispatched to America on a special mission, leaving an absence in the secretariat that had to be filled. Even Colville's two older brothers, David and Philip, both with military commissions, gave him no encouragement. David, a navy man, seemed especially hostile to the idea. "He is violently opposed to my joining the RAF," Colville wrote in his diary. "His reasons were many of them offensive (such as my practical incapacity in which he and Philip firmly, but wrongly believe) but I did not mind as I knew they were in reality based on nothing but affection and the fear that I should be killed."

Colville's resolve only grew. His goal now was to become a fighter pilot, "if humanly possible." The first step was to begin the process of getting fitted for contact lenses, an arduous venture. The lenses were made of plastic but were still "scleral" lenses that covered most of the eye and were notoriously uncomfortable. The whole affair—the fitting, the endless shaping and reshaping of the lenses, and the slow process of growing acclimated to discomfort and irritation—required stamina. Colville deemed it worthwhile.

And now that he was actually taking concrete steps toward entering the RAF, he found himself getting caught up in the romance of it all, as if his commission were already a certainty. He told his diary, "My head is full of plans for a new life in the RAF and, of course, of improbable day-dreams on the subject."

From the time of his first fitting to when he could at last wear his completed lenses would take two months.

IN THE HOUSE OF COMMONS, the members lined up in the lobby. The tellers took their positions. Only three members voted no; even Lloyd George supported Churchill's proposed resolution. The tally in the end was 447 to 3.

"Pretty good," Harold Nicolson quipped.

That night, according to Colville, Churchill went to bed "elated."

Le Coeur Encore

———

Thursday, May 8:

"Rushed up to London.

"Eric to dinner—felt v. happy

"Mummie anxious for wedding to be put off for 6
months—clearly she is not v. taken with Eric.

"Went to bed feeling perplexed—doubtful—sleepy."

Friday, May 9:

"Felt miserable—uncertain.

"Had hair done.

"Eric came & we walked round St. James' Park—
lovely day. 'Sweet lovers love the Spring'! Once
with him—somehow all fears & doubts seemed
to go. Returned to lunch happy—confident—
decided.

"Lord & Lady Bessborough to lunch—

"Families confer—

"Engagement is to be announced following Wednesday. Joy—"

Moonrise

———

I N BERLIN, JOSEPH GOEBBELS DISMISSED CHURCHILL'S SPEECH IN
the House of Commons as being full of "excuses" and devoid of information. "But no sign of weakness," he acknowledged in his diary on
Friday, May 9, adding: "England's will to resist is still intact. We shall
therefore have to continue attacking and chipping away at her power
position."

Goebbels confessed in his diary to feeling a new respect for Churchill.
"This man is a strange mixture of heroism and cunning," he wrote. "If
he had come to power in 1933, we would not be where we are today. And
I believe that he will give us a few more problems yet. But we can and
will solve them. Nevertheless, he is not to be taken as lightly as we usually take him."

For Goebbels, it had been a long and trying week, and he settled in
with his diary to take stock. There had been personnel issues to deal
with. One of his key men wanted to quit and join the army. "Everyone
wants to go to the front," Goebbels wrote, "but who is going to do the
work here?"

The war against British shipping was going well, as was Rommel's
campaign in North Africa, and the Soviet Union appeared unaware that
the German invasion was imminent. But two nights earlier, the RAF had
launched a series of heavy raids against Hamburg, Bremen, and other
cities, killing one hundred in Hamburg alone. "We shall have our hands
full dealing with it," he wrote. He expected the Luftwaffe to launch a
punishing reprisal.

He noted also that British newspapers were publishing "strong" criticism of Churchill, but he doubted this had any real significance. As best he could tell, Churchill remained firmly in power.

"How good that a difficult week ends today," Goebbels wrote. "I am tired and battle-weary.

"One can never escape from the din of it all.

"Meanwhile, the weather has turned gloriously fine.

"Full moon!

"Ideal for air raids."

IN LONDON ON FRIDAY, May 9, John Colville wrote in his diary that Eric Duncannon and his parents, the Bessboroughs, had come to the Annexe for lunch with Mary and the Churchills. Afterward, Mary announced to Colville that she was engaged.

"I was relieved to be able simply to wish her happiness," he wrote. "I had feared she might be going to ask my opinion of him."

THAT EVENING, MARY AND ERIC took a train to the village of Leatherhead, about twenty miles southwest of London, to visit the headquarters of General A.G.L. McNaughton, commander of Canadian forces in Britain. Eric was one of McNaughton's staff officers. Mary's friend Moyra, Eric's sister, was there as well, and Mary was happy to report in her diary that Moyra seemed pleased about the engagement.

Mary's confidence surged.

WITH A FULL MOON PENDING, Churchill set off for Ditchley, and a weekend that would bring that first full year of his premiership to a blazing, fantastical end.

Part Seven

—

ONE YEAR
TO THE DAY

May 10, 1941

A Beam Named Anton

L ATE ON FRIDAY NIGHT, MAY 9, A GROUP OF SENIOR NAZI OFFICIALS
and the lesser lights with whom Hitler filled his innermost circle gathered at the Berghof, in the Bavarian Alps. Hitler could not sleep. He was, by this point, plagued by insomnia. And if he could not sleep, then no one would sleep. Hitler's waiters—members of the SS, or Schutzstaffel, Hitler's elite guard—served tea and coffee; tobacco and alcohol were forbidden. A fire roared in the hearth. Hitler's dog, Blondi, an Alsatian—later known as a German shepherd—basked in the warmth and in Hitler's attention.

As always, Hitler spoke in monologues, on topics that ranged from vegetarianism to the best way to train a dog. Time advanced slowly. His guests—including Eva Braun—listened with accustomed obedience, barely sensate in the warmth and flickering light, as a freshet of words flowed past them in which they were obliged to wade. Hitler's most senior men were absent, notably Rudolf Hess, Heinrich Himmler, Göring, and Goebbels. But Martin Bormann, his ambitious private secretary, was present, savoring the growing trust showed him by his *Führer,* and aware that the night could produce a further opportunity to advance his campaign to supplant Hess as Hitler's deputy. In the course of the coming day, Bormann was to get some very good news on this score, though for Hitler and everyone else in his hierarchy, it would appear to be the worst news possible.

At about two A.M., Bormann reminded the group of the recent RAF raids on Germany, taking pains to point out that Göring's precious Luftwaffe had done little to oppose the onslaught and that the raids had gone unanswered. Germany had to respond in force, he said. Another guest, Hans Baur, Hitler's personal pilot, seconded the idea. Hitler was resistant: He wanted all resources focused on the coming invasion of Russia. But Bormann and Baur knew their chief and argued that a massive raid against London was a necessity, to save face. A raid, moreover, would help camouflage the Russian invasion by demonstrating Germany's continued commitment to conquering Britain. By dawn, Hitler was in a rage. At eight o'clock Saturday morning, he called the Luftwaffe's chief of staff, Hans Jeschonnek, and ordered a reprisal raid on London, using every available aircraft.

CLEMENTINE WAS INDEED UNHAPPY about Mary's engagement to Eric Duncannon. On Saturday, from Ditchley, she wrote a letter to Max Beaverbrook in which she confessed her doubts. That she would write to him at all, let alone about such a personal matter, was an index of the depth of her anxiety, given how much she disliked and distrusted him.

"It has all happened with stunning rapidity," Clementine wrote. "The engagement is to be made public next Wednesday; but I want you to know beforehand because you are fond of Mary—

"I have persuaded Winston to be firm & to say they must wait six months—

"She is only 18, is young for her age, has not seen many people & I think she was simply swept off her feet with excitement—They do not know each other at all."

She closed: "Please keep my doubts and fears to yourself."

That day, by chance, Mary ran into Beaverbrook as he rode horseback along a country lane. His own estate, Cherkley, was a mile and a half from the headquarters of General McNaughton's Canadian forces. "He did not seem v. pleased," Mary wrote in her diary. He telephoned her later, however, and was "v. sweet," a term that few people ever applied to Beaverbrook.

Then Pamela, who was spending the weekend at Cherkley with her young son, stopped by, bringing a gift of two brooches and some advice. "She looked grave," Mary noted.

Mary did not particularly want any advice, but Pamela delivered it anyway: "Don't marry someone because they want to marry you—but because you want to marry them."

Mary dismissed it. "I didn't pay much attention at the time," she wrote in her diary, "—and yet it stuck & I kept on thinking of it."

General McNaughton and his wife threw a small afternoon party for Mary and Eric, where the guests offered toasts to their good health. The timing of the engagement, of the party and the toasts, struck Mary as being freighted with broader meaning, for the guests, acknowledging the first-year anniversary of her father's appointment, also drank to his continued good health. "Today a year ago he became Prime Minister— what a year—it seems so long," she wrote in her diary. "And standing there with everybody around I remembered how last year I had been at Chartwell & heard Chamberlain's voice telling the world that Papa was Prime Minister. And I remembered the orchard at Chartwell— & the blossoms & daffodils shimmering through the quiet twilight & how I cried & prayed in the stillness."

She had a long talk with Eric, alone, and by day's end felt her confidence begin to falter.

THAT AFTERNOON THE RAF'S No. 80 Wing, established to track Germany's use of navigational beams and to devise countermeasures, discovered that Germany had activated its beam transmitters, indicating that a raid was likely to occur that night. Operators plotted the vectors, then notified the RAF's local "filter room," which analyzed and prioritized reports of incoming aircraft and passed them along to Fighter Command and whatever other units might find the information important. The RAF declared this a "fighter night," meaning it would assign single-engine fighters to patrol the skies over London, while restricting the firing of anti-aircraft guns to avoid bringing down friendly aircraft. The designation required a bright moon and clear skies. In a seeming paradox, on such nights the RAF ordered its twin-engine night fighters to stay at least ten miles from the designated patrol zone, owing to their resemblance to German bombers.

At five-fifteen P.M., an officer in the filter room placed a call to the headquarters of the London fire service.

"Good afternoon, sir," the officer told the fire service's deputy chief. "The beam is on London."

The transmitting station for this beam was located in Cherbourg, on the French coast, and had the code name "Anton."

Two minutes later, the deputy chief asked the Home Office to authorize the massing in London of one thousand fire trucks.

Interloper

THE WEATHER ON SATURDAY, MAY 10, SEEMED IDEAL. THERE WERE clouds over the North Sea, at sixteen hundred feet, but the skies over Glasgow were clear. The moon that night would be just shy of full, with moonrise at eight forty-five P.M. and sunset at ten o'clock. Moonlight would give him a clear view of the landmarks he had memorized from his map of Scotland.

But it was not just the weather that made the timing seem favorable. In January a member of Hess's staff who often produced horoscopes for him had forecast that a "Major Conjunction" of the planets would occur on May 10, as would a full moon. He also delivered a horoscope that revealed early May to be an ideal time for whatever personal endeavors Hess wished to pursue. The idea for the flight had come to Hess in a dream. He was now, he believed, in the hands of "supernatural forces," a notion further affirmed when his mentor, Karl Haushofer, told him about a dream of his own, in which Hess appeared to be strolling in an untroubled manner through the halls of an English palace.

Hess packed for his trip. Known to be a hypochondriac of the first order, inclined to indulge in all manner of homeopathic cures and to hang magnets above his bed, he gathered together a collection of his favorite remedies, what he called his "medicinal comforts." These included:

—a tin case containing eight ampules of drugs for relieving
    intestinal spasms and to ease anxiety, with such names as
    "Spasmalgin" and "Pantopon";
—a metal box with a hypodermic syringe and four needles;

—twelve square tablets of dextrose, with the product name
"Dextro Energen";

—two tin boxes containing thirty-five tablets of various sizes and
colors, ranging from white to speckled brown, containing
caffeine, magnesia, aspirin, and other ingredients;

—a glass bottle marked "Bayer" containing a white powder made
of sodium bicarbonate, sodium phosphate, sodium sul-
phate, and citric acid, for use as a laxative;

—a tube containing ten tablets of a mild concentration of atro-
pine, useful for colic and to ease motion sickness;

—seven bottles of aromatic brown liquid to be administered by
droplet;

—a small flask containing a solution of sodium chloride and
alcohol;

—twenty-eight tablets of "Pervitin," an amphetamine, for
maintaining wakefulness (and standard issue to German
soldiers);

—two bottles of antiseptic solutions;

—one bottle containing sixty tiny white pellets containing various homeopathic substances;

—four small boxes with twenty tablets each, labeled variously as
"Digitalis," "Colocynthis," and "Antimon.Crud";

—ten tablets of homeopathic ingredients, seven white, three
brown;

—a box marked "Aspirin" but containing opiates, motion-
sickness drugs, and soporifics; and

—a packet marked "Sweets."

He also brought along a small flashlight, a safety razor blade, and material for making earplugs.

He said goodbye to his wife and son and drove to the airfield at Augsburg, accompanied by Pintsch, his adjutant. In the cockpit he stowed a
satchel containing his medicines and elixirs and a Leica camera. He told
airport officials that he was flying to Norway; his true destination was
Scotland, specifically a landing strip eighteen air miles south of Glasgow,
825 miles from Augsburg. Once again he gave adjutant Pintsch a sealed
envelope, again forbidding him to open it until four hours had passed.
This time, as Pintsch found later, the envelope contained four letters, one
each to be delivered to Hess's wife, Ilse; to a fellow pilot whose flight kit
he had borrowed; to Willy Messerschmitt; and to Adolf Hitler himself.

At about six P.M. German time, Hess took off from the Messerschmitt Works airfield at Augsburg and made a wide sweeping turn to ensure that the aircraft was working properly; then he headed northwest, toward the city of Bonn. Next he found a key railroad junction, which told him he was on course; he then saw Darmstadt, off to his right, and soon a point near Wiesbaden where the Rhine and the Main Rivers meet. He made a minor correction in his course. The Siebengebirge, or Seven Peaks, came into view just south of Bonn. Across the Rhine from this was Bad Godesberg, which conjured for Hess pleasant memories of both his childhood and periods he had spent there with Hitler, "the last time when the fall of France was imminent."

SOMEHOW HERMANN GÖRING LEARNED of Hess's departure, and feared the worst. He may have been alerted when, just after nine o'clock that night, Hess's adjutant, Pintsch, called Luftwaffe headquarters in Berlin and asked for a navigational beam to be transmitted along a line from Augsburg to Dungavel House, south of Glasgow. Pintsch was told he could have his beam, but only until ten P.M., because all beams would be required that night for a massive raid against London.

That evening, fighter ace Adolf Galland, now in charge of his entire fighter wing, received a telephone call from Göring himself. The *Reichsmarschall* was clearly distressed. He ordered Galland to immediately get his entire fighter wing—his *Geschwader*—into the air. "With your whole *Geschwader,* understand?" Göring repeated.

Galland was perplexed. "To begin with it was already getting dark," he wrote later, "and furthermore there were no reports of any enemy aircraft flying in." He told Göring as much.

"Flying in?" Göring said. "What do you mean by 'flying in'? You are supposed to stop an aircraft flying out! The deputy *Führer* has gone mad and is flying to England in an Me-110. He must be brought down. And, Galland, call me personally when you get back."

Galland asked for details: When had Hess taken off; what course was he likely to be flying? Galland faced a quandary. The sky would be dark in about ten minutes, making it next to impossible to find another aircraft with such a head start. What's more, many Me 110s were likely to be airborne at that moment. "How should we know which was the one Rudolf Hess was flying?" Galland recalled asking himself.

He decided to comply with Göring's orders—but only in part. "Just as a token, I ordered a take-off. Each squadron leader was to send up one or two planes. I did not tell them why. They must have thought I had gone mad."

Galland consulted a map. The distance to Britain from Augsburg was extreme; even with additional fuel, Hess was unlikely to reach his goal. What's more, for a good part of the flight he would be within reach of Britain's fighter force. "Should Hess really succeed in getting from Augsburg as far as the British Isles," Galland told himself, "the Spitfires would get him sooner or later."

After a suitable interval, Galland called Göring and told him his fighters had failed to find Hess. He assured Göring that it was unlikely the deputy *Führer* would survive the flight.

AS RUDOLF HESS NEARED the northeast coast of England, he dropped his extra fuel tanks, now empty and causing needless aerodynamic drag. These fell into the sea off Lindisfarne.

AT 10:10 P.M. THAT SATURDAY, Britain's Chain Home radar defense network detected a solo aircraft over the North Sea, flying toward the Northumberland coast at about twelve thousand feet, at high speed. The aircraft was assigned an identifier, "Raid 42." Soon after this, a member of the Royal Observer Corps, Durham, heard the aircraft and plotted the sound as being about seven miles northeast of the coastal town of Alnwick, near the Scottish border. The plane began a rapid descent. Moments later, an observer in the village of Chatton, a dozen miles north, got a glimpse of the aircraft as it roared past at a mere fifty feet above the ground. The observer saw it clearly silhouetted by moonlight, identified it as an Me 110, and reported it as such.

The controller on duty at Durham dismissed this as "highly improbable." That kind of aircraft was never seen this far north, and would never have enough fuel to be able to make it back to Germany.

The observer, however, insisted his identification was correct.

The plane was next spotted by observers at two more outposts, Jedburgh and Ashkirk, who reported it to be flying at about five thousand feet. They, too, identified it as an Me 110, and notified their superiors. Their reports were forwarded to Fighter Command's No. 13 Group, which dismissed them as ludicrous. The observers had to be mistaken, the group officials assumed; probably they had spotted a Dornier bomber, which also had two engines and two tail fins and was capable of making a flight of such a great distance.

But now observers in Glasgow plotted the speed of the aircraft and found it was traveling at over three hundred miles an hour, far beyond the maximum of a Dornier bomber. What's more, an RAF night fighter—a two-man Defiant—dispatched to intercept the intruder was falling behind. An assistant group officer with the observer corps, Major Graham Donald, ordered a message sent to Fighter Command to the effect that the aircraft could not possibly be a Dornier. It had to be an Me 110. RAF officials received this message with "hoots of derision."

The aircraft, meanwhile, had flown over Scotland and exited the country's west coast over the Firth of Clyde. It then turned around and flew back over the mainland, where an observer in the coastal village of West Kilbride got a clear look at the plane as it rocketed past at a tree-pruning altitude of twenty-five feet.

The RAF still rejected the identification. Two Spitfires joined the Defiant in hunting for the intruder. Meanwhile, operators at radar stations farther to the south began watching something far more ominous. From the look of it, hundreds of aircraft were massing over the coast of France.

The Cruelest Raid

THE FIRST BOMBERS CROSSED INTO ENGLISH SKIES SHORTLY BEFORE
eleven P.M. This initial sortie consisted of twenty bombers attached to
the elite KGr 100 fire-starter group, although that night the marker fires
were pretty much a needless accessory, given the brilliant moon and clear
skies. Hundreds of bombers followed. Officially, as in past raids, the targets were to be those of military significance, including in this raid the
Victoria and West India docks and the big Battersea Power Station, but as
every pilot understood, these targets ensured that bombs would fall upon
all quarters of civilian London. Whether planned or not, during this raid,
as indicated by the pattern of damage, the Luftwaffe seemed intent on
destroying London's most historic treasures and killing Churchill and his
government.

Over the next six hours, 505 bombers carrying 7,000 incendiaries
and 718 tons of high-explosive bombs of all sizes swarmed the sky over
London. Thousands of bombs fell and ripped into all corners of the city,
but they did especially grave damage in Whitehall and Westminster.
Bombs hit Westminster Abbey, the Tower of London, the Law Courts.
One bomb sliced through the tower that housed Big Ben. To everyone's
relief, the clock's immense bell boomed just minutes afterward, at two
A.M. Fire consumed a large portion of the famous roof of Westminster
Hall, built in the eleventh century by King William Rufus (William II).
In Bloomsbury, flames raced through the British Museum, destroying an
estimated 250,000 books and devouring the Roman Britain Room, the
Greek Bronze Room, and the Prehistoric Room. Happily, as a precau-
tion, the exhibits in these rooms had been removed for safekeeping. A

bomb struck the Peek Frean biscuit factory (which now also made tank parts). Two parachute mines blew up a cemetery, scattering old bones and fragments of monuments over the landscape and launching a coffin lid into the bedroom of a nearby house. The irate homeowner, in bed with his wife at the time, carried the lid out of the house and brought it to a group of rescue workers. "I was in bed with my missus when this bloody thing came through the window," he said. "What do I do with it?"

In Regent's Park, at No. 43 York Terrace, ninety-nine members of the Group for Sacrifice and Service, the British affiliate of a California cult, gathered in an apparently abandoned house for a service held to worship the full moon. The roof was made of glass. A full dinner buffet had been laid out in the central hall of the house. At one forty-five A.M. a bomb struck, killing many of the worshippers. Rescue workers found victims dressed in white robes that appeared to be the vestments of priests. Against the white cloth, blood appeared black. The group's archbishop, Bertha Orton, a devotee of the occult, was killed. A gold cross encrusted with diamonds still hung around her neck.

IT WAS NEARLY ELEVEN P.M. The Me 110 flown by Rudolf Hess was almost out of fuel. He had only a vague idea as to where he was. After flying past the west coast of Scotland and then turning around, he again descended to a hair's-breadth altitude to get a better look at the landscape. Pilots called this "contour flying." He flew in a zigzag pattern, clearly hunting for a recognizable landmark, as his fuel dwindled. It was now dark, though the landscape below was bathed in moonlight.

Hess, realizing that he would never find the landing strip at Dungavel House, decided to bail out. He increased his altitude. After flying high enough to allow for a safe jump, he shut off his engines and opened his cockpit. The force of the onrushing wind held him pinned to his seat.

Hess remembered the advice of a German fighter commander: that in order to escape an aircraft quickly, a pilot should roll his plane over and let gravity help. Whether Hess did so or not is unclear. The plane entered a steep upward climb, at which point Hess lost consciousness. He awoke and fell from the cockpit, striking a foot on one of the plane's twin tail fins as he fell through the moonlit night.

HARRIMAN'S SECRETARY, ROBERT MEIKLEJOHN, spent that Saturday at work. Harriman left at one-thirty in the afternoon to return to the

Dorchester, "the only place where we can really get anything done," Meiklejohn wrote in his diary. Meiklejohn wound up having lunch at his desk and working until five P.M., much to his disgust. Afterward, he went to a "girl show" at the Prince of Wales Theatre called *Nineteen Naughty One*. He had hoped for something bawdy and risqué but instead got a tame vaudeville show that lasted from six-thirty until nine o'clock, after which he returned to the office to see if a reply had come to a cable Harriman had sent to the United States that morning. Meiklejohn was on his way home at about eleven o'clock when the air-raid sirens sounded. He heard gunfire, but otherwise the night was quiet, the city bright under the full moon. He reached his apartment safely.

"All of a sudden about midnight [I] heard a rain of objects on the roof and against the building and saw bright flashing blue lights through the drawn curtains," he wrote in his diary. "Took a look out and saw dozens of incendiaries sputtering around in the street and small park below, making a bluish light like electric sparks, my first close contact with incendiaries." As he watched, he heard noises in the hall and found that his neighbors were heading down to the shelter in the building's basement. A visiting airman had advised them that incendiaries were invariably followed by bombs.

"I took the hint," Meiklejohn wrote. He put on his treasured fur coat—"I didn't want it to get blitzed"—and headed downstairs to begin his first-ever night in a shelter.

Soon high-explosive bombs began to fall. At one A.M. a bomb landed just beyond a corner of the building, igniting a gas main that lit the night so brightly, Meiklejohn believed he could have read a newspaper by its light. "This caused considerable stir among those who knew what it was all about," he wrote, "because it was almost a sure thing that the bombers would concentrate on us with the fires as a target."

More incendiaries fell. "Then the bombs started coming down fast for a while, in 'sticks' of three and six that sounded like gun salvos." The upper floors of neighboring buildings caught fire. Detonations shook the building. Several times during lulls in the bombing, Meiklejohn and a trio of U.S. Army officers left the building to examine the accumulating damage, careful not to venture more than a block away.

JUST AFTER ELEVEN P.M., an observer in Eaglesham, Scotland, about twenty-five miles inland from the west coast, reported that an aircraft had crashed and burst into flames. He reported, too, that the pilot had bailed out, and appeared to have landed safely. The time was now nine minutes after eleven. To the south, hundreds of German bombers were crossing the English coastline.

The mystery pilot drifted to earth near Floors Farm, on Bonnyton Moor, where a farmer found him and took him to his cottage. The farmer offered him tea.

The pilot declined. It was too late in the day for tea. He asked for water instead.

Police arrived, and took the man to their station in Giffnock, about five air miles from central Glasgow. They locked him in a cell, which offended him. He expected better treatment, like that afforded in Germany to British prisoners of high rank.

UPON HEARING HOW CLOSE the crash site was to Glasgow, Major Donald, the assistant group officer in Glasgow, set out in his car, a Vauxhall, to locate the wreckage, telling his superiors to give the RAF a message: "If they cannot catch an Me 110 with a Defiant, I am now going to pick up the bits with a Vauxhall."

He found fragments of the plane strewn over an acre and a half. There was minimal fire, suggesting that when the aircraft crashed it was almost out of fuel. The plane was indeed an Me 110 and, what's more, appeared to be brand-new and looked as though it had been stripped of all excess weight. "No guns, bomb-racks, and surprisingly (at the time) I could find no fixed reconnaissance camera," Major Donald reported. He found a portion of the fighter's wing that bore a black cross. He put this into his car.

He drove to the Giffnock police station, and there found the German pilot surrounded by police officers, members of the Home Guard, and an interpreter. "They did not, by then, appear to be making great headway," he wrote.

The pilot identified himself as Hauptmann Alfred Horn, *Hauptmann* being the German equivalent of captain. "He simply stated that he had not been hit, was in no trouble, and had landed deliberately, with a vital secret message for the Duke of Hamilton," Major Donald reported, supplying the underscore.

The major, who spoke rudimentary German, began asking the prisoner questions. "Captain Horn" was forty-two and from Munich, a city Major Donald had visited. He said he hoped he had landed near the Duke of Hamilton's home, and pulled out a map with the location of Dungavel

House clearly marked. The airman had come remarkably close: Dungavel was only ten miles away.

Major Donald pointed out to Captain Horn that even with extra fuel tanks, the aircraft could not possibly have made it back to Germany. The prisoner said he had not planned to return, and repeated that he was on a special mission. The man had a pleasant demeanor, Major Donald wrote in his report, adding, "and he is, if one may apply the term to a Nazi, quite a gentleman."

As they spoke, Donald studied the prisoner. Something about his face struck a chord. A few beats later, Donald realized who the man was, though his conclusion seemed too incredible to be true. "I am not expecting to be believed immediately, that our prisoner is actually No. 3 in the Nazi hierarchy," Major Donald wrote. "He may be one of his 'professional doubles.' Personally I think not. The name may be <u>Alfred Horn</u>, but the face is the face of <u>Rudolf Hess</u>."

Major Donald recommended that the police take "very special care" of the prisoner, then drove back to Glasgow, where he telephoned the headquarters of the RAF sector commanded by the Duke of Hamilton and told the controller on duty that the man in custody was Rudolf Hess. "The message was somewhat naturally greeted with incredulity," according to a subsequent RAF report, "but Major Donald did his best to convince the Controller that he was in dead earnest and that the Duke should be notified at the earliest moment."

The duke met the prisoner at about ten o'clock the next morning in a room at a military hospital, to which he by now had been transferred.

"I do not know if you recognize me," the German said to the duke, "but I am Rudolf Hess."

THE BIG RAID ON LONDON continued throughout the night, until the city seemed aflame from horizon to horizon. "About five AM I took a last look around," wrote Harriman's secretary, Meiklejohn, "and saw the full moon shining red through the clouds of smoke which were reflecting the fires from the blazes below—it was quite a sight."

That morning he shaved by the glare from the burning gas main outside. His apartment was eight floors above the street.

The last bomb fell at 5:37 A.M.

A Surprise for Hitler

As COLVILLE LAY IN BED ON SUNDAY MORNING, FOR NO PARticular reason he began thinking about a fanciful novel he had read, whose plot centered on a surprise visit to Britain by Hitler himself, via parachute. The author was Peter Fleming, the older brother of Ian Fleming. Colville made note of the moment in his diary: "Awoke thinking unaccountably of Peter Fleming's book *Flying Visit* and day-dreaming of what would happen if we captured Göring during one of his alleged flights over London." It was rumored that Göring had flown over the city during one or more air raids.

At eight o'clock Colville set out from 10 Downing Street to walk to Westminster Abbey, where he planned to attend an early church service. He found a stunning spring day, with bright sun and cerulean skies, but soon encountered great shrouds of smoke. "Burnt paper, from some demolished paper mill, was falling like leaves on a windy autumn day," he wrote.

Whitehall was crowded with people, many of them merely out to see the damage, others whose blackened faces suggested they had been up all night fighting fires and rescuing the wounded. A teenage boy, one of the sightseers, pointed in the direction of the Palace of Westminster and asked, "Is that the sun?" But this glow was fire, emanating from the flames of massed blazes still burning south of the Thames.

When Colville reached the abbey, he found the way blocked by police officers and fire trucks. He approached the entrance but was stopped by a policeman at the door. "There will not be any services in the Abbey today, Sir," the officer said. Colville was struck by his quotidian tone— "exactly as if it were closed for spring cleaning."

The roof of Westminster Hall was still burning with visible flames, and gusts of smoke rose from somewhere behind it. Colville spoke with one of the firemen, who pointed to Big Ben and with satisfaction told Colville about the bomb that had passed through the tower. Despite clear signs of damage, Big Ben was indeed still marking out double British summer time, though, as was later determined, the bomb cost the British Empire half a second.

Colville walked onto Westminster Bridge, which crosses the Thames directly in front of the tower. Just to the southeast, St. Thomas' Hospital was in flames. Fires burned all along the Embankment. It was clear that the night's raid had caused deep and lasting damage of a kind the city had not experienced before. "After no previous raid has London looked so wounded the next day," Colville wrote.

On his return to 10 Downing Street, he had breakfast, then telephoned Ditchley to tell Churchill about the damage. "He was very grieved," remarked Colville, "that William Rufus's roof at Westminster Hall should have gone."

Colville walked to the Foreign Office to talk with a friend who was Anthony Eden's second private secretary, and just as he entered the office his friend said into his telephone, "Hold on a minute. I think this is your man."

ON SUNDAY MORNING, MARY and Eric set out for Ditchley, to spend the day with Clementine and Winston and the rest. The night's bombing had closed train stations, which forced the couple to take a roundabout route involving unexpected transfers. This turned the trip from a relatively quick journey into an arduous and tedious one, during which Mary's doubts became more concrete. "I became aware," she wrote, "of very definite misgivings."

Pamela's advice kept running through her mind: "Don't marry someone because he wants to marry you."

She told Eric of her concerns. He was understanding, and gentle, and did what he could to ease her anxiety. They arrived to find Ditchley full of guests, among them Averell Harriman. Immediately, Clementine took Mary into her bedroom.

IN LONDON, AT THE Foreign Office, Anthony Eden's private secretary placed his hand over the receiver and told Colville that the caller had identified himself as the Duke of Hamilton and was claiming to have news that could only be delivered to Churchill in person. The duke—if indeed the caller was a duke—planned to fly himself to the RAF's Northolt air base, outside London, and wanted to be met there by one of Churchill's men, meaning Colville, who was on duty at 10 Downing Street that day. The duke also wanted Alexander Cadogan, Eden's under-secretary, to come along.

Colville took the receiver. The duke declined to offer details but said his news was like something from a fantasy novel and involved a German aircraft that had crashed in Scotland.

"At that moment," Colville wrote, "I vividly remembered my early waking thoughts on Peter Fleming's book and I felt sure that either Hitler or Göring had arrived."

Colville again telephoned Churchill.

"Well, *who* has arrived?" Churchill asked, with irritation.

"I don't know; he wouldn't say."

"It can't be Hitler?"

"I imagine not," Colville said.

"Well, stop imagining and have the Duke, if it is the Duke, sent straight here from Northolt."

Churchill directed Colville to ensure, first, that the duke really was the Duke of Hamilton.

ON THE MORNING OF Sunday, May 11, Hitler's architect, Albert Speer, came to the Berghof to show him some architectural sketches. In the anteroom to Hitler's office, he found two nervous men, Karl-Heinz Pintsch and Alfred Leitgen, both adjutants to Rudolf Hess. They asked Speer if he would permit them to see Hitler first, and Speer agreed.

They gave Hitler Hess's letter, which he immediately read. "My *Führer,*" it began, "when you receive this letter I shall be in England. You can imagine that the decision to take this step was not easy for me, since a man of 40 has other ties with life than one of 20." He explained his motive: to try to bring about a peace settlement with Britian. "And if, my *Führer,* this project—which I admit has but very small chance of success—ends in failure and the fates decide against me, this can have no detrimental results either for you or for Germany: it will always be possible for you to deny all responsibility. Simply say I was crazy."

Speer was looking through his drawings when, he wrote, "I suddenly heard an inarticulate, almost animal outcry."

This was the start of one of the tantrums, or *Wutausbrüche,* that Hitler's men so dreaded. One aide recalled that it was "as though a bomb had hit the Berghof."

"Bormann, at once!" Hitler shouted. "Where is Bormann?"

Hitler told Bormann to summon Göring, Ribbentrop, Goebbels, and Himmler. He asked adjutant Pintsch if he knew the contents of the letter. Upon Pintsch's affirmation that he did, Hitler ordered him and his fellow adjutant, Leitgen, arrested and sent to a concentration camp. Albrecht Haushofer was arrested as well, and sent to the Gestapo house prison in Berlin, for interrogation. He was later released.

The other leaders arrived. Göring brought along his chief technical officer, who assured Hitler that it was highly unlikely that Hess would reach his destination. Navigation would be Hess's biggest problem; high winds would almost certainly drive him off course. Hess would probably miss the British Isles completely.

This prospect gave Hitler hope. "If only he would drown in the North Sea!" Hitler said (according to Albert Speer). "Then he would vanish without a trace, and we could work out some harmless explanation at our leisure." What Hitler most feared was what Churchill would do with the news of Hess's disappearance.

AT DITCHLEY, IN CLEMENTINE's bedroom, Mary now realized for the first time the depth of her mother's misgivings about her engagement to Eric. Clementine told Mary that she and Winston had grave concerns, and that she regretted letting the romance progress to this point without expressing their doubts and fears.

This was only partly true: In fact, Churchill, preoccupied with war matters, had few concerns about the engagement and was more than content to let Clementine manage the situation. Thus far that weekend, his main interests had been the prior night's air raid—which appeared to be the worst of the war—and Operation Tiger, a mission to transport a large number of tanks to the Middle East.

Clementine demanded that Mary put off the engagement for six months.

"BOMBSHELL," Mary wrote in her diary.

Mary wept. But she knew her mother was right, as she conceded in her diary: "—through my tears I became aware most clearly of her wisdom—& all the doubts—misgivings & fears I had experienced at various times during the last few days seemed to crystallize."

Clementine asked Mary if she felt certain about marrying Eric. "In all honesty," Mary wrote, "I could not say I did."

Clementine, unable to get her husband's attention, asked Harriman to talk with Mary, then went directly to Eric to tell him her decision to postpone the engagement.

Harriman took Mary into Ditchley's formal box garden, where the two walked around and around, Mary "crushed & miserable & rather tearful," Harriman trying to console her and offer perspective.

"He said all the things I should have told myself," she wrote.

"Your life is before you.
"You should not accept the first person who comes
    along.
"You have not met many people.
"To be stupid about one's life is—a crime."

As they walked and talked, she grew increasingly certain that her mother was indeed correct, but along with this she felt "more & more conscious of my own unintelligent behavior. My weakness—my moral cowardice."

She also felt relief. "What would have happened had Mummie not intervened? . . . Thank God for Mummie's sense—understanding & love."

Eric was kind to Mary, and understanding, but he was furious with Clementine. Telegrams were fired off, notifying Eric's parents, as well as others, that the engagement had been postponed.

Mary had some spiked cider, and felt better. She wrote letters until late in the night. "Went to bed crushed—humiliated but fairly calm."

But before this, she and the others all settled into the home theater at Ditchley to watch a film. Mary sat beside Harriman. The film, appropriately, was called *World in Flames*.

Blood, Sweat, and Tears

———

A S MARY SETTLED INTO HER BED THAT SUNDAY NIGHT IN THE peaceful environs of Ditchley, firefighting crews in London struggled to bring the remaining fires under control, and rescue teams dug through rubble, looking for survivors and recovering torn and broken bodies. Whether by design or accident, many bombs had failed to explode, and these kept firefighters and rescuers at bay until technicians could defuse the weapons.

In terms of treasures lost, damage done, and deaths inflicted, the raid was the worst of the war. It killed 1,436 Londoners, a record for a single night, and caused grave injury to another 1,792 people. It left some 12,000 people without homes, among them the novelist Rose Macaulay, who returned to her flat on Sunday morning to find that it had been destroyed by fire, along with everything she had accumulated in the course of her lifetime, including letters from her terminally ill lover, a novel in progress, all her clothes, and all her books. It was the loss of the books that she grieved above all.

"I keep thinking of one thing I loved after another, with a fresh stab," she wrote to a friend. "I wish I could go abroad and stay there, then I shouldn't miss my things so much, but it can't be. I loved my books so much, and can never replace them." Among the lost was a collection of volumes published in the seventeenth century—"my Aubrey, my Pliny, my Topsell, Sylvester, Drayton, all the poets—lots of lovely queer unknown writers, too." She also lost her collection of rare Baedekers ("and anyhow travel is over, like one's books and the rest of civilization"), but the single loss that caused her the greatest sorrow was her *Oxford English*

Dictionary. As she probed the ruins of her home, she found a charred page from the *H*'s. She also exhumed a page from her edition of the famed seventeenth-century diary kept by Samuel Pepys. She made an inventory of the books, at least those she could remember. It was, she wrote in a later essay, "the saddest list; perhaps one should not make it." Now and then an overlooked title would come to mind, like the familiar gesture of a lost loved one. "One keeps on remembering some odd little book that one had; one can't list them all, and it is best to forget them now that they are ashes."

The most symbolic, and infuriating, destruction in the May 10 raid occurred when a direct hit destroyed the debating chamber of the House of Commons, where Churchill just four days earlier had won his vote of confidence. "Our old House of Commons has been blown to smithereens," Churchill wrote to Randolph. "You never saw such a sight. Not one scrap was left of the Chamber except a few of the outer walls. The Huns obligingly chose a time when none of us were there."

Sunday also brought a strange and welcome calm, as recorded by a twenty-eight-year-old Mass-Observation diarist, an affluent widow with two children who lived in Maida Vale, west of Regent's Park, and saw none of the conflagration still underway in Westminster, three miles to the southeast. "I drew back the curtains on a day of sunny loveliness and perfect peace," she wrote. "The apple-trees in the garden were pink-dotted against the luscious, thick-piled whiteness of the pear-blossom; the sky was warmly blue, birds were chirruping in the trees, and there was a gentle Sunday-morning quietness over everything. Impossible to believe that last night, from this same window, everything should have been savagely red with fire-glow and smoke, and deafening with an inferno of noise."

The city braced for another attack on Sunday night, when the moon would be at its fullest, but no bombers came. And none came the next night, or the night after that. The quiet was puzzling. "It may be that they are massing on the eastern front as part of their intimidation of Russia," wrote Harold Nicolson in his diary on June 17. "It may be that their whole Air Force will be used for a mass attack on our front in Egypt. It may also be that they are equipping their machines with some new device, like wire-cutters"—to cut the cables of barrage balloons. "In any case," he concluded, "it bodes ill."

The change was immediately evident in the monthly tallies of the dead kept by the Ministry of Home Security. In May throughout the

United Kingdom, German raids killed a total of 5,612 civilians (of whom 791 were children). In June, the total plummeted to 410, a drop of nearly 93 percent; in August, to 162; in December, 37.

Oddly enough, this new quiet came at a time when Fighter Command believed it was at last getting a grip on night defense. By now, No. 80 Wing, the radio countermeasures unit, had become adept at jamming and diverting the German beams, and Fighter Command's drive to learn to fight in the dark finally seemed to be paying off. Many twin-engine night fighters were now equipped with air-to-air radar. Pilots of single-engine fighters, flying on "fighter nights," also seemed to be hitting their stride. That Saturday night, under a brilliant moon, a combined force of eighty Hurricanes and Defiants, aided by outlying anti-aircraft batteries, shot down at least seven bombers and seriously damaged a KGr 100 pathfinder, the best result thus far. From January through May, the rate at which RAF single-engine fighters intercepted German aircraft increased fourfold.

On the ground, too, there was a different attitude, this in tune with the overall feeling that Britain had shown beyond a doubt that it could endure Hitler's onslaught; now it was time to return the favor. A Mass-Observation diarist who worked as a traveling salesman wrote in his diary, "The spirit of the people seems to be moving from passive to active and rather than cower in shelters they prefer to be up and doing. Incendiaries seem to be tackled as though they were fireworks and tackling fires in top rooms with stirrup pumps is just part of the evening's work. One leader was telling me his chief trouble is to prevent people taking risks. Everyone wants to 'bag a bomb.'"

AND THEN THERE WAS HESS.

On Tuesday, May 13, Joseph Goebbels addressed the affair at his morning propaganda meeting. "History knows a great many similar examples, when people lost their nerve at the last moment and then did things which were perhaps extremely well intended but nevertheless did harm to their country," he said. He assured his propagandists that eventually the incident would recede into its historical context as one episode in the long, glorious story of the Third Reich, "even though, naturally, it is not pleasant at the moment. However, there are no grounds for letting our wings droop in any way or for thinking that we shall never live this down."

But Goebbels had clearly been rattled by the episode. "Just as the

Reich is on the point of snatching victory, this business must happen," he said at a meeting on Thursday, May 15. "It is the last hard test of our character and of our staying power, and we feel entirely up to such a trial sent to us by fate." He instructed his lieutenants to revive a propaganda line they had used before the war, which played to the myth of Hitler as a mystical being. "We believe in the *Führer*'s powers of divination. We know that anything which now seems to be going against us will turn out to be most fortunate for us in the end."

Goebbels knew, of course, that a profound deflection of public attention would soon arise. "For the moment we will ignore the affair," he said. "Besides, something is shortly going to happen in the military field which will enable us to divert attention away from the Hess issue to other things." He was referring to Hitler's imminent invasion of Russia.

In an official statement, Germany depicted Hess as an ailing man who was under the influence of "mesmerists and astrologers." A subsequent commentary called Hess "this everlasting idealist and sick man." His astrologer was arrested and sent to a concentration camp.

Göring summoned Willy Messerschmitt for a meeting and took him to task for aiding Hess. The Luftwaffe chief asked Messerschmitt how he could possibly have let an individual as obviously insane as Hess have an airplane. To which Messerschmitt offered an arch rejoinder:

"How am I supposed to believe that a lunatic can hold such a high office in the Third Reich?"

Laughing, Göring said, "You are incorrigible, Messerschmitt!"

IN LONDON, CHURCHILL DIRECTED that Hess should be treated with dignity, but also with the awareness that "this man, like other Nazi leaders, is potentially a war-criminal and he and his confederates may well be declared outlaws at the close of the war." Churchill approved a War Office suggestion that Hess be housed temporarily in the Tower of London, until a permanent accommodation could be established.

The episode clearly delighted Roosevelt. "From this distance," he cabled Churchill on May 14, "I can assure you that the Hess flight has captured the American imagination and the story should be kept alive for just as many days or even weeks as possible." In reply two days later, Churchill conveyed all he knew of the episode, including Hess's contention that though Hitler was willing to seek peace, he would not negotiate with Churchill. Hess showed "no ordinary signs of insanity," Churchill wrote. He cautioned that Roosevelt was to keep his letter confidential.

"Here we think it best to let the Press have a good run for a bit and keep the Germans guessing."

And in this, Churchill's government succeeded. Questions abounded. One newspaper quipped, "Your Hess guess is as good as mine." There was speculation that Hess wasn't really Hess but, rather, a clever double; some feared that he might even be an assassin whose true mission was to get close enough to Churchill to jab him with a poison ring. A London movie audience burst into a thunder of laughter when a newsreel announcer said that now Britain wouldn't be surprised if Hermann Göring himself arrived next.

It all just seemed too incredible. "What a dramatic episode in this whole fascinating hell!!" wrote U.S. observer General Raymond Lee in his diary. Lee found that Hess's arrival was the talk of White's, where the constant repetition of Hess's name created a strange effect, filling the club's bar, lounge, and restaurant with "sibilants," the hissing sound of repeated *s*'s.

"It sounded," Lee said, "like a basketful of snakes."

AND SO, WITH FAMILY TURMOIL, civic trauma, and Hitler's deputy falling from the sky, the first year of Churchill's leadership came to an end. Against all odds, Britain stood firm, its citizens more emboldened than cowed. Somehow, through it all, Churchill had managed to teach them the art of being fearless.

"It is possible that the people would have risen to the occasion no matter who had been there to lead them, but that is speculation," wrote Ian Jacob, military assistant secretary to the War Cabinet under Churchill and later a lieutenant general. "What we know is that the Prime Minister provided leadership of such outstanding quality that people almost reveled in the dangers of the situation and gloried in standing alone." Wrote War Cabinet secretary Edward Bridges, "Only he had the power to make the nation believe that it could win." One Londoner, Nellie Carver, a manager in the Central Telegraph Office, may have put it best when she wrote, "Winston's speeches send all sorts of thrills racing up and down my veins and I feel fit to tackle the largest Hun!"

On one of Churchill's full-moon weekends at Ditchley, Diana Cooper, wife of Information Minister Duff Cooper, told Churchill that the best thing he had done was to give people courage.

He did not agree. "I never gave them courage," he said. "I was able to focus theirs."

———

IN THE END, LONDON endured, albeit with grave injuries. Between September 7, 1940, when the first large-scale attack on central London occurred, and Sunday morning, May 11, 1941, when the Blitz came to an end, nearly 29,000 of its citizens were killed, and 28,556 seriously injured.

No other British city experienced such losses, but throughout the United Kingdom the total of civilian deaths in 1940 and 1941, including those in London, reached 44,652, with another 52,370 injured.

Of the dead, 5,626 were children.

A Weekend at Chequers

I T WAS A SUNDAY EVENING IN DECEMBER 1941, A FEW WEEKS BEFORE Christmas, and as always a host of familiar faces had made their way to Chequers to dine and sleep or just to dine. The guests included Harriman and Pamela, as well as a new face, Harriman's daughter Kathy, who turned twenty-four that day. After dinner, Churchill's valet, Sawyers, brought in a radio, so that all present could listen to the BBC's regular broadcast of the news. The mood in the house was less than buoyant. Churchill seemed downhearted, though in fact the war, for the moment, was going reasonably well. Clementine had a cold and was upstairs in her room.

The radio was an inexpensive portable, a gift to Churchill from Harry Hopkins. Churchill opened the top to turn it on. The broadcast was already underway. The announcer said something about Hawaii, then moved on to Tobruk and the Russian front. Hitler had launched his invasion in June, with a massive assault that most observers assumed would crush the Soviet army in a matter of months, if not weeks. But the army was proving more effective and resilient than anyone had expected, and now, in December, the invaders were struggling against the two eternal weapons of Russia: its sheer size and its winter weather.

Hitler was still expected to win, however, and Churchill recognized that after completing his conquest, he would turn his full attention back to Britain. As Churchill had forecast in a speech the previous summer, the Russian campaign "is no more than a prelude to an attempted invasion of the British Isles."

The BBC announcer's voice changed. "The news," he said, "has just been received that Japanese aircraft have raided Pearl Harbor, the American naval base in Hawaii. The announcement of the attack was made in a brief statement by President Roosevelt. Naval and military targets on the principal Hawaiian island of Oahu have also been attacked. No further details are yet available."

At first, there was confusion.

"I was thoroughly startled," Harriman said, "and I repeated the words, 'The Japanese have raided Pearl Harbor.'"

"No, no," countered Churchill aide Tommy Thompson. "He said Pearl River."

U.S. ambassador John Winant, also present, glanced toward Churchill. "We looked at one another incredulously," Winant wrote.

Churchill, his depression suddenly lifted, slammed the top of the radio down and leapt to his feet.

His on-duty private secretary, John Martin, entered the room, announcing that the Admiralty was on the phone. As Churchill headed for the door, he said, "We shall declare war on Japan."

Winant followed, perturbed. "Good God," he said, "you can't declare war on a radio announcement." (Later Winant wrote, "There is nothing half-hearted or unpositive about Churchill—certainly not when he is on the move.")

Churchill stopped. His voice quiet, he said, "What shall I do?"

Winant set off to call Roosevelt to learn more.

"And I shall talk with him too," Churchill said.

Once Roosevelt was on the line, Winant told him that he had a friend with him who also wanted to speak. "You will know who it is, as soon as you hear his voice."

Churchill took the receiver. "Mr. President," he said, "what's this about Japan?"

"It's quite true," Roosevelt said. "They have attacked us at Pearl Harbor. We are all in the same boat now."

Roosevelt told Churchill that he would declare war on Japan the next day; Churchill promised to do likewise immediately after him.

Late that night, at one thirty-five A.M., Harriman and Churchill sent a "MOST IMMEDIATE" telegram to Harry Hopkins. "Thinking of you much at this historic moment—Winston, Averell."

The meaning was clear to all. "The inevitable had finally arrived," Harriman said. "We all knew the grim future that it held, but at least there was a future now." Anthony Eden, preparing to leave for Moscow, learned of the attack that night in a phone call from Churchill. "I could not conceal my relief and did not have to try to," he wrote. "I felt that whatever happened now, it was merely a question of time."

Later that night, Churchill at last retired to his room. "Being saturated and satiated with emotion and sensation," he wrote, "I went to bed and slept the sleep of the saved and thankful."

Churchill worried, briefly, that Roosevelt would focus only on the Japanese, but on December 11, Hitler declared war on America, and America returned the favor.

Churchill and Roosevelt were indeed now all in the same boat. "It might be badly knocked about by the storm," wrote Pug Ismay, "but it would not capsize. There was no doubt about the end."

SOON AFTERWARD, CHURCHILL, LORD BEAVERBROOK, and Harriman set out for Washington, D.C., aboard a spanking new battleship, the *Duke of York*, at great risk and under strictest secrecy, to meet with Roosevelt and coordinate strategy for the war. Churchill's doctor, Sir Charles Wilson, came along, as did some fifty other men, ranging from valets to Britain's topmost military officials, Field Marshal Dill, First Sea Lord Pound, and Air Chief Marshal Portal. Lord Beaverbrook alone brought three secretaries, a valet, and a porter. Roosevelt worried about the risk and tried to dissuade Churchill, for indeed, had the ship been sunk, the loss would have decapitated the British government, but Churchill brushed the president's concerns aside.

Charles Wilson marveled at the change in Churchill. "He is a different man since America came into the war," the doctor wrote. "The Winston I knew in London frightened me. . . . I could see that he was carrying the weight of the world, and wondered how long he could go on like that and what could be done about it. And now—in a night, it seems—a younger man has taken his place." The fun of it all was back, Wilson saw: "Now suddenly the war is as good as won and England is safe; to be Prime Minister of England in a great war, to be able to direct the Cabinet, the Army, the Navy, the Air Force, the House of Commons, England herself, is beyond even his dreams. He loves every minute of it."

The first several days of the voyage were extraordinarily rough, even by North Atlantic standards, and forced the ship to sail at speeds as low as six knots, nullifying the hoped-for safety effect of traveling in a ship capable of moving almost five times as fast. All of the travelers were ordered to stay off the deck, as massive waves swept over the ship's low-slung hull. Beaverbrook quipped that he had "never travelled in such a large submarine." Churchill wrote to Clementine, "Being in a ship in such weather as this is like being in a prison, with the extra chance of being drowned." He took his Mothersill's to fight seasickness and gave doses to his secretaries, against the protests of Wilson, who was chary about prescribing drugs of any kind.

"The PM is very fit and cheerful," Harriman wrote. "Talks incessantly at meals." At one point Churchill held forth, at length, on the subject of seasickness—"buckets on the bridge of destroyers, etc., etc.," wrote Harriman, "until Dill who had not fully recovered turned green and almost left the table."

The battleship anchored in the Chesapeake Bay off Maryland. Churchill and his party flew the rest of the way to Washington. "It was night time," Inspector Thompson wrote. "Those in the plane were transfixed with delight to look down from the windows and see the amazing spectacle of a whole city lighted up. Washington represented something immensely precious. Freedom, hope, strength. We had not seen an illuminated city for two years. My heart filled."

Churchill stayed at the White House, as did secretary Martin and several others, and got a close-up look at Roosevelt's own secret circle. Roosevelt, in turn, got a close-up look at Churchill. The first night Churchill and members of his party spent in the White House, Inspector Thompson—also one of the houseguests—was with Churchill in his room, scouting various points of danger, when someone knocked at the door. At Churchill's direction, Thompson answered and found the president outside in his wheelchair, alone in the hall. Thompson opened the door wide, then saw an odd expression come over the president's face as he looked into the room behind the detective. "I turned," Thompson wrote. "Winston Churchill was stark naked, a drink in one hand, a cigar in the other."

The president prepared to wheel himself out.

"Come on in, Franklin," Churchill said. "We're quite alone."

The president offered what Thompson called an "odd shrug," then wheeled himself in. "You see, Mr. President," Churchill said, "I have nothing to hide."

Churchill proceeded to sling a towel over his shoulder and for the next hour conversed with Roosevelt while walking around the room naked, sipping his drink, and now and then refilling the president's glass. "He might have been a Roman at the baths, relaxing after a successful debate in the Senate," Inspector Thompson wrote. "I don't believe Mr. Churchill would have blinked an eye if Mrs. Roosevelt had walked in too."

ON CHRISTMAS EVE, CHURCHILL, with Roosevelt standing at his side, in leg braces, spoke from the South Portico of the White House to a crowd of thirty thousand people who had gathered for the lighting of the National Community Christmas Tree, an Oriental spruce that had been transplanted to the South Lawn. At twilight, after a prayer and remarks by a Girl Scout and a Boy Scout, Roosevelt pressed the button to turn on the lights. He spoke briefly, then offered the podium to Churchill, who told the audience that he felt very much at home in Washington. He spoke of this "strange Christmas Eve," and how important it was to preserve Christmas as an island amid the storm. "Let the children have their night of fun and laughter," Churchill said. "Let gifts of Father Christmas delight their play. Let us grown-ups share to the full in their unstinted pleasures"—abruptly, he lowered his voice to a deep, forbidding growl—"before we turn again to the stern tasks and formidable year that lie before us. Resolve!—that by our sacrifice and daring, these same children shall not be robbed of their inheritance or denied their right to live in a free and decent world."

He closed: "And so"—he flung his hand skyward—"and so, in God's mercy, a happy Christmas to you all."

The crowd began to sing: three carols, starting with "O Come, All Ye Faithful" and closing with three verses of "Silent Night," sung with solemnity by the massed voices of thousands of Americans facing a new war.

INSPECTOR THOMPSON WAS DEEPLY touched when, the next day, just before setting out to have Christmas dinner with the chief of Roosevelt's Secret Service detail, a maid handed him a Christmas present from Mrs. Roosevelt. He unwrapped it and found a necktie and a small white envelope with a Christmas card. "For Inspector Walter Henry Thompson—Christmas 1941—a Merry Christmas from the President and Mrs. Roosevelt."

The maid watched, fascinated, as Thompson's jaw dropped. He wrote, "I simply could not believe that the President of a nation, with his countrymen preparing to wage the greatest war in their history, could think of giving a necktie to a police officer on Christmas."

WHAT LAY AHEAD, OF course, was four more years of war, and for a time the darkness seemed impenetrable. Singapore, Britain's stronghold in the Far East, fell, and threatened also to bring down Churchill's government. The Germans drove British forces from Crete and recaptured Tobruk. "We are indeed walking through the Valley of Humiliation," wrote Clementine in a letter to Harry Hopkins. Reversal followed reversal, but by the end of 1942, the momentum of the war began to shift in the Allies' favor. British forces defeated Rommel in a series of desert battles known collectively as the Battle of El Alamein. The U.S. Navy bested Japan at Midway. And Hitler's Russian campaign slogged to a halt in mud, ice, and blood. By 1944, after the Allied invasions of Italy and France, the outcome seemed certain. The air war against Britain would briefly flare back to life with the advent in 1944 of the V-1 flying bomb and the V-2 rocket, Hitler's "Vengeance" weapons, which brought a fresh terror to London, but this was a final offensive begun for no other purpose than to cause death and destruction before Germany's inevitable defeat.

On New Year's Eve 1941, Churchill and his party—and, of course, Inspector Thompson—were aboard a train heading back to Washington, after a visit to Canada. Churchill sent a message to all asking that they join him in the dining car. Drinks were served, and as midnight arrived, he offered a toast: "Here's to a year of toil, a year of struggle and peril, and a long step forward to Victory!" Then all joined hands, Churchill taking the hands of an RAF sergeant and Air Chief Marshal Charles Portal, and sang "Auld Lang Syne," as their train tore through the darkness toward that city of light.

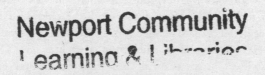

Epilogue

AS TIME WENT BY

MARY

Mary, the country mouse, became an anti-aircraft gunner assigned to the heavy-gun battery in Hyde Park. This caused her mother no small degree of anxiety, especially after an eighteen-year-old member of a Southampton battery was killed during an air raid, on April 17, 1942, the first such death of the war. "My first agonizing thought was—it might have been Mary," Clementine told her in a letter. But she also confessed to feeling "private pride that you my beloved one have chosen this difficult, monotonous, dangerous & most necessary work—I think of you so often my Darling Mouse." John Colville recalled how one evening, when air-raid sirens began to sound, "the P.M. dashed off in his car to Hyde Park to see Mary's battery at work."

Mary was promoted and by 1944, the penultimate year of the war, found herself in command of 230 female volunteers. "Not so bad at 21!" her father wrote proudly in a letter to Randolph.

Winston Junior was even more impressed. He understood that his grandfather was an important man, but it was his aunt Mary he idolized. "To a three-year-old, having a grandfather who was Prime Minister and running the entire war was a concept difficult to grasp," he wrote in a memoir. ". . . But to have an aunt who had four huge guns of her very own—that was *something*!"

———

ERIC DUNCANNON GRIEVED THE failure of his courtship, as became apparent on Saturday, September 6, 1941, when he and John Colville went shooting at Stansted Park with a group of friends.

Wrote Colville, "Eric, who was at his simplest and most charming, told me he can still think of nothing but Mary Churchill."

COLVILLE

Churchill did at last relent. On Tuesday, July 8, 1941, in the midst of a heat wave with temperatures in the nineties, John Colville stopped by Churchill's office just before his nap.

"I hear you are plotting to abandon me," Churchill said. "You know I can stop you. I can't make you stay with me against your will but I can put you somewhere else."

Colville told him he understood but added that he hoped Churchill would not do so. He showed him one of his as yet unfinished contact lenses.

Churchill told Colville he could go.

At last able to wear his lenses, Colville presented himself for another RAF medical interview and this time—"oh rapture!"—passed. Soon afterward he was sworn in as a new member of the RAF Volunteer Reserve, the initial stop on his final journey to becoming a pilot. The RAF did insist, however, that first he have two teeth filled, something his dentist had previously told him not to worry about. This took an hour.

At length, it came time for Colville's departure from 10 Downing Street, so that he could begin his training to become a fighter pilot. He could wear his contact lenses for only about two hours, and this, happily, disqualified him from serving on a bomber crew. Churchill "agreed that the short, sharp battle of the fighter pilot was far better than the long wait of a bomber crew before they reached their objective." He was, however, appalled to learn that Colville would be doing his training not as an officer but as the RAF's equivalent of an enlisted man, an aircraftman second class. "You mustn't," Churchill told him. "You won't be able to take your man."

Wrote Colville, "It had not crossed his mind that one of his junior Private Secretaries, earning £350 per annum, might not have his own valet."

On September 30, after packing his things, Colville said a private goodbye to the prime minister, in his office. Churchill was genial and gracious. "He said it must only be '*au revoir*' as he hoped I should often come back and see him." Churchill told Colville that he really should not be letting him leave, and that Anthony Eden had been annoyed at having to do so. But he conceded that Colville was doing "a very gallant thing."

As their meeting came to an end Churchill told him, "I have the greatest affection for you; we all have, Clemmy and I especially. Goodbye and God bless you."

Colville left, feeling a great sadness. "I went out of the room with a lump in my throat such as I have not had for many years."

COLVILLE DID *NOT* DIE in a fiery wreck after being shot to bits by an Me 109. He underwent his flight training and was assigned to a reconnaissance squadron flying American-made Mustangs, based in Funtington, adjacent to Stansted Park, where he contracted a case of impetigo. Lady Bessborough, Eric Duncannon's mother, invited him to stay in Stansted House, to recuperate. A few weeks later, he received a summons from Churchill.

"It is time that you came back here," Churchill told him.

"But I have only done one operational flight."

"Well, you may do six. Then back to work."

After his six sorties, he returned to Downing Street to resume his work as private secretary. As D-Day neared, he was called back to his squadron, over protests raised by the Prof that if he were captured and identified, he would prove a valuable asset to German intelligence. Churchill let him go with reluctance. "You seem to think that this war is being fought for your personal amusement," he told him. "However, if I were your age I should feel the same, and so you may have two months' fighting leave. But no more holidays this year."

It was hardly a holiday. Colville flew forty sorties over the French coast, conducting photographic reconnaissance. "It was thrilling as we crossed the Channel to look down on a sea boiling with ships of all kinds heading for the landing beaches," he wrote in his diary. "It was thrilling, too, to be part of a vast aerial armada, bombers and fighters thick as starlings at roosting-time, all flying southwards." Three times he was nearly shot down. In a lengthy letter to Churchill, he described one incident in which an anti-aircraft shell tore a large hole through one wing. Churchill loved it.

Once again Colville came back to No. 10. Prior to his RAF tenure, he had been reasonably well liked at No. 10 although never heartily loved, according to Pamela Churchill, but now that he had returned from active service, his cachet had risen. "None of us except Clemmie really liked Jock," Pamela said years later. ". . . But he then went off and joined the air force and I think that was a very smart thing to do because when he came back again, everybody, you know, was so pleased to see him." He was no longer "wet," as Mary had first judged him in the summer of 1940. "Nothing could have been less true," she conceded later.

In 1947, Colville became private secretary to Princess Elizabeth, soon to be queen. The offer came as a surprise. "It is your duty to accept," Churchill told him. During his two-year tenure in the post, Colville met and fell in love with one of the princess's ladies-in-waiting, Margaret Egerton; they married on October 20, 1948, at St. Margaret's Church, adjacent to Westminster Abbey.

Colville achieved a fame greater than any of his fellow private secretaries did when, in 1985, he published his diary, in edited form, under the title *The Fringes of Power;* the work became a touchstone for every scholar interested in the inner workings of 10 Downing Street under Churchill. He removed much personal material—"trivial entries which are of no general interest," as he put it in his preface—though anyone reading the actual handwritten diary held in the Churchill Archives Center in Cambridge will see that those trivial entries were of the utmost importance to Colville himself.

He dedicated the book to Mary Churchill, "with affection and with penitence for some of the less complimentary references to her in the early part of this diary."

BEAVERBROOK

In all, Beaverbrook offered his resignation fourteen times, the last in February 1942, when he was minister of supply. He resigned rather than take on a new post as minister of war production. This time Churchill did not object, doubtless to Clementine's delight.

Beaverbrook left two weeks later. "I owe my reputation to you," he told Churchill in a letter on February 26, his last day. "The confidence of the public really comes from you. And my courage was sustained by you." He told Churchill he was "the savior of our people and the symbol of resistance in the free world."

Churchill replied in kind: "We have lived & fought side by side through terrible days, & I am sure our comradeship & public work will undergo no break. All I want you to do now is to recover your strength & poise, so as to be able to come to my aid when I shall vy greatly need you." He credited Beaverbrook's triumph in the fall of 1940 with playing "a decisive part in our salvation." He closed: "You are one of our vy few Fighting men of genius."

And so, Beaverbrook at last departed. "I felt his loss acutely," Churchill wrote. But in the end, Beaverbrook had succeeded where he'd needed to succeed, doubling fighter output within his first three months as minister of aircraft production and, perhaps just as important, standing near at hand to provide the kind of counsel and humor that helped Churchill through his days. What Churchill most valued was Beaverbrook's companionship and the diversion he provided. "I was glad to be able sometimes to lean on him," Churchill wrote.

In March 1942, Beaverbrook felt compelled to explain to Churchill why he had made all those previous threats to resign. He acknowledged using them as a tool to overcome delays and opposition—in short, to get his way—and he believed that Churchill had understood that. "I was always under the impression," he wrote, "that, in your support for my methods, you wished me to stay on in office, to storm, to threaten resignation and to withdraw again."

The two men remained friends, though the intensity of their friendship ebbed and flowed. In September 1943, Churchill brought him back into his government as lord privy seal, a move that seemed designed mainly to keep his friend and adviser close at hand. Beaverbrook resigned from this as well, but by then Churchill, too, was leaving office. In one volume of his personal history of World War II, Churchill gave high praise to Beaverbrook. "He did not fail," he wrote. "This was his hour."

THE PROF

The Prof was vindicated.

At length Mr. Justice Singleton felt confident enough about the various statistics of German and British air strength to offer a judgment. "The conclusion at which I arrive," he wrote, in his final report in August 1941, "is that the strength of the German Air Force in relation to the Royal Air Force may be taken as roughly 4 to 3 as at the 30th November, 1940."

Meaning that all along, as the RAF fought what it believed to be an overwhelming foe, the two air forces did not differ much in terms of strength, the main variance, as Singleton now concluded, being in the numbers of long-range bombers. This comforting news came a bit late, of course, but in the end it may well be that the RAF, thinking itself the underdog by a ratio of four to one, fought better and with more urgency than might have been the case if it had shared the relative complacency of the Luftwaffe, which believed itself to be vastly superior. The report proved that the Prof's instincts had been accurate after all.

His embrace of aerial mines did not have as salutary an outcome. Throughout 1940 and 1941, he and Churchill lobbied and cajoled Air Ministry officials and Beaverbrook to produce and deploy the mines, and to make them a staple in Britain's arsenal of defensive weapons. He had few successes, many failures, and in the end, faced with increasing resistance, the mines were abandoned.

Lindemann and Churchill remained friends throughout the war, and Lindemann was a regular guest for meals—vegetarian meals—at 10 Downing Street, Chequers, and Ditchley.

PAMELA AND AVERELL

For a time, the affair between Pamela Churchill and Averell Harriman flourished. Harriman's daughter Kathy caught on to their relationship soon after her arrival in London and did not mind. The fact that she herself was several years older than her father's lover seemed not to trouble her. Kathy was not particularly close to her own stepmother, Marie, and felt no sense of betrayal.

That Kathy should grasp the reality so quickly surprised no one. The couple made little effort to disguise the affair. Indeed, at one point, for about six months, Harriman, Pamela, and Kathy shared a three-bedroom flat at 3 Grosvenor Square, near the American embassy. Churchill knew of the affair, Pamela believed, but he expressed no outward concern. If anything, so strong a bond between a member of the Churchill family and Roosevelt's personal emissary could only be an asset. Clementine did not approve but also did nothing to intercede. Randolph later complained to John Colville that his parents "had condoned adultery beneath their own roof." Beaverbrook knew of it, and loved knowing of it, and made sure that Harriman and Pamela spent long weekends at his country home, Cherkley, where Winston Junior continued to reside in the care of a nanny. Harry Hopkins knew about the affair, and so even did Roosevelt. The president was tickled.

In June 1941, Churchill sent Harriman to Cairo to assess how American aid could best buttress Britain's forces in Egypt, and asked his son,

Randolph, to look out for him. By now Randolph had been promoted to major, assigned to manage press relations at British headquarters in Cairo. He was himself conducting a love affair, this with a celebrated hostess named Momo Marriott, wife of a British general. One night, while talking with Harriman during a dinner on a chartered dhow on the Nile River, which Randolph had arranged just for the visiting American, Randolph boasted about his own affair. He had no inkling that Harriman was sleeping with his wife, even though it was a source of gossip within his circle and at White's club back in London.

Randolph's lack of awareness was evident in a letter he wrote to Pamela in July 1941, which he entrusted to Harriman to deliver to her upon his return from Cairo. The letter praised Harriman. "I found him absolutely charming," Randolph wrote, "& it was lovely to be able to hear so much news of you & all my friends. He spoke delightfully about you & I fear that I have a serious rival!"

Randolph finally learned of the affair early in 1942, while on leave. He had, by then, grown dissipated in appearance. Their marriage, already wounded by his spending and drinking and Pamela's indifference, now veered into a miasma of argument and insult. Furious battles broke out at the Annexe, during which Randolph would pick fights with Churchill. Clementine, concerned that her husband might suffer an apoplectic seizure, again banished Randolph from the house, this time for the duration of the war. By the summer, when Randolph returned to London to convalesce from injuries sustained in a car crash in Cairo, it was clear to all that the marriage could not be repaired. Evelyn Waugh, one of Randolph's clubmates at White's, wrote of Pamela, "She hates him so much she can't be in a room with him." In November 1942, Randolph left her.

Harriman moved her into an apartment of her own and paid her an annual allowance of £3,000. To disguise his role, he used an intermediary: Max Beaverbrook, who, true always to his love of human drama, was glad to do it, and worked out a scheme to camouflage the fact that Harriman was providing the money.

But this, too, was not exactly a secret. "Unlike Paris, where there was a great black market, everybody took pride in sticking pretty closely to rationing," said John Colville. "But if you dined with Pamela, you would have a five- or six-course dinner, eight or ten guests, and foods you didn't ordinarily see. My guess is that all of us around the table were sort of smirking and saying that Averell was taking good care of his girlfriend."

In October 1943, Roosevelt picked Harriman to be his ambassador to

Moscow, and the affair, inevitably, began to cool. Distance freed them both. Harriman slept with other women, Pamela with other men, including, at one point, broadcaster Edward R. Murrow. "I mean, when you are very young, you do think of things very differently," Pamela told a later interviewer.

As the war neared its end, Pamela felt a growing anxiety about what would come next. On April 1, 1945, she wrote to Harriman in Moscow: "Supposing the war ends in the next four or five weeks. The thought of it sort of scares me. It is something one has looked forward to for so long that when it happens, I know I am going to be frightened. Do you know at all what I mean? My adult life has been all war, and I know how to grapple with that. But I am afraid of not knowing what to do with life in peacetime. It scares me horribly. It's silly, isn't it?"

Years passed. Harriman went on to become U.S. secretary of commerce under President Harry Truman and later was elected governor of New York; he held various senior advisory posts in the Kennedy and Johnson administrations. He nursed grander aspirations, however—to become secretary of state, maybe even president—but these proved beyond his reach. Despite his many affairs, he remained married to his wife, Marie, and by all counts their marriage grew stronger over the years. Marie's death in September 1970 left Harriman shattered, according to Marie's daughter, Nancy. "He used to sit in her room and cry."

In 1960, Pamela married Leland Hayward, the producer and talent agent who co-produced the original Broadway version of *The Sound of Music;* their marriage lasted until Hayward's death in March 1971.

Pamela and Harriman kept in distant touch. In August 1971, they both found themselves invited to a Washington, D.C., dinner party thrown by a mutual friend, Katharine Graham, publisher of the *Washington Post.* Harriman was seventy-nine years old; Pamela, fifty-one. They spent the evening in close conversation. "It was very strange," she said, "because the moment we started talking, there were so many things to reminisce about that one really hadn't thought about for years."

Eight weeks later they married, in a private ceremony at a church on Manhattan's Upper East Side, attended by only three guests. They wanted the ceremony kept secret—but only for the moment.

Later that day, about 150 friends gathered at Harriman's nearby townhouse for what they had been told was just a cocktail party.

As Pamela walked in, she cried out to a friend, "We did it! We did it!" It had taken only three decades. "Oh Pam," another friend wrote, soon afterward, "isn't life strange!!" Their marriage endured for another fifteen years, until Harriman's death in July 1986.

THE GERMANS

At the Nuremberg trials, Hermann Göring was found guilty of an array of offenses, including war crimes and crimes against humanity. The court sentenced him to die by hanging on October 16, 1946.

In his testimony, he stated that he had wanted to invade Britain immediately after Dunkirk but had been overruled by Hitler. He told an American interrogator, U.S. air force general Carl Spaatz, that he had never liked the idea of attacking Russia. He wanted to keep bombing Britain and drive Churchill to capitulate. The timing of the Russian campaign was fatal, Göring told Spaatz. "Only the diversion of the Luftwaffe to the Russian front saved England."

To the last, Göring was unrepentant. He told the Nuremberg court, "Of course we rearmed. I am only sorry we did not rearm more. Of course I considered treaties as so much toilet paper. Of course I wanted to make Germany great."

Göring also sought to justify his systematic looting of art collections throughout Europe. While awaiting trial, he told an American psychiatrist, "Perhaps one of my weaknesses has been that I love to be surrounded by luxury and that I am so artistic in temperament that masterpieces make me feel alive and glowing inside." He claimed that all along he'd intended to donate his collections to a state museum after his death. "Looking at it from that standpoint I can't see that it was ethically wrong. It was not as if I accumulated art treasures in order to sell them or to become a rich man. I love art for art's sake and as I said, my personality demanded that I be surrounded with the best specimens of the world's art."

Investigators cataloged the works he had amassed since the war began, and counted "1,375 paintings, 250 sculptures, 108 tapestries, 200 pieces of period furniture, 60 Persian and French rugs, 75 stained glass windows," and 175 miscellaneous other objects.

The night before his execution, he killed himself with cyanide.

JOSEPH GOEBBELS AND HIS WIFE, Magda, poisoned their six youngest children—Helga, Hildegard, Helmut, Holdine, Hedwig, and Heidrun—on May 1, 1945, in Hitler's bunker as the Soviet army closed in, first directing a medical adjutant to administer a shot of morphine to each child. Next Hitler's personal doctor gave each an oral dose of cyanide. Goebbels and Magda then killed themselves, also using cyanide. An SS officer, acting on their instructions, shot them both to make certain they were dead.

Hitler had killed himself the day before.

RUDOLF HESS WAS TRIED at Nuremberg, where he avowed his continued loyalty to Hitler. "I do not regret anything," he said. He was sentenced to life in prison for his role in helping bring about the war and was assigned to Spandau Prison, along with half a dozen other German officials.

One by one the other prisoners, including Albert Speer, were released until, on September 30, 1966, Hess became the prison's sole occupant. He committed suicide on August 17, 1987, at the age of ninety-three, using an extension cord to hang himself.

MIRACULOUSLY, ADOLF GALLAND SURVIVED the war, despite a number of near-death encounters. On one day alone he was shot down twice. He achieved his final kills on April 25, 1945, when, while flying the Luftwaffe's most advanced fighter, a jet aircraft, he shot down two American bombers, bringing his score to 104. After destroying the second aircraft, he was intercepted by an American P-47. Wounded, his plane badly damaged, he managed to return to his airfield just as it came under attack, and crash-landed with bombs and bullets falling around him. He survived with only a leg injury. American forces arrested him ten days later. He was thirty-three years old. As good as his record was, it by now had been exceeded by a number of his colleagues. Two pilots accumulated more than 300 kills each, and ninety-two other men matched or exceeded Galland's record.

After first being interrogated in Germany, Galland was flown to Britain on May 14, 1945, for further questioning. This was his first visit on land. In July, his captors took him to the big air base at Tangmere, near Stansted Park, where he met the legless ace, Douglas Bader, with whom Mary Churchill had danced. Galland had met Bader earlier in the war, after Bader had been shot down and captured; Galland had insisted he be treated well.

Now Bader gave him cigars.

CHURCHILL AND THE WAR

The boy never left the man.

One morning in the summer of 1944, with the war still in full flare, Clementine, in her bed at the No. 10 Annexe, summoned to her room a teenage soldier named Richard Hill, the son of Churchill's personal secretary Mrs. Hill. A toy train set had arrived for Winston Junior, Pamela's son, and Clementine wanted to make sure all the pieces were present and that everything worked. She asked Hill to assemble it and try it out.

The package contained tracks, train cars, and two engines, which were powered by wind-up mechanisms. Hill, on his knees, began laying out the track, and as he did so, he noticed the appearance on the floor before him of two slippers bearing the monogram "W.S.C." He looked up and saw Churchill standing above, in his pale blue siren suit, smoking a cigar and closely watching his progress. Hill made a move to stand up, but the prime minister stopped him. "Carry on with what you are doing," Churchill said.

Hill completed the layout.

Churchill continued watching. "Put one of the engines on the track," he said.

Hill did so. The engine moved around the circle as its clockwork wound down.

"I see you have two engines," Churchill said. "Put the other one on the track as well."

Hill again obliged. Now two engines traveled the tracks, one behind the other.

Churchill, cigar in his mouth, got down on his hands and knees.

With obvious delight he said, "Now, let's have a crash!"

THE WAR IN EUROPE ended on May 8, 1945. Throughout the day, as the news spread through London, crowds began filling the city's squares. Cocky American soldiers threaded through the crowd, waving American flags and now and then breaking into the song "Over There." Germany's surrender was official. Churchill was to make a public speech at three o'clock from Downing Street, to be broadcast by the BBC and through loudspeakers, after which he would proceed to the House of Commons.

At the sound of Big Ben booming three o'clock, the crowd went utterly silent. The German war, Churchill said, was over. He summarized the war's course and explained how, in the end, "almost the whole world was combined against the evil-doers, who are now prostrate before us." He tempered this news with the sober reflection that Japan had yet to surrender. "We must now devote all our strength and resources to the completion of our task, both at home and abroad. Advance, Britannia! Long live the cause of freedom! God save the King!"

The staff at No. 10 made a path for him in the back garden and applauded as he walked to his car. He was touched. "Thank you so much," he said, "thank you so much."

AT BUCKINGHAM PALACE, AS the king and queen appeared on the royal balcony, a vast crowd on the Mall erupted with one fused scream of delight, and continued clapping and cheering and waving flags until the royal couple went back inside. But the crowd lingered and began chanting, "We want the king, we want the king." At length the king and queen reappeared, then stepped apart to make room for another, and out walked Winston Churchill, an immense smile on his face. The roar was explosive.

That night, even though the blackout was officially still in effect, bonfires erupted throughout London, casting the familiar orange glow of fire into the sky—except now the fires were a sign of celebration. Searchlights played on Nelson's Tower in Trafalgar Square, and in perhaps the most moving gesture of all, the searchlight operators aimed their lights at a space in the air just above the cross that topped the dome to St. Paul's Cathedral and held them there, to form a shining cross of light.

JUST TWO MONTHS LATER, in an episode of breathtaking irony, the British public voted the Conservative Party out of power, forcing Churchill's resignation. He had seemed the ideal man to run a war, less so to guide Britain's postwar recovery. Churchill was succeeded by Clement Attlee, leader of the Labour Party, which won 393 seats; the Conservatives held only 213.

The final results of the vote were reported on July 26, a Thursday; a few days later, the Churchills and some friends gathered for their last weekend at Chequers. The house filled as always. Here came Colville, Ambassador Winant, Brendan Bracken, Randolph, Mary, Sarah, and Diana, with her husband, Duncan Sandys; the Prof arrived for lunch.

The rector of the Ellesborough church, so rarely attended by Churchill, stopped by to say farewell.

That Saturday night, after dinner and after watching newsreels and a documentary about the Allied victory in Europe called *The True Glory,* the family went downstairs. Suddenly Churchill seemed downhearted. He told Mary, "This is where I miss the news—no work—nothing to do."

She poured her sadness for her father into her diary: "It was an agonizing spectacle to watch this giant among men—equipped with every faculty of mind and spirit wound to the tightest pitch—walking unhappily round and round unable to employ his great energy and boundless gifts—nursing in his heart a grief and disillusion I can only guess at."

It was "the worst moment so far," she wrote. The family played records to cheer him, first Gilbert and Sullivan, which for the first time had little effect, followed by American and French military marches, which helped a bit. Then came "Run Rabbit Run" and, at Churchill's request, a song from *The Wizard of Oz,* and these seemed at last to do the trick. "Finally at 2 he was soothed enough to feel sleepy and want his bed," Mary wrote. "We all escorted him upstairs."

She added, "O darling Papa—I love you so, so much and it breaks my heart to be able to do so little. I went to bed feeling very tired and dead inside me."

The next day, after lunch, Mary and John Colville took a last walk up Beacon Hill. It was a lovely, sun-filled day. Everyone gathered on the lawn, Clementine played croquet with Duncan, by now largely recovered from his car crash. They all signed the Chequers visitors' book—"that memorable visitors' book," Mary noted, "where you can follow the plots and stratagems of the war from the names there." In a thank-you to the estate's owners, the Lees, Clementine wrote, "Our last weekend at Chequers was sad. But as we all wrote our names in the Visitors' Book I reflected upon the wonderful part this ancient house has played in the war. What distinguished guests it has sheltered, what momentous meetings it has witnessed, what fateful decisions have been taken under its roof."

Churchill was the last to sign.

He added beneath his name a single word: "Finis."

Sources and Acknowledgments

ALTHOUGH MY MOVE TO NEW YORK AND ITS ATTENDANT 9/11 epiphany was the primary impetus for my embarking on this book, another element played an important part as well: the fact that I am a parent. As my three daughters will assure you, I am the king of fatherly anxiety, but my anxieties about my children center on the routine insults of their daily lives, like their jobs and boyfriends and the smoke detectors in their apartments, not high-explosive bombs and incendiaries falling from the sky. Honestly, how did the Churchills and their circle cope?

With that as my guiding question, I set out on what became a lengthy journey through the vast and tangled forest of Churchill scholarship, a realm of giant volumes, distorted facts, and bizarre conspiracy theories, to try to find my personal Churchill. As I've discovered with prior books, when you look at the past through a fresh lens, you invariably see the world differently and find new material and insights even along well-trodden paths.

One danger in writing about Churchill is that you'll become overwhelmed at the very start, and possibly be deterred from proceeding, by the sheer volume of work already in the public domain. To avoid this, I decided to begin with a modest amount of advance reading—William Manchester and Paul Reid's *Defender of the Realm,* Roy Jenkins's *Churchill,* and Martin Gilbert's *Finest Hour*—but then to plunge right into the archives to experience Churchill's world in as fresh a manner as possible. My particular lens meant that certain documents would be of far more use to me than to Churchill's traditional biographers—for example, lists of household expenditures at his prime-ministerial retreat, Chequers, and correspondence on how to billet soldiers on the estate's grounds without overwhelming its sewage system, a matter of significant interest at the time but not necessarily important to future writers of history.

My search took me to numerous archival depots, including three of my favorite places in the world: the National Archives of the United Kingdom, at Kew, outside London; the Churchill Archives Center at Churchill College, Cambridge; and the U.S. Library of Congress, Manuscript Division, in Washington. As my stacks of documents accumulated, I began mapping my narrative, using the so-called Vonnegut curve, a graphic device conceived by Kurt Vonnegut in his master's thesis at the University of Chicago, which his department rejected, he claimed, because it was too simple and too much fun. It provides a schema for analyzing every story ever written, whether fiction or nonfiction. A vertical axis represents the continuum from good fortune to bad, with good at the top, bad at the bottom. The horizontal axis represents the passage of time. One of the story types that Vonnegut isolated was "Man in a Hole," in which the hero experiences great fortune, then deep misfortune, before climbing back up to achieve even greater success. It struck me that this was a pretty good representation of Churchill's first year as prime minister.

With arc in hand, I set out to hunt for the stories that often get left out of the massive biographies of Churchill, either because there's no time to tell them or because they seem too frivolous. But it is in frivolity that Churchill often revealed himself, the little moments that endeared him to his staff, despite the extreme demands he placed on all. I tried also to bring to the foreground characters often given secondary treatment in the big histories. Every Churchill scholar has quoted the diaries of John Colville, but it seemed to me that Colville wanted to be a character in his own right, so I tried to oblige him. I know of no other work that mentions his bittersweet romantic obsession with Gay Margesson, which I include in part because it reminded me of a singularly pathetic phase in my own early adulthood. You won't find the story in the published version of Colville's diaries, *The Fringes of Power,* but if you compare its pages with the manuscript version at the Churchill Archives Center, as I did, you'll find each romantic installment. He dismissed these and other omissions as "trivial entries which are of no general interest." At the time he actually made them, however, the events at hand were anything but trivial. What I found so interesting about his pursuit of Gay was that it unfolded while London was aflame, with bombs falling every day, and yet somehow the two of them managed to carve out moments of, as he put it, "sufficient bliss."

Mary Churchill, too, steps forward. She loved her father very much, but also loved a good RAF dance, and thrilled at the practice of "beating up," when pilots would buzz her and her friends at treetop level. I owe special thanks to Emma Soames, Mary's daughter, who gave me permission to read her mother's diary.

I also owe a great debt to Allen Packwood, director of the Churchill Archives Center, who read a draft of the manuscript and saved me from numerous gaffes. His own recent book, *How Churchill Waged War,* proved to be an invaluable vehicle for catching up on the latest thinking about Churchill. I owe thanks also to two former directors of the International Churchill Society, Lee Pollock and Michael Bishop, who also read the manuscript and suggested all manner of corrections and adjustments, some quite subtle. Early on both gentlemen recommended a variety of resources to consult, in particular a stack of 10 Downing Street desk-calendar cards held at society headquarters in Washington, D.C. I found it singularly compelling that the card for September 1939, when the war began, is marred by a big black stain, apparently caused by the toppling of an ink jar.

As always, I owe incalculable thanks, and a supply of Rombauer char-donnay, to my wife, Chris, for putting up with me, yes, but especially for her attentive first read of my manuscript, which she returned with her usual margin notations—smiley faces, sad faces, and receding sequences of *zzzzzzz*'s. Huge thanks as well to my editor, Amanda Cook, whose margin notations were rather more eviscerating and demanding, but always smart and illuminating. Her assistant, Zachary Phillips, piloted this book through the homestretch with grace and enthusiasm, though I imagine he nearly went blind in the process owing to my terrible hand-writing. My agent, David Black, always a mensch, but also sometimes a junkyard dog, encouraged me throughout the long journey, while peri-odically plying me with red wine and great food. Julie Tate, my brilliant professional fact-checker, read the manuscript as if with a magnifying glass, hunting down misspellings, incorrect dates, bad chronologies, and misquoted quotes, in the process improving my sleep immeasurably. Thanks, also, to my friend Penny Simon, ace Crown publicist, who read an early draft, fully aware that I can never repay her for her generosity, and making that clear at every opportunity. My longtime friend and for-mer colleague Carrie Dolan, a front-page editor at *The Wall Street Jour-*

nal, also read a draft, in part while doing her absolutely favorite thing: flying in an airplane over the sea. Actually, she hates to fly, even more than me, but she claimed to like the book.

A team of resourceful, creative, and energetic souls at Random House and Crown brought this book to life and gave it a grand send-off: Gina Centrello, president and publisher, Random House; David Drake, publisher at Crown; Gillian Blake, editor-in-chief; Annsley Rosner, deputy publisher; Dyana Messina, director of publicity; and Julie Cepler, director of marketing. Special thanks to Rachel Aldrich, maestro of new media and new ways of winning the attention of distracted readers. Bonnie Thompson put the book through a rigorous final copyedit; Ingrid Sterner fixed my end notes; Luke Epplin translated my abysmal handwriting to conjure page proofs in record time; Mark Birkey oversaw it all, and produced a book. Chris Brand designed a killer jacket, and Barbara Bachman made the book's interior pages into beautiful things.

I owe particular thanks to my three daughters for helping me keep perspective amid the routine trials of daily life, which pale in comparison to the awful things that Churchill and his circle had to deal with every day.

ONE PARTICULAR SOURCE OF original documents deserves special notice: *The Churchill War Papers,* collected and published by the late master of Churchill history, Martin Gilbert, as a vast appendix to his multivolume biography of the prime minister. I made extensive use of volumes 2 and 3, whose telegrams, letters, speeches, and personal minutes together total 3,032 pages. Another invaluable source, for matters beyond romance, was Colville's *Fringes,* primarily the first volume, which provides a wonderful sense of life at No. 10 Downing Street during the war. I came across many terrific secondary works. Among my favorites: Andrew Roberts's *"The Holy Fox,"* a biography of Lord Halifax; John Lukacs's *Five Days in London, May 1940;* Lynne Olson's *Troublesome Young Men;* Richard Toye's *The Roar of the Lion;* Lara Feigel's *The Love-Charm of Bombs;* and David Lough's *No More Champagne,* a financial biography of Churchill and one of the most original works of Churchillian scholarship to emerge in the last decade.

In the following notes I cite and credit mainly material that I have quoted from original documents or secondary sources; I've also cited things that seem likely to strike readers as novel or controversial. I do not, however, cite everything. Episodes and details that are well-known and fully documented elsewhere, and material whose source is obvious, such as certain clearly dated diary entries, I have chosen not to annotate in order to avoid end-matter bloat. Having said that, I have salted the notes with little stories that did not make the final draft but that for one reason or another seem to demand retelling.

BLEAK EXPECTATIONS

3 **The first of these occurred:** Overy, *Bombing War*, 20.

3 **One immense German bomb:** "Examples of Large German Bombs," Dec. 7, 1940, HO 199/327, UKARCH. Also, "Types of German Bombs and Mines," Jan. 3, 1941, HO 199/327, UKARCH. The precise weight of a Satan bomb before rounding was 3,970 pounds.

3 **"I think it is well":** Fort, *Prof,* 130; Overy, *Bombing War,* 14–15.

3 **Britain's civil defense experts:** Süss, *Death from the Skies,* 407.

4 **"It was widely believed":** Colville, *Fringes of Power,* 1:20; Harrisson, *Living Through the Blitz,* 24, 39.

4 **"London for several days":** Ryan, *Bertrand Russell,* 146; Field, "Nights Underground in Darkest London," 13.

4 **The Home Office estimated:** Harrisson, *Living Through the Blitz,* 24.

4 **bury people in shrouds:** "Mortuary Services," Department of Health, Scotland, March 1940, HO 186/993, UKARCH.

4 **"For mass burial":** Ibid.; Süss, *Death from the Skies,* 409.

4 **Special training was to be provided:** "Civilian Deaths due to War Operations," Department of Health, Scotland, Feb. 28, 1939, HO 186/1225, UKARCH.

4 **The code name for signaling:** Stansky, *First Day of the Blitz,* 101, 102.

4 **Towns and villages took down street signs:** "World War II Diary," 49, Meiklejohn Papers; Bell, "Landscapes of Fear," 157.

4 **The government issued:** Basil Collier, *Defense of the United Kingdom,* 69; Longmate, *Air Raid,* 78.

5 **London's mailboxes received:** Ziegler, *London at War,* 73; Ogden, *Life of the Party,* 77.

5 **Strict blackout rules:** "World War II Diary," 15, Meiklejohn Papers.

5 **The full moon:** Longmate, *Air Raid,* 74; Manchester and Reid, *Defender of the Realm,* 104.

5 **"The atmosphere is something more":** Nicolson, *War Years,* 77, 84, 91.

PART ONE: THE RISING THREAT

CHAPTER 1: THE CORONER DEPARTS

12 **"I drove behind":** Thompson, *Assignment,* 164.

12 **"I suppose you don't know":** Wheeler-Bennett, *King George VI,* 444n. For more on the king's feelings toward Churchill, see ibid., 445–46.

12 **"You have sat too long":** Olson, *Troublesome Young Men,* 294; Andrew Roberts, *"Holy Fox,"* 196. (Three exclamation points appear in Olson; Roberts includes only one, at the end of the sentence. It does, however, seem to have been an exclamatory moment.)

13 **"a dirty old piece of chewing gum":** Olson, *Troublesome Young Men,* 306.

13 **"rogue elephant":** Andrew Roberts, *"Holy Fox,"* 209.

13 **"I accepted his resignation"**: Wheeler-Bennett, *King George VI,* 443–44. Wheeler-Bennett makes a tiny adjustment to the king's phrasing. The actual entry is rendered thus: "unfai[r]."

13 **He made this duly clear**: Andrew Roberts, *"Holy Fox,"* 208.

13 **"I sent for Winston"**: Wheeler-Bennett, *King George VI,* 444.

14 **"You know why"**: Thompson, *Assignment,* 164–65.

14 **"In my long political experience"**: Winston Churchill, *Their Finest Hour,* 15.

14 **"At last I had the authority"**: Pawle, *War and Colonel Warden,* 39.

15 **"It sets up an almost"**: Thompson, *Assignment,* 183.

15 **Once, while walking**: Hickman, *Churchill's Bodyguard,* 116–17.

CHAPTER 2: A NIGHT AT THE SAVOY

17 **"a succession of wild shrieks"**: Soames, *Clementine Churchill,* 264.

17 **"very effervescent"**: "World War II Diary," 342, Meiklejohn Papers.

17 **"She's a very intelligent girl"**: Kathleen Harriman to Mary Harriman Fisk, July 7, 1941, Correspondence, W. Averell Harriman Papers.

18 **"Mary the mouse"**: Purnell, *Clementine,* 152.

18 **"England's greatest security risk"**: *Daily Mail,* Sept. 4, 2019.

18 **"No hell could be so bad"**: Ibid. The *Daily Mail* uses "this bad," but a number of other published sources agree it was "so bad."

18 **"London social life"**: Soames, *Daughter's Tale,* 143.

19 **"Emerging from streets"**: Ibid., 145–46.

19 **"rather fancied"**: Ibid., 153. Decades later, Major Howard's ancestral home, Castle Howard, in Yorkshire, would be the setting for a popular public television adaptation of Evelyn Waugh's *Brideshead Revisited.*

19 **"Danced almost exclusively"**: Diary, May 9, 1940, Mary Churchill Papers.

19 **"While Mark & I were dancing"**: Ibid., May 10, 1940.

19 **"A cloud of uncertainty"**: Ibid.

19 **"The Happy Zoo"**: Soames, *Daughter's Tale,* 111–12.

20 **"I suspected him—rightly"**: Ibid., 153.

20 **"I thought the Churchill girl"**: Colville, *Fringes of Power,* 1:140.

21 **Colville had been schooled**: For details about Colville's upbringing, see his *Footprints in Time.*

21 **"One of Hitler's cleverest moves"**: Colville, *Fringes of Power,* 1:129.

21 **"He may, of course"**: Ibid., 141.

22 **"There seems to be"**: Manuscript Diary, May 11, 1940, Colville Papers. Colville's original entry differs greatly from that published in *Fringes of Power,* 143–44. This reference is omitted.

22 **"I am filled with amazement"**: Dockter and Toye, "Who Commanded History?," 416.

22 **"I cannot yet think"**: Wheeler-Bennett, *King George VI,* 446.

22 **"I hope Winston"**: Lukacs, *Five Days in London,* 67.

22 **"I have seldom met"**: Ibid.

22 **"W.C. is really the counterpart"**: Olson, *Troublesome Young Men,* 328.

23 **"If I had to spend"**: Lukacs, *Five Days in London,* 81.

23 **"My wish is realized"**: Gilbert, *War Papers,* 2:2–3.

23 **The second letter**: Ibid., 3.

CHAPTER 3: LONDON AND WASHINGTON

24 **"Sit down, dear boy":** Gilbert, *War Papers*, 2:70–71.

25 **"Apparently," Ickes said:** Lukacs, *Five Days in London*, 72n.

26 **"When I was shown into his office":** Sumner Welles, Memorandum, March 12, 1940, FDR/Safe. Clearly Welles was exaggerating when he called it a twenty-four-inch cigar. At least one hopes so.

26 **At one point Kennedy repeated:** Maier, *When Lions Roar*, 213. Chamberlain phrased it differently: "His judgment has never proven to be good."

26 **"I could have killed him":** Andrew Roberts, *"Holy Fox,"* 268.

CHAPTER 4: GALVANIZED

27 **"Heaven help us":** Gilbert, *War Papers*, 2:13.

27 **"It was as though":** Wheeler-Bennett, *Action This Day*, 220.

28 **To Colville's astonishment:** Ibid., 50.

28 **In the course of transcribing:** Nel, *Mr. Churchill's Secretary*, 37.

28 **"There's always that cigar":** Ibid., 29.

28 **"It is slothful":** Ismay, *Memoirs,* 169. Churchill paid particular attention to the code names chosen for secret operations, according to Ismay. The names could not be glib or frivolous. "How would a mother feel if she were to hear that her son had been killed in an enterprise called BUNNY HUG?" Ismay wrote. Ibid., 187.

28 **"Anything that was not":** Wheeler-Bennett, *Action This Day*, 24–25.

29 **The effect, Brooke observed:** Ibid., 22.

29 **"The eyes, wrinkling nose":** Colville, *Winston Churchill and His Inner Circle*, 161.

30 **"Poor people, poor people":** Ismay, *Memoirs*, 116.

30 **"bleed and burn":** Wheeler-Bennett, *Action This Day*, 198.

30 **The raid killed four people:** Overy, *Bombing War*, 239.

30 **"I have nothing to offer":** Gilbert, *War Papers*, 2:22.

30 **"a brilliant little speech":** Colville, *Fringes of Power*, 150.

31 **"if possible today":** Gilbert, *War Papers*, 2:30–31.

31 **First would come:** Shirer, *Berlin Diary*, 274.

31 **"We have been defeated":** Winston Churchill, *Their Finest Hour*, 42.

32 **"if necessary, we shall continue":** Churchill to Roosevelt, cable, May 15, 1940, FDR/Subject.

32 **"I am not certain":** Gilbert, *War Papers*, 2:69.

32 **"The best of luck to you":** Kennedy, *American People in World War II*, 21.

33 **"none of us could believe it":** Gilbert, *War Papers*, 2:54.

33 **"It would not be good":** Winston Churchill, *Their Finest Hour*, 50. Also in Gilbert, *War Papers*, 2:62.

33 **"This means denuding":** Colville, *Fringes of Power*, 1:154.

33 **Upon their engagement:** Wrigley, *Winston Churchill*, 113.

34 **"finished, flawless beauty":** Carter, *Winston Churchill*, 171.

34 **She and Churchill kept:** Purnell, *Clementine*, 48.

34 **It was to Bonham Carter:** Carter, *Winston Churchill*, 173.

34 **"flayed him verbally":** Soames, *Daughter's Tale*, 156.

34 **"Clemmie dropped on him":** Purnell, *Clementine*, 177.

34 **"I was most ashamed":** Soames, *Daughter's Tale*, 156.

34 **"You ought to have cried":** Colville, *Fringes of Power*, 1:157.

35 **"Whatever Winston's shortcomings"**: Ibid.

35 **"I speak to you"**: Gilbert, *War Papers*, 2:83–89. See also Toye, *Roar of the Lion*, 45–47. Toye's book provides the often-surprising backstory to Churchill's greatest speeches.

36 **"Of 150 house-to-house"**: Toye, *Roar of the Lion*, 47.

36 **"It was terrible flying weather"**: Diary, May 22, 1940, Mary Churchill Papers.

37 **"I have become his doctor"**: Moran, *Churchill*, 5.

37 **"dressed in the most brilliant"**: Colville, *Fringes of Power*, 1:162.

37 **He was about to take**: Purnell, *Clementine*, 162.

38 **"the inevitable, egregious Sawyers"**: Colville, *Fringes of Power*, 2:216.

38 **"so pneumatic as to suggest"**: Thompson, *Assignment*, 173.

38 **"The one firm rock"**: Andrew Roberts, *"Holy Fox,"* 211.

CHAPTER 5: MOONDREAD

39 **"The object of this paper"**: "British Strategy in a Certain Eventuality," May 25, 1940, War Cabinet Papers, CAB/66/7, UKARCH.

40 **"the greatest target"**: Clapson, *Blitz Companion*, 27.

40 **"Take a good look"**: Dalton, *Fateful Years*, 329.

42 **As one American visitor put it**: Memorandum, May 6, 1943, Writings File, Memoirs, W. Averell Harriman Papers.

42 **"Beaverbrook enjoyed being provocative"**: Cowles, *Looking for Trouble*, 112.

43 **"a violent, passionate, malicious"**: Lee, *London Observer*, 79. Lee also, on page 54, refers to Beaverbrook as looking "dwarfish and prickly." After meeting him in the spring of 1941, Kathleen Harriman likened him to a caricature from the satirical magazine *Punch:* "Small, baldish, big stomach and from there he tapers down to two very shiny yellow shoes. His idea of sport is to surround himself with intelligent men, then egg them on to argue and fight among themselves." Kathleen Harriman to Mary Harriman Fisk, May 30, 1941, Correspondence, W. Averell Harriman Papers.

43 **"the Toad"**: Andrew Roberts, *"Holy Fox,"* 265.

43 **"the Beaver"**: I came across this nickname in numerous sources, for example, in Chisholm and Davie, *Beaverbrook*, 339, 356, 357, 371, and Colville, *Fringes of Power*, 2:83.

43 **"My darling"**: Smith, *Reflected Glory*, 66.

43 **"Max never seems"**: Moran, *Churchill*, 7.

43 **"He's like a man"**: A.J.P. Taylor, *Beaverbrook*, 411.

43 **"Some take drugs"**: Purnell, *Clementine*, 194.

43 **"believe in the Devil"**: Maier, *When Lions Roar*, 211.

43 **"It was as dark a picture"**: Farrer, *Sky's the Limit*, 11.

44 **"They are all captains"**: Ibid., 33.

44 **"Tell Thomson that Hitler"**: A.J.P. Taylor, *Beaverbrook*, 424.

44 **"For god's sake, hurry up"**: Farrer, *G—for God Almighty*, 53.

45 **"But there is one thing"**: Minute, Churchill to Beaverbrook, [date barely legible, but appears to be July 8, 1940], Prime Minister Files, BBK/D, Beaverbrook Papers.

45 **From time to time**: Thompson, *Assignment*, 129. It is perhaps worth noting that Thompson in 1943 shot himself in the leg accidentally, after his pistol snagged

a piece of upholstery. He recovered, and Churchill accepted him back. "I have no doubts about you whatever, Thompson," Churchill said, by Thompson's account. "You are a most careful person. Carry on as before." Ibid., 214–15.

45 **he embedded a capsule:** Manchester and Reid, *Defender of the Realm*, 124.

46 **"You will have to get the Buick":** Nicolson, *War Years*, 88.

46 **"unstained heaven of that perfect summer":** Ziegler, *London at War*, 82.

47 **"In the case of air raids":** Hinton, *Mass Observers*, 191.

CHAPTER 6: GÖRING

48 **27,074 soldiers dead:** Boelcke, *Secret Conferences of Dr. Goebbels*, 59.

48 **"fatal error":** Kesselring, *Memoirs*, 60. See also the head of Army High Command General Franz Halder's incredulous diary entry, which concludes, "Finishing off the encircled enemy army is to be left to air force!!" Halder, *War Diary*, 165.

48 **"The task of the Air Force":** Trevor-Roper, *Blitzkrieg to Defeat*, 27–29.

49 **"When I talk with Göring":** Speer, *Inside the Third Reich*, 211.

49 **"In his childhood games":** Air Ministry Weekly Intelligence Summary, No. 51, Aug. 23, 1940, AIR 22/72, UKARCH.

49 **On the side, Göring ran:** "The Göring Collection," Confidential Interrogation Report No. 2, Sept. 15, 1945, Office of Strategic Services and Looting Investigative Unit, T 209/29, UKARCH. This is an impressive and detailed account of Göring's personal looting campaign. The breadth of the operation, and the depth of his corruption, is breathtaking. Material cited in this paragraph can be found on pages 7, 14, 15, 16, 18, 19, 25, 28, 35.

50 **Paintings hung from the walls:** Speer, *Inside the Third Reich*, 214.

50 **Every year his underlings:** Ibid., 385.

50 **One German general:** Dietrich von Choltitz Interrogation, Aug. 25, 1944, WO 208/4463, UKARCH.

51 **"despite rumors to the contrary":** "Hermann Göring," Interrogation Report, Military Intelligence Service, U.S. Ninth Air Force, June 1, 1945, Spaatz Papers.

51 **"Where Hitler is distant":** Shirer, *Berlin Diary*, 468.

51 **"We swore by the *Führer*":** Baumbach, *Life and Death of the Luftwaffe*, 55.

51 **"small clique of sycophants":** "The Birth, Life, and Death of the German Day Fighter Arm (Related by Adolf Galland)," Interrogation Report, 28, Spaatz Papers.

51 **"Göring was a man":** Ibid.

51 **"Beppo Schmid," Galland said:** Conversation between Galland and Field Marshal Erhard Milch, June 6, 1945, transcript, Spaatz Papers.

CHAPTER 7: SUFFICIENT BLISS

53 **He was in love:** John Colville's often despairing entries about Gay Margesson can be found in his original handwritten diary in the Colville Papers at the Churchill Archives Centre, but the saga, save for a few glancing references, is omitted from the published version, *The Fringes of Power*.

53 **"She did so with an ill-grace":** Manuscript Diary, May 22, 1940, Colville Papers.

54 **The sun emerged:** Ibid., May 26, 1940.

55 **"Only a few fishing boats":** Lukacs, *Five Days in London*, 140.

CHAPTER 8: THE FIRST BOMBS

56 **"In these dark days":** Directive to Ministers, May 29, 1940, Prime Minister Files, BBK/D, Beaverbrook Papers.

57 **"I am convinced":** Dalton, *Fateful Years*, 335–36. See a slightly different, and less graphic, version in Andrew Roberts, *"Holy Fox,"* 225.

57 **John Martin:** Wheeler-Bennett, *Action This Day*, 154, 156.

57 **Inspector Thompson recalled:** "Private Life of a Prime Minister," MEPO 2/9851, UKARCH.

58 **"How wonderful it would be":** Colville, *Fringes of Power*, 1:171.

58 **"were treated with respect":** Wheeler-Bennett, *Action This Day*, 144.

58 **"Wars are not won":** Gilbert, *War Papers*, 2:243.

58 **As the House roared:** Halle, *Irrepressible Churchill*, 137; Maier, *When Lions Roar*, 256. Maier's version reads, "And if they do come, we shall hit them on the head with beer bottles, for that is all we shall have to fight them with!"

58 **"It was now that my love":** Soames, *Daughter's Tale*, 157.

58 **One young navy man:** Toye, *Roar of the Lion*, 70.

58 **"I feel so much":** Nicolson, *War Years*, 94.

58 **He instructed her:** Ibid., 89–90.

59 **Clementine noted:** Pottle, *Champion Redoubtable*, 224–25.

59 **David Lloyd George:** Toye, *Roar of the Lion*, 53.

59 **The next day:** Ibid., 54–55.

59 **"Churchill's speech yesterday":** Ibid., 55.

CHAPTER 9: MIRROR IMAGE

60 **"It brings me to the fact":** Lukacs, *Five Days in London*, 192–93n.

CHAPTER 10: APPARITION

61 **"People who go to Italy":** Colville, *Fringes of Power*, 1:177.

61 **"He was in a very bad temper":** Ibid.

61 **"He would turn on":** Thompson, *Assignment*, 217.

61 **"He has been accused":** A.J.P. Taylor, *Beaverbrook*, 657.

62 **"Pitch dark":** Cadogan, *Diaries*, 296.

62 **"The black heavy clouds":** Cockett, *Love and War in London*, 93, 95.

62 **"on and on and on":** Spears, *Fall of France*, 150. In a letter dated May 30, 1940, America's ambassador to France, William Bullitt, told President Roosevelt, "In case I should get blown up before I see you again, I want you to know that it has been marvelous to work for you and that I thank you from the bottom of my heart for your friendship." Goodwin, *No Ordinary Time*, 62.

62 **"an angry Japanese genie":** Spears, *Fall of France*, 161.

63 **The empire's preparedness:** Kennedy to Hull, cable, June 12, 1940, FDR/Safe.

PART TWO: A CERTAIN EVENTUALITY

CHAPTER 11: THE MYSTERY OF SWAN CASTLE

68 **"was to unite against":** Fort, *Prof,* 232.

68 **"I think he was probably":** Ibid., 329.

68 **"d–dirty l–little Jew":** Birkenhead, *Prof in Two Worlds,* 68.

68 **"His memory was not":** Colville, *Winston Churchill and His Inner Circle,* 48.

69 **"Peach at luncheon":** Fort, *Prof,* 12.

69 **"The fact that she knew":** Birkenhead, *Prof in Two Worlds,* 16.

69 **"His foreign connections":** Fort, *Prof,* 208.

70 **"beautiful brain":** Colville, *Winston Churchill and His Inner Circle,* 46.

70 **"Does this mean anything to you?":** Jones, *Most Secret War,* 135. See 135–50 for Jones's engaging account of his detective work.

70 **The town had a famous castle:** Anne was queen for all of six months, until the marriage was annulled for lack of consummation. "As you know, I liked her before not well," Henry confided to Thomas Cromwell, "but now I like her much worse." This romantic episode can be found in Robert Hutchinson's *Thomas Cromwell* (New York: St. Martin's Press, 2007), 253.

72 **"I have never met":** Harrod, *Prof,* ?.

72 **"I do hate it when he goes":** Diary, June 13, 1940, Mary Churchill Papers.

72 **"extremely stern and concentrated":** Spears, *Fall of France,* 199. See ibid., 198–220, for Spears's richly detailed account of that fateful meeting in Tours.

73 **By way of further preparation:** See Jones, *Most Secret War,* 135–50.

74 **"Tell me," he said:** Ibid., 137.

75 **"He was as obstinate":** Ismay, *Memoirs,* 173.

75 **"Stop that dripping":** Fort, *Prof,* 216.

75 **"There seems some reason":** Lindemann to Churchill, note, June 13, 1940, F107/17, Lindemann Papers.

76 **"This seems most intriguing":** Jones, *Most Secret War,* 137.

76 **"It was looking cool":** Pottle, *Champion Redoubtable,* 224.

76 **There was much to arrange:** "No. 10 Downing Street: Expenditure, 1935–1936," Ministry of Works Report, WORK 12/245, UKARCH.

77 **"The Chamberlains have left":** Diary, June 15, 1940, Mary Churchill Papers.

77 **"Mummie has given me":** Ibid., June 18, 1940.

78 **"To watch him compose":** Colville, *Fringes of Power,* 1:337.

78 **"I understand all your difficulties":** Gilbert, *War Papers,* 2:337–38.

78 **"If words counted":** Colville, *Fringes of Power,* 1:183.

CHAPTER 12: THE GHOSTS OF DULL PEOPLE

80 **"One would sit":** Nel, *Mr. Churchill's Secretary,* 60–61.

80 **"A police officer":** Thompson, *Assignment,* 3.

81 **"Apart from these":** Elletson, *Chequers and the Prime Ministers,* 49–50.

81 **"Happy Prime Ministers":** J. Gilbert Jenkins, *Chequers,* 7.

81 **"Ye houres doe flie":** Ibid., 130.

81 **Rembrandt's *The Mathematician*:** When Lee bought it, the painting was thought to have been done by Rembrandt himself. Later research determined that it

was painted by one of his students, Gerbrand van den Eeckhout. Major, *Chequers,* 128.

82 **"God made them as stubble"**: Elletson, *Chequers and the Prime Ministers,* 25–26.

82 **"full of the ghosts of dull people"**: Ibid., 59, 61–62.

82 **"Here I am"**: Soames, *Clementine Churchill,* 256. Churchill used the abbreviation "wd" in his letter, instead of "would."

82 **"My mother took"**: Fort, *Prof,* 164–65.

82 **"I always rather dreaded"**: Ibid., 165.

83 **Colville took the news**: Colville, *Fringes of Power,* 1:184.

83 **"silent, grumpy and remote"**: Andrew Roberts, *"Holy Fox,"* 186.

83 **"Always remember, Clemmie"**: J. Gilbert Jenkins, *Chequers,* 122.

83 **"The war is bound"**: Colville, *Fringes of Power,* 1:184.

84 **"It was light"**: Ibid.

84 **"Tell them . . . that"**: Ibid.

84 **As the coal ends of cigars**: It is unclear just how many cigars Churchill smoked per day, and how many he actually smoked to the end. "He will light a cigar immediately after breakfast," Inspector Thompson observed, "but by lunchtime the same cigar may be only half finished, having been relighted innumerable times and quite as often abandoned soon after. He chews cigars, he doesn't smoke them." The relighting process involved a good deal of smoke and fire. "One of the permanent mental pictures I have of Mr. Churchill is of the relighting of his cigar," wrote his secretary Elizabeth Layton (later Mrs. Nel). She described the sequence: "A pause in whatever he was doing: the flame from a very large match jumping up and down, while clouds of blue smoke issued from his mouth: then a hasty shake of the match to extinguish it, and on with the job." Expended cigars, or those Churchill deemed substandard, wound up tossed into the nearest hearth. The near-constant dormancy of his cigars prompted General Ian Jacob, assistant secretary to the War Cabinet, to observe, "As a matter of fact he didn't really smoke at all." See Thompson, *Assignment,* 251; Nel, *Mr. Churchill's Secretary,* 45; Wheeler-Bennett, *Action This Day,* 182.

84 **"a flood of eloquence"**: Colville, *Fringes of Power,* I:184–85.

85 **"It was at once"**: Ibid., 183.

CHAPTER 13: SCARIFICATION

86 **"looking just like"**: Colville, *Fringes of Power,* 1:185.

86 **"provided, but only provided"**: Gilbert, *War Papers,* 2:346.

87 **"What a change"**: Jones, *Most Secret War,* 138.

87 **"some rather nebulous"**: Ibid.

87 **"I may be wrong"**: Ibid., 139.

87 **"that such investigation"**: Fort, *Prof,* 261.

87 **"Let this be done without fail"**: Ibid., 262.

88 **"He was doubtless considering"**: Colville, *Fringes of Power,* 1:189.

88 **"I wish to repeat"**: Gilbert, *War Papers,* 2:359.

88 **Home intelligence reported**: Addison and Crang, *Listening to Britain,* 123.

88 **"Poor France!"**: Cockett, *Love and War in London,* 100.

88 **"Personally," the king wrote**: Wheeler-Bennett, *King George VI,* 460.

89 **"I don't mind telling you"**: Cadogan, *Diaries*, 299.

89 **"The newspapers have got quite"**: Winston Churchill, *Their Finest Hour*, 194.

89 **"The withholding of the news"**: Addison and Crang, *Listening to Britain*, 271.

90 **"In the pursuit of anything"**: Ismay, *Memoirs*, 180.

90 **"Today," he began**: Beaverbrook to Churchill, June 16, 1940, BBK/D, Beaverbrook Papers.

CHAPTER 14: "THIS QUEER AND DEADLY-GAME"

92 **Churchill spoke of parachute troops**: Gilbert, *War Papers*, 2:360–68.

93 **"Some suggested he was drunk"**: Toye, *Roar of the Lion*, 59.

93 **"Whether he was drunk"**: Ibid.

93 **"Experience of the campaign"**: "Urgent Measures to Meet Attack," Report by the Chiefs of Staff, June 19, 1940, CAB 66/8, UKARCH.

94 **When he got to his office**: Jones, *Most Secret War*, 144.

94 **"holding out his hand"**: Nel, *Mr. Churchill's Secretary*, 30.

95 **"Any chortling by officials"**: Fort, *Prof*, 227; Ismay, *Memoirs*, 172; Gilbert, *War Papers*, 2:402.

96 **"Make one million"**: Fort, *Prof*, 227.

96 **"bellowing at him"**: Ibid., 242.

96 **"Love me, love my dog"**: Ibid.

97 **Jones sensed the tension**: Jones, *Most Secret War*, 145.

97 **"Would it help"**: Ibid.

97 **"one of the blackest moments"**: Jones, *Most Secret War*, 153.

98 **"there was a general air"**: Winston Churchill, *Their Finest Hour*, 385.

98 **"the load was once again lifted"**: Jones, *Most Secret War*, 153.

99 **"All I get from the Air Ministry"**: Ibid., 146.

99 **"the principles of"**: Winston Churchill, *Their Finest Hour*, 386–87.

100 **"Had I, after all"**: Jones, *Most Secret War*, 148.

100 **But that Friday**: Lough, *No More Champagne*, 288–89. David Lough's *No More Champagne* is an excellent account of how Churchill struggled financially through much of his career.

101 **First, Bufton reported**: Jones, *Most Secret War*, 148–49.

CHAPTER 15: LONDON AND BERLIN

102 **"A wrathful & gloomy"**: Diary, June 23, 1940, Mary Churchill Papers.

102 **With France quelled**: Boelcke, *Secret Conferences of Dr. Goebbels*, 60.

103 **"Well, this week"**: Ibid.

CHAPTER 16: THE RED WARNING

104 **"the awful problem"**: Cadogan, *Diaries*, 306.

104 **"The German Government"**: "Battle Summary No. 1: Operations Against the French Fleet at Mers-el-Kebir (Oran), July 3–6, 1940," Appendix A, ADM 234/317, UKARCH.

104 **The clause as later published**: Ibid.

105 **"Ask half a dozen"**: Gilbert, *War Papers*, 2:415.

105 **"The night is very still"**: Cockett, *Love and War in London,* 109.

105 **"Many people did not"**: Addison and Crang, *Listening to Britain,* 154.

105 **"an intention to land"**: Gilbert, *War Papers,* 2:433n3.

106 **"this should be done"**: Ibid., 452–53; Lindemann to Churchill, minute, June 30, 1940, F108/21, Lindemann Papers.

106 **"Supposing lodgments were effected"**: Gilbert, *War Papers,* 2:444–45.

106 **"Much thought,"** he wrote: Note, "Home Defense," June 28, 1940, War Cabinet Papers, CAB 66/9, UKARCH.

106 **She reported that a member:** Clementine to Winston, June 27, 1940, CSCT 1/24, Clementine Churchill Papers.

CHAPTER 17: "TOFREK!"

108 **After one weekend:** Gilbert, *War Papers,* 3:555.

109 **"But, no!" he wrote:** Elletson, *Chequers and the Prime Ministers,* 108–9.

110 **"I thought Randolph"**: Colville, *Fringes of Power,* 1:207.

110 **"His coughing is like"**: Smith, *Reflected Glory,* 57.

110 **"was anything but kind"**: Colville, *Fringes of Power,* 1:207.

111 **"Pam was terribly"**: Ogden, *Life of the Party,* 69.

111 **"She's a wonderful girl"**: Kathleen Harriman to Mary Harriman Fisk, May 30, 1941, Correspondence, W. Averell Harriman Papers.

111 **"She passed everything"**: Ogden, *Life of the Party,* 123.

111 **"I expect that he"**: Ibid., 86.

111 **"All you need"**: Ibid., 85.

111 **"One of the secrets"**: Sarah Churchill, *Keep on Dancing,* 18.

111 **"One to reproduce"**: Wheeler-Bennett, *Action This Day,* 264.

111 **"Combative,"** according to one: Purnell, *Clementine,* 139.

111 **He once pushed:** Readers will find all three incidents in ibid., 88, 115.

112 **When he was nine:** Ibid., 182.

112 **"Your idle & lazy life"**: Winston Churchill to Randolph Churchill, Dec. 29, 1929, RDCH 1/3/3, Randolph Churchill Papers.

112 **Churchill loved him:** Colville, *Winston Churchill and His Inner Circle,* 36.

112 **"as his personality developed"**: Soames, *Clementine Churchill,* 315.

112 **"It was indeed generous"**: Gilbert, *War Papers,* 2:231.

113 **"You must get"**: Ogden, *Life of the Party,* 69.

113 **"Are you listening?"**: Winston S. Churchill, *Memories and Adventures,* 6.

113 **The three found themselves:** Colville, *Fringes of Power,* 1:208–9.

114 **"It is a curious feeling"**: Ibid., 209–10.

CHAPTER 18: RESIGNATION NO. 1

115 **The letter began:** Beaverbrook to Churchill, June 30, 1940, BBK/D, Beaverbrook Papers.

115 **John Colville guessed:** Colville, *Fringes of Power,* 1:214.

116 **"Dear Minister"**: Gilbert, *War Papers,* 2:454.

116 **"I will certainly not neglect"**: Young, *Churchill and Beaverbrook,* 150.

CHAPTER 19: FORCE H

117 **The Royal Navy was poised:** All references to the Mers el-Kébir episode are drawn from "Battle Summary No. 1: Operations Against the French Fleet at Mers-el-Kébir (Oran), July 3–6, 1940," ADM 234/317, UKARCH. It's a literate and dispassionate recounting, full of excerpts from original documents, and thus wholly chilling. For some reason—possibly convenience—most secondary sources use the name Oran when referring to the incident, but in fact the main action was at Mers el-Kébir.

118 **He called the matter:** Manchester and Reid, *Defender of the Realm,* 107; Martin, *Downing Street,* 14. Martin omits the words "and painful."

119 **"The Germans will force":** Young, *Churchill and Beaverbrook,* 153.

120 **The war in the west:** Koch, "Hitler's 'Programme' and the Genesis of Operation 'Barbarossa,'" 896.

120 **"Britain's position is hopeless":** Halder, *War Diary,* 230.

120 **"the plan to invade England":** Trevor-Roper, *Blitzkrieg to Defeat,* 33.

122 **"There was nothing for it":** Ismay, *Memoirs,* 149.

122 **"The action was sudden":** Winston Churchill, *Their Finest Hour,* 233–34.

123 **Churchill paced his office:** Colville, *Fringes of Power,* 1:215.

124 **"It is so terrible":** Diary, July 3, 1940, Mary Churchill Papers.

124 **"I leave the judgment":** Gilbert, *War Papers,* 2:474.

124 **"Fortified":** Nicolson, *War Years,* 100.

124 **"This is heartbreaking":** Colville, *Fringes of Power,* 1:216.

124 **The Home Intelligence survey:** Addison and Crang, *Listening to Britain,* 189.

124 **"an act of sheer treachery":** Manchester and Reid, *Defender of the Realm,* 110.

125 **"I am sure it cut him":** Ismay, *Memoirs,* 150.

125 **"To this," Pamela recalled:** "My Memory of the Lunch in the Downstairs Flat . . . ," n.d., Churchill Family and Mary Soames File, Pamela Harriman Papers.

125 **Clementine glared at Churchill:** Inspector Thompson dreaded this look and was all too familiar with it. He knew his own constant presence could be annoying, "far more trying and importunate than protective, at least to her," and he respected how she kept this displeasure to herself. "She did, however, have an icy way she could look at a man when things went to the snapping point of endurance, and on these occasions I always wished I could disappear till she could recover." Thompson, *Assignment,* 15.

CHAPTER 20: BERLIN

126 **In July, Hitler met:** Stafford, *Flight from Reality,* 14, 156–57.

127 **"What more can I do?":** Ibid., 14.

127 **"Britain has really revealed":** Boelcke, *Secret Conferences of Dr. Goebbels,* 63.

127 **Anticipating his remarks:** Ibid., 65.

127 **On July 3, a report:** "Evacuation of Civil Population from East, South-East, and South Coast Towns," July 3, 1940, War Cabinet Memoranda, CAB 66/8, UKARCH.

128 **"Information from a most reliable":** "Imminence of a German Invasion of Great Britain," Report by the Joint Intelligence Sub-committee, July 4, 1940, Appendix A, War Cabinet Memoranda, CAB 66/9, UKARCH.

128 **"I have the impression":** Colville, *Fringes of Power,* 1:218.

128 **"a bad look-out":** Ibid., 216.

CHAPTER 21: CHAMPAGNE AND GARBO

129 **"In the intervals"**: Manuscript Diary, July 10, 1940, Colville Papers. This is one of what Colville called his "trivial" entries, which he omitted in the published version of his diary.

CHAPTER 22: HAVE WE SUNK SO LOW?

130 **"exactly the color of blood"**: Panter-Downes, *London War Notes,* 62.

130 **"Yes," she said, "I shall not go down"**: Nicolson, *War Years,* 100.

130 **A government pamphlet**: Panter-Downes, *London War Notes,* 71.

130 **By now the Foreign Office**: Numerous such telegrams can be found in Roosevelt's papers, in the President's Secretary's Files, FDR/Diplo. For example, July 13 and 14, 1940.

131 **"very jolly and noisy"**: Soames, *Daughter's Tale,* 169.

131 **On one occasion**: Diary, Aug. 5, 1940, Mary Churchill Papers.

132 **"Have we really sunk"**: Cockett, *Love and War in London,* 124.

132 **"It shouldn't be allowed"**: Ibid., 119.

132 **"callous Oxford accent"**: Addison and Crang, *Listening to Britain,* 229.

132 **"a considerable majority"**: Ibid., 231.

132 **"The majority of decent citizens"**: Panter-Downes, *London War Notes,* 79.

132 **"the bringing down"**: Addison and Crang, *Listening to Britain,* 231.

132 **"After all," he told an interviewer**: Gilbert, *War Papers,* 2:533.

133 **"The naming of a whole squadron"**: Farrer, *Sky's the Limit,* 78.

133 **By May 1941**: Ibid., 79.

134 **The people appeared"**: Beaverbrook to Churchill, minute, Jan. 31, 1941, BBK/D, Beaverbrook Papers.

134 **"It will do the players"**: Farrer, *Sky's the Limit,* 81.

134 **" 'On Preparations for a Landing' "**: Trevor-Roper, *Blitzkrieg to Defeat,* 34.

CHAPTER 23: WHAT'S IN A NAME?

136 **A small but pressing crisis**: Ogden, *Life of the Party,* 100; Smith, *Reflected Glory,* 71.

CHAPTER 24: THE TYRANT'S APPEAL

137 **"like a happy child"**: Shirer, *Berlin Diary,* 363. Shirer calls Göring's retreat "Karin Hall"; for the sake of consistency, I've changed it to Carinhall.

137 **"The Minister emphasizes"**: Boelcke, *Secret Conferences of Dr. Goebbels,* 67.

137 **"So wonderful an actor"**: Shirer, *Berlin Diary,* 362.

138 **First Hitler ran through**: See transcript of the speech in *Vital Speeches of the Day,* 6:617–25, on www.ibiblio.org/pha/policy/1940/1940-07-19b.html.

138 **"Throughout Hitler's speech"**: Shirer, *Berlin Diary,* 363–64.

139 **"One bomb on the Kroll Opera House"**: Galland, *The First and the Last,* 8.

139 **Galland's journey to this moment**: Details of Galland's upbringing and career can be found in his autobiography, *The First and the Last,* and in materials relating to his postwar interrogations by U.S. Air Force officials. See especially the May 18, 1945, transcript of one interrogation and the more comprehensive report, "The Birth, Life, and Death of the German Day Fighter Arm (Related by Adolf Galland)," Spaatz Papers.

140 **the Messerschmitt Me 109:** The fighter is often referred to as the Bf 109, after its original manufacturer, Bayerische Flugzeugwerke. Overy, *Battle of Britain,* 56.
141 **"Let me tell you what":** Manchester and Reid, *Defender of the Realm,* 129–30.
141 **The various officials present:** Shirer, *Berlin Diary,* 362.
142 **"I do not propose to say":** Colville, *Fringes of Power,* 1:234.
142 **"We shall not stop fighting":** Andrew Roberts, *"Holy Fox,"* 250.
142 **"Mistrust must be sown":** Boelcke, *Secret Conferences of Dr. Goebbels,* 70.
142 **"At the right moment":** Ibid., 74.

CHAPTER 25: THE PROF'S SURPRISE

143 **Churchill was in high spirits:** Gilbert, *War Papers,* 2:580.

CHAPTER 26: WHITE GLOVES AT DAWN

146 **"the effect of which":** Winston Churchill, *Their Finest Hour,* 406.
147 **"Nothing must now be said":** Gilbert, *War Papers,* 2:667.
147 **"The next six months":** Winston Churchill, *Their Finest Hour,* 398.
147 **In May, a military maneuver:** Goodwin, *No Ordinary Time,* 49.
147 **"Against Europe's total war":** Ibid., 52.
148 **"this minor and easily remediable factor":** Churchill to Roosevelt, cable, July 31, 1940, FDR/Map.
149 **"no chance of passing":** Goodwin, *No Ordinary Time,* 142.
149 **"I was driven all through the day":** A.J.P. Taylor, *Beaverbrook,* 446.
150 **The first night began:** For a full account of the episode, see Interview Transcripts, July 1991, Biographies File, Pamela Harriman Papers. Also, Ogden, *Life of the Party,* 95–97.

CHAPTER 27: DIRECTIVE NO. 17

152 **"The German Air Force":** Boelcke, *Secret Conferences of Dr. Goebbels,* 37–38.
152 **"For the first time":** Otto Bechtle, "German Air Force Operations Against Great Britain, Tactics and Lessons Learnt, 1940–1941" (lecture, Feb. 2, 1944), AIR 40/2444, UKARCH.
153 **He expected little resistance:** Indeed, at the end of 1942 a captured Luftwaffe officer would tell his interrogators that if German intelligence reports were correct, the RAF and Allied air forces possessed "minus 500 aircraft." See "Intelligence from Interrogation: Intelligence from Prisoners of War," 42, AIR 40/1177, UKARCH.
153 **"Göring refused to listen":** "The Birth, Life, and Death of the German Day Fighter Arm (Related by Adolf Galland)," Interrogation Report, 15, Spaatz Papers.

CHAPTER 28: "OH, MOON, LOVELY MOON"

154 **"To do our work":** Gilbert, *War Papers,* 2:636.
155 **Anti-tank mines:** Colville, *Fringes of Power,* 1:251.
155 **"The First Sea Lord fell":** Ibid., 252.
156 **Saturday morning brought:** Ibid., 253–54.
156 **"Oh, Moon, lovely Moon":** Ibid., 254.
157 **"Today they painted them":** Shirer, *Berlin Diary,* 373.

PART THREE: DREAD

CHAPTER 29: EAGLE DAY

161 **At dawn on Tuesday**: Baker, *Adolf Galland*, 109–11; Basil Collier, *Battle of Britain*, 70–71; Basil Collier, *Defense of the United Kingdom*, 184–88; Bekker, *Luftwaffe Diaries*, 151; Overy, *Battle of Britain*, 62–63.
162 **"Everything beyond was practically"**: Galland, *The First and the Last*, 18.
164 **"At Luftwaffe HQ, however"**: Ibid., 24.

CHAPTER 30: PERPLEXITY

166 **"The question everyone is asking"**: Colville, *Fringes of Power*, 1:261.
167 **"Our view is that we are two friends"**: Winston Churchill, *Their Finest Hour*, 409–10.
167 **"The transfer to Great Britain"**: Ibid., 404.
168 **Galland dove headlong**: Baker, *Adolf Galland*, 110.

CHAPTER 31: GÖRING

170 **"There's more than a hundred"**: Baker, *Adolf Galland*, 157.
170 **"I have known him"**: "War Diary of *Kampfgruppe* 210," Appendix to Interrogation Report 273/1940, AIR 40/2398, UKARCH.

CHAPTER 32: THE BOMBER IN THE PASTURE

171 **"Don't speak to me"**: Ismay, *Memoirs*, 180.
171 **"RAF exploits continue to arouse"**: Addison and Crang, *Listening to Britain*, 331.
171 **"This was to be the day"**: Cadogan, *Diaries*, 321.
172 **"While our eyes are"**: Gilbert, *War Papers*, 2:679.
172 **A British intelligence report**: Air Ministry Weekly Intelligence Summary, No. 51, Aug. 23, 1940, AIR 22/72, UKARCH.
173 **"The setting was majestic"**: Cowles, *Looking for Trouble*, 423–24.
173 **One Luftwaffe bomber pilot**: Basil Collier, *Battle of Britain*, 88–89.
173 **"So, you see," she scolded**: Nicolson, *War Years*, 111. William Shirer, in his diary, described the sound of shrapnel from exploded anti-aircraft shells: "It was like hail falling on a tin roof. You could hear it dropping through the trees and on the roofs of the sheds" (389).
174 **"one thinks every noise"**: Cockett, *Love and War in London*, 148.
174 **"With this gorgeous moon"**: Ibid., 143.
174 **When Colville arrived**: Colville, *Fringes of Power*, 1:264–65.
175 **As it happened, the plane**: Air Interrogation Reports, 237/1940 and 243/1940, AIR 40/2398, UKARCH. Report 237 notes the bomber's markings: "Blue Shield with a White Starfish in the Centre, Yellow patch in centre of Starfish. Upper wing dark green, under wing grey."
175 **In the course of the war**: Bessborough, *Enchanted Forest*, 118. Lord Bessborough's son and his co-author, Clive Aslet, published an engaging portrait of Stansted House and of English country life, titled *Enchanted Forest: The Story of Stansted in Sussex*. Here one can learn a multitude of things, among them the fact that one of the stained-glass lights in the east windows of the house is a depiction of the Ark of the Covenant, a nifty detail if ever there was one (80). Also,

one learns about the early tactic of making a "Resurrection Pie" to create the illusion that a host had prepared more foods for a meal than was actually the case—"a homely dish composed of promiscuous fragments, which was intended merely to swell the number of dishes on the board, but otherwise to be ignored" (73).

CHAPTER 33: BERLIN

177 **"The important thing now"**: Boelcke, *Secret Conferences of Dr. Goebbels*, 78–79. Goebbels came up with a particularly cunning way to further generate unease within Britain, by amplifying already widespread fears that fifth columnists were hard at work paving the way for invasion. He commanded his director of external broadcasting to achieve this by inserting "mysterious-sounding but well thought-out messages" into regular programming, these crafted to sound like what one might imagine the secret communications of spies would sound like, "thereby keeping alive the suspicion that we are getting in touch with members of the Fifth Column in Britain." One can only imagine a British family listening to such a broadcast on a Sunday evening. "How so very odd—why did that news reader just say porridge for the sixth time?" Ibid., 79.

CHAPTER 34: OL' MAN RIVER

180 **"It is curious"**: Colville, *Fringes of Power*, 1:266.
180 **"We feel that the material loss"**: Upward to Churchill, Aug. 20, 1940; Beaverbrook to John Martin, Aug. 26, 1940, Correspondence, BBK/D, Beaverbrook Papers.
180 **"We have already many interruptions"**: Beaverbrook to Churchill, Aug. 27, 1940, BBK/D, Beaverbrook Papers.
181 **"Undoubtedly," he said**: Gilbert, *War Papers*, 2:697.
182 **"On the whole"**: Colville, *Fringes of Power*, 1:267.
182 **Their mother, Edith Starr Miller**: Miller, *Occult Theocracy*, 8. Miller also wrote a kind of cookbook, published in 1918, called *Common Sense in the Kitchen*, to show how best to reduce food waste at home, tailoring her advice for a "household of 12 servants and 3 masters." See Edith Starr Miller, *Common Sense in the Kitchen: Normal Rations in Normal Times* (New York: Brentano's, 1918), 3.
182 **"very attractive and refreshing"**: Colville, *Fringes of Power*, 1:99n.

CHAPTER 35: BERLIN

184 **"The collapse of England"**: Overy, *Battle of Britain*, 87.
184 **"a piece of carelessness"**: Basil Collier, *Battle of Britain*, 95.

CHAPTER 36: TEATIME

185 **His enemies made him out**: Fort, *Prof*, 233; Birkenhead, *Prof in Two Worlds*, 167, 272–73; Note, "*Mrs. Beard*: An old woman . . . ," June 4, 1959, A113/F1, Lindemann Papers. See the rest of the long saga of the former nurse—and her increasing fiscal demands—at F2–F15. For other examples of the Prof's charitable deeds, see files A114–18.

185 **The one universal balm:** For various references to tea, see Overy, *Battle of Britain*, 45–46; Stansky, *First Day of the Blitz*, 138; Harrisson, *Living Through the Blitz*, 78; Wheeler-Bennett, *Action This Day*, 182–83.
186 **"The wisdom of a 2 ounce tea ration":** Fort, *Prof*, 217.

CHAPTER 37: THE LOST BOMBERS

187 **On the night of:** Bekker, *Luftwaffe Diaries*, 172; Basil Collier, *Battle of Britain*, 95; Colville, *Fringes of Power*, 1:270.
188 **"This," he said, his voice deep:** I found Murrow's broadcast at www.poynter .org/reporting-editing/2014/today-in-media-history-edward-r-murrow -describes-the-bombing-of-london-in-1940/. I've punctuated these excerpts to reflect how I heard it, though transcripts available elsewhere may vary.
188 **"It is to be reported":** Bekker, *Luftwaffe Diaries*, 172.
189 **"I suppressed a horrid fantasy":** Cockett, *Love and War in London*, 159.

CHAPTER 38: BERLIN

190 **"The Berliners are stunned":** Shirer, *Berlin Diary*, 388.
190 **One rumor making the rounds:** Ibid., 397.
190 **"Unofficial measures are to be":** Boelcke, *Secret Conferences of Dr. Goebbels*, 82.

CHAPTER 39: AH, YOUTH!

191 **"Now that they have begun":** Colville, *Fringes of Power*, 1:270.
192 **"I stood in the garden":** Ibid., 271.
192 **"I would not be anywhere":** "Home Opinion as Shewn in the Mails to U.S.A. and Eire," Sept. 5, 1940, War Cabinet Papers, CAB 66, UKARCH.
193 **"Ah '*la jeunesse*'":** Diary, Aug. 26, 1940, Mary Churchill Papers.
193 **She read them the works:** Soames, *Daughter's Tale*, 167.
193 **"I am indulging":** Ibid., 171.
194 **"It makes me glad":** Ibid., 172.
194 **"It was thrilling":** Diary, Aug. 28, 1940, Mary Churchill Papers.
194 **"I always thought my daffodils":** Andrew Roberts, *"Holy Fox,"* 268; Maier, *When Lions Roar*, 251.
194 **"unkind but deserved":** Andrew Roberts, *"Holy Fox,"* 268.
195 **"Nobody knows the trouble":** Beaverbrook to Churchill, Sept. 2, 1940, Correspondence, BBK/D, Beaverbrook Papers.

CHAPTER 40: BERLIN AND WASHINGTON

197 **Hess and Haushofer spoke:** Stafford, *Flight from Reality*, 82.
197 **"As you know":** Ibid.
198 **"We haven't had a better":** Goodwin, *No Ordinary Time*, 149.
198 **As one American officer put it:** Goodhart, *Fifty Ships That Saved the World*, 194.

CHAPTER 41: HE IS COMING

199 **"Mr. Churchill," he said:** Manchester and Reid, *Defender of the Realm,* 152.

199 **"When they declare":** Shirer, *Berlin Diary,* 396.

200 **At Carinhall in the peaceful:** Reproduced in Richard Townshend Bickers, *The Battle of Britain: The Greatest Battle in the History of Air Warfare* (London: Batsford, 2015). Also, see online "Plan of Attack," doc. 43, Battle of Britain Historical Society, www.battleofbritain1940.net/document-43.html.

200 **Göring told Goebbels:** Overy, *Bombing War,* 88.

201 **German scientists had developed:** Wakefield, *Pfadfinder,* 7–12.

202 **The group's zone of operations:** Ibid., 45.

CHAPTER 42: OMINOUS DOINGS

203 **"PM warmed up":** Alanbrooke, *War Diaries,* 105.

CHAPTER 43: CAP BLANC-NEZ

205 **"There were no limits":** "The Göring Collection," Confidential Interrogation Report No. 2, Sept. 15, 1945, 3, 4, 9, and, in attachments, "Objects Acquired by Goering," Office of Strategic Services and Looting Investigative Unit, T 209/29, UKARCH.

206 **"This moment is a historic one":** Bekker, *Luftwaffe Diaries,* 172; Feigel, *Love-Charm of Bombs,* 13. Remarks quoted in Garry Campion, *The Battle of Britain, 1945–1965: The Air Ministry and the Few* (Basingstoke, U.K.: Palgrave Macmillan, 2019). For a ready resource, see Battle of Britain Historical Society, www.battleofbritain1940.net/0036.html.

PART FOUR: BLOOD AND DUST

CHAPTER 44: ON A QUIET BLUE DAY

210 **"It was so lovely":** Diary, Sept. 7, 1940, Mary Churchill Papers.

211 **"At first we couldn't see":** Cowles, *Looking for Trouble,* 434–35.

211 **"I'd never seen so many":** Stansky, *First Day of the Blitz,* 31–32.

212 **"It was the most amazing":** Ziegler, *London at War,* 113.

212 **"We all became conscious":** Stansky, *First Day of the Blitz,* 33–34.

213 **Harold Nicolson, in his diary:** Nicolson, *War Years,* 121.

213 **"What struck one":** Stansky, *First Day of the Blitz,* 53.

213 **"the purgatorial throng":** Feigel, *Love-Charm of Bombs,* 129.

214 **"Thick clouds of smoke":** Cowles, *Looking for Trouble,* 435.

214 **When dropping their biggest:** "More About Big Bombs," Interrogation Report 592/1940, Sept. 22, 1940, AIR 40/2400, UKARCH.

214 **"A blazing girdle":** Overy, *Bombing War,* 87.

214 **"an appalling shriek":** Cockett, *Love and War in London,* 165.

214 **"the deep roar":** Cowles, *Looking for Trouble,* 439.

214 **"an acute irritation":** Feigel, *Love-Charm of Bombs,* 53.

214 **"The bombs are lovely":** Wyndham, *Love Lessons,* 113–16.

215 **"I recognized one head":** Stansky, *First Day of the Blitz,* 72.

215 **"The day," he said:** Adolf Galland Interrogation, May 18, 1945, Spaatz Papers.

215 **"let himself be carried away"**: Kesselring, *Memoirs*, 76.
216 **"It was, I think, inconceivable"**: Farrer, *G—for God Almighty*, 62.

CHAPTER 45: UNPREDICTABLE MAGIC

217 **"The destruction was"**: Ismay, *Memoirs*, 183.
218 **"Morale rose immediately"**: Gilbert, *War Papers*, 2:788–89.
218 **"he was in one of his most"**: Ismay, *Memoirs*, 184.
218 **"Apparently indiscriminate bombing"**: "Diary of Brigadier General Carl Spaatz on Tour of Duty in England," Sept. 8, 1940, Spaatz Papers.
219 **"anybody who imagined"**: Ismay, *Memoirs*, 184.
220 **"dangerously exposed to enemy"**: Young, *Churchill and Beaverbrook*, 152.
220 **"It was high-handed"**: Farrer, *Sky's the Limit*, 61.
220 **"I had the opportunity"**: Stafford, *Flight from Reality*, 83.
221 **"Buz! Take notice"**: Ibid., 141.
221 **"I think of you all"**: Diary, Sept. 8, 1940, Mary Churchill Papers.
222 **"The 'ordering' of my life"**: Soames, *Daughter's Tale*, 173.
222 **"He gave me such"**: Diary, Sept. 11, 1940, Mary Churchill Papers.
222 **"We cannot tell," he said**: Gilbert, *War Papers*, 2:801–3.
223 **"largely wild and uncontrolled"**: "Air Defence of Great Britain," vol. 3, "Night Air Defence, June 1940–December 1941," 56, 66, AIR 41/17, UKARCH.
223 **"a momentous sound"**: Feigel, *Love-Charm of Bombs*, 15.
223 **"Tails are up"**: Martin, *Downing Street*, 25.
223 **"The dominating topic"**: Addison and Crang, *Listening to Britain*, 414.
224 **"the severest bombing yet"**: Shirer, *Berlin Diary*, 401.

CHAPTER 46: SLEEP

225 **"to smash as much glass"**: Gilbert, *War Papers*, 2:834.
225 **"People living near guns"**: Addison and Crang, *Listening to Britain*, 418.
225 **"It's not the bombs"**: Harrisson, *Living Through the Blitz*, 102.
226 **A survey found**: Ibid., 105.
226 **"Conversation was devoted"**: Cowles, *Looking for Trouble*, 440.
226 **On the night of September 27**: Harrisson, *Living Through the Blitz*, 112. Field, "Nights Underground in Darkest London," 44n17, notes that in November 1940 only about 4 percent of Londoners sheltered in the tube "and equivalent large shelters." In October 1940, Home Intelligence quoted a Mass-Observation study that found about 4 percent of Londoners used public shelters. One major reason people gave for not using tube stations as shelters was "fear of being buried." Home Intelligence Weekly Report for Sept. 30–Oct. 9, 1940, INF 1/292, UKARCH.
226 **"A very formidable discontent"**: Overy, *Bombing War*, 147.
226 **Many more Londoners**: Harrisson, *Living Through the Blitz*, 112. The estimate of 71 percent, derived from a Mass-Observation study, appears in the Home Intelligence Weekly Report for Sept. 30–Oct. 9, 1940, INF 1/292, UKARCH.
227 **"We looked at each other"**: Wheeler-Bennett, *King George VI*, 468.
227 **"It was a ghastly experience"**: Ibid., 469.
227 **"I'm glad we've been bombed"**: Ibid., 470.
227 **"Everything looks like an invasion"**: Alanbrooke, *War Diaries*, 107.
228 **"We must expect"**: Gilbert, *War Papers*, 2:810.

CHAPTER 47: TERMS OF IMPRISONMENT

229 **The room was imbued:** J. Gilbert Jenkins, *Chequers,* 26–30, 120–21; Soames, *Daughter's Tale,* 176–77.

229 **the match as "monstruous":** J. Gilbert Jenkins, *Chequers,* 28.

230 **"Mummie had ordered":** Diary, Sept. 15, 1940, Mary Churchill Papers.

230 **"the last day":** Ibid., Sept. 14, 1940.

231 **"the weather on this day":** Winston Churchill, *Their Finest Hour,* 332.

231 **The family took seats:** Ibid., 333–37.

232 **"What losses should we not suffer":** Ibid., 336.

233 **"It was repellent":** Ibid., 336–37.

233 **"How sweet everyone is":** Diary, Sept. 15, 1940, Mary Churchill Papers.

CHAPTER 48: BERLIN

234 **"We lost our nerve":** Interrogation of General A. D. Milch, Transcript, May 23, 1945, Spaatz Papers.

234 **"a vulgar little man":** Air Ministry Weekly Intelligence Summary, No. 51, Aug. 23, 1940, 7, AIR 22/72, UKARCH.

235 **"to ascertain":** Boelcke, *Secret Conferences of Dr. Goebbels,* 91.

CHAPTER 49: FEAR

236 **"This is the twentieth century":** Diary, Sept. 21, 1940, Mary Churchill Papers.

237 **Her father ordered:** Gilbert, *War Papers,* 2:862.

237 **"My darling, you must realize":** Interview Transcripts, July 1991, Biographies File, Pamela Harriman Papers.

238 **"The night," he wrote, "was cloudless":** Colville, *Fringes of Power,* 1:292–93.

CHAPTER 50: HESS

239 **The letter was a curious one:** Stafford, *Flight from Reality,* 21, 88–89, 160–63. A copy of the letter is in "The Capture of Rudolf Hess: Reports and Minutes," WO 199/328, UKARCH.

CHAPTER 51: SANCTUARY

240 **"proclaims the enemy's entire abandonment":** Gilbert, *War Papers,* 2:839.

241 **"Alive":** Kathleen Harriman to Mary Harriman Fisk, June n.d., 1941, Correspondence, W. Averell Harriman Papers.

241 **Audiences edged toward tears:** Panter-Downes, *London War Notes,* 26. The pianist's trick with the orange is mentioned in Fort, *Prof,* 49.

241 **"Walked out into the light":** Cockett, *Love and War in London,* 188.

241 **"I lay there":** Harrisson, *Living Through the Blitz,* 81.

242 **"Finding we can take it":** Cockett, *Love and War in London,* 195.

242 **"I am getting a burying-phobia":** Ibid., 175.

242 **"Siren Stomach":** Wyndham, *Love Lessons,* 121.

243 **"If you would also":** Elements of this saga reside in the Churchill Archives Centre, at CHAR 1/357, Winston Churchill Papers.

243 **The Chequers Trust:** For the cost overrun, see "Chequers Household Account,"

June–Dec. 1940, and C. F. Penruddock to Kathleen Hill, March 25, 1941; Hill to Penruddock, March 22, 1941, CHAR 1/365, Winston Churchill Papers. The file contains numerous other accountings, for other periods. Regarding the chauffeurs, see Elletson, *Chequers and the Prime Ministers*, 107.

244 **One Chequers order:** See "Wines Installed in Cellar at Chequers, 23rd October, 1941," and related correspondence, CHAR 1/365, Winston Churchill Papers.

245 **At least one brand:** Andrew Roberts, *"Holy Fox,"* 292.

245 **"Greetings to our nightly companions":** Süss, *Death from the Skies,* 314; *Swiss Cottager,* Bulletin Nos. 1–3, digital collection, University of Warwick, mrc -catalogue.warwick.ac.uk/records/ABT/6/2/6.

246 **"From its high windows":** Cooper, *Trumpets from the Steep,* 44.

247 **"Experts agree," the brochure proclaimed:** Ziegler, *London at War,* 135.

247 **"reminiscent of a transatlantic crossing":** Andrew Roberts, *"Holy Fox,"* 248.

247 **"Edward only takes three minutes":** Ibid., 247.

247 **"Between 6 and 6:30":** Cooper, *Trumpets from the Steep,* 68.

247 **"They wandered about":** Cowles, *Looking for Trouble,* 441.

248 **"Everyone talked to everyone else":** Ibid., 442.

248 **"We decided that":** Field, "Nights Underground in Darkest London," 17; Overy, *Bombing War,* 146; "On This Day: Occupation of the Savoy, 14th September 1940," Turbulent London, turbulentlondon.com/2017/09/14/on-this -day-occupation-of-the-savoy-14th-september-1940/.

248 **After one raid set:** Ziegler, *London at War,* 122–23.

249 **Early in the war, the zoo:** Nicolson, *War Years,* 120; "Animals in the Zoo Don't Mind the Raids," *The War Illustrated* 3, No. 4 (Nov. 15, 1940). See also, "London Zoo During World War Two," Zoological Society of London, Sept. 1, 2013, www .zsl.org/blogs/artefact-of-the-month/zsl-london-zoo-during-world-war -two.

249 **"Among the heaps of brick":** Harrisson, *Living Through the Blitz,* 82.

249 **"No one wanted to be alone":** Cowles, *Looking for Trouble,* 441.

249 **"Every night next week":** Kathleen Harriman to Mary Harriman Fisk, June n.d., 1941, Correspondence, W. Averell Harriman Papers.

249 **"For the young it was":** Stansky, *First Day of the Blitz,* 170–71.

250 **"The normal barriers":** Ogden, *Life of the Party,* 122.

250 **"only one complete for me":** Cockett, *Love and War in London,* 186.

250 **"I have never in all my life":** Ziegler, *London at War,* 91.

250 **He had come close:** Fort, *Prof,* 161–63.

250 **"Now come on":** Ibid., 163.

CHAPTER 52: BERLIN

251 **In the first three months:** Overy, *Bombing War,* 97.

252 **"The Fat One promised":** Galland, *The First and the Last,* 37.

253 **Night bombing, the airman said:** Shirer, *Berlin Diary,* 411–13. British intelligence made it a point to take cooperative prisoners on tours of London, even to the theater, to show them how much of the city had survived the bombing. "Prisoners saw for themselves that London was not lying in ruins as they had been led to believe," states an intelligence report on the process. Seeing this shook their confidence in what their leaders had been telling them and often made them more cooperative. "Intelligence from Interrogation: Intelligence from Prisoners of War," 10, AIR 40/1177, UKARCH.

Another intelligence report presents an excerpt of a conversation between two prisoners recorded by British interrogators eavesdropping through microphones, in which one prisoner says, "I still can't understand that London still exists!"

"Yes," the other says, "it is inexplicable, though I was driven all round the outer districts, but . . . more must have been smashed up!" Special Extract No. 57, WO 208/3506, UKARCH. (Interestingly, this file was kept secret until 1992.)

253 **"An airplane carrying Hitler"**: Shirer, *Berlin Diary*, 448.
253 **"an unmistakable wave of optimism"**: Boelcke, *Secret Conferences of Dr. Goebbels*, 97.
254 **"must expect to find himself"**: Ibid., 98.

CHAPTER 53: TARGET CHURCHILL

255 **"striding along the middle"**: Wheeler-Bennett, *Action This Day*, 118.
255 **"One thing worries me"**: Gilbert, *War Papers*, 2:818–19.
256 **"It may be fun for you"**: Pottle, *Champion Redoubtable*, 228.
256 **"When I was at Chequers"**: Lee to Neville Chamberlain, April 4, 1940, PREM 14/19, UKARCH.
256 **"I don't know how to fire a gun"**: Ogden, *Life of the Party*, 95; Winston S. Churchill, *Memories and Adventures*, 10; Pamela C. Harriman, "Churchill's Dream," *American Heritage*, Oct./Nov. 1983.
257 **Compounding Ismay's worries**: Ismay to P. Allen, Aug. 29, 1940, PREM 14/33, UKARCH.
258 **Sewage could be a problem**: Ismay to General Sir Walter K. Venning, Aug. 8, 1940, "Protection of Chequers," pt. 3, WO 199/303, UKARCH.
258 **"These would provide"**: J. B. Watney to GHQ Home Forces, Sept. 22, 1940, and "Note for War Diary," Sept. 14, 1940, "Protection of Chequers," pt. 3, UKARCH.
258 **One detailed assay**: "Report on Cigars Presented to the Prime Minister by the National Tobacco Commission of Cuba," Oct. 14, 1941, CHAR 2/434.
258 **"Gentlemen," he said**: Gilbert, *War Papers*, 3:1238.
259 **The Prof, he told Churchill**: Ibid., 1238n.
259 **"The Professor thought"**: Colville to Churchill, June 18, 1941, CHAR 2/434, Winston Churchill Papers.
259 **"The sirens, it must be admitted"**: Farrer, *Sky's the Limit*, 63.
260 **"The decision might"**: Beaverbrook to Churchill, June 26, 1940, BBK/D, Beaverbrook Papers.
260 **"It was the appearance"**: Farrer, *Sky's the Limit*, 65.
260 **"Beaverbrook is a man"**: Ibid., 63.
261 **In one memorandum**: Lindemann to Churchill, minute, Aug. 14, 1940, F113/19, Lindemann Papers.
261 **"In my view burning oil"**: Lindemann to Churchill, Aug. 20, 1940, F114/12, Lindemann Papers.
262 **"Another victory for evacuation"**: Home Intelligence Weekly Report for Sept. 30–Oct. 9, 1940, INF 1/292, UKARCH.
262 **"I don't see how"**: Diary, Sept. 26 and 27, 1940, Mary Churchill Papers.
262 **"All today seemed overcast"**: Ibid., Sept. 27, 1940.
263 **"I cannot feel"**: Gilbert, *War Papers*, 2:902.

263 **The dinner was in full sway:** Diary, Oct. 8, 1940, Mary Churchill Papers; Soames, *Daughter's Tale,* 179–80.

264 **"I've told you five times":** Interview Transcript, July 1991, Biographies File, Pamela Harriman Papers.

264 **"Winston Churchill Junior arrived":** Diary, Oct. 10, 1940, Mary Churchill Papers.

264 **Pamela's husband, Randolph:** Interview Transcript, July 1991, Biographies File, Pamela Harriman Papers; Ogden, *Life of the Party,* 100; Smith, *Reflected Glory,* 72.

264 **"Will they do us any damage":** Colville, *Fringes of Power,* 1:307.

265 **"Certainly there is a danger":** Ibid., 309.

265 **"Probably, they don't think":** Ibid.

266 **"It is quite a business":** Nicolson, *War Years,* 128–29.

266 **"I have always been":** Roy Jenkins, *Churchill,* 640.

266 **"Max knows how":** Chisholm and Davie, *Beaverbrook,* 445.

CHAPTER 54: SPENDTHRIFT

267 **"Yes," Pamela assured him:** Interview Transcript, July 1991, Biographies File, Pamela Harriman Papers.

267 **One day during a shopping trip:** Ibid.; Ogden, *Life of the Party,* 92.

268 **"Instead of this":** Winston Churchill to Randolph Churchill, Oct. 18, 1931, RDCH 1/3/3, Randolph Churchill Papers.

268 **"as I really cannot run the risk":** Winston Churchill to Randolph Churchill, Feb. 14, 1938, RDCH 1/3/3, Randolph Churchill Papers.

268 **"She was wonderfully comforting":** Interview Transcript, July 1991, Biographies File, Pamela Harriman Papers.

268 **"What a shock it was":** Ogden, *Life of the Party,* 102–3.

269 **"Oh! Randy everything would be so nice":** Winston S. Churchill, *Memories and Adventures,* 14.

269 **"It is a very good thing":** Pamela Churchill to Randolph Churchill, Sept. 17 and 18, 1940, RDCH 1/3/5 File no. 1, Randolph Churchill Papers.

270 **"Please darling pay":** Pamela Churchill to Randolph Churchill, Sept. 9, 1940, RDCH 1/3/5 File no. 1, Randolph Churchill Papers.

270 **"I know it is difficult":** Pamela Churchill to Randolph Churchill, [n.d., but likely late Oct. 1940], RDCH 1/3/5 File no. 2, Randolph Churchill Papers.

270 **"We have no gas":** Pottle, *Champion Redoubtable,* 230.

270 **"They heard the bomb":** Nicolson, *War Years,* 121.

270 **"Where is Nelson":** J. Gilbert Jenkins, *Chequers,* 146.

271 **In London that following Saturday:** Colville, *Fringes of Power,* 1:318.

272 **"I believe that I can do it!":** Ismay, *Memoirs,* 175; Elletson, *Chequers and the Prime Ministers,* 110.

CHAPTER 55: WASHINGTON AND BERLIN

273 **"When your boy":** Sherwood, *Roosevelt and Hopkins,* 198.

274 **"I have said this before":** Ibid., 191.

274 **"a very difficult situation for Germany":** Kershaw, *Nemesis,* 336.

275 **"The decisive thing":** Overy, *Battle of Britain,* 98.

275 **"For the first time"**: "Air Defense of Great Britain," vol. 3, "Night Air Defense, June 1940–December 1941," 82, AIR 41/17, UKARCH. The report uses the phrase "small propositions," surely an unintended substitute for "proportions."

CHAPTER 56: THE FROG SPEECH

277 **The ministry sent**: Gilbert, *War Papers*, 2:979.
277 **"frog speech"**: Toye, *Roar of the Lion*, 80.
277 **"He relished the flavor"**: Ibid., 81.
277 **"On my knees"**: Ibid.
278 **"Frenchmen!"**: Gilbert, *War Papers*, 2:980–82.
278 **"Tonight Papa spoke"**: Diary, Oct. 21, 1940, Mary Churchill Papers.
278 **"heavy sentences for radio offenders"**: Boelcke, *Secret Conferences of Dr. Goebbels*, 108.
279 **"in the long run"**: "Intelligence from Interrogation: Intelligence from Prisoners of War," 42, AIR 40/1177, UKARCH.

CHAPTER 57: THE OVIPOSITOR

280 **"It looks all right"**: Goodwin, *No Ordinary Time*, 189.
280 **"It is the best thing"**: Nicolson, *War Years*, 126.
280 **"Glory hallelujah!!"**: Diary, Nov. 6, 1940, Mary Churchill Papers.
280 **"This does not mean"**: Gilbert, *War Papers*, 2:1053–54.
281 **"Would you kindly find out"**: Ibid., 1147.
281 **"I trust this unlikely accident"**: Lindemann to Churchill, Nov. 1, 1940, F121/1, Lindemann Papers.
282 **"Professor Lindemann implies"**: Portal to Churchill, Nov. 5, 1940, PREM 3/22/4b, UKARCH.
282 **A navy salvage squad**: Wakefield, *Pfadfinder*, 67.
282 **"It is a very great pity"**: Lindemann to Churchill, Nov. 13, 1940, PREM 3/22/4b, UKARCH.
283 **"Pray make proposals"**: Churchill to Ismay, Nov. 18, 1940, PREM 3/22/4b, UKARCH.
283 **The airplane had been lost**: Ismay to Churchill, Nov. 21, 1940, PREM 3/22/4b, UKARCH.
283 **Lost in this acerbic interchange**: See Wakefield, *Pfadfinder*, 64–67, for a detailed account of the pilot Hans Lehmann's very bad night.

CHAPTER 58: OUR SPECIAL SOURCE

All the official intelligence reports and memoranda that I used to tell the story of the Coventry attack in this chapter and the one following may be found in the file "German Operations 'Moonlight Sonata' (Bombing of Coventry) and Counter-plan 'Cold Water,'" AIR 2/5238, in the National Archives of the United Kingdom. Ever since the attack, conspiracy-minded souls have sought to prove that Churchill knew all about it but did nothing, in order to avoid revealing the secret of Bletchley Park. However, the documentary record, declassified in 1971, makes it clear that Churchill on that night had no idea Coventry was the target.

289 **"apolaustically"**: Colville, *Winston Churchill*, 85.

289 **Growing impatient:** As Inspector Thompson put it, "He could no more stay out of a raid than he could sit still in a debate in Parliament." Thompson, *Assignment*, 126.

CHAPTER 59: A COVENTRY FAREWELL

292 **"We could almost have read":** Longmate, *Air Raid,* 73.
292 **"The air was filled":** Ibid., 79.
293 **"After a time":** Ibid., 102.
293 **Her seven-year-old said:** Ibid., 109.
293 **"The complication with bomb lacerations":** Ibid., 105.
293 **"During the course of my training":** Ibid., 106.
294 **"The whole interior":** Ibid., 95.
294 **"When we went out":** Donnelly, *Mrs. Milburn's Diaries,* 66.
294 **Now came scenes of horror:** Süss, *Death from the Skies,* 412; Longmate, *Air Raid,* 156.
295 **"It is greatly regretted":** Longmate, *Air Raid,* 223.
295 **"The roots of the Air Force":** A.J.P. Taylor, *Beaverbrook,* 454.
295 **"He'd asked Coventry's workers":** Longmate, *Air Raid,* 196.
296 **"since the night was so clear":** "Note on German Operation 'Moonlight Sonata,'" and Counter-plan 'Cold Water,'" 2, AIR 2/5238, UKARCH.
296 **"Oh dear!" she cried:** Longmate, *Air Raid,* 202.
296 **A team of Mass-Observation researchers:** Harrisson, *Living Through the Blitz,* 135.
297 **"The strangest sight of all":** Ibid., 134.
297 **"No means of defense":** Longmate, *Air Raid,* 212.
297 **"exceptional success":** Boelcke, *Secret Conferences of Dr. Goebbels,* 109.
297 **"The reports from Coventry":** Fred Taylor, *Goebbels Diaries,* 177.
298 **"The unpredictable consequences":** Kesselring, *Memoirs,* 81.
298 **"The usual cheers":** Bekker, *Luftwaffe Diaries,* 180.

CHAPTER 60: DISTRACTION

299 **"Mounted on two":** Diary, Nov. 17, 1940, Colville Papers.
299 **"I enclose a sketch":** Pamela Churchill to Randolph Churchill, Nov. 19, 1940, RDCH 1/3/5 File no. 2, Randolph Churchill Papers.
300 **"Having no false dignity":** Colville, *Fringes of Power,* 1:379.
300 **The child was round:** Gilbert, *War Papers,* 2:1002.
301 **"As it was *my* birthday":** Elletson, *Chequers and the Prime Ministers,* 107.
301 **"I have never forgotten":** Cowles, *Winston Churchill,* 327.
301 **"I am not now the man":** Beaverbrook to Winston Churchill, Dec. 2, 1940, BBK/D, Beaverbrook Papers.
302 **"As I told you":** Churchill to Beaverbrook, Dec. 3, 1940, BBK/D, Beaverbrook Papers.

CHAPTER 61: SPECIAL DELIVERY

303 **"The Prime Minister said":** Gilbert, *War Papers,* 2:1169.

304 **"I have not been able"**: Churchill to Sinclair et al., Dec. 9, 1940, G 26/1, Lindemann Papers.

304 **"Surely there is"**: Churchill to Sinclair et al., Jan. 12, 1941, G 35/30, Lindemann Papers.

305 **"It's horrible"**: Gilbert, *War Papers,* 2:1204.

305 **"As we reach the end"**: Churchill to Roosevelt, Dec. 7, 1940, FDR/Diplo. Also in FDR/Map.

306 **"Another victim for Christian Science"**: Andrew Roberts, *"Holy Fox,"* 272.

306 **"Orangeade and Christian Science"**: Cooper, *Trumpets from the Steep,* 69.

306 **"Papa in very bad mood"**: Diary, Dec. 12, 1940, Mary Churchill Papers.

306 **"Since we aimed"**: Gilbert, *War Papers,* 2:1217.

307 **"I didn't know for quite awhile"**: Sherwood, *Roosevelt and Hopkins,* 224.

CHAPTER 62: DIRECTIVE

308 **"How do I feel"**: Cockett, *Love and War in London,* 181–82.

CHAPTER 63: THAT SILLY OLD DOLLAR SIGN

309 **"I don't think there is"**: Sherwood, *Roosevelt and Hopkins,* 225.

310 **"ploughing under every fourth"**: Ibid., 229.

CHAPTER 64: A TOAD AT THE GATE

311 **"There was nothing"**: A.J.P. Taylor, *Beaverbrook,* 58.

312 **"He returned to Churchill"**: Andrew Roberts, *"Holy Fox,"* 275.

313 **"the shock effect"**: Hylton, *Their Darkest Hour,* 107.

313 **"to say that their mental health"**: James R. Wilkinson to Walter H. McKinney, Dec. 27, 1940, FDR/Diplo.

313 **The blackout invariably**: Harrisson, *Living Through the Blitz,* 313.

314 **"Blinds must be kept"**: Cockett, *Love and War in London,* 149.

314 **"Used to smoke occasionally"**: Ibid., 140.

315 **What Clementine found**: Clementine Churchill to Winston Churchill, Jan. 3, 1941; "The 3-Tier Bunk," "Sanitation in Shelter," "Shelters Visited in Bermondsey on Thursday December 19th 1940," all in PREM 3/27, UKARCH.

Along these lines, here is a nice breakfast story: Earlier in the fall, the journalist Kingsley Martin visited the massive Tilbury shelter in the East End, a margarine warehouse that nightly drew up to fourteen thousand people. He then wrote a graphic essay about the experience, titled "The War in East London." The shelter's inhabitants—"Whites, Jews and Gentiles, Chinese, Indians and Negroes"—paid little attention to sanitation, he wrote. "They urinate and defecate in every part of the building. The process is helped by the convenience of the margarine in cardboard cases which can be piled up into useful mounds behind which people can dig themselves in and sleep and defecate and urinate in comfort." He did not know whether this margarine had then been distributed to food markets in the city, but wrote that "the dangers of thousands of people sleeping on London's margarine is obvious enough."

More toast anyone? PREM 3/27, UKARCH.

317 **"Now is the time"**: Churchill to Home Secretary et al., March 29, 1941, PREM 3/27, UKARCH.
317 **"Furious," he wrote**: Cadogan, *Diaries*, 342.
317 **"I looked up and saw"**: Ibid., 343.
317 **"He was very unhappy"**: Wheeler-Bennett, *King George VI*, 520.

CHAPTER 65: WEIHNACHTEN

319 **"When will that creature"**: Fred Taylor, *Goebbels Diaries*, 179–80.
319 **"It seems that the English"**: Ibid., 208.
319 **"The German Armed Forces"**: Trevor-Roper, *Blitzkrieg to Defeat*, 49.
320 **"No strip dancers"**: Boelcke, *Secret Conferences of Dr. Goebbels*, 112.
320 **He warned his lieutenants**: Ibid., 110.
321 **"A lot of work"**: For this succession of diary entries, see Fred Taylor, *Goebbels Diaries*, 201, 204, 215, 217, 209.
321 **An idea came to Hess**: Stafford, *Flight from Reality*, 126, 127.

CHAPTER 66: RUMORS

323 **As Christmas neared**: For these rumors, and many others, see Home Intelligence Weekly Reports for Sept. 30–Oct. 9, 1940; Oct. 7–Oct. 14, 1940; Jan. 15–Jan. 22, 1941; Feb. 12–Feb. 19, 1941, all in INF 1/292, UKARCH. Regarding the Wimbledon rumor, see "Extract from Minute by Mr. Chappell to Mr. Parker, Sept. 23, 1940," HO 199/462, UKARCH.

CHAPTER 67: CHRISTMAS

326 **He gave the king**: Colville, *Fringes of Power*, 1:383.
326 **"There may not be"**: Lee, *London Observer*, 187.
326 **"Apparently," wrote John Martin**: Martin, *Downing Street*, 37.
326 **"A busy Christmas"**: Colville, *Fringes of Power*, 1:383.
326 **"But it gave me a pang"**: Diary, Dec. 24, 1940, Colville Papers.
327 **"I know what your wife"**: Colville, *Winston Churchill and His Inner Circle*, 110.
327 **"The great gloomy hall"**: Soames, *Daughter's Tale*, 185.
328 **"For once the shorthand writer"**: Martin, *Downing Street*, 37.
328 **"This was one of the happiest"**: Diary, Dec. 25, 1940, Mary Churchill Papers.
329 **"The gloomiest Christmas Day"**: Nicolson, *War Years*, 131.
329 **"The pubs were all full"**: Wyndham, *Love Lessons*, 166.

CHAPTER 68: EGGLAYER

330 **No balloons rose**: Basil Collier, *Defense of the United Kingdom*, 274.

CHAPTER 69: AULD LANG SYNE

331 **"I believe that the Axis"**: Sherwood, *Roosevelt and Hopkins*, 228.
332 **"Roosevelt," he wrote**: Fred Taylor, *Goebbels Diaries*, 222.
333 **"This may help us"**: Cadogan, *Diaries*, 344.

333 "Remember, Mr. President": Gilbert, *War Papers*, 2:1309.

334 "Sometimes I hate the big city": Fred Taylor, *Goebbels Diaries*, 223.

334 In the Cabinet War Rooms: Martin, *Downing Street*, 37; Colville, *Fringes of Power*, 1:386.

PART FIVE: THE AMERICANS

CHAPTER 70: SECRETS

339 "What a nice wintry morning": Lee, *London Observer*, 208.

340 "Nothing can exceed": Churchill to Beaverbrook, Jan. 2, 1941, BBK/D, Beaverbrook Papers.

340 "I am not a committee man": Beaverbrook to Churchill, Jan. 3, 1941, BBK/D, Beaverbrook Papers.

341 "My dear Max": Churchill to Beaverbrook, Jan. 3, 1941, BBK/D, Beaverbrook Papers.

341 "Mademoiselle Curie": Gilbert, *War Papers*, 3:2–3.

342 "With the beginning": Ibid., 4–6.

342 "The P.M. has circulated": Colville, *Fringes of Power*, 1:387.

342 "sank up to his ankles": Ibid.

343 "At one time": Singleton to Churchill, Jan. 3, 1941, F125/12, Lindemann Papers.

343 "I did not want to join": Beaverbrook to Churchill, Jan. 6, 1941, BBK/D, Beaverbrook Papers.

343 "I have not the slightest": Gilbert, *War Papers*, 3:35.

344 "You must not forget": Churchill to Beaverbrook, Jan. 7, 1941, BBK/D, Beaverbrook Papers.

344 "The truth is that they both": A.J.P. Taylor, *Beaverbrook*, 465.

345 "Who?": Sherwood, *Roosevelt and Hopkins*, 234.

345 Brendan Bracken called: Colville, *Fringes of Power*, 1:393.

345 "as he snuggled": Ibid., 392.

345 "Oh! I wish you were here": Pamela Churchill to Randolph Churchill, Jan. 1, 1941, RDCH 1/3/5 File no. 3, Randolph Churchill Papers.

CHAPTER 71: THE ELEVEN-THIRTY SPECIAL

346 "He was as unlike": Ismay, *Memoirs*, 213–14.

346 "His was a soul": Gilbert, *War Papers*, 3:58.

347 "A rotund—smiling—red-faced": Ibid., 59.

348 "I tried to be reasonably aloof": Diary, Jan. 10, 1941, Colville Papers.

349 "It is so dreadfully dark": Donnelly, *Mrs. Milburn's Diaries*, 72.

349 "feeling strange—country-cousinish": Diary, Jan. 11, 1941, Mary Churchill Papers.

350 "embarrassed officials would often": Soames, *Clementine Churchill*, 385–86.

350 "Dinner at Ditchley": Colville, *Fringes of Power*, 1:395.

351 "We seek no treasure": Gilbert, *War Papers*, 3:68–69; Colville, *Fringes of Power*, 1:396.

351 "Heavens alive": Gilbert, *War Papers*, 3:69.

352 "which with all its salutes": Colville, *Fringes of Power*, 1:397.

352 "The people here are amazing": Sherwood, *Roosevelt and Hopkins*, 243.

CHAPTER 72: TO SCAPA FLOW

355 **"When?" Wilson asked:** Moran, *Churchill*, 6.
356 **The train carried:** Nel, *Mr. Churchill's Secretary*, 78.
356 **"We both felt Beaverbrook":** Andrew Roberts, *"Holy Fox,"* 280.
356 **"Lord and Lady Halifax":** Lee, *London Observer*, 224.
357 **"He looked miserable":** Ismay, *Memoirs*, 214.
357 **"We really had a pleasant time":** Lee, *London Observer*, 225.
358 **"came beaming into the breakfast car":** Gilbert, *War Papers*, 3:86.
358 **"The smile faded":** Ibid., 86–87.

CHAPTER 73: "WHITHER THOU GOEST"

359 **"There was much discussion":** Martin, *Downing Street*, 42.
359 **"The land is bleak":** Lee, *London Observer*, 226.
360 **"I wanted Harry to see":** Ismay, *Memoirs*, 214.
360 **"Excuse me, sir":** Sherwood, *Roosevelt and Hopkins*, 246.
361 **"There was no noise":** Lee, *London Observer*, 227.
361 **"One of the projectiles":** Martin, *Downing Street*, 40; Sherwood, *Roosevelt and Hopkins*, 250.
361 **"I was careful to avoid":** Ismay, *Memoirs*, 215.
362 **"But there was no escape":** Ibid., 216.
362 **"I suppose you wish":** Ibid.; Moran, *Churchill*, 6.
363 **"He knew what it meant":** Moran, *Churchill*, 6.
363 **"I found her charming":** Diary, Jan. 18, 1941, Colville Papers.
364 **"Oh yes," Hopkins told one valet:** Sherwood, *Roosevelt and Hopkins*, 255.
365 **"He gets on like":** Gilbert, *War Papers*, 3:165.

CHAPTER 74: DIRECTIVE NO. 23

366 **On Thursday, February 6:** Trevor-Roper, *Blitzkrieg to Defeat*, 56–58.
366 **"The decision to attack":** "Hermann Göring," Interrogation Report, Military Intelligence Service, U.S. Ninth Air Force, June 1, 1945, Spaatz Papers.
367 **"We've got England":** Interrogation Report, Generals Attig, Schimpf, et al., May 20, 1945, Spaatz Papers.
367 **"Nothing leaked out":** Kesselring, *Memoirs*, 85.

CHAPTER 75: THE COMING VIOLENCE

368 **"My dear Prime Minister":** Gilbert, *War Papers*, 3:191.
369 **"made some people's flesh creep":** Home Intelligence Weekly Report for Feb. 5–12, 1941, INF 1/292, UKARCH.
369 **Churchill opened by offering:** Gilbert, *War Papers*, 3:192–200.
370 **called it "insolent":** Fred Taylor, *Goebbels Diaries*, 229.
371 **"I could not have a better":** Wheeler-Bennett, *King George VI*, 447, 849.
371 **"How many bombs":** Gilbert, *War Papers*, 3:224.
372 **"We must begin persuading":** Ibid., 225.
372 **"The need for sustained":** Telegrams, Jan. 21 and 23, 1941, BBK/D, Beaverbrook Papers.
372 **"Sunny day like spring":** Wyndham, *Love Lessons*, 171.

372 **"Well, it is hell"**: Interview Transcripts, July 1991, Biographies File, Pamela Harriman Papers.

CHAPTER 76. LONDON, WASHINGTON, AND BERLIN

374 **"This bill has to pass"**: Conant, *My Several Lives*, 253–55.
375 **"It is impossible"**: "Memorandum for the Chief of Staff," War Department, March 3, 1941, Spaatz Papers.
375 **On March 5 he issued**: Trevor-Roper, *Blitzkrieg to Defeat*, 58–59.

CHAPTER 77: SATURDAY NIGHT

377 **"slim grey beautiful"**: Wyndham, *Love Lessons*, 160.
377 **"the least melancholy"**: Graves, *Champagne and Chandeliers*, 112.
377 **"I don't know why"**: Ibid., 115.
378 **"He has established"**: Fred Taylor, *Goebbels Diaries*, 260.
378 **One important factor**: Goodwin, *No Ordinary Time*, 213.

CHAPTER 78: THE TALL MAN WITH THE SMILE

379 **"An extraordinary meal"**: Averell Harriman, Memorandum to self, March 11, 1941, "Harriman Mission," Chronological File, W. Averell Harriman Papers.
380 **The U.S. Navy had no plans**: Ibid.
381 **"No one has given me"**: Ibid.
381 **"cheap old bastard"**: Smith, *Reflected Glory*, 259.
382 **Just two days earlier**: Gilbert, *War Papers*, 3:320–24.

CHAPTER 79: SNAKEHIPS

Charles Graves's *Champagne and Chandeliers*, a biography of the café, provides a vivid and detailed account of the bombing on pages 112–25. The National Archives of the United Kingdom holds a map made by investigators that shows the layout of the club and the locations of injured guests and bodies, and includes this notation: "Six persons were found dead still sitting at table. They had no superficial injuries." HO 193/68, UKARCH.
383 **"I do find London shops"**: Diary, March 8, 1941, Mary Churchill Papers.
384 **He set off at a run**: Graves, *Champagne and Chandeliers*, 116.
385 **"The men, almost all in uniform"**: Ziegler, *London at War*, 148.
385 **"It is my sister's birthday"**: Graves, *Champagne and Chandeliers*, 121.
385 **"It seemed so easy to forget"**: Diary, March 8, 1941, Mary Churchill Papers.
386 **"Wilkins and I tried to lift"**: Graves, *Champagne and Chandeliers*, 118–19.
387 **"Oh it was so gay"**: Diary, March 8, 1941, Mary Churchill Papers.
388 **"Recalling it now"**: Soames, *Daughter's Tale*, 191.

CHAPTER 80: BAYONET QUADRILLE

389 **"a draught of life"**: Gilbert, *War Papers*, 3:331.
389 **"Our blessings from the whole"**: Ibid., 332.
389 **"Papa not at all well"**: Diary, March 9, 1941, Mary Churchill Papers.
390 **"The evening remains"**: Alanbrooke, *War Diaries*, 145.

390 **"To bed at the record hour"**: Colville, *Fringes of Power,* 1:433.

390 **"Luckily PM decided"**: Alanbrooke, *War Diaries,* 144–45.

390 **"There will be worse"**: Fred Taylor, *Goebbels Diaries,* 262.

CHAPTER 81: THE GAMBLER

391 **"There was very high gambling"**: Waugh, *Diaries,* 493.

391 **"Poor Pamela will have to"**: Smith, *Reflected Glory,* 75.

391 **"Anyway," he concluded**: Interview Transcripts, July 1991, Biographies File, Pamela Harriman Papers.

392 **"I mean, that was the first"**: Ibid.

392 **"I won't advance Randolph"**: Ibid.

393 **"Not as glamorous"**: Clarissa Eden, *Clarissa Eden,* 58.

393 **"She combined a canny eye"**: Ibid., 59.

394 **"because I couldn't really tell Clemmie"**: Interview Transcripts, July 1991, Biographies File, Pamela Harriman Papers.

CHAPTER 82: A TREAT FOR CLEMENTINE

395 **The list was like something**: "Atlantic Clipper Passenger List," New York–Lisbon, March 10–12, 1941, "Harriman Mission," Chronological File, W. Averell Harriman Papers; Harriman, *Special Envoy to Churchill and Stalin,* 19.

396 **Anyone who peeked**: "World War II Diary," 2, Meiklejohn Papers.

396 **"Mr. Harriman in a rash moment"**: Meiklejohn to Samuel H. Wiley, April 16, 1941, "Family Papers," W. Averell Harriman Papers.

397 **"We were prepared"**: Martin, *Downing Street,* 42.

398 **"Our fliers are talking of"**: Fred Taylor, *Goebbels Diaries,* 268.

399 **"I was surprised to see"**: Harriman, *Special Envoy to Churchill and Stalin,* 21.

399 **"You shall be informed"**: Ibid., 22.

399 **"The weekend was thrilling"**: Diary, "Monday & Tuesday," March 17–18, 1941, Mary Churchill Papers.

400 **"Will have to move out"**: "World War II Diary," 10, Meiklejohn Papers.

400 **"Most impressive thing"**: Ibid., 12.

401 **"Mr. Harriman achieves"**: Meiklejohn to Knight Woolley, May 21, 1941, Public Service, Chronological File, W. Averell Harriman Papers. Harriman also was subject to episodes of dyspepsia, an arcane term for heartburn and indigestion.

402 **"Young man," Churchill said**: Niven, *Moon's a Balloon,* 242.

402 **"a meal and a laugh"**: Niven to Harriman, March 16, 1941, "Harriman Mission," Chronological File, W. Averell Harriman Papers.

402 **"Mr. Harriman was too cagey"**: Christiansen to Harriman, March 19, 1941, "Harriman Mission," Chronological File, W. Averell Harriman Papers.

402 **"Of course," Owen wrote**: Owen to Harriman, March 19, 1941, "Harriman Mission," Chronological File, W. Averell Harriman Papers.

403 **"For g. sake tell your father"**: Kathleen Harriman to Marie Harriman, March 19 [n.d., but likely 1942], Correspondence, W. Averell Harriman Papers.

CHAPTER 83: MEN

404 **"the strides which"**: Anthony Biddle to Franklin Roosevelt, April 26, 1941. FDR/Diplo.

404 **"A fantastic climb"**: Gilbert, *War Papers,* 3.369.

405 **"the mortuary men"**: "Air Raid Casualties," April 3, 1941, Metropolitan Police Report, MEPO 2/6580.

406 **"Dearest," she wrote:** "'Dearest, I Feel Certain I Am Going Mad Again': The Suicide Note of Virginia Woolf," *Advances in Psychiatric Treatment* 16, no. 4 (July 2020), www.cambridge.org/core/journals/advances-in-psychiatric-treatment /article/dearest-i-feel-certain-i-am-going-mad-again-the-suicide-note-of -virginia-woolf/8E400FB1AB0EEA2C2A61946475CB7FA3.

406 **While flying over Chequers:** C. R. Thompson to Hastings Ismay, March 26, 1941, Protection of Chequers, pt. 3, WO 199/303, UKARCH.

407 **"A sleeping bag"**: "Your Anderson Shelter This Winter," PREM 3/27, UKARCH.

407 **"If we can't be safe"**: Memorandum, "Yesterday evening . . . ," May 1, 1941, PREM 3/27, UKARCH.

408 **"good looking in rather"**: Diary, March 28, 1941, Mary Churchill Papers.

408 **"He's marvelous"**: Ibid.

409 **The secretary had brought:** "World War II Diary," 15, Meiklejohn Papers.

409 **"I saw the best-looking man"**: Interview Transcripts, July 1991, Biographies File, Pamela Harriman Papers.

410 **"Minister of Midnight"**: Channon, *"Chips,"* 385.

410 **"Yesterday was a grand day"**: Gilbert, *Finest Hour,* 1048.

410 **"has spent much of the weekend pacing"**: Colville, *Fringes of Power,* 1:440.

411 **"All day we felt jubilant"**: Diary, March 30, 1941, Mary Churchill Papers.

PART SIX: LOVE AMID THE FLAMES

CHAPTER 84: GRAVE NEWS

415 **"Snow—sleet—cold"**: These various diary entries can be found at the indicated dates in Mary's diary. Mary Churchill Papers.

416 **"a place to be held"**: Gilbert, *Finest Hour,* 1055.

416 **"Let me have meanwhile"**: Gilbert, *War Papers,* 3:460.

416 **"I am told"**: Ibid.

417 **In a gloomy speech:** Ibid., 470. For the speech, see ibid., 461–70.

417 **"The House is sad"**: Nicolson, *War Years,* 162.

417 **"the extent to which"**: Harriman to Roosevelt, April 10, 1941, "Harriman Mission," Chronological File, W. Averell Harriman Papers.

418 **"If one could really completely"**: Diary, April 9, 1941, Mary Churchill Papers.

418 **"You know Duncan"**: Winston Churchill to Randolph Churchill, June 8, 1941, CHAR 1/362, Winston Churchill Papers.

419 **"The devastation in parts of the town"**: Diary, April 11, 1941, Mary Churchill Papers.

419 **"The firing of the rockets"**: Colville, *Fringes of Power,* 1:443.

420 **"Rather strained pale faces"**: Diary, April 12, 1941, Mary Churchill Papers; Soames, *Daughter's Tale,* 193.

420 **"Yes, sir!" the desk manager said:** Thompson, *Assignment,* 215–16.

420 **"He has the root"**: Diary, April 12, 1941, Mary Churchill Papers.

421 **"What did you say?"**: "War Reminiscences," 12, Oct. 13, 1953, Memoirs, Harriman Recollections, W. Averell Harriman Papers.

421 **"It was quite extraordinary"**: Soames, *Daughter's Tale,* 193.

422 **"Many of those here today"**: Gilbert, *War Papers,* 3:480.

422 **"They have such confidence"**: "War Reminiscences," 12, Oct. 13, 1953, Memoirs, Harriman Recollections, W. Averell Harriman Papers.

423 **"will favorably affect"**: Gilbert, *War Papers,* 3:486n1.

423 **"Deeply grateful for"**: Ibid., 486.

423 **"That's what I hope"**: Colville, *Fringes of Power,* 1:444.

424 **"whatever happens we do"**: Clementine Churchill to Harriman, April 15, 1941, "Harriman Mission," Chronological File, W. Averell Harriman Papers.

424 **"Thrilled," he telegraphed**: Averell Harriman to Kathleen Harriman, April 15, 1941, W. Averell Harriman Papers.

424 **"We're all dying to know"**: Smith, *Reflected Glory,* 90.

424 **Gloom settled over meetings**: As Alexander Cadogan noted in a series of diary entries, beginning April 7, 1941: "V. gloomy." "Altogether gloomy." "Rather gloomy." Cadogan, *Diaries,* 370.

CHAPTER 85: SCORN

425 **"Churchill should be pilloried"**: Boelcke, *Secret Conferences of Dr. Goebbels,* 143.

425 **"Hitler was outraged"**: Below, *At Hitler's Side,* 93; Fred Taylor, *Goebbels Diaries,* 311.

426 **"I set special importance"**: Gilbert, *War Papers,* 3:502.

CHAPTER 86: THAT NIGHT AT THE DORCHESTER

427 **eleven thousand tons of cheese**: Roosevelt to Cordell Hull, April 16, 1941, FDR/Conf.

427 **"Standing on the roof"**: Greene, *Ways of Escape,* 112.

428 **"I had quite a disagreeable walk"**: Colville, *Fringes of Power,* 1:445.

428 **"More scary than actual explosions"**: "World War II Diary," 23, Meiklejohn Papers.

429 **"All this time"**: Lee, *London Observer,* 244.

429 **Nine blocks away**: In *Life of the Party,* Christopher Ogden relies on, and amplifies, Pamela's own recollections to place this dinner in the Dorchester apartment of Lady Emerald Cunard, a celebrated London hostess (118–20). During this period, however, Lady Cunard was not in England. Sally Bedell Smith, in *Reflected Glory,* offers a more convincing account (84–85). See also Anne Chisholm's *Nancy Cunard,* which puts Cunard on an island in the Caribbean at the time the dinner party took place (159, 261). It should be noted, however, that the end result was the same.

430 **"Well, would you"**: Interview Transcripts, July 1991, Biographies File, Pamela Harriman Papers.

430 **"A big bombing raid"**: Smith, *Reflected Glory,* 85.

430 **"London looks bleary-eyed"**: Colville, *Fringes of Power,* 1:445.

430 **"Needless to say"**: Smith, *Reflected Glory,* 85.

CHAPTER 87: THE WHITE CLIFFS

431 **The RAF "Egglayers":** Lindemann to Churchill, April 17, 1941, F132/24, Lindemann Papers.
432 **He was told, however:** Colville, *Fringes of Power,* 1:449.
433 **"For the first time since war":** Ibid., 472.

CHAPTER 88: BERLIN

434 **"The effect is devastating":** Fred Taylor, *Goebbels Diaries,* 332.
434 **"He is said to be":** Ibid., 331.
434 **"What a glorious spring day":** Ibid., 335.

CHAPTER 89: THIS SCOWLING VALLEY

435 **"That's all we're really good at!":** Cadogan, *Diaries,* 374.
435 **"I have come back":** Gilbert, *War Papers,* 3:548.
435 **"His statement that morale":** Toye, *Roar of the Lion,* 95.
436 **In a "MOST SECRET" directive:** Gilbert, *War Papers,* 3:556.
436 **"The failure to win":** Ibid., 577.
437 **"The battle over intervention":** Fred Taylor, *Goebbels Diaries,* 337.
437 **"Their great fear":** Ibid., 340.
438 **"My dear Excellency":** Gilbert, *War Papers,* 3:577.
439 **"In a later letter to Hitler":** Quoted in Stafford, *Flight from Reality,* 142; "Studies in Broadcast Propaganda, No. 29, Rudolf Hess, BBC," INF 1/912, UKARCH.

CHAPTER 90: GLOOM

440 **"I have taken the decision":** Beaverbrook to Churchill, April 30, 1941, BBK/D, Beaverbrook Papers.
440 **"anxious to see the war":** Panter-Downes, *London War Notes,* 147.
441 **"The hammering must":** Colville, *Fringes of Power,* 1:452.
441 **"Personally I am not downcast":** Kimball, *Churchill and Roosevelt,* 180.
442 **"It seems to me":** Gilbert, *War Papers,* 3:592.
442 **"We must not be too sure":** Ibid., 600.
442 **It was true that the destroyers:** In the end, the record of the fifty destroyers that Roosevelt gave to Britain was a mixed one. At least twelve collided with Allied ships, five of them American. The Royal Canadian Navy received two of the destroyers and in April 1944 tried to give them back. The U.S. Navy declined.
　　But the ships did their part. Their crews rescued a thousand sailors. One, the *Churchill,* named for an ancestor of the prime minister, provided escort service for fourteen convoys in 1941 alone. The destroyers brought down aircraft, sank at least six submarines, and helped capture one U-boat intact, which the Royal Navy then commissioned into its own fleet.
　　As the war progressed, the American destroyers fell out of service. A dozen served as targets to train pilots in maritime warfare. Eight, including the *Churchill,* were transferred to the Russians, along with a ninth, to be scavenged for spare parts.

On January 16, 1945, the *Churchill,* rechristened *Dejatelnyj*—in English, *Active*—was torpedoed and sunk by a U-boat while escorting a convoy through Russia's White Sea. The ship's captain and 116 members of the crew were lost; 7 survived.

For the best account of all this, see Philip Goodhart's *Fifty Ships That Saved the World.* The title is hyperbolic, but the story is a good one.

442 **"Mr. President," Churchill wrote:** Gilbert, *War Papers,* 3:600.
442 **"a world in which Hitler dominated":** Colville, *Fringes of Power,* 1:453.

CHAPTER 91: ERIC

444 **"The cold is incredible":** Nicolson, *War Years,* 165.
444 **"It has a good psychological effect":** "World War II Diary," 56, Meiklejohn Papers.
444 **"Everything is very late":** Colville, *Fringes of Power,* 1:454.
445 **"How is it that":** Gilbert, *War Papers,* 3:596.
446 **"He dictates messages":** Fred Taylor, *Goebbels Diaries,* 346.
447 **"It was obvious":** Colville, *Fringes of Power,* 1:454.

CHAPTER 93: OF PANZERS AND PANSIES

450 **"There is much that I would like":** *Hansard,* House of Commons Debate, May 6 and 7, 1941, vol. 371, cols. 704, 867–950.
450 **"He sat down":** Channon, *"Chips,"* 303.
451 **"He hates criticism":** Kathleen Harriman to Mary Harriman Fisk, Feb. 10, 1942, Correspondence, W. Averell Harriman Papers.
451 **"I feel very biteful":** Pottle, *Champion Redoubtable,* 236.
452 **"from the very first moment":** Nicolson, *War Years,* 164.
453 **"It was the sort of speech":** *Hansard,* House of Commons Debate, May 6 and 7, 1941, vol. 371, cols. 704, 867–950.
453 **"He thinks it of value":** Harriman to Roosevelt, May 7, 1941, Public Service, Chronological File, W. Averell Harriman Papers.
455 **"He is violently opposed":** Colville, *Fringes of Power,* 1:483.
455 **"My head is full of plans":** Ibid., 465.
455 **"Pretty good":** Nicolson, *War Years,* 164.

CHAPTER 95: MOONRISE

457 **"But no sign of weakness":** Fred Taylor, *Goebbels Diaries,* 355.
458 **"How good that a difficult week":** Ibid., 358.
458 **"I was relieved":** Colville, *Fringes of Power,* 1:457. In his published diary, Colville omits the last two words of the sentence: "of him." A minor thing, but interesting all the same.

PART SEVEN: ONE YEAR TO THE DAY

CHAPTER 96: A BEAM NAMED ANTON

461 **Late on Friday night:** Richard Collier, *City That Would Not Die,* 24–25, 26, 28.
462 **"It has all happened":** Soames, *Daughter's Tale,* 194.

463 **In a seeming paradox:** Basil Collier, *Defense of the United Kingdom,* 271.
463 **"Good afternoon, sir":** Richard Collier, *City That Would Not Die,* 44.

CHAPTER 97: INTERLOPER

The National Archives of the United Kingdom, one of the most civilized places on the planet, possesses vast holdings on the Hess saga, some opened to researchers only quite recently. These contain all the detail anyone could wish for, but here too, as with the Coventry story, the files will disappoint the conspiracy-minded among us. There was no conspiracy: Hess flew to Britain on a mad whim, without the intercession of British intelligence. I derived my account from the following:

- FO 1093/10.
- "The Capture of Rudolf Hess: Reports and Minutes," WO 199/328.
- WO 199/3288B. (Opened in 2016.)
- AIR 16/1266. (Originally ordered closed until 2019, but opened sooner, by "Accelerated Opening.")
- "Duke of Hamilton: Allegations Concerning Rudolf Hess," AIR 19/564.
- "Studies in Broadcast Propaganda, No. 29, Rudolf Hess, BBC," INF 1/912.

464 **"supernatural forces":** Speer, *Inside the Third Reich,* 211; Stafford, *Flight from Reality,* 168.
464 **Hess packed for his trip:** "Report on the Collection of Drugs, etc., Belonging to German Airman Prisoner, Captain Horn," FO 1093/10, UKARCH. Horn was the code name temporarily assigned to Hess.
466 **"With your whole *Geschwader*":** Toliver and Constable, *Fighter General,* 148–49; Galland, *The First and the Last,* 56; Stafford, *Flight from Reality,* 135.
467 **At 10:10 P.M. that Saturday:** Report, "Rudolf Hess, Flight on May 10, 1941, Raid 42.J," May 18, 1941, AIR 16/1266, UKARCH.
467 **The plane was next spotted:** Ibid.; Note, "Raid 42J," Scottish Area Commandant to Commandant Royal Observer Corps, Bentley Priory, May 13, 1941, AIR 16/1266, UKARCH.
468 **"hoots of derision":** "Prologue: May 10, 1941," Extract, AIR 16/1266, UKARCH. This is a lucid, detailed, dispassionate account by the author Derek Wood; a copy is lodged in the Air Ministry's files.

CHAPTER 98: THE CRUELEST RAID

470 **"I was in bed":** Richard Collier, *City That Would Not Die,* 157.
470 **In Regent's Park:** Ibid., 159–60; Ziegler, *London at War,* 161.
470 **Hess remembered the advice:** Stafford, *Flight from Reality,* 133.
471 **"All of a sudden":** "World War II Diary," 33, Meiklejohn Papers.
471 **Just after eleven P.M.:** Report, "Rudolf Hess, Flight on May 10, 1941, Raid 42.J," May 18, 1941, AIR 16/1266, UKARCH. In the same file, see "Raid 42J—10/5/1941," No. 34 Group Centre Observer Corps to Royal Observer Corps, Bentley Priory, May 13, 1941; and "Prologue: May 10, 1941," Extract. See also "The Capture of Rudolf Hess: Reports and Minutes," WO 199/328, UKARCH.
472 **"If they cannot catch":** "Prologue: May 10, 1941," Extract, AIR 16/1266.

472 **"No guns, bomb-racks"**: Report, Major Graham Donald to Scottish Area Commandant, Royal Observer Corps, May 11, 1941, AIR 16/1266, UKARCH. Also, "Prologue: May 10, 1941," Extract, AIR 16/1266.

472 **"He simply stated"**: Report, Major Graham Donald to Scottish Area Commandant, Royal Observer Corps, May 11, 1941, AIR 16/1266, UKARCH.

473 **"I do not know if you recognize"**: Stafford, *Flight from Reality*, 90.

473 **"About five AM I took"**: "World War II Diary," 35, Meiklejohn Papers.

CHAPTER 99: A SURPRISE FOR HITLER

474 **"Awoke thinking unaccountably"**: Colville, *Fringes of Power*, 1:457; Fox, "Propaganda and the Flight of Rudolf Hess," 78.

475 **"Hold on a minute"**: Colville, *Fringes of Power*, 1:459.

475 **"I became aware"**: Diary, May 11, 1941, Mary Churchill Papers.

476 **"At that moment"**: Colville, *Fringes of Power*, 1:459.

476 **"Well, *who* has arrived?"**: Colville, *Footprints in Time*, 112.

476 They gave Hitler Hess's letter: Speer, *Inside the Third Reich*, 209.

476 **"My *Führer*,"** it began: Douglas-Hamilton, *Motive for a Mission*, 193, 194.

476 **"I suddenly heard"**: Speer, *Inside the Third Reich*, 209, 210.

477 **"BOMBSHELL,"** Mary wrote: Diary, May 11, 1941, Mary Churchill Papers.

CHAPTER 100: BLOOD, SWEAT, AND TEARS

479 **"I keep thinking"**: Feigel, *Love-Charm of Bombs*, 151–57.

480 **"Our old House of Commons"**: Winston S. Churchill, *Memories and Adventures*, 19. The Foreign Office undersecretary, Alexander Cadogan, had a different view: "I don't care about that. I wish it had got most of the Members." Cadogan, *Diaries*, 377.

480 **"I drew back the curtains"**: Harrisson, *Living Through the Blitz*, 275.

480 **"It may be that they"**: Nicolson, *War Years*, 172.

480 The change was immediately evident: "Statement of Civilian Deaths in the United Kingdom," July 31, 1945, HO 191/11, UKARCH.

481 **"The spirit of the people"**: Harrisson, *Living Through the Blitz*, 274.

481 **"History knows a great many"**: Boelcke, *Secret Conferences of Dr. Goebbels*, 162, 165.

482 **"How am I supposed to believe"**: Stafford, *Flight from Reality*, 131.

482 **"From this distance"**: Roosevelt to Churchill, [likely date is May 14, 1941], FDR/Map.

483 **"Your Hess guess"**: Panter-Downes, *London War Notes*, 148.

483 **"What a dramatic episode"**: Lee, *London Observer*, 276.

483 **"It is possible that the people"**: Wheeler-Bennett, *Action This Day*, 174–75.

483 **"Only he had the power"**: Ibid., 236.

483 **"Winston's speeches send"**: Toye, *Roar of the Lion*, 8.

483 **"I never gave them courage"**: Cooper, *Trumpets from the Steep*, 73.

CHAPTER 101: A WEEKEND AT CHEQUERS

485 **"The news," he said**: Harriman, *Special Envoy to Churchill and Stalin*, 111–12.

486 **"We looked at one another"**: Winant, *Letter from Grosvenor Square*, 198.

486 **"It's quite true"**: Harriman, *Special Envoy to Churchill and Stalin*, 112. Roosevelt

repeated the sentiment in a telegram dated December 8, 1941, in which he tells Churchill, "Today all of us are in the same boat with you and the people of the Empire and it is a ship which will not and cannot be sunk." Roosevelt to Churchill, Dec. 8, 1941, FDR/Map.

486 **"Thinking of you much"**: Gilbert, *War Papers,* 3:1580.

486 **"The inevitable had finally"**: Harriman, *Special Envoy to Churchill and Stalin,* 112.

486 **"I could not conceal"**: Anthony Eden, *Reckoning,* 331.

487 **"Being saturated and satiated"**: Gilbert, *War Papers,* 3:1580.

487 **"It might be badly knocked"**: Ismay, *Memoirs,* 242.

487 **"He is a different man"**: Moran, *Churchill,* 9–10.

488 **"never travelled in such"**: Martin, *Downing Street,* 69.

488 **"Being in a ship"**: Winston Churchill to Clementine Churchill, December n.d., 1941, CSCT 1/24, Clementine Churchill Papers.

488 **"The PM is very fit"**: Harriman, Memorandum to self, "Trip to U.S. with 'P.M.,' December 1941," W. Averell Harriman Papers.

488 **"It was night time"**: Thompson, *Assignment,* 246.

488 **"I turned," Thompson wrote**: This story is told by different figures in different ways, but all have the same denouement. Ibid., 248; Sherwood, *Roosevelt and Hopkins,* 442; Hallo, *Irrepressible Churchill,* 165.

489 **"Let the children"**: For background details, see Hindley, "Christmas at the White House with Winston Churchill." I watched a British Pathé news-reel of the speech, which I found on YouTube at www.youtube.com/watch?v=dZTRbNThHnk.

489 **"I simply could not believe"**: Thompson, *Assignment,* 249.

490 **"We are indeed walking"**: Hastings, *Winston's War,* 205.

490 **"Here's to a year of toil"**: Thompson, *Assignment,* 257.

EPILOGUE: AS TIME WENT BY

491 **"My first agonizing thought"**: Soames, *Daughter's Tale,* 232–33.

491 **"the P.M. dashed off"**: Colville, *Fringes of Power,* 2:99.

491 **"Not so bad at 21!"**: Winston S. Churchill, *Memories and Adventures,* 32.

491 **"To a three-year-old"**: Ibid., 26–27.

492 **"Eric, who was at his simplest"**: Colville, *Fringes of Power,* 1:523.

492 **"I hear you are plotting"**: Ibid., 490.

492 **"It had not crossed his mind"**: Wheeler-Bennett, *Action This Day,* 60.

493 **"I went out of the room"**: Colville, *Fringes of Power,* 1:533.

493 **"It is time that you came back"**: Ibid., 2:71.

493 **"You seem to think"**: Ibid., 84.

493 **"It was thrilling"**: Ibid., 116.

494 **"None of us except Clemmie"**: Interview Transcript, July 1991, Biographies File, Pamela Harriman Papers.

494 **In all, Beaverbrook offered**: A.J.P. Taylor, *Beaverbrook,* 440.

494 **"I owe my reputation"**: Young, *Churchill and Beaverbrook,* 230.

494 **"We have lived & fought"**: Ibid., 231.

495 **"I was glad"**: Ibid., 325.

495 **"I was always under"**: Ibid., 235.

495 **"The conclusion at which"**: Singleton to Churchill, [ca. Aug. 1941], G 36/4, Lindemann Papers.

496 **Randolph later complained:** Smith, *Reflected Glory,* 106.

497 **One night, while talking:** Winston S. Churchill, *Memories and Adventures,* 247.

497 **"I found him absolutely charming":** Ibid., 20.

497 **"She hates him so much":** Waugh, *Diaries,* 525.

497 **"Unlike Paris, where there was":** Smith, *Reflected Glory,* 111.

498 **"I mean, when you are very young":** Interview Transcript, July 1991, Biographies File, Pamela Harriman Papers.

498 **"Supposing the war ends":** Ibid.

498 **"He used to sit":** Smith, *Reflected Glory,* 260.

498 **"It was very strange":** Note, "William Averell Harriman," Biographies and Proposed Biographies, Background Topics, Pamela Harriman Papers.

498 **"We did it!":** Smith, *Reflected Glory,* 265.

498 **"Oh Pam":** "Barbie" [Mrs. Herbert Agar] to Pamela Digby Harriman, Sept. 19, 1971, Personal and Family Papers, Marriages, Pamela Harriman Papers.

499 **"Only the diversion":** "Interrogation of Reich Marshal Hermann Goering," May 10, 1945, Spaatz Papers.

499 **"Of course we rearmed":** Overy, *Goering,* 229.

499 **"Perhaps one of my weaknesses":** Goldensohn, *Nuremberg Interviews,* 129.

499 **Investigators cataloged the works:** "The Göring Collection," Confidential Interrogation Report No. 2, Sept. 15, 1945, 174, Office of Strategic Services and Looting Investigative Unit, T 209/29, UKARCH.

499 **Joseph Goebbels and his wife:** Kershaw, *Nemesis,* 832–33.

500 **"I do not regret":** Douglas-Hamilton, *Motive for a Mission,* 246.

500 **He achieved his final kills:** Baker, *Adolf Galland,* 287–88, 290–92.

501 **The package contained:** Winston S. Churchill, *Memories and Adventures,* 31.

502 **"Thank you so much":** Hastings, *Winston's War,* 460.

502 **Searchlights played on Nelson's Tower:** Nicolson, *War Years,* 459.

503 **"This is where I miss the news":** Soames, *Daughter's Tale,* 360–61.

503 **"Our last weekend":** Elletson, *Chequers and the Prime Ministers,* 145.

503 **"Finis":** Soames, *Daughter's Tale,* 361.

Bibliography

ARCHIVES AND DOCUMENT COLLECTIONS

Beaverbrook, Lord (Max Aitken). Papers. Parliamentary Archives, London.

Burgis, Lawrence. Papers. Churchill Archives Center, Churchill College, Cambridge, U.K.

Churchill, Clementine (Baroness Spencer-Churchill). Papers. Churchill Archives Center, Churchill College, Cambridge, U.K.

Churchill, Mary (Mary Churchill Soames). Papers. Churchill Archives Center, Churchill College, Cambridge, U.K.

Churchill, Randolph. Papers. Churchill Archives Center, Churchill College, Cambridge, U.K.

Churchill, Winston. Papers. Churchill Archives Center, Churchill College, Cambridge, U.K.

Colville, John R. Papers. Churchill Archives Center, Churchill College, Cambridge, U.K.

Eade, Charles. Papers. Churchill Archives Center, Churchill College, Cambridge, U.K.

Gallup Polls. ibiblio.org. University of North Carolina, Chapel Hill.

Gilbert, Martin. *The Churchill War Papers*. Vol. 2, *Never Surrender, May 1940–December 1940*. New York: Norton, 1995.

————. *The Churchill War Papers*. Vol. 3, *The Ever-Widening War, 1941*. New York: Norton, 2000.

Hansard. Proceedings in the House of Commons. London.

Harriman, Pamela Digby. Papers. Library of Congress, Manuscript Division, Washington, D.C.

Harriman, W. Averell. Library of Congress, Manuscript Division, Washington, D.C.

Ismay, General Hastings Lionel. Liddell Hart Center for Military Archives, King's College London.

Lindemann, Frederick A. (Viscount Cherwell). Papers. Nuffield College, Oxford.

Meiklejohn, Robert P. Papers. Library of Congress, Manuscript Division, Washington, D.C.

National Archives of the United Kingdom, Kew, England (UKARCH).

National Meteorological Library and Archive, Exeter, U.K. Digital archive: www
.metoffice.gov.uk/research/library-and-archive/archive-hidden-treasures/
monthly-weather-reports.

Roosevelt, Franklin D. Papers as President: Map Room Papers, 1941–1945
(FDR/Map).

Roosevelt, Franklin D. Papers as President: The President's Secretary's File, 1933–
1945. Franklin D. Roosevelt Presidential Library & Museum. Digital collection: www.fdrlibrary.marist.edu/archives/collections/franklin/?p=collections/
findingaid&id=502.

———. Confidential File (FDR/Conf).

———. Diplomatic File (FDR/Diplo).

———. Safe File (FDR/Safe).

———. Subject File (FDR/Subject).

Spaatz, Carl. Papers. Library of Congress, Manuscript Division, Washington, D.C.

BOOKS AND PERIODICALS

Addison, Paul. *Churchill on the Home Front, 1900–1955*. London: Pimlico, 1993.

Addison, Paul, and Jeremy A. Crang, eds. *Listening to Britain: Home Intelligence Reports
on Britain's Finest Hour, May to September 1940*. London: Vintage, 2011.

Adey, Peter, David J. Cox, and Barry Godfrey. *Crime, Regulation, and Control During the Blitz: Protecting the Population of Bombed Cities*. London: Bloomsbury,
2016.

Alanbrooke, Lord. *War Diaries, 1939–1945*. London: Weidenfeld & Nicolson, 2001.

Allingham, Margery. *The Oaken Heart: The Story of an English Village at War*. 1941.
Pleshey, U.K.: Golden Duck, 2011.

"The Animals in the Zoo Don't Mind the Raids." *War Illustrated*, Nov. 15, 1940.

Awcock, Hannah. "On This Day: Occupation of the Savoy, 14th September 1940."
Turbulent London. turbulentlondon.com/2017/09/14/on-this-day-occupation
-of-the-savoy-14th-september-1940/.

Baker, David. *Adolf Galland: The Authorized Biography*. London: Windrow & Greene,
1996.

Baumbach, Werner. *The Life and Death of the Luftwaffe*. New York: Ballantine, 1949.

Beaton, Cecil. *History Under Fire: 52 Photographs of Air Raid Damage to London Buildings,
1940–41*. London: Batsford, 1941.

Bekker, Cajus. *The Luftwaffe Diaries*. London: Macdonald, 1964.

Bell, Amy. "Landscapes of Fear: Wartime London, 1939–1945." *Journal of British Studies* 48, no. 1 (Jan. 2009).

Below, Nicolaus von. *At Hitler's Side: The Memoirs of Hitler's Luftwaffe Adjutant, 1937–
1945*. London: Greenhill, 2001.

Berlin, Isaiah. *Personal Impressions*. 1949. New York: Viking, 1980.

Berrington, Hugh. "When Does Personality Make a Difference? Lord Cherwell and
the Area Bombing of Germany." *International Political Science Review* 10, no. 1
(Jan. 1989).

Bessborough, Lord. *Enchanted Forest: The Story of Stansted in Sussex*. With Clive Aslet.
London: Weidenfeld & Nicolson, 1984.

Birkenhead, Earl of. *The Prof in Two Worlds: The Official Life of Professor F. A. Lindemann, Viscount Cherwell*. London: Collins, 1961.

Boelcke, Willi A., ed. *The Secret Conferences of Dr. Goebbels: The Nazi Propaganda War,
1939–43*. New York: Dutton, 1970.

Booth, Nicholas. *Lucifer Rising: British Intelligence and the Occult in the Second World War*. Cheltenham, U.K.: History Press, 2016.

Borden, Mary. *Journey down a Blind Alley*. New York: Harper, 1946.

Bullock, Alan. *Hitler: A Study in Tyranny*. New York: Harper, 1971.

Cadogan, Alexander. *The Diaries of Alexander Cadogan, O.M., 1938–1945*. Edited by David Dilks. New York: Putnam, 1972.

Carter, Violet Bonham. *Winston Churchill: An Intimate Portrait*. New York: Harcourt, 1965.

Channon, Henry. *"Chips": The Diaries of Sir Henry Channon*. Edited by Robert Rhodes James. London: Phoenix, 1996.

Charmley, John. "Churchill and the American Alliance." *Transactions of the Royal Historical Society* 11 (2001).

Chisholm, Anne. *Nancy Cunard*. London: Sidgwick & Jackson, 1979.

Chisholm, Anne, and Michael Davie. *Beaverbrook: A Life*. London: Pimlico, 1993.

Churchill, Sarah. *Keep on Dancing: An Autobiography*. Edited by Paul Medlicott. London: Weidenfeld & Nicolson, 1981.

Churchill, Winston. *The Grand Alliance*. Boston: Houghton Mifflin, 1951.

———. *Great Contemporaries*. London: Odhams Press, 1947.

———. *Their Finest Hour*. Boston: Houghton Mifflin, 1949.

Churchill, Winston S. *Memories and Adventures*. New York: Weidenfeld & Nicolson, 1989.

Clapson, Mark. *The Blitz Companion*. London: University of Westminster Press, 2019.

Cockett, Olivia. *Love and War in London: The Mass Observation Wartime Diary of Olivia Cockett*. Edited by Robert Malcolmson. Stroud, U.K.: History Press, 2009.

Collier, Basil. *The Battle of Britain*. London: Collins, 1962.

———. *The Defense of the United Kingdom*. London: Imperial War Museum; Nashville: Battery Press, 1995.

Collier, Richard. *The City That Would Not Die: The Bombing of London, May 10–11, 1941*. New York: Dutton, 1960.

Colville, John. *Footprints in Time: Memories*. London: Collins, 1976.

———. *The Fringes of Power: Downing Street Diaries, 1939–1955*. Vol. 1, *September 1939–September 1941*. London: Hodder & Stoughton, 1985.

———. *The Fringes of Power: Downing Street Diaries, 1939–1955*. Vol. 2, *October 1941–1955*. London: Hodder & Stoughton, 1987.

———. *Winston Churchill and His Inner Circle*. New York: Wyndham, 1981. Originally published in Britain, under the title *The Churchillians*.

Conant, James B. *My Several Lives: Memoirs of a Social Inventor*. New York: Harper & Row, 1970.

Cooper, Diana. *Trumpets from the Steep*. London: Century, 1984.

Costigliola, Frank. "Pamela Churchill, Wartime London, and the Making of the Special Relationship." *Diplomatic History* 36, no. 4 (Sept. 2012).

Cowles, Virginia. *Looking for Trouble*. 1941. London: Faber and Faber, 2010.

———. *Winston Churchill: The Era and the Man*. New York: Harper & Brothers, 1953.

Dalton, Hugh. *The Fateful Years: Memoirs, 1931–1945*. London: Frederick Muller, 1957.

Danchev, Alex. "'Dilly-Dally,' or Having the Last Word: Field Marshal Sir John Dill and Prime Minister Winston Churchill." *Journal of Contemporary History* 22, no. 1 (Jan. 1987).

Davis, Jeffrey. "Atfero: The Atlantic Ferry Organization." *Journal of Contemporary History* 20, no. 1 (Jan. 1985).

Dockter, Warren, and Richard Toye. "Who Commanded History? Sir John Colville, Churchillian Networks, and the 'Castlerosse Affair.'" *Journal of Contemporary History* 54, no. 2 (2019).

Donnelly, Peter, ed. *Mrs. Milburn's Diaries: An Englishwoman's Day-to-Day Reflections, 1939–1945*. London: Abacus, 1995.

Douglas-Hamilton, James. *Motive for a Mission: The Story Behind Hess's Flight to Britain*. London: Macmillan, 1971.

Ebert, Hans J., Johann B. Kaiser, and Klaus Peters. *Willy Messerschmitt: Pioneer of Aviation Design*. Atglen, Pa.: Schiffer, 1999.

Eden, Anthony. *The Reckoning: The Memoirs of Anthony Eden, Earl of Avon*. Boston: Houghton Mifflin, 1965.

Eden, Clarissa. *Clarissa Eden: A Memoir, from Churchill to Eden*. Edited by Cate Haste. London: Weidenfeld & Nicolson, 2007.

Elletson, D. H. *Chequers and the Prime Ministers*. London: Robert Hale, 1970.

Farrer, David. *G—for God Almighty: A Personal Memoir of Lord Beaverbrook*. London: Weidenfeld & Nicolson, 1969.

———. *The Sky's the Limit: The Story of Beaverbrook at M.A.P.* London: Hutchinson, 1943.

Feigel, Lara. *The Love-Charm of Bombs: Restless Lives in the Second World War*. New York: Bloomsbury, 2013.

Field, Geoffrey. "Nights Underground in Darkest London: The Blitz, 1940–41." *International Labor and Working-Class History*, no. 62 (Fall 2002).

Fort, Adrian. *Prof: The Life of Frederick Lindemann*. London: Pimlico, 2003.

Fox, Jo. "Propaganda and the Flight of Rudolf Hess, 1941–45." *Journal of Modern History* 83, no. 1 (March 2011).

Fry, Plantagenet Somerset. *Chequers: The Country Home of Britain's Prime Ministers*. London: Her Majesty's Stationery Office, 1977.

Galland, Adolf. *The First and the Last: The Rise and Fall of the German Fighter Forces, 1938–1945*. New York: Ballantine, 1954.

Gilbert, Martin. *Finest Hour: Winston S. Churchill, 1939–41*. London: Heinemann, 1989.

Goldensohn, Leon. *The Nuremberg Interviews: An American Psychiatrist's Conversations with the Defendants and Witnesses*. Edited by Robert Gellately. New York: Knopf, 2004.

Goodhart, Philip. *Fifty Ships That Saved the World: The Foundation of the Anglo-American Alliance*. London: Heinemann, 1965.

Goodwin, Doris Kearns. *No Ordinary Time: Franklin and Eleanor Roosevelt: The Home Front in World War II*. New York: Simon & Schuster, 1994.

Graves, Charles. *Champagne and Chandeliers: The Story of the Café de Paris*. London: Odhams Press, 1958.

Greene, Graham. *Ways of Escape*. New York: Simon & Schuster, 1980.

Gullan, Harold I. "Expectations of Infamy: Roosevelt and Marshall Prepare for War, 1938–41." *Presidential Studies Quarterly* 28, no. 3 (Summer 1998).

Halder, Franz. *The Halder War Diary, 1939–1942*. Edited by Charles Burdick and Hans-Adolf Jacobsen. London: Greenhill Books, 1988.

Halle, Kay. *The Irrepressible Churchill: Stories, Sayings, and Impressions of Sir Winston Churchill*. London: Facts on File, 1966.

———. *Randolph Churchill: The Young Unpretender*. London: Heinemann, 1971.

Harriman, W. Averell. *Special Envoy to Churchill and Stalin, 1941–1946*. New York: Random House, 1975.

Harrisson, Tom. *Living Through the Blitz*. New York: Schocken Books, 1976.

Harrod, Roy. *The Prof: A Personal Memoir of Lord Cherwell*. London: Macmillan, 1959.

Hastings, Max. *Winston's War: Churchill, 1940–45*. New York: Knopf, 2010.

Hickman, Tom. *Churchill's Bodyguard*. London: Headline, 2005.

Hindley, Meredith. "Christmas at the White House with Winston Churchill." *Humanities* 37, no. 4 (Fall 2016).

Hinton, James. *The Mass Observers: A History, 1937–1949*. Oxford: Oxford University Press, 2013.

Hitler, Adolf. *Hitler's Table Talk, 1941–1944*. Translated by Norman Cameron and R. H. Stevens. London: Weidenfeld & Nicholson, 1953.

Hylton, Stuart. *Their Darkest Hour: The Hidden History of the Home Front, 1939–1945*. Stroud, U.K.: Sutton, 2001.

Ismay, Lord. *The Memoirs of General the Lord Ismay*. London: Heinemann, 1960.

Jenkins, J. Gilbert. *Chequers: A History of the Prime Minister's Buckinghamshire Home*. London: Pergamon, 1967.

Jenkins, Roy. *Churchill*. London: Macmillan, 2002.

Jones, R. V. *Most Secret War: British Scientific Intelligence, 1939–1945*. London: Hodder & Stoughton, 1978.

Kendall, David, and Kenneth Post. "The British 3-Inch Anti-aircraft Rocket. Part One: Dive-Bombers." *Notes and Records of the Royal Society of London* 50, no. 2 (July 1996).

Kennedy, David M. *The American People in World War II: Freedom from Fear*. Oxford: Oxford University Press, 1999.

Kershaw, Ian. *Hitler, 1936–1945: Nemesis*. New York: Norton, 2000.

Kesselring, Albert. *The Memoirs of Field-Marshal Kesselring*. Novato, Calif.: Presidio Press, 1989.

Kimball, Warren F. *Churchill and Roosevelt: The Complete Correspondence*. Vol. 1. Princeton, N.J.: Princeton University Press, 2015.

Klingaman, William K. *1941: Our Lives in a World on the Edge*. New York: Harper & Row, 1988.

Koch, H. W. "Hitler's 'Programme' and the Genesis of Operation 'Barbarossa.'" *Historical Journal* 26, no. 4 (Dec. 1983).

———. "The Strategic Air Offensive Against Germany: The Early Phase, May–September 1940." *Historical Journal* 34, no. 1 (March 1991).

Landemare, Georgina. *Recipes from No. 10*. London: Collins, 1958.

Lee, Raymond E. *The London Observer: The Journal of General Raymond E. Lee, 1940–41*. Edited by James Leutze. London: Hutchinson, 1971.

Leslie, Anita. *Cousin Randolph: The Life of Randolph Churchill*. London: Hutchinson, 1985.

Leutze, James. "The Secret of the Churchill-Roosevelt Correspondence: September 1939–May 1940." *Journal of Contemporary History* 10, no. 3 (July 1975).

Lewin, Ronald. *Churchill as Warlord*. New York: Stein and Day, 1973.

Longmate, Norman. *Air Raid: The Bombing of Coventry, 1940*. New York: David McKay, 1978.

Lough, David. *No More Champagne*. New York: Picador, 2015.

Lukacs, John. *Five Days in London, May 1940*. New Haven, Conn.: Yale University Press, 1999.

Mackay, Robert. *The Test of War: Inside Britain, 1939–1945*. London: University College of London Press, 1999.

Maier, Thomas. *When Lions Roar: The Churchills and the Kennedys*. New York: Crown, 2014.

Major, Norma. *Chequers: The Prime Minister's Country House and Its History*. London: HarperCollins, 1996.

Manchester, William, and Paul Reid. *Defender of the Realm, 1940–1965*. Vol. 3 of *The Last Lion: Winston Spencer Churchill*. New York: Bantam, 2013.

Martin, John. *Downing Street: The War Years*. London: Bloomsbury, 1991.

Matless, David. *Landscape and Englishness*. London: Reaktion Books, 1998.

Miller, Edith Starr. *Occult Theocracy*. Abbeville, France: F. Paillart, 1933.

Moran, Lord. *Churchill, Taken from the Diaries of Lord Moran: The Struggle for Survival, 1940–1965*. Boston: Houghton Mifflin, 1966.

Murray, Williamson. *Strategy for Defeat: The Luftwaffe, 1933–1945*. Royston, U.K.: Quantum, 2000.

Nel, Elizabeth. *Mr. Churchill's Secretary*. London: Hodder & Stoughton, 1958.

Nicolson, Harold. *The War Years, 1939–1945: Diaries and Letters*. Edited by Nigel Nicolson. Vol. 2. New York: Atheneum, 1967.

Niven, David. *The Moon's a Balloon*. New York: Dell, 1972.

Nixon, Barbara. *Raiders Overhead: A Diary of the London Blitz*. London: Scolar Press, 1980.

Ogden, Christopher. *Life of the Party: The Biography of Pamela Digby Churchill Hayward Harriman*. London: Little, Brown, 1994.

Olson, Lynne. *Troublesome Young Men*. New York: Farrar, Straus and Giroux, 2007.

Overy, Richard. *The Battle of Britain: The Myth and the Reality*. New York: Norton, 2001.

———. *The Bombing War: Europe, 1939–1945*. London: Penguin, 2014.

———. *Goering: Hitler's Iron Knight*. London: I. B. Tauris, 1984.

Packwood, Allen. *How Churchill Waged War: The Most Challenging Decisions of the Second World War*. Yorkshire, U.K.: Frontline Books, 2018.

Panter-Downes, Mollie. *London War Notes, 1939–1945*. New York: Farrar, Straus and Giroux, 1971.

Pawle, Gerald. *The War and Colonel Warden*. New York: Knopf, 1963.

Phillips, Paul C. "Decision and Dissension—Birth of the RAF." *Aerospace Historian* 18, no. 1 (Spring 1971).

Pottle, Mark, ed. *Champion Redoubtable: The Diaries and Letters of Violet Bonham Carter, 1914–1945*. London: Weidenfeld & Nicolson, 1998.

Purnell, Sonia. *Clementine: The Life of Mrs. Winston Churchill*. New York: Penguin, 2015.

Roberts, Andrew. *"The Holy Fox": The Life of Lord Halifax*. London: Orion, 1997.

———. *Masters and Commanders: How Four Titans Won the War in the West, 1941–1945*. New York: Harper, 2009.

Roberts, Brian. *Randolph: A Study of Churchill's Son*. London: Hamish Hamilton, 1984.

Ryan, Alan. *Bertrand Russell: A Political Life*. New York: Hill & Wang, 1988.

Sherwood, Robert E. *Roosevelt and Hopkins: An Intimate History*. New York: Harper, 1948.

———. *The White House Papers of Harry L. Hopkins*. Vol. 1. London: Eyre & Spottiswoode, 1949.

Shirer, William L. *Berlin Diary: The Journal of a Foreign Correspondent, 1934–1941*. 1941. New York: Tess Press, 2004.

Showell, Jak Mallman, ed. *Führer Conferences on Naval Affairs, 1939–1945*. Stroud, U.K.: History Press, 2015.

Smith, Sally Bedell. *Reflected Glory: The Life of Pamela Churchill Harriman*. New York: Simon & Schuster, 1996.

Soames, Mary. *Clementine Churchill: The Biography of a Marriage*. Boston: Houghton Mifflin, 1979.

———. *A Daughter's Tale: The Memoir of Winston and Clementine Churchill's Youngest Child*. London: Transworld, 2011.

———, ed. *Speaking for Themselves: The Personal Letters of Winston and Clementine Churchill*. Toronto: Stoddart, 1998.

Spears, Edward. *The Fall of France, June 1940*. Vol. 2 of *Assignment to Catastrophe*. New York: A. A. Wyn, 1955.

Speer, Albert. *Inside the Third Reich*. New York: Macmillan, 1970.

Stafford, David, ed. *Flight from Reality: Rudolf Hess and His Mission to Scotland, 1941*. London: Pimlico, 2002.

Stansky, Peter. *The First Day of the Blitz: September 7, 1940*. New Haven, Conn.: Yale University Press, 2007.

Stelzer, Cita. *Dinner with Churchill: Policy-Making at the Dinner Table*. New York: Pegasus, 2012.

———. *Working with Churchill*. London: Head of Zeus, 2019.

Strobl, Gerwin. *The Germanic Isle: Nazi Perceptions of Britain*. Cambridge, U.K.: Cambridge University Press, 2000.

Süss, Dietmar. *Death from the Skies: How the British and Germans Survived Bombing in World War II*. Oxford: Oxford University Press, 2014.

Taylor, A.J.P. *Beaverbrook*. New York: Simon & Schuster, 1972.

Taylor, Fred, ed. and trans. *The Goebbels Diaries, 1939–1941*. New York: Putnam, 1983.

Thomas, Martin. "After Mers-el-Kébir: The Armed Neutrality of the Vichy French Navy, 1940–43." *English Historical Review* 112, no. 447 (June 1997).

Thomas, Ronan. "10 Downing Street." *West End at War*. www.westendatwar.org.uk/page/10_downing_street.

Thompson, Walter. *Assignment: Churchill*. New York: Farrar, Straus and Young, 1955.

Toliver, Raymond F., and Trevor J. Constable. *Fighter General: The Life of Adolf Galland*. Zephyr Cove, Nev.: AmPress, 1990.

Toye, Richard. *The Roar of the Lion: The Untold Story of Churchill's World War II Speeches*. Oxford: Oxford University Press, 2013.

Treasure, Tom, and Carol Tan. "Miss, Mister, Doctor: How We Are Titled Is of Little Consequence." *Journal of the Royal Society of Medicine* 99, no. 4 (April 2006).

Trevor-Roper, H. R., ed. *Blitzkrieg to Defeat: Hitler's War Directives, 1939–1945*. New York: Holt, Rinehart, 1965.

Tute, Warren. *The Deadly Stroke*. New York: Coward, McCann & Geoghegan, 1973.

Wakefield, Ken. *Pfadfinder: Luftwaffe Pathfinder Operations over Britain, 1940–44*. Charleston, S.C.: Tempus, 1999.

Wakelam, Randall T. "The Roaring Lions of the Air: Air Substitution and the Royal Air Force's Struggle for Independence After the First World War." *Air Power History* 43, no. 3 (Fall 1996).

Waugh, Evelyn. *The Diaries of Evelyn Waugh*. Edited by Michael Davie. London: Phoenix, 1976.

Wheeler-Bennett, John, ed. *Action This Day: Working with Churchill*. London: Macmillan, 1968.

———. *King George VI: His Life and Reign*. London: Macmillan, 1958.

Wilson, Thomas. *Churchill and the Prof*. London: Cassell, 1995.

Winant, John G. *A Letter from Grosvenor Square: An Account of a Stewardship*. London: Hodder & Stoughton, 1948.

Wrigley, Chris. *Winston Churchill: A Biographical Companion*. Santa Barbara, Calif.: ABC-CLIO, 2002.

Wyndham, Joan. *Love Lessons: A Wartime Diary*. Boston: Little, Brown, 1985.

Young, Kenneth. *Churchill and Beaverbrook: A Study in Friendship and Politics*. London: Eyre & Spottiswoode, 1966.

Ziegler, Philip. *London at War, 1939–1945*. London: Sinclair-Stevenson, 1995.

Index
